Art Nouveau Glass

The Gerda Koepff Collection

Art Nouveau Glass

The Gerda Koepff Collection

Edited by
Helmut Ricke and Eva Schmitt

With contributions by
Susanne Brenner,
Brigitte Leonhardt and Nobuo Tsūji

Prestel
Munich · Berlin · London · New York

Front cover: Vase with woodland scene, Daum Frères, 1903/4, cat. no. 104
Back cover: *top row, from left to right*: Vase with underwater scene, Emile Gallé, *c.* 1900,
cat. no. 45; Covered vase with mount, Eugène Rousseau, *c.* 1885–89, cat. no. 5; 'Le Scarabée'
(beetle) flacon, Daum Frères, 1899, cat. no. 91; 'Eucalyptus' vase, Daum Frères, 1897, cat. no. 79;
bottom row, from left to right: Vase with cuckoo and primroses, Emile Gallé, *c.* 1899 / 1900,
cat. no. 46; Vase with red begonias, Muller Frères, *c.* 1919–25, cat. no. 124; 'Libellules' footed
vase, Emile Gallé, 1904, cat. no. 60

The present volume is a revised edition of the original German book,
Art Nouveau Glas: Die Sammlung Gerda Koepff, published in 1998.

Photographic Credits
The photographs reproduced in this volume were taken by *Walter Klein*,
with the following exceptions:

Service régional de l'inventaire générale en Lorraine, Nancy:
Gilles André: pp. 197 (bottom), 200 (bottom), 203 (top), 238 (top)
Daniel Bastien: pp. 59 (top and bottom left), 65 (both bottom images), 178 (both),
180, 182 (both) 183 (bottom), 186 (bottom), 190 (bottom right), 191 (both centre images),
194 (both), 203 (bottom centre), 204 (both bottom images), 205 (bottom), 208 (centre),
211 (bottom), 218 (bottom right), 221 (bottom), 223 (bottom); 224 (top), 226 (bottom),
236 (bottom), 238 (bottom)
Gérard Coing: pp. 58 (bottom right), 60 (1–12), 62 (1–4, 6), 63, 64 (1–4, 6),
65 (both top images), 193 (bottom), 198 (bottom), 208 (bottom), 214 (bottom right),
216 (bottom), 218 (bottom left), 222 (bottom right), 224 (bottom centre), 232 (top), 236 (top)
Alain George: pp. 59 (top right), 61 (top), 62 (centre), 62 (5), 184 (bottom), 208 (bottom)
Musée de l'Ecole de Nancy, Nancy:
Jean-François Brabant: pp. 212 (bottom), 235 (bottom)
Y. Fleck, Meisenthal: p. 74
Horst Kolberg, Neuss: p. 27 (top)
Rheinisches Bildarchiv, Cologne: pp. 278–86
Service photographique du musée d'Orsay, Paris: pp. 25, 26 (both)
Laurent Sully-Jaulmes, Paris: p. 27 (bottom)
Jan Svoboda and Gabriel Urbánek, Prague: p. 28

The Library of Congress Cataloguing-in-Publication data is available;
British Library Cataloguing-in-Publication Data: a catalogue record for this book is available
from the British Library; the Deutsche Bibliothek holds a record of this publication
in the Deutsche Nationalbibliografie; detailed bibliographical data can be found under:
http://dnb.ddb.de

© **Prestel Verlag, Munich · Berlin · London · New York 2004**

Prestel books are available worldwide.
Please contact your nearest bookseller or one of the following Prestel offices
for information concerning your local distributor:

Prestel Verlag
Königinstrasse 9, 80539 Munich
Tel. +49 (89) 38 17 09 - 0; Fax +49 (89) 38 17 09-35

Prestel Publishing Ltd.
4 Bloomsbury Place, London WC1A 2QA
Tel. +44 (020) 7323-5004; Fax +44 (020) 7636-8004

Prestel Publishing
900 Broadway, Suite 603, New York, N.Y. 10003
Tel. +1 (212) 995-2720; Fax +1 (212) 995-2733

www.prestel.com

Translated from the German by Jane Smith (pp. 7–250, 285–87, 293–331)
and from the French by David Radzinowicz (pp. 251–73, 288)
Edited by Michele Schons
Designed by Zwischenschritt, Rainald Schwarz, Munich
Typeset by Michael Hempel, Munich
Originations by ReproLine Mediatem, Munich
Printed and bound by Fotolito Longo, Bolzano

Printed in Italy on acid-free paper

ISBN 3-7913-3021-7 (English edition)
ISBN 3-7913-1923-X (German edition)

Contents

Foreword

The documentation in book form of important private collections, especially those hitherto virtually unknown, is bound to interest the public. At Gerda Koepff's express wish, however, the catalogue of her collection was not to be merely treated to a lavishly illustrated volume. A committed connoisseur, she decided to bequeath the superlative pieces she had acquired over decades of knowledgeable collecting to a museum, a decision that provided an ideal occasion to subject the collection to scholarly study, based on the latest research done in the field. In so doing – apart from ensuring that her treasures would be presented as they deserve to be – she would be providing scholarship with a fresh look at, and new approaches to, the subject of Art Nouveau glass. The book was, in short, to be a thoroughly grounded study of a private collection and not simply a feast for the eyes. We have done our best to meet both requirements.

When one considers the wealth of publications dealing with Art Nouveau glass that has appeared since the 1980s, however, writing a new book on it might at first appear a rather daunting task. Yet by treating the subject in depth, the authors have, in most cases, realized that a great deal of study at an advanced level remains to be done if the subject is to be completely elucidated. The essays and catalogue texts in this volume do not claim to be more than a small further step in this direction. Still considerable new knowledge and clarification of what had been believed to be thoroughly covered have resulted from this undertaking.

This is true of both the production and the importance of these factories, workshops and retail outlets in Paris: Appert Frères, Eugène Rousseau, Auguste Jean and Eugène Michel, and especially Daum Frères in Nancy, whose archives were made available for intensive study. It has, therefore, been possible to come much closer to untangling the seemingly intractable problem of determining which designers worked for which factories and when, and to place the dating of individual models, long a moot question as far as Daum was concerned, on a firmer footing than was previously possible. The archival material in the 'Sources' section of this volume will be an invaluable aid to scholars and to all other users.

This book is, on the lines of our 1997 publication *Italian Glass, 1930–1970*, again the product of a collaborative effort. Helmut Ricke wrote the commentaries on Emile Gallé's glass and his design drawings and the introduc-tory essays conveying an overview; he also compiled the 'Sources' section in the Appendix and was responsible for the conception of the book. The lion's share of the extensive archival research fell to Eva Schmitt. She is the author of the catalogue texts dealing with the pieces grouped under the heading of 'Paris before 1900' as well as the glass of Daum, Muller Frères and Paul Nicolas. Working in archives and libraries, mainly in Paris and Nancy, but also in smaller towns, she built up the foundation for her introductory essays and provided the material for the 'Manufacturers and Artists' section in the Appendix. In addition, she compiled the 'Selected Bibliography' and the 'Glossary of Technical Terms'.

Susanne Brenner brought the detailed knowledge acquired in preparing her dissertation on Désiré Christian to the catalogue entries and the texts on Burgun, Schverer & Co., Vallerysthal and Désiré Christian prepared by Eva Schmitt, and contributed an essay of her own to the book.

We are indebted to Brigitte Leonhardt, not only for many inspiring discussions, but also for her essay on the reception of Emile Gallé's work in Germany and, in this connection, her probing analysis of the Symbolist aspects of his work.

We were fortunate, indeed, at the suggestion of Patrizia Jirka-Schmitz, in having been able to involve Christine Mitomi, Japanologist in Hamburg, in the project. Christine Mitomi not only provided an excellent translation into German – on which the English is based – of the essay written by Nobuo Tsūji, Director of the Chiba Prefecture Museum, but also contributed substantially to clarifying the links between Art Nouveau glass and East Asian art by furnishing us with a great deal of specific information on these ties.

Ultimately, however, the work on this book and its results are due solely to the collector, Gerda Koepff. She took the step from the private sphere, to which collecting after all belongs, to the public, and linked this step with an act that, apart from representing the time-honoured practice of patronage of the arts, is the most encouragingly active approach imaginable to supporting museum work.

There is nothing haphazard about the Gerda Koepff Collection. It is the deliberate work of a personality, a person whose thoughts and feelings are reflected in it. In the wider context of a museum collection it makes excellent sense and is enormously enriching to keep such an ensemble together as shaped by an entirely individual viewpoint and make it permanently accessible to the public.

It is a great pleasure for us to be able to dedicate this volume to Gerda Koepff.

Helmut Ricke   Eva Schmitt

Acknowledgements

Without the unstinting aid of our French colleagues in museums, libraries and archives, the copious research required for this book would certainly have produced inadequate results, or would have remained piecemeal at best. We are extremely grateful for such kind assistance, for we are well aware that being granted permission to consult sources not yet evaluated is by no means a matter of course. This is especially true of the archive material relevant to Daum Frères in Nancy.

In Paris we are indebted particularly to Christiane Filloles of the Archives Départementales de la Ville de Paris for her untiring personal commitment. The same holds for our friend Jean-Luc Olivié, as well as Véronique Ayroles at the Centre du Verre of the Musée des Arts Décoratifs. At the Musée d'Orsay Philippe Thiébaut and Marie-Madeleine Massé have been extremely helpful as were Anne-Laure Carré and Christiane Delpy at the Musée National des Techniques; Brigitte Belorgey at Sageret publishers; Dany Sautot, Pascaline Pascal and Alphonse Goberville at the museum and archives of the Cristallerie de Baccarat, Paris and Baccarat; Janine Milliard at the Photothèque of the Archives Municipales de Meudon and Tamara Préaud at the Archives de la Manufacture de Sèvres.

In Nancy thanks are due first and foremost to Mireille Bouvet, Jacques Guillaume and Pascal Thiébaut at the Service Régional de l'Inventaire de Lorraine. We also wish to extend our thanks to Valerie Thomas and the archivist Françoise Sylvestre at the Musée de l'Ecole de Nancy, who have been extremely helpful; Martine Mathias, Francine Roze and René Cuénot at the Musée Lorrain; Béatrice Salmon at the Musée des Beaux-Arts; Michèle Renson and Bernard Hanry at the Archives Municipales de la Ville de Nancy; Martine Heuraux-Chatelain of the Etat civil de la Ville de Nancy; as well as Christophe Bardin, who has now finished his dissertation on Daum Frères at the Université II, Nancy.

Our particular thanks go to the Société SAGEM, Paris, now owners of Daum, for so generously permitting us to publish so many photographs of drawings and materials from their archives free of charge. At the Archives Municipales de Lunéville we found Joël Moris and Martine Krummenacker very supportive as was Frédéric Morillon of the Service Patrimoine Expositions de la Ville de Vierzon.

At the Corning Museum of Glass, Corning, NY, our colleague Susanne Frantz readily made pieces available to us and Gail Bardhan of the Rakow Library at Corning provided us with invaluable support.

Yoriko Mizuta, Curator of the Hokkaidō Museum of Modern Art in Sapporo, was unswerving in her efforts to help us in the difficult search for the numerous Japanese publications that have appeared recently on Art Nouveau and Jugendstil glass and in transcribing the titles.

Susanne Netzer at the Kunstgewerbemuseum, Berlin, Ursula Lienert and Thomas Berg at the Museum für Kunst und Gewerbe, Hamburg, and Karin Rühl at the Glasmuseum Frauenau aided us by giving us last-minute permission to reprint photographs and information on their collections. Help was also forthcoming from Helena Brožková at the Museum of Applied Arts, Prague, Constanza Arvani-Kotta at the library of the Schule für Gestaltung, Zurich, Harald Riege at the Augustiner Museum library in Freiburg im Breisgau, Imke Mees at the Museum für Ostasiatische Kunst library in Cologne and especially Anne-Marie Katins and Marianne Dunas at the library of the museum kunst palast in Düsseldorf.

In botanical questions Werner Gelius-Dietrich of the Botanical Institute at Düsseldorf University placed his specialist knowledge of the field at our disposal. Joseph Jurt, Professor of Philosophy at the Albert-Ludwigs University, Freiburg im Breisgau, tracked down references on Robert de Montesquiou, which had been virtually untraceable. Bernd Hakenjos of the Hetjens-Museum, Düsseldorf, gave us valuable pointers on many issues related to Emile Gallé.

We wish to extend our heartfelt thanks to those who contributed essays and worked on compiling the catalogue entries, as well as to Ute Ricke-Immel and Hans Schmitt, who helped edit the texts, to the translators – Jane Smith and David Radzinowicz – and to the copy editor, Michele Schons.

The burden of bringing this work to publication fell to the lot of Gabriele Ebbecke, who mastered the task with unshakeable calm and without ever losing her sense of humour. It has been a delight to work with her and Rainald Schwarz, who has designed the book so skilfully and imaginatively.

For their prompt and unfailing assistance in revising the book for the English-language edition we are additionally indebted to our colleagues and friends in France and Germany: Meike Annuss, Altonaer Museum, Hamburg; Christian Cau, Archives Départementales de Bordeaux; Frédérique Desmet, Archives Municipales de Châlon-en-Champagne; Hendrik Eder, Staatsarchiv Hamburg; Yvon Fleck, Meisenthal; François Le Tacon, Ludres; Nathalie Tailleur, Musée des Beaux-Arts, Nancy, and Agnès Vatican, Archives Municipales de Bordeaux.

H. R. and E. S.

Thoughts on the Collection: A Conversation with Gerda Koepff[*]

When, as an outsider, one looks in retrospect at Gerda Koepff and her collection, everything seems easy to understand. On the one hand, one sees an active woman – jointly responsible for both the administration and workforce of a large family business, educated and interested in art and culture – and, on the other, an extraordinary collection of Art Nouveau glass that she established. One falls prey to hackneyed notions. Obviously a dream has come true here, a retreat has been created, a possibility for counteracting the tough world of business, something to draw on as a source of fresh energy. One imagines that the businesswoman has also brought prudent planning to bear on the private activity of collecting, keeping results and goals clearly in view.

Yet such cliché-ridden thoughts often prove deceptive. I know, dear Frau Koepff, that things have developed rather differently in your case. Since this chapter in your life is virtually closed now, we might perhaps try to sum it up. What was your motivation then and how did everything begin?

I can't really give a straight answer to that. I didn't decide to collect; it just happened. I saw six little Bohemian vases in delicate colours that I liked as a set and I wanted to give them to my mother as a birthday present, but she gave them right back to me. To her generation, Art Nouveau was tantamount to kitsch.

I subsequently bought several vases without any particular intention; our big new living room provided lots of space for decorative objects. So a rather indiscriminate hotchpotch was assembled, consisting of enamelled Gallé vases, plus some etched with a hydrangea motif, Joseph-Gabriel Argy-Rousseau's 'spider', one or two Daum objects, some Lötzes and a very fine piece by Christopher Dresser. My interest was awakened and deepened when a Munich dealer in Jugendstil, using his pieces as examples, demonstrated the differences between, and distinctive characteristics of, the individual glass artists and explained the techniques they employed.

I began to see – and to buy! Nothing was further from my mind than establishing a collection conceived and built up according to plan as a welcome distraction from professional life. It just started off purely and simply as fun and aesthetic delight in beautiful objects and a general preference for Art Nouveau glass.

Then, one day, I was offered a large *jardinière* (cat. no. 87) and several other pieces from the estate of a well-known silversmith, Nicolaus Trübner. The glass was by Daum, with silver mounts by Trübner. There were links between the Daum brothers and Trübner through visits to the most important exhibitions in France. At one time Daum had made glass so that it could be mounted, or even had to be. The *jardinière* is a particularly splendid piece, both the glass and the Trübner mount. I bought it and this represented a decisive step towards collecting.

In our house I was able to display this showy, highly ornamental ensemble appropriately and to great effect, but not later in my small flat. The Karlsruhe Landesmuseum seemed to me to be just the right place for Trübner since he was an artist from Baden, so I loaned the pieces from his estate to it.

Then began a more intensive involvement, at first with Daum, then with Emile Gallé and the Ecole de Nancy. Now I wanted to know, to understand, to see more accurately and be able to discriminate, so I began to study specialist publications. A sort of intellectual challenge grew out of this preoccupation, accompanied by a decision to acquire important pieces. I wanted to have them around me, to keep seeing them from different angles and pick them up. Their exquisiteness is revealed only when you see and touch them.

For a long time I made no attempt to contact museums, probably because I was unconsciously afraid they would try to influence me and make me lose my nerve. Somehow it was a highly individual process, as I realized afterwards – with one exception: quite soon after acquiring a particularly interesting Daum vase I looked up Professor Dr. Brigitte Klesse, then director of the Museum für Angewandte Kunst in Cologne, and this contact grew into an exchange of ideas that was important to me.

What then happened might be called 'learning by doing' – with each new piece I was better able to recognize typical features, distinguishing characteristics and similarities. It is impossible from the outset to predict what a process of this kind may lead to and to plan it. Living with the collection caused questions, focal points and, very gradually, a sense of direction to emerge.

Something important, therefore, evolved almost as if by chance. Nevertheless, was the desire there from a certain point to give things more shape – to find something like a concept for the collection?

I was forced to limit myself when I moved into a smaller flat and so I decided to concentrate on Art Nouveau. When I acquired the Trübner estate around 1968, the Daum brothers' work was still completely overshadowed by Emile Gallé in the eyes of most experts and on the art market. I thought – once I was acquainted with the Trübner pieces – they were unjustly undervalued. The more I saw of the Daums' work the more I was convinced of the quality of the workmanship and its value as art.

Earlier on I had studied the influence of Japonism on French Art Nouveau, on Gallé and especially Rousseau. My eye had perhaps been schooled in East Asian forms and motifs – on some fine pieces of porcelain and bronzes in my parents' home.

I also intended my collection to demonstrate the paramount importance of Gallé's work and his personality for the time, but I also consciously decided to concern myself with other glass artists and artisans, with their own styles, as independent craftsmen and as highly skilled artists, each in his own right.

The collection has three focal points: Gallé, Daum and Rousseau. Eugène Michel, Burgun, Schverer & Co. and Désiré Christian are each represented by several works that clearly show how important they are – even when compared with the 'big names'. There will always be gaps in my collection, whether I want this to be so or not. I have no Gallé or Daum pieces with historical subject matter, hardly any landscapes or portrait pieces. Realistic subject matter didn't seem to fit in with my conception of the collection; I also have the space for only a few large vases.

I didn't have an ideal of a complete collection. At some point I had the feeling of having reached the end; the collection had a look. And that was where I wanted to stop. Because everything has just grown the way it is, I couldn't have done anything else.

Some wishes have remained unfulfilled. I would dearly love to have particular pieces by Philippe-Joseph Brocard and Philippe Wolfers. I was unexpectedly able to make a wish come true with a vase by Alphonse-Georges Reyen. In addition, three other vases, illustrated here, by Gallé, Michel and Escalier de Cristal, were important to me to round off the collection.

Art Nouveau glass marks the close of an era – both the apogee and the end of an upper-middle-class culture and it shows all the symptoms of a far-reaching crisis. If I have understood you correctly, your point of departure has always been the fascination exerted by the individual object. Above and beyond that, do you feel any sort of kinship with the fin de siècle *and its intellectual atmosphere?*

My way to Art Nouveau glass was not through an inner relationship with the art and exponents of that over-refined society. It was the glass I was interested in. That was what made me want to find out about the intellectual side and the conditions that gave rise to it. I read Proust – with great enjoyment – but I wouldn't have wanted to live in that world. I wouldn't have been a Proustian figure in a lace dress, strolling idly about under a parasol musing on lines from Victor Hugo! The decadence, the over-refinement, dandyism, the unrealistic attitudes to the world that shaped the *fin de siècle* are foreign to me. Good glass was made as luxury items, but it isn't merely as such that they express their era. In the sur-

roundings in which they are displayed in my home, in light, unadorned rooms, they are far removed from the ambience of their own era. They are no longer part of a splendid decorative scheme and setting; they are works of art in their own right. All the qualities of craftsmanship and art are displayed; the pieces aren't standing in a showcase in a dimly lit room. You can pick them up, study and enjoy even the most minute detail. As individual works of art they have an emotional value that is both timely and timeless. What makes them so special for me is that you don't need a bridge to the *fin de siècle* to be enthralled by them.

Collectors can afford to have this highly subjective attitude. The collection is also, however, to be viewed from an art-historical point of view. In the scholarly essays in this volume the links with *fin de siècle* literature and the visual arts must also be addressed and shown.

Gallé was bound up as an artist with a particular circle in society and a prevailing attitude to life even though there was that other side, the crafts and entrepreneurial aspect. This is particularly true of the most beautiful and technically sophisticated Gallé pieces, his representations of bats, butterflies and cicadas as denizens of the night that can be linked in their symbolic significance to the literature of the period as quotations. The dragonfly plays a special role because it's ambivalent. It's not just fascinating because of its iridescent beauty; it's also a cruel insect. It's a symbol of the enigmatic, cruel femme fatale cultivated at that time in poetry and the fine arts. From Gallé's Dragonfly Woman to Fernand Khnopff's panther-woman – fear and seduction differ only in nuances.

The material has quite obviously played an important role in your decision for Art Nouveau glass. Glass is evidently to you a unique artistic medium.

There's no simple answer to the question of why I decided on Art Nouveau or Jugendstil glass. My decision back then was linked with glass as a material and vice versa. It was Art Nouveau glass that made me start collecting systematically. Perhaps I do really have a special relationship with glass: I can't explain it. I would never have collected silver or porcelain, but would have liked to collect East Asian art or carpets or textiles. As for glass, it needn't be Art Nouveau; it could be modern glass as well. In Art Nouveau glass I see a development leading to modern glass via the increased freedom in the handling of glass as a material.

In my family home there were some pieces of antique furniture together with good modern utilitarian and decorative objects: Bampi cache-pots, Karlsruhe majolica and Murano vases. We children had the fragile Bimini glass animals on a shelf. Decorative objects mean more to me than pictures; I have an eye and a memory for objects.

Alphonse-Georges Reyen, Paris
Vase with lady's-slipper and
butterfly, 1904
H 21 Ø 12.1 cm
Signature: *A Mlle Goury / Souvenir
amicale / A. Reyen / 1904*, drypoint
etched on the underside

Light brown smoky glass over
irregular blue, inclusions of
streaky pink, green and opaque
lemon yellow, dark brown
overlay. On the inner wall matt
etching with traces of trailing
prunts, some of which are blue-
tipped, flowing down from the
rim and etched in shallow relief.
Decoration on the outer wall
in double relief etching on a
ground finely textured to
resemble bark; relief engraved
and polished like the outer wall.

of its distinctive transparent character, thereby acquiring more freedom in design and formal potential. Gallé then arrived at the 'alienation effect' by dirtying it and creating patina. He even went a step further by handling glass like wood. *Marqueterie de verre* is an intarsia technique he also used for his furniture. The transformation of glass as a material opens up possibilities for new designs and forms. Glass is no longer just a material for vessels but also for works that are so close to sculpture that they can't be called vases. It has taken on a new quality.

Gallé went this way very resolutely in his late work. My bowl with a foot and raised applications (cat. no. 61) is a prime example of this sculptural approach to form. It and similar works represent the height of Gallé's work in a development from which the freer handling of the material in modern glass derives.

Daum, Michel, Christian et al. adhered more to convention and tradition: their pieces in glass remained vessels. However, glass as a material was markedly changed by Daum. Fused-in powdered glass and above all the fused-on incrustations in various layers and colours created a new effect typical of Daum glass. The high-quality workmanship attained by Gallé in his marquetry glass is matched by Daum's *intercalaire* glass. The enamel painting on different layers of overlay creates a unique spatial effect. An enigmatic mood is evoked by a beauty that gives these pieces a lofty status of their own.

Rousseau and Michel retained the transparency of glass for parts of their vases, thus creating a distinctive effect through the contrast with the casing and applications.

Yet, apart from the handling of the material, there are thematic groupings in the collection that are, of course, in part on account of artists' preferences at the time but also partly reflect your own way of seeing things. What focal points have emerged from the process of collecting?

I have tried to arrive at contexts and links via individual pieces in order to make themes recognizable. That took a great many steps from piece to piece. Not until then was there anything like planning or a targeted search for objects that might show either a line of development or a shift in focus.

All Art Nouveau artists depicted flowers and plants. There are noticeable preferences for large flowers, such as the lotus, waterlilies, lilies, the iris, wisteria and orchids. In the work of Daum more modest flowers, such as wood hyacinths, wood anemones, liverwort and bleeding heart, also occur. All these, be they large or small, are more than decoration; they are, from a botanical point of view, accurately rendered. The symbolic content of the individual flowers, such as chrysanthemums, the iris or the lotus, was taken over in part from East Asia but is also typical of the time. Wild flowers, especially the Lorraine thistle, stand for love of country

Escalier de Cristal, Paris
Cylindrical vase with dragon's-wort, c. 1885 (?)
H 29.4 Ø 14.9 cm
Signature: *Escalier de Cristal Paris*, matt engraved on the underside

Thick-walled colourless glass with three colourless vegetal applications and fine deep intaglio cutting and engraving.

Talking with you I keep noticing that you are more interested in the technical possibilities of working in glass than other collectors seem to be. The question of how something is done is just as important for you as what it expresses. You evidently consider the possibilities of the material as being part of the content and form.

That is certainly not entirely wrong. For Art Nouveau glassmakers early glass was clear glass with a surface decoration either in enamel or ground and cut. These limited design possibilities were soon overcome by depriving glass in part of its transparency with *mouches* ('seeds', or minute air bubbles), streaks, metal leaf and fused-in colour. The development of casing made it possible to decorate both the surface and the batch. Cutting the casing also created depth and perspective.

In a further step to opaque glass and especially to the various types of hardstone glass, glass was deprived

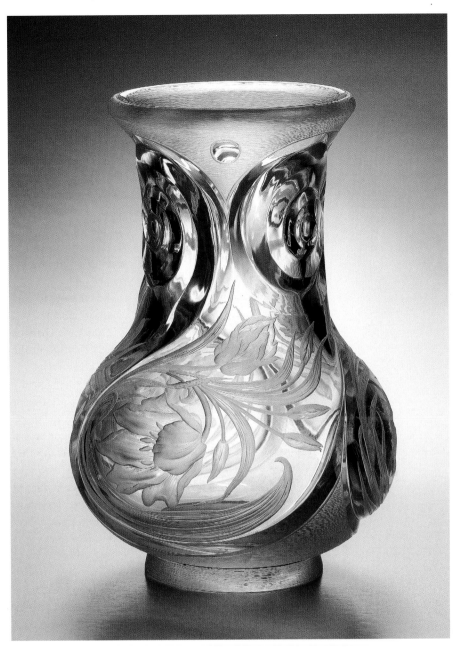

The love of nature and the native flora that links the members of the Ecole de Nancy is not expressed in decoration alone. With great empathy and botanical precision these pieces capture the shape of a flower, part of a flower or its fruit. The flower appears on the vessel wall in the decoration, often in various stages of development. My collection contains several examples of this: for instance, the columbine vase (cat. no. 41), the vase called 'Les Bleuets' (cornflowers; cat. no. 42) or the Gallé 'datura' study (cat. no. 38), a Daum vase in the form of a poppy seed capsule (cat. no. 103), a waterlily bud (cat. no. 93), a snapdragon flower (cat. no. 110) or an ornamental gourd (cat. no. 118). This melding of form and decoration certainly doesn't just fulfil a formal or aesthetic function, but also expresses the artists' profound yet unsentimental feeling for nature – as is the botanical precision with which plants and flowers are depicted by Gallé, even though they have symbolic and emotional content.

The symbolic plane is relatively easy to decode with floral motifs. Things aren't quite so simple with underwater scenes.

The first thing that made me want to buy Gallé *aquatique* vases was the high quality of the glass. I can't quite grasp the meaning of water as a symbol as it is expressed for Gallé and his era in literature, music and the visual arts. Such symbolic content is probably revealed only after total immersion in how art was experienced then. With pieces of such exceptional quality, and they include the *aquatiques*, I admire the work of the glassmaker, the craftsman, just as much as I do the glass artist's. Still, the artisan's skill isn't the sole explanation for the magic, the secret of these and many other pieces. For all the consummate workmanship of the Daum pieces, they don't match the inexplicable aura and freedom of Gallé.

Your collection is noticeably shaped by pieces with a Chinese or Japanese background.

Like all works of art from the latter half of the nineteenth century, Art Nouveau glass was decisively influenced by the impact made on European art by the fine and decorative arts of the Far East. This influence is one of the most deeply rooted in French glass, which is readily apparent in the forms, motifs and symbols taken over from it or, indirectly, in the new way of seeing things. I have found it fascinating to show this in my collection. All Rousseau and Ernest Léveillé pieces show this influence. Gallé, too, took over elements of East Asian art early on, for instance, mounts, classical bronze forms.

Eugène Michel, Paris
Vase with iris, carnation and crown imperial (*Fritillaria imperialis*), c. 1900
H 22.8 Ø 16.1 cm
Signature: *E. Michel* (underlined from M to h), engraved on the underside

Colourless glass with floor attached. Decorated with three polished arcs and spirals in mitre cutting, with a single printy cut between each; in the lower zone and on the rim partly matt ground with horizontally positioned hatching in line engraving. The floral motifs in sophisticated intaglio cutting with line engraving. For a design by Ernest Léveillé, published in 1902 (without further references), on the same model see Duncan, *Salons*, 1998, p. 304.

and natural beauty and, after the loss of Lorraine to Germany in 1871, also carry political connotations. Toxic and intoxicating plants form a special group: the poppy in numerous variants, the autumn crocus, etc. Some pieces suggest opium dreams. Intoxication-induced imagery and dreams were part and parcel of what artists experienced at the time.

Often flowers are shown on the body of a single vase at different stages of its development: as a bud, in full bloom or fading, thus symbolizing transience. They express the melancholy feeling of waxing and waning that was so widespread in *fin de siècle* art. Here, too, I prefer reality, the beauty of plants and flowers, to what they symbolize. Gallé, gardener and botanist: I'd love to have seen the flower beds he had laid out in front of his workshop, also for his staff to study.

Emile Gallé, Nancy
Vase with scabiosa blooms,
c. 1893/94
H 26.8 Ø 8.7 cm
Signature: *Cristallerie de Gallé
à Nancy* in contour drawing of
an orchid, also honeycomb
texturing and *modèle et décor
déposés* on the underside of the
floor, drypoint etched and
painted with dark red flat
colour; above it round sticker
with: *EMILE GALLÉ NANCY.
PARIS No. 723* in black print
(numerals handwritten in
black ink)

Green glass, inner wall matt
etched, decoration on the
outer wall in simple, low relief
drypoint etching and in painting
with dark red flat colour, gold
and opaque enamels in white,
light green, purple, honey
yellow and salmon pink.

They accompany him throughout his work. The Far East had a formative influence on Art Nouveau glass.

That is also why I have incorporated a group of late Gallé vases with bronze mounts in my collection. I tend to find silver mounts irritating because of the gloss of the silver, but even more because they are superficially supposed to make the glass 'more precious', often without assimilating the mood of the glass. It's a different matter altogether with bronze and wooden mounts, which enhance the object, support the effect it creates as an integral part of the whole. I managed, at an auction in Monaco, to acquire a portfolio with sketches by Gallé. It contains the designs for the bronze mounts of my vases in meticulous drawings.

Now we have heard something about the focus of the collection and the conception underlying it. I should also be interested to know how the decision to buy was reached in individual cases. Who helped you and according to what criteria were decisions taken?

Why and how I bought a particular piece? Never really spontaneously – except in the very beginning – but rather on the basis of seeing it together with pieces I already had after I had a 'picture' of how my collection might look. At the beginning deciding wasn't such a straightforward process. Later I wanted to clarify my ideas on the development individual glass artists had gone through and not just according to stylistic or formal characteristics. The large number of new or typical techniques also had to be demonstrated. With time an overview of an artist's oeuvre was distilled from elements of the individual pieces. What are exciting are pieces that don't look familiar, are exceptional, somehow 'different'. They're the ones I keep returning to.

Quality is evaluated according to neutral criteria as far as technique and workmanship are concerned. This sort of knowledge can be learnt. The quintessence eludes understanding: it's a blend of instinct and intuition with a highly personal aesthetic idea that is rooted in the collector's personality and can scarcely be explained. That is the crux of all collections.

I could never be preoccupied with the collection as a distraction from the daily grind of work. I had to be free, with an open mind, in order to be receptive to a new piece and acquire it. Some of my most important pieces came to me in this way, because my receptivity to their aura wasn't disturbed by externals. Even though some things are best left to felicitous coincidence, one does need the support of Art Nouveau dealers and intermediaries. How well does he empathize with the plans and ideas for a collection and the collector as an individual, his or her personal style and taste? Many important pieces in my collection are indebted to this joint understanding. I am grateful for bonds of friendship that have grown out of years of such cooperation. Here I should

especially like to mention Pier-Carlo Casati, who has a fine nose for what is distinctive about my conception and my taste and to whom I owe some very fine pieces.

My friends Brigitte Leonhardt and Wolfgang Ehrlich are the 'co-creators' of this collection. Art Nouveau brought us together more than twenty years ago and will remain our never-ending story. Through our talks a red thread has gradually emerged in collecting and so has my decision to establish a collection systematically. They have contributed substantially to ensuring that my collection has assumed its present 'look' through an acquisitions policy. I am indebted to their mediation in finding the appropriate place in which the collection can continue to have the impact I want it to: the Glasmuseum Hentrich in Düsseldorf's museum kunst palast.

You have touched on what is certainly not a routine decision, to bequeath your collection to a museum designated in your will and thus make it permanently accessible to the public. What hopes and expectations are linked for you with this decision?

The feeling gradually grew on me that something of value and significance in its own right had developed with the collection, something that ought to remain intact. I have never even considered selling it myself or having my daughter do so. I have my doubts about whether the collection can spark off a more broad-based discussion of Art Nouveau – except in specialist circles. Of course it can be an aesthetic pleasure if viewers have a feeling for the sensitivity, for the sophisticated tastes of this period.

It isn't important to me to become well known to the public through this decision. What does matter a great deal to me, however, is what will happen to the collection in future. Not only that it is seen but above all the way it is exhibited, the arrangement and grouping of the pieces, so that something of the idea underlying the collection – which I didn't develop until I was already collecting – becomes clear. My hope for this book is a thoroughly grounded, accurate description of the individual pieces and scholarly essays that will broaden knowledge of Art Nouveau and elucidate it through the collection. There are still some 'blank spaces'!

* Helmut Ricke spoke with Gerda Koepff for the preparation of this volume.

Helmut Ricke

Art Nouveau Glass: Origins, Sources, Developments

In the course of the nineteenth century the decorative arts in Europe became increasingly dominated by mechanization and industrialization. If one seeks the theoretical basis of this vehemently debated change, one finds it, on the one hand, in the demand for methods of craftsmanship that would do justice to the materials used and, on the other, in a reversion to work of past eras that was deemed exemplary. As with the other visual arts, especially contemporary architecture, the decorative and applied arts were, almost without exception, under the sway of historicism, which involved borrowing from whatever great European style happened to be fashionable at a given time. As the furnishings of middle-class and aristocratic dwellings, such products contributed considerably to shaping the self-image of an era that viewed history as a revitalizing force and, as such, one that might be studied. Moreover, an intense, albeit romantically transfigured, feeling – increasingly reinforced by the emergence of nation states – was evolving that creating something new might be possible only on the foundations laid by the achievements and experiences of earlier generations.

The atmosphere of uncertainty resulting from the intellectual and social upheavals of the time led to a reappraisal of the values of past eras, which were invoked with admiration. An attempt was made – at least in the decorative and applied arts – to uphold these rediscovered standards with the new means available through science and technology, the ultimate aim being to surpass them wherever possible.

Following the 1851 Great Universal Exhibition in London, the first of its kind, artists throughout Europe began to create objects that met the highest design standards, drawing on period styles. The new standards advocated by historicism, which were primarily directed at consummate workmanship, informed the decorative arts in the latter half of the nineteenth century. Around 1880 these standards represented the point of departure for a second step, a highly distinctive art commensurate with the aesthetic ideals of the time – a 'new art', or Art Nouveau.

Reassimilation of the art of the past had attained a dynamic of its own by the 1860s. Together with movements aligned with European styles, Middle Eastern and Indian art served as models, as was unmistakably the case in France, for instance in the work of Philippe-Joseph Brocard,[1] as did occasionally ancient Egyptian art

and, as a growing trend, works from the Far East. In these currents of exoticism, fascination with what was unknown and foreign replaced the old and the familiar. Priority was now given to what was distinctive and no longer to what was amusingly decorative and entertainingly bizarre – as in eighteenth-century chinoiserie designs – and it became the object of serious study. For the first time in relatively recent history, the underlying assumption of Western cultural superiority, which had previously been taken for granted, was called into question. The reaction of the art world was enthralment rather than rejection. With the European stance as questionable as it was, the Far Eastern way of viewing things became revelation, linked with hopes of escape from the prevailing aesthetic crisis.

The influence of Japanese art on French painting, such as that of Edouard Manet and the Impressionists on down to Henri de Toulouse-Lautrec, Paul Gauguin and Vincent van Gogh, need not be gone into here.[2] Since Japan had taken part in the 1862 International Exhibition in London, after opening its doors to trade with the West in 1854, a flood of objects in wood, lacquer, ivory and bronze and an especially large number of Japanese coloured woodcuts had conveyed some impression of the sophisticated art of that Far Eastern country. With designs based on line, the free handling of the picture plane as a value in its own right, with compositions often arranged along diagonals and extremely taut yet always balanced and harmonious, Japanese art exerted a profound influence on European painting and graphic art. A genuine attempt was made to understand the artistic principles underlying Japanese art, which was not only the subject of artistic investigation, but also of scholarly inquiry, which had become highly specialized by the 1870s.[3]

Starting from different assumptions and true to their essence, the decorative arts did not approach the phenomenon of East Asia in the same way as the fine arts did. Here knowledge of Chinese vessels, which had been imported to Europe without interruption since the seventeenth century, had provided a foundation. The same holds for Japanese porcelain, which was imported by the Dutch – although in more limited quantities – via the Dutch East India Company or their trading post on Dejima in Nagasaki Bay.[4]

From the 1860s avid collectors became increasingly interested in earlier Chinese and Japanese art outside the classic areas of porcelain and fine china, and soon became adept at evaluating it by sophisticated means. The brothers Edmond and Jules de Goncourt, doyens of the contemporary intellectual scene, possessed, for instance, a large collection of East Asian *objets de vertu*, which the salon culture of the time made well known in cultured circles. The collections amassed by Samuel Bing, Philippe Burty, a connoisseur of porcelain, and others also belong in this context. Some of these collec-

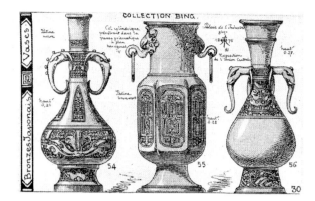

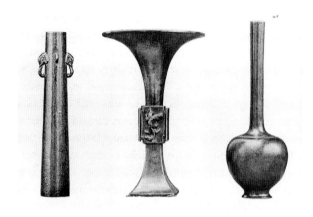

tions had even been documented in books by the 1870s and 1880s.[5] The writings of Rutherford Alcock on the occasion of and following the 1862 International Exhibition in London were widely read. Other early writings include the publications of George Ashdown Audsley and James L. Bowes on Japanese ceramics.[6]

A rich repertoire of forms was, therefore, available to craftsmen working in the East Asian style. The same holds for ornamentation, which no longer had to draw on the traditional decor of eighteenth-century Chinese porcelain or contemporaneous Japanese wares. A revival of the small figures or purely ornamental surface design typical of chinoiserie soon proved to be a dead end, playing virtually no role in the departures of the 1860s. New impulses provided by Japanese carved lacquer, textiles, bronze vessels, sword decoration and other objects proved of far greater consequence.

The crucial impetus, however, was furnished here, too, by prints, with new ideas being gleaned largely from Japanese coloured woodcuts. Unlike painting, however, which from the outset strove to reach a deeper understanding of Japanese art, the reception of the woodcut in the applied arts was at first restricted primarily to the mere adoption of motifs. The quintessence of Japanese art had not yet been grasped. In the 1870s the decoration of contemporary faience based on Japanese models tended to look like a paratactic, rather alien afterthought and Japanese forms were arbitrarily transferred to ceramics from different contexts. Occasional attempts to enhance small-scale European landscapes on ceramics or glass by including the framing elements, motifs and dec-

oration characteristic of the Japanese graphic arts also tended to produce unsatisfactory results. This is true of work by firms such as J. Vieillard & Cie. and of Emile Gallé's ceramics as well as some of his early glass.[7]

In glass, Eugène Rousseau and artists working for Escalier de Cristal, a company run by Pannier Frères, were the first to assimilate the East Asian style with convincing results (cat. nos. 1–9, 16, 17). Even they, however, still approached their work in the same way as contemporaries who were biased towards European art: they regarded the relatively free modification and new interpretation of traditional East Asian art as their task and personal achievement.

The unknown designer of the vase in cat. no. 9, for one, borrowed the form of his vessel from either Chinese or Japanese ceramics. Its simple shape, interrupted by two glossy, metallic-looking elephant-head handles is quite common. Handles of this kind, symbols of peace and strength, also occur in East Asian bronzes (illus. left). The classic form of such ceramic vessels features a baluster-shaped body, which is square in section, with a round mouth and foot.[8] The French designer took over this formal principle, but decorated his vessel with a frame of the kind used on Japanese Arita or Imari porcelain, which he filled with a figurative motif. This, in turn, derives from a Hokusai woodcut, which the designer had not seen in the original, but which he must have admired in the standard work on Japanese art of 1883 by Louis Gonse.[9] The decorative programme is augmented with a freely engraved lotus flower, leaf decoration and tall grasses. The elephant and lotus recall Buddhist cult vessels. Since all these interlinked elements are of East Asian origin, Western eyes might receive the impression of aesthetic unity. To the Japanese viewer, however, this vase would surely represent a hotchpotch of misconstrued and arbitrarily deployed ornamental elements, which, divested of their content, have been reduced to a purely decorative status.

A similar case in point is a vase by Auguste Jean (cat. no. 15). The decoration consists of grasses and flowers, which, as a direct quotation that is highly reminiscent of Japanese brocade, is typical of Japanese autumnal arrangements, occurring in various materials on implements and vessels of different kinds.[10] The outsize fish shown snapping at an insect does not belong in this context. Breaking with the reticent calm of the original autumnal decoration, which suggests transience and farewell, here the fish, depicted in the flora growing on the banks of a stream or pond, is a reinterpretation.

Particularly impressive combinations of elements from different contexts were the forte of both François Eugène Rousseau, who must surely be regarded as the most skilled French glass artist among those in the nineteenth century who first adopted East Asian motifs, and his successor, Ernest Léveillé. The principal motif on a monumental vase with a leaping carp (cat. no. 5) bears a

Double carp, China, Ch'ien Lung (1735–96), light green jade with brown flecks, cut and ground
H 19 W 10.5 cm
Museum für Kunst und Gewerbe, Hamburg

close resemblance to the Hokusai woodcut on which it was modelled, yet its handling of material is obviously associated with work in carved red lacquer. What is new here is the successful attempt, made by exploiting the physical properties of glass, to convey an impression of water and thus show the fish, despite the use of false colour, in its natural habitat. A distinctive and attractive aspect is the combination of a vase shaped by East Asian influences with a mount, possibly made by a different hand and added c. 1890, whose forms recall those of the Rococo. It represents a highly original revitalization of the close ties forged in the latter half of the eighteenth century between East Asian and European art.

The reinterpretation of Chinese small sculpture and vessels of semi-precious stones or pieces of rough jade (illus. below) as ornamental vases or *jardinières* in coloured glass typical of many designs by Rousseau and Léveillé (cat. nos. 6, 7) changed their original character as precious, coveted objects to items that brought good luck. These valuables have become part of the decor in luxurious bourgeois homes and satisfy collectors' desire for objects with an exotic look and feel. Yet these pieces do not give the impression of being mere imitations in a cheaper material. On the one hand, the development of new types of glass similar to semi-precious stones, on which Emile Gallé was hard at work,[11] represented to his contemporaries a triumph of modern science and glass technology they greatly appreciated. On the other hand, Rousseau and Léveillé succeeded admirably in lending their objects a distinctive character and doing justice to the material by rendering apparent the process by which they were made from molten, ductile glass.

In the hands of these same designers, a modest, stringently simple bamboo vase of the kind used in Japan to decorate rooms for the tea ceremony was translated into glass (cat. no. 8), becoming an ornamental object in its own right, a showpiece to be displayed in elegantly decorated European drawing rooms. Its original purpose, effectively serving the ends of simplicity but only in conjunction with other objects, was, however, reversed. This manner of dealing with models from East Asia is also reflected in the way a motif widespread in China, the double carp (illus. top left), was reinterpreted in Europe.[12] Objects by Pannier Frères and their circle turned vessels redolent of symbolic connotations or small sculptures executed in rock crystal and jade, of a type that even today are given in China as wedding presents to bring good fortune, into showy decorative vases (cat. nos. 16, 17).

When considering the first generation of glass art influenced by East Asian art in a broader context, one must not overlook, apart from the artistic aspect, the market issue of supply and demand, which should never be underestimated when dealing with the applied and decorative arts. Since the 1860s the craze for East Asian art had assumed all the characteristics of a fashion move-

ment, cutting a broad swathe through a receptive public. Since original pieces from China and Japan were hard to come by and virtually unaffordable, the need arose for – not cheap, but far more reasonably priced – substitutes in the Far Eastern style. Glass was the ideal material for satisfying these consumer desires.[13] New colouring methods based on systematic chemical research as well as inventive glassmaking techniques, such as press moulding – adopted at progressive factories, such as Appert Frères – were the means by which the desired colours and textures were achieved. The Far Eastern-inspired pieces by Rousseau and Léveillé, Pannier Frères, Baccarat, Auguste Jean, among others, became greatly admired, indeed highly sought-after luxury items.

A substantial part of Emile Gallé's early work can thus be classified without qualification (cat. no. 21).[14] The remaining market segments were covered by the glass made in the late 1870s and early 1880s. Gallé's production ranged from forms in the antique manner and Romantic borrowings from the Middle Ages via Renaissance quotations (cat. no. 19), Baroque cups and objects in the Rococo and Louis Seize styles to oriental-inspired decoration and fantasy creations with an Egyptian look.[15]

The only approach productive for the development of Art Nouveau glass art, however, was the exoticism moulded by East Asian influences that originated in Rousseau's circle and was taken up by Gallé. All that remained was for the step to be taken from the superficial adoption of motifs to a genuine understanding of the principles underlying the Far Eastern – primarily Japanese – conception of form and design.

Emile Gallé's key role in these developments as a pioneering artist is undisputed. During the 1880s he gradually emancipated himself from adapting Far Eastern motifs for solely decorative purposes (cat. nos. 19–21), an approach that still informed the celebrated carp vase he made for the 1878 Exposition Universelle in Paris (illus. p. 27, bottom). By combining such motifs with the newly developed oxide fusion techniques (cat. no. 20) and glass imitating semi-precious stones, he conceived a formal idiom that reflected a Japanese concept of nature and way of seeing. In 1889 he presented the results of his studies to the public as a major part of his contribution to the Paris Exposition Universelle.

Times of aesthetic uncertainty are often marked by a reversion to the safe ground of natural models. Accordingly, in Gallé's new pieces, elements of naturalism, which had been latent in the applied arts since mid-century and which informs some of Charles Gallé's work, were now combined with a notion of animate nature that sought to discover its inner being. With Gallé setting a pioneering example, the profound relationship between Japanese art and nature, i.e., the changing seasons, the cycles of growth and decay, of birth and death, had a far greater impact on the French decorative and

Vase in the form of a hollow tree stump, China, Ch'ing dynasty (eighteenth/nineteenth century), rock crystal, cut and ground
H 14 cm
Musée Cernuschi, Paris

Dish with bat, Japan, Satsuma, mid-nineteenth century, blown, cut and polished
H 10.4 W 13.2 L 18.1 cm
Suntory Museum, Tokyo

Vase of cased glass, China, Ch'ien Lung (1735–96), formerly in the Kunstgewerbemuseum, Berlin. From *Kunstgewerbeblatt* 1 (1885): 44

Chinese glass vases, formerly in the Kunstgewerbemuseum, Berlin. From *Kunstgewerbeblatt* 1 (1885): 40

applied arts than on contemporary painting, drawing and the graphic arts. This linkage represents the core of the main current in Art Nouveau, which is rightly called the 'genre Gallé'.

Everything else grew out of this deepened understanding of nature. It became the point of departure of poetic Symbolism formulated in Nancy, thus ultimately reinforcing the claim insistently made by Gallé that pieces representing the pinnacle of the decorative arts should be evaluated as original achievements of great art with all its potential for expression. This contention, which Gallé was not alone among his contemporaries in advancing, was certainly grounded in essentials on the Japanese conception of art, to which the Western distinction between the fine and the applied arts was foreign and which drew its evaluation criteria solely from the semantic content, the expressive powers and the standard of workmanship distinguishing a work of art.

There is no concrete evidence of Gallé having been inspired by Japanese glass art. With a stretch of the imagination one could view the mid-nineteenth-century bat dish in the Suntory Museum, Tokyo (illus. above, left), as anticipating Art Nouveau ideas. This dish, however, is, in turn – as Japanese glass art of the late Edo and early Meiji periods generally was – strongly under the sway of Western influence. Moreover, the bat motif establishes only a superficial link with the iconography of Gallé's repertoire of forms and pieces such as this must have been virtually unknown in nineteenth-century Europe.

However, Japan is in any case not the sole East Asian source of inspiration for Art Nouveau glass art. Beginning in the 1870s the Kunstgewerbemuseum in Berlin had, with Max von Brandt, the Imperial German envoy in Peking, as its intermediary, amassed an extensive collection of ancient and contemporary Chinese glass. By 1884, following the acquisition of a small group of eighteenth-century pieces, the collection comprised nearly four hundred objects and was the only one of its kind in Europe.[16] Since virtually nothing was known of this ancillary branch of Chinese art until then, Arthur Papst took the occasion of the most recent acquisitions to reproduce some of the pieces in the first issue of *Kunstgewerbeblatt*, the decorative arts monthly he edited from 1885. They were accompanied by information that he had for the most part gleaned from reading the imperial reign period marks on them and also owed to the collector von Brandt.[17]

No sooner had the article appeared than Gallé seems to have set off for Berlin to study the pieces.[18] The wide variety of forms represented by the pieces assembled in Berlin was probably of secondary importance to him (illus. below). In this respect not too many surprises were in store for him since these shapes were already known from pottery and porcelain. What must have lured Gallé were the illustrations showing two vessels, which today seem to anticipate the Art Nouveau pieces he would later create. In them he is likely to have found the answers to many of the questions he had had in the mid-1880s. The slender vase with plants and fluttering butterflies (illus. left), in particular, might at first glance be mistaken for one of the exquisitely cut 1890s Gallé studio pieces. The decoration on the neck and the foreign-looking double scroll between the plants are all that is recognizably East Asian about the piece.

His encounter with the originals may have been disappointing for the artist. Fortunately, one of the vases reproduced by Papst has been preserved. It does not quite match the expectations raised by the illustration (illus. p. 21). In a direct comparison the stark contrast between the light ground and the dark decoration makes the original look rather dry and less sensuously expressive. Nonetheless the vase, with its distinctive character – emphatically underscored by the wooden base – would seem to have served as a prototype for the work done by Gallé from the late 1890s. This observation applies to the combination of a body composed of swirling leaf forms with pronounced floral applications and especially to the conception of the vase as a free-standing sculpture,

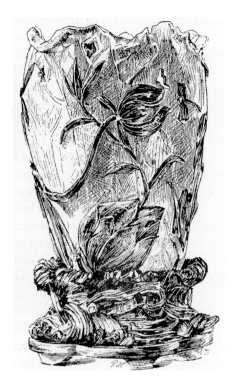

Left: Vase of cased glass on wooden stand, China, Ch'ien Lung (1735–96). From *Kunstgewerbeblatt* 1 (1885): 41

Right: The original cut and polished vase. H 15 cm Staatliche Museen zu Berlin – Preussischer Kulturbesitz. Kunstgewerbemuseum

which informed Gallé's late work. The lotus buds, flowers and leaves, which on the Chinese vase have sacral connotations, were similarly used by Gallé to decorate the extensive 'étrennes' group, conceived as New Year's presents for 1897/98.[19] Pieces of this type differ markedly from the bulk of what he produced during those years, suggesting a direct reference to Chinese models.

The general character of thick-walled Chinese vases, which, as virtually verbatim quotations, tend to follow the rules governing the cutting and working of semi-precious stones and jade, corresponds only to a limited extent with the design principles informing Western glass art, which, by contrast, developed from the process of glass-blowing. Consequently, their somewhat stiff, even harshly angular contours probably impressed Gallé less than their striking colouring. They would have re-affirmed Gallé's interest as a technician in the possibilities afforded by cased glass. Although he lost little time in leaving the influence of Chinese glass models behind in the studio pieces of the late 1880s, the studies he conducted in Berlin in 1885 had an unmistakable impact on the 1890s serial work, especially the factory-made glass from 1900 onwards. In design, the inexpensive, serially produced ware of this period is based largely on the principle of coloured decoration on a light ground (illus. p. 22, top).

All his working life, however, Gallé continued to draw on Japanese art as the crucial source of inspiration for his studio pieces. A small vase decorated with waterlilies in the Koepff Collection (cat. no. 23) incorporates the elements he used after 1889. In its reticent form, recalling Chinese designs, in its rejection of spectacular decoration in favour of a concise state-ment and in its inclusion of 'empty', albeit formed, space, this piece goes beyond most extant Gallé glass. It would, in fact, have been unthinkable without the knowledge of Japanese art. The principal motif, consisting of a bud and a wilting waterlily, has been depicted almost modestly. A detailed depiction of a waterlily in full bloom has been hidden from the uninitiated eye, on the underside of the vase. The result is a highly personal piece, aimed at the individual viewer – made to be picked up and turned around, felt and touched. Only in this way are the tactile qualities of its texture and the semantic content revealed as belonging to a *vase de tristesse*.

Even in the handling of the material this glass represents a consistent new departure. Any attempt to do justice to the physical properties of glass *qua* material in the conventional sense has been deliberately eschewed. Instead, the bluish purple mass tone looks black. Transparency has been deployed only in a few places to make the metal filing inclusions under the flowers on the wall glow mysteriously, as if from unfathomed depths. Unlike the piece made for the 1884 Exposition Universelle in Paris, content now took precedence over decoration, which merely did justice to the material. Even the utter denial of the material could no longer be precluded should this serve to heighten the expressive force of a piece. Thus a major principle of nineteenth-century crafts theory has been rejected and the step towards Art Nouveau taken.

Once the quintessential principles of Japanese art had been grasped and assimilated, the practice of taking over motifs as direct quotations from prints or other models receded into the background in Gallé's work. Japanese art does, nonetheless, always remain present on an almost subliminal level. It came to the fore sporadically, in unconcealed allusions, and involved a free handling of the repertoire of Japanese themes and motifs that were by then widespread in art and generally accessible.

Without diminishing the originality of his creations, quotations of this kind from Japanese art flash into view time and again when examining Gallé's work. Many of his forms (e.g., cat. nos. 28, 32, 45) bear witness to this in, for example, occasional free variations on Sino-Japanese bronzes in the form of slender sleeve vases, sacral vessels of the *gu* type or the narrow-necked vases from which he developed the 'Soliflore' type (illus. p. 18, bottom; see also cat. nos. 48, 35, 44, for further examples). For the basic idea of his fish vase (cat. no. 49) Gallé is likely to have once again reverted to East Asian models: see the 'Vase antique chinois, en bronze' in Philippe Burty's work published in 1866, *Chefs-d'œuvre des arts industriels: Céramique, verrerie et vitraux, émaux, métaux, orfèvrerie et bijouterie, tapisserie* (illus. p. 23, bottom right), with which Gallé was surely acquainted. One is also occasionally reminded of Japanese carved lacquer (cat. nos. 36, 37), of effects produced by oxblood glazes (cat. no. 54), of the

Left: Vase, overlay on a white ground, China, Ch'ien Lung (1735–96)

Right: Vase, Emile Gallé, serially produced, Nancy, c. 1900–1904, etched and acid-polished H 24.2 cm

Both museum kunst palast, Düsseldorf – Glasmuseum Hentrich

Covered vessel, terracotta, Japan, second half of nineteenth century. From Bing, *Formenschatz*, 1888–91, vol. 3, pl. ED

spontaneous handling characteristic of calligraphic brushwork (cat. no. 50) or of jade, in his jade imitations of the 1880s (cat. no. 30).

Certain image types, such as underwater scenes (cat. nos. 45, 52, 59), recall woodcuts from Hokusai's *manga* or have been preformulated in Japanese *objets de vertu*.[20] However, motifs that are direct quotations from Japanese art, such as the sword guards (*tsuba*) on a beaker vase (cat. no. 51), which evolved as a vessel form from the brush-washer, were, as a rule, reserved for serial production.[21] Pictorial types transferred from Chinese to Japanese art, such as the widespread bird on a flowering branch (cat. no. 46), occasionally give rise even in the fine 'grand genre' pieces to direct pictorial quotation (illus. left),[22] although these are exceptions.

Interestingly, Gallé once again approached Japanese art – albeit on a different plane and from a different angle – in his highly sculptural late work. His late dishes and vases developed from powerfully modelled leaf shapes (cat. no. 61)[23] appear less startling when one compares them with Japanese bronze vessels of the type publicized as early as 1888 by Bing (illus. p. 23, top). Similarly, designs such as the root-shaped feet of a covered vessel (illus. left) do not appear until the late work.[24] It would seem that Gallé needed to put a decade behind him before he could accept, understand and implement in his own work certain phenomena characteristic of the East Asian manner of rendering natural forms. Once this step had been taken, however, he achieved a degree of assimilation and transformation of Japanese art never attained by any of his contemporaries or successors.

Looking at Art Nouveau glass art in context and as a whole, one receives the impression that the influence of

Japanese art, recognizable as it is, is only rarely unmediated. On the contrary, it was usually filtered through Gallé's work before it made an aesthetic impact. Frequently the clue pointing to East Asia is now almost undetectable, as is the case with Désiré Christian's work, to take one example. He translated impulses received from Gallé – not from Japan – into a highly personal, in part expressive, although awkward, idiom nonetheless notable for a bold handling of colour. Nor did factories such as Burgun, Schverer & Co. or Vallerysthal model their gourd vases (cat. no. 75) directly on Japanese prototypes[25] but rather on the pieces conceived by Gallé or Daum (cat. no. 118).

The range of Gallé's main competitor in Nancy, Daum Frères, is wider than that of smaller factories working in this manner. The importance of Gallé's pioneering work is beyond question, yet these companies invariably strove to give their wares a distinctive appearance. This was made possible in serial production by the development of sophisticated techniques for fusing layers of glass strewn with powdered glass and in fine pieces by means of the 'intercalaire' technique, by which this was done. Such pieces equal Gallé's best work in their atmospheric, evocative qualities (see, for instance, cat. no. 104).

In exploring the possibilities of Japanese art, emulators, too, sought the direct route, bypassing Gallé. Pieces like the frequently reproduced Hanzan *inro*[26] or coloured woodcuts, such as a depiction of a poppy plant with a bud, a wilting flower and a seed-capsule (illus. p. 23, bottom left and centre), must have been studied directly at Daum. The superb translation of such studies into glass, as evinced by the poppy seed-capsule (cat. no. 103) or vases (cat. nos. 107, 98) secured Daum an unassailably unique position within the Ecole de Nancy, although it was dominated by Gallé.

Eugène Michel in Paris undoubtedly also personally studied Japanese models, to which he had easy access. His pond landscapes (cat. nos. 11, 12, 14), in particular, reveal his familiarity with East Asian art, yet at the same time furnish proof of pronounced independence. The Michel vase with black chrysanthemums (cat. no. 13) also bears the stamp of Japanese influence. Although it echoes Gallé's *gravures noires*, it could not possibly be mistaken for Gallé's work.

Gallé's death left glass art in France bereft of the driving force behind it. For all that, it would certainly mean misjudging matters to see in it the cause of the ensuing abrupt decline in interest in the Art Nouveau, which amounted virtually to a collapse. His contemporaries must have realized in the early years of the new century that the highly sensitive Symbolism, bound up with natural phenomena, of which Gallé was the leading exponent, was ultimately the expression of a dying era, more aptly characterized by such terms as 'fin de siècle' than by the optimistically forward-looking 'Art Nouveau'.

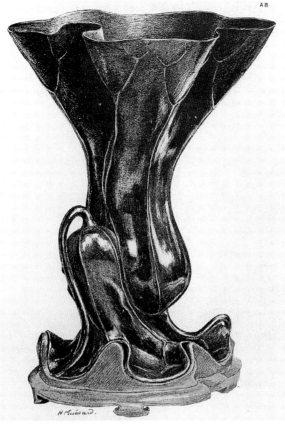

artistic substance and creative powers informing late Art
Nouveau were no longer adequate to transmit to the
new century the fresh impulses called for by the times – a
situation that other contributors to the development,
such as Louis Comfort Tiffany in New York or Lötz
Witwe in southern Bohemia, had to come to terms with
in 1905.

With its burgeoning approaches to social reform, its
tendency to functionalism and formal allegiance to Josef
Hoffmann and the Viennese circle, with the Werkbund
movement that grew out of this, the Art Nouveau of the
German-speaking countries, known as Jugendstil, and
the potential for renewal inherent in it, was on an incom-
parably grander scale. The future lay in deliberately
abandoning the 'great' glass art that Gallé had led to a
lonely pinnacle of achievement in favour of artistic
design manufactured serially. The course it took would
be increasingly determined, alongside the traditional
European glassmaking centres, by new centres such as
Sweden and Finland, the Netherlands and Italy.

Beginning with the Empire period style and continuing
on through the various forms taken by historicism via
exoticism – primarily relating to Japan – a steady development took place that marked both the culmination
and the end of Art Nouveau.

The 'genre Gallé' would remain, despite all his efforts
at renewal and the splendour of the achievement it represented, quintessentially a nineteenth-century bourgeois art. As such it managed to inspire only a late reflection in the ornamental luxury products of Art Deco. The

Notes

1 See, for instance, Bloch-Dermant 1980, pp. 22–27; Hilschenz-Mlynek and Ricke 1985, pp. 47–51; and Schmitt, *Sammlung Silzer*, 1989, pp. 40–43.

2 For the multifarious phenomena that constitute japonism see Wichmann, *Japonisme*, 1981, and, as the best succinct overview, Paris, *Japonisme*, 1988, both with further references.

3 See the comprehensive bibliography in Paris, *Japonisme*, 1988, pp. 334–39.

4 The European notion of East Asian art was for centuries shaped by the Chinese and Japanese decorative arts. However, only in exceptionally rare instances were the products sold in Europe regarded in their countries of origin as fine works of art. Instead they tended to be viewed there as rather mediocre wares intended for export that had been adapted to what was presumed to be, and actually accorded with, European tastes. This holds for both forms and decoration.

5 Such collections were not infrequently reproduced in books, representing part of the striving for theoretical validity by leading art historians; see, for instance, E. Reiber, *Le Premier Volume des Albums-Reiber: Bibliothèque portative des arts du dessin* (Paris, 1877), with illustrations showing objects from the collections amassed by H. Cernuschi, S. Bing et al. See also Wichmann, *Japonisme*, 1981, pp. 11–12.

6 See R. Alcock, *Catalogue of the Works of Industry and Art sent from Japan* (London, 1862); idem, *Art and Industry in Japan* (London, 1878); and G. A. Audsley and J. L. Bowes, *Keramic Art of Japan* (Liverpool and London, 1875).

7 See *J. Vieillard & Cie.: Eclectisme et Japonisme: Catalogue des céramiques et des dessins: Catalogue réalisé dans le cadre de l'exposition 'Vieillard à Bordeaux'*, exh. cat., Musée des Arts Décoratifs, Bordeaux (Bordeaux, 1986). On Gallé see Munich, *Nancy 1900*, 1980, pp. 51, 194–95; Paris, *Gallé*, 1985, pp. 105, 126; for examples in glass, see ibid., p. 161, and Hilschenz-Mlynek and Ricke 1985, p. 159.

8 See, for instance, R. L. Hobson, *Chinese Pottery and Porcelain*, vol. II (London, 1915), p. 242, pl. 124, fig. 2, and p. 268. I am indebted to Christine Mitomi for pointing out these links.

9 See Gonse 1883, vol. I, p. 288, illustrated here as cat. no. 9.

10 See, for instance, the brocade on a gold ground in *Nô: Gewänder und Masken des japanischen Theaters*, trans. Christoph Langemann, exh. cat., Museum Rietberg, Zurich; Museum für Kunst und Gewerbe, Hamburg; Linden-Museum, Stuttgart (Stuttgart, 1993), nos. 1, 7, 8, and the decoration on a box for writing utensils and a sutra case in J. Orange, *A Small Collection of Japanese Lacquer* (Yokohama, 1910), pls. 19 and 10 (Christine Mitomi kindly drew my attention to these publications).

11 See Gallé's observations on this subject informed by a positive belief in progress, in his comments on his submissions to the 1884 and 1889 Exposition Universelle in Paris, in the 'Sources' section of the Appendix.

12 See, for instance, Wichmann, *Japonisme*, 1981, p. 123, fig. 293.

13 'Here traditional art techniques also esteemed as "valuable" were poured effectively into industrial production orientated towards the tastes of the times, which showed no respect for what had been handed down from time immemorial but rather continually explored new methods of manufacture and constantly stimulated the market with surprising effects [...] No other material succeeded as well as glass in imitating the texture and feel of mottled jade and other semi-precious stones, of enamel, gold and mother-of-pearl intarsia in lacquer or metal or rare flambé glazes on Asian ceramics.' Imparted in writing by Christine Mitomi, Hamburg.

14 See also Hilschenz-Mlynek and Ricke 1985, no. 184, 'Tête de monstre japonnais', and no. 186.

15 See Paris, *Gallé*, 1985, pp. 151–52.

16 More than three hundred pieces were acquired in 1879, of which seventeen have survived. The 1884 acquisition comprised twenty-one pieces, of which four survived the burning of the Berlin Palace in the Second World War (I am indebted to Susanne Netzer of the Kunstgewerbemuseum, Berlin, for this information), including the original vase reproduced here. Four smaller groups had been donated before 1884 to the Ethnographisches Museum, Berlin; the Österreichisches Museum für Angewandte Kunst, Vienna; the Museum für Kunst und Gewerbe, Hamburg; and the Victoria & Albert Museum, London. For more on von Brandt's activities as a collector see H. Butz, 'Max von Brandt: Ein Diplomat als Sammler chinesischer Kunst', *Museums Journal* 1, no. 14 (January 2000): 79–81, printed on the occasion of the exhibition organized by the Museum für Ostasiatische Kunst at the Kunstgewerbemuseum, Berlin, 4 January–2 April 2000.

17 A. Papst, 'Chinesische Glasarbeiten', *Kunstgewerbeblatt* 1 (1885): 40–45, with six illustrations, one of which is a colour plate.

18 Gallé travelled in April 1885; see Paris, *Gallé*, 1985, p. 71. Whether Papst's essay on Chinese glass actually occasioned his trip to Berlin or whether Gallé had planned to go there anyway for other reasons is not known. In the context of his remarks made on jade carving and Chinese glass in a travel report published in 1916, Peter Jessen, the second director of the Kunstbibliothek, Berlin, mentioned Gallé's visit to Berlin. He recalled, "how, as a young assistant, I once opened up the sensational collection of such glass at the Museum of Applied Arts for the Master of Nancy, and how he studied it piece by piece for two weeks long, which is something that no German glassmaker had ever asked to do; Berlin is where he learned the rudiments of the technique that he took the world by storm with." See P. Jessen, 'Reisestudien VII: China – Volkstum und Werkkunst', *Kunstgewerbeblatt* 28, n.s. (1916/17): 157–64, esp. 163.

19 See Hilschenz-Mlynek and Ricke 1985, nos. 232–34.

20 See, for instance, the little receptacle bearing an underwater scene, in *Le Magasin pittoresque* (1874): 373, illustrated in Paris, *Japonisme*, 1988, p. 87, and the woodcut with an underwater scene of marine fauna in Hokusai's *manga*, vol. XV, posthumously published in 1878.

21 See the many variants of sparrows and bamboo with snow, for which numerous models occur in Bing's repertoire of forms. Employees in the studios often had recourse to Hokusai's *manga* or other pattern books – apart from the dominant plant motifs – as a source of inspiration for their variants of insects, bats, swallows, etc.

22 See, for instance, the birds on a flowering cherry branch in Bing, *Formenschatz*, 1888–91, no. 14, pl. AJF.

23 See the dish that has become famous as the 'Rhubarb Leaf', *Art of Gallé* 1988, no. 21, and the vases in the shape of flower calyces with applications, Paris, *Gallé*, 1985, nos. 145–46.

24 Gallé used such designs primarily in his late sculptural vessels with underwater decoration; see, for instance, the 'Hypocampes' jug decorated with seahorses, the sea anemone vase or the vase with a landscape and sculptural tree trunks, Corning 1984, nos. 34–35 and 16.

25 See the Bizen-ware pottery gourd bottle in Bing, *Formenschatz*, 1888–91, no. 24, pl. BEH.

26 This piece is reproduced not only in Gonse 1883, but also in Bing, *Formenschatz*, 1888–91, no. 12, p. 150.

Eva Schmitt

Paris: Between the 1867 and 1900 Expositions Universelles

The crucial milestones in the development leading up to the emergence of Art Nouveau glass were the exhibitions held at the Union Centrale in the Palais de l'Industrie[1] in 1874 and 1884 as well as the Expositions Universelles of 1878 and 1889 in Paris, where the leading glassmakers found a forum. Impulses emanating from these major events were reinforced and underscored by the reporting that accompanied them, which highlighted both the art-historical background and the artistic potential of technical innovations.

Vital contributions to the new glass design were made by the distinguished artists and retailers François Eugène Rousseau (1827–1890) in Paris (illus. below) and Emile Gallé (1846–1904) in Nancy, who at that time were working out the fundamentals of their individual, pioneering glass idiom. Among those close to them who played roles that should not be overlooked in the early phase up to 1884 were the Cristallerie de Baccarat, with an outlet in Paris, the retailer and distributor Emile-Augustin Pannier (1828–1892) and his venerable and renowned company, Escalier de Cristal, as well as the craftsmen Philippe-Joseph Brocard (c. 1840–1896) and Ste Marie François Augustin Jean (1829–1896), called simply Augustin or Auguste Jean. The quest for artistic innovation was facilitated by the technical advances made by the reputable firm of Appert Frères. Their inventions and facilities were largely indebted to the

Eugène Rousseau (1827–1890), aged fifty-five. Reproduction of a photograph taken in 1882

achievement of the gifted engineer Léon-Alfred Appert (1837–1925). Active in the family business since 1857, he managed it jointly with his brother from 1865.[2]

The situations from which Rousseau and Gallé started out were – despite similarities in their family environments – as different as the results on show in the 1884 exhibition held at the Union Centrale in Paris. Both had been familiarized with the field, especially faience design, through their work for the businesses specializing in porcelain, pottery and glass operated by their fathers. Unlike Rousseau, Gallé's creativity as a designer is obviously closely bound up with a thorough grounding in his craft and his technical knowledge. Both skills enabled him to draw on a virtually inexhaustible reservoir of expressive forms and this advantage was reinforced by collaboration with his artist colleagues.

Nothing has been ascertained about Rousseau's training. After taking over his father's business in 1855 at the age of twenty-eight, he made his first public appearance at the 1862 International Exhibition in London. The faiences he showed there were mainly neoclassical in design and executed by several craftsmen. To carry out the work that followed in the *pâte-sur-pâte* technique of painting on porcelain, he hired Marc-Louis-Emmanuel Solon (1835–1913), who co-signed these pieces using Milès as his *nom d'artiste*.[3] Even at this stage the considerable differences in approach to Gallé's are apparent, which would later have a bearing on glass design. His success with a dining service boasting motifs taken from Japanese colour woodcuts – Rousseau had designed them in collaboration with the draughtsman Félix Bracquemond (1833–1914)[4] – at the 1867 Exposition Universelle in Paris catapulted Rousseau into the ranks of contemporary avant-garde designers although he was also represented at this exhibition by a large group of historicist designs.[5]

The decision Rousseau soon afterwards took to explore the potential of glass as material may well have been linked with the recognition he won at the exhibition.[6] His beginnings as a glass designer are obscure; indeed the artist, who was known for his discretion and reticence, did not even tell his family about what he was doing.[7] The first two Rousseau pieces in glass with painted underwater scenes to be sold were acquired by the Victoria & Albert Museum, London, in 1869.[8] The first of the many professional contacts he could have made at this time were with employees of Appert Frères, Paul Bitterlin and Jules Dopter as well as the glass restorer and painter Philippe-Joseph Brocard and the engraver Eugène Michel.

Appert Frères, like Bitterlin, one of the most reputable firms of its kind in Paris and environs,[9] produced basic materials and glaze pigments for making pottery, porcelain, enamel and glass. Contact with Rousseau might even date from the period when he was working on ceramics.

Established in 1855 by Paul Bitterlin as a refinery for hollow and flat glass at 127, rue de l'Université, and from 1861 the largest business of its kind in Paris, it had, by its own account, the capacity to produce decoration using techniques such as engraving, etching and painting. Rousseau must have met Bitterlin through the Union Centrale,[10] particularly since the latter had been awarded honourable mention and a gold medal at the 1863 and 1865 Union Centrale exhibitions. Jules Dopter, also a member of the Union Centrale, had a similar but smaller business specialized in etching glass and making stained-glass windows for ecclesiastical buildings. Both workshops could have taken over the painting on Rousseau's early, still small-scale pieces.[11]

Brocard's reputation as an outstanding glass painter rested on his having presented the first perfect replicas of mosque lamps, at the 1867 Exposition Universelle in Paris. He and his colleagues must also be considered as possible candidates for executing Rousseau's painting on glass since there is evidence of business links between them.[12]

Only twenty when he embarked on what would be years of collaboration with Rousseau, the glass cutter Eugène Michel had been in Paris since 1868. His elder sister, Eléonore, had petitioned successfully for his exemption from national service since, as the only surviving male member of the family, he bore the main responsibility for keeping his widowed mother and his sister in Lunéville.[13]

1874

Rousseau first presented a glass collection at the 1874 exhibition mounted by the Union Centrale des Beaux-Arts Appliqués à l'Industrie in Paris. It was reported on by Philippe Burty, editor of the journal *La Presse* and author of *Chefs-d'œuvre des arts industriels*, published in Paris in 1866.[14] Like Rousseau's fellow artists and colleagues, Solon and Bracquemond, Burty belonged to 'Jing-Lar', a circle formed in the late 1860s by artists and collectors who were Japan enthusiasts.[15] Much in demand as an art critic, he was among the key authors in Paris to advocate and accelerate the development of Japanese-inspired design in the applied and decorative arts. At that exhibition Rousseau had shown 'porcelain and stoneware, tableware and vases after Japanese models as well as engraved crystal glass in the manner in which rock crystal is cut'. However, the terse, rather ambiguous descriptions of the exhibits in the catalogue and Burty's account convey hardly any idea of the specifications of individual designs: '[…] After all, his pieces in glass are among the best, not to mention the brilliance that his cowled glasses or his cups lend to luxurious tables; we deem little vases square in section and wheel-engraved decoration in hollow relief as rivalling the cut crystal of the Orient […].'[16]

A first interpretation of what were known as *verres coulés* alludes to glass with trailing prunts applied in blue

Cristallerie de Baccarat
Pair of vases, 1878
Private collection

Emile Gallé, Nancy
'La Carpe' vase, 1878
Musée des Arts Décoratifs,
Paris, inv. no. 86 OA

and representations of a school of fish after the 1832 colour woodcut by the Japanese artist Hiroshige, which Rousseau had used for his 1867 service.[17]

1878

The vase type with engraved, painted foliage and fish as well as blue trailing prunts (illus. p. 26) – aptly described by Rousseau and critics as tears of blue glass ('des larmes de verre bleu') – was undoubtedly represented among the exhibits at the 1878 Exposition Universelle. A tentative idea of Rousseau's unusual approach to glass design can be gleaned from these accounts of the exhibition and the first museum acquisitions. They also include vases in colourless or smoky glass decorated with intaglio engraving like rock crystal and / or moonscapes, bamboo shoots (cat. no. 1), underwater scenes (similar to cat. no. 2 for purposes of comparison) and peacock feathers.[18] The same Paris exhibition also featured work by the renowned Cristallerie de Baccarat and the young Emile Gallé with Japanese-inspired designs on transparent colourless or coloured glass. Baccarat executed the decoration in intaglio engraving (illus. above) whereas Gallé preferred painting (illus. right). This would suggest that these pieces are indebted to Rousseau's Japanese-inspired pieces of 1874, especially when one considers the lofty status enjoyed in interested specialist circles by the first Union Centrale exhibition after the Franco-

Prussian War of 1870/71 and the ensuing praise from Philippe Burty. In the official account of the 1878 Exposition Universelle, products made by the large factories and technical innovations were given priority, including the new iridescent glass by Auguste Jean, which has been erroneously attributed to his son.[19] Jean, who had been awarded several distinctions for his 'inventiveness' as a ceramist, had worked on glass design at Appert Frères since declaring insolvency in 1876 and had had his experiments with iridescent glass surfaces patented in 1877: 'This process involves adding silver nitrate or acetate and bismuth acid in varying quantities – depending on the hue desired – to the glass, crystal glass or coloured glass batch, making it melt into the batch or creating a sleeve for casing the glass, as for ordinary manufacture. As soon as the object has been formed it is reheated and exposed to smoke produced by burning dung or the like in order to cause the reaction [reduction firing], which creates the beautiful metallic sheen.'[20]

An example of this early output is a vase bought in 1880 by the Prague Museum of Applied Arts (illus. p. 28).[21] From a formal standpoint already extremely bold, this piece is entirely coated with a translucent yet speckled iridescent pinkish lavender layer that is bluish grey when held up to the light. Without knowledge of the process employed, one might be tempted to describe it as lustre. The speckled look might have been created by fusing the compounds directly on to the molten glass. The striking trailing prunts of blue glass Jean used may have been inspired by Rousseau's vases, which were also executed at Appert Frères and presumably even by the same glassmaker, who was especially gifted at this technique. Rousseau no longer exhibited his designs with trailing prunts of blue glass after 1878.

Auguste Jean, Paris
Vase, 1877/80
Museum of Applied Arts,
Prague, inv. no. 142

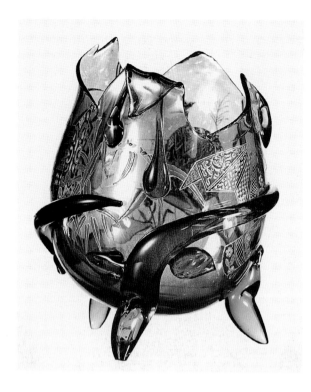

The Cristallerie de Pantin Monot Père et Fils & Stumpf, on the other hand, did produce similar work modelled on Jean's after that date and some of it was formally very close to his designs.[22]

Presumably inspired by the iridescent colouring, which he interpreted as lustre, Gallé used it to add a sophisticated touch to the pieces painted with fused colours he showed at the 1884 Exposition Universelle in Paris. Brocard and Gallé are given only brief, albeit apposite, mention in the 1878 Exposition Universelle report. Brocard, whose style is evaluated as an 'imitation of Oriental glass' is, however, also regarded as an 'innovator in painting with fused colour'. Gallé's style is described as a 'borrowing of some principles of Japanese art in conjunction with engraving and painting', which was, however, even then viewed as the 'harbinger of a development that can achieve outstanding results'.[23] The commentary on Rousseau, who is evaluated together with Lahoche-Pannier (Escalier de Cristal), is quite detailed. The two retailers and distributors were regarded as the leading Paris specialist dealers who 'on the one hand nurtured their customers' taste in glass design and, on the other, ensured an interesting variety of products through close collaboration with the glassmakers.'[24] Whereas Lahoche-Pannier is praised as a distributor for Venetian and French glass factories, the personal commitment shown by Rousseau as a designer is underscored in connection with the following descriptions of his work: '[...] imitations of rock crystal or smoky quartz, which he has had made after Chinese prototypes, decorating them with engraving in the grand manner. He applies blue trailing prunts to colourless or green glass, engraves these pieces with foliage or fish and paints them with translucent smalt pigments. M. Rousseau achieves

delightful effects by transferring to glass elements of decoration that the Chinese and Japanese apply to clay, wood and bronze by means of enamel and lacquer, gold and silver [...].'[25]

None of the accounts of the 1878 Exposition Universelle, however, mentions Rousseau's first large exhibit in 'strass',[26] which Jules Henrivaux called a 'veritable tour de force' in his account of the 1889 Exposition Universelle after having seen it again the same year at Boucheron's, a reputable jeweller.[27]

1884

The Union Centrale mounted its eighth exhibition in 1884. Focusing on the theme of 'Stone, Wood (construction), Pottery and Glass' (La Pierre, le Bois [construction], la Terre et le Verre), it 'marked, with the successes of Rousseau and Gallé, the onset of the dazzling renewal in glass, which, after decades in the doldrums, would go on to triumph brilliantly in Art Nouveau.'[28] Gallé was hailed as the great talent, the 'event at this exhibition'. Appealing to the prevailing tastes, his Islamic-looking and East Asian-inspired pieces with imitations of intaglio cutting on rock crystal and medieval motifs reflected 'the analytical experiential values of a creative historicism,' which had emerged by 1878. Edmond Bazire's rave review culminated in the prophetic statement: 'This work is complete and, in material expression and composition [...], literary. All this is very French and no one beyond our borders would even attempt to rival it. All that will happen is that it will be copied. To sum up my opinion of M. Gallé, I should like to say he is a scholar, an artist and a poet.'[29]

Eugène Rousseau, given only marginal mention by the same author in his account of the exhibition, had attained the zenith of his career with his ground-breaking collection. The bodies of his pieces, which bore a striking resemblance to gemstones, his bold colours and occasionally powerful designs as well as the use of state-of-the-art glass technology by Appert Frères made the artist far ahead of his time (illus. p. 29). He was able to handle forms in thick-walled 'strass' glass, creating vessels recalling cut gemstones, by applying an invention of Léon Appert's patented in 1880 as 'glass blown with mechanically compressed air'.[30] Rousseau was, therefore, the first – a generation ahead of René Lalique[31] – to use the industrial process of blowing with compressed air to make glass objects. It was exceptionally well suited to the manufacture of his thick-walled, large vessels, which boasted relief decoration or were angular in shape since their surfaces could be completely worked over by means of hot and cold techniques[32] and the handling of various inclusions, including crizzelled or crazed (crackle) textures, did not betray the technique of manufacture at first glance. The attractiveness of a precious-looking opaque or *strass craquelé* body was even considerably enhanced by means of unusual

colour combinations in the casing layers. Rousseau was bold enough to deploy strong colours and contrasts, which underscored the decidedly sculptural quality of his vessels. Although his forms and decoration were often direct quotations from the Renaissance or Sino-Japanese art, Rousseau still succeeded in conveying a new standard in design that was at once austere and bold. This was glass as art, far removed from all conventional notions of the obliging decorative arts. The innovative status of these pieces, which made an impact comparable with the sudden fame Rousseau achieved with his celebrated service of 1867, would not be revealed in full until the 1889 Exposition Universelle five years later.[33] One of the few to appreciate his aesthetic achievement as early as 1884 was the art critic Louis de Fourcaud: 'M. Eugène Rousseau commands our respect and deserves our gratitude in several respects. He is an entrepreneur and the son of an entrepreneur; he has become an artist at his own risk with all the perils that this entails and, what is more, he is a demiurge, by virtue of his exquisite taste and his initiative [...]. For twenty years now we have watched him on his way to becoming a ceramist and glassmaker, sketching, combining, experimenting, determining the models of tomorrow [...]. The very day he turned to glass he became a distinguished glassmaker [...]. He possesses a heightened sense of what is precious in glass: the form he chooses, be it Japanese or not, is invariably one that shows his

marvellous material at its best. Everything becomes gem-like in his hands. The glass blushes with a rosy tint on contact with gold oxide, is spattered with a gush of blood where copper oxide has left its mark, borrows from manganese the violet translucency of the amethyst or brings into play the yellow of silver stain, like a golden oil, in its luminous crazing. Nothing more attractive can be seen in the Palais de l'Industrie than M. Rousseau's showcase, iridescent and austere, worthy of a museum.'[34]

In stark contrast with this rave review was the rejection expressed, albeit indirectly and without giving names, by Gallé as well as the critic reporting on Group 4 (glass, enamels, mosaics), Edmond Bazire. Gallé's essay, written at the request of Victor Champier, editor of the *Revue des Arts Décoratifs*, and prefacing the reports on the exhibition, contains the following statements: '[...] Indeed, to inflict opacity on crystal means extinguishing the beautiful eyes that the light of heaven would imbue. Tricking glass out in an unsophisticated manner with forms borrowed from opaque materials, such as stone and bronze or grainy ones such as wood – shapes and decoration that do not underscore its actual properties but instead precisely the opposite qualities – represents infidelity on the part of the artisan, which is a disgrace to his craft in particular and to art in general. It amounts to a violation of the material. A craftsman owes it respect [...].'[35]

It is now almost impossible to uncover the background of the publication of Gallé's views and Bazire's exhibition reporting. Apart from some remarks of a polemical nature coupled with dubious assertions revealing ignorance of the subject, Bazire's account not only emphasizes the artistic achievement of Brocard and Gallé; it also contains observations that can be a covert reference to Rousseau's exhibits. On Brocard he writes: '[…] Others dream of covering the glass. He, however, strives to leave it its character. When he applies an enamel, he retains its transparency […]. He has grasped the incomprehensible: that glass is not meant to be opaque and that its supreme quality is its translucency […].' On Appert: '[…] this industrialist has made his name by abolishing free glass-blowing right in his studio. He has introduced mechanical glass-blowing, which was originally Bontemps's idea […]. I repeat, M. Appert is full of – I should almost like to say is puffed up with – good intentions. But, as experience shows, it would seem that his good intentions hardly produce anything, especially in decoration, but superfluous results.' On Gallé: 'All his forms have the advantage of being taken from nature. He does not distort his moulds in a grotesque manner […].'[36]

The opinions subsequently expressed by Louis de Fourcaud and other members of the jury represent a brusque correction of the unjustified criticism of Appert Frères. The suspicion lingers that Rousseau, associated as he was with Appert Frères and years ahead of his time, may well have been the victim of intrigues behind the scenes. The decision taken by Rousseau a year later to turn over his work and his business to Ernest Léveillé might have something to do with this.[37] After taking over all the wares and moulds for making pottery and glass, Léveillé collaborated with Rousseau on designing glass. He continued to use the hard, gemstone-like body of opaque coloured glass or transparent glass with inclusions, crizzelling and/or casing developed by Rousseau (cat. nos. 5–7), which was also the material preferred by Eugène Michel, who worked for them (cat. nos. 11–14). From 1885 to 1889 Rousseau was mainly responsible for designs and variations on them, whereas Léveillé added decoration variants of his own, such as the underwater scene with fish and a dense growth of marine flora (cat. no. 5) or the new decor of cut spiralling tendrils.[38]

1889

In his 1889 exhibition report Henrivaux emphasized that the combination of acid-etching and engraving used by Rousseau and Léveillé to decorate cased glass was new. It would also be emulated in Nancy in the years to come.[39] At the 1889 Exposition Universelle their new work, some of it fitted out with 'rich mounts in gold and silver', was widely acclaimed, although by then several glassmakers had been working on the 'type of decoration imitating precious stones, introduced by Rousseau in 1884'.[40]

Chief among them was Emile Gallé. After encountering initial resistance and openly expressed criticism, he succeeded in creatively exploiting the revolutionary means of expression introduced by Rousseau in 1884 so that he presented an extremely diverse collection of a high aesthetic standard. 'It was no longer a question of transparency, rendering visible the steps used in crafting or fidelity to the material as such. On the contrary, all new models strove to cover up the fact that this was glass; they were imitations of hardstones in opaque coloured glass, with the main emphasis laid on jade, amber and alabaster.'[41]

Auguste Jean was not able to participate in this major exhibition because, in 1883, he was forced to register his second insolvency, caused by his obsessive preoccupation with glass.[42] His last patent specification, Bulletin no. 196013, dated 12 February 1889, reads: 'Teinter ou métalliser le tout ou en partie le verre, cristal et tout ce qui a rapport à la verrerie et à la céramique en général, dans le cours de la fabrication ou une fois les pièces terminées, par le vaporisateur ou tout autre appareil à vent, ayant pour base l'air', referring to the use of a spraying device operated by compressed air for colouring or rendering iridescent ceramics or glass while it was being made at the furnace or before reduction firing in the muffle kiln (cat. no. 15). This process, as developed by Jean, was again far ahead of its time. It would not be used in glassmaking in France until after the First World War, when it was taken up by Marcel Goupy in Paris and by others.

Following Rousseau's death, in 1890, Léveillé and Michel also turned increasingly to the floral motifs Gallé was so fond of as well as to such innovations as his engraving black glass, whose textured surface was created by high-relief cutting (cat. no. 10). The productive influence the leading glassmakers of Paris and Nancy had on each other can be traced in numerous cases.[43] Trend-setting designs from Paris included the spiralling tendril decoration in powerful mitre grinding developed before 1889 from Chinese models[44] and, above all, the lacustrine imagery in false colours that was executed in cased glass and developed by Rousseau before 1884 (illus. p. 29, left) as well as further developments of this by Eugène Michel (cat. nos. 11, 12), which were still inspiring Daum Frères in 1908 (cat. no. 117). A complex motif was Rousseau's underwater scenes, which had been interpreted variously since the 1870s. Although the close link to Japanese models was still apparent in these works, they reveal heightened atmospheric qualities. A high point of this development is the cased glass created in collaboration with Léveillé (cat. nos. 4, 5), which spawned numerous interpretations of the underwater theme by Gallé and Daum Frères (cat. no. 88). This theme had a special symbolic status in Gallé's oeuvre (cat. nos. 33, 45, 49, 52, 59), revealing a parallel development in design to the work of Rousseau and Léveillé, such as the 1889 Gallé vase called 'Le Martin-pêcheur' (The Kingfisher).[45] Echoes of Léveillé's decoration featuring a serpent amid tropical vegetation or a corn-cob surrounding a vessel shape – exhibited at the Salon du Champ-de-Mars in 1896 and 1897, respectively – can be found, for instance, in a footed vase in the form of a corn-cob made by Emile Gallé c. 1899/1900 and models created by Daum Frères for the 1903 Paris exhibition mounted by the Ecole de Nancy with a serpent motif in high relief or yet another vase by the same company, shaped like a corn-cob.[46]

The stagnation and gradual decline of what had been trend-setting Paris Art Nouveau glass design was apparent by the 1889 Exposition Universelle.[47] Compared with Gallé's teeming imagination, the continuing insistence on showcasing the physical properties of glass as developed years before by Rousseau could at best spark off a tired déjà vu reaction, in spite of the relatively high quality of both design and execution. Gallé's genius was revealed in the way he assimilated fresh impulses in design, which in most instances he reinterpreted. Boundlessly creative, he used all sources available to him, drawing especially on his knowledge of the natural sciences, including botany, chemistry and glass technology.[48] Since he had devoted himself to such studies along with his craft early on, he was able to exploit all the knowledge he had acquired in his designs and explain it in detail to the employees who were to execute them. Today Rousseau's vital contribution to the development of Art Nouveau glass is uncontested. He ranks as an artist with Gallé, whose meteoric rise as a designer was triggered off by the encounter with Rousseau's work.

Notes

1 Founded on the private initiative of industrialists, artists, writers, entrepreneurs and collectors 'to cultivate beauty in the utilitarian and to safeguard the unity of art and crafts', the association had attracted attention as early as 1861 with its first exhibition. Its instigators founded the Union Centrale des Beaux-Arts Appliqué à l'Industrie in Paris in 1864, which made a substantial contribution to the development of design in Art Nouveau glass through numerous events and exhibitions. François Eugène Rousseau was a founding member and was active in the organization: see Schneck 1988, pp. 3–5; Schneck 1990, p. 449.

2 No in-depth studies have been conducted on the meeting of kindred spirits that characterized the collaboration of Rousseau with the Appert Frères factory. The only hint of this is in the obituary for Rousseau written by Victor Champier in 1890: see V. Champier, 'Nécrologie Eugène Rousseau: Céramiste et verrier', Revue des Arts Décoratifs 11 (1890–91): 90. Evidence of the collaboration between Auguste Jean and Appert Frères is furnished by the records documenting his second insolvency in 1883: see Archives Départementales de la Ville de Paris, D 11 U 3/1090, no. 13397.

3 There is an extensive discussion of this in Karin Schneck's master of arts thesis: see chapter entitled 'Rousseau Fayencen'. 1. Historicizing enamel painting. The 1862 London International Exhibition. 2. Neoclassical pâte-sur-pâte painting. Collaboration with Marc-Louis Solon. 3. Japanese-inspired enamel paint-

ing done by means of lithographic printing. Félix Bracquemond's designs for the 'Service Rousseau', see Schneck 1988, pp. 9–23.

4 The dining service known as the 'Service Rousseau' is a design milestone of Japonism in France. It was still being produced until about 1938 by his successors, Léveillé and Harant & Guignard. On the story of its creation see Paris, Rousseau, 1988.

5 This shows that Rousseau also arrived at unusual solutions in this genre, aptly described as follows by the German writer Wilhelm Hamm: 'His exhibition includes faience with painting on unfired glaze, luxury porcelain with painted reliefs, vessels with underglaze painting fired in the glost [second, vitrifying] fire, a banquet service, etc. All these things have been handled with a great deal of taste and richly fitted out; at the same time they strive for originality of form, sometimes of course in a rather bold, almost eccentric manner. On the whole, however, one may acclaim the Rousseau porcelain pieces as excellent work and count them among the best in the French section although it is so richly stocked with exhibits.' See W. Hamm, Illustrirter Katalog der Pariser Industrie-Ausstellung von 1867 (Leipzig, 1868), p. 128 with illustrations.

6 Rousseau and Bracquemond were acclaimed by art critics. As a retailer, Rousseau was not eligible for the official distinction he deserved. The Lebeuf & Milliet factory in Creil-Montereau, which executed his work, was awarded a gold medal. For further excerpts from the exhibition report by Philippe Burty see Schneck 1988, pp. 19–20.

7 See Champier (note 2), p. 87.

8 For a reference to their destruction see Schneck 1988, p. 25, and Schneck 1990, p. 451.

9 Both were awarded the distinction 'Notable Commerçant de Département de la Seine' and its framed seal 'N. C.' was added to the firm name: see Almanach du Commerce 1868, p. 830; Sageret 1867, p. 192; 'Dossier Légion d'Honneur Appert, Léon-Alfred', Archives Nationales F12 5082; 'Lettre d'Appert Frères au Ministre de l'Agriculture et du Commerce, le 26 Juillet 1878', p. 1.

10 Paul Bitterlin, Philippe Burty and Eugène Rousseau belonged to the group of early active founding members of the Union Centrale (annual dues 100 Frs), who were distinguished in the roll of members as 'cofondateur' (co-founders) by a 'C' appended to their names: see Le Beau dans l'utile: Histoire sommaire de l'Union Centrale des Beaux-Arts Appliqués à l'Industrie suivi des rapports du jury de l'exposition de 1865 (Paris, 1866), pp. 19–20, 63–64.

11 For extensive information on both businesses see Sageret 1867, p. 192, and ibid. 1875, pp. 281, 460. Whether the engravings noted by Bitterlin as 'gravures sur verres' were engravings executed with engraving tools such as the wheel or whether acid-etching was meant is linguistically unclear.

Production concentrated on acid-etched flat glass for windows, panels, mirrors, lighting, etc. Moreover, Bitterlin also made hydrofluoric acid, which is used in acid-etching.

12 The inventory of wares drawn up when Rousseau turned his business over to Léveillé in 1885 contains, written virtually throughout in lower case letters – usually also for names such as appert or reyen – glass described as brocard, with inconsistently formulated brief descriptions: '18 vases divers, renaissance colorié, renaissance brocard [...]; 5 vidercomes divers; marguerite feu de fond or, émail de brocard [...]; 32 vases divers [...] éléphant fumé craquelé emaillés brocard, [...] 2 lampes diverses arabe de brocard [...]'. Brief as they are, these entries do reveal that Rousseau sold work by Brocard and commissioned painting with smalt colours from him: see Archives Nationales, Minutier Central, LXVI, 1689, 16 December 1885, Vente de matériel et marchandises par M. Rousseau à M. et Mme Léveillé, pp. 9–10. It might be possible to interpret the word 'brocard' as a term for a pattern recalling the fabric brocade (brocart) when one takes incorrect spelling into consideration, yet is impossible for stylistic reasons.

13 The conscription roll drawn up in 1868 mentions as his profession 'Graveur sur Cristaux à Paris' (Engraver on Crystal in Paris). The address given as 4, rue du Château, is that of his mother in Lunéville. The 1870 roll lists as his Paris address 237, rue St-Denis, and as his profession 'Tailleur sur Cristaux' (Crystal Cutter) with the remark: 'exempté, fils unique de veuve' (exempt, only son of a widow), with the contradictory additional entry: 'Bon pour la mobile' (eligible for the garde mobile, a guards regiment): see Archives Municipales de Lunéville, Classe de 1868, Série H1 1868, no. 97; ibid., 'Tableaux de recensement des classes 1866–1870', Canton Nord, Série H1, Section 29, nos. 21/37. A check of the relevant registry office in Paris revealed no mention of Michel but does show a Letheux as a landlord with furnished rooms for rent, who, without names being mentioned, was responsible only for changes in lodgers: see registry office 237, rue St-Denis, Archives Départementales de Paris, D1P4, 1862, no. 1000.

14 *Chefs-d'œuvre des arts industriels: Céramique, verrerie et vitraux, émaux, métaux, orfèvrerie et bijouterie, tapisserie* (Paris, 1866). Reading this work on the historical development of arts and crafts must have represented a wellspring of stimulating ideas for some of the aforementioned designers of the day. On Burty's membership of the Union Centrale see note 10.

15 Schneck 1988, p. 17, n. 42, with reference to J.-P. Bouillon, '"A Gauche": Note sur la société du Jing-Lar et sa signification', *Gazette des Beaux-Arts* 91, no. 120 (1978): 107–18.

16 '[…] Enfin, ses verreries sont de premier choix, et sans parler de l'éclat que ses verres coulés ou ses coupes apportent aux tables luxueuses, nous signalerons comme rivalisant avec les cristaux taillés de l'Orient, des portebouquets carrés, gravés à la roue, les uns en creux, les autres au contraire laissant à l'ornement son relief […].' See P. Burty, *Rapport présenté par le jury de la IVe section art appliqué à la céramique et à la verrerie, Union Centrale des Beaux-Arts Appliqués à l'Industrie* (Paris, 1875), pp. 8, 13, and Schneck 1988, pp. 30, 129, n. 84–85. The interpretation of 'portebouquets carrés' must remain uncertain for the time being. It is questionable whether they can be interpreted as the angular cup/dish forms with decorative fields engraved by Rousseau in the Sino-Japanese manner used for rock crystal (see Schneck 1988, pp. 31–32), particularly since Rousseau also used vase forms that were square in section. The obsolete term 'portebouquet', meaning little receptacles that could be hung up or attached to something, was still widely used in the late nineteenth century for vases that held little bouquets. The extract quoted above from the 1874 Union Centrale catalogue runs: 'Porcelaines et faïences d'art. – Porcelaines pâtes rapportées. Services de table et vases, inspirations japonaises. – Cristaux gravés, imitation de cristaux de roche' (Art porcelain and faience. – Engraved crystal, imitating rock crystal). See *Union Centrale des Beaux-Arts Appliqués à l'Industrie, Quatrième Exposition 1874: Catalogue des œuvres et des produits modernes exposés au Palais de l'industrie* (Paris, 1874), p. 104.

17 Schneck 1988, pp. 30–31, and ibid. 1990, p. 451. If this is so, it would support the hypothesis that Rousseau was having work done at Appert Frères even before 1874. Auguste Jean also used blue applied decoration, which was much more emphatic, for the blanks that he also had made at Appert Frères from 1877. There was apparently a glassmaker there who was particularly skilled in this technique. In the 1885 inventory drawn up on the occasion of his turning his business over to Léveillé, Rousseau used the more apt description 'à larmes' (with tears) for vessels with trailing prunts: see Archives Nationales, Minutier Central, LXVI, 1689, 16 December 1885, *Vente de matériel et marchandises par M. Rousseau à M. et Mme Léveillé*, pp. 10, 11, 13 (also 15 'vases plats à larmes' [shallow vessels with tear-shaped prunts]).

18 Schneck 1990, pp. 451–52.

19 Didron and Clémendot 1880, p. 33. Attribution to the son rests on the circumstance that Auguste Jean was at first refused and his new pieces in glass were accepted only at the instigation of his son, Maurice; see inquiries about participating in the 1878 Exposition Universelle, Archives Nationales F21 3367–3368.

20 'Ce procédé consiste à ajouter dans la composition du verre, du cristal ou du verre de toute couleur du nitrate d'argent ou azetate d'argent et de l'acide de bismuth en plus ou moins grande quantité selon les tons que l'on veut obtenir, faire fondre en masse ou faire une couverte pour doubler le verre comme pour la fabrication ordinaire, aussitôt que la pièce est faite et formée la faire rechauffer et la passer dans la fumée produite avec du fumier ou toute autre sorte de fumée la réaction s'opère et produit de beaux réflets métalliques.' Patent specification of 30 April 1877, Bulletin no. 118301, 'Verre métallisé'. The text of the patent specification leaves several precise possibilities for carrying out the technical process, which have not been completely clarified. In the case of the Prague piece, when one looks through it, the bluish grey tinge characteristic of bismuth, which may also be produced by the addition of silver, is discernible rather than the yellowish tinge that might be expected from silver stain.

21 J. Brožova, *Historismus umělecké řemeslo 1860–1900* (Crafts 1860–1900), exh. cat., Museum of Applied Arts (Prague, 1975), vol. I, p. 218, no. 322, illus. in vol. II.

22 The factory donated an azure vase with two applied lizards and a butterfly to the Conservatoire Nationale des Arts et Métiers in Paris in 1880. An almost identical one in greyish green smoky glass also bearing the signature of Auguste Jean is in the Silzer Collection; see Paris, *Arts Métiers*, 1908, p. 265, no. 9400-0000, and E. Schmitt, *Europäisches Jugendstilglas aus der Glassammlung Silzer/Leihgabe Deutsche Bank*, exh. cat., State Tretyakov Gallery (text in Russian) (Moscow, 1991), no. 5, illus. p. 23. It has not been clarified whether there was a link between Jean and the Cristallerie de Pantin. It is also conceivable that the specialized glassmaker transferred to the Cristallerie de Pantin after Appert switched to the manufacture of pressed glass, using the process developed by Léon Appert.

23 Didron and Clémendot 1880, pp. 14, 33.

24 The two are known to have collaborated but this has not yet been researched and analyzed. Quite a few models bearing both signatures exist and it is known that they used the same shapes. They also include the vase form with a high shoulder used by Rousseau and Léveillé, which Pannier Frères exhibited with an ormolu bronze serpent mount as late as the 1900 Exposition Universelle: see Bascou and Thiébaut, Orsay, 1988, no. OAO 513, illus. p. 181.

25 '[…] Imitations de cristaux de roche blancs ou enfumés qu'il fait fabriquer sur des types chinois, en les décorant de gravures de grand style. Sur des pièces de verre blanc ou vert, il ajoute des larmes de verre bleu, et les grave de feuillages ou de poissons peints avec des émaux translucides. M. Rousseau obtient des effets charmants en transportant à la verrerie des éléments de décoration imités de ceux que les Chinois et les Japonais appliquent, au moyen de l'émail, de la laque, de l'or et de l'argent, sur la terre, le bois et le bronze […].' See Didron and Clémendot 1880, p. 43.

26 'Strass' is the term for simulated diamonds made of cut glass with a high lead content and is named after its inventor, an eighteenth-century Paris jeweller: see Garnier 1886, p. 339. Strass is the very dense glass used for simulated precious stones with a lead content of 53%: see A. Sauzay, *La Verrerie depuis les temps les plus reculés jusqu' à nos jours*, with revisions and additions by A. Jacquemart, 3rd ed. (Paris, 1876), pp. 187–88. 'Strass' as Rousseau used the term also meant clear glass with inclusions: see Paris, *Arts Métiers*, 1908, p. 276, nos. 10604–5. 'Strass craquelé' meant, as used by Rousseau, strass glass with a crizzelled or crazed texture, which was produced by submerging a piece in water at the furnace while it was being made: see ibid. no. 10605.

27 'Une pièce, remarquée en 1878, fut créée par Rousseau, qui figurait encore cette année à l'exposition de M. Boucheron, pièce de strass de grande dimension qui fut considerée en 1878 comme un véritable tour de force' (A piece noted in 1878 was

created by Rousseau, who again this year figured prominently at the exhibition mounted by M. Boucheron with a large-scale piece in strass, which was considered a veritable tour de force in 1878): see Henrivaux 1889, p. 172.

28 Hakenjos 1982, p. 118.

29 'L'œuvre est complète, et dans son expression matérielle et dans sa composition [...] littéraire. Tout cela est très Français, et personne, hors des frontières, n'essayerait de rivaliser. On copiera, voilà tout. Pour résumer mon opinion sur M. Gallé, je dirai ceci: c'est un savant, un artiste, un poète.' See E. Bazire, 'La Verrerie et la cristallerie', *Revue des Arts Décoratifs* 5 (1884–85): 194.

30 Léon Appert may have tested his process as early as 1878 on the large piece of 'strass' glass mentioned by Henrivaux (see note 27).

31 René Lalique, who began experimenting with glass in 1890, was advised by Léon Appert and Jules Henrivaux: see Schmitt, Zurich II, 1995, p. 305.

32 Among the hot-glass techniques is application, which requires the glass to be heated at the furnace, thus subjecting the surface to localized melting so that it is automatically smoothed by what is known as fire polishing. Rousseau's range of cold techniques included engraving, cutting and acid-etching. Until 1884 Rousseau may have had his pieces pre-etched and then had the traces left by the etching completely removed. Etching in conjunction with engraving is presented in the report on the Exposition Universelle as a procedure for decorating glass introduced by Léveillé: see Appert and Henrivaux 1893, p. 355.

33 Jules Henrivaux's report expatiates on Rousseau's work and his merits. The term 'œuvre d'art', 'work of art', is used here for the first time in connection with his glass: see Henrivaux 1889, p. 172, and Appert and Henrivaux 1893, pp. 354–55.

34 'A des titres différents, M. Eugène Rousseau a forcé notre estime et mérite notre gratitude. Celui-ci est marchand, fils de marchand; il est devenue artiste à ses risques et périls et, qui mieux est, créateur, par la finesse de son goût et son initiative. [...] Depuis vingt ans, nous le voyons sur la brèche, céramiste et verrier, dessinant, combinant, essayant, fixant des modèles du lendemain [...]. Du jour où il s'est adonné au verre, il a été verrier personnel. [...] Il possède, au degré suprême, le sens du précieux dans les vitrifications: la forme qu'il choisit, japonaise ou non, est toujours celle qui mettra le mieux en valeur sa matière magique. Tout devient gemme entre ses mains. Le verre s'empourpre d'un suc de rose au contact de l'oxyde d'or, s'éclabousse d'un jet de sang là où l'oxyde de cuivre l'est venu marquer, emprunte au manganèse la transparence violette de l'améthyste ou laisse jouer le jaune d'étain, pareil à une huile dorée, dans ses craquelures lumineuses. On ne pouvait rien voir de plus attirant, au palais de l'Industrie, que la vitrine de M. Rousseau, chatoyante et sévère, et digne d'un musée.' See L. de Fourcaud, 'Rapport général', *Revue des Arts Décoratifs* 5 (1884–85): 259–60, pl. 258 a.

35 '[...] Oui, infliger au cristal l'opacité, c'est éteindre les beaux yeux où pénétrait la lumière du ciel. Affubler indifféremment le verre de formes empruntées à des matières opaques, telles que la pierre, le bronze, ou fibreuses comme le bois, formes et parures qui ne jaillissent pas de ses qualités, mais de propriétés contraires à celles qui le caractérisent, c'est une infidélité de l'artisan, c'est un outrage à son art en particulier, à l'art en général. C'est violer la matière. L'ouvrier lui doit le respect [...].' See E. Gallé, 'Sur le décor du verre', *Revue des Arts Décoratifs* 5 (1884–85): 7.

36 On Brocard: '[...] D'autres songent à couvrir le verre, lui s'évertue à lui laisser ses valeurs. Quand il applique un émail, il réserve une transparence. [...] Il a compris cette chose incomprise que le verre n'est pas destiné à devenir opaque, et que sa qualité suprême, c'est sa translucidité [...].'
On Appert: '[...] ce fabricant s'est fait une réputation en supprimant, dans son atelier, le soufflage direct. Il a institué le soufflage mécanique, dont Bontemps avait eu le premier l'idée. [...]

Je le répète, M. Appert est pétri, je dirai même: soufflé de bonnes intentions. Mais, par expérience, il semble que ses bonnes intentions ne produisent guère, en matière décorative principalement, que des résultats superflus.'
On Gallé: '[...] Toutes ses formes ont cet avantage d'être tirées d'éléments naturels. Il ne tourmente pas bizarrement ses moules.' See E. Bazire, 'La Verrerie et la cristallerie', *Revue des Arts Décoratifs* 5 (1884–85): 191–92.

37 For the records documenting the sale of the business to Léveillé see Archives Nationales, Minutier Central, LXVI, 1689, 16 December 1885, *Vente de matériel et marchandises par M. Rousseau à M. et Mme Léveillé*.

38 The vases given by Léveillé in 1889 to the Conservatoire Nationale des Arts et Métiers in Paris bear the inscription 'Fabrication de M. E. Léveillé': see Paris, *Arts Métiers*, 1908, p. 276, nos. 11536, 11537.

39 Appert and Henrivaux 1893, p. 355. Antonin Daum started using the more economical combination of acid-etching and engraving, which is more suitable for serial production, from the outset of the manufacture of glass art at Daum Frères, from 1889/90, and varied it at will.

40 Henrivaux 1889, p. 172.

41 Hakenjos 1982, p. 127.

42 In 1876 Auguste Jean must have been first forced into insolvency as a consequence of the Franco-Prussian War of 1870/71 and the ensuing rebellion of the Communards: see Archives Départementales de Paris, 'Rapport Faillite Jean 13 Avril 1876', D11U3, 813, no. 997. Like Gallé, he was a technically skilful, inventive artist and was probably the first to register an application for a patent, on 8 November 1872, as Bulletin no. 97101, 'Application de la galvanoplastie à la décoration de tous les produits de la céramique'. In it he specifies the most permanent method of making non-conductive (necessary for galvanically applied decoration) surfaces, such as pottery, faience and porcelain, conductive. Had he extended this patent application at the same time to include glass, the Austrian firm of Gebrüder Feix in Albrechtsdorf would not be regarded as the inventors of galvanically applied decoration on glass, for which they were awarded a distinction in 1889: see Appert and Henrivaux 1893, p. 355. After insolvency in 1876 Jean turned to glass design and again invested on a lavish scale in new studio buildings and furnaces. Like the insolvency report of 1883, the report of 1876 contains an exhaustive biography of Auguste Jean although, compared with other sources, the information in it is occasionally erroneous: see Archives Départementales de Paris, 'Rapport Faillite Jean 27 Mars 1883', D11U3, 1090, no. 13397.

43 This, too, remains to be studied in depth.

44 Gallé took over this decoration as a direct quotation, an exception for him: see Hilschenz-Mlynek and Ricke 1985, pp. 180–81, nos. 208–9.

45 Hilschenz-Mlynek and Ricke 1985, p. 169, no. 194.

46 On Gallé see Thiébaut, *Dessins*, 1993, illus. p. 178; on Daum see Paris 1903, illus. n.p.; Paris, portfolio, 1903, pl. 17, no. 4.

47 Indicated in the report, which begins as follows: '[...] Ces objets, nouveaux comme décorations, indiquent que cet art peut encore se développer, "s'affiner" [...]' (These new objects, *qua* ornaments, indicate that this art still has scope to develop, to 'become more sophisticated'). See Appert and Henrivaux 1893, p. 355.

48 Gallé, *Ecrits*, 1908, pp. 293–301.

Victor Prouvé, *Emile Gallé in his Studio*, 1892, oil on canvas, 150 x 98 cm. Signed bottom right: 'Cordial Hommage à l'Excellent artiste Emile Gallé. Nancy, Victor Prouvé Xbre 1892'. Musée de l'Ecole de Nancy, Nancy

Helmut Ricke

Emile Gallé:
A Brief Appraisal*

Few artists' personas have been determined by a single painting to the extent that Emile Gallé's has. Hardly any book on Art Nouveau – and the present volume is no exception – can get by without reproducing that famous picture of the master in his studio (illus. p. 34) that was painted in October 1892 by his friend, occasional employee and companion throughout his career, Victor Prouvé. Even today this painting looks – quite rightly so – somehow more authentic than the numerous extant photographs showing the founder of the Ecole de Nancy at different ages.

The painting reflects the way contemporaries saw Gallé and presumably also tallied, for the most part, with his own idea of himself. Gallé, depicted in a pictorial space that is not specifically defined, yet informed by spiritual and intellectual qualities, seems to dissolve in an aureole over the table at which he is seated to heighten the drama of the creative act: the artist awaiting inspiration, the creative spark. Portrayed as a sensitive, highly strung man wearing garments that almost resemble a priest's cassock, he sets about his task with the utmost concentration, his pen apparently poised to capture in writing or a sketch the still inchoate idea forming in his mind's eye.

The scene at the centre is – according with Symbolist ideas of art – surrounded by objects rife with connotations. Coloured glass vases of various shapes and sizes indicate the field of endeavour to which Gallé unstintingly devoted himself from the late 1880s onwards. The figure portrayed is not the designer of fine ceramics or the most outstanding creator of Art Nouveau intarsia furniture but rather a glass artist, from whose hands marvels of his craft emerged to enchant an entire era.

The type of work to be done on the vessels surrounding him on the spacious work surface has, however, deliberately been left indeterminate. Is the vase in his left hand a blank that has just been procured from the glassworks so that he can entice from it its potential for decoration before handing it over to the engraver ready to receive it and carry out the designer's detailed instructions in the studio? Is Gallé musing over a correction, a variation or perhaps even the next model or is he listening to the voice of the glass to receive the answer to questions he has asked?

Twining tendrils, foliage and flowers, placed as if casually in the vessels or strewn about the work top, illustrate the forces on which all endeavours in this space are centred – the diverse phenomena of nature, her cycle of growth and decay, her symbolic powers over all living things, including humankind.

Then there are a great many sheets of paper spread about, an unusually dominant motif. They refer to the enormous amount of planning, designs, written notes and fleetingly executed sketches that were so crucial to the artist's work. To one side lies a book – a sign of intellectual preoccupations, not only knowledge and scholarship but also, perhaps first and foremost, letters and poetry.

The portrait of the man himself confirms what we know, or believe we know, about him. Prouvé has portrayed him warts and all: pale, with a tendency to nervous hyperactivity and certainly not an easy person to deal with. This portrait makes him look less attractive than he is in many contemporary photographs (illus. p. 39, top). The sitter's prominent nose is shown entirely in profile so that it becomes the dominant facial feature, indeed accentuating the forceful intensity of his expression, which is concentrated in his fixed, almost piercing gaze. The frail leanness, the almost haggard quality, which was the artist's distinguishing characteristic, is emphasized. At the same time this portrait has captured a flexible and vivid intellect. Prouvé has succeeded magnificently in rendering in visual terms a man who, albeit not the slave of his feelings, nonetheless acts intuitively and is receptive. His extraordinary sensitivity is expressed in the hand holding the vase, concentrated, as it were, in the long, slender fingers. There is something almost palpably obsessive in the sitter's concentration on what he is doing. The impression is created that this was a driven man, incessantly demanding too much of himself – probably aware that his life would not be an overly long one – and given over entirely to his artistic aims, which were linked with the loftiest ambitions for himself and his staff.

This is the quality – Gallé's absolutely uncompromising dedication to his art – that Prouvé, a kindred spirit, wanted to capture for posterity. It is certainly the side of this complex personality that has had permanency, ensuring Gallé his place in the history of turn-of-the-century art.

Still the painting, in representing this versatile, prolific and talented man as a dreamer, a visionary utterly caught up in creativity, captures only one side of the artist. One can imagine other portraits of him. He might just as plausibly have been portrayed as a prudent, farsighted entrepreneur in his factories, a man who was fully aware of the responsibilities he bore for a workforce of several hundred and still growing, a manager who knew how to exploit the commercial viability of serial production without – at least as far as he is concerned – coming into conflict with his artistic aims.[1] Another facet of his personality that does not seem to fit with the notion of an artist lost in an idealistic dreamland is the hard-headed economic journalist Gallé also was, com-

Left: Emile Gallé's father,
Charles Louis Edouard Gallé
(1818–1902), c. 1865

Right: Emile Gallé in 1867, aged
twenty-one

mitted to fostering foreign trade and against absurd export regulations and customs practices.[2]

Depicting Gallé as a scholar and writer in his study would also have been an approach worthy of Prouvé's commitment to his subject. The writings published by Gallé as a botanist and herbalist, not to mention a landscape architect, mineralogist, art theorist and public-relations adept in his own cause in themselves represent a not insubstantial life's work.[3] If that were not enough, there is a voluminous correspondence, which to this day has yet to be subjected to thorough study and represents far more than a running commentary on his daily work routine.[4]

Yet another painting might portray him as a scientist, a chemist experimenting with glazes or as an expert glass technician surrounded by his staff, who possessed the basic knowledge and skills needed for any stage of production so that he always appeared in the glassworks as well as the refining studios as an unassailable authority. Instructions for working, written in his hand and sounding very practical and authoritative, exist as well as precise guidelines for production and recommendations for everyday application, which amply furnish telling evidence of this side of his personality.[5]

What would, on the other hand, be misleading would be a portrait in which Gallé is depicted actually performing a specific task connected with his craft, such as painting or engraving glass. For all his profound insight into the aesthetic potential of these decorating techniques

and his knowledge in employing them to best effect, hands-on experience was not his strong point.[6] Even in drawing, a medium he had dabbled in since his school days and intensively pursued during his years of training and travel before 1867, he can scarcely be said to have attained more than amateur status for all his connoisseurship. Consequently, to realize his ideas and execute many of his designs, he had the good sense to rely on the professional skills of employees, such as Louis Hestaux, Auguste Herbst and Paul Nicolas, or the designers Désiré Christian and Eugène Jacques Kremer, who were bound by contract to his firm in the Meisenthal workshops of Burgun, Schverer & Co.[7] Even for the illustration of his botanical works he preferred to rely on these experts' superior skills.[8] The artistic medium he felt most at home with was cursory watercolour sketches. In them he succeeded admirably in putting across the ideas that spontaneously occurred to him, in quick, sweeping brushwork and an extraordinarily attractive palette.[9]

It would also have been a daunting task to portray him as the driving force behind his Nancy workshops, of which he was the guiding spirit, whose ideas pervaded an entire region and went far beyond it. Nevertheless Prouvé's painting does hint at this side of his personality.

Another portrayable facet would have been Gallé as an eloquent public speaker, committed to human rights. For years he used these skills unstintingly in the cause of Captain Dreyfus, a Jew who had been the victim of injustice, wrongly accused of divulging military secrets.

A suitable pose might also have been found to portray the ardent patriot and model Frenchman that Gallé was. As a chevalier and, from 1900, commander of the Legion of Honour, he would also have cut a good figure.

The quality most obviously missing from the portrait is his passion for studying the native flora of Lorraine in his garden or an exotic plant only recently introduced from the Far East or an unfamiliar species of orchid.[10] A portrait along these lines would reveal Gallé as an inward-directed person who withdrew from the demands made on him daily by all his commitments to contemplate the essentials of life – and that meant to him nature, as the basis of all life and the wellspring of creativity. In portraying this quality, one would presumably come closest to capturing the quintessence of Gallé's personality, informed by religion of a decidedly Protestant tinge, which in the course of his life turned into an equally deeply felt pantheism.

Contemporary photographs can indeed go some way towards replacing all these missing pictures, some of them revealing affinities with the Prouvé painting. One – dominated by huge acanthus leaves in front of a window – shows Gallé in profile as he sits writing, emphasizing all the more clearly his chaotic surroundings, whether as a result of his activities or a determining factor in the course he will take (illus. p. 40, top).

Others trace the course of Gallé's development as a man and an artist. In an early photograph of him, at twenty-one (illus. p. 36, right), he already looked back on a broad-based course of study and training in all the diverse fields that interested him: studies in Germany, travels to several countries and intensive on-the-job training at the Meisenthal glassworks of Burgun, Schverer & Co. in neighbouring Alsace. It shows a young man lost in thought yet nonetheless eager in 1867 to find a niche of his own in the family business under the watchful eye of a demanding yet benevolent father (illus. p. 36, left), where he can break new ground for himself and the firm.

Still rather unformed yet fine-featured and idealistic, he is then shown at twenty-four as a volunteer in the 23rd Regiment of the Line in the 1870/71 Franco-Prussian War (illus. above). He was yet to have the experience, even though he was spared service on the front, that would mould his political views and shape his patriotic attitude. The annexation of neighbouring Alsace-Lorraine in the Frankfurt Treaty was a blow to him. The impact it had had on him was reflected most noticeably in the work he produced in the 1870s and 1880s, although his stance never was that of a simplistic nationalist. Gallé, after all, mastered the German language and all his life maintained both business and private contacts with France's neighbour to the east.

A photograph of Gallé and his young wife, Henriette, née Grimm (illus. p. 38), records his integrated status in the bourgeois society of his native city, revealing a man

on a comfortable footing with the higher classes and documenting a marriage that would produce four daughters. All his life Gallé saw himself as part of this society, in which he – through membership of associations or assumption of honorary office – always strove to play an establishment role. Nothing was further from his mind than to strike bohemian poses. Seriousness of purpose, a sense of responsibility and awareness of the artist's duty to educate and his moral mission informed his way of life.

Photographs of the Gallé family are rare, yet occasional remarks made in his correspondence, dedications and presents indicate that his private life meant a great deal to Emile Gallé. Henriette played an active role in her husband's life. A prime example is her whole-hearted support for his endeavours in the Dreyfus Affair.[11]

Photographs became rarer in the years that followed. Again one's imagination supplies the missing pictures – snapshots of situations characteristic of this particular life, ones that shaped it: Gallé talking to Tokuzo Takashima, for instance, a Japanese forestry expert who studied in Nancy from 1885 to 1888. Thanks to his talent as a draughtsman, the provincial art scene in Nancy was given a close-up view of the East Asian conception of art and design.[12] Another would be of Gallé in 1885 studying the von Brandt collection of Chinese cased glass in the Kunstgewerbemuseum, Berlin. Still other snapshots would show the artist in company with distinguished contemporaries, dining with Edmond de Goncourt at

Emile Gallé and his wife,
Henriette, née Grimm, in 1875,
shortly after marrying

lifted his head and shoulders above a host of contemporaries. One must read his notes on his submissions to the 1884 and 1889 Expositions Universelles[14] in order to grasp and appreciate how unique this combination of talents was.

In 1889 Gallé was confronted with the task of consolidating the success he had achieved, expanding it as a firm foundation from which to launch a broad-based realization of his ideas. He eagerly took up this challenge and drove his projects forwards, only to overtax his physical powers in the end. Announced in his 1889 *Notices d'Exposition* and accompanied by the critical remarks of such aristocratic, elitist contemporaries as Robert de Montesquiou,[15] his programme for serial production was so successful that it led to a considerable broadening of this range, culminating in his terminating the collaboration in 1894 with his principal manufacturer, Burgun, Schverer & Co. in Meisenthal,[16] and building viable factories of his own in Nancy.

These years also saw him enter the glittering world of the 'fine arts'. The applied and decorative arts were henceforth recognized, even by the public at large, as being of equal status as painting and sculpture, say, and accorded a commensurate annual forum from 1892 in the Champ-de-Mars Salon exhibitions. The realization of contributions to these ambitious competitions, the commissions urged on him by members of Paris high society, the commissions connected with state visits or commemorative gifts at anniversary celebrations, etc., for all of which Gallé rightly felt responsible, increasingly took up his time and energy. At the same time his responsibilities for his expanding workshops and factories were also growing.

He had found what would be his mature, 1890s style by 1889, yet it was not enough for Gallé simply to draw on the forms and decoration conceived for this exhibition and vary them. He made a point of exploring the potential of coloured overlay, applying it both to serially produced wares and introducing it in his better studio pieces (cat. nos. 28, 29, 31, 32). And floral decoration was increasingly assuming the symbolic dimension that turns reproduction into image, a step that he presented as his agenda and professional creed in a lecture held at the Académie de Stanislas, Nancy, in 1900.[17]

Statements of a highly personal nature increasingly inform the outstanding Gallé pieces in the 'grand genre' and the 'série riche' – his own terms for the luxury pieces produced at his workshops. Melancholy and awareness of the transience of all things are reflected in his *vases de tristesse* (cat. nos. 23, 37, 51). In these pieces Gallé demonstrates consummate skill in exploiting the results of chemical and technical experiments to heighten artistic expression.

Gallé's intellectual horizon and poetic leanings are increasingly disclosed in works that are poetry pure and simple – *verres parlantes* – adorned almost unnecessarily

his house, conversing with Marcel Proust, an admirer of his, with Robert de Montesquiou or Anna de Noailles, Countess Greffulhe, whom he revered and whose salon he frequented, with the idolized actress Sarah Bernhardt or with Loïe Fuller, the dancer who was the talk of all Paris.[13] All these photographs were either never taken or have not come to light.

What is perhaps the finest portrait photograph of Gallé was taken in the year that saw his major breakthrough: his success at the 1889 Exposition Universelle in Paris (illus. p. 39, top). It reveals him as self-confident, assured and self-sufficient, a law unto himself – a man who is at the height of his creative powers yet is still striving to attain the still distant goals of his dreams. This is the time in which he saw everything he had striven for confirmed, when he was acclaimed and encouraged from all sides. The 1870s and early 1880s were the years during which he explored his potential, experimenting with historicism and eclecticism (cat. no. 19) and now they lay behind him. His study of Japanese and Chinese art and the impulses he received from Rousseau and his Paris circle (cat. nos. 20, 21) bore fruit and nature was by now uncontestedly the focus of his work. Minerals and flora, supplemented by entomological and marine fauna motifs, now shaped the appearance of his pieces. The dual nature of this artist, who knew how to turn his profound knowledge of glass technology and natural science into instruments for realizing grand ideas of design,

with lines of verse from poets Gallé particularly admired.[18] Yet the interplay of the poetry of glass and that of the written word meant far more to Gallé than witty aperçus, as is shown when the two engage in a kind of dialogue (cat. no. 44). Other pieces from those years reflect the fascination exerted on Gallé and his contemporaries by the fledgling science of oceanography and the discoveries it brought to light. The mysteries of the sea, only partly decoded and still alluringly dangerous, inspired Gallé's underwater scenes, which are suffused with movement, a mood of hovering unreality and, on occasion, even a menacing quality (cat. nos. 33, 45, 52).

The portrait photograph for which Gallé sat in 1895, when he was forty-nine (illus. right), seems to be marked more by the exertions of those years than the successes. Gallé looks drawn, tense, almost aggressive. Yet this photograph shows him on the threshold of his mature work. The years between 1895 and 1900 would see the creation of works linked with his name as unparalleled masterpieces.

Apart from a lifelong urge to cross borders and conquer new artistic territory while advancing glass technology, the challenge of participating in the Paris Exposition Universelle planned to celebrate the turn of the century must indeed have been a crucial driving force. The years from 1897 were definitively shaped by this event and by the task he set himself of once again asserting himself and consolidating his own position, possibly even of surpassing the expectations his contemporaries had of him, which could not have been anything but high.

This is the period in which Gallé developed the techniques of marquetry and patinage, which fulfilled his need for devising ever-new sophisticated means of expression. Gallé found possibilities for enhancing the

originality of his designs and heightening his powers of expression in interlayering and overlaying different colours, mixing different types of batch, which is technically very difficult, enclosing streaky veils of air bubbles and artificially induced impurities, working with glass that is not fully in the molten state and experimenting with the artistic potential of surface textures so unusual that they had, up to then, been considered rejects by glass-blowers.

The photograph taken of him in his studio in 1898/99 (illus. p. 40, top) captures the mood of that stage of his career. Unmistakably echoing the 1892 Prouvé painting, this photograph, because it is so much more detailed, conveys a more realistic impression of the artist in his working environment. The photograph looks both poetic and artistic without, however, appearing arranged or posed. It would seem to have been used as the model for a painting done by Gallé's workshop foreman, Louis Hestaux (illus. p. 41), showing the artist writing. Painted in the manner of seventeenth-century minor Dutch painters, its composition features the subject backlit by a window. Whether the petty bourgeois idealization emanating from this picture does justice to Gallé's personality is a moot question. The painting cannot have been executed before 1899, yet it reveals nothing of the artist's actual physical and mental state at the time. It is likely, or at least not impossible, that it was painted after the photograph but not until Gallé was dead, as an idealizing tribute paid by his closest colleague.

Emile Gallé in 1895, aged forty-nine

Emile Gallé in his studio,
c. 1898/99

With the prospect of the turn-of-the-century exhibition before him, Gallé's work became more noticeably orientated towards the meaning underlying externals – towards symbolic content, mood and atmospheric qualities. Pieces such as 'La Nature' (cat. no. 47), created for the 1900 Exposition Universelle, exemplify this endeavour.

Gallé's submissions to that exhibition both summarize his career and represent its acme. Alongside 1890s ideas that he now perfected, the marquetry pieces represented current work. The development that would take place in the final years of his life was also foreshadowed (cat. no. 52). Once again honoured with the Grand Prix and made a commander of the Legion of Honour, Gallé celebrated the turn-of-the-century Exposition Universelle as a personal triumph. Yet when one looks at the only extant photograph from that year (illus. below), little is apparent of the elation one might expect. On the contrary, an almost insecure-looking man gazes rather reluctantly out of it. Virtually nothing is left of the energy that made even the 1895 photograph so evocatively powerful. Vigorous activity seems to have yielded to inward-directedness and a pensive mood.

This is a man who, although showing the signs of advancing terminal illness, was nonetheless about to embark on conceiving works that would break through yet another aesthetic barrier. In his late vessels and objects he turned increasingly to exploiting the sculptural potential of glass, questioning the conventional assumptions underlying vessel shapes. Under his supervision, the glass-blowers in Nancy now began to model the hot glass batch like clay. The cutters and engravers handled the applied decoration like sculpture. Ambivalent in expression, often beautiful yet just as often men-

Emile Gallé in 1900, aged fifty-four

acing (cat. nos. 59, 61), almost aggressive yet invariably of the most extreme intensity, these pieces mark the last step towards art in glass. No trace remains of the utilitarian function of the serviceable object. Of consummate workmanship, these pieces mark the end, a zenith that cannot conceivably be surpassed.

Even when one takes into consideration the limits of a medium like photography, subject as it is to the vagaries of external influences so that it does not allow all too profound conclusions to be drawn about the psychological and physical state of the subject portrayed, the sequence of portrait photographs taken of Emile Gallé – in view of the facts and sources available on his life and work – gives a plausible and authentic overview of his career, revealing something of his character, his strengths and weaknesses and his world-view.

Yet something eludes understanding: character traits and personal secrets that no photograph or painting can disclose, the depths of Gallé's character, the reasons why he was so prolific and so versatile, the heights to which his ambition spurred him to attain – at least in his final years – his often histrionic self-stylization, his premonitions of death and paralyzing depression.[19] What remains is the picture of a man driven incessantly by his creative powers, whose life ended early yet not before fulfilment. This was a man who, with all his other talents, was quintessentially an artist – one who gave a final viable expression to the closing nineteenth century.

Helmut Ricke

Louis Hestaux, *Portrait of Emile Gallé, c.* 1900 or after 1904, oil on canvas, 48 x 31 cm. Signed: 'L. Hestaux'. Musée Lorrain, Nancy

Notes

* There did not seem much point in providing an extensive survey of Emile Gallé's life and work in the present book. For that readers are referred to several excellent accounts: Hakenjos 1982; Garner 1976; Zurich 1980; and Paris, *Gallé*, 1985. Since, on the other hand, Gallé is so central to the Koepff Collection, this essay shall focus on the artist's personality as it is shown in the various extant paintings and photographs of him.

For a commentary on Gallé's career from a contemporary point of view see the address of Charles de Meixmoron de Dombasle in the 'Sources' section of this volume. For facts on the history of the firm and the development of the factory see the survey of 'Manufacturers and Artists' in the present book.

1 See the comments made by Gallé on his serially produced wares, published as *Applications industrielles: Vulgarisation artistique*, in conjunction with his notes on his contribution to the 1889 Exposition Universelle in Paris; see Gallé, *Ecrits*, 1908, pp. 348–49, translated into English in the 'Sources'.

2 See, for instance, Emile Gallé, *Considérations à propos de notre commerce extérieur* (Nancy, 1884).

3 On Gallé's published writings see Gallé, *Ecrits*, 1908; overview in Hakenjos 1982, pp. 861–69, and in Paris, *Gallé*, 1985, pp. 310–11.

4 This is especially true of Gallé's correspondence with the leading men of letters of his day, such as Robert de Montesquiou, which is now in the Bibliothèque Nationale in Paris, but has hitherto been studied mainly by Montesquiou scholars; see Hakenjos 1982, p. 674, n. 1387.

5 See excerpts from the correspondence in the Chambon Collection at The Corning Museum of Glass, translated into English in the 'Sources'.

6 Gallé seems to have personally had a hand in painting faience only in his early years, while working for his father at the St-Clément factory, where he himself designed rustic, comical or conventionally historicist decoration for it. These pieces do not indicate any particular talent for handling brush and paint.

7 See on this the confidential contract of collaboration concluded between Gallé and the Meisenthal glassworks in 1885, translated into English in the 'Sources'.

8 See Gallé's sketches, which may be even more awkward because of the onset of his illness, for his study of native orchids and the way Nicolas handled them, in Le Tacon 1995, pp. 92–93, and Pertuy 1984.

9 See the colour sketches for glass in Thiébaut, *Dessins*, 1993, pp. 36, 37, which were presumably intended, with written pointers, as conceptual notes for the workshop. A single sheet of this kind is in the Chambon Collection at The Corning Museum of Glass, but bears no written notes.

10 The photograph taken *c.* 1890 of Gallé posing in his garden, reproduced in Charpentier et al., 1987, p. 73, can only begin to close the gap.

11 Gallé had a lady's secrétaire made as a present for his wife on this occasion, with the dedication 'To my courageous wife, Henriette Gallé, commemorating the patriotic struggles for the principles of humanity, justice and liberty. May 1899. Emile Gallé, treasurer of the French League for the Defence of Human and Civil Rights'; see Garner 1976, p. 123.

12 See Le Tacon 1995, pp. 38–42.

13 For more on this aspect of Gallé see, in particular, the very lively description in the chapter entitled 'Le Chef des Odeurs Suaves' in Garner 1976, pp. 111–30.

14 See Gallé, *Ecrits*, 1908, pp. 302–17, translated into English in the 'Sources', and pp. 332–53, with a translated excerpt also in the 'Sources'. The complete text has been published in English in Corning 1984, pp. 181–89.

15 See the remarks made by the Robert de Montesquiou in his essay on goldsmiths and glass artists, published in *Roseaux pensants* (Paris, 1897), translated into English in the 'Sources'.

16 Collaboration with the Meisenthal glassworks goes back to the period when Charles Gallé was managing director. Around 1884 disputes broke out between the partners, which were resolved by the conclusion of a contract with Gallé, the factory and the head decorator, Désiré Christian, as signatories; translated into English in the 'Sources'.

17 See the address and the reply of president Meixmoron de Dombasle, translated into English in the 'Sources'.

18 The quotations on Gallé's pieces were not universally admired by contemporaries; some found them superfluous. See on this Gallé's comments on his submission to the 1898 Salon, translated into English in the 'Sources'.

19 The importance that taking drugs – addressed prudently yet certainly not as something unusual for the time – may have had for Gallé in his work as an artist will probably never be clarified; see Garner 1976, pp. 141–42.

Brigitte Leonhardt

Emile Gallé, Symbolism and Art Criticism in Germany

'La matière est pour nous matière à poésie'

Emile Gallé as viewed by German art critics

'The material is to us the stuff of poetry': this quotation from the Lorraine poet Emile Hinzelin is a metaphor for Emile Gallé's artistic agenda. The latter chose this verse as the 'title' of a display case in which he showed work at the Eighth International Art Exhibition in Munich in 1898.[1]

That was not the first time Gallé had exhibited work in Germany. The year before he had been represented with glass creations at the celebrated Glass Palace Exhibition in Munich and at the International Art Exhibition in Dresden. In 1897 he also opened his own retail outlet, at 38 Kaiserstrasse in Frankfurt am Main, to facilitate contact with German customers and the directors of the recently founded museums for the decorative and applied arts. His most important submission to any German exhibition was an entire interior, replete with furnishings and appointments, at the First Art and Applied Arts Exhibition in Darmstadt in 1898, in which he was the only non-German artist to participate. As the commentary in the catalogue explains, 'so many artworks by Emile Gallé–Nancy, […] are shown for the first time in Germany […]: a wide variety of furniture in the French style with rich intarsia decoration […], primarily floral and plant motifs with butterflies […], and, most notably, the finely wrought pieces in glass of coloured batch with representations worked from or into them by means of cutting, etching and engraving.'[2] He presented 113 exhibits in what was known as the Purple Room.[3]

That Gallé was so much better represented than other artists, many of whom showed only a single painting and at most fifteen works, indicates how highly valued his work was. This is especially remarkable when one considers the unmistakable nationalist objectives of that particular exhibition: '[…] in order to awaken in the public a sense of Germanness and German character in modern art'.[4] Gallé appears to have been satisfied with his sales in Germany[5] even though he does write that the public's interest tended to lie in 'mediocre wares'.[6] Was this owing to scarce financial resources, a general lack of interest in glass art or limited press coverage in Germany?

Although he was so well represented at exhibitions in Germany and had received so many awards since 1889 at exhibitions in France and abroad, reporting on Gallé's work remained limited to short reviews until 1900. He was generally acknowledged for having revived the art of glassmaking, yet scarcely any informed reviews of his work appeared in art journals. The texts generalized, often beginning with a positive view of glass art and ending with critical remarks on utility glass lacking functionality. It was not until 1899 that a longer report, on Ecole de Nancy glass, was printed in the journal *Dekorative Kunst* with six pages of illustrations, some of them in colour. The article deals primarily with the relationship of glass art to utility glass. The 'sublime poetry' of Gallé's vases is praised, but the author seems to have considered the manufacture of reasonably priced utility glass more important: 'With the indefatigable energy characteristic of a MORRIS, he [Gallé] defied the public at large at the last international exhibition to win the recognition he so rightly deserved […].' He does, however, dilute his praise with criticism: 'This prestige has long concealed the other side of the coin from us. Whereas luxury glass has developed into all sorts of sophisticated guises, utility glass has continued to be utterly neglected.'[7]

The specialist press shows a far more positive response. Gustav Pazaurek, probably the most important turn-of-the-century glass expert, published several articles on Gallé. In his famous book entitled *Moderne Gläser*, published in 1901, he covered Gallé's work extensively. The book's endpapers, which consist of a colour reproduction of three Gallé vases, can be viewed as a tribute to the artist. In an introductory essay Pazaurek outlines the most recent trends in modern glass art, emphasizing the importance of Gallé's work compared with Karl Koepping's delicate ornamental glass, which was positively received in France as well: 'Two representatives of other styles who have already set trends and are at the forefront of modern glass art production are immeasurably more important, viz. Gallé of France and Tiffany, an American.'[8] In a separate chapter on the Ecole de Nancy, Pazaurek has a great deal to say in praise of Gallé, singling out his pioneering role as a model for other glassmakers, not just in Nancy but worldwide. Pazaurek admires Gallé's technical inventiveness and his skill at taking up impulses received from East Asian models and turning them into a style distinctively his own. Above all, he points out that cost-intensive techniques, such as casing and marquetry, are employed as a means of translating 'poetic ideas' into the medium of glass, and not just for the sake of demonstrating virtuosity in handling them. He does, however, refer rather sarcastically to 'the deeper meaning underlying Gallé's intentions, [which] one might not always be able to decipher were not supplementary quotations provided as didactic aids'.[9]

This last sentence refers to a debate about the quotations from poetry that has cropped up time and again, not just in Germany but in the French press as well.

Leopold Gmelin also referred to this discussion in his review of the exhibition, which was printed in 1897 in the journal *Kunst und Kunsthandwerk*: 'Opponents of "programme music" will reproach him for providing so many of his pieces with the words of poets or the like, which also set the basic mood of the decoration [...]'.[10] With criticism focusing so frequently on these quotations, the questions arise as to what these verses signify and whether they are acceptable at all in the applied arts. To shed light on this poetic and literary aspect of Gallé's work it will be necessary to discuss the position it occupies on the fraught continuum between the fine and the applied arts.

In the wake of the art reform movements that swept the late nineteenth century, many artists who had originally trained as painters, including Peter Behrens, Henry van de Velde and Richard Riemerschmid, no longer saw their vocation in fine art but rather in decorating everyday, utilitarian objects. They advocated abolishing the borders between the fine and the applied arts, and called for a synthesis of both. Their ideal was art and design pervading all aspects of life so that a *Gesamtkunstwerk*, a total work of art, might be created. A consequence of this stated aim was a change in exhibition style and the opening of the Salons and art exhibitions to the applied arts. The first noticeable impact it had in Germany was in 1897, when a separate section for *Kleinkunst* (*objets de vertu*) was established at the aforementioned art exhibition in the Glass Palace. Gallé's pieces were shown in these exhibition rooms together with furniture and utilitarian objects designed in the 'modern style'. The decorative and applied arts now had access to the sacred halls of the fine arts, but they continued to be separated.

The term *Kleinkunst* begs the question of double meaning: is the classification a qualitative one, based on the physical properties and aesthetic qualities of materials, or is it quantitative, depending on the size of the objects in question? If one compares the exhibits in this group, size actually does seem to be the criterion by which they are assigned to it: mirrors, salt cellars and beakers are listed. Does the second aspect – the artistic or aesthetic side – derive, as it were, as a logical consequence from the first? Viewed from the angle of distinguishing clearly between 'fine art' and the 'applied arts', the literary 'titles' on Gallé vases would seem to represent a deliberate crossing of boundaries, to the closely related art of poetry, more specifically, lyric poetry. In the discussion about the *Gesamtkunstwerk* and synaesthetic effects centring on Richard Wagner's aesthetic objectives, the verses on vases boldly challenge art critics and connoisseurs to reflect not only on the categorization of the fine arts but also on the relationship between language and the fine arts. Critics, however, avoid this daunting hermeneutic task, pointing instead to the tradition of linking verse with objects intended as gifts and with glasses bearing mottoes, or to the 'moods' these are meant to create.

From Symbolism to the enigmatic nature of art

The turn of the century saw some painters placing an ever-greater distance between themselves and the fine arts to design functional objects 'in good taste' for serial production. Emile Gallé went in the opposite direction. He did not, however, view himself as a producer of luxury glass objects that would arouse admiration because they were aesthetically perfect and finished with the utmost sophistication as has often been claimed disparagingly in the press. On the contrary, his objective was to address people's interest in knowledge and self-knowledge. With his quotations from poetry he refers to the polysemic, enigmatic aspect of his works. By making his shapes indeterminate and, *c.* 1900, increasingly sculptural, he also freed his objects visually from their originally utilitarian function as vases and bowls. This enigmatic ambivalence between poetry and aesthetic object exacts an entirely different response: attention is diverted from the ornamental appearance of these works to a deeper level of meaning. Gallé was aiming at art, not the decorative and applied arts. Thoughts, 'ideas' are at the core of many of his quotations: 'Aimons l'Idée avec tous ses aspects: Puissance, Verité, Liberté, Paix, Justice, Innocence' (Let us love all aspects of the Idea: Power, Truth, Liberty, Peace, Justice, Innocence).[11]

Ideals and abstract ideas, such as justice and truth, are philosophical criteria; they cannot be represented in a 'concrete' form but must be translated to the symbolic plane. Unlike symbols, however, allegories are always associated with a specific semantic content. Gallé, on the other hand, always sought an 'open-ended' form of representation that was polysemic and not fixed so that he could express his artistic intentions in a sophisticated way. The problem with polysemic statements aiming at transcendence lies in their being difficult for viewers to understand. Gallé's works were, as we have said, presented in the sections for *Kleinkunst* and the applied arts rather than the fine arts rooms. Perception is always affected by context, that is, by prior knowledge and environmental conditions. In the *Kleinkunst* section of the exhibition visitors' attention was directed primarily at the usefulness and overall aesthetic effect of the objects exhibited in it. In referring to poetry, Gallé provided viewers with a second plane of reception and response, thus stimulating intellectual activity that went beyond merely acknowledging mimetic reproduction.

In so doing, he was using a 'trick' that could not be verified until the twentieth century, when empirical studies dealing with viewer and reader response were conducted in the epistemological context of reception theory. Literary and philosophical texts in particular have been found to provoke interpretations that generate meanings when dealing with the symbolic and transcendent content of works of art.[12] Gallé was probably not completely aware of the impact he made, but he did know exactly what reception problems arose when his objects were viewed under such conditions. That this was so is indicated by his great 'need to impart', with which he 'sought to trigger as many associations as possible in everyone viewing his works', as Pazaurek sarcastically remarks in his book.[13] In order to prevent himself from being neatly pigeon-holed, Gallé wrote copious descriptions of what he intended with his submissions.[14]

How strongly visitor reception at the 1897 Glass Palace exhibition was moulded by traditional notions of art – and undoubtedly still is today – is amusingly described by an art critic who was a contemporary of Gallé's: 'One day, in 1897, at the Munich Glass Palace, I became enthusiastic about an extraordinarily elegant couple who were conversing extremely knowledgeably but without being pompous about pictures and sculpture. [...] they were trying to understand and this meant a great deal. Consequently, I became convinced that these were people who were visiting the exhibition not for appearance's sake, because it was fashionable to do so, but because they had developed a certain feeling for beauty. Now, however, making their way to the Salons in the left wing, [...] they went through one or two of them until the beautiful lady turned up that little nose of hers and uttered one disparaging word: "junk room", before they vanished.

This junk room contains neither pictures nor sculpture [...]. Each "piece of junk" was, on the other hand, genuine art in the best sense of the word; it included lovely pieces of furniture by Berlepsch [and] wonderful glass by Emile Gallé [...].'[15]

Gallé's works were presented in just such 'junk rooms'. As a result, it is only too clear why he used all the means at his disposal to convey his intentions as an artist. Numerous contemporary biographies emphasize that Gallé was not concerned with beauty but instead wanted to express his 'ideas on art'. Why were these scarcely recognized by German art critics despite all the information provided? In refusing to address the content of his works, they indirectly denied him the right to claim that these are works of art. Is this because art critics tend to think in categories? Does the traditional classification by material that assigns glass to the applied arts preclude any claims to it having fine art status or is this rejection directed at the unintelligibility of the literature quoted? The writer and art critic Roger Marx described Gallé's work as '[...] unfathomable like a mysterious temple that no one enters without awe and bewilderment. Grace and beauty are only the outer garment. In the depths of the consecrated interior glows the flame of the spirit.'[16]

Oddly enough, the Romantic poetry of Victor Hugo crops up again and again in this connection, yet Charles Baudelaire is hardly ever mentioned by German art critics, even though most of the quotations on Gallé's works are from him.[17]

In the final third of the nineteenth century, after the fall of the Second Empire, an intensive discussion got underway in France about Symbolist literature and the work of Victor Hugo, who did not return from exile until 1871. In their quest for a new art form independent of models from the past, artists turned to modern literature. Baudelaire became the model for the 'modern artist'. The poetry of *Les Fleurs du mal* best expresses this search for new content:

It cheers the burning quest that we pursue,
Careless if Hell or Heaven be our goal,
Beyond the known world to seek out the New![18]

Gallé went through a phase of intensive experimentation with the forms of Egyptian, Persian and East Asian art, but by 1886 his work shows a stylistic reorientation. In his search for new forms of aesthetic expression, he studied the works of the Symbolists around Stéphane Mallarmé and especially Baudelaire. As François-Thérèse Charpentier has verified, Gallé owned an 1884 edition of Baudelaire's *Les Curiosités esthétiques* and an 1882 edition of *Les Fleurs du mal*.[19] From today's standpoint it is probably impossible to ascertain whether his intensive preoccupation with literary Symbolism inspired him to seek a new formal idiom or whether he found aesthetic principles in literature that corresponded to his own.

Although at the time there were numerous literary groups and circles printing their multifarious aims in their self-published journals, they were united by the desire to combat 'naturalism' and the prevailing positivist world-view that led to 'the world being disenchanted' (Max Horkheimer). However, in a *Symbolist Manifesto* published in 1886, Jean Moréas wrote that 'Symbolist poetry' should not be an end in itself.[20] 'Form as the manifestation of an idea' was what Gallé aspired to. A characteristic feature of Symbolism is its allusion to a truth or a vital force that does not reveal itself directly but can be inferred only through analogies and correspondences. Baudelaire formulated this principle in a sonnet, 'Correspondances', defining it as the analogy between the visible world and an invisible one, which come together to form a whole encompassing all the senses (synaesthesia).

Correspondences
Nature's a temple where each living column,
At times, gives forth vague words. There Man advances
Through forest-groves of symbols, strange and solemn,
Who follow him with their familiar glances.

As long-drawn echoes mingle and transfuse
Till in a deep, dark unison they swoon,
Vast as the night or as the vault of noon –
So are commingled perfumes, sounds, and hues.

There can be perfumes cool as children's flesh,
Like fiddles, sweet, like meadows greenly fresh,
Rich, complex, and triumphant, others roll

With the vast range of non-finite things –
Amber, musk, incense, benjamin, each sings
The transports of the senses and the soul.[21]

It is up to the artist to reveal in the work of art the analogies existing between nature and humankind. The correspondences thus disclosed include all sensory percepts: scents, colours, sounds. Wagner's music consequently became Baudelaire's foremost model: '[...] for he has, through the "interaction" of several of the arts [...] wrought art to its most lofty synthesis and consummate perfection'.[22]

He lets himself be carried away when describing these reciprocal analogies in a passage on the 1861 performance of *Tannhäuser* in Paris. Summing up the experience once again, he refers directly to 'Correspondances', closing the paragraph by quoting the first two lines: '[...] for it would indeed be astonishing should sound "be unable" to evoke colour, should colours "be unable" to convey the idea of a melody and should sound and colour be unsuited to express thoughts; since things have always imparted meaning by corresponding analogies [...].'[23] A similar enthusiasm for Wagner had gripped most Symbolists in France. Gallé, too, was among this host of Wagnerians. He expressed his reverence in art with 'Le Saint Graal et son Tabernacle', an ensemble consisting of a wooden tabernacle with variegated marquetry work and a glass chalice. It was reproduced in several contemporary publications, including Louis de Fourcaud's biography of the artist.[24]

Although 'Correspondances' was written as early as mid-century, it came to represent an agenda and a source of inspiration to all Symbolist artists. Gallé, too, who professed Symbolist leanings in numerous writings, referred both directly and indirectly to this poem. It became his aesthetic guideline, the red thread running through his work. His pieces in glass, at once reproduction and transformation of nature, represent this universal unifying principle in subtle symbolism. 'In its aesthetically fascinating quality and consummate beauty, both aimed at by Baudelaire in lyric poetry, his glass

attains that transcendental plane "of mastering the language of flowers and mute things".'[25]

Like Mallarmé in poetry, Gallé wanted to reproduce ideas in his works 'and at the same time evoke the sensations aroused by those ideas'.[26] He found this universal language of symbols in the most minute natural phenomena: in grasses and wild flowers, whose exquisite fragility and vulnerability he expressed with infinite sensitivity on his vessels. As a nature-lover, he was imbued with this *analogie universelle*. He was, however, not always understood by his intellectual friends in Paris: his subtle allusions and analogies often escaped them. Although Robert, Count Montesquiou, himself wrote Symbolist verse[27] and dedicated a poem, 'Loggia', to Gallé, he reacted with sarcasm when Gallé invited him to dinner and 'decorated what was otherwise an elegant table with a plant that would have been better suited to the crannies of an old wall.'[28]

By 1885 Gallé had found his own personal form of artistic expression in Symbolist representation. The symbol became an essential element of his art. Apart from Montesquiou, his best interpreters were such Symbolist poets as the Frenchman Roger Marx.

Art reception as a process of metamorphosis
At the 1889 Exposition Universelle in Paris Gallé presented a vase entitled 'Les Carnivores' (i.e., carnivorous orchids) and decorated it with a line from the French Romantic poet Alfred de Musset: 'je récolte en secret des fleurs mystérieuses' (I secretly pick mysterious flowers).[29] This line disclosed the enigma of the glass creations that were now appearing: tribute paid to nature's mysteries. The floral motifs and verses became aesthetic stimuli referring viewers to the analogies hidden behind appearances in order to make them 'more finely tuned and sensitive', as Pazaurek put it.[30]

The subject Gallé chose for his inaugural address to the Académie de Stanislas, Nancy, in May 1900 was 'Symbolic Decoration'. He did not, however, define the term 'symbol' as such, but instead sought an analogy in the metamorphosis of the humble dung beetle into the 'sacred scarab' of Egyptian art. Admiringly he described the creative powers of the artist as 'inventor', who, recognizing in the appearance of this lowly beetle the 'reflection of an august image', accordingly created an 'artistic, cosmographic, religious and prophetic' symbol.[31] Referring to the floral symbols he so often used, he explained that the rose was no more amorous than the peony and 'the violet no more modest than the opium poppy'.[32] Taking these associations linked with plants as examples, he referred both to the process by which the artist creates symbols, which are the 'soul of a work of art', as he put it, and the necessary process through which viewers create meaning by association. Gallé's statement addresses the quintessence of Symbolist art theory: that, since symbols never have a fixed content or meaning, the entire gamut of ideas and emotional states can unfold in them. Not meant to be a static, predetermined nexus of meanings and content, the work of art exacts active, constantly reflective behaviour of viewers, which encompasses all levels of reaction: thought, feelings, moods. As a result, viewers can never be sure of their interpretations. In describing the process of interpretation Theodor W. Adorno claimed that a work of art is never 'resolvable'.

Gallé's attempt to spark off this process of association in viewers is most readily recognizable in the objects created from 1895 onwards, in the highly charged relationship between their mimetic and indeterminate qualities. In these pieces the vessel forms became freer and more sculptural. Motifs partly dissolve into abstract areas of colour (cat. no. 50) or fuse with vessel shapes to form a visual whole (cat. no. 38).

These new, for the most part thick-walled, objects were not, however, universally admired. The generally positive obituary of Gallé penned by Emil Hannover begins with criticism of them: 'When one remembered him as he was in 1889 and then saw him again in 1900, one felt disappointed for a moment [...] his exhibition of cut glass in 1900 was not only presented more dramatically than accords with our more sober northern tastes; one could not deny that his new pieces made a less powerful impression [...].'[33]

The 'change in perspective' intended by Gallé, which was to enhance receptivity to the physical properties of glass, which make it not only appear fragile and translucent but, like abstract symbols, can manifest themselves in many 'guises', was either not recognized or not accepted. The Symbolist poet Robert de Montesquiou defended these works from such criticism, arguing that a 'spiritual synthesis of all natural elements' was symbolized in the 'hardstone imitations'.[34] The following examples demonstrate that even traditional vessel forms, freed from their utilitarian functions, assume new shades of meaning. I should like to show how the *vases de tristesse* and *vases aquatiques* bear witness to the symbolization process, that is, the translation of idea into art form.

Vases de tristesse and vases aquatiques

It is doubtful whether the *vases de tristesse* are really about 'the continual and emotional commemoration of the dead in visual memory', as Hakenjos writes.[35] The frequent use of this type associated with political content would instead tend to suggest a universally valid statement. The reasons for creating 'mourning vases' may be legion: the artist's awareness that he had a life-threatening illness, his deep discouragement at political setbacks, such as the annexation of Alsace and northern Lorraine, his fruitless endeavours in the Dreyfus Affair or the expression of an outlook on life tinged with melancholy, one that is inherent in all artistic expression of the time.

The symbolic reference to mourning is transmitted in these vases via the emotionally tinged moods with which they are imbued and the symbolism of the decoration (cat. no. 23). The dominant colours are those associated with mourning and melancholy: black, dark grey, purple and dark blue. The body is usually solid, stained opaque in the batch, and forms are round with soft contours. Moreover they feature hardly any motifs that suggest movement. The decoration rarely runs round the vessel but is instead positioned at the centre of the vase as its focal point – an indirect manner of directing viewers to the contemplative semantic content.

There is another *vase de tristesse* in the Koepff Collection (cat. no. 44). In some respects it does not fulfil the criteria outlined above, yet it can still be viewed as a 'mourning vase'. It is a prime example of polysemic representation in art. The 'title' of the vase is a quotation from the Belgian poet Maurice Maeterlinck: 'Petits sourires et grandes larmes' (Small smiles and large tears).[36] The body of the vessel is of transparent glass overlaid with a delicate silvery white patina. The two outsize trailing prunts resembling trickling tears are the first recognizable sign of mourning. The slender neck of the vase is partly cased with purple glass. Purple, the colour of communion with the soul and penance as well as mourning, contrasts with the amber casing of the body. The brilliance of the golden yellow is heightened by the silvery metal filings fused between the casings. This provides the first key to interpreting the piece: golden yellow, the symbol of light and truth, is 'overshadowed' by mourning. The floral motif, an iris – also a symbol of light – with wilting petals, cut in deep relief, supports this interpretation, for it is shown hanging upside down. The colour contrast between bluish purple and golden yellow is striking. This fraught relationship indicates a conflict, for which the iris could be a visual metaphor. The iris, or fleur-de-lis, is a heraldic attribute of the Bourbon monarchy, with its lanceolate leaves symbolizing military might. Thus political and legal connotations are clearly alluded to, particularly since the vase was made at the time of the Dreyfus Affair. Taken together with the incised line from Maeterlinck, the vase becomes a polysemic metaphor for grief.

The contrasting concepts of 'smiling' and 'tears' in the Maeterlinck quotation could be interpreted as suggesting that the hope of truth should not be abandoned, just as the purple casing on the neck of the vase still allows a small part of the silvery white glass (the symbol of enlightenment) to shine through. As a universal statement constituting a synthesis of the two symbols mentioned, the vase might represent grief that justice has not won out or, in more generalizing terms, that the quest for truth is always hazardous.

The search for truth and justice was a main theme for Gallé, one that he repeatedly referred to as the goal of his artistic endeavours. In a letter to Victor Champier he wrote: 'You ask me what I am sending to the [1898] Salon. […] my most humble observation that, in art as in life, the best thing is truth and the most beautiful is light.' And he goes on to quote some verses from the *verres parlantes* he intends to submit to the exhibition: 'You know very well that I have wings, O truths' and 'We shall at last rise to the light'.[37]

The same semantic content yet with a more pronounced political bias informs a *vase de tristesse* Gallé presented to the Countess Anna de Noailles. This vase, also decorated with irises cut in deep relief, is cased with red and purple glass to create a dichroic effect. Depending on the angle of incidence of light shining on it, purple, the colour of mourning, or red, the colour of war gods, is the predominant tint. The engraved Maeterlinck device makes an unequivocal statement: 'All souls are willing but one must make a start. Why not dare to be the one that begins […].'[38] With this 'symbolic allusion' Gallé was asking Anna de Noailles for her support in the Dreyfus Affair.

As these examples clearly show, Gallé was not concerned with accurately reproducing nature with the means available to him. He aimed at creating overarching nexes of meaning and content. The plants are metaphors, which in turn are deployed analogously with other metaphors. It is up to the viewer to decode this referential field. The symbols used are always polysemic. They are 'overdetermined', as Arnold Hauser puts it, and continually recur in new semantic contexts.

What has not been taken into account in interpretations is the emotional content that is opened up to each viewer. Yet personal access to the work of art is the most important criterion of interpretation in Symbolist art for, in order to reproduce 'ideas', the emotions (*émotions*) associated with them must be elicited at the same time.[39]

The symbols are linked 'partly with conscious, partly with unconscious associations of ideas'. An individual's past experiences allow for 'different meanings' to be attributed to a single object.[40] The work is to be approached through mimesis but viewers must find their own access to it. This will become particularly clear in the object described in the following.

The motifs on the vases hitherto discussed can be decoded by means of their traditional iconographic background. The same does not apply, however, to a glass plate in the Koepff Collection graced with *aquatique* motifs, a round, ornamental charger featuring depictions of an octopus and seashells (cat. no. 59). Gallé's striving to enter into an 'inner dialogue' with viewers through ambiguous images is particularly apparent here, largely owing to the emotional and cognitive perceptual processes that they at once elicit.

When looking at this plate, one's attention is involuntarily drawn to two glass cabochons in iridescent brown at its centre. Distinctly recalling a pair of eyes, they draw the viewer's gaze as if by magic. This effect is enhanced by the irregular streaks of light yellow fused into an intervening layer of glass. The plate looks as if lit at the centre by a source of artificial light. In seeking identifiable pictorial elements, one spots the octopus tentacles, which seem to float above the ruffled surface of water. But one's gaze is again arrested by dense green and brown swirls and specks glowing out of the depths. Interpretations surface, only to vanish. Are the glossy reflections offsetting the matt texture of the octopus, complete with raised textures, seashells or stones? Refracted in the bright, transparent outer edge of the plate, the light picks out details that were initially invisible: tiny white specks that seem to be moving like fish in a sandwiched layer. Swirls of dark green and brown draw one's gaze down into the depths. Changes in perspective accelerate in the alternation of identifiable and abstract forms. When the plate is turned and moved, the light is refracted on the narrow edges of the octopus tentacles. Colour flares up to illuminate new, deeper picture planes; white flecks with a tinge of orange recall marine shells lapped by waves, as if dancing. The eye plunges down ever deeper into this enigmatically seething vortex. With each new image caught by the light interpretations continue to shift: wavy lines become fish and vanish. One's vision blurs with the incessant change in perspective; the octopus, seaweed and shells begin to move. One almost seems to hear the whisper of waves gradually swelling, only to break in dazzles of light. This is a continuous process of metamorphosis.

The longer one looks at the object the more blurred boundaries seem to become. The transparency of the glass dissolves the picture plane, which seems to float in an imaginary space. The theme of this glass plate – the sea as a metaphor for the source of all living things, for the cycle of waxing and waning – is revealed as an unmediated emotional experience through the process of reception rather than through an intellectual process of analytic reflection triggered off by recognizable images. The basic form chosen, the circle as the universal symbol of infinity and synchronicity, is perceived in the viewer's subjectivity as an *analogie universelle*. Boundlessness is experienced in an endless process of seeing.

In his glass pieces Gallé constantly plays with the physiological and psychological laws governing perception. A masterly combination of glass techniques and skilful exploitation of the material's physical properties – transparency contrasting with subtle gradations of colour and the positive-negative effect created by cutting and etching techniques – evokes an impression of movement. Put in metaphysical terms: it provides evidence of time and space.

This process is set in motion by the layering of multiple pictorial structures, the simultaneous perception of surfaces and linear forms (e.g., the contours of the octopus) and the use of colour to create the effect of depth; a continuous and never-ending shift between recognition and non-recognition is the result. The principle of polysemy is for the most part technically realized, namely through the 'multiple layering' of glass casing to suggest spatial depth.

Gallé's objective of eliciting experience of nature via associative imagery rather than direct imitation reveals striking parallels with Piet Mondrian's intention of generating experience of nature through equivalent pictorial experience. In works from around 1915, such as *Composition No. 10*, he initiates a similar process solely by means of the line and the spatial effect of colour. Mondrian saw the artistic act of evoking nature 'not in reproducing nature but instead in initiating a visual process, [the] attempt to design a visual equivalent to the experience of nature. Nature is thought of as a processually fecund *natura naturans* rather than as a fact that can be unequivocally reproduced.'[41]

If, on the other hand, one remains in the nineteenth-century context of the Gallé plate, startling analogies can be made of the visual associations induced by Richard Wagner's music, which Baudelaire described in the passage on *Tannhäuser* quoted above with reference to Franz Liszt: 'It begins with the melody like the "broad, shimmering surface of water, with a pervasive ethereal haze" […], horns and bassoons come in to repeat the melodies for the fourth time "with dazzling brilliance and play of colour" as if, at this instant, the matchless sacred form (the Holy Grail) had appeared in "all its glowing, radiant majesty before our dazzled eyes". Yet the "bright glitter and sparkle", which is gradually heightened to such a "violent excess of sunlight", soon fades away to a "celestial gleam".'[42]

Gallé, like his employees, was keen to develop sophisticated new technical processes in order to create such synaesthetic effects in his own work. What he wanted to demonstrate was neither artificiality as such nor consummate technical mastery of working glass. On the contrary, he used his knowledge of chemistry, botany and physiology to lend artistic form to his ideas.

He succeeded in doing so by taking advantage of optical illusion, for instance, the transformation of images caused by light alternatively shining through them or on them or adding new picture planes, which are not discernible at first glance. Minute details are often revealed as motifs loaded with connotative meaning. One must look closely at the Dragonfly Bowl (cat. no. 60), for instance, to see that the delicate streak of brown glass behind the dragonfly's body is its shadow and not a chance stain in the glass. Deploying a wide variety of such subtle artistic inventions, Gallé sought to create an atmosphere addressed to all the senses. Illusionist effects ensured that images remained indeterminate. Gradations and nuances informed his idea of design – as in the celebrated Paul Verlaine poem 'Art poétique':

For still we want the nuance
Not the colour, nothing but the nuance!
Ah! the nuance alone affiances
Dream to dream, flute to horn![43]

Light puts the finishing and crowning touch to his pieces. This is one of the reasons why Gallé preferred small works to large, showy ones. Small-scale pieces lend themselves best to attentive, contemplative study because one can slowly turn them round and over to follow the play of light, changes in colour and perspective, the continual appearance of new interpretations. Not until its visual and tactile qualities have been simultaneously 'grasped' is the whole polyphony of a Gallé work revealed. The philosopher Johann Gottfried Herder describes the perception of sculpture as a 'feeling hand' checks and supplements the 'deceiving eye' to probe the unity of form and content. This sensory and psychological process of profound contemplation becomes almost palpable in Victor Prouvé's celebrated portrait of Gallé (illus. p. 34).

Something of this ambiguous, polysemic quality is also evident in the serially produced objects made until 1904. This attests to Gallé having been the driving artistic force in the creation of his oeuvre. Although the serially produced objects were executed with the same technical perfection even after 1904, the 'nuances' are missing. Decoration no longer has a referential function, is no longer symbolic or metaphorical but has reverted to the mimetic reproduction of nature.

Transformation through memory

In design Gallé deliberately gambled everything on the viewer's imagination and ability to supplement percepts. Viewers were to complete the work of art in their mind's eye just as the artist created his work by using his powers of imagination. However, an analytic process preceded the imaginative act, literally 'breaking down a new work into its components' before it could be created by an act of 'transformation': 'Elle est l'analyse, elle est la synthèse' (It is analysis and synthesis), is how Baudelaire described this process.[44] Analogous to the creative process in art, the reception process involves a continual interplay of analysis and synthesis. Representation is always only a tiny, microscopic detail of a universal, yet the laws governing both are of universal validity. Gallé symbolizes this by using 'blurred' contours,

Brigitte Leonhardt

produced, for instance, by multiple casings of coloured and colourless glass to engender a visually indefinable space between the pictorial content as the inner world, and the outer world, or by using 'cut out' decoration, which encourages viewers to fill in the empty space with their imaginations.

What prompts this incessant search for meaning initiated by a work of art has been termed 'intentionality of consciousness'. It is the premise on which meaningful experience and understanding are based. The work of art activates this 'spontaneous act of seeing' by eschewing unambiguous, immediately decodable nexes of meaning and content. Polysemic images and the resistance to direct connotative allusions encourage viewers to discover ever smaller, previously undiscerned and scarcely perceptible details of the image – literally, to analyze. Resistance lures viewers on a voyage of perceptual discovery analogous to the study of nature, which is revealed only in small doses, both to the probing eye of the natural scientist and the intent gaze of the plant enthusiast. Seeing or perceiving is here far more than an act of recognition. The sum of our experiences and memories is reactivated in this nonutilitarian way of seeing: it links past and present by way of imagining a new reality. Just as in Proust's novel *A la Recherche du temps perdu*, the taste of 'madeleines' (sponge cakes) dipped in tea infused with lime-tree blossoms evokes an instantaneous childhood memory, the reception of these glass objects represents a spontaneous revival of feelings, thoughts and long-forgotten images. These are moments of spontaneous recollection, for Proust moments of the greatest happiness: 'Only an instant from out of the past?'[45] Since memory contains the experience of a new self, it 'releases the inherent, albeit usually hidden, essence of all things and our true self, which has sometimes seemed dead for a long time [...], awakens to new life.'[46] It marks the beginning of the new rather than a completed past. 'Whereas works of art open themselves to observation, at the same time they confuse the viewer as to the distance [from the work] of the mere spectator; he realizes the truth of the work as that which should also be the truth about himself. This moment of transition is art at its most supreme.'[47]

Both Proust and Gallé devoted themselves to nature with a scientific interest. They viewed it from complementary angles. Proust turns to people, analyzing them with the '[...] curiosity of a scientist observing insects or plants,'[48] as André Maurois observed. He quotes one of the many similes in Proust: 'On the beach at Baalbek I saw the old ladies [...] who the young women I knew would, like a plant with flowers ripening at different times into fruits, one day have to become.'[49] The work of both Proust and Gallé originates in the analysis of nature. Proust must have recognized in Gallé's work the passion they shared. As his biographers have written, Proust was fascinated by the powers of imagination, by their transformation into art. He 'was particularly receptive to the layered moods and secrets in which Gallé's works are shrouded and to their evocative powers. He was impressed by the number of interpretations each of these works allowed.'[50] Proust commissioned a great many bespoke pieces from Gallé as presents for friends, evidently more than Gallé was able to handle.[51]

The idea of aesthetics and art shared by Emile Gallé and Marcel Proust lies in the conception of the duality of these opposing experiential horizons of expectations. Linking up with the hermeneutics of memory, they refer to the possibility of an 'actualized life' (Adorno) while also calling for pre-existing structures as metaphors for self-incurred limitation to be unmasked. In this they refer to the defence mechanisms in our thinking and our unreflected acceptance of what is imposed on us by everyday life. 'That works of art have something to say yet in the same breath conceal it is to name the enigmatic character' of art.[52] They thus give rise to a never-ending search for interpretations. In denying the possibility of any one particular insight, they open up a wide range of potential interpretations.

The work of art as an enigma. The Symbolists used this construct to oppose the positivist world-view of their day. The inability and unwillingness to understand Symbolist art – attitudes that, incidentally, are not restricted to the turn of the century – can, therefore, be read as the aesthetic distance between Symbolism and an adversarial world-view. The Symbolist semantic content of Gallé's work was inaccessible to his contemporaries because they entertained the positivist notion of art, which requires that the work of art make a single, unequivocal and generally intelligible statement. This is clearly illustrated in the stance adopted by Wilhelm von Bode (1845–1929), director general of the Berlin museums, in an article in *Pan* magazine (1899) arguing against Symbolism as follows: '[They] believe that the charm or the value of art lies in the very riddles it poses for beholders.' He counters by imposing the obligation of ensuring that the statements made by art are generally intelligible: 'Allegorical, symbolic [...] representations are only tolerable and justifiable if their content is also the common property of all beholders, if everyone can immediately understand it.'[53] He thus defines the meaning and content of allegories and symbols as the conventional, unambiguous relationship between representation and the statement it makes. However, the significance of the art of any period lies in its expressive content being multidimensional.

Emile Gallé attached no importance to making generally valid statements in his work. Anticipating instead an individual, highly personal dialogic response to it, he wanted to 'effect' as well as 'affect' as can be inferred from so many of his writings and political activities.

In an article entitled 'La Pensée et l'art d'Emile Gallé' (1910), which deals with Gallé's artistic objectives, Gaston Varenne writes: 'In his view, art had a task to perform that was more lofty than merely creating beauty and delighting people. Art was supposed instead to appeal to the heart and the soul rather than the senses; above all it had to be powerfully expressive rather than simply ornamental.'[54] The writer's use of the terms 'soul' and 'heart' means that he is not just addressing feelings but wants to 'set something in motion'. Because Gallé insisted that 'works of art are enigmas', he counted on the viewer's powers of imagination. His works raise questions, but refuse to give clear answers. Moreover, in rejecting unequivocal nexes of content and meaning, he makes us realize that there can be no absolute truth in art or even in everyday life. Gallé lived by the same maxim as Baudelaire: 'L'imagination est la reine du vrai, et le "possible" est une des provinces du vrai' (The imagination is the sovereign queen over what is true and what is 'possible' is a province of what is true).[55]

Notes

1 Munich 1898, p. 45.

2 Gallé's work was sold by the Frankfurt furnishing and decorating firm Seyd & Sautter; see Darmstadt 1898, p. 12.

3 Ibid., pp. 12 and 16–17. The prices listed for glass art range from 30 to 1350 marks.

4 Ibid., p. 9.

5 The journal *Deutsche Kunst und Dekoration* lists the sales made at the Darmstadt exhibition: 'Grand Duke Ernst Ludwig bought 1 vase.' Further sales: 'a small cupboard, 2 small tables, a chair, music stand, desk, console, urn with pedestal and 4 vases'.

6 Thérèse Charpentier, 'La Clientèle étrangère d'Emile Gallé', in *Stil und Überlieferung in der Kunst des Abendlandes: Akten des 21. Int. Kongresses für Kunstgeschichte in Bonn 1964*, vol. 1: *Epochen europäischer Kunst* (Berlin, 1967), pp. 256–64.

7 *Dekorative Kunst* 3 (1899): 100–101.

8 Pazaurek 1901, p. 3.

9 Ibid., pp. 85–86.

10 *Kunst und Kunsthandwerk* 47 (1897/98): 55–56.

11 Pazaurek 1901, p. 86.

12 The relationship between the context and the reception of art has been verified in empirical studies of texts of varying content. This trans-subjective process does not take place with purely informative texts, such as those consisting of biographical information; in such cases, reception remains largely limited to identifying the mimetic qualities of a work of art. See Wolfgang Ehrlich and Brigitte Leonhardt, *Empirische Untersuchung zur Kunstrezeption* (MS) (Heidelberg, 1981).

13 Pazaurek 1901, p. 86.

14 See his letters on the exhibition, such as the one addressed to Champier, in 'My Submissions to the Salon', translated into English in the 'Sources'.

15 'Baltazar, das Kunstgewerbe oder die angewandte Kunst', *Prawda* (Warsaw) 16 (1901): 321; 27, p. 333. Reprinted in Julian Marchelewski, *Sezession und Jugendstil: Sozialdemokratische Kritik um 1900* (Dresden, 1974), p. 53.

16 Munich, *Nancy 1900*, 1980, p. 44.

17 See F.-T. Charpentier, 'L'Art de Gallé a-t-il été influencé par Baudelaire?', *Gazette des Beaux-Arts* 61 (1963): 367–68.

18 'Nous voulons, tant ce feu nous brûle le cerveau, / Plonger au fond du gouffre, Enfer ou Ciel, qu'importe? / Au fond de l'Inconnu pour trouver du nouveau!': 'Le Voyage', in *Les Fleurs du mal*, ed. E. Starkie, 8th ed. (Oxford, 1970), no. CXXVI, p. 140; for the English see *Poems of Baudelaire: A Translation of 'Les Fleurs du mal'*, ed. Roy Campbell (London, 1952), p. 176.

19 Charpentier (note 17). The first edition of the collected poems as *Les Fleurs du mal* was published in 1857, but Baudelaire did not become famous until the 1880s, after his death in 1867.

20 Josef Theisen, *Die Dichtung des Französischen Symbolismus* (Darmstadt, 1974), p. 3.

21 'La Nature est un temple où de vivants piliers / Laissent parfois sortir de confuses paroles; / L'homme y passe à travers des fôrets de symboles / Qui l'observent avec des regards familiers. // Comme de longs échos qui de loin se confondent / Dans une ténébreuse et profonde unité, / Vaste comme la nuit et comme la clarté, / Les parfums, les couleurs et les sons se répondent. // Il est des parfums frais comme des chairs d'enfants, / Doux comme les hautbois, verts comme les prairies, / – Et d'autres, corrumpus, riches et triomphants, / Ayant l'expansion des choses infinies, / Comme l'ambre, le musc, le benjoin et l'encens, / Qui chantent les transports de l'esprit et des sens': 'Correspondances', in *Les Fleurs du mal* (note 18), no. IV, p. 7; for the English see Campbell, p. 8.

22 Charles Baudelaire, *Sämtliche Werke/Briefe*, ed. Friedhelm Kemp and Claude Pichois (Munich, 1989), vol. 7, p. 94.

23 Ibid., vol. 7, p. 97.

24 Fourcaud 1903, p. 53.

25 Hakenjos 1982, p. 361.

26 Guy Michaud, *La Doctrine symboliste (Documents)* (Paris, 1947), p. 337.

27 See Montesquiou's text translated into English in the 'Sources'.

28 Garner 1976, p. 118.

29 Munich, *Nancy 1900*, 1980, p. 84.

30 Pazaurek 1901, p. 85.

31 Emile Gallé, 'Symbolic Decoration', translated into English in the 'Sources'.

32 Ibid.

33 Emil Hannover, 'Emile Gallé', *Kunst und Künstler* 3 (April 1905): 290–97.

34 Garner 1976, p. 126; this layer of meaning is also discussed in Hakenjos 1982, p. 363.

35 Hakenjos 1982, p. 295.

36 Gallé developed this type of vase with a globular body and a long, thin neck to hold single flowers, especially orchids.

37 See note 14.

38 Garner 1976, p. 118, illus. in Bloch-Dermant 1980, p. 64.

39 See Theisen (note 20), p. 40.

40 Hans H. Hofstätter, *Symbolismus und die Kunst der Jahrhundertwende* (Cologne, 1978), p. 45.

41 Richard Hoppe-Sailer, 'Bilderfahrung und Naturvorstellung bei Cy Twombly', in Max Imdahl (ed.), *Wie eindeutig ist ein Kunstwerk* (Cologne, 1986), p. 103.

42 Baudelaire (note 22), vol. 7, p. 96.

43 'Car nous voulons la nuance encore / Pas la couleur, rien que la nuance! / Oh! La nuance seule fiance / Le rêve au rêve et la flute au cor!': translated from the German in Theisen (note 20), pp. 38–39.

44 Johannes Kleinstück, *Der Gott, der uns entweicht: Baudelaire und die Romantik* (Stuttgart, 1992), p. 120.

45 Marcel Proust, *A la recherche du temps perdu*; translated into English from the German, *Auf der Suche nach der verlorenen Zeit* (Frankfurt, 1979), p. 3942.

46 Ibid., p. 3943.

47 Theodor W. Adorno, *Ästhetische Theorie* (Frankfurt, 1981), p. 401.

48 André Maurois, *Auf den Spuren von Marcel Proust* (Frankfurt, 1982), p. 212.

49 Ibid.

50 Garner 1976, pp. 115–16.

51 See ibid., p. 117.

52 Adorno (note 47), p. 182.

53 Wilhelm von Bode, 'Die bildenden Künste beim Eintritt in das neue Jahrhundert (gegen den Symbolismus)', *Pan* 5 (1899): 264.

54 Gaston Varenne, 'La Pensée et l'art d'Emile Gallé', *Mercure de France* 86 (1910): 31.

55 Baudelaire, quoted in Kleinstück (note 44), p. 119.

Nobuo Tsūji

The Glass Masterpieces of Emile Gallé and their Affinity with Japanese Art

A reply in a letter to my friend, Dr. Helmut Ricke

Yoriko Mizuta of the Hokkaidō Museum of Modern Art has asked me to describe how the forms and decorations of Art Nouveau glass strike me, as a Japanese art historian. For this I feel extremely honoured. My field of specialization is the history of Japanese painting and I unfortunately have no specialist knowledge of late nineteenth-century European art or Art Nouveau glass. I am therefore merely an amateur who greatly admires and is interested in Emile Gallé's work. In the following I shall give the impressions I have gained from examining particular pieces and should count myself fortunate indeed were this to be sufficient for you.

In the past few decades the interest shown by the Japanese public in Emile Gallé's work has increased considerably. Thanks to the Hokkaidō Museum of Modern Art, the Suntory Museum in Tokyo, the Kitazawa Museums in Nagano and Suwa and other institutions, the public now has access to outstanding collections throughout Japan.

What are the reasons for this growing enthusiasm for Art Nouveau glass? First and foremost the 'Japanese' character of the motifs and decoration on the vessels. Yet this quality is not all that makes this glass attractive to the Japanese.

Art Nouveau glass, and Emile Gallé's work in particular, reflects a way of thinking and approaching life, a distinct visionary aesthetic rooted in the world-view of the closing nineteenth century, which occasionally manifests itself in pervasive, almost obsessive Symbolism or aestheticism. It is this aspect that elicits such a positive response in Japanese art-lovers who have had the opportunity of familiarizing themselves with twentieth-century Western art.

The peculiarly 'Japanese quality' with which its decorative forms and *fin de siècle* motifs are tinged is what makes Art Nouveau glass so fascinating to the Japanese. I should like to go into this in more depth by taking as examples works that have been reproduced in books.

Three publications are available to me. The first is your catalogue to the exhibition of works from the Kunstmuseum Düsseldorf, which was shown at seven Japanese museums in 1991–92.[1] The second is the catalogue to the 1984 exhibition entitled 'Emile Gallé: Dreams into Glass' at the Corning Museum of Glass[2] and the third is the catalogue of the exhibition devoted to Gallé at the Palais du Luxembourg in Paris in 1985–86.[3]

Vases constitute the bulk of Gallé's work. The rest consists of shallow dishes or bowls (*coupes*) and other vessel types. Although the vase stems from a Western formal tradition that can be traced back to ancient Greece, many variants have been tried out. The shape of the slender bamboo cane for a single flower spray, the tall tea-urn form, the shape of a gourd, the brush-washer form, which has, however, been widened at the bottom to roughly the shape of an octopus pot,[4] etc. – these are all extraordinary pieces that deviate from normal Western vase forms. What makes them interesting is their use of Japanese or Chinese formal idioms.

The surface decoration is another feature that arouses feelings of familiarity in the Japanese. Representations on some vases derive from Greek mythology or Western iconographic tradition. Most, however, bear motifs of flora (flowers, grasses and trees) or fauna (insects and small animals) and have been conceived in a highly distinctive manner. Such representations deviate from the traditional stylized floral motifs[5] in their naturalism, with asymmetric representations of individualized flowers, grasses, trees or insects. The illusionist effect of plasticity is enhanced by the use of hot-working techniques for applying these motifs to vessel surfaces. The practice of placing a single motif on a blank background results in something resembling book illustrations of fauna, though not clinically rendered, 'dead' specimens. On the contrary, they are very much alive; some creatures would even seem to be hunting prey.

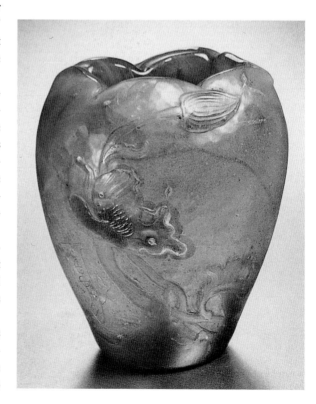

Emile Gallé, Nancy
'Les Anémones' vase, *c.* 1897/98

Gallé is said to have learnt of such motifs and techniques from Japanese art, yet I wonder whether it is possible to localize specific sources of inspiration. In order to go into this issue in depth, one would have to subject the material actually available to Gallé and his contemporaries to thorough study.

Ukiyo-e, i.e. colour woodcuts depicting scenes from the Yoshiwara brothel quarter, Hokusai's *manga*,[6] or sketchbooks, illustrated books and bound series of pictures by other *ukiyo-e* masters or painters of other Japanese schools as well as lacquer, porcelain, *inrō* (medicine boxes) and catalogued objects shown at international exhibitions, the illustrations in *Le Japon artistique*, the journal founded by Samuel Bing, works by exponents of Japonism who were his contemporaries and innumerable other sources – were all this to be studied, some idea might be gained of just how vast and varied this body of material is, yet this is beyond my capabilities. Tokuzō Takashima, a Japanese who spent several years in Nancy, has recently attracted attention. However, what is known about the role he may have played in the transmission process is certainly far from sufficient. All that I can provide, therefore, are arbitrary associations and comparisons based on my study of individual pieces, even though conjectures may arise from this. I shall try to proceed step by step and will first turn to floral designs.

Gallé's floral designs are distinguished by the faithfulness to natural models. However, the elements are structured in an oscillating rhythm. A further characteristic is that Gallé does not show plants in their entirety. Instead, with the aid of free cutting, he developed a method of showing them in perspective, as if viewed either from above or below. The vivid expressiveness of these plants and the way in which the elements are interwoven reveal the Art Nouveau canon of forms, yet such elements also occur in Japanese painting as well as the Japanese decorative and applied arts. Gallé would, therefore, have certainly found rich sources of inspiration there. The decoration of the 'Anémones' vase (illus. p. 52) is a prime example.

The stem of the flower applied to the side forms a large wave recalling the Hokusai colour woodcut 'Poppies' (illus. below). Although Gallé's image does depart in some respects from the model – the single flower has become a bud, the interior of the flowers is different and the leaves have been reduced in scale – it seems quite obvious that this is a highly skilful variation on a Hokusai original.

This is just one example of his use of a specific Japanese model. However, this cannot be so readily assumed to be true of many of Gallé's other floral designs. A vase decorated with birds on snow-covered bamboo[7] definitely sports a motif taken from Far Eastern painting – in my opinion, possibly from those conventional works painted by commercial artists from the early Meiji era shown at the Paris Exposition Universelle of 1889. More importantly, however, is that, were Gallé's motifs merely copies of Japanese art, the Japanese would be bound to find this tedious, no matter how skilful his techniques.

Yet they do not find them dull. In fact what makes Gallé's works so charming is that he, as an exponent of French *fin de siècle* art, handled his models sensitively, translating them into something formally different, which must be appreciated as such.

The wisteria blossoms he was so fond of are, of course, gems from the repertoire of the *Rimpa* school;[8] however, the way in which Gallé has made individual flowers pirouette and bend like ballerinas is unparalleled. A depiction of wisteria in one volume of Hokusai's *manga* may have been his inspiration,[9] yet, if Gallé really was inspired by this fleeting sketch, his handling of it would make his powers of imagination and intuition seem brilliant indeed.

As it is, plants in Gallé's work – both stems and flowers – form an undulating wavy band in harmony with all the other elements. I assume that Gallé learned this type of movement and dynamics from the expressive qualities revealed by plants in Japanese pictures. Plants by Sakai Hōitsu[10] and painters of the *Rimpa* school he revived in the nineteenth century are distinguished by a spontaneous handling that captures the flowers, foliage or tendrils in a lively manner.

I have already touched on Hokusai's dynamic conception of plant images shown in his sketchbooks or prints

Katsushika Hokusai, 'Poppies', colour woodcut

'Carp', woodcut from vol. 13 of Hokusai's *manga* (sketchbooks)

tic, looking like neither flora nor fauna, so he dedicated a work to it. A look at this vase is instructive if one wants to know what he may have found so interesting about Japanese representations of plants. He was concerned with this marine creature as living form and the fantastic world it evoked rather than its scientific classification. The enchanting mushroom-shaped glass objects evoke probably explains his fondness for them. A few days ago I saw a group of these large glass mushrooms in the Kitazawa Museum and they left a lasting impression on me. There is no comparable motif in Japanese art.

Gallé's favourite subjects were fish and insects, which he combined with plant motifs. The transparent glass surface of a large vessel from the Musée des Arts Déco-ratifs in Paris, which has been exhibited in Japan, is decorated with a black carp (illus. p. 27, bottom) and is a copy of a motif in the thirteenth volume of Hokusai's *manga*[13] (illus. left). Nonetheless examples like these, which obviously derive from Japanese models, are rare indeed. Gallé turned to Japanese art for inspiration rather than a mere catalogue of forms.

When looking at Gallé's work, one notices that he liked particular kinds of insects and depicted them time and again. Butterflies and dragonflies are the most notable of these, followed by a creature that is not entomological – the frog.[14] Unfortunately, I do not know what role these insects and small fauna have played in the traditions of European art. I am, however, generally familiar with how butterflies, dragonflies and frogs are handled in Chinese and Japanese art. To be sure, they do not look back on a particularly long history as motifs. Only very few butterfly designs are known from the Tang dynasty[15] or the Nara and Heian periods[16] in Japan. The grotesque forms of such insects probably did not accord with the tastes of the aristocracy.

Pictures teeming with butterflies, dragonflies and other insects as well as frogs and small fauna began to appear during the period following the Tang dynasty,[17] continuing in the Sung (Song) era[18] and on into the Ming period,[19] as a new variant of the classic image of flowers and birds together with grasses and insects. Grasses and insects as subject matter, including realistic representations of marsh and moor flora and fauna so prevalent in the southern Chinese provinces,[20] as well as the closely related pictures of lacustrine plants and fish (algae, fish, crayfish and crabs as well as molluscs in water, as they are encountered in Art Nouveau glass objects), were highly popular in Japan, too, because they were novel and utterly different from the conventional, albeit widely admired, representations of lovely flowers and magnificent birds. From the Edo period[21] the Japanese intelligentsia and some Japanese painters studied Chinese botany.[22] In addition, illustrated European handbooks showing flora and fauna were introduced through the trading port of Nagasaki. These circumstances combined to promote the 'naturalistic representation of

with the classical floral and bird motifs. With a masterly sweep of the brush, Hiroshige,[11] too, although famous for his tranquil landscapes, makes his birds and flowers excitingly vibrant. Gallé was inspired by such forcefulness of expression, but his rendering of motifs is more emphatically dynamic than his Japanese models, as is shown by the wisteria blooms mentioned above. Further, I imagine that the physical properties of molten glass, its viscosity and ductility, may be particularly suited to the creation of such organic forms. Representing plants in motion, writhing like fauna, is an integral part of the formal canon of *fin de siècle* European art.

In this connection, I find an extraordinary vase with sea anemones as its theme[12] extremely interesting. A coelenterate from the depths of the sea, the sea anemone was long known only from fossils and aroused Gallé's interest because it was so mysterious and fantas-

Kitagawa Utamaro, 'Poppies and butterflies', colour woodcut

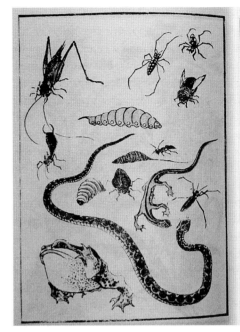
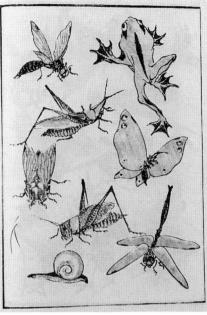

'Small animals and insects', woodcut from vol. 1 of Hokusai's *manga* (sketchbooks)

sions) by Kubo Shumman (illus. below),[26] who was born in the same year as Utamaro, are delightful images of butterflies executed with precision and a consummate mastery of colour.[27] The first volume of Hokusai's sketchbooks, from the following generation, also contains lively fold-out illustrations showing plants and animals.

In the Edo period, in which Hokusai also lived, it was Sakai Hōitsu who revived the traditions of the ornamental Kyōto school of which Ogata Kōrin was a leading exponent. Pictures of flowers and grasses were an integral part of the repertoire of the *Rimpa* school (Tawaraya Sōtatsu, Ogata Kōrin and their circle), known for formal painting. Oddly enough, however, there are hardly any representations of insects in the work of this school. This rejection of insects seems to be a relic of the aesthetic cultivated by the Kyōto nobility.

Yet, in Hōitsu's day, insects were popular elsewhere and were accordingly chosen as motifs (illus. above, left). His series of works entitled *satsuga chō* (Various Trifles) features a wide variety of butterflies, water beetles and small carp (*medaka*) snapping at flower petals that have fallen into a pond (illus. p. 56, top) and similar motifs. Interestingly, the same little fish are encountered in Gallé's work.[28] On the lower rim of one vessel tadpoles are shown turning into frogs. I know of no rendering of this metamorphosis by a Japanese painter. However, the humorous treatment of the motif on a tea-bowl featuring a group of little frogs assembled at a pond for a concert of croaking depicted in a narrow band – like a belt – at the centre[29] is reminiscent of Kawanabe Gyōsai's frogs.[30] Although I do not know whether Gallé was acquainted with Gyōsai's frogs, he may well have been.

This is not the place to expatiate further on how Japanese art was introduced into Gallé's work. What has struck me most when examining the plants and insects on his pieces is how consummately the European *fin de siècle* aesthetic informs the work of that period. As previously mentioned, a great many impulses received from Japanese painting and other art forms are discernible in his depictions of animals and plants, but the world expressed in them is foreign to me. His orchid petals, like his starfish bowl feet, make me think of small, creeping living things. I also link this same connotation of lower forms of life in motion with his 'autumn maple' and 'lilies',[31] yet hardly any examples of Japanese painting evoke similar associations. To a certain extent Hokusai's plants could be called exceptions to the rule. Similar elements also occur in the work of Itō Jakuchū,[32] an eighteenth-century painter who worked in Kyōto. Incidentally, Jakuchū owes his current popularity to the fact that he established a style resembling Art Nouveau in eighteenth-century Japan.

Turning from Gallé's plants to his insects, one encounters an entirely different world. A stunning display of virtuosity, these representations of various kinds

insects and small fauna in their habitats', which became increasingly popular in art from the eighteenth century onwards.

Nowadays the word 'naturalistic' (Jap. *shasei*) is used to describe Western sketches 'from nature'. However, it has been used from time immemorial in China for the realistic reproduction of flora and fauna shown living in their natural habitats. Maruyama Ōkyo[23] is regarded as a master of 'naturalistic representation' and his works teem with insects of all kinds. Kitagawa Utamaro,[24] known for his beautiful portraits of women, worked 'naturalistically' in his youth. His book *ehon mushi erami* (Selection of Pictures of Insects, published in 1788)[25] shows dragonflies and butterflies on poppies in masterly compositions (see p. 54, bottom). The *surimono* (prints in a roughly square format commemorating special occa-

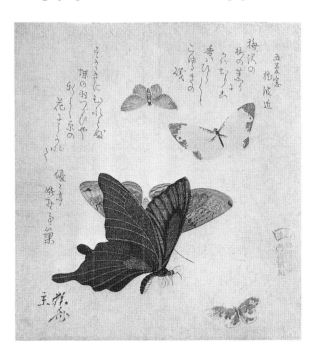

Kubo Shumman, *surimono* (commemorating special occasions), colour woodcut

of works of art. This is the quality that is so attractive to most Japanese art-lovers. His striving to subvert the dichotomy of utilitarian object and work of art to create an aesthetic *Lebensraum* that is lyrically expressed through the medium of glass fills us with profound admiration. Behind it lies the goal of realizing 'Le Japon artistique', an undertaking begun by Vincent van Gogh that culminated in the dreamworld that is late nineteenth century Japonism. Ironically, while all this was going on in Europe, Japan was doing its utmost to shake off tradition and replace it with everything that represented Western achievement and a Western way of life.

Art Nouveau is not at all unfamiliar to the Japanese. Even in the Meiji period the Art Nouveau style was brought back by painters who had studied in France. Japanese painting and Japanese art in general subtly assimilated these impulses. In 1904, the year Gallé died, Fujishima Takeji,[33] who worked in the Western manner, painted *Butterflies* (illus. below), which is clearly influenced by Art Nouveau.

Now, even though this text is probably not very well organized, I should be happy indeed if you can make something of it. I am indebted to you for the hours of pleasure I spent immersed in Art Nouveau while leafing through the catalogues.

Notes compiled by Christine Mitomi, Hamburg

of dragonfly, butterfly, moth, cricket and stag beetle evoke the duality of symbolism and life. The golden eyes of the dragonflies are aglow, lending them an almost demonic quality (cat. no. 60).

One cannot avoid mentioning the superlative handling of colour that is a hallmark of Gallé's glass objects. He combined techniques, such as casing, vapour coating to create iridescence or etching to achieve highly sophisticated effects. His richly imaginative visions, recalling paintings of Odilon Redon, are heightened by the play of light.

Gallé has left the utilitarian object far behind – his works are exhibition pieces that have attained the status

Notes

1 Sapporo 1991.
2 Corning 1984.
3 Paris, *Gallé*, 1985.
4 See Corning 1984, no. 21.
5 Literally *karakusa*, the floral tradition since the Tang dynasty.
6 Katsushika Hokusai (1760–1849): painter, illustrator and master of *ukiyo-e* and conveying different moods in landscapes; Hokusai, who was prolific all his life, left as his legacy an incredibly wide-ranging oeuvre. His working life was twice as long as that of any of his celebrated contemporaries: after training as a designer of colour woodcuts, he turned to *ukiyo-e*. Although he acquired expertise in traditional Japanese painting (*Rimpa* and other schools), he also experimented boldly with imported styles and techniques (perspective). He is, of course, famous for such series as the *Views of Mount Fuji* as well as his images of waterfalls, bridges, ghosts, birds and much more. His *manga*, or sketchbooks, which were published from 1814 to 1834, achieved world renown, which has lasted down to the present day.
7 Sapporo 1991, no. 20, and Hilschenz-Mlynek and Ricke 1985, no. 255.
8 *Rimpa* (= *Rin* school): ornamental, formal and stringently stylized school of painting that grew out of the tradition established by Ogata Kōrin (1658–1716) and Tawaraya Sōtatsu (seventeenth century).
9 Has yet to be verified.
10 Sakai Hōitsu (1761–1828), from an old princely family, received a thorough grounding in painting, calligraphy, classical Japanese literature and poetry. From 1800 he devoted himself to painting in the manner of the *Rimpa* school, which owed its renewed popularity in the nineteenth century to him.

Fujishima Takeji, *Butterflies*, 1904

11　Andō Hiroshige (1797–1858): *ukiyo-e* master of the late Edo period, renowned especially for his landscapes with skilfully composed scenes suffused with tranquillity and aesthetic harmony. He is best known for his series entitled *Fifty-Three Stations of the Tōkaidō Highway* (*tōkaidō gojūsantsugi*), the old trade route between Kyōto and Edo.

12　Corning 1984, no. 33.

13　Has yet to be verified.

14　In Japan frogs and even snakes are traditionally classified as *mushi*, i.e. insects; see Utamaro, *hon mushi erami* (*Songs of the Garden*).

15　Tang (618–907).

16　Nara (712–93) and Heian (794–1186).

17　Wū dái (907–60).

18　Sung (Song) (960–1279).

19　Ming (1368–1644).

20　Provinces south of the River Yangtze.

21　Edo (1603–1868).

22　Illustrated natural history deriving from pharmacology.

23　Maruyama Ōkyo (1733–1795): the founder of the Maruyama-Shijō school, which remained active into the nineteenth century. From an impoverished background, he studied the eclectic painting of the Kanō school but developed an utterly distinctive style after studying on his own imported Chinese works, Western engravings of the type on which the style of the Nagasaki school was based, etc. The enormous popularity of his work did, however, prevent him from progressing beyond a certain point.

24　Kitagawa Utamaro (1753–1806): the master of the four-colour *ukiyo-e* woodcut. He did not restrict himself to classical poses in his portrayals of celebrated beauties and courtisans, in which his subjects represent parodies of gods, poets, etc., but showed them in their everyday surroundings. His portraits were innovative in their individualization and beauty, yet adhere to the classical stylization of *okubi-e* portraits. He attained a mastery of composition in space, colour and line in the classical *ukiyo-e* that was never to be surpassed (before Prussian Blue was introduced as a colour in 1829).

25　*Utamaro: Songs of the Garden*, exh. cat., The Metropolitan Museum of Art, New York (London, 1984). Comical short poems (*kyōka*) in the form of parodies of poetry contests engaged in by pairs of insects spouting forth on such themes as love, with masterly representations of the contestants depicted in a setting of wild flowers and grasses.

26　Kubo Shumman (1757–1820): studied *kanga*, i.e. classical Chinese painting, and *ukiyo-e*; famed as the author of five-line comic poems (*kyōka*) and an erudite man of letters.

27　From the series of butterflies reproduced as a luxury edition of New Year's prints for members of the Kasumi-ren literary club and entitled *Gunchō gafū*. See Schmidt and Kuwabara, *Surimono: Kostbare japanische Farbholzschnitte aus dem Museum für Ostasiatische Kunst, Berlin* (Berlin, 1990), figs. 84–85.

28　See Corning 1984, no. 32.

29　See Paris, *Gallé*, 1985, no. 56.

30　Kawanabe Gyōsai (1831–1889): also known as Kyōsai. Studied *ukiyo-e* and the painters of the Kanō school, i.e. Chinese paintings of birds and flowers, preferred by the ruling warlords from the Murōmachi era (1333–1568) to the Edo era (1600–1868). Known for his art-historical studies and socially critical caricatures, he was extraordinarily prolific. He took part in the international exhibitions in Vienna (1873) and Paris (1878). The English architect Josiah Conder was among his numerous pupils.

31　See Sapporo 1991, nos. 12, 30, and Hilschenz-Mlynek and Ricke 1985, nos. 202, 321.

32　Itō Jakuchū (1726–1800): born into an affluent merchant family in Kyōto, he became acquainted with the painting of the Kanō school (flowers and birds as well as monumental landscapes in a showy, formal style) via contact with the Shōkokuji Temple. Known for his obsessively detailed, naturalistic representations of exotic birds based on both Western botanical and zoological works and studies from nature. His masterpiece is a series of thirty votive hanging scrolls featuring flowers, birds and fish for the Shōkokuji altar room (now owned by the Imperial Family).

33　Fujishima Takeji (1867–1943): studied Japanese painting (*Nihonga*) before turning to Western oil painting in Tokyo, which he taught from 1896 in the newly established department of Western painting at Tokyo Fine Arts and Music University. He travelled for study purposes in France and Italy from 1905 to 1910.

Eva Schmitt

Daum Frères: Stepping out of Gallé's Shadow

It is rather difficult to compare the artistic achievements of the Emile Gallé and Daum Frères glassworks since they were founded under completely different conditions.[1] Gallé took as his point of departure his own individual ideas of art, which, thanks to his success, led to serially produced factory wares marked by a high standard of craftsmanship. Antonin Daum, on the other hand, had come from the simplest kind of factory glass production, but strove to improve the quality of his work by taking a crafts approach.[2] The two factories did not reach a standard that might be termed similar enough for purposes of comparison until developments had led to market forces ensuring stiff competition between them. Proof that Gallé was often the guiding spirit of Daum's designs does not, however, provide sufficient grounds for a negative evaluation of the latter, especially since Gallé himself derived inspiration from the work of contemporary glass artists. During the long phase of searching for his own style, he was preoccupied, among other things until the mid-1880s, with the pioneering

Daum Frères, sales catalogue of 1891, pl. 22

work of Eugène Rousseau in Paris. As it developed further under Rousseau's successor, Ernest Léveillé, and his engraver, Eugène Michel, to embrace colour schemes and decoration (cat. nos. 88, 117), it also exerted an influence on Daum that should not be underestimated. Rousseau's design principle entailing the use of glass as a precious-looking material was taken over by both Gallé and Daum. As far as the industrial manufacture of the glass of both is concerned, it is just as easy to make a case for inspiration going the other way, from Daum to Gallé. From the outset of his glass-art production, in 1891, Antonin Daum had used relief etching of floral decoration on coloured and overlay glass as a basic and standard manufacturing method.[3] Gallé's serial production methods at that time were still very elaborate, entailing repeated firings of painting in colour enamels and lustre, precious metals and stains, which were only in part supplemented by etched designs. He himself did not begin to use similar relief etching on serially produced coloured or overlay glass until after 1894 in his own factory in Nancy.[4] The growing competition between the Gallé and Daum factories brought forth remarkable achievements in Art Nouveau glass. Recognized as the equal of the Gallé factory from the 1900 Paris Exposition Universelle onwards, Daum Frères effortlessly succeeded Gallé after his death in 1904 in leading the market in glass design. At the Gallé glass-

Antonin Daum

works it proved impossible to compensate for the loss of Gallé, who was a charismatic and dominant artist, no matter what his tried and tested employees might accomplish in design. Furthermore, under the management of Henriette Gallé, the innovative line of luxury glass was discontinued. Only etched serially produced wares continued to be made and the tediously simple process of making them inexorably led to a lowering of aesthetic standards.

The initial situation of Antonin Daum's improved product line (illus. below, left) can be inferred from the first factory catalogue, issued in 1891. The names of the historicist models introduced in it reflect the period styles on which the designs for these sets of glasses and vases are in part based: 'Régence', 'Louis XIII', 'Charles VII', 'Henri II'. The early decorative programmes include quite a large number of symbolic devices taken from local and national heraldry – the cross of Lorraine, the thistle and the Bourbon fleur-de-lis – and such conventional motifs as garlands, initials, ivy, clover, violets, scrolling tendrils, sprays of flowers, wild flowers, a spider in its web, crickets on blades of grass and banderoles bearing mottoes. The fine, intricately detailed motifs are partly etched, engraved and painted in colour enamels or burnish gold,[5] the ground is cut in facets and polished (illus. below, right). Meticulous execution cannot, however, conceal the discrepancy between the products and the claim to high artistic standards implicit in the

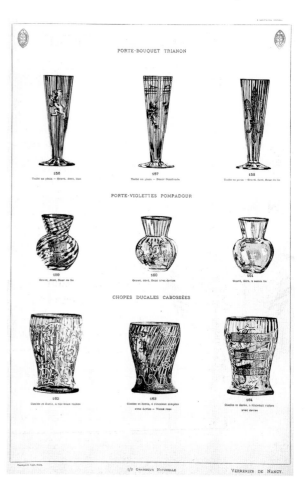

Left: Daum Frères, sales
catalogue, plate showing
models from 1891 to 1894 and
'Egg' model no. 1388, added in
1898

Right: Exhibits for the 1893
Chicago World's Columbian
Exposition

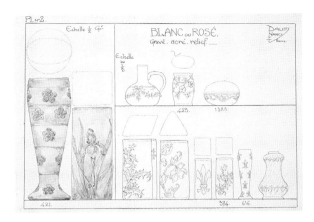

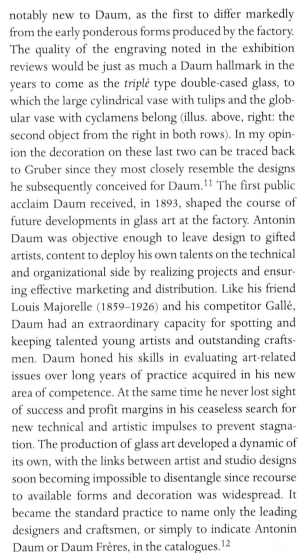

Anonymous drawing, model
no. 613, 'Lampe arabe' (Le Jour)
(Arabian lamp [the day]), 1893

catalogue title 'Verreries Artistiques de Nancy: Créations de 1891'. Antonin Daum recruited a division responsible for a line in glass art from 1891, which created some editions of vases with etched decoration in bold relief combined with engraving and painting in burnish gold (illus. above, left) in preparation for the Chicago World's Columbian Exposition in 1893. Comparison of the Chicago exhibits (illus. above, right) and the models launched in the 1891 catalogue (illus. p. 58, right), which were presented at the factory before despatch, reveals that some objects featured more boldly conceived decoration than had been usual before 1891. An article written for a local periodical in March 1893 amounts to a rave review. It goes into the technical achievements as well as the colour schemes[6] and introduces the creator of the new designs, the painter Jacques Gruber.[7] The most recent research on the artist, conducted by Christophe Bardin, who could find no signed drawings by him except for his illustrations in the 1897 Brussels catalogue, has shown that contemporary accounts were far from correct in attributing to Gruber all models presented. On the contrary, the exhibits for Chicago reflect a variety of experiments rather than a unified new departure in decoration.[8] Consequently, it is almost impossible to pick out Gruber's specific contribution to the Chicago World's Columbian Exposition. First of all, he knew virtually nothing about glassmaking when he started at Daum, whereas Antonin Daum and his select group of staff working on the exhibition pieces had by then had two years of experimentation behind them. It should not be forgotten, however, that the painters or engravers recruited by Daum as glass decorators would certainly have been able to adapt their decoration and to improve it simply on the basis of instructions issued orally. The official report on the Chicago World's Columbian Exposition devotes an extensive description to a model designated 'Lampe arabe' (Arabian lamp; illus. left), featuring a heraldic eagle with outspread wings (*alérion* in heraldry).[9] This model, important for further Daum editions with heraldic motifs, and the emblem itself as well as its arrangement are revealed as borrowings from Emile Gallé's pieces in the oriental style (1884–89) with intricately etched ornamental fields.[10] The shape is notably new to Daum, as the first to differ markedly from the early ponderous forms produced by the factory. The quality of the engraving noted in the exhibition reviews would be just as much a Daum hallmark in the years to come as the *triplé* type double-cased glass, to which the large cylindrical vase with tulips and the globular vase with cyclamens belong (illus. above, right: the second object from the right in both rows). In my opinion the decoration on these last two can be traced back to Gruber since they most closely resemble the designs he subsequently conceived for Daum.[11] The first public acclaim Daum received, in 1893, shaped the course of future developments in glass art at the factory. Antonin Daum was objective enough to leave design to gifted artists, content to deploy his own talents on the technical and organizational side by realizing projects and ensuring effective marketing and distribution. Like his friend Louis Majorelle (1859–1926) and his competitor Gallé, Daum had an extraordinary capacity for spotting and keeping talented young artists and outstanding craftsmen. Daum honed his skills in evaluating art-related issues over long years of practice acquired in his new area of competence. At the same time he never lost sight of success and profit margins in his ceaseless search for new technical and artistic impulses to prevent stagnation. The production of glass art developed a dynamic of its own, with the links between artist and studio designs soon becoming impossible to disentangle since recourse to available forms and decoration was widespread. It became the standard practice to name only the leading designers and craftsmen, or simply to indicate Antonin Daum or Daum Frères, in the catalogues.[12]

Jacques Gruber (illus. p. 61, centre) was, until the 1895 Brussels Spring Exhibition, the sole designer at Daum Frères. His designs for bespoke pieces and his influence on serial production, *fantaisie courante*, are concentrated between 1893 and 1895. This was a period that saw the factory engaged in major exhibitions, including the 1894 Exposition d'Art Décoratif et Industriel Lorrain in Nancy, where Daum competed against Gallé for the first time; the annual Salon de Nancy, organized by the Société Lorraine des Amis des Arts (illus. pp. 60, 62; cat. no. 87); and the Exposition Universelle in Lyons, where Daum

1–10 Works shown at the exhibition
'Art Décoratif et Industriel Lorrain',
Nancy, June/July 1894

Exhibits for the 1895 industrial exhibition in Bordeaux

Opposite: 1–10: Exhibits for the Art Décoratif et Industriel Lorrain exhibition, Nancy, June/July 1894:

1 'Sagittaires ou Libellules et flèches d'eau' (sagittaria or dragonflies and arrowhead)
2 'Aurore coupe d'orchidée' (dawn, orchid cup)
3 'Pavots noirs' (black poppies)
4 'Pensées sombres et pensées folles' (sombre thoughts and foolish thoughts)
5 'Le Chevalier au Cygne Rêve d'Elsa, Lohengrin 1er acte' (the knight of the swan dreaming of Elsa, *Lohengrin*, 1st act)
6 'Cyclamens' (appartenant à M. Haller)
7 'Urne iris' (iris urn)
8 'Cornet aigle et serpent' (Verreries de fantaisie) (cornet eagle and serpent; fantasy glass)
9 'Fiole de pervenche' (Verreries de fantaisie) (periwinkle flask; fantasy glass)
10 'Douce amère' (Verreries de fantaisie) (bitter-sweet; fantasy glass)
11 'Ronces et épines' (brambles and thorns), exhibit for the Société Lorraine des Amis des Arts XXXIe Exposition, Nancy, 1894
12 'Cyclamens', exhibit for Bordeaux, 1895

Jacques Gruber

Henri Bergé

was awarded its first gold medal. The firm's first major distinction, a *diplôme d'honneur*, was conferred in 1895 at the 13ème Exposition de l'Industrie et des Beaux-Arts, des Arts Industriels et de l'Art Ancien in Bordeaux. In addition, Daum joined forces with Gruber by participating in three art exhibitions in 1895, in Brussels – La Libre Esthétique, Toison d'or at Maison d'art – and in Remiremont. Unfortunately, it has not been possible to locate the catalogue issued by Daum on the occasion of the 1895 exhibition in Bordeaux.[13] It would be an important document supporting more precise attribution of designs to Gruber. Starting with the few assured designs by the artist, one can define some characteristic criteria underlying his approach to design. His floral motifs are marked, even in recurring ornamental patterns, by dynamic, free-flowing movement and an emphasis on line. Second, the natural vertical arrangement of plant motifs is broken up by leaves, flowers or stems extending into the horizontal. Third, climbing plants and tendrils are frequently shown hanging, in diagonals or in swags, surrounding the body of the vessel. Furthermore, adherence to botanical criteria to make the plants depicted identifiable is often rejected in favour of ornamental solutions. Moreover, Gruber's favourite forms tended to be of oriental origin, in particular the bottle-shaped vase later regarded as being characteristic of Daum (cat. nos. 78, 80) and known as the 'berluze', which has been attributed to Gruber although it ultimately derives from Gallé's form for 'Les Hirondelles' (1889). Gruber's more or less creative borrowings from Gallé during his early years in Nancy are in fact easy to trace. There is evidence of them in his glass designs for Daum as well as his furniture designs for Louis Majorelle. His preference for literary quotations or titles,[14] which place the object in an

intellectual context,[15] is yet another feature taken over from Gallé. After 1894, however, Gruber did not work as much for Daum. By the 1895 exhibitions in Brussels (La Libre Esthétique) and Bordeaux (illus. pp. 59 and 61, top), when Gruber was the sole designer at Daum, most of the pieces shown were ones that had been on display at the 1893 Chicago World's Columbian Exhibition or in Nancy in 1894. Even the Daum catalogue illustrated by Gruber for the 1897 Brussels Exposition Internationale contains in separate illustrations (illus. p. 62) only the models he designed between 1893 and 1895, except for the new figurative Gruber vase 'L'Heure calme'. Since Gruber's success with his 1894 'Rêve d'Elsa' vase, he had been noticeably more preoccupied with figurative motifs, which were not immediately taken over for Daum lines. Gruber showed eight of these designs at the 1900 Paris Exposition Universelle for Daum Frères yet most of them dated from 1894 to 1897. Gruber, who was a friend of Daum's,[16] had been teaching at the Ecole des Beaux-Arts in Nancy since December 1893. He was also increasingly preoccupied with designing furniture and book-bindings. One of his early designs for Louis Majorelle had led to a breakthrough for Majorelle, too, at the 1984 L'Art Décoratif et Industriel Lorrain exhibition in Nancy.[17] From 1897 Gruber designed flat-glass panes with etched overlay adorned with floral decoration, which he integrated into his furniture designs. In 1898 he collaborated with Majorelle's smithy to produce the first non-electrical table lamp made of wrought iron and glass, which in turn marked the launching of a new line, produced jointly by Daum and Majorelle. That year Gruber turned to leaded windows, a field in which he developed a distinctive signature.[18] As prolific and versatile as he now was, he apparently was no longer willing to tie himself exclusively to Daum, whose demands on designers were multiplying rapidly.

The collaboration between Daum and Majorelle began in 1894, when Daum ordered exhibitions furniture. They subsequently participated jointly in exhibition and shared advertisements. Majorelle also exhibited Daum glass regularly in his showrooms. Daum returned to the Majorelle workshop for the production of lamps with wrought-iron bases, which began in 1899. The fruitful collaboration between the two grew considerably in scale by launching electric lamps in 1900, which were considerably improved in appearance and construction from 1903 by Louis Majorelle's designs. From 1916 Majorelle designed the wrought-iron bases and mounts for the *vases ferronnés*, into which *verre de jade* glass was blown.[19]

Since Gruber tended to work only sporadically for Daum, the latter hired a second artist, the painter Henri Bergé (illus. left), in 1895.[20] Daum also established a drawing school at the factory to promote the training and education of apprentices in order to maintain standards of craftsmanship. In 1897 Gruber and Bergé were placed jointly in charge of the firm's schooling programme[21]

and also named as the leading Daum designers in the catalogue for the Brussels Exposition Internationale. It is safe to assume that Bergé supervised the apprentices from the outset since Gruber was initially harshly criticized by Jules Larcher, his predecessor and boss, when he studied at the Ecole des Beaux-Arts in Nancy.[22] When Bergé started to work for Daum, the serially produced range at Daum Frères was still relatively modest and limited mainly to sets of glasses and dessert services. It was gradually broadened by the repeated use of, and variations on, decoration, techniques and forms that had already proved successful. The cost of making the wood and metal moulds was so high that re-using forms had always been standard practice in the glass industry and Daum was no

exception. Bergé, who first had to familiarize himself with glassmaking, created numerous new designs up to the 1897 Exposition Internationale in Brussels, in which Daum was the only French glass factory to participate. Daum had commissioned a sequence of photographs showing special models for this important event and some of these were included in the firm's catalogue (illus. above, cat. no. 80). A photograph of Louis Majorelle's new exhibition display table was published in the German periodical *Dekorative Kunst* in 1898, which had a great deal to say in praise of that 'table that is so practical and in such good taste'.[23] In addition, the sequence of photographs shows a set of new models (illus. p. 64), which also illustrated an article in the same magazine, in

1899.[24] The article led to the immediate enhancement of Gallé's status.[25] Among the illustrations to this article was the unusual 'Gourde en forme d'ancolie' vase (illus. p. 64, no. 5), which had been purchased by the king of Belgium.[26] Another variant of this model is shown in the photograph of the Majorelle table (see note 22) mentioned above. Since the two vases have the same basic shape where the foliate decoration is located, it may not be out of place to conjecture that this is one of the first Daum models known to have been *soufflé-moulé* (mould-blown) (similar enough for comparison to cat. no. 93).[27] The 1897 exhibits also include three models by the well-known ceramist Edmond Lachenal: the large vase (cat. no. 82), there no. 871 and designated 'Gourde camée triplé Narcisses' (gourd, cameo-cut, double-cased, narcissi), a bottle-shaped vase, no. 36, 'Fiole à long col niel-lée' (nielloed long-necked flask), and a later serially produced model, a dish with two handles, no. 1096, 'Vasque à deux anses à décor de nénuphars' (dish with two handles and waterlily decoration). Around 1903 Lachenal also designed sets of glasses for Daum, which were shown at the Georges Petit gallery in Paris.[28] Another special exhibit was represented by six designs designated 'Veilleuses' (night lights). The term can be interpreted as standing for little (bedside-table) lamps, although it might also simply be the name chosen for a particular model along the lines of the model name 'Lampe arabe' (illus. p. 59, bottom). The 'Veilleuse' type is represented by five lavishly engraved works, including 'Le Lis' (illus. p. 64, no. 4).[29] Should these be examples of the little lamp type so popular then, they would have burnt either oil or candles since the factory presented its first five electric lamps

at the 1900 Paris Exposition Universelle as a sensational novelty.[30] The enormous success in Brussels represented the financial and artistic breakthrough for which Daum had waited so long in the struggle for official recognition. When it came, it came with a vengeance: two *diplômes d'honneur*, two gold medals and six medals awarded to staff members. Unfortunately, the detailed attributions have not yet been disentangled and consequently prevent a definitive statement to be made on the extent to which Bergé contributed to this sudden success. Whatever the case, in Bergé Daum had certainly found the reliable artist he had so long sought to employ. This was a designer who was willing to be a good team-worker entirely at the service of the factory, subordinating his achievement to the group effort. Daum himself was in an entirely different position in the family business and was often taken for a designer. He even participated in numerous exhibitions under that heading.

It was, however, Bergé who, although building in his first decade as a designer (1895–1905) on Jacques Gruber's achievements, created Daum's naturalistic Art Nouveau style, one that emphasized the decorative and was retained in essentials until 1914.[31] Unfortunately, Bergé's real contribution to design at Daum during his early years there, 1895–97, before he embarked on the systematic study of botanical drawing, cannot be satisfactorily studied because records are so scarce. Apart from his regular work as a designer and teacher at Daum, Bergé executed hundreds of botanical drawings, landscape studies and even occasional sketches of animals as designs for models and decoration, all of them attesting eloquently to his gift for keen observation of nature and his ability to translate it faithfully into drawings. This is why his standing plant motifs nearly always meet all criteria for accurate botanical identification. Unlike Gruber's linear style of draughtsmanship, Bergé tended to emphasize the handling of surfaces. Bergé has been criticized for his naturalistic approach and even reproached with eschewing the personal viewpoint and being reluctant to leave out any 'detail, even when devoid of beauty'.[32] From the present-day standpoint, however, an aesthetic stance is recognizable in Bergé's skilfully objective handling, which was intended to sharpen the viewer's eye by presenting nature as it was and thus instilling respect for all natural phenomena. This objective, scientific approach to draughtsmanship, which was employed for purely decorative purposes, ensured that Bergé and Gallé, with his polysemic Symbolism, were poles apart. It is Bergé's naturalism that distinguishes Daum glass from that of Gallé and other manufacturers and demonstrates its independence from them.

That independence is revealed in the variegated collection Daum Frères put together for the 1900 Paris Exposition Universelle. Like Emile Gallé, they were awarded the same high distinction, the Grand Prix. Two techniques claimed to be new appear in the Daum

1

2

3

4

1 'Iris urne' (iris urn)

2 'Marronnier automne' (autumn chestnut)

3 'Cruche orchidée' (orchid jug)

4 'Le Lis veilleuse jaspée' (the lily, marbled night lamp)

5 'Gourde en forme d'ancolie' (gourd in the shape of a columbine)

6 'Chrysanthème de Lemoine'

5

6

catalogue illustrated by Bergé: decoration between layers, *intercalaire*,[33] and fusing coloured powdered glass between layers and on surfaces, *couleurs tachtées* (flecked colours), also simply termed *vitrification*. Experimentation with both techniques increased from 1899. They altered Bergé's decoration by layering colours or creating false colours, contributing substantially, especially in the early trial pieces (cat. nos. 89, 90, 97), to facilitating freedom of design, so much so that this led to setting trends. A major group of Impressionist landscape decoration appeared in the catalogue under the heading 'Morning and evening mists – various aspects of nature – the forest – the valley – the pond – the sea, etc., landscapes fused under translucent coatings, shaded, clouded and blurred at the engraving wheel.'[34] These landscapes, some of them merely suggested, encased in layers of glass, are fascinating indeed in the way they enigmatically evoke the moods in Romantic paintings (cat. nos. 92, 97, 104). Even when translated into simplified versions for serial production (cat. no. 101), they must be regarded as some of the factory's great achievements in design. Daum Frères owed its enormous success at the 1900 Paris Exposition Universelle to the untiring efforts of its leading designer, Henri Bergé, and to Antonin Daum, who, for his part, had realized that investment in new technical processes would vastly enrich design. To the pieces featuring *triplé* overlay with engraving introduced in 1893 a large collection of *martelé* glass was added, featuring a ground pattern that looks as if it has been hammered, a process devised in 1896. This texturing also goes back to Emile Gallé, who used it as early as 1884 to enliven isolated surface areas and, with it, had developed scope for new expressive potential in engraving.[35] Unlike Gallé, however, Daum created a homogeneous impression with the *martelé* technique, like Eugène Michel's engraving in Paris (cat. nos. 10–14), by covering the entire ground of his vessels with fine texturing. Daum Frères presented the *martelé-triplé* group in a separate album, which had been prepared as a sample book for the Paris Exposition Universelle. As rare and precious as individual pieces (cat. no. 99) may seem, when observed as a group these designs look rather schematic (see comparative illus. in cat. no. 99). As he had done for the 1897 Brussels Exposition Internationale, Antonin Daum again included designs by artists from outside the firm. Apart from the models by Gruber mentioned above, which were not in the least new, there were some highly ornate pieces (cat. nos. 91, 110) after ceramic designs by the sculptor Ernest Bussière (illus. p. 63), who had had them made by Keller & Guérin in Lunéville since 1895. Of all Bussière's forms, only a slightly simplified variant (cat. no. 110) was taken over for serial production. The influence his notions of form had on Daum models is apparent in the objects and vessels modelled on plant forms and in the *soufflé-moulé* pieces.

The Daum style achieved by 1900 through the efforts of Henri Bergé and Antonin Daum continued to develop along the same lines until the Ecole de Nancy exhibitions in Paris in 1903 and in Nancy in 1904. Most of the one-off pieces shown at those exhibitions (cat. nos. 103 and 104) are of outstanding workmanship and this high standard was often retained in the luxury glass editions. Among these superb pieces are those with engraved insect applications (illus. below, left) and others with single flower or leaf motifs (illus. p. 64, nos. 1–4), which were also made as *intercalaire* decoration (cat. nos. 98, 100, 102, 103) until 1904. It had been planned to use this elaborate technique for serial production and some designs were even included in the catalogue of models (illus. below, right). The process was, however, simply too costly, even for bespoke pieces. After 1900 Daum made more use of the marquetry technique patented by Gallé in 1898, albeit in simplified form. From 1903 it was integrated into Daum's serially produced luxury line as *lamellé ciselé* (lamellar wheel-engraved) or *ciselé sur plaque* (wheel-engraved on veneer patches) (cat. nos. 107, 108) and was still being used for lines introduced after the First World War (cat. nos. 120, 121). Unlike Gallé, Bergé used this technique to create vibrant colour contrasts. No longer in harmony with the subtle Art Nouveau colour tones, they anticipate as early as 1904 the glowing colours of the 1920s.

Late in 1903 Antonin Daum hired Victor Amalric Walter (1870–1959) to adapt for special use the *pâte de verre* technique, which Walter had developed jointly with his teacher, Gabriel Lévy. Bergé left his stamp on this area, too, by conceiving numerous designs. This new process, initially known as *pâte céramique*, was first implemented in 1909 for small objects, *pâte de verre* panes and windows at the Exposition Internationale de l'Est de la France Nancy 1909. The glass produced by Daum Frères up to 1914 is distinguished by a rich palette created by strewing coloured glass powder over surfaces and fusing them, either between layers of glass or on the outer walls of vessels. An endless variety of batch blends, to some of which a white powder with silver compounds[36]

in harmonizing tints (cat. nos. 79, 98, 99, 103) was added, made it possible to develop a great many more or less elaborate decorative schemes for serial production. They were more varied than the serially produced etched overlay pieces by Gallé. After 1906 the naturalistic Ecole de Nancy style began to die out, even in Nancy. Bergé's consistent naturalism was criticized for the first time (see note 32). Antonin Daum began to make more use of the young designers Emile Wirtz (1884–1953) and Charles Schneider, who had trained in the factory as Bergé's pupils and were at that time still largely under his influence. Their designs did not, however, lead to breakthroughs in product design, a development that would not set in until 1919.

The work done by the brothers Charles (1881–1953) and Ernest (1877–1937) Schneider at Daum Frères between 1898 and 1913 has been for the most part clarified by Christophe Bardin.[37] Charles Schneider began an apprenticeship as an engraver at Daum Frères around 1898, training in draughtsmanship at the same time under Bergé. Until 1904 he also studied painting and drawing at the Ecole des Beaux-Arts in Nancy. In 1904–6 a bursary from the city of Nancy enabled him to continue his studies in Paris at the Ecole Nationale des Beaux-Arts. Afterwards he returned to Daum, where he signed the same artisan's contract as Bergé had. Charles Schneider was awarded a *diplôme d'honneur* in Nancy in 1909 and in Brussels in 1910. His brother, Ernest Schneider, who had originally trained to be a teacher, no longer practised that profession by the time he was hired at Daum in 1903 to help out with Antonin Daum's complex management. He appears, like Antonin Daum before him, in what was really an administrative capacity, as a designer in the Daum exhibition catalogues from 1904 and received awards as a craftsman: a silver medal at Liège in 1905 and a *diplôme d'honneur* in Nancy in 1909 and in Brussels in 1910. Antonin Daum held his work in such high esteem that in 1910 he promised to make him managing director of the Daum warehouse in Paris.

Left: Daum Frères, model catalogue, plate from 1903, editions with insect applications

Right: Daum Frères, model catalogue, plate from 1901 with *intercalaire* models

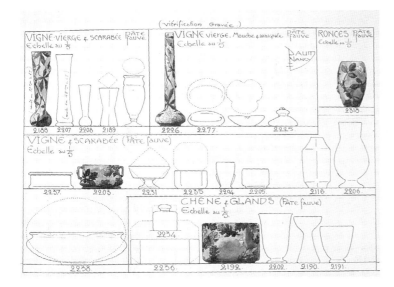

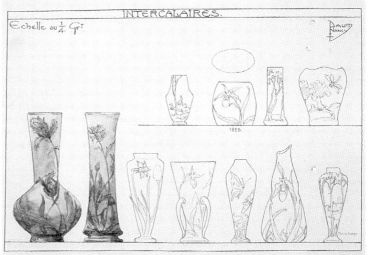

However, the Schneider brothers left Daum in 1913 to found a glass factory of their own, at Epinay-sur-Seine.[38]

The leading role in glass design played by Daum Frères after Emile Gallé's death in 1904 does not stand comparison with the ranking of Gallé and his firm during his lifetime. Its reputation was inextricably linked with Gallé's personal achievements as a designer who, as such, was irreplaceable. Serial production at Gallé, on the other hand, did not develop to the extent that it did at Daum. Although the serially produced Gallé models were initially elaborate and still conveyed an impression of individuality in design, they became increasingly banal by being reduced to etching on overlay. Daum Frères, by contrast, had developed in the opposite direction by virtue of having consistently invested more in serial production. This care paid dividends in the form of innovative editions, both broad-based and catering for different markets and distinguished by variety and quality of design. Antonin Daum expressed the difference between the handmade art object and the industrially produced object very aptly in a lecture entitled 'Les Industries d'art à Nancy': '[...] First the definition of the "art object": or the object "of art, strictly speaking", means a type created and executed by a single artist, a precious one-off piece, for practical purposes useless, to be showcased under glass; – then the object "of industrial art", which may also be an edition object conceived by an artist and manufactured by a different industrialist – or an object produced by a man who is both the artist who creates and the manufacturer who executes and who creates an edition with a team, large or small, of closely linked collaborators, artisans and technicians? It is the latter type that has been adopted by the Nancy studios and is one of the main secrets of their strength [...].'[39]

Notes

1 Compared with Daum, Gallé conceived considerably more pieces specially for exhibitions in order to showcase high-quality design: see Bardin 2002, vol. 2, p. 440.

2 The first account given of the development of the Daum Frères factory emphasizes this approach: 'MM. Daum entreprirent alors une fabrication de fantaisies plus étendue, sans avoir encore, si nos souvenirs sont exacts, la prétention d'appeler artistique une production tout industrielle. Il semblait qu'ils se proposassent seulement de produire dans les meilleures conditions possibles d'économie, de rendement et d'extension, une catégorie de marchandises qui plussent au grand nombre et ne coûtassent pas trop cher. C'était là un point de vue purement industriel [...]' (Messers Daum then undertook to enlarge the range of fantasy articles in production without as yet, if our recollection is accurate, having any pretensions to calling an entirely industrially produced range art. It would seem that they intended only to produce, under the most economical, lucrative and line-extending conditions possible, a category of merchandise that would please only a large number of customers and would not be too expensive. That is a purely industrial point of view [...]'). See Rev. Est, Daum, 1894, p. 7.

3 The design principle entailing the combination of decoration in relief etching with engraving had in turn – according to a contemporary account – been introduced by Ernest Léveillé at the 1889 Paris Exposition Universelle: see Appert and Henrivaux 1893, p. 355.

4 A contemporary account in which the two firms are compared describes the situation in detail. It also establishes that Daum was able to produce 'an extraordinary variety of effects' (des effets étrangement variés) with his relief etching: see Rev. Est, Daum, 1894, p. 8.

5 The technical terminology occurring in the firm's own records – ciseler for wheel engraving and graver for etching – was used as early as in the 1891 sales catalogue. The stippled parts of heraldic decoration are etched and recur in later models (illus. p. 58, right). The basic requirements for all finishing and decorating techniques in glass had been established by 1889: see Bardin 2002, pp. 118 and 198.

6 Among the earliest colours were red, green, black, pinkish lavender (mauve), pearl grey and smoky colours: see E. Gouttier-Vernolle, 'Verrerie Lorraine', Lorraine Artiste (March 1893): 202. The palette reveals, except for black, a noticeable affinity with that used by Rousseau and Léveillé in Paris. Gallé had promoted black in 1889.

7 '[...] il convient de féliciter le jeune artiste, au goût décoratif si développé, au talent si sûr, qui a donné les dessins de ces jolies choses: nous avons nommé M. Gruber [...]' ([...] it is fitting to congratulate the young artist who conceived the designs for these beautiful things with such a highly developed taste in decoration and such assured talent: we have made mention of M. Gruber [...]'): see E. Gouttier-Vernolle, 'Verrerie Lorraine', Lorraine Artiste (March 1893): 201–3.

8 Bardin 2002, vol. 1, pp. 123–30.

9 Krantz 1894, pp. 28–29.

10 See Hilschenz-Mlynek and Ricke 1985, p. 161, no. 180.

11 The cyclamen motif occurs on a two-handled vase with the rare addition to the signature, Compositon de Jacques Gruber 1896: see Zurich, Wühre 9, 1986, no. 10.

12 This process can be followed in the information on the annual exhibitions mounted by the Société Lorraine des Amis des Arts in Nancy. The two events with Jacques Gruber in 1894 furnish even more detailed information on his designs. From 1895 Henri Bergé and Gruber appear as designers without further information on the exhibits. From 1898 designers are no longer named. Not until 1904 is there a list of the most important staff members, including the foremen, without, however, attributing individual pieces to them. From 1909 to 1911 mention is made chiefly of Antonin Daum: see Nancy 1894, pp. 21, 109, nos. 636–44; Nancy, Art Décoratif, 1894, p. 32, nos. 189–213; Nancy 1895, p. 120, no. 722; Nancy 1897, p. 133, no. 667; Nancy 1898, p. 141, no. 708; Nancy 1901, p. 145, no. 780; Nancy 1904, p. 39, nos. 44–48, pls. LVI–LVII, colour pl. n.p.; Nancy 1910, p. 120, no. 456; Nancy 1911, p. 44, no. 371; Lafitte 1912, pp. 36, 38, 473, 873, pls. VIII, XX.

13 Bardin 2002, vol. 1, p. 142, n. 76–77.

14 Gruber's interest in literature must also be viewed in connection with his cousin, Ferdinand Baldensperger, who later became professor of literature in Strasbourg. They did their national service together in Nancy: see J.-L.Vallières, 'Jacques Gruber: Le Régénérateur du vitrail', La Vie en Alsace (1936): 8.

15 Among Gruber's earliest models with a quotation is a bottle-shaped vase made in 1893 bearing the words 'Le deuil violet des colchiques G. Deschamps': see Bascou and Thiébaut, Orsay, 1988, p. 68, no. OAO 292. It is illustrated in the Daum catalogue for the 1897 Brussels Exposition Internationale (illus. p. 62, no. 1). For the titles of the early designs see the captions accompanying the illustrations on pp. 60ff. in the present volume.

16 Antonin Daum was, with Jules Larcher, a witness at Gruber's marriage on 9 May 1902 to the painter Suzanne Elisa Jeanne Jagielski (b. 1874): see marriage certificate, Mairie de la Ville de Nancy, 1902, Gruber and Jagielski, no. 327.

17 Gruber's table 'La Source', which was presented at the 1894 exhibition in Nancy, is still thought to mark the stylistic turnaround in Louis Majorelle's work: see Duncan 1991, pp. 28–29.

18 Gruber's first design for a lamp is a table lamp, 'Eglantine' (wild rose), which the staff gave to Antonin Daum as a wedding present in March 1898: see Brussels, *Gruber*, 1983, p. 33; both the furniture and windows were on display at the annual exhibitions in Nancy: see Nancy 1897, p. 133, nos. 668–69; Nancy 1898, p. 142, nos. 715–18.

19 Bardin 2002, vol. 1, pp. 102–5, 268–71, 460.

20 The contact was perhaps arranged by Gruber. He and Jules Larcher were witnesses at Henri Bergé's marriage to Anne Marie Joséphine Rougieux in Nancy on 20 March 1897: see marriage certificate Bergé and Rougieux, Archives Municipales de la Ville de Nancy, Mariages 1897, no. 163.

21 Mention is first made of training at Daum Frères in 1897 in a lengthy article written on the occasion of a visit to the firm by Henri Boucher, Minister of Trade and Industry, Post and Telegraph: 'Le personnel employé dans les ateliers d'art est en grande partie formé à l'usine même où fonctionne, à l'usage des apprentis, une école de modelage et de dessin gratuite sous la direction de MM. Jacques Gruber et Henri Bergé dont les noms doivent être mentionnés à titre de collaborateurs [...]' (The personnel employed in the art studios is trained mainly at the factory itself, where a school of modelling and design is operated free of charge for apprentices under the supervision of the two employees Jacques Gruber and Henri Bergé, who have already been mentioned by name as co-workers [...]'). See *Rev. Est*, Daum, 1897, pp. 5–6.

22 Bardin 2002, vol. 1, pp. 88–89, n. 87–94.

23 'Moderne kunstgewerbliche Ausstellungen', *Dekorative Kunst* I, no. 1 (1898): 37. The photographs of Marjorelle's new exhibits displayed on the table are not kept in the Daum archives.

24 The article makes a point of giving Gallé and Daum the credit they deserve but makes no bones about deprecating their glass art as élitist: 'While the luxury glass developed into all the sophisticated refinements imaginable, utility glass was entirely neglected. The very amateurs who admired Gallés and Daums were content with only what was necessary, with the use of the hackneyed models of decadent make, and the artists in turn, who made these objets d'art as a sideline, were the industrialists responsible for these mass-produced wares; indeed, unfortunately, this line was not a sideline but art was sidelined and one invariably received the same answer when this contradiction in terms was remarked on: only because we can market the rubbish en masse are we able to achieve something better in our leisure hours, which we make no money on [...].' '[...] Gallé has made vases in whose sublime poetry an unparalleled dignity inheres; Daum, on the other hand, has managed with relatively less effort to lend his vases genuine beauty, which aims more at simplicity, and seems to us to be destined to industrialize this area in the right way [...].' See 'Die Kristallglaskünstler Nancys', *Dekorative Kunst* III, no. 3 (1899): 101, illus. Daum, pp. 126–27, colour pl. n.p. [128a, 129a].

25 '[...] Les auteurs de l'article (M. G. et J.) entre plusieurs louanges, regrettent que M. Gallé ne dépense ses qualités qu'au profit exclusif du bibelot de luxe. C'est un reproche très mal fondé, auquel répond notre collaborateur E. Hinzelin dans la partie de ce numéro consacrée à "l'Art en Lorraine"' ([...] The authors of the article (M. G. and J.), amid praises, regret that M. Gallé has squandered his skills entirely to the benefit of luxurious knick-knacks. This is a reproach that is very much without basis in fact, to which our collaborator, E. Hinzelin, replies in the part of this issue dedicated to "Art in Lorraine"'). See *Lorraine Artiste* (March 1899): 5. The message of the article, which was published in German, essentially boils down to the following: 'The least of his creations are those of a sharply observant intellect, which miss nothing, of a noble heart, which is receptive to all emotions.' See E. Hinzelin, 'L'Art en Lorraine', *Lorraine Artiste* (April 1899): 19.

26 'Die Kristallglaskünstler Nancys' (note 24), illus. p. 126; E. Hinzelin, 'L'Art en Lorraine', *Lorraine Artiste* (March 1899): illus. p. 3; Bardin 2002, vol. 1, p. 147, n. 90.

27 The term *soufflé-moulé* signifies 'mould-blown', i.e. blowing into a form with relief design on its walls in which the blowpipe cannot be 'trundled' (rotated) and the entire glass form or most of it is created, with the impressed relief, in a single stage. This process had always been used at Daum and the surface was usually reworked with etching or engraving. If the engraved 'Gourde en forme d'ancolie' vase had been thus preformed, Bergé may have designed it, because this shape derives directly from that of the columbine bud and must, therefore, be the work of a very shrewd observer of natural forms. Moreover, the shape of the vase, which tends to be static compared with the ceramic forms created by Ernest Bussière (illus. p. 63), is consistent with Bergé's handling of sculptural form and design.

28 E. Belville, 'Daum, Lachenal, Majorelle à la Galerie Georges Petit', *L'Art Décoratif* (January 1904): 33; Bardin 2002, vol. 1, p. 102, n. 153–54.

29 Brussels, *Daum*, 1897; Brussels, catalogue, 1897, no. 3: 'Le Lis' (illus. p. 64, no. 4); no. 8: 'Chardon vert' (green thistle); no. 437: 'Clématites bleues' (blue clematis); no. 445: 'Larmes et pavots' (tears and poppies); and in the subsequent order of 13 July 1897, no. 769: 'Chrysanthème'.

30 Paris, *Daum*, 1900, p. 31, illus. pp. 24–25; Pazaurek 1901, pp. 97–98, illus. nos. 86–87.

31 Bardin 2002, vol. 1, pp. 91, 93, 150, 154, 170, 213.

32 The first criticism appeared in 1906 on the occasion of a competition advertised by Alphonse Cythère, Société des Produits Céramiques de Rambervillers, in the *Bulletin des Sociétés artistique de l'Est*; a harsher critique is contained in a 1925 article on Victor Amalric Walter of 1925: excerpts in Bardin 2002, vol. 1, p. 214.

33 Research conducted by Susanne Brenner, Berne, on Désiré Christian, formerly head of the decoration studio at Burgun, Schverer & Co., has suggested new links with the Daum Frères patents on sandwiched decoration (*Zwischenschichtdekor*): see biography of Désiré Christian in the Appendix.

34 'Les brumes – matinales et vespérales – divers aspects de la nature – la Forêt – la Vallée – l'Etang – la Mer etc., paysages vitrifiés sous couvertes translucides, ombrées, nuagées et estompées à la roue de graveur': see Paris, *Daum*, 1900, p. 23, nos. 276–78, 349, 351, 352, 354.

35 E. Schmitt, 'Emile Gallé: Theoretiker und Schöpfer impressionistischer Gravurgestaltung – wegweisend bis heute', in *Festschrift für Brigitte Klesse*, issued by the Förderer des Museums für Angewandte Kunst, Cologne, formerly the Overstolzengesellschaft (Berlin, 1994), pp. 153–57.

36 From 1893 Antonin Daum made use of striking colours as well as strewing glass powder with silver content over the surface of the vessel to produce an iridescent finish.

37 C. Bardin, 'Autour de la coupe au serpent, le rôle des frères Schneider à la manufacture Daum', in B. Chavanne and N. Tailleur, *Schneider une verrerie au XXe siècle*, exh. cat., Musée des Beaux-Arts de Nancy (Nancy, 2003), pp. 23–39.

38 The idea for the new, brilliant palette implemented from 1904 was presumably the Schneider brothers', especially since this palette continued to play a key role in their own product range after 1919.

39 '[...] D'abord la définition de "l'objet d'art": objet "d'art proprement dit", c'est à dire type crée et exécuté par un seul artiste, pièce précieuse et unique, pratiquement inutile, à mettre sous vitrine; – puis, l'objet "d'art industriel", qui peut être lui-même un objet d'édition conçu par un artiste et fabriqué par un industriel différent, – ou l'objet produit par l'homme qui est tout ensemble l'artiste qui crée et le fabricant qui exécute et qui édite avec un concours plus ou moins nombreux de collaborateurs intimement liés, ouvriers d'art et techniciens? C'est ce dernier type qui est adopté par les Ateliers de Nancy et qui est un des principaux secrets de leur force [...].' See J.-A. Daum, 'Les Industries d'art à Nancy avant et depuis la guerre', in *Mémoires de l'Académie Stanislas, Années 1924–1925*, vols. XXII, LXXV (Nancy, 1925), p. 56.

Susanne Brenner

Désiré Christian:
Between Meisenthal
and Nancy

Born on 23 May 1846 in Lemberg, Lorraine, France, Désiré Jean Baptiste Christian apparently worked even in his youth at the Meisenthal glassworks. In May 1863 the firm of Burgun, Schverer & Cie. made an advance payment to him, when he – according to the firm records – was about to leave for Paris.[1] We do not know whether he only visited his aunt, who is said to have lived in Paris, or whether he was absent from Meisenthal for quite some time. He may have received further training in glass painting near Paris. Depending on when he completed his training as a glass painter, he must have started working for the Gallé-Reinemer workshop at Burgun, Schverer & Cie. sometime between 1861 and 1867, for the two firms began collaborating in 1860/61. Between 1867 and 1870 Christian is thought to have first encountered Emile Gallé, the son of Charles Gallé-Reinemer, in Meisenthal – an assumption based on Gallé's biographical data, for in 1867 he had taken up a regular, leading position as a designer in his father's firm. His work involved taking short trips to the firm's business partners in Meisenthal and St.-Clément. Later encounters with Gallé and collaboration with him seem to have had a formative influence on Christian's work. Mathieu Burgun, at the time director of Burgun, Schverer & Co., admitted in a letter dated 1 January 1885[2] that Christian's artistic sense had developed under the 'inspiration' of Gallé. Further, the letter indicates that Christian at first worked solely for Burgun, Schverer & Co. and that they had placed him at Gallé's disposal on a commission basis. Burgun also mentions an impasse from which Christian had been extricated. It is not known just what the difficulties were and what years Burgun is referring to.

Collaboration between Meisenthal and Nancy *c.* 1885

The contract concluded in 1885

A handwritten contract, concluded on 4 January 1885, regulated the collaboration between Burgun, Schverer & Co. in Meisenthal and Désiré Christian and Emile Gallé in Nancy.

Désiré Christian and family, *c.* 1890. From left to right: Désiré, Armand, Juliane and Marie

Under the terms of the contract, Christian retained his position and committed himself – to both Gallé and Burgun and Schverer – 'not to place his skills and knowledge at the service of any third party'.[3] The specific examples mentioned in the contract as pertinent are 'the invention of [technical] processes and improvements in enamels or to other applications on glass fired in a muffle kiln'.[4] In this connection, however, Christian reserved the right to use his own inventions himself. The relevant passage in the contract is highly restrictive: 'if he were to come upon an innovation that, being offered to the parties, were to be declined by both, then, in that case only, he will be free to do with it as he sees fit'.[5]

It can be inferred from the written guarantees, which were evidently regarded as having become necessary, that the parties to the contract were at that time commercially interdependent. Gallé depended on reliable delivery of products from Meisenthal.[6] He also depended on the firm and its employees not using their knowledge for their own purposes or revealing it to third parties. Gallé had evidently issued an ultimatum in 1884 that the decoration studio and Christian in particular should work exclusively for him. In a letter written to Gallé even before the contract was concluded, Burgun states that he could never have imagined that Gallé would one day require that Christian or his pupils might no longer be employed by Burgun, Schverer & Co. in their workshops.[7] Gallé was unable to get his way. Christian and his studio also continued to execute work on commission for Burgun, Schverer & Co.

Only four years before the above contract had been concluded, Christian seems to have been managing director of a studio. A document recording considerable sums paid to Christian for decoration executed in the months from July 1881 to June 1882[8] furnishes evidence on the one hand that Christian did a great deal of work for Gallé at this time. On the other, the sums mentioned suggest that Christian was not the only person involved with this work and that those working with him were paid by Christian as head of the workshop.

In this capacity, Christian was responsible for its organization and the practical side of collaboration with Nancy. That this was so can be inferred from undated instructions for corrections addressed to him in which Gallé wrote: 'On the basis of the ones here, I note that the workshop has not fully grasped this decor'.[9] Interestingly, a document issued in January 1885 – work regulations, as it were, intended for the pottery decoration workshop in Raon L'Etape – also allows specific conclusions to be drawn about the organization of the decoration workshop in Meisenthal.[10] The 'chef d'atelier' was invested with supervisory powers in the workshop and in particular the supervision of decoration work. He was responsible for ensuring that no design or model left the workshop and that all work was executed 'at the expense of the house'. His tasks also included determin-

ing the pay employees were to receive. Further instructions refer to the organization of the workshop and ensuring the availability of materials needed for decoration. Some of the correspondence between Meisenthal and Nancy that has been preserved also implies that Christian was assigned such tasks. In it such matters as the procurement of materials (e.g., gold leaf) or pricing are discussed and detailed instructions for corrections indicate Christian's responsibility for ensuring that decoration was executed and quality standards were maintained. The following statement suggests that Christian received all documentation with instructions for the pieces to be produced: 'M. Emile believes he has left his files – the duplicates of the documents that were left behind for the workshop – with M. Christian'.[11] It must remain a moot question whether the records mentioned refer to descriptions in writing of models, profiles of models, watercolours and some trial pieces, which are mentioned in instructions preserved in the Chambon Collection. In any case the collaboration between Meisenthal and Nancy seems to have run so smoothly in 1892 that new models were created on the basis of written instructions and drawings. Corrections were issued in writing and orally by Gallé whenever he visited Meisenthal.[12] Letters with suggestions for improvements in decoration were addressed to Christian. Orders for blanks to be processed at Nancy were addressed either to the director of Burgun, Schverer & Co. or to the managing director in charge of the furnaces.[13]

The extent to which Christian was involved in the production of glass art, for which he was responsible in Gallé's studio, at the Meisenthal glassworks is unclear. Presumably his tasks also included supervising the decoration done in that glassworks. That they did is suggested by a precise set of instructions for a 'coupe 49' that has come down to us, presumably dating from 1892, which was made under Christian's supervision.[14] These instructions reveal that whoever wrote them (Gallé or an employee of his in Nancy) had already prepared *taches* ('blobs', i.e., 'prunts'; possibly also pieces for intarsia) for an important object[15] and was going to send them by post to Meisenthal so that they could be worked according to precise instructions. The drawings were to be sent back so that the *taches* could be referred to again when the engraving was done. All three variants described were to be made to ensure that at least one good piece resulted. They were made in this case according to Gallé's instruction[16] and the elaborate article was produced at Meisenthal, with preliminary work and finishing done at Nancy. Christian was responsible in Meisenthal for ensuring that Gallé's ideas were realized.[17] The written instructions from Nancy attest to a clear conception of the objects in glass as well as sound technical knowledge of how they were to be made.

Glass painters, engravers and important glassmakers in Meisenthal

A photograph gives a good idea of the size of the Meisenthal decoration workshop under Désiré Christian's management in the 1890s.[18] It shows, apart from Christian and his son, Armand, four grown and four young men as well as four women and girls. The girls were probably employed at the Meisenthal workshop to do acid-etching and pack the wares for shipment.[19] Unlike the workmen, Armand Christian is not wearing working clothes. It is not yet known what his function in the workshop was.

The following men over the age of twenty-five[20] lived in Meisenthal at that time and worked there as glass painters: Joseph Schmitt (1855–1912), Nicolas Schmitt (1823–1892), Joseph Basilius Winckler (b. 1859) and François Christian (b. 1863).[21] Of the young glass painters employed there, Eugène Jacques Kremer (1867–1941) and Alfred Jean-Marie Schaeffer (b. 1869) are known by name. There were only a few engravers, although numerous glass grinders and cutters, at Meisenthal in 1890/91. The engravers included Emile Maas (b. 1864), Joseph Maas (1867–1904) and Antoine Walter (b. 1856). The 1903 electoral roll lists Eugène Kremer's younger brothers, Felix Kremer (b. 1874) and Luzian Kremer (b. 1876), as an engraver and a glass painter, respectively. The two were presumably still serving their apprenticeships in the 1890s, with Luzian Kremer probably apprenticed to Désiré Christian. The glassmakers Joseph Stenger (1849–1916) and Georg Franckhauser (1843–1900) probably also acquired their glassmaking skills in art while collaborating with Gallé or Christian.

Burgun, Schverer & Co., Meisenthal, c. 1895

Distinctions for the firm and three employees

A year after Gallé had moved glass production entirely to Nancy, Désiré Christian was awarded his first personal distinction at the 1895 Strasbourg Industrial & Applied Arts Exhibition. He was mentioned with praise as a master painter and employee of Burgun, Schverer & Co. The two glassmakers Joseph Stenger and Georg Franckhauser were also awarded employee certificates with distinction.[22] Burgun, Schverer & Co. was awarded a certificate of honour with a medal by the jury at the 1895 Strasbourg Industrial and Applied Arts Exhibition, which was the top award given there.

The journal of the Bavarian Applied Arts Association wrote: 'We are confronted with the supreme achievements in the applied arts at the exhibition in glass, where the palm has been awarded to Burgun, Schverer & Co., Meisenthal Glass Factory, Lemberg Station, Lorraine. Apart from some replicas of antique Venetian or Middle Eastern glass, which were, incidentally, excellent, and the "current articles" shown in the special pavilion, the works by this firm are entirely on modern ground and are at the same time veritable works of art; all glass-finishing techniques, cutting and engraving, painting inside and out, casing overall or in part, polishing and matt etching are handled here in the freest possible manner. [...] Forms recall Arabian antiques or Japanese ideas, some without any echoes of what is familiar [...] those objects representing combinations of various techniques are particularly enigmatic.'[23]

Glass from Meisenthal c. 1895 – Patent for painting between casings (sandwich glass)

Replicas of Venetian glass: Pieces in this category were created after models. A glass dish once bought in Strasbourg and now missing was a copy of a Venetian piece dating from the first half of the fifteenth century in the Slade Collection in South Kensington, London. When it was purchased, in 1895, it was noted as being a copy.[24] The museum at Veste Coburg is also in the possession of a cup that is modelled on an original from the above collection.[25]

Glass art: Most of the pieces of glass art bought about 1895 are embellished with painting or colour fused between layers of casing. Surfaces are frequently acid-etched and some of the decoration between the layers of casing has been echoed in fine relief and in part painted with flat colour or enamelled.[26] The signature *B.S & Co/ Meisenthal* is inscribed on the arm of a cross of Lorraine with a thistle entwined around it. On an amber-coloured glass with diamond-point engraving, enamel and gold painting, the signature *B.S & Co / Meisenthal* is inscribed on a stylized thistle bloom – as on the above-mentioned Coburg cup, in the Venetian style. The three letters *DC A* occasionally occur in both signature types,[27] indicating that Désiré Christian had a hand in the decoration.

The process for sandwiching painting between body and glass sleeve, which was developed in the Meisenthal decoration workshop and was used on objects by Burgun, Schverer & Co. and D. Christian & Sohn, was patented in Strasbourg by Burgun, Schverer & Co. – earlier than has hitherto been assumed[28] – shortly after the firm's successful exhibition in Strasbourg in 1895.[29] The patent is made out to Burgun, Schverer & Co., Meisenthal. Inventors are not named in it – nor are rights granted in it to any individuals or businesses. Christian nonetheless would later use the technique for his own purposes.

Current articles: These are probably unsigned articles, tableware, acid-etched and engraved crystal and cased or flashed glass.

Home of Désiré Christian
and family, in the 'Strumpf',
Meisenthal

Désiré Christian between 1895 and 1899

If one can rely on the accuracy of lists in the civic registry-office records indicating shareholders who always met in person and by proxy for the general shareholders' meeting of the Meisenthal glassworks – a limited partnership with shares as a subsidiary of Burgun, Schverer & Co. – Désiré Christian was living in Nancy in the autumn of 1896 and two years later in Vallerysthal.[30] This would cast doubts on the usual assumption that he became self-employed in Meisenthal in 1896. Unfortunately, however, there is no evidence of Christian having lived in Nancy at that time; he still could have worked for Gallé or even Daum Frères there. There is no proof in the official catalogue of the 1897 Strasbourg Exposition d'Art that Christian participated in that exhibition under his own name.[31] At best he could have been represented as an employee of a participating firm, such as Burgun, Schverer & Co. Meisenthal, Gallé or Daum, Nancy, or the Vereinigte Glashütten Vallerysthal. Nor is there any confirmation that Christian was hired by the Vereinigte Glashütten von Vallerysthal & Portieux in 1898. It is nevertheless conceivable that, during the period in which Charles Spindler, Bruno Paul and F. A. Otto Krüger were invited to Vallerysthal from Munich to design for the firm,[32] Christian, too, was hired there. More than one mention was made of Christian's links with Vallerysthal.[33] As is well known, pieces similar in body and decoration occur with the signatures of both Christian and Vallerysthal.[34]

The firm of D. Christian & Sohn, Meisenthal, Lorraine

The decoration workshop

A muffle kiln and the colourful stained-glass window in the house once lived in by Désiré Christian and his family still bear witness to the glass-decoration workshop and the firm headquarters of D. Christian & Sohn (illus. left and p. 74). Between 1891 and 1896 Désiré Christian bought meadows and property in several stages in the 'Strumpf', where he later built his own house. A promissory note for more than 3000 marks registered in September 1899 attests to a fairly substantial investment. If he did invest this money in his business, this was probably at a time when Christian – after the first flush of success in Munich – either established a workshop with a muffle kiln or hired more workmen.

Founding of the firm, Products, Trade

The date on which the firm of D. Christian & Sohn, Meisenthal, Lorraine was founded is unknown. The first pieces were probably produced for sale under this name towards the close of 1898. The firm is mentioned by name in 1899,[35] 1900 and 1902 on the occasion of the annual Munich Exhibition and in 1900 as participating in the Paris Exposition Universelle as well as in exhibitions in St Petersburg in 1901, in Turin in 1902, in St. Louis, Missouri, in 1904 and in Dresden and Metz in 1906. The name and a factory mark (capital C with a cross of Lorraine; aligned with the C: on the left D, on the right F, below A) were entered in the glass industry roll for the first time in January 1903.[36] The mark was not used very frequently but was in use prior to that date, also as a signature.

A letter dated 1 May 1906 on the firm's original letterhead, 'Christian frères & fils, Meisenthal', changed by hand to 'D. Christian & fils', proves that a firm called 'Gebrüder Christian & Sohn' existed.[37] This firm name was never used at the above-mentioned exhibitions, yet it was referred to as the former firm name by Paul Schulze in 1906.[38] On the aforementioned letterhead the following products are offered for sale: 'Cristaux et Céramique d'art / objets d'art d'après dessins spéciaux / Pièce pour Monture / Service de table et Liqueur' (Art Crystal and Pottery / art objects after special designs / A piece for

Mounting/Table and Liqueur Service). Unlike the entry in the 1903 roll of the German glass industry, where 'Art glass and artistic faience, fantasy things after special drawings, articles to be mounted, [a] table service'[39] are listed, this sheet also mentions liqueur services. Apart from the glass art, it is not known what the artistic faience, fantasy articles or table services by the firm of Christian were like, and articles for mounting on stands are rare. Christian also sold early Gallé glass made in Meisenthal: a scent flacon to the Württembergisches Landesmuseum, Stuttgart, in April 1904;[40] a dish, a tumbler and a vase to the Musée des Arts Décoratifs, Strasbourg, in July 1905.[41] In 1906 D. Christian & Sohn was represented at the Lorraine Pottery Exhibition in Metz with a variety of products made by other firms: four 'old Gallé' vases, 'pottery from Diemeringen, engraved and enamelled in the Moorish style' (including three vessels designated 'Fayence Gallé'), twenty 'old Meisenthal' objects and three 'pieces of antique glass'.[42] 'Very early work by Emile Gallé' was exhibited at the Kaiser Wilhelm-Museum, Krefeld, in 1906. Paul Schulze made a point of emphasizing that this glass was owned by the firm of 'Désiré Christian & Sohn in Meisenthal, Lorraine'.[43]

The decoration workshop staff

A photograph, which probably shows the workshop team at D. Christian & Sohn about 1900, provides information on the size of the firm (illus. below). Désiré and his wife, Juliane Lina Christian, their son, Armand Antoine, and their daughter, Marie Augustine, are seated on chairs in the foreground while behind them stand a woman and four men in light-coloured aprons. Two of the men are presumably François Pierre Christian and Joseph Schmitt, possibly also Johann Nicolaus Illig, although it is not clear whether he was employed on a permanent basis as an engraver in this workshop team.

François Pierre Christian (b. 1863). François is said to have gone to Paris with his two brothers in 1870/71 because of the Franco-Prussian War (see biography under 'Manufacturers and Artists' in the Appendix). In 1882 he stayed in Aubervilliers – possibly to train there at the Verreries d'Aubervilliers.[44] In 1890 he lived in Meisenthal, where he is registered as a porcelain or glass painter. He probably worked at first for the Meisenthal decoration workshop and in his brother's workshop from about 1898 until about 1905. François apparently left Meisenthal during his brother's lifetime and moved to Cologne. More pieces bear his signature than was previously assumed; he also presumably did some designing.

Johann Nicolaus Illig (b. 1879). Illig trained as an engraver in St-Louis. About 1900 he worked on objects

Désiré Christian and family with workmen, *c.* 1900

ably date from the firm's early years. These techniques were later used merely to ensure the continuation of a particular product line. Elaborate cased pieces,[49] some partly cased, with intricate engraving and sophisticated colour schemes date from a later period. These pieces are presumably linked with the procurement of blanks from St-Louis (cat. no. 72).

Decoration with figurative representations, such as allegorical scenes,[50] animal motifs, lacustrine and forest scenes[51] as well as ornamental decoration in enamel colours can often be verified as belonging to the early years,[52] with floral motifs predominating. This last was used throughout the firm's existence, either in combination with other motifs or frequently also as individual motifs, some of them highly stylized.

When considering how brief the firm's existence was, many different signatures were used. The following signatures have been verified for the early years: *D. Christian* signatures in floral motifs;[53] *D. Christian, Meisenthal*, possibly the painted firm seal,[54] and an etched signature in a stylized thistle bloom.[55] According to the latest research, objects with the following signatures and marks must be later: *F. Christian* (cat. no. 74), *Geb. Christian* (cat. no. 72) and the sticker (cat. no. 70). It is, however, not yet possible to date objects by signatures such as *DC*, *D. Christian, Meisenthal, Loth.*, *D. Christian, Meisenthal, Lorraine*, *AD Christian, Meisenthal, Lothr.*, etc.

to be exhibited by D. Christian & Sohn at the Paris Exposition Universelle of the same year, receiving an award for them. In 1902 he emigrated to America, working as an engraver for several firms in Corning, New York. His employment at Christian & Sohn was, therefore, limited to between 1899 and 1902.

Armand Antoine Christian (1874–1953) is mentioned as a son of Désiré Christian's in the firm's names from its foundation. His function within the firm is unknown. Described in 1891 as still unemployed, the young man was, according to Françoise-Thérèse Charpentier,[45] sent by D. Christian to the 'école professionelle de Nancy'. In January 1907, before his father's death, Armand is listed on the electoral roll as a 'factory official'. At B S & Co. managing directors, treasurers, bookkeepers and supervisory personnel were called factory officials. It is not known whether Armand worked as an artisan or artist.

Joseph Schmitt (1855–1912) was married to Désiré Christian's sister, Melanie. No pieces signed by Schmitt are extant. Nevertheless glass signed *F. Christian* and *Geb. Christian* formerly from the family estate indicate close ties between him and the firm of D. Christian and Christian Brothers.[46]

Products – Aids in dating works

Products made by D. Christian & Sohn, Meisenthal, within a period of roughly seven years vary widely in style. Several people designed and executed the decoration. Apart from glass art, utility glass was also made.[47]

As for dating Christian glass art, only some general remarks can be made regarding the painting with enamel colours (cat. no. 70) and sandwiched decoration.[48] Pieces with marquetry (intarsia) work (cat. no. 71) prob-

Contemporary reviews

Contemporary reviews of Christian pieces shown at the 1899 annual Munich Exhibition[56] often link them with Gallé glass: 'D. Christian und Sohn, Meisenthal (Lorraine), are now trying to step into Gallé's shoes in the Glass Palace by carving in relief thick-walled cased pieces in coloured cased glass and indeed he is achieving quite remarkable things in so doing, even though he is still quite a long way from overtaking Gallé [...].'[57] Even as late as 1901 Gustav E. Pazaurek emphasized that Christian's 'preference for Gallé [...] is not limited solely to technique and occasional recourse to his method of decorating but [...] also [...] extends to the addition of inscriptions in the Gallé manner and – which is most telling – even in the French language, such as "fumer et plaisir".'[58]

The reasons for the noticeable similarities between Meisenthal and Gallé glass were made public not long after the twentieth century was ushered in. The *Strassburger Neueste Nachrichten*, for instance, proclaimed on the occasion of an exhibition mounted by the Gesellschaft der Kunstfreunde (Art-Lovers' Association): 'Glass art of all kinds is made by Meisenthal. Two firms, Burgun-Schverer and Christian, are represented with their wares. The more remarkable is the former, which for many years was sole supplier of glass art to Gallé-Nancy.'[59]

In the catalogue accompanying the First International Exhibition for the Modern Decorative Arts in

Turin (1902), Christian is called 'a former Gallé employee'.[60] This time his pieces are warmly received, by Leopold Gmelin: 'Among the higher-quality glass art, the pieces by Des. Christian, Meisenthal (Lorraine), are particularly noteworthy. For anyone who takes the trouble to study these works (we except, of course, the usual pieces made for everyday use) will be astonished at how much laborious technique, casing, application, undercutting [to reveal the lower layers] had to be united here to bring forth those delightful atmospheric qualities that can only be expressed in glass.'[61] The considerable achievement of Christian as a firm is also acclaimed in the journal *Kunstgewerbe in Elsass Lothringen*: 'Among the other products of the Reich's decorative arts, which are only sparsely represented, the luxury pieces in polychrome glass by D. Christian and Meisenthal stand out [...].'[62]

D. Christian & Sohn, Meisenthal were awarded a silver medal for outstanding achievement at the 1900 Paris Exposition Universelle and a second silver medal in St Petersburg in 1901. The firm was awarded a certificate of recognition at the First International Exhibition for the Modern Decorative Arts in Turin and the gold medal at the 1904 World's Fair in St. Louis, Missouri.

Summary

While working with Emile Gallé, Désiré Christian probably started out as a painter of decoration but later became head of the decoration workshop. Gallé had a formative influence on the development of Christian's skills as an artist. Long and intensive collaboration created a working climate in which the workshop was able to adapt forms and interpret decoration, variations and corrections. It is highly unlikely, however, that designs for new Gallé models were made in Meisenthal. Some preliminary work and finishing – such as elaborate engraving – was done at Nancy even during the period covered by the contract between Meisenthal and Nancy.

In 1890 the Meisenthal workshop employed about fourteen workmen, who did not, however, work solely for Gallé. Decoration designed and executed for Burgun, Schverer & Co. also originated there. The glass art shown in 1895 at the Strasbourg Industrial and Applied Arts Exhibition was decorated at the Meisenthal workshop headed by Christian. Many of these pieces have sandwiched gold painting or enamel painting. Surfaces are often decorated with etching in delicate relief, some of which traces the decoration between the layers of casing. Various types of decoration occur in combination.

Little is known until 1899 about Désiré Christian's further career, after the contract with Gallé was terminated. He is likely to have worked on commission, even outside Meisenthal. The actual date on which Christian founded his own firm is unknown; the firm is, however, first verifiably recorded in 1899 under the name D. Christian & Sohn, Meisenthal. From then on the name is represented by pieces shown at various trade fairs and exhibitions, even after Désiré Christian's death. In 1900 four workmen and a woman were employed by D. Christian & Sohn. About 1903–6 the broad range of wares included glass art and artistic faience, fantasy objects after special designs, articles for mounting on stands and table services. Christian also sold early Gallé objects, probably before 1904 and later as well as glass art from Meisenthal and some 'antique' glass in 1906. The present state of scholarship permits only a chronology – and a sketchy one at that – of the glass, especially the art glass (which often bears Christian signatures), made by the house of Christian.

Notes

1 Musée du Verre et du Cristal, Meisenthal. 'Journal B.S. et CO. [from] 1861 [...] Compte d'avance / 10 n / versement à Christian en partant p. Paris / 60 [...]' (Advance payment / 10 n / made to Christian on leaving for Paris / 60 [...]).

2 Musée d'Orsay, fonds Gallé, Paris. Letter from Mathieu Burgun to Emile Gallé, 1 January 1885.

3 Musée d'Orsay, fonds Gallé, Paris. Contract concluded on 4 January 1885. '[...] et s'engage envers les deux parties à ne pas user de son art et de son savoir envers un tiers'. See also the 'Sources'.

4 Ibid. '[...] soit comme invention de procédés et de perfectionnement d'emaux et d'autres applications sur le verre et cuits au feu de moufle'. See also the 'Sources'.

5 Ibid. '[...] et qu'après l'avoir présentée aux parties contractantes, ces derniers refusant de les accepter, il sera libre d'en faire ce que bon lui semble'. See also the 'Sources'.

6 On Gallé's successes in 1884 see Zurich 1980, p. 22.

7 Musée d'Orsay, fonds Gallé, Paris. Letter of 1 January 1885.

8 Traub, *Christian*, 1978, p. 29: 'payé à Christian pour le décor Gallé' (paid to Christian for the Gallé decoration).

9 The Corning Museum of Glass, Corning, NY, Chambon Collection. 'Je remarque, d'après celles qui sont ici que l'atelier n'a pas compris ce décor'. See also the 'Sources'.

10 Charpentier 1984, p. 147. 'Règlement de l'atelier et instructions pour les chefs d'atelier' (Regulations Governing the Workshop and Instructions for the Heads of the Workshop).

11 The Corning Museum of Glass, Corning, NY, Chambon Collection. 'Mr Emile croit avoir laissé chez Mr Christian son dossier, Duplicata de celui laissé pour l'atelier'. See also the 'Sources'.

12 Gallé's visits are recorded until 1888 in the 'Roll of Foreigners Staying in the Community'; anticipated and past visits by Gallé to Meisenthal are mentioned in documents contained in the Chambon Collection.

13 The Corning Museum of Glass, Corning, NY, Chambon Collection. Letter of 1890; see also the 'Sources'. Joseph Burgun was the managing director of the furnaces in 1891. See 'Nebenakten zur Fabrikstatistik' (Ancillary Documents on Factory Statistics), Archives Départementales, Strasbourg.

14 The Corning Museum of Glass, Corning, NY, Chambon Collection.

15 The *taches* are probably little pieces of glass for *marqueterie de verre*.

16 The Corning Museum of Glass, Corning, NY, Chambon Collection. Other models were made entirely in Meisenthal.

17 The Corning Museum of Glass, Corning, NY, Chambon Collection. 'Piece of wood veneer sent to Meisenthal – intended to be interpreted in decoration 77.'

18 Klesse, *Funke-Kaiser* I, 1981, p. XXXI, fig. 47.

19 Archives Départementales, Strasbourg, 'Jahresbericht der kaiserlichen Gewerbeaufsichtsbeamten für den Bezirk Lothringen für das Jahr 1896' (Annual Report of the Imperial Commercial Supervisory Official for Lorraine District, Year 1896). The Corning Museum of Glass, Corning, NY, Chambon Collection. Letter to Christian, containing packing instructions '[...] prévenez les Dames emballeur s.v. plaît' ([...] Please inform the ladies to pack).

20 Archives Départementales, Saint-Julien-les-Metz. Meisenthal electoral roll 1890/91, 1893. Men were eligible to vote from the age of twenty-five. Ergänzte Lebensdaten nach Meisenthal 1999, pp. 20, 22–23.

21 Joseph Schmitt was married to Melanie Christian (1850–1927), a sister of Désiré Christian's. Nicolas Schmitt was probably Joseph Schmitt's father. François was Désiré Christian's youngest brother.

22 Archives Départementales, Strasbourg. Strassburger Industrie & Gewerbeausstellung Strassburg 1895 i.E. Ausstellungskorrespondenz (Strasbourg Industrial & Applied Arts Exhibition, Strasbourg in Alsace: Exhibition Correspondence).

23 'Die Industrie- und Gewerbeausstellung zu Strassburg im Elsass', *Zeitschrift des bayerischen Kunstgewerbevereins in München* (1895): 73.

24 Musée des Arts Décoratifs, Strasbourg, inv. no. 5373 (whereabouts unknown), description in book in which acquisitions were entered (*Eingangsbuch*), purchased November 1895.

25 Kunstsammlung, Veste Coburg. Cup in the antique Venetian manner. Cobalt glass, etched, painted in enamel and gilt, inv. no. a. S. 5108/90. See also Clementine Schack von Wittenau, *Alte Glaskunst* (Cologne, 1973), p. 294, the *Catalogue of the Collection Formed by Felix Slade* (London, 1871) and Traub, *Christian*, 1978, pp. 50–51.

26 Musée d'Art Moderne, Strasbourg. Four interesting objects, decorated mainly with floral motifs, executed in the variety of techniques described: vase, inv. no. 5369, H 15 cm, cased glass with painting sandwiched between the layers and etched surface. Decoration: plants and insects. Signature *B S & Co./ Meisenthal* in a cross of Lorraine; thistle. Globular vase, inv. no. 5372, H 15 cm. Cased glass, coloured inclusions, painting sandwiched between the layers. Decoration: pansies. Signature *B S & Co./Meisenthal* in a cross of Lorraine with thistle and *DC A*. Vase, inv. no. 5370, H 15.8 cm. Amber-coloured glass, polished, painted in enamel and gold, engraved. Decoration: peacocks. Signature *B S & Co.* in stylized thistle bloom. Vase, inv. no. 5371, H 14.5 cm/15 cm. Cased glass, painting sandwiched between the layers, enamel painting, partly iridescent. Decoration: grapes. Signature *B S & Co./Meisenthal* in a cross of Lorraine with thistle.

Württembergisches Landesmuseum, Stuttgart: vase, inv. no. 3817, purchased January 1896, H 15 cm. Cased glass, etched, flat painting and painting between the layers. Decoration: butterflies and grasses. Signature *B S & Co./Meisenthal* in a cross of Lorraine with thistle and *DC A*.

Kunstgewerbemuseum, Berlin: vase, inv. no. 1896.14. Cased glass with fused-in colour. Decoration: etched, partly copper oxide stain, designs cut within contours, contours gilt. Decoration: iris and reed-mace. Signature formerly on underside factory mark *B S & Co.*

27 See notes 25 and 26.

28 Schmitt, *Sammlung Silzer*, 1989, p. 52.

29 Patent no. 92709 from the Kaiserliches Patentamt (Imperial Patent Office), Berlin: 'Process for making painted hollow-glass objects / Patented in the German Empire from 21 February 1896.' See also the 'Sources'.

Patent 264948, République Française, Paris. 'Brevet d'Invention [...] pour la décoration d'objets en verre creux / Pièces déposé [...] du 13 Mars 1897' (Patent [...] for decoration of objects in hollow glass / Pieces registered [...] from 13 March 1897).

30 Archives Départementales, Saint-Julien-les-Metz. Roll of shareholders at general meeting on 24 September 1896: 'Désiré Christian, domicile Nancy, is present and represented with 7 shares.'/Roll of general meeting of 23 September 1898: 'Désiré Christian, domicile Vallerysthal, is present and represented with 9 shares.'

31 Archives Départementales, Strasbourg, *Catalogue de l'Exposition d'art Strasbourg – Novembre 1897*.

32 *Dekorative Kunst: Illustrierte Zeitschrift für angewandte Kunst* (Munich) III (1899).

33 Schmitt, *Sammlung Silzer*, 1989, p. 322.

34 Museum kunst palast, Düsseldorf – Glasmuseum Hentrich: vase in the form of a calabash (gourd), Hilschenz-Mlynek and Ricke 1985, no. 23, signature *D. Christian, Meisenthal, Loth.*; vase, ibid., no. 539, signature *Vallerysthal*. See also Klesse, *Funke-Kaiser* I, 1981, p. 480, no. 369: vase, Vallerysthal, similar piece for comparison in a private collection, with signature *D. Christian, Meisenthal*; decoration: see Stenger 1988, p. 138, dish, Vallerysthal.

35 *Offizieller Katalog der Münchner Jahres-Ausstellung 1899 im königlichen Glaspalast*, no. 6, August 1899.

36   Verzeichnis der deutschen Glasindustrie (Roll of the German Glass Industry), Coburg, January 1903.

37   Archives Départementales, Saint-Julien-les-Metz. Documentation of the 1906 Lorraine Pottery Exhibition.

38   Paul Schulze, 'Erstlingsarbeiten Emile Gallés', *Werkkunst* (October 1905–6): 236. Schulze points out that the firm earlier went under the name of Christian frères & fils.

39   See note 36.

40   Württembergisches Landesmuseum, Stuttgart, inv. no. G 4173.

41   Musée d'Art Moderne, Strasbourg (formerly Musée des Arts Décoratifs): glass dish, inv. no. 6371 (whereabouts unknown), thick opaque glass with prunts and gold decoration (Gallé); glass beaker, inv. no. 6372 (whereabouts unknown), etched, parcel gilt Renaissance decoration – rosette prunts and enamel painting (Gallé); glass vase, inv. no. 6370 (whereabouts unknown), golden butterflies on a green patterned ground, Japanese pattern, labelled *Gallé à Nancy*.

42   A broken seventeenth-century Bohemian double glass / a flask (1812) / a beaker (1825), Münzthaler make.

43   See Schulze (note 38).

44   Musée du Verre et du Cristal, Meisenthal. Envelope addressed to F. Christian, Aubervilliers, Paris. Postmarked: 'Lemberg, 14.12.82'. On the Verreries d'Aubervilliers see Schmitt, Zurich II, 1995, p. 268.

45   Charpentier 1984, p. 146.

46   Objects now in the Musée du Verre et du Cristal, Meisenthal.

47   Strasbourg, exh. cat., 1901. The other exhibits were a Rhine wine glass, a tobacco-stopper and six little liqueur glasses. Utilitarian objects were also exhibited in Turin in 1902, *Kunst und Handwerk* (1901/2): 331: 'We except, of course, the usual pieces made for everyday use.'

48   Museum für Kunst und Gewerbe, Hamburg: vase, inv. no. 1900.354. Cased glass, painting sandwiched between the layers, powder inclusions, contour and inner drawing undercut, stipple engraving. Decoration: orchid panicles and lady's slipper flower. Acquired at the 1900 Paris Exposition Universelle. Signature cut in high relief *Christian/D.* on the flower.
Württembergisches Landesmuseum, Stuttgart: vase and cover, inv. no. G 28973. Painting sandwiched between the casing, enamel painting, partly stipple engraved, partly etched. Acquired in 1902. Signature *D. Christian, Meisenthal, Lothr.*

49   Württembergisches Landesmuseum, Stuttgart: dish (Nycotina), inv. no. G 4172; vase (thistle), inv. no. G4171. Multiple casing, particoloured casing, yellow silver stain, intricate engraving. Acquired 7 April 1904. The dish (Nycotina) used to have an adhesive label from D. Christian & Sohn, Meisenthal; the vase (thistle), without a signature, was bought at the same time. Similar pieces for comparison can be found in the museum kunst palast, Düsseldorf – Glasmuseum Hentrich, Hilschenz-Mlynek and Ricke 1985, no. 24; Musée d'Art Moderne, Strasbourg, inv. no. 55.974.0.1078, 55.974.0.1079; Liberec, inv. no. S 1475/KI 192; Hessisches Landesmuseum, Darmstadt, Kg 64:68/*Kunst und Handwerk* (1906/7): 93–94.
In a report on the third Kunstgewerbeausstellung in Dresden, in 1906: reference to Christian's ground/cut cased glass, which was on an equal footing within the Strasbourg group of exhibits with Spindler's intarsia work.

50   Arwas 1987, p. 61.

51   Traub, *Christian*, 1978, pp. 66–67, figs. 18–19.

52   Strasbourg 1901. Information given on decoration and techniques: peacocks, dragonflies, waterlilies, reeds, Ricinus (castor-oil plant), orchids, fuchsia, seaweed, wild grapes; metallic crystal, cased, decoration sandwiched between the layers, cameo cutting. Two-handled vessels: 'L'Eté' (Summer) and 'La Vigne' (The Vine) (see Arwas 1987, p. 61).

53   See note 48.

54   Firm seal: capital 'C' with a cross of Lorraine aligned with the 'C': on the left 'D', on the right 'F', below 'A'.

55   Musée d'Art Moderne, Strasbourg: vase, inv. no. 55.974.0.1080, formerly 6573. Painted peacock decoration sandwiched between the casings.

56   See note 35: 'Christian, D. & Sohn, Meisenthal, Lorraine, is represented with glass art in crystal (2463–77).'

57   *Kunst und Handwerk* (1899/1900): 60.

58   Pazaurek 1901, pp. 91–92.

59   *Strassburger Neueste Nachrichten*, 13 July 1901.

60   Catalogue from the First International Exhibition for the Modern Decorative Arts, Turin, 1902: '[…] e il lorenese Cristian di Meisenthal, veccio operaio di Gallé, di questo poeta del vetro […]' ([...] and Christian of Meisenthal, a native of Lorraine, formerly employed by Gallé, that poet of glass [...]).

61   *Kunst und Handwerk* (1901/2): 331.

62   *Kunstgewerbe in Elsass Lothringen* (1902/3): 40.

Catalogue

General remarks on the catalogue entries

Turn-of-the-century French glass art is, as a rule, mould-blown with a dilated rim; the underside is carefully ground out spherically and polished. No special mention is made of these features in the catalogue entries. The term 'freely formed' indicates that the forming process was preceded by blowing once or repeatedly into a shaper or mould. The designation 'on the underside' refers to the underside of a vessel.

'Thick-walled' signifies a minimum wall thickness of 0.5 cm. Unless otherwise indicated, the dimensions given are of the body, not the decoration running round a vessel, the mounts or the applications.

Colour layers are described from the interior to the exterior, from bottom to top or from left to right. The term 'band' indicates a colour zone running horizontally round the body; 'strip' is used for a vertical one. All colours mentioned are transparent; turbidity is described by the terms 'opaque', 'semi-opaque' or 'opalescent'. White is always opaque. Colours are given in accordance with the terminology used for precious stones.

'Same model' or 'same decoration' also denotes the same colouring. The term 'relief' signifies raised decoration. 'Engraving' refers to cutting on the surface. 'Vessel matt etched' describes matt etching of the walls inside and out.

The production dates given are taken from the literature cited. They do not represent verified dates on the pieces themselves.

Daum Frères

The research conducted by Christophe Bardin at the Daum archives has shown that specific attribution of individual designs for decoration to the paramount designers of the early phase, Jacques Gruber and Henri Bergé, remains problematic since no signed drawings by Gruber, with the exception of the few illustrations in the catalogue to the 1897 Brussels Exposition Internationale, are extant. One must, on the other hand, bear in mind that verbal influence can be brought to bear on a design or be conveyed without a drawing, especially when those executing the designs are such skilled and experienced craftsmen as the head of the Daum decoration studio and his subordinates. The influence exerted by the two artists on decoration at the factory is inestimable. The forms, by contrast, played a minor role at Daum since the firm, as was then usual, continued to use and re-use models once created and only rarely took over forms conceived by artists, for special exhibition pieces. To indicate the contributing artists, the following expressions are used in the catalogue:

'Influenced by Gruber' refers to designs for editions from the Daum studio, the quality of which improved between 1893 and 1895, when Gruber, as sole designer, was largely responsible for the special pieces made for exhibition. 'After Gruber or Bergé' refers to decoration or designs executed between 1895 and 1897, which cannot definitively be attributed to one or the other of these artists. 'After Bergé' refers to decoration that evidently derives from Bergé's botanical drawings or was created between 1897 and 1906, when Bergé was alone as head designer, or to later decoration that reveals significant correspondences with a botanical study by Bergé.

Abbreviations

auct. cat.	auction catalogue
coll. cat.	collection catalogue
D	depth
exh. fl.	exhibition flier
exh. rep.	exhibition report
H	height
W	width
‡	cross of Lorraine
Ø	diameter

Paris before 1900

1

'Bambou' vase

Signature: *E. Rousseau Paris*
engraved on the underside
Design: Eugène Rousseau,
Paris; execution: Appert
Frères, Clichy
1877/78

Light smoky brown glass,
mould-blown, rim ground
flat, bevelled and polished.
Decoration in rock crystal engraving, painting in opaque
enamels and burnishing gold:
a bamboo cane with two off-
shoots, interrupted by a broad
band with dense, opaque blue
arabesques and recurring pattern of stylized thistles in
white with fine dark dots.

H 31.3 W 14.2 D 13.7 cm

Luxury edition. In China and
Japan bamboo symbolizes
truthfulness, a noble character
and pliancy as well as powers of
resistance. In China the symbol
has more, widely different
meanings, such as longevity,
child-like love and winter: see
Cooper 1978, p. 17; Lurker
1985, p. 506. The design was
first introduced at the 1878
Paris Exposition Universelle.
Listed in the inventory of cast-
iron models sold by Rousseau
to Léveillé in 1885 is an object
described as a 'Vase bambou'.
The complete list of wares that
follows contains entries for a
pair of relatively expensive
vases designated 'gravé bambou émaux', which fits the
description of the present vase,
estimated at 90 Frs, and a group
of twenty-four different vases
estimated at 139 Frs, which
includes nineteen vessels referred to as 'bambou' vases.
As these are inexpensive,
they are either undecorated
exemplars (blanks) of the

present model or other vases
in the shape of bamboo: see
Archives Nationales, Minutier
Central, LXVI, 1689, 16
December 1885, *Vente de
matériel et marchandises par M.
Rousseau à M. et Mme Léveillé*,
pp. 6, 10, 12; see also cat. no. 8.

A model of the same size and
with the same decoration (inv.
no. 16, H 27 cm) was acquired
by the Musée des Arts Décoratifs, Paris, in 1879: see Polak
1962, fig. no. 3; Schneck 1988,
p. 36, fig. 37. For a larger
version of the same model
(H 40 cm), with dated signature, see Bloch-Dermant 1980,
p. 34. For a variant with different decoration on the shoulder,
called a 'Modèle bambou',
see Bascou and Thiébaut,
Orsay, 1988, p. 190, no. OAO
965 (H 28.3 cm). For a smaller
variant with painted bamboo
decoration (H 25.3), signed
Escalier de Cristal and dated
c. 1874–78, see Schmitt, Zurich
II, 1995, p. 41, no. 57.

The painted design recalls a
rich textile pattern that was
highly prized in Japan, known
as *sarasa*, a batik or chintz fabric imported from India, Persia,
Siam or Java, which was also
made in Japan as *wa-sarasa* (we
are indebted to Christine Mitomi for this information).

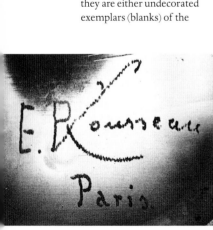

2

'Plat à tête de chimère' vase

Signature: *E. Rousseau Paris*
engraved on the underside
Design: Eugène Rousseau,
Paris; execution: Appert
Frères, Clichy
c. 1880

Light brown smoky glass,
mould-blown with com-
pressed air, two moulded
chimaera heads backed with
gold leaf applied hot, rim
ground flat, bevelled and
polished. Decoration in high
relief and deep-cut rock crystal engraving with predominantly a linear design on the
interior: ornamental field
suspended above a stylized
underwater scene featuring
a large fish, plants and stones
as well as an amoeba-like
creature on the reverse.
The ormolu bronze mount
takes the form of bamboo
shoots.

H 29.2 W 18.1 D 11.2 cm
(including applications and
mount)

A one-off piece or from a very
limited luxury edition featuring
this decoration. This 'Vase plat
à tête de chimère' (Flat-sided
vase with chimaera head) is listed in three numbered sizes,
including the moulds for the
applications to match, in the
inventory of cast-iron moulds
sold by Rousseau to Léveillé in
1885: see Archives Nationales,
Minutier Central, LXVI, 1689,
16 December 1885, *Vente de
matériel et marchandises par M.
Rousseau à M. et Mme Léveillé*,
p. 6. Rousseau's calling the
application, which resembles
a lion's head, a chimaera head
would seem to be based on an
image of this mythical beast
from Greek mythology, which
was regarded as a symbol of
the powers of darkness: see
Lurker 1985, pp. 118, 177–78.
Since, however, Chinese
straight-sided jars that are
quadrilateral in section may
have served as the model for
this unusual vase shape and
comparable applications are
often encountered on Sino-
Japanese vessels, the application resembling a lion's head
could be interpreted as the
Sino-Japanese lion-like 'fabulous animal' (the 'shi shi'),
symbolizing strength and
courage: see E. Herzog et al.,
*Staatliche Kunstsammlungen:
Historismus – Angewandte Kunst
im 19. Jahrhundert*, coll. cat.
(Kassel, 1987), vol. 2, p. 204,
no. 476; Düsseldorf, *Netsuke*,
1994, p. 126.

The ornamentation above
the fish motif was used several
times by Rousseau on *jardinières* and vases and has been
interpreted as the Japanese tor-
toiseshell pattern: see Schneck
1988, p. 32. It might also be the
'peau de lion' (lion's skin) used
by Rousseau in the above-mentioned inventory to characterize a vase or *jardinière* mould
since virtually the same patterns occur as lion-skin decoration on 'lion (shi shi)' *netsuke*
from the first half of the nineteenth century: see Düsseldorf, *Netsuke*, 1994, nos. 275,
283. Dishes and vases adorned
with the same ornamental
fields or reserves can be found
in the Hokkaidō Museum
of Modern Art, Sapporo
(inv. no. 86288), The Corning
Museum of Glass, Corning,
NY (inv. no. 79.3.153), and the
Walters Art Gallery in Baltimore, MD (inv. no. 47.377):
see Schneck 1988, p. 32,
n. 92–94, figs. 32–33.

The form is one often used by
Rousseau and Léveillé: cf. cat.
no. 3. The dating to *c.* 1880 is
based on the first patent application, 'Soufflage du verre par
l'air comprimé mécanique-
ment', submitted by Léon-
Alfred Appert for glass-blowing
by means of mechanically
compressed air, which made it
possible to produce large,
straight-sided or relief vessels
without difficulty: see L. Appert,
'Le Verre', *Revue des Arts Décoratifs* 5 (1884–85): 447–50;
Appert and Henrivaux 1893,
pp. 390–91. For the history of
Appert Frères see the 'Manufacturers and Artists' section in
the Appendix.

For a similar, if not the same,
model see Lausanne 1973,
no. 146. For the same form,
with slightly yellow-tinged
glass, without a neck and
decoration with Rousseau's
signature, see Sammlung Silzer
2003, no. 237.

3
'Plat à tête de chimère' vase

Signature: *E Rousseau Paris*
needle etched on the underside
Design: Eugène Rousseau,
Paris; execution: Appert Frères,
Clichy
c. 1880–84

Yellow-tinted glass with strewn powder melted in between layers in pink and dark red, overlaid with gold-leaf particles; mould-blown with compressed air, two moulded chimaera heads backed with gold foil and applied while the metal was in a molten state; inside wall crazed. Rim ground flat, bevelled and polished.

H 20.4 W 10.9 D 8.2 cm

Luxury edition, relatively frequently encountered, still executed under Eugène Léveillé in this technique, called 'strass craquelé', which Rousseau first presented to the public at the 1884 Union Centrale exhibition in Paris. On the design and date see cat. no. 2. A variant of the model was donated by Rousseau in 1884 to the Conservatoire National des Arts et Métiers, Paris, with specifics on the physical properties of the coloured inclusions of copper filings in yellow and red, the colour of which was achieved by repeated heating at the furnace gloryhole: see Paris, *Arts Métiers*, 1908, p. 276, no. 10604; Bloch-Dermant 1980, p. 31. A jug donated in 1885 had additional gold particles in 'strass craquelé' glass: see Paris, *Arts Métiers*, 1908, p. 276, no. 10605.

For further exemplars of this model, dating from *c.* 1884, see Hilschenz-Mlynek and Ricke 1985, p. 366, no. 487; Schneck 1990, p. 457, no. 6; for a piece with Léveillé's signature and one without see Klesse, *Funke-Kaiser* I, 1981, nos. 243, 439, illus. pp. 333, 551; Yoshimizu 1983, no. 616; E. Herzog et al., *Staatliche Kunstsammlungen: Historismus – Angewandte Kunst im 19. Jahrhundert*, coll. cat. (Kassel, 1987), vol. 2, p. 204, no. 476; Cappa 1991, no. 702; Klesse, *Funke-Kaiser* II, 1991, pp. 68–69, nos. 95–96. For a model with stress crack and intact cap see Polak 1962, illus. no. 5; *Sammlung Silzer* 2003, no. 238. For variants with

landscape and hare see Bloch-Dermant 1980, p. 35; with landscape and geese see Klesse, *Funke-Kaiser* I, 1981, no. 438, illus. p. 551.

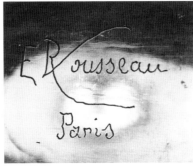

4
Rod-shaped vase

Signature: ... *EAU-LEVEILLE* ... *USSMANN*
Remains of a sticker on the underside, with greyish black print
Design: Ernest Léveillé and Eugène Rousseau, Paris; execution: Appert Frères, Clichy *c.* 1885–89

Semi-opaque, light grey glass with two streaks on either side of the vase, formed by inclusions in brick red powdered glass and a copper compound (black with bluish green haloes), opaque sand-coloured overlay; freely formed, lip fused. Bottom ground and polished, traces of pontil mark visible. Decoration in simple relief etching with rough, speckled etched ground, interior markings in needle etching and engraving. Walls, including matt-etched lip, polished. Underwater scene with pondweed, scallops and fish.

H 12.5 Ø 5.5; 5.2 cm

Luxury edition; not made in the present form as often as the wide version in the shape of a flattened flask. Form and colour were taken over from Rousseau. The detailed underwater scene, designed by Léveillé, as he himself indicated, recalls Japanese carved lacquer, yet the composition is too compressed for Japanese design (kindly imparted by Christine Mitomi). It differs from Rousseau's interpretations of East Asian models in that Léveillé strove for atmospheric effects in his scenes.

The date of the sticker, *c.* 1885–89, is confirmed by the donation of a flattened flask-shaped vase with the same dec-

oration to the Conservatoire National des Arts et Métiers, Paris, in 1889. Léveillé described that vase as one of his own: see Paris, *Arts Métiers*, 1908, p. 276, no. 11537. The design is generally dated later – *c.* 1890–95 – presumably because Léveillé's exhibition lists for those years contain recurrent entries for similar showpieces, including several for Liège in 1895: see *Exposition d'art appliqué* (Liège 1895), no. 408; for a variant of the same shape without information on the colour, acquired by Léveillé in 1895, see Brussels 1965, no. 49; a variant with pronounced bulges can be found in The Corning Museum of Glass, Corning, NY, inv. no. 743.1 56. For the same decoration on flattened flask form, like that in the Conservatoire National des Arts et Métiers, see Bloch-Dermant 1980, p. 40 (no information on colour); Klesse, *Funke-Kaiser* I, 1981, no. 244, illus. p. 333; Yoshimizu 1983, no. 610; Klesse, *Funke-Kaiser* II, 1991, p. 69, no. 97; Schmitt, Zurich II, 1995, p. 108, no. 175.

5

Covered vase with mount

Signature: *E. Rousseau Paris*
needle etched on the underside
Design: Eugène Rousseau,
Paris; execution of glass:
Appert Frères, Clichy; mount:
Escalier de Cristal of Pannier
Frères & Cie., Paris
c. 1885–89

Colourless glass with inclusions of glass powder (pink, green chromium aventurine, opaque yellow, light bluish grey, white, copper ruby red with striking colours in brown and black), multiple dippings with opaque copper ruby reddish brown; mould-blown with compressed air, rim ground, bevelled and polished, foot-rim ground flat, rough matt. Decoration in simple relief etching, almost the entire wall worked over in polished fine cutting and engraving: underwater scene with leaping carp; on the back waves, stylized aquatic plants, including lotus.

H 48.5 W 22.8 D 18.2 cm
(including mount)

A one-off or limited-edition piece. The carp motif is the Sino-Japanese symbol of masculine strength, courage and perseverance in battle: see Cooper 1978, p. 89; Lurker 1985, p. 195. It may have been modelled on a colour woodblock print by Taito hitsu, the pseudonym of

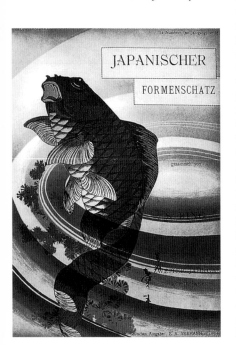

Katsushika Hokusai (1760–1849). For the first state (1816) see W. Boller, *Hokusai: Ein Meister des japanischen Holzschnitts* (Stuttgart, 1955), pl. 7. The sheet was slightly modified around late 1890 by Samuel Bing for the cover of issue 8 of his journal *Le Japon artistique: Japanischer Formenschatz* (illus. below) and was, therefore, in wide circulation. The design of the vase in the Koepff Collection, however, definitely predates the publication of that issue. The form has not yet been assigned to any of the registered but only in part numbered cast-iron moulds sold by Rousseau to Léveillé in 1885: see Archives Nationales, Minutier Central, LXVI, 1689, 16 December 1885, *Vente de matériel et marchandises par M. Rousseau à M. et Mme Léveillé*, pp. 5–6.

Both the form and the decoration differ from two related models with underwater scenes published in 1889 and 1902 and attributed to Ernest Léveillé. The account of the 1889 Paris Exposition Universelle describes a large, technically similar-sounding vase with fish. This vase, standing on a simple base, was acquired by the Musée National de la Céramique in Sèvres (inv. no. 9207): see Champier 1889–94, vol. 2, n.p.; Henrivaux 1889, p. 173; Appert and Henrivaux 1893, p. 355; Seoul 1986, no. 31; Schneck 1988, fig. 79. The second variant, published in 1902, from the private collection of Edmond Taigny, has a similar mount to that of the vase in the Koepff Collection. According to the 1902 report, Taigny had his mount designed and made in 1890 by Pannier Frères (Escalier de Cristal) in Paris. His covered vase, first attributed to Rousseau, then to Léveillé in the article, boasts a far more stylized version of the carp motif but has the same bulging shoulder form as the

vase shown by Léveillé at the 1889 Paris Exposition Universelle: see M. Demaison, 'Les Montures des Vases', *Art & Décoration* XI (1902): 203, illus. p. 205. The covered vase in the Koepff Collection was in any case designed to stand on a mount, to which the roughly ground edge of the foot-rim attests. It dates, like the two published variants, to between 1885 and 1889, the phase during which Rousseau collaborat-

ed with Léveillé, who would become his successor. The well-known firm Escalier de Cristal of Pannier Frères et Cie. had also begun to market Rousseau's glass in the 1880s; this circumstance suggests Rousseau may well have worked with Pannier Frères. Comparison of the two mounts reveals some differences. Consequently, Taigny may have had his mount modelled in 1890 on one at

Pannier Frères (possibly even the present vase).

Lit.: Yoshimizu 1983, no. 131; Yoshimizu 1988, p. 48.

6

Small *jardinière*

Signature: *E Leveillé Paris 1889*
diamond-point engraved on
the underside
Design: Ernest Léveillé and
Eugène Rousseau, Paris; executed: Appert Frères, Clichy
1889

Opaque glass, multiple casing
in light jade green, freely
blown and shaped; the superimposed uppermost layer
irregularly pulled and pincered, partly with twisted
relief; rim of opening sheared,
triangular aperture. Decoration underscores form in
grooves cut and polished in
ribbing.

H 11.8 Ø 19.1; 9.6 cm

Luxury glass from a limited
edition. The design goes back
to Eugène Rousseau, who first
exhibited a model in Paris in
1884 with lacquer-red overlay
inspired by jade finds with Chinese carving: Brunhammer
1976, p. 289, no. 461; Seoul
1986, no. 37; Schneck 1990,
p. 455, no. 5; Tokyo, Paris selection, 1991, p. 28, no. 21; The
Corning Museum of Glass,
Corning, NY, inv. no. 623.112
(signed and dated 1884). The
jardinière in the Koepff Collection was, as the signature
shows, exhibited at the 1889
Exposition Universelle in Paris.
There is another exemple in
the collection of the Danish
Museum of Decorative Art,
Copenhagen, which is dated
1900: see Polak 1962, fig. 7A.

7

'Tronc d'arbre' vase

Signature: *E Léveillé 74 B^ard Haussmann Paris* diamond-point engaved on the under-side
Design: Ernest Léveillé and Eugène Rousseau, Paris; execution: Appert Frères, Clichy
c. 1885–90

Yellow tinted, thick-walled glass, partly with powdered glass inclusions (white, partly under gold ruby pink) and metallic compounds in dark green and ochre (striking colours). The last layer of overlay ends approximately a centimetre below the rim. The vessel is freely blown and shaped. The wall has been formed by pincering three times and with threading, which has been drawn up and cut off at the base with pincers and formed into a branch with three applied pattern-moulded little leaves of yellow-tinted glass; the inside wall is heavily crazed. The veining of the leaves executed in polished fine cutting.

H 18.5   Ø 8.9; 8.5 cm (including applications)

Limited-edition luxury glass. The design of this vase in the shape of a hollow tree stump can be traced back to rod-shaped vessels made by Eugène Rousseau. Inspired by similar Chinese forms carved from stone, he conceived this design as early as *c.* 1882 / 83: see Schneck 1988, pp. 44–45, n. 122, p. 60, illus. no. 43. In inventory of wares sold to Léveillé the model called 'Tronc d'arbre' appears twice in groupings of vases, for instance in amethyst tint: see Archives Nationales, Minutier Central, LXVI, 1689, 16 December 1885, *Vente de matériel et marchandises par M. Rousseau à M. et Mme Léveillé*, p. 10.

Léveillé presumably varied this model for only a short while. He, his successors, Harant & Guignard, and Eugène Michel, who worked for both, frequently used and modified the basic form with different overlays: cf. cat. no. 13.

For a Rousseau model in colourless glass with bluish green, red and brown inclusions and stylized applied decoration in the form of a tree and a figure see Munich 1972, no. 1189; Schneck 1988, illus. no. 43. For a variant by Léveillé with branch applications, dating from *c.* 1890, see Bloch-Dermant 1980, p. 43; Hilschenz-Mlynek and Ricke 1985, no. 422. For a variant with the same colour scheme but without applied decoration, bearing Léveillé's signature and dating from *c.* 1895, see Schmitt, *Sammlung Silzer*, 1989, p. 196, no. 104, illus. p. 197; *Sammlung Silzer* 2003, no. 204.

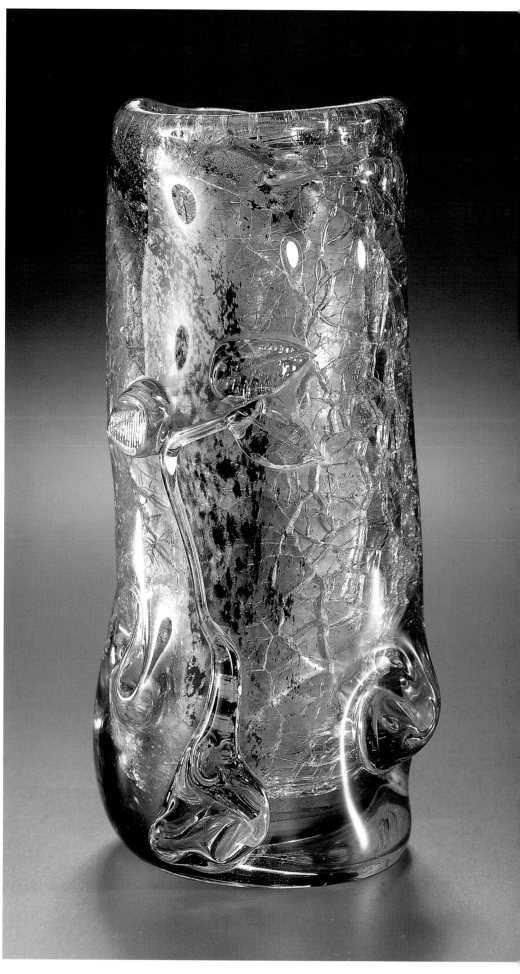

8

**Vase in the form of
segmented bamboo cane**

No signature
Attributed to Eugène Rousseau
Execution: attributed to Appert
Frères, Clichy
c. 1880–84

Colourless, slightly yellow-
tinged glass with two strips
opposite each other, created
by inclusions in gold leaf
and powdered glass in pink
and dark red; mould-blown
with compressed air. Rim
ground flat, bevelled and
polished.

H 18.7 Ø 5.5; 5.3 cm

A limited edition made from
batches typical of Rousseau and
Léveillé, ranging from smoky
brown to purple in 'strass
craquelé'. Attribution to one or
the other of the two artists
depends in part on the signatures, which cannot be authen-
ticated. For the attribution to
Rousseau see Arwas 1987,
p. 269; Okuoka and Mizuta,
Sapporo selection, 1990, no. 27;

Cappa 1991, no. 701; for the
attribution to Léveillé see
Bloch-Dermant 1980, p. 43; on
dating see cat. no. 3.

The attribution to Rousseau
rests on his predilection for
incorporating Sino-Japanese
forms and motifs into his
works: see Schneck 1988, p. 53,
n. 152, illus. no. 54. It would
also furnish an explanation
for further versions, with the
Léveillé signature. On the
other hand, the complex, rather
unstable-looking form does
not accord with Rousseau's
composed, concentrated conception of form. The inventory
of all cast-iron moulds and
wares sold by Rousseau to Léveillé in 1885 contains a group
of nineteen reasonably priced
vases designated 'bambou'.
Unless this refers to a blank for
a large 'bambou' vase, similar
small vases shaped like bamboo cane might be meant:
cf. cat. no. 1.

The glass pieces made by
Appert Frères and their collaboration with Paris designers
has yet to be studied in depth.

9

Vase with mounted elephant heads

Signature: *Escalier de Cristal Paris* painted on the underside in gold
Retailer: Escalier de Cristal of Pannier Frères et Cie., Paris
Design and execution: unknown
c. 1883–85

Colourless glass, freely formed, walls flattened bilaterally; rim ground flat, bevelled and polished. Decoration in shallow rock crystal engraving: lacustrine plants with lotus flower and leaves; on the lower wall *martelé* texture; on front and back two slightly depressed picture reserves, in low relief etching, painted with matt opaque flat colours and burnish gold. On the front the god Hotei as an itinerant singer and musician, next to him another lute, a *shamisen*; on the back stylized aquatic plants with lotus flowers and leaves. Two ormolu bronze elephant-head handles.

H 22.4 Ø 14; 10.6 cm

Luxury edition, presumably a limited one. The motif of the god Hotei making music is a detail from a Katsushika Hokusai

(1760–1849) woodcut. It is reproduced in the frequently cited book on Japanese art by Louis Gonse (illus. below, right), whose date of publication, 1883, has been used as a point of reference for dating this design: see Gonse 1883, vol. I, p. 288. Hotei, one of the seven Japanese deities of happiness, symbolizes generosity. He is often depicted with a fat belly and a sack as his attributes: see Düsseldorf, *Netsuke*, 1994, p. 56, nos. 36–41. The elephant is a symbol of strength and wisdom in both India and China: see Cooper 1978, p. 44; Lurker 1985, p. 155.

The bronze handles were presumably made in one of the Paris studios that worked for Escalier de Cristal of Pannier Frères et Cie.: see Thiébaut 1988, p. 83. For the same motif, integrated into the decorative

programme of a flat-walled vase by Escalier de Cristal that is quadrilateral in section, see auct. cat. Sotheby's Belgravia (London, 1976), 31 March – 1 April 1976, p. 4, no. 5.

10

Vase with black chrysanthe-mums

Signature: *E. Michel*
engraved on the lower wall;
Escalier de Cristal Paris
engraved on the underside
Design: attributed to Eugène
Michel, Paris; retailer:
Escalier de Cristal, Paris;
blank: unknown
c. 1892

Colourless glass, cased in
black (dark red); rim slightly
dilated and matt engraved.
Outer foot-rim, like the wall,
matt engraved. Decoration in
matt, partly polished high
relief and line engraving: seascape with crescent moon
and three upright black
chrysanthemums in different
phases of growth, the stems
cut off and floating.

H 28.9 Ø 12.5 cm

A one-off piece or from a
limited luxury edition. The
nocturnal seascape with black
chrysanthemums conveys a
mood of melancholy and lone-
liness. The three developmen-
tal phases of the plant
symbolize phases of life. The
chrysanthemum is a Japanese
imperial emblem signifying
longevity and good fortune.
In China, however, this is only
one interpretation of this complex symbol, where it can also
stand for autumn, retirement
and scholarship as well as harvest, wealth, happiness and
comfort: see Cooper 1978,
p. 32; Lurker 1985, p. 507.

Definite attribution of the
design is not possible at present
since only some of the activities engaged in by Pannier
Frères, the proprietors of
Escalier de Cristal, have been
studied: see Thiébaut 1988.
The addition of the retailer's
signature may indicate either
that he designed it or influenced its design, or merely a
collaboration between artist
and retailer. As an aid to dating,
two vases of the same form but
different decoration (H 30.5
cm), signed *Escalier de Cristal*,
inv. nos. 7292 and 7308, can be
cited that were bought by the
Musée des Arts Décoratifs,
Paris, in 1892. That year Michel
also engraved pieces cased in

black for Léveillé: see Tokyo,
Paris selection, 1991, p. 49,
no. 46. The idea of engraving
black casing goes back to Emile
Gallé, who presented it in 1889
as one of his new techniques,
in his *Notices d'exposition*:
'La gravure des couches noires
est venue achever mon œuvre'
(Engraving black casing has
put a finishing touch on my
work): see Gallé 1908, p. 336.
Unlike the dynamic engraving

technique advocated by Gallé
for emphasizing textures in
bold relief, which exploits the
artistic effects of both line and
pure surface texture, Michel
usually championed classic
engraving techniques that produced uniform surfaces: see
cat. nos. 11–14. For Michel this
vase with its black chrysanthemums is, as far as the engraving
is concerned, unusually close
to Gallé's new approach.

11

Vase with pond scene

Signature: *E. Michel*
engraved on the underside
Design and execution: Eugène
Michel, Paris; blank: unknown
c. 1898–1904

Colourless glass with sporadic, in part overlapping, powdered glass inclusions in opaque light blue, white, bluish green, pink and cobalt blue under two layers of casing in bluish green and purplish red; applied foot and three pronounced knops of colourless glass; rim dilated and matt engraved. The decoration consists of a lacustrine scene with arrowhead (*Sagittaria*) and three white waterlilies, almost completely in the round, in various phases of development; executed in high relief, intaglio and line engraving, partly polished; the engraved applications in places strongly undercut.

H 19.8 Ø 11.8 cm

A one-off piece or from a limited luxury edition. Among Michel's best-known motifs and most outstanding achievements in design are his atmospheric pond scenes with waterlilies in the foreground, which in Western art often take the place of the Far Eastern lotus motif. The artist must have been familiar with the symbolic meaning of the lotus since he was for years one of the closest collaborators of Rousseau, an expert on East Asia. One of the most frequently occurring motifs in Art Nouveau glass, it was taken over from Egyptian and East Asian art. As a seminal Buddhist symbol, the lotus has numerous meanings, ranging from the sum of all spiritual revelations (the thousand-petalled lotus), purity, beauty, reincarnation, immortality, the universe, the points of the compass, the sun and moon to the vital centres of the human body (chakras): see Cooper 1978, pp. 112–14; Lurker 1985, p. 410. In his coloured pond scenes Michel creates the shimmering atmosphere that can be experienced in summer at the edge of a

body of water. His brilliantly handled overlay engraving reveals the most subtle colour nuances and includes the skilful use of intaglio and cameo engraving as well as the carving of applications that are virtually in the round to achieve an inimitable effect of spatial depth that is utterly enthralling. For a baluster-shaped vase with the same colour scheme and a pond, iris and white waterlily

applications see Mannoni n.d. [1986], p. 42, and cat. no. 12. A chronology of the pieces designed by Michel himself has not yet been reconstructed. For a pond scene with waterlilies in relief engraving on various vessel forms see Waltraud Neuwirth, *Das Glas des Jugendstils: Sammlung des Österreichischen Museums für angewandte Kunst, Wien* (Munich, 1973), pp. 372–73, no. 219 (dating

from *c.* 1898; purchased 1899); Bloch-Dermant 1980, pp. 42, 44; dating from *c.* 1895–1900: see Hilschenz-Mlynek and Ricke 1985, p. 329, no. 448; Ricke 2002, no. 262, illus. p. 169.

Lit.: Bloch-Dermant 1980, p. 42.

12

Vase with aquatic plants

Signature: *E. Michel*
engraved on the lower wall
Design and execution: Eugène
Michel, Paris; blank: unknown
c. 1898–1904

Colourless glass with sporadic, partly overlaid, powdered glass inclusions in white, bluish green, pink and cobalt blue under two layers of overlay in light yellow and bluish green; on the inner wall banded crazing; two pronounced applied knops of colourless glass. Rim ground flat, interior ground and polished, outside matt engraved. Decoration in matt, partly polished high relief, intaglio and line engraving, in places the applications are boldly undercut: pond scene with iris, arrowhead (*Sagittaria*) and two white waterlilies almost entirely in the round.

H 29.7 Ø 17.5; 16.6 cm

A one-off piece or from a limited luxury edition; cf. cat. no. 11. For the same applied waterlilies on a flask-shaped vase with pond scene and reed-mace (cat's tail) with the same colour scheme, dating from *c.* 1900, see Mukai, *Hida Takayama*, 1997, p. 105.

Lit.: Zons 2002, cat. no. A 3, p. 169, illus. p. 91.

13

Rod-shaped vase

Signature: *E. Michel*
engraved on the lower wall;
HG (ligated) engraved on
the underside
Design: attributed to Eugène
Michel, Paris; retailer: Harant
& Guignard, Paris; blank:
unknown
c. 1898–1904

Semi-opaque, light greyish
green glass with sporadic,
partly superimposed glass
powder inclusions in white,
blue, green and pink under
a dark purple cased layer;
freely formed, the inner wall
pushed out with a hook; rim
dilated, pulled up in three
places, outside partly matt-
carved. Concave floor ground
and polished. Decoration
consisting of three swirling
orchid plants with one bud
and two large flowers in bold
relief; executed in relief
engraving, the ground entirely worked over in fine matt
carving.

H 20 Ø 8.8; 8.3 cm
(including applications)

Luxury edition, presumably a
limited one. The addition of
the retailer's signature may
either refer to his having designed the piece or influenced
the design, or merely to collaboration between artist and
retailer. A precursor of this
design, which unites forming
at the furnace with engraved

decoration, is the 'Feuilles de marronnier' vase exhibited in Paris in 1893, which Michel engraved for Léveillé: see Bascou and Thiébaut, Orsay, 1988, p. 160, no. OAO 308, illus. p. 161. For further models with this bold relief, in which the design links form and decoration with applications, dating from *c.* 1898, see Tokyo, Paris selection, 1991, p. 49, no. 47. The floral decoration is very similar to that of a Philippe Wolfers design for a flask-shaped vase shown at the 1897 Brussels Exposition Internationale: see exh. rev. in *Art & Décoration* 2 (1897): 360. The first mention of Michel as an engraver for Harant & Guignard is crucial to establishing the date: see E. Molinier, 'Les Arts du Feu: Salons de 1898', *Art & Décoration* 3 (1898): 191. It is, however, also possible that engraving was still being done for Harant & Guignard in Michel's studio, which his widow ran after his death, until 1911. For an unsigned vase that is wider at the bottom and features iris decoration, with the same metal, see Schmitt, *Sammlung Silzer*, 1989, p. 254, no. 135, illus. p. 255; *Sammlung Silzer* 2003, no. 207.

14

Vase with fish and shell applications

Signature: *HG* (ligated) engraved, *Le Rosey Paris* diamond-point engraved on the underside
Design: attributed to Eugène Michel, Paris; retailer: Harant & Guignard, Paris; blank: unknown
c. 1898–1904

Opaque, light greyish green glass with sporadic, partly superimposed glass powder inclusions in blue, white, green and red, partly brown under three layers of overlay in colourless, green and purplish red; two pronounced humps and a knop of opaque, light greyish green glass fused on to the vessel in the molten state. The decoration is in high relief, intaglio and polished line engraving, the applications partly undercut: underwater scene with pondweed and three scallop shells below the rim, with two fish and a scallop almost entirely in the round.

H 14.6 Ø 11.9; 10.9 cm (including a fish application)

A one-off piece or from a limited luxury edition. Michel developed a distinctive signature as an artist in his underwater scenes, which sets him apart from all other glass artists. On the attribution with retailer signature and the dating see cat. no. 13.

15

Vase with trailing prunts

Signature: *A Jean*
painted on the underside in
opaque rust-red flat colour
Design and execution:
Ste Marie François Augustin
Jean, Paris; blank: Appert
Frères, Clichy
c. 1885–88

Light purple glass, freely
formed, solid light purple
applied base, wall flattened
bilaterally; eight applied
prunts: bulging applied ring,
pulled upwards and notched
in several places on the edge
of the rim. Decoration painted in opaque enamel in light
greyish green, pink, purple,
blue, white and grey, opaque
rusty red flat colours, bright
gold and pinkish violet, partly
sprayed lustre: pond scene
with leaping carp snapping at
a grasshopper and aquatic
plants, such as iris, arrowhead
(*Sagittaria*) and white and
yellow waterlilies.

H 23 Ø 23.2; 13.1 cm
(including applications)

A one-off piece or from a
limited luxury edition. The representation has been rendered
in false colours reminiscent of
poster painting. The incorporation of the trailing prunts in the
overall design has lent the
painted scene in the Japonist
manner remarkable depth.
Middle and Far Eastern motifs
influenced Jean's decoration.
Paintings such as this – tending
to narrative representation –
are, on the other hand, rare. On
the Sino-Japanese symbol of
the leaping carp see cat. no. 5.

Owing to a lack of documentation, a chronology of Jean's
designs has yet to be reconstructed. The artist was intensively preoccupied with glass
from 1877 to 1888. The dating
can be established by consult-
ing Jean's third patent (1889), in
which he describes spraying on
substances to induce iridescence with a compressed-air
spraying device. Jean's second
patent (1877) describes the
reduction firing of glass with
traces of silver and bismuth to
create other iridescent surfaces.
It has not been ascertained

whether the artist still painted
on glass after moving to Vierzon, France, in 1888. There is
a fish on an early Gallé vase,
dating from 1878–80, in the
Juken Museum of Art, Hiroshima; see Takeda and Olivié
1996, no. 1, which is similar
enough for comparison.

16

Double carp vase

Signature: *E. Gallé*
(not authentic) needle etched
on the underside
Design and execution:
unknown, Clichy
c. 1875–85

Thick-walled, colourless glass, mould-blown with compressed air and subsequently formed at the furnace, with two flattened applications of solid colourless glass. Wall, rim and bottom entirely worked over by grinding and polishing, drawing within contours in polished printy cutting as well as painting in opaque flat colours and bright gold. The inner wall is noticeably notched under the two applied fins; it is perforated, presumably accidentally, on one of the fins. This mishap might have occasioned the piece to be painted.

H 28.4 W 14.1 D 8.4 cm

Luxury glass edition, presumably a limited one. The signature is not authentic. The double carp is the Chinese symbol of the union of lovers: see Cooper 1978, p. 89. Several measurements that tally with one another despite differences in decoration and finishing prove that the same mould for mould-blowing was used for both variants, the present one and cat. no. 17.

The painting of the present vase is very similar to that of the carp on the little dish in the Koepff Collection (cat. no. 18). The painting on the double carp designed by Gallé illustrated below (Kitazawa Museum, Suwa) bears the same swimming carp motif as the vase in 'clair de lune' blue glass acquired in 1879 by the Musée des Arts Décoratifs, Paris: see Bloch-Dermant 1980; Tokyo 1974, no. 4; Garner 1976, p. 40; Paris, *Gallé*, 1985, p. 158, no. 68.

Lit.: Duncan and de Bartha 1984, fig. 30.

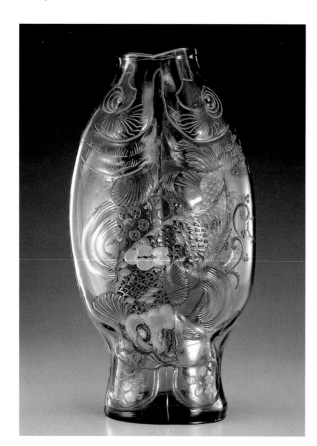

17

Double carp vase

Signature: *E Rousseau*
(not authentic) engraved on
the underside with flexible
shaft
Design and execution:
unknown
c. 1875–85

Thick-walled, colourless
glass, mould-blown with
compressed air and subse-
quently formed at the furnace, two flattened applications of solid colourless glass.
Surface entirely worked over
and polished, within the
contours polished prismatic
cutting and printies; foot-rim
ground flat for the mount.
Ormolu bronze foot, possibly
of Asian origin (nineteenth
century), attached with putty.
The inner wall beneath the
two fin applications is noticeably notched due to the
mould seams.

H 30.3 W 16.6 D 11.4 cm
(including applications and
mount)

Luxury edition, presumably a
small one. The signature is
spurious. The popular shape of
the double carp was also interpreted by others, including
Cristallerie de Baccarat, who
produced three different versions in 1878 alone: see Cristallerie de Baccarat 1878 and 1879
model catalogue, model nos.
2253, 2252 and 2269 (illus.
right). There is also a faience
vase of the same form in the
Koepff Collection (illus.
above), of unknown make (H
28.5 W 15.3 D 9.4 cm, marked
on the underside with an
impressed stamp *84*).

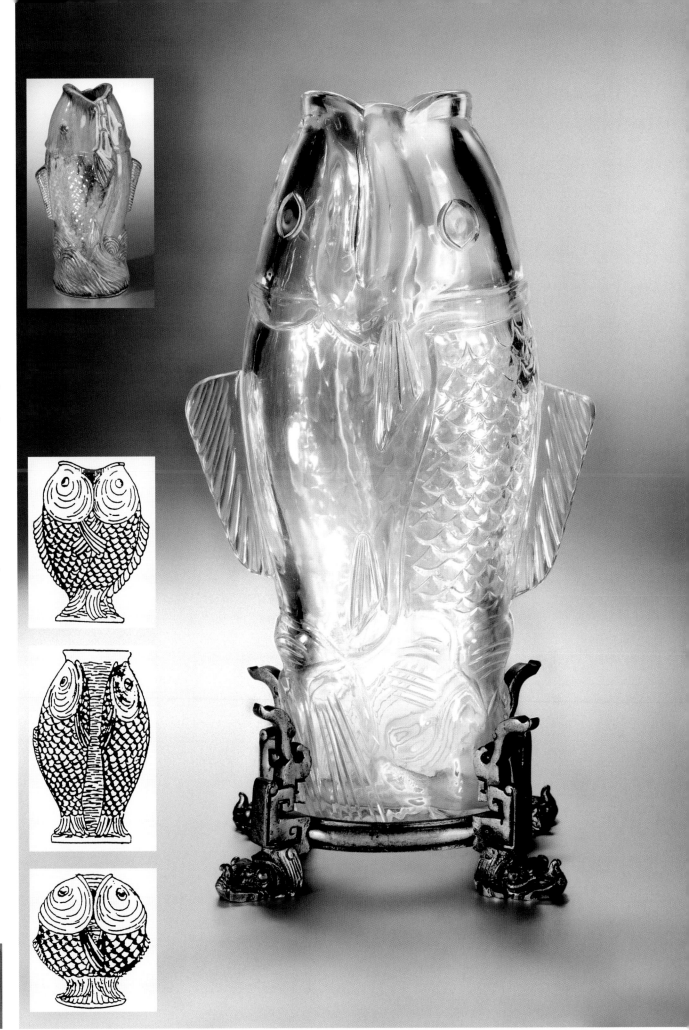

18

Dish with bronze mount

Signature: *E. Leveille E Rousseau Paris* (not authentic) engraved with flexible shaft on the underside
Design and execution: unknown
c. 1875–85

Colourless glass, freely formed, rim dilated, cut and polished; where the dish meets the mount rough ground. Underside and outer wall ribbed throughout and polished; on the upper side decorated with two bamboo canes and a leaping carp painted in opaque flat colours; markings and contour lines in bright gold. Ormolu bronze mount in the form of a twig with a crouching rat.

H 4.6   W 24.6   D 22.8 cm (including mount)

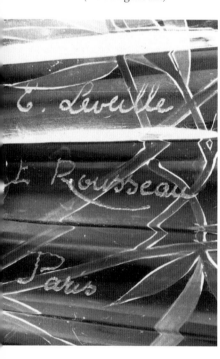

From a luxury edition. The rat is the first symbol in the Chinese zodiac: Cooper 1978, p. 148; Düsseldorf, *Netsuke*, 1994, p. 138. On bamboo and carp motifs see cat. nos. 1 and 5.

The signature is spurious. The attribution to Eugène Rousseau and Ernest Léveillé, as indicated by the signature, is highly unlikely since, during their collaborative phase, from 1885 to 1890, Rousseau had long since shifted his focus to etched and engraved cased glass and 'strass craquelé'. Similar pieces with paintings would be conceivable in his early phase from about 1868 to 1878. This piece may have been sold by such firms as Escalier de Cristal of Pannier Frères et Cie. or Edmond Enot in Paris, both known for their ormolu bronze mounts.

Emile Gallé

19

Footed vase

Signature: *E. Gallé fec ͭ·*
Nancy. no. 221 finely engraved
on the underside
Emile Gallé, Nancy
Engraved decoration: attributed to Victor Prouvé; execution: Burgun, Schverer & Co.,
Meisenthal
c. 1880–84

Honey-tinted yellow glass
with sporadic black, yellow
and white granule inclusions;
foot and stem applied, threading round the neck. Grooves
in polished line engraving on
foot and neck; decoration in
part slightly polished intaglio
engraving: an elf with bare
torso floating in a seated position and wearing a long, flowing garment; a dragonfly hovering above her; on the back
three more dragonflies, two
of them with superimposed
bodies.

H 14.3 Ø 7.9 cm

The profile of the vessel makes
it look as if it had been made on
the lathe. It is still firmly rooted
in the tradition of historicist
design, drawing on Renaissance
forms. Recalling semiprecious
stones, the physical properties
of the material make it contrast
sharply with the delicate, lyr-
ical mood of the engraving.

This piece is part of a large
group of wide-ranging shapes,
each of which was made only
in limited numbers. The most
seminal example, a footed bowl
(dating from 1886) reminiscent
of sixteenth-century Lombard
work in rock crystal, can be
admired in the Württembergisches Landesmuseum,
Stuttgart: see Munich, *Nancy
1900*, 1980, no. 180; Zurich,
Gallé, 1980, no. 27.

Victor Prouvé was probably
responsible for the figurative
decoration; see the similar

figure and comparable style of
a vase in the Musée d'Orsay,
inv. no. OAO 1000, Paris, *Gallé*,
1985, no. 81, with the original
sticker, on which is written
Prouvé and N1, and the 'L'Escar-
got des Vignes' footed bowl,
Paris, *Gallé*, 1985, no. 82, bearing an inscription that explicitly
refers to Prouvé as the designer
of the figurative decoration.

Similar pieces were shown at
the 1889 Exposition Universelle
in Paris, although the material
was handled differently and the
decoration was less delicate
and more intricately engraved,
incorporating striking dark
pigments and powdered glass
inclusions or black layers of
casing: see, for instance, Corning 1984, no. 2; Yoshimizu
1985, nos. 127–29; Paris, *Gallé*,
1985, nos. 90, 94, among others.

For an example with the same
shape as the present piece, with
torn foil inclusions, see auct.
cat. Drouot Paris, 13 November 1974, no. 52; for another,
decorated with relief engraving, see Bloch-Dermant 1980,
p. 67.

Pieces clearly revealing formal
affinities with the present one
were also made with plant
motifs: see Hilschenz-Mlynek
and Ricke 1985, no. 190. As late
as 1892 Mme Carnot, the wife
of the then French president,
was presented by the Nancy
chapter of the Union des
Femmes de France on the occasion of a visit to Nancy with a
piece that is virtually identical
in both shape and size with the
present piece: sold at auction
on 27 November 1991 at the
Hôtel Drouot in Paris and since
then in the collection of the
Musée de l'Ecole de Nancy, inv.
no. 991.24.1.

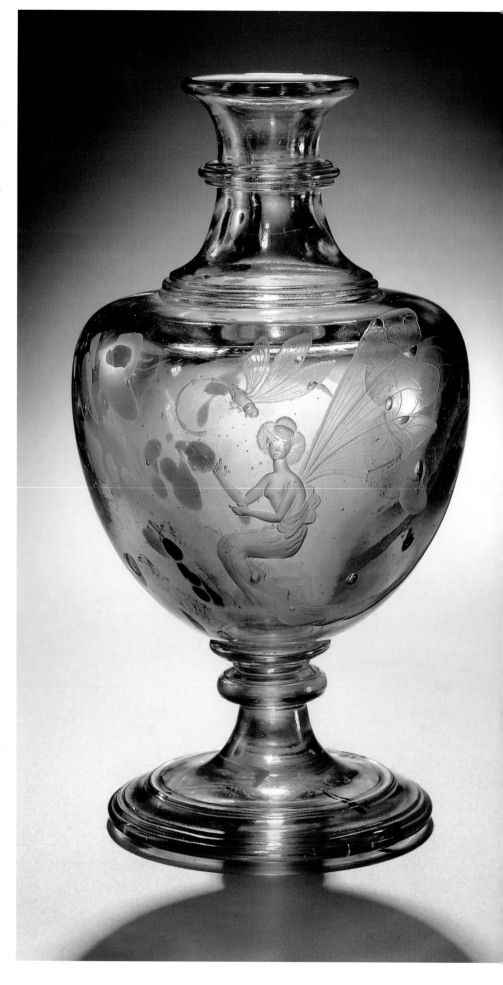

20

Vase

Signature: *E. Gallé fec^{t.}* *Nanceiis no. 170* engraved on the underside, also on the wall, *e ‡ g* in polished engraving below flying insect
Emile Gallé, Nancy
Execution: Burgun, Schverer & Co., Meisenthal
*c.*1880–84

Colourless glass with inclusions of bluish green metallic compounds and pinkish mauve splinters. Rim ground flat, bevelled and polished. Decoration for the most part line engraving, polished in places: a fly, a wispy blade of grass with several shoots, an insect with long antennae bent back; the blades of grass decoration partly continues on the side faces.

H 12.2   W 6.4   D 5.6 cm

Formerly Anne Marie Gillion-Crowet Collection, Brussels

A studio piece. Corresponds to the way Gallé handled material in the 1880s yet the overall formal impression made also recalls the work of Rousseau. It furnishes evidence of Gallé's preoccupation with the Paris scene at that time and its close links with Japanese prints: see, for instance, cat. no. 15. Similar vases, so simple in form, are rare indeed in Gallé's oeuvre.

Lit.: Grover 1970, no. 227.

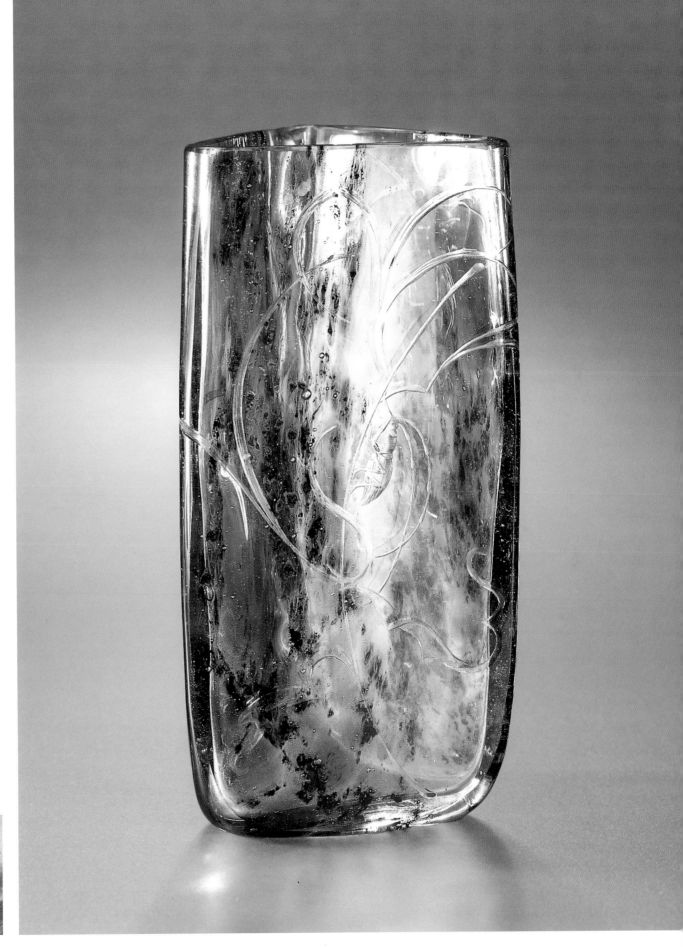

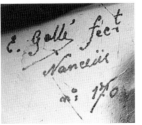

21

Bowl on Chinese stand

Signature: *E ‡ G Emile Gallé de Nancy inv^t et f^t*
engraved on the underside
Emile Gallé, Nancy
Execution: Burgun, Schverer & Co., Meisenthal
c. 1884–89

Thick-walled, smoky brown glass, black metallic-compound inclusions on front and back and surrounded by irregular, fine-grained, white reticulated patterns. Free-blown, applied foot of same metal; asymmetric rim, slightly indented on one side. Pointed oval foot surface ground flat and polished. Decoration in polished, partly matt engraving: on the front a double helix and matt leaf-vein motif; on the vessel head a spiral, on the back *martelé* texturing.

Gilt bronze mount consisting of five cast pieces held together by screws, presumably of Asian origin (nineteenth century).

H 15.2 W 17.3 D 11.5 cm (including mount)

An infrequently occurring vessel type. This bowl is related to the 1880s line in simulated hardstone ware; the form reflects the haphazard character of bowls cut from pieces of such natural and valuable materials.

According to Christine Mitomi this might also be a translation of the libation vessel form, which was made of rhinoceros horn.

22

Vase with a pair of dragonflies

Signature: *E. Gallé Nancy fec ͭ. No 180* incised in diamond-point engraved on the underside

Design and execution: Studio Burgun, Schverer & Co., Meisenthal for Emile Gallé, Nancy
c. 1885–90

Light green glass with dense dark red and yellow granule inclusions with opaque reddish brown striking colours; rim partly matt etched as a result of matt etching of the inner wall. Polished concave floor. Decoration: two dragonflies flying towards each other, between sunbursts; simple relief etching on glossy ground. Polychrome painting in opaque enamels, reddish brown opaque flat colours, bright gold and lustre.

H 20.3 Ø 9.2 cm

Reminiscent of Japanese lacquer intarsia with mother-of-pearl inlay, this vase is part of the elaborate studio output. For a similar piece, in a private collection in Cologne, see Klesse 1982, p. 38, fig. 65; for a basin with the pair of dragonflies, in a Japanese private collection, see Yoshimizu 1985, fig. 85. For the same motif, but reversed and on faience, shown by Gallé at the 1889 Paris Exposition Universelle, see Tokyo, *Gallé*, 1980, no. 76; *Gallé* 1985, no. 59.

This piece attests to the close ties between the Burgun, Schverer & Co. factory and Gallé, who commissioned work from it. The lower dragonfly, only slightly modified, has been preserved as a draw-ing on tracing paper with perforations left by the needle used for tracing, in the Chambon Collection at The Corning Museum of Glass (illus. below, right). The drawing is part of a large collection of work materials of unknown provenance found in the Meisenthal factory studio.

A study in colour of a similar pair of dragonflies and a variant of the upper dragonfly on tracing paper are in a Meisenthal private collection and are linked with Christian's employee Eugène Kremer: see Klesse 1982, pp. 37–38.

Gallé probably had little to do with the design and production of this piece. The conservative shape points to the Meisenthal glassworks as does the gold-tooled sunburst known from Japanese textiles, which is a distinguishing feature, used for many of the vases produced by that firm from the mid-1890s onwards: see cat. nos. 64–65.

The motif of two dragonflies was also occasionally used by the Vallerysthal factory: see Klesse, *Funke-Kaiser* I, 1981, no. 371; Klesse 1982, p. 38. That factory maintained close ties with Burgun, Schverer & Co. In 1898 Désiré Christian lived in Vallerysthal and possibly worked for a short time as a designer and consultant for the glass factory.

23
Vase with waterlilies

Signature: *Emile Gallé*
engraved on the underside,
surrounded by a miniature
landscape with a blooming
waterlily cut in relief
To the right, above the name,
a spurious date was added
later: *1889*
Emile Gallé, Nancy
Execution: Burgun, Schverer
& Co., Meisenthal
c. 1892/93

Colourless glass, subjected
to multiple dippings in purple
glass; white flakes, powder
and mica in places fused
beneath the colourless top
layer. Decoration in relief
engraving on the front: a
pond is suggested with two
waterlilies adorning the wall –
one as a growing bud, the
other in full bloom, bent
towards the left – and one
waterlily in full bloom on the
underside (illus. below, left).
The ground, including the
rim and floor structured with
fine, in places lightly polished, cutting and *martelé* texturing.

H 14.7 W 12.6 D 8.8 cm

Formerly Robert Walker Collection, Paris

A rare example of the studio-
produced *vases de tristesse*.
Markedly reticent decoration
based on Japanese woodcuts.

The date can be identified as
later and not authentic because
it is engraved in a shallow technique, different from that used
for the signature and the
image, and is awkwardly handled. Signatures on the underside featuring a motif taken
from the overall decorative
programme of a piece have
been verified in Gallé's work as
early as the 1880s – also for the
1889 Paris Exposition Universelle – but were used more
frequently, with minute details
as in this vase, primarily
between 1892 and 1895. They
occur less often after the mid-
1880s. Gallé had the decoration
and several variants registered
c. 1892 (see illus. far right).
A drawing clearly borrowed
from Hokusai's *manga* (sketchbooks) was sold at auction in

1982 as lot no. 60 in an undated batch: see Sotheby's Monaco 1982, no. 55, no illus.

The date of the drawings,
now in the Corning Museum
of Glass, Corning, NY, is verified by the use of one of these
sketches for a Gallé vase dated
1892; see Hilschenz-Mlynek
and Ricke 1985, no. 199.

For another example, virtually identical in shape and size
but with more detailed decoration on the front, yet modelled on the same pattern, see
Newark 1989, p. 85; auct.
cat. Sotheby's Monaco, 4 April
1993, no. 17, n.d.

Lit.: Garner 1976, p. 135;
Bloch-Dermant 1980, p. 79.

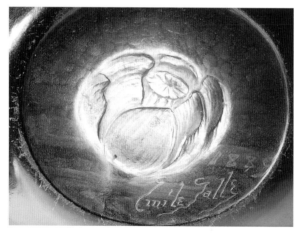

24

Bowl with gilt mount

Signature: *E Gallé a Nancy*
needle etched on the underside
Emile Gallé, Nancy
Execution: Burgun, Schverer
& Co., Meisenthal, mount:
unknown
1892/93

Light brown smoky glass, four
round prunts of the same
material as well as two light
green trailing prunts. Foot-rim
and inner wall matt etched.
Decoration in simple, shallow
etching, painted over with
opaque and transparent enamel in white, honey brown –
partly on bright gold – and
dark brown flat color: stylized
symmetrical leaf ornament on
a white-speckled ground with
finely striped, dark brown
hatching.

Gilt metal mount, cast and
chased; four mother-of-pearl
discs collet-set like baroque
pearls.

H 10.9 W 14.7 D 13.3 cm
(including mount)

A virtually identical but unmounted example was acquired
on 20 May 1893 by the Musée
des Arts Décoratifs, Paris, for
70 Frs from Gallé personally at
the Salon exhibition of that year
(illus. as no. 6 there), inv. no.
7651: see Tokyo, *Gallé*, 1980, no.
30; Yoshimizu 1985, fig. 84. For
another exemplar, also unmounted, from the Anne Marie
Gillion-Crowet Collection, Brussels, see Grover 1970, fig. 201.

In Gallé's oeuvre this vase represents the end of a series of pieces
influenced by Islamic decoration; compare the cut decoration on ninth and tenth-century
glass from Iran, which features
similar details combined with
hatching, in, for instance, A. von
Saldern, *Kataloge des Kunstmuseums Düsseldorf: Glas*, vol. III:
*Glassammlung Hentrich: Antike
und Islam* (Düsseldorf, 1974),
nos. 401, 402 and 411.

A case could also be made for
the decoration deriving from
Chinese art: see, for instance,
the *taotie* motif, reproduced in
H. Brinker, 'Zur archaischen
Bronzekunst', in *China, eine
Wiege der Weltkultur: 5000 Jahre
Erfindungen und Entdeckungen*,

exh. cat., Roemer-Pelizaeus
Museum, Hildesheim (Mainz,
1994), figs. 42, 43 (kindly
imparted by Christine Mitomi,
Hamburg).

For a variant of both the shape
and the decoration, with
cicadas in flight and butterflies
on a pronouncedly concave
neck, see Suzuki, *Kitazawa*,
1996, no. 92; auct. cat. Ader
Picard Tajan, Tokyo 20 November 1990, no. 144. A vase in
Marx 1911, p. 241, also belongs
to this group.

Emile Gallé

25
Rod-shaped vase

Signature: *Gallé Modèle et décor déposés Compos*[t.] in reddish brown paint on the underside
Emile Gallé, Nancy
Execution: Burgun, Schverer & Co., Meisenthal or Nancy
c. 1895

Light aquamarine glass with applied purplish blue bottom, mould-blown; rim with three indentations. Concave matt-etched floor, with glossy flower in low relief at centre. Decoration: stem and leaves of the common house-leek (*Sempervivum*) as well as three scattered groups of individual blooms and buds executed alternately in deep and needle etching and painting with bright gold, opaque and transparent enamels, powdered gold and matt enamel. On the inner wall also stylized blooms and parts of plants in simple, low relief etching, the lower two-thirds with a matt ground.

H 22.1 Ø 7.3 cm

Elegant serially produced ware. This vase belongs to the rather late group of vessels decorated in enamels. All techniques of painting Gallé described as early as 1884 and 1889 have been employed, including *émaux bijoux* (jewelling) with powdered gold on enamel or polished gold under enamels. Moreover, the intricate detail recalls works from the 1880s and the shape has also been verified for 1884. Yet the signature would seem to suggest the 1890s. A further argument for the later date is the circumstance that, on 5 April 1895, Gallé applied for the protection of a decoration drawing on which this vase may have been directly modelled (illus. p. 113, top).

The drawing was bought at
auction by The Corning Museum of Glass, Corning, NY, in
1982 as part of a series of sixty
sheets. It is listed as no. 49; see
auct. cat. Sotheby's Monaco
1982, no. 27. In Gallé's marginal note the sheet is, like nos.
48–54, described as 'Compositions végétales diverses
mêmes observations (i.e., pour
applications décoratives [...] sur
toutes matières, pour objets et
formes de modèle, gravure
chimique, gravure au touret
sur le cristal & le verre, impression, peinture, photogravure,
photographie, email de relief
ou à plat, etc.).' ('Diverse vegetal compositions with the same
observations.' This refers to the
addition to earlier numbers
'for use in decoration [...] on
all materials, for objects and
moulds, etching, wheel-
engraving on crystal and glass,
stamping, painting, photo-
engraving, relief or flat enamelling, etc.')

There are very few comparable
pieces. For the decoration on a
vase in the same colour scheme
but of different shape see *Emile
Gallé*, exh. cat., Navio Museum
of Art, Osaka (Osaka, 1987),
no. 46.

26

Rod-shaped vase with iris

Signature: *Cristallerie de Gallé à Nancy Modèle et décor déposés* in both shallow and deep etching on the underside
Emile Gallé, Nancy
c. 1895–97

Smoky yellow glass with irregular, opaque overlay in light bluish grey with a greenish tinge; rim with three indentations. Decoration: on the front two irises; in the lower zone, running round the vase, additional outlines of small irises. Relief etching executed in two phases on fine-grained matt ground, which is lightly polished up to the middle of the wall; sparse veining executed in needle etching.

H 18 Ø 6.3 cm

Serially produced. Gallé added the iris motif, derived from the iris and flag plants of Japanese colour woodcuts so widely circulated by Samuel Bing's *Japon artistique* and other publications quite late to his repertoire of images.

The irregularly indented, etched rim of this vase is a decorative element characteristic of Gallé's Meisenthal partner, Burgun, Schverer & Co.

Lit.: Zons 2002, cat. no. A 5, p. 169, illus. p. 94.

27
Rod-shaped vase with drawn rim

Signature: *Gallé* in deep etching on the underside
Emile Gallé, Nancy
1895–97

Colourless glass, with fine-grained white patinage inclusions, orange-yellow casing, overlaid with trails of vitrified red powdered glass; cased in colourless glass. Freely blown and formed, an applied vertical colourless prunt with white powdered glass melted into it; rim pulled to one side and fused with the colourless application. Ground and polished concave floor.

H 20.9   Ø 5.3 cm

This vase combines the simulated hardstone metal of the 1880s (agate) with the symbolic interpretation of plants that distinguishes Gallé's late work. The static principle of the mineral kingdom is linked with the dynamic burgeoning and growth in nature.

For a more slender and taller variant without brownish inclusions yet with the addition of etched and then engraved woodbine (honeysuckle) decoration that used to be in the Funke-Kaiser Collection, Cologne, see Klesse, *Funke-Kaiser* I, 1981, no. 192. For yet another exemplar, without etching, see Bloch-Dermant 1980, p. 111; auct. cat. Sotheby's Monaco, 13 October 1991, no. 39.

On the late group of hardstone adaptations see Hilschenz-Mlynek and Ricke 1985, nos. 216–18, with further references.

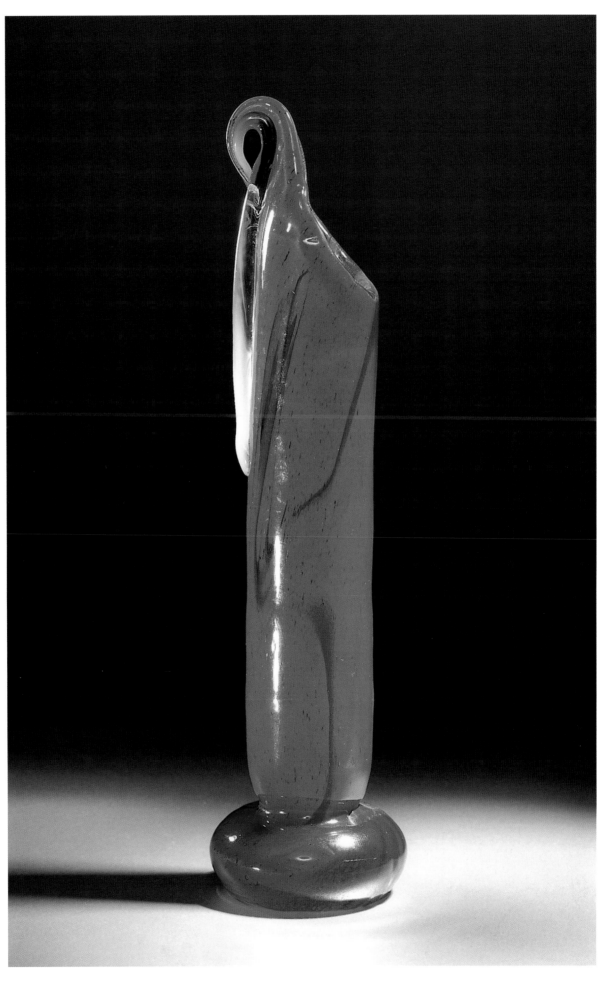

28

Vase with Turk's cap lily

Signature: *Cristallerie de Gallé Nancy* on the underside, deeply etched and partly engraved
Emile Gallé, Nancy
c. 1895–97

Semi-opaque, light bluish grey glass with a slight green tinge, opaque oxblood overlay, surface dark brown (striking colour). Wall flattened on two sides. Rim bevelled and slightly polished. Concave matt-ground floor; traces of the pontil mark discernible. Decoration: Turk's cap lily with bloom and bud in simple relief etching, surface engraved; on the back cloud-like formations bordered in dark red.

H 17.7 W 12.1 D 9.5 cm

A fine studio piece, of which quite a few variants were made. Forms of this kind, developed from the calabash and partly inspired by East-Asian models, appear in Gallé's work with other colour schemes and decoration variants: see, for instance, Klesse, *Funke-Kaiser* I, 1981, no. 132. For the present version see auct. cat. Christie's Geneva, 28 November 1982, no. 303; Duncan and de Bartha 1984, fig. 172; auct. cat. Drouot Paris, 5 April 1995, no. 29, etc.

The Turk's cap lily decoration executed in sealing-wax red on an opalescent ground was often used and varied *c.* 1895–97 on studio pieces of various shapes: see, for instance, Hilschenz-Mlynek and Ricke 1985, nos. 211–14, with further references.

Vase with Turk's cap lily

Signature: *Cristallerie de Gallé Nancy* in deep etching on the underside and *Modèle et décor déposés* needle etched Emile Gallé, Nancy
1895–97

Colourless glass, white streaks throughout, opaque oxblood overlay, surface dark brown (striking colour). Wall flattened on two sides. Polished floor, with partly carved texture and traces of pontil mark discernible. Decoration: on the front Turk's cap lily flower and leaves, etched in one stage; flower surface matt engraved. Below and next to the flower touches of polished *martelé* cutting; on the lower left wall single flower with bow-like, inwardly curled petals. On the back cloud-like formations in opaque brick red, partly red-rimmed, tinged a smoky dark grey in thin layers.

H 21.1 W 11.3 D 8.4 cm

Part of the stylish group of studio pieces to which cat. no. 28 belongs. Several similar examples of the present variant exist. For a vase in the Munich Stadtmuseum with very similar metal see Munich, *Nancy 1900*, 1980, no. 220, illus. p. 87, where further pieces from this group are illustrated. See also Blount 1968, fig. 71; auct. cat. Ader Picard Tajan, Monte Carlo, 16 December 1978, no. 285, etc.

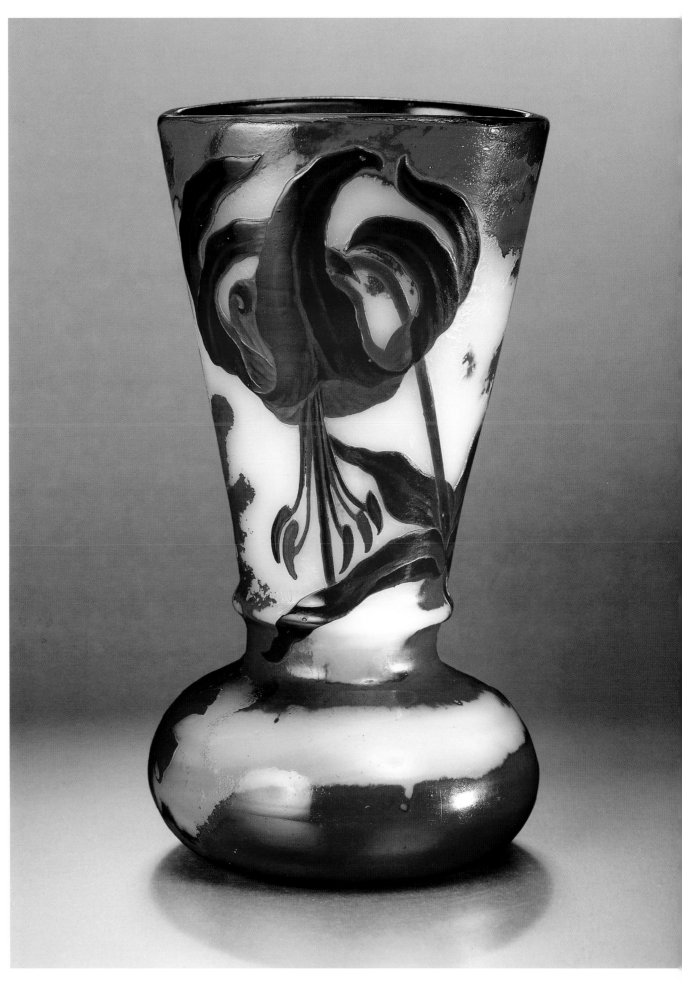

30

**Beaker-shaped vase
with bat**

Signature: *à Robert de
Montesquiou pour Virgile les
chauves-souris E. Gallé Nancy*
engraved on the back
outside wall
Emile Gallé, Nancy
c. 1895–97

Colourless glass with powdered glass in opalescent
white melted in and on to
the surface. Upper wall flattened on two sides. The concave floor centre is ground
matt. Decoration on the
front: full moon, trailing
clouds and a bat, wings
spread, clinging to a branch;
on the back trailing clouds
and a dedication. Executed
in shallow relief engraving;
ground, including rim,
engraved with fine, in part
lightly polished, variously
textured carving.

H 14.4 W 9.8 D 7.8 cm

This piece was dedicated to
Robert, Count Montesquiou-
Fézensac (1855–1921), a fre-
quenter of Paris Salons and
man of letters with whom
Gallé developed a friendship
between 1889 and the late
1890s. Through him Gallé
made some important con-
tacts in Parisian high society:
see Garner 1979, pp. 111–12.
By 1890 Gallé had designed
the small 'Urne funéraire
d'Ariel' with bats and dedicated it to Robert de Montesquiou: see Hilschenz-
Mlynek and Ricke 1985, no. 196.

The inscription refers to
'Virgile', a poem in Mon-
tesquiou's *Les Chauves Souris*
(The Bats), published in 1893.
Incorporating an original line
of verse from Virgil, the poem
describes an evocatively
atmospheric landscape, which
evidently impressed Gallé.

Bats as symbols of the night
and the dark sides of the soul
assumed a special role in Gallé's personal iconography
from the late 1890s onwards –
which holds true for *fin de siècle* art in general. For further
examples see Garner 1976, pp.
122–23, as well as cat. nos. 53
and 54 here.

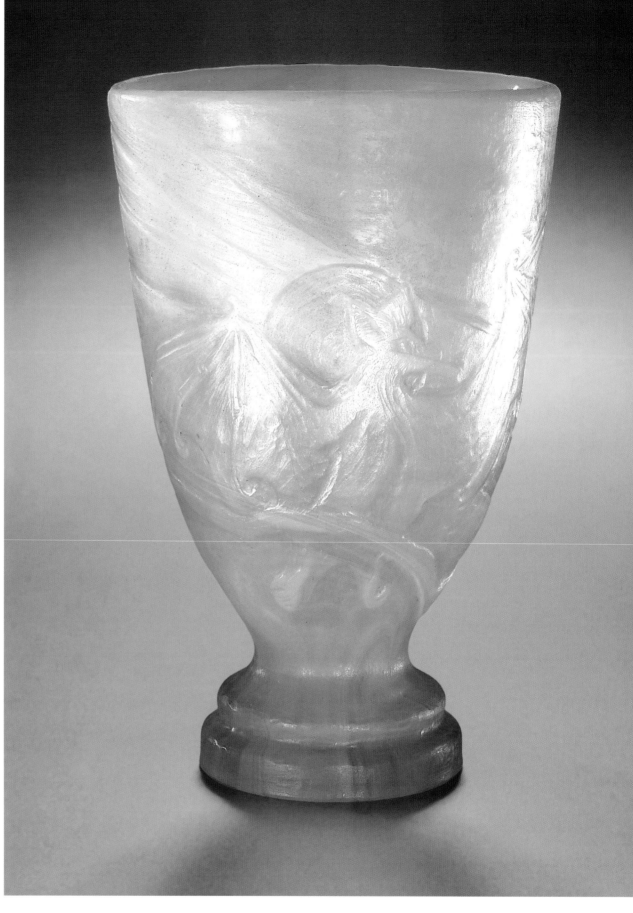

In the present piece a gloomy
colour scheme, which might at
first glance seem more appropriate to the subject matter, has
been deliberately eschewed.
Apart from the more usual
emphasis in Europe on the sin-

ister aspects of bat symbolism,
Gallé was also aware of the
positive role played by this animal, as a harbinger of good fortune, in Chinese and Japanese
iconography: see Hakenjos
1982, pp. 181–82. The physical

properties of the material
used for this vase, recalling
white jade, which was particularly prized and valuable, are
in keeping with the positive
iconography.

31
Vase with autumn crocuses

Signature: *Gallé* engraved on the outer wall
On the underside remains of a sticker with blue print:
... TION 1933 ... ATIFS
Emile Gallé, Nancy
c. 1895–97

Colourless glass with double casing in opaque pink and light bluish mauve; on the back, below the rim, a cabochon-like knop in opaque pink and light bluish mauve backed with dark inclusions. The body of the vessel is flattened on two sides. Concave floor ground and polished.

Decoration: autumn crocuses in various stages of blooming and fading, relief etching and relief engraving. Ground, including the rim, engraved with carving and *martelé* texture, some parts lightly polished; its horizontal hatching continues, sketchily executed, on the inner wall to suggest a horizon.

H 15.5 W 9.4 D 6.5 cm

Formerly Henri Hirsch Collection, Nancy

The late-blooming autumn crocus, which flowers before its leaves appear, was a favourite motif of Gallé's. Symbolizing hope and vulnerability or transience, but also the danger of beauty's deadly poison, it recurred in many guises, particularly in the marquetry pieces he created between 1897 and 1900.

This elaborately engraved vase from the Hirsch Collection is a harbinger of a large output of 'grand genre' pieces. Additional colour effects have been eschewed, with the colour of the flower determining the overall colour scheme of the decoration.

The sticker provides evidence that the vase was loaned by the Hirsch Collection in 1933 to the exhibition 'Le Décor de la vie sous la IIIe République de 1870 à 1900', mounted by the Musée des Arts Décoratifs in the Pavillon de Marsan at the Musée du Louvre, Paris: see Paris 1933, p. 182, no. 1439 – 'Petit vase aplati en cristal doublé d'un

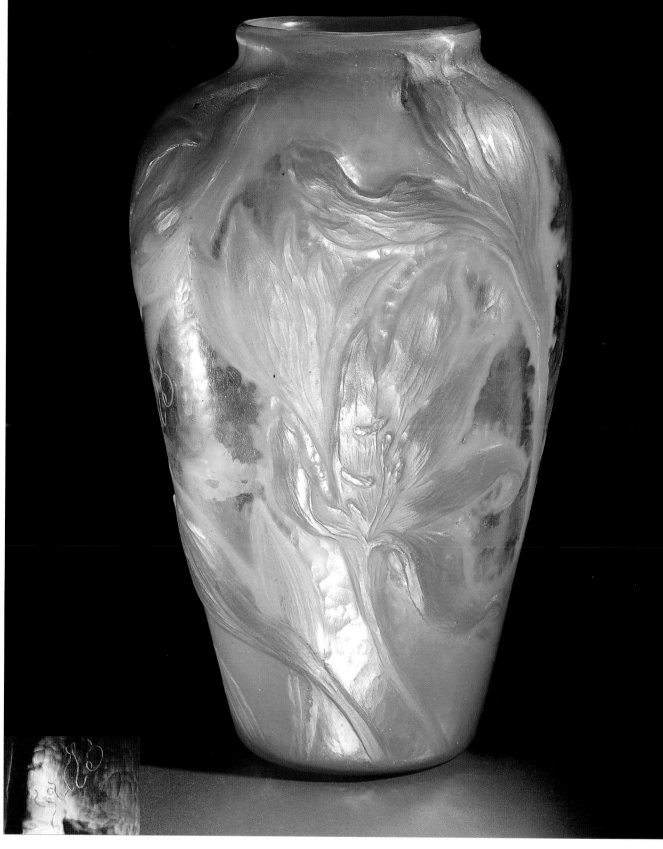

couche de verre rose portant un décor de "Veilleuses" (Colchiques), gravé à la roue. Signé' (Small flattened vase in crystal cased in pink glass boasting 'meadow saffron' (*Colchicum*), wheel-engraved. Signed).

The previous owner of the vase, Henri Hirsch, a high-ranking administrative official in Nancy, was one of Gallé's most important clients. The celebrated 'Vitrine aux libellules' (dragonfly glass cabinet; 1904), now in the Musée

d'Orsay, and the 'Aube et crépuscule' (sunrise and sunset), a bed now in the Musée de l'Ecole de Nancy – Gallé's most important late works, if not his greatest pieces of furniture – were created for Henri Hirsch: see Paris 1985, nos. 167–68.

For a somewhat larger but identically shaped variant with different decoration see Yoshimizu 1988, p. 33.

Lit.: Darmstadt 1999, illus. p. 306.

32

Baluster-shaped vase with woodbine (honeysuckle)

Signature: *Gallé* engraved on the lower outer wall in double-lined writing
Emile Gallé, Nancy
c. 1896–98

Colourless glass with triple overlay in white, yellow and pink; blown into a sixteen-ribbed optic mould. Decoration: woodbine (honeysuckle: *Lonicera*) tendrils, flowers and leaves traced in low relief etching and worked over in finely modelled engraving on the entire surface; the ground is textured with delicate carving.

H 23.8 Ø 9.7 cm

An elaborate studio piece, superlatively engraved. The dynamism of the plant with its tendrils twining in all directions matches the movement achieved in the ground in the upper and lower part of the vase by the use of the ribbed optic mould.

The simple, classical vase form and the eschewal of extraneous colour effects at once restrain and harmoniously offset the variegated, teeming motif.

For a slightly more slender example of this rare model see auct. cat. Christie's Geneva, 12 May 1991, no. 228. For a further variant see the *Documentation Gallé* of the Musée d'Orsay, no. 100491.

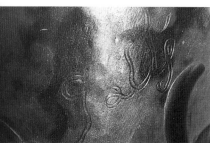

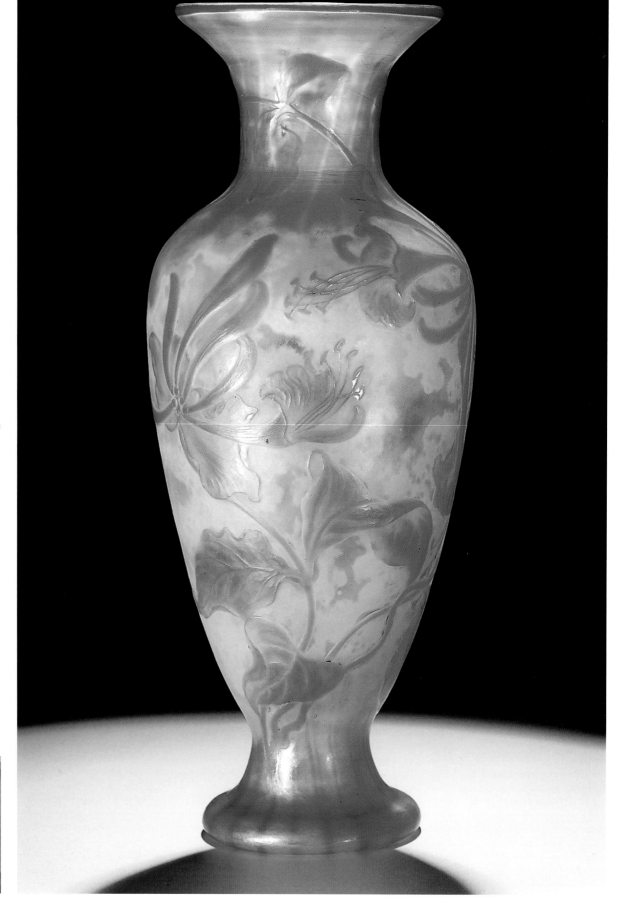

33
Vase with underwater decoration

Signature: *Gallé* engraved on the outer wall, on the underside a damaged sticker with black print: *CRISTALLERIE D' ART. MILE GALLÉ ...ARIS,* handwritten in black ink: *85804*
Emile Gallé, Nancy
c. 1895–1900

Colourless glass with scattered, partly overlapping blue powder and metallic-compound green and rusty red inclusions; rim freely formed, splayed outwards in two places and inside partly matt engraved.

Underwater decoration with pondweed, two water snails and a shell in variously polished relief engraving; the ground, including the underside, entirely textured with homogeneous carving.

H 25.6 W 11.7 D 8.2 cm

An elaborate studio piece. The form, suggesting that of a fish, is similar to designs bearing floral motifs yet is exceptional among pieces with underwater decoration.

For a variant identical in form with dynamic inner structure and intricate engraving in a London private collection see Yoshimizu 1985, no. 156; Newark 1989, p. 96.

34

Rod-shaped vase with a lady under trees

Signature: *Gallé* in relief engraving on the outer wall
Emile Gallé, Nancy
c. 1890–1900

Colourless glass, the upper wall vertically indented in four places. Decoration: lady in a long dress, with a train, under an apple or orange tree, holding a fruit in her hand; lightly polished relief engraving; the entire wall, including the underside and rim, worked over with broad *martelé* texture. Vessel matt inside.

H 20.4 Ø 7.2 cm

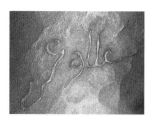

A one-off piece that is highly unusual for Gallé's mature work, which, as a rule, did not feature figurative representations of people. The image develops unrelated to the shape of the vessel within an almost square pictorial reserve on the outer wall. Its only link with the vessel appears to be the carved texture of the surrounding surface.

Despite its unusual appearance, there is no reason to doubt that this piece originated in Gallé's studio in Nancy.

For extant depictions of this kind, which may have served as models for similar pieces in ceramic and glass, see the drawing in the Persian manner (*c.* 1889) in the Musée d'Orsay, Paris (illus. below): Thiébaut, *Dessins*, 1993, p. 99; this drawing has been translated into enamel painting on a vase in Cappa 1991, fig. 331.

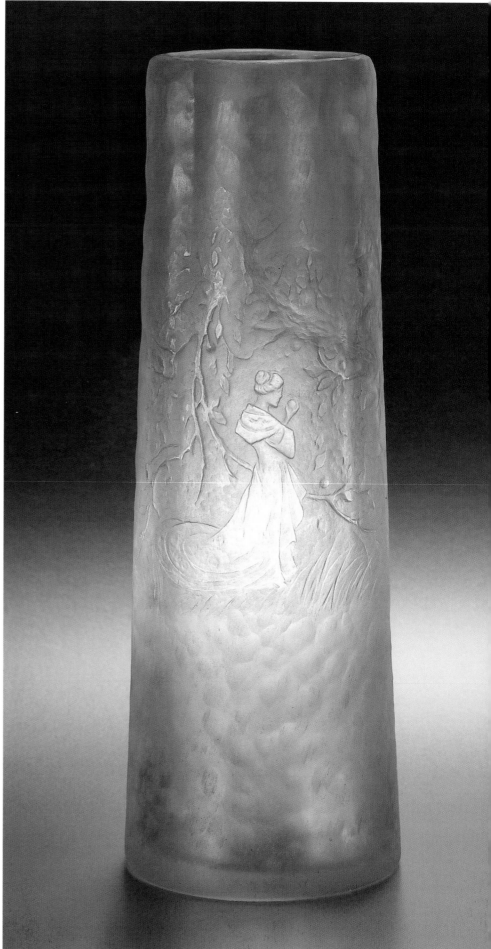

35
'Datura' vase

Signature: *Gallé 1889*
needle etched low on the
outer wall
Signature not authentic
Emile Gallé, Nancy
c. 1898

Colourless glass with finely
textured, white patinage
inclusions, overlaid with four
patches of fused-on purple
glass, silver leaf and partly
cased, in the lower half in
purple, drawn out in several
places, in the upper half in
yellow. Mould-blown into a
six-piece flower mould; two
applied knops of colourless
glass backed with gold leaf
and reddish purple powdered
glass.

Rim ground and polished,
as is the footed rim and the
partly ground outer wall.
Concave matt ground floor
centre. Both beetle knops
engraved and lightly pol-
ished.

H 21.2 W 12.7 D 11.1 cm

This vase is a play on the shape
of ancient Chinese ritual
bronzes of the Gu type (Shan-
Yin and early Chou dynasties),
yet the upper part is transformed into a stylized flower.
A model with several verified

exemplars, also shown at the
1900 Paris Exposition Universelle (now in the Musée des
Arts Décoratifs, Paris: illus., for
instance, in *Gallé's Gallé* 1993,
no. 18), belongs stylistically
and formally to early Gallé
marquetry models. This is
confirmed by a sheet with
sketches and writing in the
artist's hand, which is in the
Musée d'Orsay, Paris (illus.
below, left); see Thiébaut,
Dessins, 1993, p. 31. Dated
1er Janvier 1898, the sheet shows
several identifiable 'Série riche
1ère' models, which went into
production that year. The
'Datura' (Solanée) model on
the sheet is marked as no. 700.

The present piece is formally
incomplete since the petals
are merely suggested. This
may have been an originally
unsigned trial piece. Although
deceptively well forged, the
signature is nevertheless obviously not authentic. This is
revealed by its ostentatious execution, the date given, which is
too early for this piece, as well

as the lack of additional information, such as the artist's
first name, place of execution
(à Nancy) and the cross of
Lorraine typical of early Gallé
signatures. The engraving on
the cabochons may also have
been added later.

For complete versions of this
model see Hilschenz-Mlynek
and Ricke 1985, no. 276, with
further references. For what is
presumably the best preserved
example see Garner, *El Fituri*,
1982, no. 28; for a variant with
primroses on the shaft ring see
ibid. no. 29; for the preliminary

sketch for it in the Musée
d'Orsay (illus. right) see
Thiébaut, *Dessins*, 1993, p. 123.
For further exemplars see auct.
cat. Sotheby's London, 4
March 1988, no. 15; *Art of
Gallé* 1988, no. 8, etc.

Lit.: Duncan and de Bartha,
1984, fig. 114.

36

Rod-shaped vase with bronze foot

Signature: *GaLLé* vertically on the outer wall, engraved and picked out in gold
Emile Gallé, Nancy
c. 1898

Dark green glass casing over yellow. Marquetry decoration consisting of an opaque yellow flower and a transparent yellow patch over precious metal leaf and red powdered glass; mould-blown in the shape of a stylized segment of bamboo cane; rim pinched. Decoration: branching stem with flowers and leaves of a dahlia, partly in deep intaglio engraving, which incorporates all metal melted into and fused on to the surface. Tree bark texture in simple etching, matt and partly glossy ground. The casing on the inner wall has been removed in places in frosted matt shallow engraving.

Mounted on a bronze base with dark brown patina: 'Fausse renoncule' (lesser celandine).

H 27.4 Ø 6.4 cm
W 10.2 D 9.9 cm
(including mount)

This model is a studio piece that is fairly frequently encountered yet invariably with different decoration. A variant was shown at the 1900 Paris Exposition Universelle in the 'Repos dans la solitude' display case: see Paris, *Gallé*, 1985, p. 304.

For comparable pieces see Hilschenz-Mlynek and Ricke 1985, no. 250; auct. cat. Drouot Paris, 20 May 1988, no. 117; Arwas 1987, p. 127; auct. cat. Sotheby's London, 17 June 1988, no. 79 (both without needle etching).

Gallé registered the foot on 5 March 1898. The drawing has been donated by Gerda Koepff to the Museum für Angewandte Kunst, Cologne; see illus. here p. 280, pl. 15.

Lit.: J. Bloch-Dermant, 'Emile Gallé et la marqueterie de verre', *L'Estampille*, no. 108 (April 1979): 11.

37
'Toujours bonheur' vase

Signature: *Emile Gallé ‡*
engraved low on the outer wall
Silver mount: on foot-rim and
below the ferrule
Hallmarks: hexagon with M (?)
Al and head of Minerva
Emile Gallé, Nancy
1898

Green casing over yellow,
powdered glass melted on in
streaks, overlaid with two
opaque light green mar-
quetry patches. Ground and
polished floor. Inner wall
matt etched. Decoration: two
upright branching plants, as
in cat. no. 36, on bark texture
in relief etching and intaglio
engraving, lightly polished,
incorporating the two marquetry patches.

Two-piece silver-gilt mount
with dark red and opaque
blue cabochons in notched
collet settings. The stylized
foot decoration is foliate;
above the rim in decorative
lettering *TOUJOURS*, which
continues in the links of the
longer pendant with *BON-
HEUR*.

H 33.4 Ø 15 cm

A studio piece. The decoration
was developed from that on
cat. no. 36. For an unmounted
companion-piece see Duncan
and de Bartha 1984, fig. 138.
For further exemplars see
Charpentier et al. 1987, p. 173;
Arwas 1987, p. 173, which is
identical with no. 63 in *Art of
Gallé* 1988.

The form exists with different
decoration: see, for instance,
Klesse, *Funke-Kaiser* I, 1981,
no. 179; auct. cat. Drouot Paris,
17 December 1971; *Art of
Gallé* 1988, nos. 39, 65; for new
acquisitions of the Koepff Collection see here 'Thoughts on
the Collection', esp. illus. p. 14.

The model had to be altered
to accommodate the silver
mount. Although it remains a
moot question whether the
mount was designed by Gallé's
studio, its linear decoration
would make this seem unlikely.

38
'Datura' vase

Signature: *Gallé Etude*
engraved on the lower wall,
picked out in gold
Emile Gallé, Nancy
c. 1898

Purple overlay on colourless glass with fine-grained white powdered glass inclusions over large areas. Several threads of silver-stain yellow glass worked into the outer wall and drawn up into pointed leaves. Body of vessel freely formed; an orange yellow, applied knop backed with gold leaf and silver alloy compounds fused on. Outer wall matt as a consequence of inadvertent reduction firing and matt firing during the glassmaking process.

Cast bronze foot with dark brown patina.

H 25.5 Ø 9.7 cm

Gallé made several forays into ambitious vase forms developed from the exotic datura flower and executed in elaborate techniques. For a variant in a low-grade steel mount see auct. cat. Drouot Paris, 1 June 1990, no. 87; for a variant with a different base, cut leaf and fine needle etching see auct. cat. Nouveau Drouot Paris, 20/21 May 1987, no. 74; Sun Kurino 1995, no. 62. For a lamp formally similar to this exemplar see Suzuki, *Kitazawa*, 1996, no. 4; for a version with an undulating fused-on glass foot see: Duncan and de Bartha 1984, fig. 138; *Art of Gallé* 1988, no. 55, etc.

The present examples would seem to be a unique version. Two rather small, burst air bubbles are probably what caused it to be classified as an *étude*.

Lit.: Darmstadt 1999, cat.

39
Vase with morning glories
(bindweed)

Signature: *Gallé* needle etched and picked out in gold vertically on the outer wall and *Gallé* cast into the underside of base
Emile Gallé, Nancy
1898–1900

Colourless glass with white overlay and marquetry decoration – five purple flowers with five green leaves attached to two branching tendrils executed in etching and then carved in relief and partly polished; the ground entirely engraved with carving and *martelé* texture. The preliminary etching is discernible only in a few places.

Mounted on cast bronze base with dark brown patina 'Végétation'.

H 28 W 9.1 D 9.1 cm

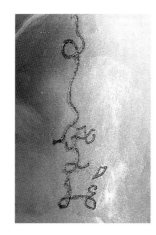

This model belongs to a rather small group of marquetry pieces that owe the impact they make to their white ground. Isolating the decoration creates an alienation effect while drawing attention to the painstakingly executed details of the floral surface design.

Pieces of this kind were shown as early as 1897, at the Champ-de-Mars Salon: see *Revue des Arts Décoratifs* 17 (1897): 342. For several models exhibited at that Salon the following year see Gallé 1898, pp. 144–45. For further pieces see Paris, *Gallé*, 1985, nos. 114–15; Newark 1989, p. 67; auct. cat. Sotheby's New York, 26 November 1993, no. 292, etc. Gallé showed a piece from this group at the 1900 Exposition Universelle in Paris in the 'Le repos dans la solitude' display case: see Paris, *Gallé*, 1985, p. 55.

Gallé registered the base on 5 March 1898. The design drawing has been donated by Gerda Koepff to the Museum für Angewandte Kunst, Cologne; illus. here p. 280, pl. 16.

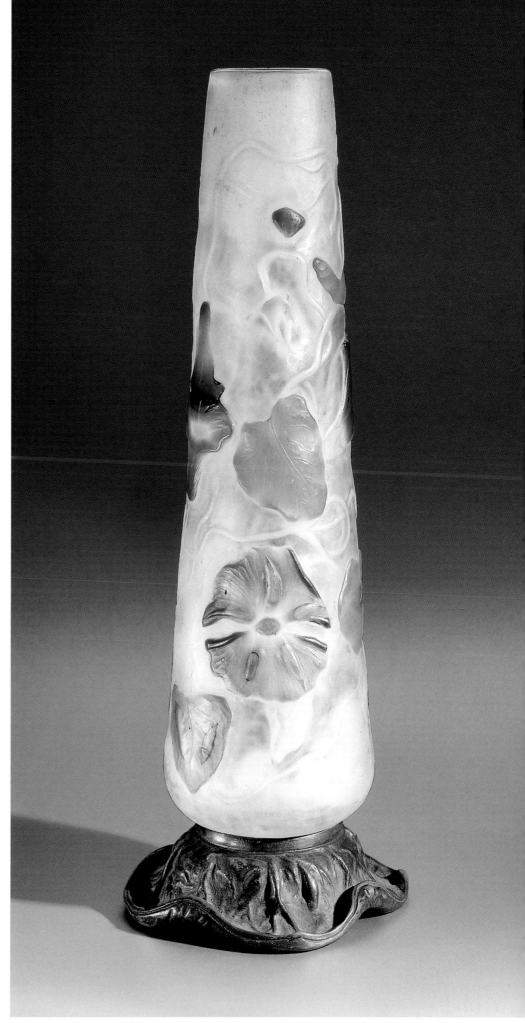

40

Vase with columbine

Signature: ‡ *E Gallé* in line
engraving on the lower outer
wall
Emile Gallé, Nancy
1898

Patinage with fine air bubbles
and several larger air bubbles
below the rim on a colourless
ground. Orange yellow overlay blown out; in the bottom
half double part casing in
dark purple and mauve. Marquetry decoration in dark
purple and orange yellow
consisting in threading and
patches, partly backed with
silvery foil. Decoration:
columbine stem and off-
shoot, with leaves, bud and
flower; on the back stem with
three leaves carved in fine-
matt relief. Lozenge-shaped
rim ground, bevelled and
polished.

Cast bronze mount with
brown patina 'Aquilegia',
screwed on to the vase.

H 26.7 W 10.7 D 6.3 cm

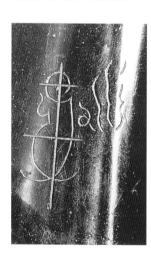

A marquetry model executed
several times, first shown in
1898 at the Champ-de-Mars
Salon of the Société Nationale
des Beaux-Arts: see Gallé 1898,
p. 148; *Dekorative Kunst 3*
(1899): 128; *L'Art Décoratif*
(March 1905): 136. For a piece
that is recognizable in the
illustration showing the 'Les
Granges' display case at the
1900 Paris Exposition Universelle see Paris, *Gallé*, 1985,
p. 54. For a parallel piece, in the
Musée de l'Ecole de Nancy,
see *Plaisir de France*, no. 405,
1972/73, p. 58. Others tend to
have ended up in Japanese collections. For some in a private
collection and in the Kitazawa
Museum, Suwa-shi, see
Yoshimizu 1985, figs. 178–79;
Gallé's Gallé 1993, no. 48; Suzuki, *Kitazawa*, 1996, no. 171; Sapporo, *Gallé*, 2000, nos. 60, 61.
For examples in the Suntory
Museum of Art, Tokyo, see
Gallé's Gallé 1993, no. 47; *Gallé
et Toulouse-Lautrec*, 1995, p. 48,
no. 32. For those in the Daimaru Museum, Tokyo, see
Tokyo, *Style floral*, 1988, no. 28;
auct. cat. Ader Picard Tajan,
Hotel Okura, Tokyo, 3 April
1990, etc.

Gallé registered the base –
specially designed for this
model, with prong-like lateral
supports formed by the
curled, horn-like spurs of the
columbine – on 5 March 1898.
The drawing has been donated
by Gerda Koepff to the Museum für Angewandte Kunst,
Cologne; illus. here p. 280,
pl. 14. The columbine motif
appeared as early as 1892, on a
vase de tristesse for the Société
Nationale des Beaux-Arts
Salon, in Gallé, *Ecrits*, 1908,
p. 126, no. XIV.

In 1902 Gallé used the vessel
type again at the Société
Nationale des Beaux-Arts Salon
for a variant with a fused glass
base, magnolia decoration and
a 'Peau de cristal' surface. The
engraved date – 1898–1902 –
refers to the re-use of the form:
see Hilschenz-Mlynek and
Ricke 1985, no. 295.

Lit.: Darmstadt 1999, cat.
no. 318.

41

Footed vase with columbine

Signature: *Gallé* in double line engraving on the outer wall
Emile Gallé, Nancy
1898–1900

Colourless body with milky pink and yellow-tinged casing; blown into an eight-piece ribbed optic mould. Marquetry decoration consisting of columbine leaves, flower and bud in yellow, colourless, light green and reddish brown under yellow overlay, all on a white ground, partly worked into the wall. The foot cased in dusty pink was made separately and fused on; four fused-on solid columbine spurs of colourless glass with greyish brown, slightly iridescent powdered glass fused on. The green leaves, the columbine flower and the bud semi-matt, the ground round the flower engraved with *martelé* texture. Foot hollow, pontil mark ground and polished, leaving a concavity.

H 28 Ø foot 6.4 cm

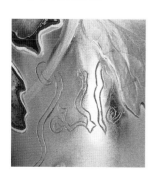

The vases with columbine decoration, representing variations in form on the flower itself with its horn-like spurs, are among the most successful marquetry models. They were made in various sizes and diameters.

The mount in the Koepff Collection represents the most slender version, which was circulated most widely and made in several variants.

For further models of the type in the Koepff Collection see the Musée de l'Ecole de Nancy collection, Nancy, inv. no. 002.9.1; Garner, *El Fituri*, 1982, no. 49; Suntory 1983, no. 1; *Art of Gallé* 1988, nos. 88–89; Newark 1989, p. 69; auct. cat. Sotheby's London, 25 October 1991; auct. cat. Drouot Montaigne, Paris, 2 October 1992, no. 196. For those in the Suntory Museum of Art, Tokyo, see Tokyo, *Gallé*, 1980, no. 95; *Gallé et Toulouse-Lautrec* 1995, pp. 40–41, no. 28; *Gallé's Gallé* 1993, no. 46; Sapporo, *Gallé*, 2000, no. 64, etc.

For a similar model, but with a livelier profile and more elongated points on the mouth as well as more slender columbine spurs that are applied higher up, see Duncan and de Bartha 1984, fig. 110; auct. cat. Christie's Geneva, 8 May 1983, no. 344; Sun Kurino 1995, no. 35, etc.

The columbine motif appears as early as 1892, on a *vase de tristesse* for the Société Nationale des Beaux-Arts Salon, in Gallé, *Ecrits*, 1908, p. 126, no. XIV. For the columbine decoration see drawing no. 33 for the registration of 5 March 1898, illus. here p. 284. Gallé also registered a lamp with the flower-shaped foot on 1 July 1902; on this and for further parallel forms and variants see Hilschenz-Mlynek and Ricke 1985, no. 272.

Lit.: Nancy 1999, cat. no. 102, illus. p. 299.

42

'Les Bleuets' (cornflowers) footed vase

Signature: *Gallé* engraved on the outer wall
Emile Gallé, Nancy
1898–1900

Colourless glass cased with dusty pink. Sixteen vertical threads – colourless core, dipped in white and amber – were laid into the mould to fuse with the surface when the glass was blown in. Marquetry of opaque, milky green stems and three cased pieces in white beneath bluish purple, carved into cornflowers. One has been cut down to the white ground. The blue flowers are accompanied by three lanceolate leaves, matt with shallow engraving. The vertical threads between the petals were removed with the engraving tool. The separately blown and fused-on hollow foot is tinted light amber and slightly opalescent with milky mauve powdered glass and pigment inclusions, which have become green (striking colour) on the surface and are full of air bubbles. The rim has been pinched. The foot-rim ground flat and polished.

H 20.2 Ø 11.7 cm

Mould-blown vessels bearing fruit, flowers or buds are infrequently encountered in the marquetry pieces. Once dubbed 'the artichoke', the shape of the vase echoes that of the cornflower bud. The actual name is verified by the inscription on an exemplar in the Philadelphia Museum of Art, Philadelphia, PA: *Les bleuets la trouvaient belle: Victor Hugo*: see *La Gloire de Victor Hugo*, exh. cat., Galeries Nationales du Grand Palais, Paris (Paris, 1985), no. 930.

There are comparatively few verified parallels. One variant of this model was shown in the 'Les Granges' display case at the 1900 Paris Exposition Universelle: see Paris, *Gallé*, 1985, p. 54. For further examples, in the Felix Marcilhac Collection, Paris, see Garner 1976, p. 157;

Munich, *Nancy 1900*, 1980, no. 245, illus. p. 95; *Art of Gallé* 1988, no. 81, etc.

Lit.: Dr. Heuser & Co, *Miscellanea* 4, no. 2 (April 1971); Darmstadt 1999, cat. no. 306.

43
Rod-shaped vase with iris

Signature: *Gallé* in partly raised, partly sunk engraving on the outer wall
Emile Gallé, Nancy
1898–1900

Light smoky brown glass with white patinage full of fine streaks and seeds (minute air bubbles) melted in. In the lower zone partly cased in yellowish brown, diagonal and wavy inclusions of purple, dark and light yellow threading. Polychrome marquetry decoration – iris and leaves – formed of partly superimposed, melted on and worked in sections of threading and patches in purple, light green, yellowish brown and white, partly with powdered glass inclusions. The decoration is emphasized by shallow relief engraving; the ground, including the rim and floor, engraved with carved and *martelé* texturing.

H 21.2 Ø 7.6 cm

The shape represents a reversion to Gallé's standard repertoire of forms in the 1880s. Representations of iris or flags, on the other hand, are quite rare on marquetry models. A very similar example was published as early as 1899: see *La Lorraine Artiste* 17 (1899): 5. Another is recognizable in the picture of the 'Les Granges' display case at the 1900 Paris Exposition Universelle: see Paris, *Gallé*, 1985, p. 54.

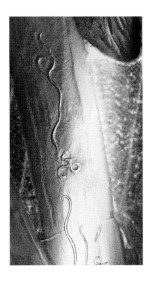

For a very similar piece, donated by David Nillet in 1933 to the Musée des Arts Décoratifs, Paris, see Tokyo, *Gallé*, 1980, no. 48. For a further variant see auct. cat. Sotheby's New York, 26 and 27 November 1993, no. 297. For a vase different in form but with the same decoration see Duncan and de Bartha 1984, fig. 131. The model was also produced in simpler techniques – acid-etched and polished: see, for instance, auct. cat. Ketterer, Munich, 16 November 1984, no. 51.

Lit.: Zons 2002, cat. no. A 6, p. 170, with illus.

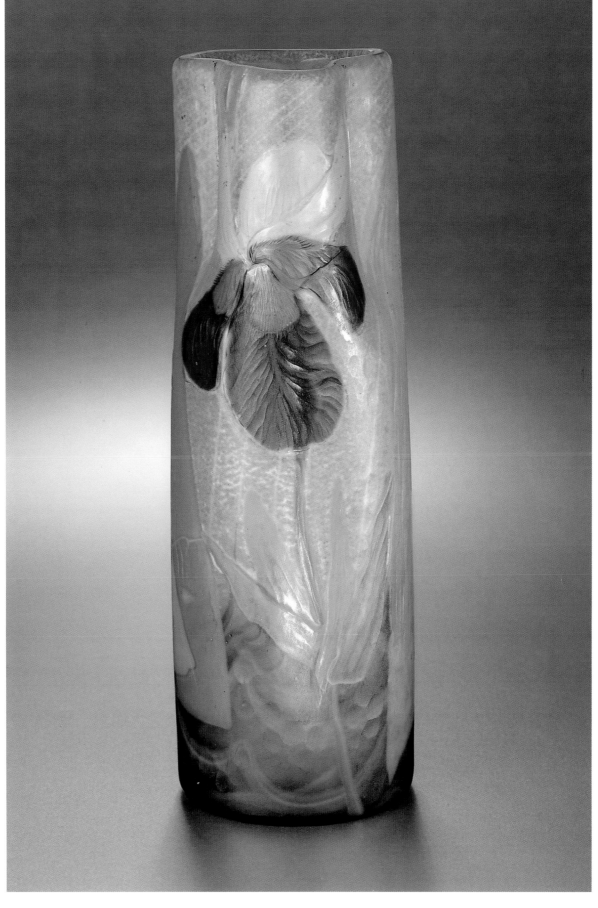

44

'Petits sourires et grandes larmes' vase

Signature: *Gallé* engraved in relief on the lower outer wall
Emile Gallé, Nancy
1898–1900

Colourless glass with fine-grained white patinage melted in throughout and full of seeds (minute air bubbles), superimposed fused-on silvery metal foil, partly cased – in the lower third in dark yellow, in the upper half purple as well as a purple glass patch above the foil inclusions. On the neck two trailing prunts of colourless glass with silver compounds melted on.

Decoration in variably polished relief engraving: irises hanging upside down, the ground partly worked over in a *martelé* texture. Two more leaves on the back of the neck. In the lower half clouds and the inscription *Petits sourires et grandes larmes* (Small smiles and large tears).

H 54.7 W 17.6 D 14.9 cm

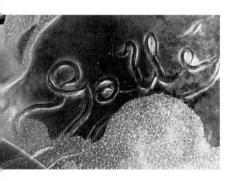

The form of this rather rare marquetry model is a variation on a long-necked type common at the time, which Gallé made shortly before 1900 in different versions – usually as a long-necked flask on a bronze base. The impression of lightness created by the narrow, tubular neck is counteracted by the heaviness of the trailing prunts, gathering volume as they trickle down, and the drooping irises. Add the quotation from the Belgian Symbolist Maurice Maeterlinck and the overall effect is one of melancholy, making this piece a *vase de tristesse*.

Similar pieces can be found in the Ise Collection: see *Exhibition of Art Nouveau Glass*, exh. cat., Art Gallery, Toyama-shi (Toyama, 1990), no. 9; further exemplars in Duncan and de Bartha 1984, no. 151 b; auct. cat. Drouot Montaigne, Paris, 16 November 1993, no. 64, all bearing the same inscription, another, without the inscription, in auct. cat. Enghien Lyons, 26 October 1980, no. 23. For a variant with a shorter neck and without foil inclusions see *Art of Gallé* 1988, no. 27.

Lit.: Darmstadt 1999, cat. no. 327; Nancy 1999, cat. no. 101, illus. p. 175.

45

Vase with underwater scene

Signature: *Gallé* engraved in relief on the outer wall
Emile Gallé, Nancy
c. 1900

On colourless glass yellowish brown and white streaks of coloured granules or splinters drawn diagonally and alternating with fine grey seed (air bubble) patinage. The floor partly cased in brownish red. Black patches applied to surface. The entire surface and floor textured with engraving. Decoration: various types of marine flora, including stipes of oarweed and bladder wrack, and three different seashells and snails in meticulously modelled relief. The greyish black seaweed continues in the colour of the ground on the underside of the floor, which is textured with carving.

H 13.5 Ø 11.5 cm D 9.3 cm

This vase represents a reversion to the repertoire of classically simple East Asian forms Gallé was so fond of varying: see, for instance, Hilschenz-Mlynek and Ricke 1985, no. 210. It is a superlative small studio piece. A typical collector's item, the vase must be looked at close up, held in one's hand and turned around in good light. The atmospheric qualities of the motifs are then revealed – flowing water, plants floating in it, motionless marine life and the reflection of light falling on the scene from outside – as a mysterious, unfathomable aesthetic whole.

For a second model, with the same shape but slightly different decoration, see auct. cat. Jean Claude Anaf, Lyons, 27 November 1990. For pieces of this kind shown at the Ecole de Nancy exhibition in Paris see Paris 1903, 2nd ser., pl. 5, no. 3, and Zurich 1980, no. 136.

46

Vase with cuckoo and primroses

Signature: *Gallé* engraved in relief on the right narrow face
Emile Gallé, Nancy
c. 1899/1900

White streaks drawn diagonally in green glass. Marquetry of overlay patches – opaque dark purple and mauve, yellow, transparent yellowish brown, partly backed in white; on the back a large patch of overlay in white and oxblood with partly melted-on silver compounds (striking colours). Rim ground and bevelled. Marquetry decoration – a cuckoo perched on the branch of an apple tree with buds and flowers, primroses – carved in high relief. On both sides, the floor and the upper half of the back are fine matt cut with *martelé*

texture; in the lower part a mountain landscape is suggested.

H 12 W 14.6 D 6.3 cm

Not many variants of this elaborately wrought vase were made. Gallé's contemporaries, however, seem to have considered it to be quite typical of his late work. A similar piece was used to illustrate both Gustav E. Pazaurek's obituary of Gallé in *Mitteilungen des Nordböhmischen Gewerbemuseums* XXII, no. 3 (1904): 77, and the obituary in *Deutsche Kunst und Dekoration* (October 1904): 137. For another version of this model see *Art of Gallé* 1988, no. 37,

which is the same piece in Yoshimizu 1992, no. 55. Gallé rarely used this type of marquetry decoration. For a vase similar in conception see Garner, *El Fituri*, 1982, no. 35.

The preliminary colour sketch of this model is in the Musée d'Orsay (illus. below): see Thiébaut, *Dessins*, 1993, p. 124. Like other drawings of such exceptional pieces, it shows the leeway allowed glassmakers and engravers in execution.

Japanese-inspired, the image is enlivened by the colour contrast between the two main motifs, which achieve a harmonious balance by being tied into the surface, with the picture reserve framed. Gallé used similar motifs for intarsia on furniture: see P. Thiébaut, 'Un meuble aux ombellifères d'Emile Gallé au Musée des Beaux-Arts de Lyon', *La Revue du Louvre* 4 (1990): 299–306; Thiébaut, *Dessins*, 1993, p. 186.

The form is a truncated version of a type used in the early 1880s: see, for instance, Hilschenz-Mlynek and Ricke 1985, no. 183, which in turn originated in the forms used for Japanese lacquer boxes and bronze vessels – see, for instance, Bing, *Formenschatz*, 1888–91, vol. 15, pl. AFI – and was adapted in France for pottery jars and jugs: see Jacqueline du Pasquier, *Jules Vieillard & Cie.: Eclectisme et Japonisme*, exh. cat. (Bordeaux, 1986), no. 128.

Lit.: *Sammeln* 10 (1984): 18; Duncan, *Salons*, 1998, p. 40.

47

'Nature' bowl

Signature: *Gallé* engraved on
the outer wall
Emile Gallé, Nancy
1900

On a colourless body milky
yellow, slightly bubbly casing,
blown out in the lower section, partly cased in dark purple with scattered melted-on
silver compounds, halfway
up the purple lower zone
partly cased in orange yellow.
Freely applied in low relief:
yellow-tinged greyish white
leaf or tree canopy shapes
with a speckled, slightly iridescent surface created by
melting on silver compounds
(striking colours).

H 14.1 Ø 23.5 cm

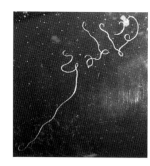

The model is a small version
of the central piece in the
'Repos dans la solitude' display
case at the 1900 Paris Exposition Universelle. Gallé called
it 'La Grande Communion de
la nature' and it is now in the
Musée Municipal de Cognac:
see Paris, *Gallé*, 1985, no. 129,
with further references. An
exemplar of the small version
was exhibited in the same showcase: see Thiébaut, *Dessins*,
1993, p. 141; Paris, *Gallé*, 1985, p.
304. The present piece was published as early as 1901 by Gustav
E. Pazaurek (illus. above, right).

This model links elements of
atmospheric landscape with a
stylized tree in a symbolic representation of nature bordering on complete abstraction. It
rapidly became so popular that
a comparatively large number
of copies and variants was produced. There were, however,
not many copies of the large
model (approx. 43 cm in diameter): see auct. cat. Enghien
Lyons, 29 March 1987, no. 10.
For pieces in the Daimaru
Museum, Tokyo, see Tokyo,
Style floral, 1988, no. 46. A large
footed variant is reproduced in
Marx 1911, p. 248.

There are several exemplars of
the small version, including the
one in the Koepff Collection:
see, for instance, Musée de
l'Ecole de Nancy, Charpentier
et al. 1987, p. 91; for a piece
with the inscription *Venez, cher-
chons un site solitaire et prenons
un peu de repos* (Come, let us
seek out a solitary spot and

take some rest) see auct. cat.
Drouot Paris, 13 November
1974, no. 48; auct. cat. Drouot
Paris, 24 March 1988, no. 76;
auct. cat. Sotheby's New York,
11 June 1992, no. 42; Yoshimizu
1992, no. 51; Mukai, *Hida
Takayama*, 1997, p. 117.

Both the motif and the
abstract conception of landscape were used at the 1900
Paris Exposition Universelle
for a number of large vessels:
see, for instance, the 'Paysage
de verre' vase, illustrated in
Revue des Arts Décoratifs, no. 11

(1900); for a variant in the
Count Foulon de Vaux Collection see Duncan and de Bartha
1984, p. 127.

Lit.: Pazaurek 1901, p. 87,
fig. 78; Garner 1976, p. 139;
Duncan and de Bartha 1984,
no. 140; Duncan, *Salons*, 1998,
p. 218 (illus. from Pazaurek).

48
Rod-shaped vase with bronze foot

Signature: *Gallé 1900* needle etched on the lower outer wall and *Gallé* cast beneath the base
Emile Gallé, Nancy
1900

Colourless glass over light smoky brown body; purple threading drawn into shapes like ears of grain and dense, fine-grained white inclusions under a layer of smoky brown glass with white powdered glass fused on or deliberately induced decomposition in places. Polychrome marquetry decoration of thread segments and patches, melted on and worked in; some of the patches made of overlay glass on a ground of white.

Decoration: clover, wildflowers and ears of grain, accentuated by partly frosted etching and engraving.

Mounted on a cast bronze foot with dark brown patina: 'Végétation'.

H 25.2 Ø foot 9.1 cm

A rather rare variant of the marquetry technique. The rough surface is a result of Gallé's experimentation with creating new textures, which he called 'Peau de cristal' (glass pelt). For related pieces see, for instance, Duncan and de Bartha 1984, fig. 151 a; Suzuki, *Kitazawa*, 1996, no. 162; for an inferior version without a foot see *Art of Gallé* 1988, no. 18; for a truncated variant in the Museum für Angewandte Kunst, Cologne, see special issue of the *Kölner Museums-Bulletin: 100 Jahre Museum für Angewandte Kunst – 100 Jahre Mäzenatentum* (1988): 19.

Gallé registered the foot on 5 March 1898. The drawing has been donated by Gerda Koepff to the Museum für Angewandte Kunst, Cologne: see illus. here on p. 280, pl. 16.

Lit.: Nancy 1999, cat. no. 120, illus. p. 301.

49
Vase with freshwater fish motifs

Signature: *Gallé* engraved on the outer wall
Emile Gallé, Nancy
c. 1899/1900

Thick-walled vessel of colourless glass with sandwiched casing in milky light greyish green, in the lower zone pigment inclusions and powdered glass in greys, browns, greens and dark reds with air bubbles and mica particles throughout. Three striking applications of colourless glass, partly cased in white and reddish brown (the sturgeon), in grey (the trout) and streaked with mauve and purple (the pike). The body of the vessel shaped with fine-matt cut grooves, the fish heads engraved in relief and ground fine-matt.

H 18.8 Ø 17 cm

A one-off 'grand genre' piece revealing an entirely new approach to the representation of aquatic fauna. The emphasis on atmospheric qualities and mood – here a riparian scene after a rain – has been retained, yet more is depicted than an underwater scene. What is represented is the surface of a river, broken through by the heads of three fish. The forcefully plastic quality of modelling distinguishing these three freshwater fish – a sturgeon, a pike and a trout – anticipates Gallé's late work. Gallé's conception of form and design may have been inspired by an ancient Chinese bronze vase from the collection of the Duchesse de Morny (illus. p. 23, bottom right), reproduced in Philippe Burty's book *Chefs-d'œuvre des arts industriels*, with

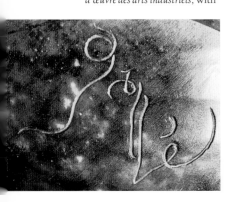

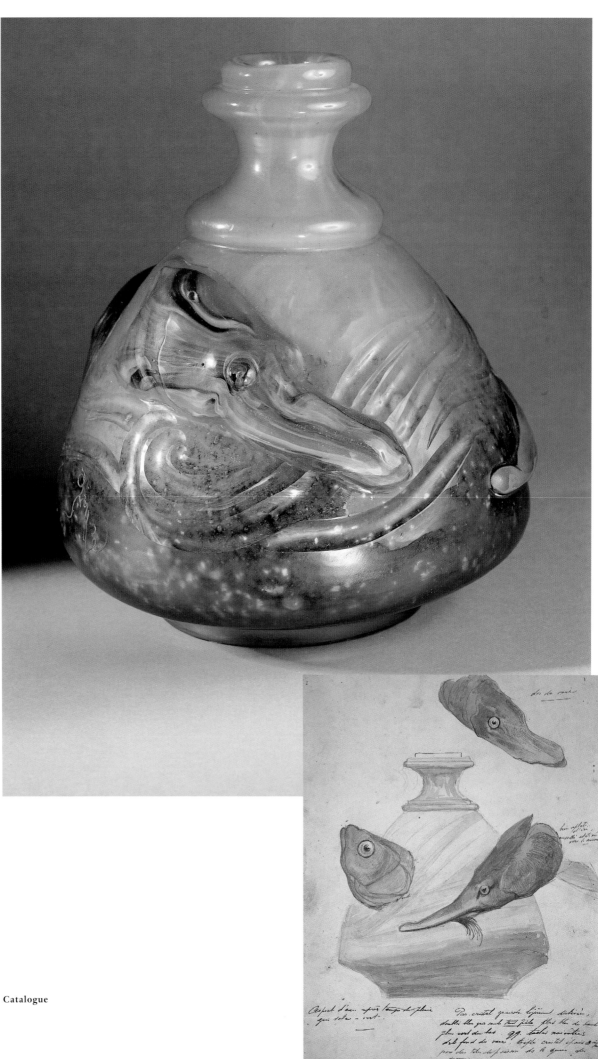

fish decoration that is almost fully in the round, especially since the author, a well-known connoisseur of Asian art, makes a point of going into the unusual plasticity figuring in the design of this bronze vase: see Burty 1866, p. 403, with illus.

The preliminary sketch in the Musée d'Orsay (illus. p. 138, bottom right) furnishes instructions for execution, which accurately describe the technique and colour scheme to be used:

Top: *dos de vase* (back of vase). Next to the sturgeon's head: *bien aplati / d'ici, / collé et étiré / vers le museau* (well flattened / from here, / fused and drawn out / towards the jaws).

Bottom left: *Aspect de l'eau après temps de pluie / gris salevert* (The appearance of water following rain / dirty grey green).

Bottom right: *Par.[aison] cristal graissée légèrement déclinée* [?], / *doublée bleu gris saule tout pâle plus bleu du haut / plus vert du / bas. Qq.* [Quelques] *taches noirâtres / d*[an]*s le fond du vase, triplé cristal épais 3 mm / pose des têtes de poisson d*[an]*s le genre des and têtards* (Muddy parison slightly declined [= held at an angle], / cased bluish grey willow, more blue at top / more green / at bottom. Some blackish patches / in the floor of the vase, triple glass overlay 3 mm thick / pose of fish heads in the manner of tadpoles): see Thiébaut, *Dessins*, 1993, p. 180.

The mention of tadpoles must refer to the model featuring the metamorphosis of tadpoles to frogs, which was designed for the 1889 Paris Exposition Universelle and made again in several variants shortly before 1900: see, for instance, Corning 1984, no. 32.

Lit.: *L'Oeil: Revue d'Art*, no. 320 (March 1982): 58; *Sammeln* 10 (1984): 18; Duncan and de Bartha 1984, fig. 115; Marshall 1990, p. 148; Duncan, *Salons*, 1998, p. 232; Darmstadt 1999, cat. no. 342.

50

Vase

Signature: *Gallé* in line
engraving on the outer wall
Emile Gallé, Nancy
c. 1900–1902

Colourless glass with sandwiched casing in slightly
opalescent milky greenish
grey and superimposed
fused-on flower-shaped glass
patches in beige with dark red
overlay, on the back in brownish black; dipped in colorless
glass; inclusions of strewn silica grains under the last thin
layer. Air bubbles surround
the grains. Freely blown and
formed, oval in section.

H 19.6 W 13.8 D 10 cm

A rare model without any
finishing or applied decoration.
The deliberately haphazardly
strewn cased-in decoration
of simplified flower and bud
motifs recalls magnolias at first
glance, yet are open to other
interpretations. The aim of the
design is to evoke an impression of the threat of a sudden
wintry cold spell to burgeoning
life.

A related vase is in a photograph of the 1900 Paris Exposition Universelle: see Nicolas
1900/1901, February 1901,
p. 53; reproduced in Duncan
and de Bartha 1984, fig. 130.
Similar in form and with a
comparable ground, it also
features marquetry applications that take the form of
underwater motifs.

Another vase from this small
experimental group is the sil-
ver-mounted Bonvallet exemplar: see M. Demaison, 'Les
Montures de Vases', *Art &
Décoration* (1902): 206.

51

Beaker-shaped vase with tsuba (sword guard)

Signature: *Gallé* engraved low on the outer wall
Emile Gallé, Nancy
c. 1900

Colourless glass with fine-grained, whitish, melted-in patinage with seeds (minute air bubbles) and crazed texture. Double casing in light blue and opaque dark grey; sporadic flecks of brown. Decoration: three Japanese sword guards (*tsuba*) with iris, mistletoe and grasses surrounded by spiralling foliate tendrils with enclosed floral rosettes (a Japanese textile pattern); relief and needle etching, supplemented in places by line and matt engraving.

H 16.6 Ø 9.3 cm

A common form with different decoration schemes, some of them intricately engraved, most of which are *vases de tristesse*: see, for instance, Tokyo, *Gallé*, 1980, nos. 64–65; Yoshimizu 1985, no. 144; Suzuki, *Kitazawa*, 1996, nos. 181–82. Gallé exhibited one model in the 'Le Repos dans la solitude' showcase at the 1900 Paris Exposition Universelle: see Paris, *Gallé*, 1985, p. 304.

The triple *tsuba* motif was used particularly often on vases of this shape, albeit usually with a simple greyish brown overlay: see Hilschenz-Mlynek and Ricke 1985, no. 281, dated 1900, with further references; see also two exemplars in auct. cat. Drouot Richelieu, Paris, 2 June 1989, nos. 79–80, etc. Its encased patinage and light blue inner casing make the piece in the Koepff Collection stand out among the numerous vases in this group.

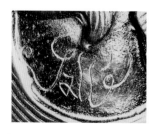

52

Vase with underwater decoration

Signature: *Gallé* etched in relief on the outer wall, 7 engraved on the underside
Emile Gallé, Nancy
1900

Colourless glass with glittering silver inclusions (presumably mica), oxblood overlay and fused-on silver compounds, gleaming in all the tints of striking colours, ranging from light blue to opaque ochre yellow. Applications: freely formed sea-fish handle (John Dory), colourless, tinted amber with silver stain; shell, white with dusty pink overlay; shell, light beige with dusty pink streaks; starfish in grey and beige tones with an opaque light blue centre. Between the applications simple etched decoration in low relief consisting of various species of seaweed as well as an engraved sea snail and shell. Matt carving from the rim and continuing on to the inner wall. Floor ground with faint carving.

H 12.9 Ø 11.2 cm

Bears witness to continued efforts to achieve new designs with marine decoration. The underwater scene with kelp, seaweed and seashells is linked with surface effects evoking associations of sea spray or foam. The sculptural application emphasize the emphatically tactile quality of the vessel at the expense of atmospheric qualities.

Numerous variants exist. For those in the Anne Marie Gillion-Crowet Collection, Brussels, see Grover 1970, no. 302; for those in the M. Manukian Collection, see Bloch-Dermant 1980, p. 72; Garner 1976, p. 92; for particularly detailed variants see auct. cat. Sotheby's Monaco, 23 June 1979, no. 50; Garner, *El Fituri*, 1982, no. 61; for exemplars in Japanese private collections see Tokyo, *Gallé* 1980, no. 99; Yoshimizu 1985, figs. 159–60; for those in the Daimaru Museum, Tokyo, see Tokyo, *Style floral*, 1988, no. 34; auct. cat. Sotheby's New York, 10 and 11 March 1989, no. 112; for those in the Suntory Museum of Art, Tokyo, see *Gallé's Gallé* 1993, no. 32; *Gallé et Toulouse-Lautrec* 1995, p. 72, no. 50; for those in the Hida Takayama Museum of Art see Mukai, *Hida Takayama*, 1997, p. 116; Sapporo 2000, cat. nos. 106–7, etc. A simplified but elongated version was issued in 1901 in a limited edition for the 'Amis du Bibelot' association: see Paris, *Gallé*, 1985, p. 42.

53

Footed vase with bats

Signature: *Gallé*
engraved on the foot
Emile Gallé, Nancy
c. 1900

Colourless glass covering the body (with silver content) and yellow quadruple casing in white; yellow, red and black as well as silver compounds melted on throughout, in places reduced to metallic silver precipitation. Rim pinched . Floor ground and matt-etched. Simple etched relief decoration: four geometric window ornaments, in the upper section four stylized bats in different phases of flight, contours in matt prismatic or step engraving, the ground for the most part worked over with engraving, partly in finely textured carving.

H 41.8 Ø 19.8 cm

A late version of the bat motif in a particularly striking colour scheme (see here cat. nos. 30 and 54). The framing element suggests an architectural context, perhaps a tower and parapet, while the colour of the ground evokes a crepuscular mood. In the bat representa-

tions naturalistic details have been eschewed; the motif is reduced to a silhouette-like contour. This has made it possible to achieve a mysterious alienation effect with the skilfully deployed textural properties of the greyish metallic reduction-fired silver com-

pounds. The model was made in a limited edition. Only a few similar pieces are extant: see auct. cat. Enghien Lyons, 28 October 1979 – practically identical in size but with a deep blue tinge to the silver compounds melted on to the surface.

In its overall appearance – red compounds casing and reduced silver compounds – this vase closely resembles the celebrated large lamp with a Joan of Arc battle scene after Victor Prouvé (for the design see Thiébaut, *Dessins*, 1993, p. 57), now in the Sun Kurino Museum in Atami, Japan: see Sun Kurino 1995, pp. 19–20.

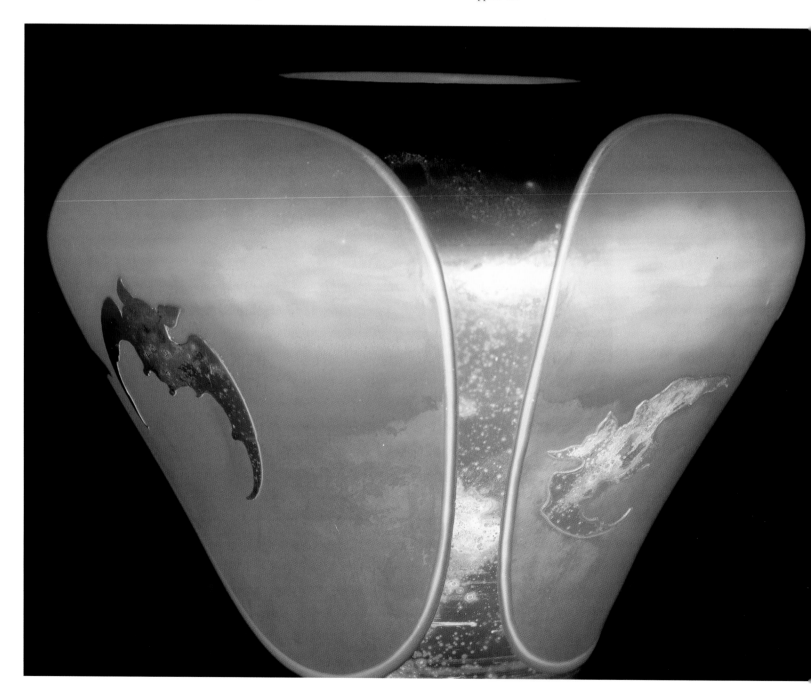

54
Club vase with bats

Signature: *Gallé* in engraving on the lower outer wall and vertically in relief engraving on the underside
Emile Gallé, Nancy
c. 1900

Red, semi-opaque casing over colourless glass with salmon-tinted inner layer and inclusions of white grainy particles melted in densely throughout; on the surface silver compound, which has in places been reduced to metallic precipitation. Freely formed, the upper part of the wall flattened on two sides, rim pinched. The foot-rim ground flat, floor centre textured with matt carving. Decoration: on the front one bat, on the back two between clouds as silhouettes with no drawing within the contours; ground partly engraved with fine carving.

H 19　W 7.3　D 6 cm

This vase is associated with the technical experiments to which Gallé repeatedly returned from the 1880s: see, for instance, the vase inscribed *Etude de matière,* Hilschenz-Mlynek and Ricke 1885, no. 230.

For further examples of the creative possibilities afforded by reduction-firing of silver compounds on coloured glass, which, depending on how highly concentrated they are, can trigger off metallic precipitation, see cat. nos. 38, 44, 47, 52, 53, 56, 58.

Lit.: J. Bloch-Dermant, *Guidargus de la verrerie* (Paris, 1985), p. 213.

55
Vase with gentian, morning glories and cicada

Signature: *Gallé* engraved in relief on the lower outer wall
Emile Gallé, Nancy
c. 1900–1902 or Gallé successor

Colourless glass over blown-out blue and metallic compound inclusions, blue powdered glass of non-uniform grain and particles of gold leaf. Floor ground fine matt. Decoration: an arrangement of gentian, morning glories, a cicada in flight and a snail on a large leaf; executed in powerful, partly polished relief engraving, extensive areas of the ground worked over to create a coarse, blurred, *martelé* texture.

H 29.4 Ø 10.7 cm

The consummate engraving does not match the dynamic, subtle cutting technique of the

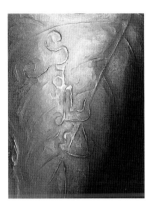

years preceding 1900 but instead exploits the full gamut of sophisticated modelling techniques made possible by relief cutting. The uniformity of register achieved in the handling of the various plants together with a snail and a flying cicada is remarkable. It can be assumed that, during Gallé's last years, his studio was given a great deal of leeway in the conception of such decoration from the inventory of forms and

model drawings available to it in order to meet the demand for fine engraving. Gallé personally tended to be more interested in exploring marquetry techniques and highly sculptural work during those years.

A fairly large number of pieces from this high-relief group are reproduced in Hilschenz-Mlynek and Ricke 1985, nos. 296–303. Since the present piece does not bear the simple

signature characteristic of this group, it was probably made shortly before or after 1900, although a much later date in the Gallé style is also conceivable.

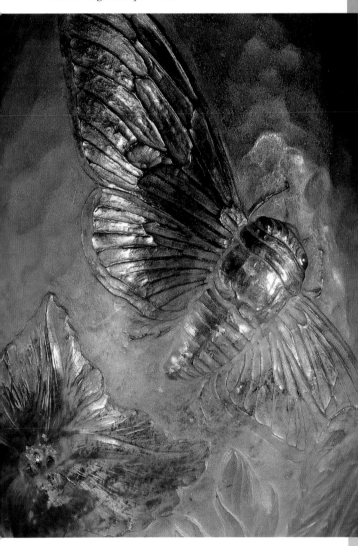

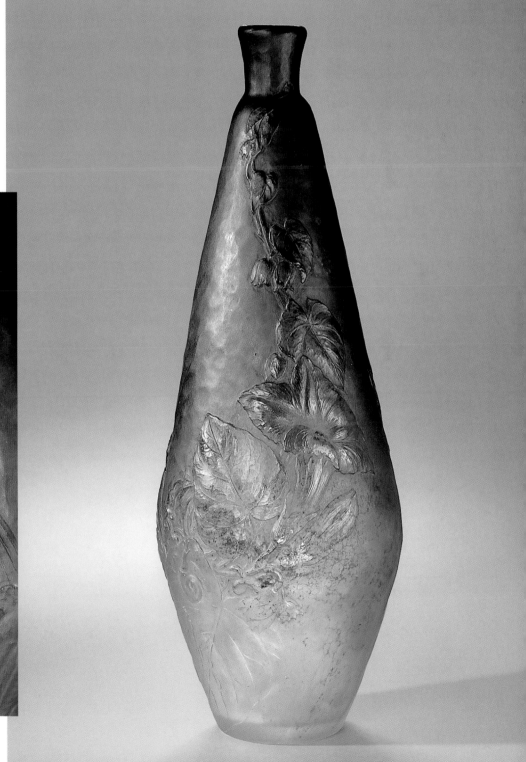

56

Vase with pasque flowers

Signature: *Gallé* engraved in relief on the outer wall
Emile Gallé, Nancy
c. 1900–1902

In colourless glass fine grey patinage, shading to black in the coarser particles; melted in pigments and powdered glass in blue, purple, orange and grey, cased in thin, milky greyish white. On the floor amber-coloured casing, silver compounds partly fused on (striking colours). Applications in deep purple and colourless with white and green. Floor carved fine-matt. Decoration: pasque flowers elaborately carved, against a matt *martelé* ground.

H 13.4 W 8.9 D 7.1 cm

This model represents a combination of the sculptural design principle informing Gallé's late work and elaborate relief engraving pushed to its technical limits. The potential for enlivening the decoration with striking inclusions and the creation of mysterious effects in the wall, which suggests an unfathomable depth, has been exploited to the full.

Even though the floral decoration can be identified with the aid of the preliminary sketch for cat. no. 57 as the flower and bud of the common European pasque flower (*Pulsatilla vulgaris*), the underlying intention is not a botanically accurate reproduction of a particular plant. Instead it is a generalizing statement about the process of budding and flowering, which reflects the idea of beauty unfolding. On the formation of the flowers see also *Art of Gallé* 1988, no. 79.

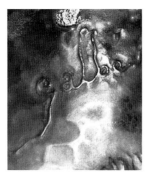

57

Vase with hazel catkins

Signature: *Gallé* in line
engraving on the outer wall
Emile Gallé, Nancy
c. 1900–1902

Pigment inclusions and powdered glass in purple, bluish
green, dark red and black
melted into a colourless body,
air bubbles and metallic inclusions; cloudy, milky grey
overlay and opaque greyish
brown casing; brownish
green overlay in part on the
floor. Two applications in
blue and deep purple. Floor
ground, with carved texture.
Decoration: hazel catkins,
pasque flower buds and trees
suggesting a landscape; in
relief etching and semi-matt
relief engraving, the entire
surface with a matt *martelé*
texture.

H 13.4 W 8.8 D 7.1 cm

This vase almost perfectly
exemplifies the ideals realized
in cat. no. 56. For an extant preliminary sketch of this piece
see Sotheby's Monaco, 4 April
1993, no. 40, now in the Musée
de l'Ecole de Nancy, which features the principal elements of
the composition (illus. below).

The present piece strays fur-
thest from the drawing of the
three versions of the model
known. Close to the sketch,
although not directly reproducing it, is the Claudius Côtes
bequest version, which went
to the Musée des Beaux-Arts,
Lyons, in 1961: see *Bulletin des
Musées et monuments Lyonnais* 1
(1989): 24–25; C. Briend, *Les
Objets d'Art: Musée des Beaux-
Arts de Lyon* (Lyons, 1993), p. 90,
no. 135. In this version sculptural applications have been
eschewed; sophisticated relief
cutting is developed on the surface. The inner wall is accentuated by metal inclusions and
the overall impression created
is one of delicacy and atmospheric effects.

The plant represented can be
identified from the drawing, in
which the flowers and the
feathery leaves reveal it to be

the common European pasque
flower. The motif recurs several times in Gallé's late work:
see, for instance, Takeda and
Olivié 1996, no. 15; *Gallé et
Toulouse-Lautrec* 1995, p. 62,
no. 43.

The motif is rendered more
boldly on a version in the Neu-
mann Collection, Château de
Gingins: see Corning 1984, no.
29, the same as Duncan and
de Bartha 1984, fig. 55 c;
Yoshimizu 1985, fig. 73; *Art of
Gallé* 1988, no. 78; Bartha,
Collection Neumann, 1993, p. 99.
The sculptural effect is more

pronounced yet the engraving is much cruder in detail.
Closely related to this version
is another exemplar without
hazel catkins but with the
motif of the pasque flower
growing up out of the floor of
the vase: see *Art of Gallé*, 1988,
no. 79.

The vase in the Koepff Collection goes far beyond the other
known variants in its sculptural
effects, yet the engraving is not
nearly as sophisticated. What
is new in this version is the
limitation to only two stages
of bud, which could not be

identified as a pasque flower
without knowledge of the
drawing and the other versions
of the motif. The suggestion
of a wooded landscape on the
narrow face of the vase is
another feature that sets it
apart from the other variants.

58

Lamp with landscape and swallows

Signature: *Gallé* etched in relief on the shade and low on the shaft
Emile Gallé, Nancy
c. 1900–1904

Colourless glass over milky yellow-tinged white body; triply cased in milky yellowish white, orange red shading into brown and black; silver compounds irregularly fused on and reduced in places to metallic precipitation. The shoulder of the foot has been formed so that it is oval in section.

Shade: Decoration – ten swallows in flight – etched in relief in one stage.

Foot: Decoration – a landscape with a pond and copses – etched in two stages. Almost the entire ground carved to a fine-matt texture. The tip of the shade and foot-rim ground fine-matt.

Original brass mount with new lamp-holders

H 56 cm (including mount)
Foot 36; shade 15.5 cm
Ø foot 14.5; shade 28.4 cm

One of the most successful serially produced luxury wares with widely variable decoration, this lamp was in production long after Gallé's death.

The additional effects achieved by silver reduction and the meticulous working over with cutting make the exemplar in the Koepff Collection stand out from the rest of the range. For the same model in conventional acid-etching and without silver reduction see, for instance, auct. cat. Sotheby's London, 19 December 1986, no. 130; for a model with light silver reduction see *La Gazette du Hôtel Drouot*, no. 22 (1 June 1990); for further variants see Franzke 1987, cat. no. 83, illus. in picture section; auct. cat. Drouot Paris, 13 and 14 November 1996, no. 60.

Loaded as it is with connotative associations, the combination of birds on the shade suggesting the sky with a landscape on the foot was varied considerably: see the widespread combination of an Alpine landscape with soaring eagles, Hilschenz-Mlynek and Ricke 1985, no. 349. Other widely circulated combinations are trees with butterflies, irises on the foot and dragonflies on the shade, etc. For the swallow motif in Gallé's work see also the designs registered in 1898: nos. 3, 6, 7; here pp. 278–79.

Lit.: Darmstadt 1999, illus. p. 308.

59
Plate with octopus

Signature: *Gallé* deeply etched
on the underside
Emile Gallé, Nancy
c. 1902–4

Colourless glass with flecked
white inclusions; irregular
glass granules with a silver
content or splinters in honey
yellow shading to brownish
black melted into the underside. On the upper surface
five dark yellow applications
backed with foil and powdered glass in reds and browns:
three large (scallop shell and
seashells) and two small ones
(the eyes of the octopus).
Decoration etched in two
stages; the fine-matt ground
has been textured with carving. The shape of the octopus
freely follows the streaks on
the underside of the plate.
The applications cut, en-
graved and lightly polished.

H 4.7 Ø 27.7 cm

Possibly a one-off piece. This
plate is related to the material
studies Gallé conducted in
1902/3 in connection with the
creation of 'La Soude' (soda), a
vase commissioned as a present
from the Belgian chemicals concern Solvay & Cie. to a branch
on its thirtieth anniversary. The
firm produced the carbonate of
soda that Gallé needed as a
batch ingredient at Dombasle-
sur-Meurthe. The body of that
vase matches the octopus plate
in that it consists of yellow-
tinged glass with opaque yellowish brown streaks and sports
trailing prunts with white inclusions intended to represent
soda: see Hakenjos 1982, p. 299;
Art of Gallé 1988, no. 72, and
illus. of no. 61; Le Tacon, *Solvay
Gallé*, 2000, p. 35, cat. no. 61.

The vivid material with its
strongly contrasting streaks was
used for another free variation
on the underwater decoration;
turbulent entwined bands
underscore the octopus tentacles. Gallé was interested in
octopuses as part of underwater scenery as early as 1884;
see Gallé, *Ecrits*, 1908, p. 303;
see English translation in the
'Sources'.

Lit.: Darmstadt 1999, cat.
no. 320.

60

'Libellules' footed vase

Signature: *Gallé* engraved in relief on the outer wall
Emile Gallé, Nancy
1904

Colourless glass with streaky yellow (silver compunds) and reddish purple inclusions, partly with striking colours in greyish brown; white overlay in part, blue and green applications form the dragonfly bodies and eyes with foil inclusions. Separately made foot of colourless glass with irregular yellow inclusions (silver compounds). Body ground matt, inside and outside, rim carved. Dragonfly and suggested twig matt engraved, partly polished. Head and base of wing of a second dragonfly in shallow relief cutting beneath the first dragonfly. Floor concave, ground matt.

H 14.1 W 17 D 14 cm

The last important model by Gallé, designed shortly before he died. This bowl illustrates all the essential characteristics of his late work. With its inclusions, its inner dynamic and its unfathomable depths, the material has become the vehicle for an idea. It represents a last definitive statement on the enigmatic quality and the ambivalence of beauty and menace, which for the *fin de siècle* were indissolubly linked with insects, especially the dragonfly.

The exquisitely delicate use of the streaky brownish inclusions to suggest the tint of the dragonfly wings is particularly striking. A brown streak positioned inside the wall with deliberate precision evokes a second dragonfly, which seems to blur in an indeterminate haze. The large dragonfly in the foreground is similarly accompanied by a coloured inclusion, which creates the effect of a shadow on the surface of water or suggests the insect's reflection. For the relationship between body and the foot see here cat. no. 61.

There are two versions of this particular model. The more elaborate one is distinguished

by a taller foot with a knop set with volutes and shells. The most elaborate model of this group, in the Musée de l'Ecole de Nancy, boasts an additional waterlily decoration engraved in relief on the foot: see Paris, *Gallé*, 1985, p. 25, no. 147; Nancy 2001, pp. 78–79. Other exemplars can be found in The Corning Museum of Glass, Corning, NY: see Corning 1984, no. 23; the Musée d'Art et d'Histoire (Musée Ariana), Geneva: see Zurich 1980, no. 147; the Conservatoire National des Arts et Métiers, Paris: see Bloch-Dermant 1980, p. 84; Arwas 1987, p. 113; and the Sun Kurino Museum, Atami, Japan: see Sun Kurino 1995, pp. 10–13 (illus. below).

The simpler version represented by the piece in the Koepff Collection was published at the time it was produced: see J. Henrivaux, 'Emile Gallé', *L'Art Décoratif* 7 (1905): 125; *La Lorraine Artiste* (January 1905): 22. The following variants are extant, most of them in Japan: Tokyo 1974, no. 1; Neumann Collection, Château de Gingins, dated 1904, and in the original casket: see Garner 1976, pp. 94–95; Bartha, *Collection Neumann*, 1993; F. W. Nees Collection, Wiesbaden: see Hakenjos 1982, cat. no. 286; Kitazawa Museum, Suwa-shi: see Yoshimizu 1985, no. 264; *Gallé's Gallé* 1993, no. 63; Suzuki, *Kitazawa*, 1996, no. 202 with comparison to a piece of the same form but with different decoration; private collection, Japan: see Yoshimizu 1985, no. 263; Musée de l'Ecole de Nancy: see Charpentier et al. 1987, p. 175; Japanese art market: see *Belle des Belles: Beauty of Glass: Art Nouveau*, exh. cat. (Tokyo, 1991); *Gallé et Toulouse-Lautrec* 1995, p. 80, no. 57; Musée Lyon: see C. Briend, *Les Objets d'Art*,

exh. cat., Musée des Beaux-Arts de Lyon (Lyons, 1993), p. 91.

A variant with a smooth rim, a ring below the rim and a higher cup wall is documented in *Documentation Gallé* of the Musée d'Orsay, Paris, no. 6793.

Shortly before he used it on the footed bowls, Gallé also deployed the motif of the

dragonfly, appearing on a menacing scale, to decorate the wall of a conical vase, of which several exemplars are extant: see, for instance, Garner 1976, p. 121; Corning 1984, no. 24; Zurich 1980, no. 53. The motif accompanied him in his work from the 1889 Exposition Universelle in Paris, where he showed a narrow-

necked flask-shaped vase with a dragonfly modelled on the outer wall in *gravure noire*, which appears to be swooping down on prey: see, for instance, Paris, *Gallé*, 1985, no. 96. A rare variant on a bronze pedestal was made *c.* 1898 and another in needle etching: see Sun Kurino 1995, pp. 15, 68.

61

Footed bowl

Signature: *Gallé*
engraved in relief on the
underside of the bowl
Emile Gallé, Nancy
c. 1903

Colourless glass with inclusions and irregularly drawn
out trailing yellow prunts
(silver compounds) and
bright red glass granules or
cullet splinters. The cup of
the bowl is freely blown and
formed, the wavy rim curves
inwardly and is indented

outwardly. Applications of
white, incompletely melted
glass mixed with grains of silica or soda to create a mottled
effect. Separately made foot

of the same metal as the
vessel. Bottom of the foot
adorned with shallow carving
and polished.

H 16.9   Ø 18.5 cm

One of the most widespread
models characteristic of Gallé's
late style, which was predominantly sculptural. A comparatively large number of these
were made and known by what
might – to some perhaps –
seem a misnomer: 'Feuille de
chou' (cabbage leaf).

The combination of a lively,
organic free form with a strin-

gently moulded foot that looks
as if it has been turned on the
lathe creates a dynamic effect
that enhances the expressivity
of the form while at the same
time encompassing it. Being
placed on a pedestal monumentalizes the form, elevating
it from what seems to have
grown haphazardly to the universal symbolic plane.

The most elaborate version
known is in the Neumann Collection in Switzerland. The
inside of the cup is decorated
with a butterfly and two dragonflies are engraved in relief
inside the rim: see Bloch-Dermant 1980, p. 88, 94; Zurich
1980, no. 140; Bartha, *Collection
Neumann*, 1993, p. 75.

For further exemplars in the
Alain Lesieutre Collection,
Brussels, see Garner 1976,
p. 117; Duncan and de Bartha
1984, fig. 99; in the Musée
d'Orsay, Paris, see Paris, *Gallé*,
1985, no. 142, and further
examples; Newark 1989, p. 71;
auct. cat. Drouot Paris, 17
November 1989, no. 31; Marshall 1990, p. 149; auct. cat.
Sotheby's London, 4 June 1993,
no. 31; and the Hida Takayama
Museum of Art, see Mukai,
Hida Takayama, 1997, p. 121.

A variant on a metal pedestal is
in the Musée d'Art et d'Industrie de Roubaix, Legs Sélosse
1924.

Gallé used applications in
this form with inclusions of
unmelted grains for his 'La
Soude' (soda) model (illus. left):
see cat. no. 59. This design
principle was prefigured in
1900 in models with inclusions
of glittering metal filings or
mica: see, for instance, Garner,
El Fituri, 1982, no. 57; Corning
1984, no. 9, etc.

Lit.: Darmstadt 1999, cat.
no. 321.

62

Bowl with lotus flowers

Signature: *GALLÉ* etched into the floor of the cup
Emile Gallé, Nancy
1920s

Colourless glass over blown-out blue body double-cased in blue and green. Decoration: two concentric circles with a concentric zigzag pattern, opened lotus flowers flanked by two half-open ones on the two protruding handles; inside simple deep etching, on the outer wall and floor etched twice in high relief, the wall ground and polished throughout. Rim ground, bevelled and polished; floor concave.

H 7.9 Ø 38 cm
(including handles)

A rare model with lotus decoration in the Egyptian style known from numerous vases: see, for instance, Klesse, *Funke-Kaiser* I, 1981, no. 206; Garner 1976, p. 97; auct. cat. Drouot Paris, 21 November 1988, no. 57.

Pieces from this group have occasionally been dated to the 1890s and associated with the Egyptianizing models made for the 1884 Exhibition in Paris – see, for instance, Hilschenz-Mlynek and Ricke 1985, no. 181 – or the small-scale stemmed lotus goblets *c*. 1890–95 – see, for instance, Bloch-Dermant 1980, p. 73 – on this see 'Jugendstilglas in München: Ägyptischer Gallé', *Antiquitätenzeitung* 23 (1986): 607.

However, in the present instance the Art Deco conception of form noticeably informs the decoration.

This late reversion to the lotus motif may have been inspired by Gallé's son-in-law, Paul Perdrizet, who helped to manage the business after 1904. A specialist in Middle Eastern studies, Perdrizet went to Egypt several times and, according to René Dézavelle, a decorator in the Gallé outlets during the 1920s, brought back decoration samples from his trips: see 'The History of the Gallé Vases', *Glasfax Newsletter* 8, no. 6 (September 1974): 54.

For the only hitherto known parallels, albeit with a pink ground, see *Antiquitätenzeitung*, 23 (1986): 607, fig. 1. Charles Legras also launched models similar in character during the 1920s: see auct. cat. Drouot Paris, 31 February 1992, no. 80.

Lit.: Duncan and de Bartha 1984, fig. 260.

63

Lamp

Signature: *Gallé* above the rim
of the shade and over the foot,
needle etched in double lines
Emile Gallé, Nancy
1920s

Colourless glass over milky
yellowish white body with
orange red casing. Dark blue
granules or splinters fused
on and drawn out in threads
to run irregularly round the
foot; on the lower rim of the
shade also in yellowish white
and red, drawn almost horizontally to encompass the
screen, colourless dipped
layer. The tip of the shade
ground and polished.
Original mount with new
lamp-holders.

H 51 (including mount)
foot 35 shade 15.5
Ø foot 14.8 shade 25.4 cm

This model is one of the best
in the late range produced
by Gallé's firm. A reversion to
the glass batches recalling the
hardstone of Gallé's early
work is combined with simple,
functional form to create a
modern product for its time.

The factory produced slightly
globular, large vases that
had the same colour scheme
and material composition
and structure: see Hilschenz-
Mlynek and Ricke 1985,
no. 371. The same lamp form
was also made with conventional etched decoration: see,
for instance, auct. cat. Sotheby's London, 7 November
1973, no. 270.

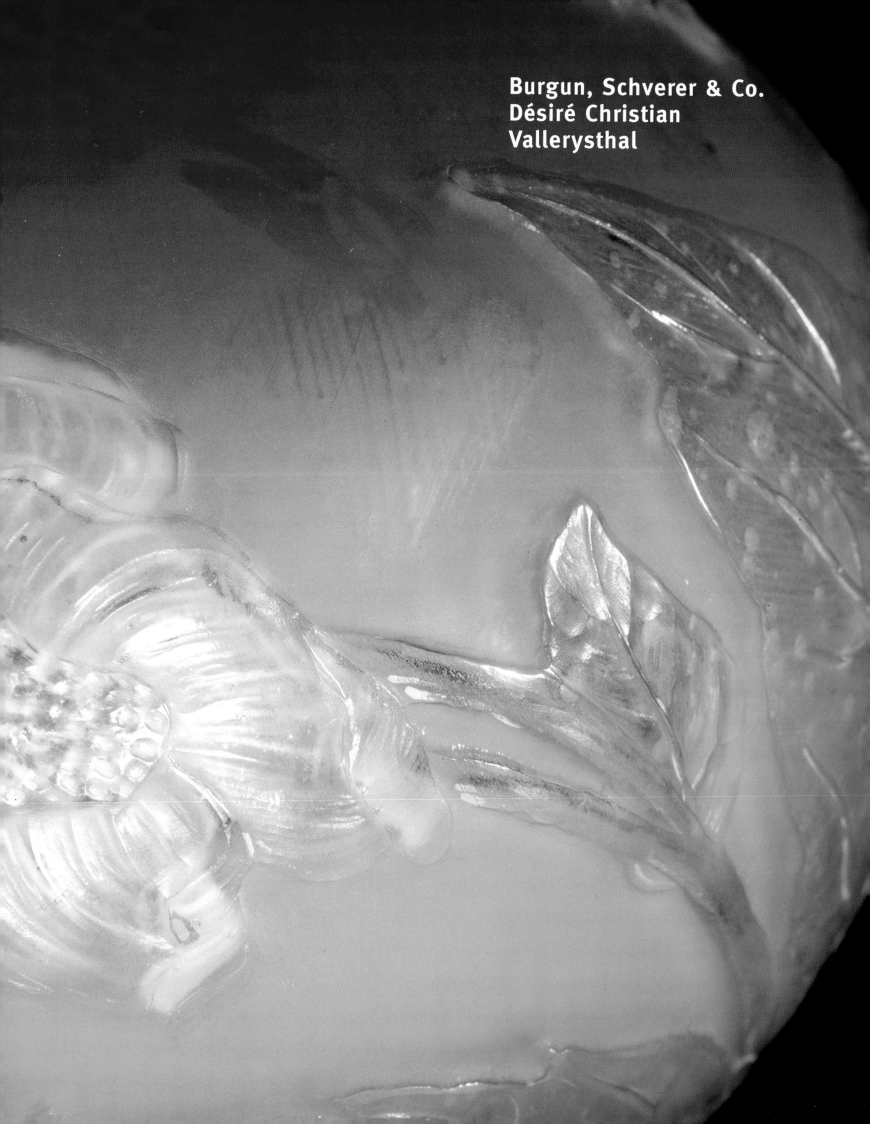

Burgun, Schverer & Co.
Désiré Christian
Vallerysthal

64

Jardinière

Signature: thistle, *B S & Co.*, banderole inscribed *VERRERIE D' ART DE LORRAINE* and *déposé* in reddish brown flat colour on the underside
Burgun, Schverer & Co.
Meisenthal, Lorraine
c. 1896

Honey yellow glass with sporadic inclusion of green metallic compounds and opaque ochre overlay; rim ground flat, bevelled and polished. Decoration in simple relief etching with fine matt etched ground and painting in opaque enamels, reddish brown flat colour, bright gold and lustre: motifs based on those of Walter Crane in *Echos of Hellas*.

H 11.3 W 15.1 D 15.0 cm

A small edition. For the same form and similar decoration type, in the Landesmuseum, Mainz, see Venzmer and Mendelssohn, Mainz, 1990, pp. 52–53. For the same form, with floral decoration sandwiched between layers of casing, such as hibiscus or a 'Bleeding Heart', see auct. cat. Christie's London, March 1982, no. 154A.

The representations on the front are borrowed from a Walter Crane illustration showing the chorus of women from the chapter 'The Story of Orestes, Act III, Scene II, "The Furies"'; on the back a vignette from 'Act I, Agamemnon', same chapter, both in George C. Warr, *Echos of Hellas: The Tale of Troy & The Story of Orestes from Homer & Aeschylus with Introductory Essay & Sonnets by Prof. George C. Warr M.A. presented in 82 Designs by Walter Crane* (London, 1887). Further references to Crane's illustrations can be found in Klesse, *Funke-Kaiser* I, 1981, pp. XXXV–XXXVII; Hilschenz-Mlynek and Ricke 1985, p. 53; Venzmer and Mendelssohn, Mainz, 1990, pp. 52–53, 268–69.

A small edition of vases with a peacock frieze and floral bands taken from a Walter Crane wallpaper design (see Hilschenz-Mlynek and Ricke 1985, p. 53, no. 13) probably derives from the *Echos of Hellas* edition. A piece from this small edition, now in the Musée d'Art Moderne, Strasbourg, was purchased in 1895. The circumstance that this type of decoration borrowed from Walter Crane illustrations also occurs on glass by Gallé and from Vallerysthal may have something to do with Désiré Christian's having worked for various firms between 1896 and 1899.

Lit.: Traub, *Christian*, 1978, pp. 78–79.

65

Vase

Signature: thistle with
B S & Co., banderole inscribed
with *VERRERIE D'ART DE
LORRAINE* and *déposé*
painted in shell gold on the
underside
Burgun, Schverer & Co.
Meisenthal, Lorraine
c. 1896

Honey yellow glass with
sporadic inclusions of green
metallic compounds and
opaque ochre overlay;
applied foot of same metal.
Decoration in simple relief
etching with fine matt etched
ground and elaborate painting in bright gold under transparent enamels – *émaux
bijoux* (jewelling) – in opaque
enamels, flat colours in reddish brown and black, bright
gold as well as lustre: mytho-
logical motifs rendered in the
antique style.

H 22.0 Ø 9.4 cm

Small edition. The same
model is in the Musée du Verre,
Meisenthal, inv. no. AN 28709.
For the same form, with floral
decoration, see ibid., inv.
no. AN 29113, and Arwas 1987,
p. 53.

Decoration with figurative
representations and mytho-
logical subject matter was
executed in numerous variants
on glass in a wide variety of
forms by the Burgun, Schverer
& Co. glassworks in Meisenthal. The source of the model
for this piece has not yet been
traced.

Although often dated to
c. 1890, objects with mytho-
logical scenes of this kind were
probably not made before
c. 1896. The signature was used
from 1896 onwards: see
Hilschenz-Mlynek and Ricke
1985, p. 52; Schmitt, *Sammlung
Silzer*, 1989, p. 54.

66

Bottle with silver mount

Signature: thistle with
B S & Co., banderole inscribed
with *VERRERIE D'ART DE
LORRAINE* and *déposé*
in gold on the underside.
Several, for the most part illegible, hallmarks struck on the
mount: including a head of
Minerva on the stopper; on
the foot part of a lozenge with
a jug and *V*
Burgun, Schverer & Co.
Meisenthal, Lorraine
1896–1903

Colourless glass over light
green body and inclusion of
colourless threading with
dark red powdered glass
irregularly fused on; sandwiched decoration in enamel
painting cased in colourless
glass: 'bleeding hearts'.
Concave floor ground and
polished. Decoration with
additional relief and matt
etching, relief and *martelé*
surfaces engraved and lightly
polished; contours traced in
bright gold. Solid stopper of
colourless glass. Knop, neck
and floor originally silver-gilt
mounted.

H 11.3 Ø 7.7 cm

Small edition. The colour
scheme is typical of numerous
works by this firm. The 'bleeding heart' decoration occurs on
a variety of other vessel forms:
see Venzmer and Mendelssohn, Mainz, 1990, pp. 58–59;
auct. cat. Christie's London,
March 1982, no. 154A.

The mount was made in
France, presumably by the
same firm (*M jug V*) that supplied mounts for Daum: see
cat. no. 100.

67

Vase

Signature: thistle with
B S & Co., banderole with
*VERRERIE D'ART DE
LORRAINE* and *déposé*
painted in gold on the
underside
Burgun, Schverer & Co.
Meisenthal, Lorraine
1896–1903

Opaque yellowish green
glass with blown-out reddish
pink overlay; sandwiched
decoration in enamel painting under colourless casing:
two branching Christmas
roses (*Hellebore*) with three
buds and four blooms. Decoration done in additional relief
etching on a matt-etched
ground, relief and *martelé*
areas painstakingly engraved
and lightly polished, contours
traced with bright gold.

H 28.9 Ø 16.5 cm

Small edition, neck sometimes
varied.

Lit.: Traub, *Christian*, 1978,
p. 110 and cover.

68
Vase

Signature: thistle with
B S & Co., banderole with
*VERRERIE D'ART DE
LORRAINE* and *déposé*
painted in gold on the
underside
Burgun, Schverer & Co.
Meisenthal, Lorraine
1896–1903

Yellowish green glass with
multiple layers of inclusions
consisting of pulled colourless splinters with dark red
powdered glass fused on.
Sandwiched decoration in
enamel painting under
colourless casing: white lupin
and forked stem with white
monkshood blooms. Rim and
floor ground flat, bevelled
and polished. Decoration
supplemented by relief and
matt etching; relief and
martelé surfaces engraved and
lightly polished; contours
traced with bright gold.

H 15.8 W 7.6 D 7.5 cm

Produced in great numbers.
For the same decoration, on a
different form, see Schmitt,
Zurich II, 1995, p. 78. For the
same form, in honey-yellow
glass with figurative representations, similar enough to cat.
nos. 64 and 65 for comparison,
see auct. cat. Sotheby's Monaco, Oct. 1987, no. 122. Similar
vases, square or rectangular in
section, belonged in 1891 to the
repertoire of forms drawn on
by Daum Frères in Nancy.

This vase was classified as
being of inferior quality, presumably because of the large
air-bubble inclusions, and was
consequently not finished and
decorated to the high standard
of the factory's best ware.

Lit.: Traub, *Christian*, 1978, p. 97.

69

Long-stemmed vase

Signature: thistle with
B S & Co., banderole with
*VERRERIE D'ART DE
LORRAINE* and *déposé*
diamond-point engraved on
the underside
Burgun, Schverer & Co.
Meisenthal, Lorraine
c. 1900/1901

Colourless glass with opaque,
fawn to greyish yellow overlay; flaring lip pulled up on
two places, worked over with
carving and, like the floor,
polished. Matt etched inside;
decoration in simple relief
etching, surface in low-relief
engraving; the ground, including the foot-rim, covered
with engraved texturing;
relief lightly polished: a poppy plant with an open and a
wilted bloom as well as three
seed capsules. The preliminary etching is discernible only
in places, with the aid of a
magnifying glass.

H 41.5 Ø 12.5 cm

Small edition. For more on
such tall vase forms, which
were evidently used almost
exclusively in combination
with this technique and colour
scheme, see Musée du Verre,
Meisenthal, AN 29117, AN
29622; see also Venzmer and
Mendelssohn, Mainz, 1990,
pp. 64–65. There are shorter
vessels done in a similar technique in the Mainz Landesmuseum and the museum kunst
palast, Düsseldorf – Glasmuseum Hentrich: see Venzmer and
Mendelssohn, Mainz, 1990,
pp. 63–65; Hilschenz-Mlynek
and Ricke 1985, p. 56.

Burgun, Schverer & Co.
showed imitations of Chinese
jade vases (see Pazaurek 1901,
p. 121) at the 1900 Paris Exposition Universelle. According to
Pazaurek, the firm reverted
to Gallé models in launching
this edition and imitated Chinese cut jade (nephrite) vases.
'Some of these greyish yellow
and leek-green vessels had a
positively Chinese-looking
wooden stand at the Paris
Exposition.' In 1901 two jade-
coloured vases were exhibited:
'596. Vase, jade-coloured,
orchids'; '603. Vase, jade-
coloured, apple blossom': see
Strasbourg 1901, pp. 97–98.

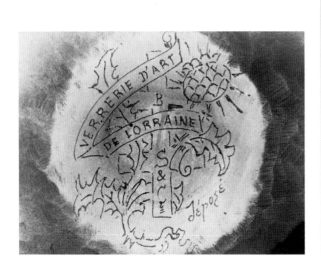

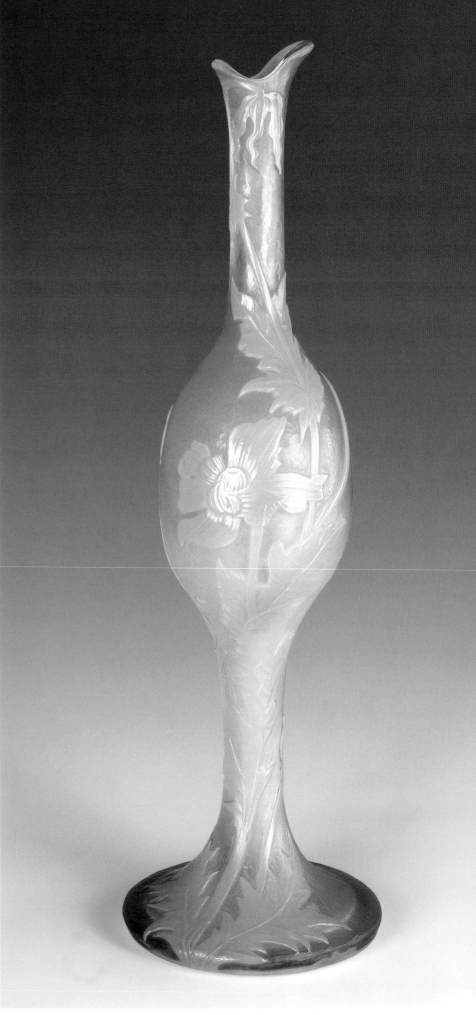

70

Small footed bowl

Signature: *D. Christian*
diamond-point engraving
under the foot-rim;
silvery sticker: thistle
D. CHRISTIAN & SOHN
Meisenthal LOTHRINGEN
Design: Désiré Christian for
Désiré Christian
Meisenthal, Lorraine
c. 1878 or 1898–1904

Thick-walled, colourless
glass, four knops and a solid,
separately formed foot of
colourless glass fused on.
Rim ground flat, bevelled and
polished. Decoration in polished olive and sharp-strap
cutting: border round the top
of the foot and below the
rim; grooves run round the
outer wall and in cruciform
arrangement; four cubelike
applications. On the inner
and outer walls symmetrical
arabesques painted in opaque
enamels in rusty red, black,
white and light blue; contours and applications in
polished gold.

H 6.7 Ø 12.2 cm

Presumably a one-off piece.
The form is the same as that of
'Les Quatre Saisons' bowl with
figurative engraving and less
elaborate enamel decoration,
which Gallé showed at the 1878
Paris Exposition Universelle
(illus. right), acquired by the
Musée des Arts Décoratifs,
Paris, in 1879: see Tokyo, *Gallé*,
1980, no. 2, and mention in
Gallé, *Ecrits*, 1908, p. 312. Christian may have owned this piece
from the 1870s and added his
company signature later. The

fact that he occasionally traded
in early Gallé glass *c.* 1906
would seem to support this
conjecture; see here p. 72. The
signature on the present bowl
may be an indication that
Christian claimed the 1878
design as his own after Gallé's
death.

Alternatively, Christian may
have used the early Gallé
form as a blank on which to
paint. Glass with enamel decoration was also sold *c.*1900 by
D. Christian & Sohn: see Pazaurek 1901, p. 121: 'Christian &
Sohn [...] produce – apart
from still widely marketable

glass in the Venetian or Moorish style – glass art [...].' Enamelling was important even on
the work done earlier by Christian for Gallé: see the contract
concluded in 1885 between
Gallé, Christian and Burgun,
Schverer & Co.: in Thiébaut,
Dessins, 1993, p. 30; translated
into English in the 'Sources'
section of the Appendix. Under
its terms Christian pledged not
to pass on inventions related
to perfecting enamelling techniques to third parties. The
enamel range of Gallé glass
was praised for its richness in
1884 and described in 1889
as having been perfected:
see Gallé's *Notices* of 1884,
translated into English in the
'Sources' section of the Appendix, and Zurich 1980, pp. 22–23.

71

Vase with tulip decoration

Signature: *D. Christian Meisenthal Loth.* diamond-point engraved on the underside
Design: Désiré Christian for Désiré Christian Meisenthal, Lorraine
c. 1900

Colourless glass over three layers of yellowish green glass casing with white powdered glass inclusions; green overlay, in places dark red patches and four green segments of threading fused on; vessel wall flattened bilaterally. Oval foot-rim ground flat and matt. Marquetry decoration on one side: a standing tulip, worked over in low-relief etching with a glossy, partly line-etched ground; the motif in lightly polished engraving with carved texture.

H 18.0 W 9.2 D 7.6 cm

Small edition. For the same model, with a different colour scheme, see auct. cat. Christie's Geneva, 17 Nov. 1991. Hardly any other marquetry work by Christian is known. Floral motifs consisting of standing plants that look as if they were cut flowers, with the flower emphasized, represent a design principle frequently occuring in Christian glass. Although the tulip motif is rare, it is mentioned as the decoration of an object by Burgun, Schverer & Co. from *c.* 1901: see Strasbourg 1901, p. 97.

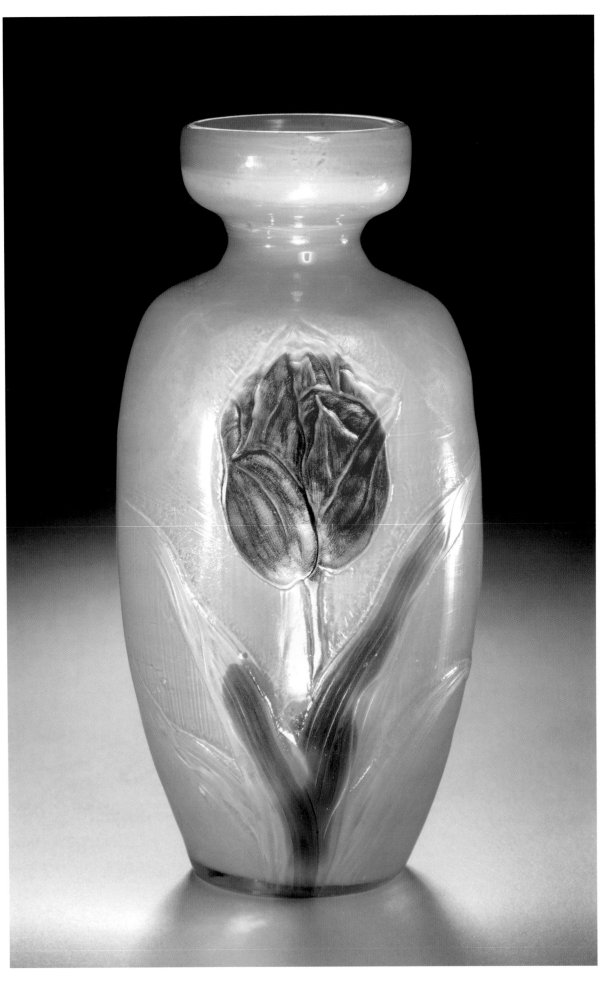

72
Vase with magnolia branches

Signature: leaf and
Geb = Christian Meisenthal
Lothr = engraved on the
underside
Design: Désiré or François
Christian for Désiré Christian
Meisenthal, Lorraine
c. 1904

Colourless glass with triple
casing in white, reddish pink
and light green. The layers
have been pulled vertically
with a hook. The decoration
in lightly polished intaglio
engraving, which in places
goes down to the white layer:
one magnolia branch each
on front and back.

H 18.9 Ø 11.4 cm

Small edition. For the same
model, with signature
F. Christian Meisenthal Loth, see
auct. cat. Sotheby's Monaco,
April 1987, no. 117. For the
same shape, with different decoration, see Venzmer and
Mendelssohn, Mainz, 1990,
pp. 66–67; Munich, *Nancy 1900*,
1980, p. 356. For the same
decoration, on a different form,
see Musée du Verre, Meisenthal, inv. no. AN39006. The
form occurs relatively frequently; the decoration varies,
and is sometimes also etched.

Similar magnolia decoration
also occurs on other vessel
shapes. According to Schmitt,
Sammlung Silzer, 1989, cat.
no. 18, the blanks for all objects
drawn on for comparison here
were procured from St-Louis.
This raises the question of
whether Christian procured
all technically sophisticated
blanks from St-Louis from
1903 onwards (when Burgun,
Schverer & Co. began to produce predominantly hand-
blown and pressed utility glass).

Lit.: Nancy 1999, cat. no. 29,
illus. p. 64.

73

Bottle-shaped vase

Signature: *D Ch* engraved on
the lower outer wall
Design: Désiré or François
Christian for Désiré Christian
Meisenthal, Lorraine
c. 1903/4

Colourless glass triply cased
in white, reddish pink and
light green, the layers pulled
with a hook, partly over large
areas of the surface, and deep
enough to invert them; neck
freely formed, rim fused.
Decoration in shallow, lightly
polished relief engraving; on
the front a Venus's slipper
(lady's-slipper), on the back
iris and anemones.

H 21.0 Ø 10.8 cm

A one-off piece or from a small
edition. In Christian's work the
technique of ripping open casings with the angle-iron or dis-
placing or inverting layers by
pulling them with a hook can
be quite frequently observed:

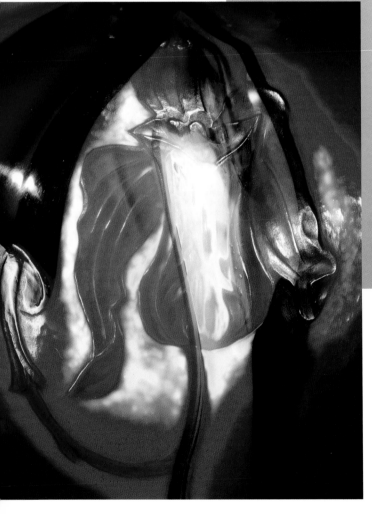

see here cat. no. 72; Schmitt,
Sammlung Silzer, 1989, cat.
nos. 17 and 18, Venzmer and
Mendelssohn, Mainz, 1990,
p. 67; *Sammlung Silzer* 2003,
nos. 25 and 28. The technique
seems to have been used from
1903/4 onwards and may be
connected with the procurement of blanks from St-Louis:
see cat. no. 72.

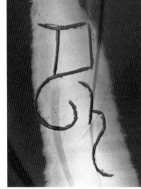

74
Footed vase

Signature: *F. Christian* and
Meisenthal Lothr. engraved on
the underside
Design: François Christian
for Désiré Christian
Meisenthal, Lorraine
c. 1904/5

Colourless glass with light
green overlay and on one side
fused-on yellow and red marquetry patches, one above the
other; foot of solid colourless
glass with light green casing,
fused on and freely formed;
rim dilated and fine-matt cut
on the outside. Concave floor
centre cut in fine-matt texturing, matt etching inside vessel. Decoration in shallow
relief etching and in places
slightly polished, low-relief
engraving; supplemented by
occasional *martelé* reserves in
lightly polished engraving:
a squash or courgette (gourd-
like plant) with its flowers
and fruits.

H 25.6   Ø 9.6 cm

Small edition. For the same
decoration, on a different form,
see auct. cat. Drouot Richelieu
1990, no. 165; for decoration
similar enough for comparison,
on a different form, see
Venzmer and Mendelssohn,
Mainz, 1990, p. 68; Klesse,
Funke-Kaiser I, 1981, cat. no. 33.
Pieces of similar metal and
processing are usually signed
Geb. or *F. Christian, Meisenthal,
Lothr.* The floral motifs adorning this group (poppies, pansies, courgette flowers)
are represented in life-like
arrangement.

The same vase shape exists
with opaque casings in different colours – technically comparable to cat. nos. 72 and 73 –
with decoration consisting of
the flowers and leaves of
nicotea, a member of the
tobacco family, signed *Geb.
Christian Meisenthal Lothringen.*

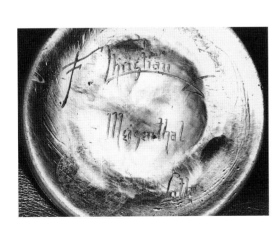

75
Bottle-gourd vase

Signature: *Vallerysthal*
Leaf in relief, writing in needle
etching on the underside
Verreries Réunies de
Vallerysthal et Portieux
Vallerysthal, Lorraine
c. 1898/99

Light green glass with ochre
inclusions, some of them
embedded in large scales,
dark red overlay; neck freely
formed, with light green
threading applied below the
rim and pulled down to
writhe about the body of the
vessel like a snake. Concave
floor ground, polished and
etched like the wall. Decoration in low relief needle etching on satin matt ground and
painted in silver stain, bright
gold and transparent enamels
in pink, light green and
colourless: a twining gourd
vine and two fluttering butterflies.

H 21.1 Ø 10.2 cm

Small edition. For the same
form, with the signature
D. Christian, Meisenthal, Loth,
see Hilschenz-Mlynek and
Ricke 1985, pp. 60–61. For
similar metal with signature
Vallerysthal, probably from
the same edition, see ibid.,
pp. 410–11. The similarities
between the pieces mentioned
above suggest Désiré Christian's links with the Vallerysthal glass factory. Further, vase
no. 369 in Klesse, *Funke-Kaiser* I,
1981, as well as the existence
of a piece similar to it in form
and decoration and signed by
D. Christian, would seem to
confirm this assumption. Collaboration between Désiré
Christian and Vallerysthal may
have been limited to the years
1898/99, for Christian lived in
Vallerysthal in 1898: see pp. 73,
77, n. 30.

76

Covered vessel

Signature: *Vallerysthal*
painted in brown flat colour
on the underside with a
contour drawing of an orchid
Verreries Réunies de Vallerysthal et Portieux
Vallerysthal, Lorraine
c. 1900

Colourless glass with opaque
pink casing and two fused-on
red patches; rim pinched, two
applied handles of colourless
glass. Oval concave floor
centre polished. Decoration
in gradations of relief and
needle etching on a roughly
etched ground with relief-
etched flecked pattern and
supplemented with painting
in silver stain, opaque and
transparent enamels, flat
colours and bright gold: on
front, back and cover a floating spray of orchids (*Encyc-
lia*), with five, four and one
bloom, respectively; on the
handles a dense, intricately
detailed rosette pattern.

H 21.7 W 18.7 D 17.0 cm

A one-off piece. Possibly commissioned or made specially
for exhibition.

The unusual form is a borrow-
ing from Chinese tea urns.
Gallé used similar forms: see
Bloch-Dermant 1980, p. 98.
Rudimentary handles of this
type are known to have existed
on archaic bronze vessels in
China (kindly imparted by
Christine Mitomi).

Daum Frères

77

'Platane' (Plane-tree)
jardinière

Signature: *Daum ‡ Nancy*
painted in burnished gold
on the underside
Influenced by Gruber, Nancy
1894

Colourless glass over opalescent body in white with
silver content; lip pulled into
three points and pinched into
a trefoil. Decoration in simple
relief etching on a slightly
glossy, grainy ground, markings within contours in
shallow needle etching; relief
painted with rust red flat
colour and burnish gold: twig
from a plane-tree with fruits;
around the lip symmetrical,
lively ribbon with winged
fruits motif repeated three
times.

H 13.9 ⌀ 21.9 cm

Serially produced. Model no.
727, 'Boule cabossée, aurore,
platane' (Indented bowl, dawn,
plane-tree), from the 'Opale
fondu, gravé, doré en plein'
(opal cast, etched, completely
gilded) edition: see *Daum Cat.
aquar.* I (without model number; illus. right); *Daum Tarif* I,
unsigned drawing (illus. above).

As a design, 'Platane' differs
markedly from earlier models
produced by the Daum studio
in being more generously conceived and in taking into account the vessel's form. The
technical side of production,
including the choice of colours,
was determined by Antonin
Daum in the firm's early glass
series. Later drawings by Henri
Bergé relating to the 'Erable'
(maple) and 'Platane' motifs
do not include studies of the
fruits. For the same model,
dating from *c.* 1895, see Sterner
1969, M. Daum Collection,
no. 9; Daum Dossier S.R.I.L.,
no. 54005444. For examples
dating from 1894, see Nancy,
Daum II, 1978, no. 10, not illus.;
Pétry and Maury, *Daum*, 1989,
p. 174, no. 44 (Musée des
Beaux-Arts, Nancy). For the
model with a silver stand, dating from 1894, see Sapporo,
Daum, 1980, no. 7; for the same
decoration, on a biconoidal
vase, see ibid. no. 6.

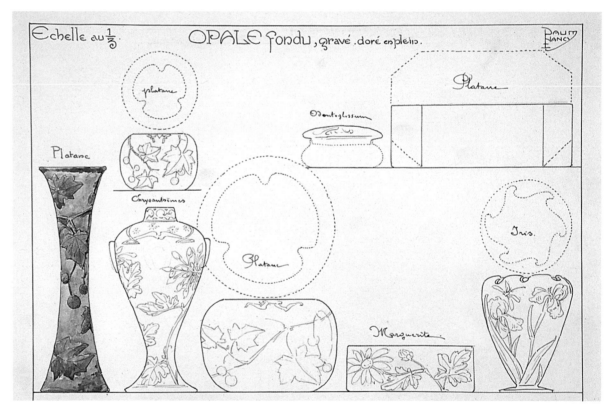

78

Bottle-shaped 'pois de senteur' (sweet pea) vase

Signature: *Daum ‡ Nancy*
painted in burnished gold
on the underside
Influenced by Gruber, Nancy
1894

Colourless glass over pink
body cased with semi-
opaque, light greyish green
glass in white with silver
content; wall flattened and
deeply indented on two
sides; applied, freely formed
foot of colourless glass.
Decoration in simple relief
etching on a matt, rough
ground with glossy, shallow
mottled relief; lines within
the contours in needle etching and foot covered in burnish gold: tendrils and pods
of a species of sweet pea.
Silver-gilt engraved mount
with four sweet pea designs.

H 32.7 W 16.7 D 9 cm
(including mount)

Serially produced. Model no.
728, 'Fiole annelée, pois de
senteur' (ring flask, sweet
pea), from the 'Ivoire et rose' edition, in the model catalogue
in the 'Opale décor gravé et
doré' (opal decoration etched
and gilded) line: see *Daum
Cat. aquar.* I (illus. p. 182, bottom), *Daum Tarif* I, unsigned
model drawings (illus. right
and p. 182, top).

The designer and maker of
the unsigned mount are unknown. The motif is referred
to in the Daum archives as
'Pois de senteur', 'Pois' or
'Pois fleur' and is, botanically
speaking, not always accurately depicted. For variants with
pinnate leaves see cat. no. 86.
An early version with rounded
leaves adorns a bottle-shaped
vase of 1894, model no. 688,
recorded in the archives with
contradictory information
on technique: 'doublé violet
ou rouge au cuivre, fond
blanc givré' (cased purple or
copper red, frosted white
ground) and 'noir et bleu':
see *Daum Cat. aquar.* I; *Daum
Tarif* I; *Daum Album* I, pl. 45.
It was evidently executed in
both techniques: see Zurich,
Wühre 9, 1986, no. 6.

The term used for the form, *fiole*, denotes the type of bottle-shaped vase derived from Middle Eastern models, with a markedly long, thin neck, which was used by Gallé as early as 1889 and introduced at Daum in 1893 by Gruber with his celebrated 'Le deuil violet des colchiques' model (the lavender mourning of autumn crocuses, illus. p. 62, no. 1): see Bascou and Thiébaut, Orsay, 1988, p. 68, no. OAO 292. The present model was usually executed in this version yet was, according to the catalogue of models, intended for an edition in opal glass without casing or overlay. It belongs to, among others, the exhibition edition 'Verreries & cristaux de fantaisie' made for the 1897 Brussels Exposition Internationale: see Brussels, *Daum*, 1897, nos. 34–222; Brussels, catalogue, 1897, no. 76. Bergé later drew botanical studies of various types of peas and vetches, most of which are in the Musée de l'Ecole de Nancy collection and some in the Daum archives. For the same model, unmounted, see Daum, Dossier S.R.I.L., no. 54005639; Bloch-Dermant 1980, p. 152; Pétry and Maury, *Daum*, 1989, p. 67, no. 57; Bacri 1993, p. 45; Karlsruhe, *Daum*, 1995, no. 43.

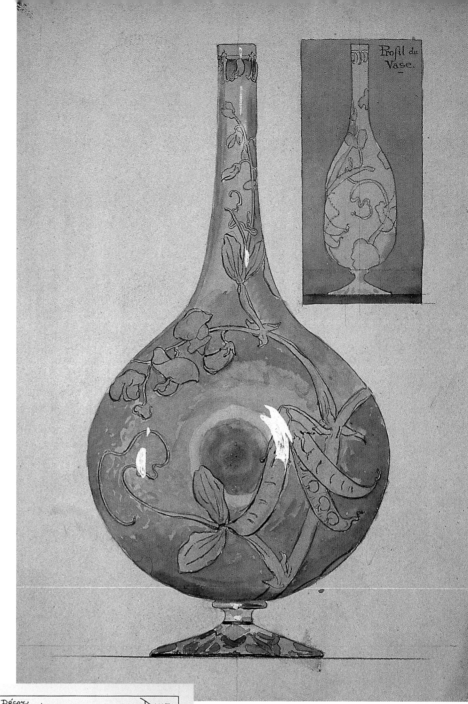

79

'Eucalyptus' vase

Signature: *Daum Nancy ‡*
engraved on the underside
After Gruber or Bergé, Nancy
1897

Colourless glass over opalescent, blown-out light blue body cased in violet black. Decoration in relief engraving; ground and floor entirely worked over with engraving, upper wall textured with carving and *martelé*: two eucalyptus twigs with one flower and three seed capsules. No preliminary etching discernible.

H 23.2 Ø 19.7 cm

Two exemplars, made specially for the 1897 Brussels Exposition Internationale. The 1897 handwritten list indicates that, owing to high demand, the number of exhibits was doubled during the exhibition and reveals that two vases bearing the 'Eucalyptus' motif fetched prices as high as 250 and 220 Frs, which was not unusual for elaborately engraved exhibition pieces. The first is entered in the catalogue with no additions to the description; a second order of 6 July 1897 is indicated by the form designation 'gourde', which is applicable to the present vase: see Brussels, *Daum*, 1897, no. 444; Brussels, catalogue, 1897, nos. 444, 718. It is difficult, however, to attribute this model specifically to one of the two designers because records are lacking. The shape of the vessel, a variation on the bud form, is striking, as is the dynamism with which the plant decoration is depicted close up. Both features are typical of Bergé's late designs. The black overlay, inspired by Gallé's engravings on black glass in 1889, occurs in 1894 on Gruber's 'Pavots noirs' (black poppies) model for Daum (illus. p. 60, no. 3), which was not listed under the heading of 'Fantaisie' for editions: see Nancy, *Art Décoratif*, 1894, no.192. The form of the vase in turn is close to Bussière's 'Marronnier' (chestnut), a ceramic vase (illus. p. 63, top centre) executed by Keller & Guérin in Lunéville. Gruber used a slightly modified version of it, years

later in his 1909 design for a window with glass-blowing as its theme for the Société Industrielle de l'Est: see Nancy 1911, p. 44, no. 388, illus. n.p. The motif itself does not recur at Daum until 1913, in the 'Verreries gravées en triple couches de verre, eucalyptus' (glass engraved in three layers of glass, eucalyptus) edition (illus. below), featuring dangling eucalyptus twigs in natural colours on a red and yellow ground. Reversion to previously employed forms and motifs, whose design could be reinterpreted, is characteristic of the production from *c.* 1910 to 1914. One result of this practice was that the 1897 vase model with an altered lip was entered as model no. 4043 in the 1913 edition: see *Daum Cat. aquar.* I; *Daum Tarif* I.

Lit.: Darmstadt 1999, cat. no. 348.

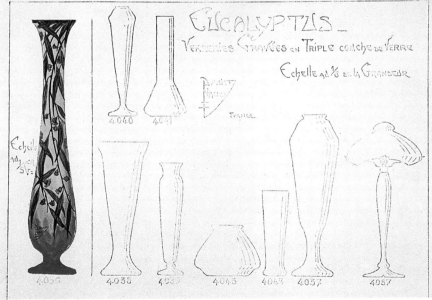

80

Bottle-shaped 'chardons' (thistles) vase

Signature: ‡ *DAUM NANCY*
engraved on the underside
Studio Antonin Daum, Nancy
1897

Thin-walled, colourless glass
casing over a streaked body
with inclusions of pink splinters and opalescent white
powdered glass with silver
content, with a large silver or
platinum leaf inclusion on
one side; freely formed, wall
slightly indented in four places; pontil mark not ground
off. Contours of decoration
needle etched and painted
with black flat colour as well
as gold, the inner surface
painted with matt flat colour:
four standing thistles, spiralling tendrils (presumably large
periwinkle) at the lip.

H 40   W 10.7   D 10.7 cm

Bottle-shaped vase no. 472,
'Fiole jaspé à paillons décor
chardons' (streaked flask, with
foil, thistle decoration). Bearing an unusual signature, this
vase is referred to as a technical
trial piece, 'Essais divers', in
the catalogue for the 1897
Brussels Exposition Internationale: see Brussels, *Daum*,
1897, nos. 469–83; Brussels,
catalogue, 1897, no. 472; *Daum
Tarif* I. It features in a photograph of exhibits in the Daum
catalogue produced for the
Brussels Exposition (illus.
below), without any dis-
cernible decoration: see Brussels, *Daum*, 1897, n.p. Antonin
Daum and his studio played an
important role in such experiments as creative technicians.
The term 'jaspé' is used as early
as 1895, for model no. 787, to
designate streaky colouring
created by fusing-on glass splinters. They are here evidently
combined with inclusions of
powdered glass, which the
factory presented at the 1900
Paris Exposition Universelle
as *couleurs tachetées* (mottled
colours): see Paris, *Daum*,
1900, p. 10. New to the range
were the inclusions of torn precious metal leaf, called *paillons*.
After 1920 the techniques
in combination are called
'Verreries marbrées pailletées
d'or' (marbled glass foiled
with gold) or *verre de jade*.

Attribution of the design to
either Jacques Gruber or
Henri Bergé is impossible
because the decoration is so

modest. The *fiole* form refers to the bottle-shaped vase type derived from Middle Eastern vases with markedly long, thin necks, which was used by Gallé as early as 1889 and introduced at Daum in 1893 by Gruber with his celebrated 'Le deuil violet des colchiques' (the lavender mourning of autumn crocuses) model (illus. p. 62, no. 1).

81

'Jacinthe' (hyacinth) jug

Signature: ‡ *DAUM NANCY 32*
engraved on the underside
After Gruber or Bergé, Nancy
c. 1895–98

Colourless glass over opalescent body in white with silver content cased with pink; handle of the same glass applied; lip freely formed. Decoration in relief engraving; ground and floor entirely engraved in *martelé* and carved texturing and slightly polished: two stylized stalks, forking below the handle, of a variety of hyacinth, a symmetrical linear ornament with a stylized bloom on the shoulder and neck. No preliminary etching discernible.

H 40.6 W 14.3 Ø 10.8 cm

Specially made piece or from a small luxury edition. Lack of documentation makes it difficult to attribute this piece to one of the two designers. A striking feature is the uniform hyacinth decoration and the shape of the jug, which echoes the flower shape. By 1894 Jacques Gruber had introduced the hyacinth motif in his showpiece 'Jacinthes mauves', which he presented at the Nancy Exhibition: see Nancy, *Art Décoratif*, 1894, no. 207. The 1894 price list designates the elaborately worked model no. 646 as 'Porte bouquet jacinthes': see *Daum Tarif* I. The jug shape was evidently used for several different but elaborate decorations and techniques. It features in a photograph of exhibits in the Daum catalogue produced for the 1897 Brussels Exposition (see cat. no. 80) and was listed in 1899 as model no. 1421, 'Cruche élancée, triplée bleue, Iris' (slender jug, double-cased in blue, iris), in the 'Triplé bleu, fond camée' (double-cased blue, cameo ground) edition (illus. below): see Brussels, *Daum*, 1897, illus. n.p.; *Daum Cat. aquar.* I ; *Daum Tarif* I; *Daum Album* I, pl. 11. For the same vessel shape, with different decoration executed in different techniques and dating from *c.* 1900, see Blount 1968, p. 73, no. 99; Cappa 1991, no. 172 a; Bacri 1993, p. 70.

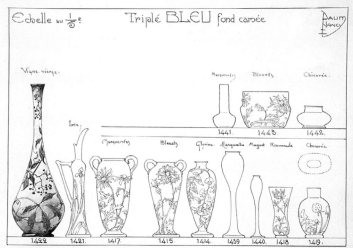

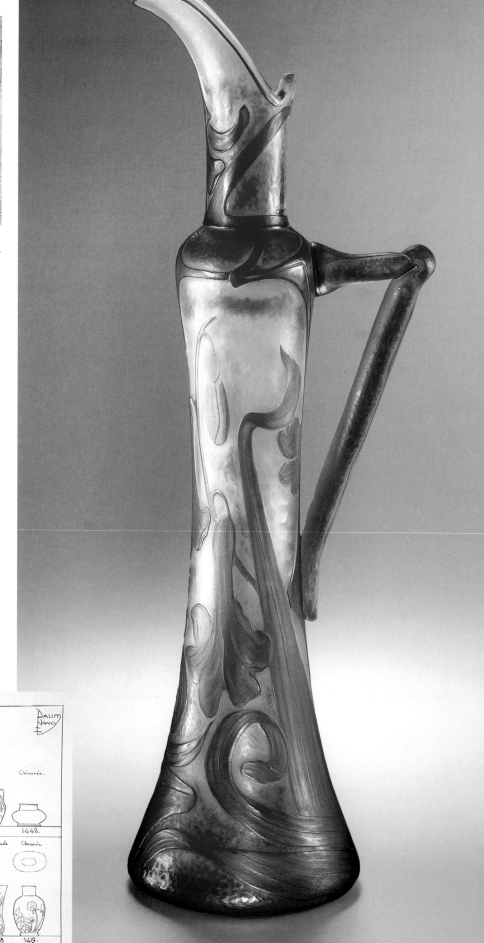

82

Broad-shouldered 'Narcisses' vase

Signature: *Daum Nancy ‡ d' après Lachenal* engraved on the underside
Design: Edmond Lachenal, Paris, 1897

Colourless glass over blown-out white body double-cased in pink and bluish green. Decoration in double relief etching on a matt, rough ground; relief entirely worked over in low-relief engraving: two pairs of narcissi, bending towards each other in different configurations, one flower snapped off.

H 33 Ø 14.6 cm

Presumably a one-off piece. 'Gourde camée triplé – Narcisse –' (gourd, cameo, double-cased): see Brussels, catalogue, 1897, no. 871. The notes in the handwritten exhibition list for the 1897 Brussels Exposition Internationale were drawn on to date this piece. They consist of a tiny outline sketch next to the vase shape, designated as 'Gourde Lachenal triplé' and the sole entry with narcissus decoration, for delivery on 20 September 1897. Lachenal's design for Daum represents a further development and simplification of his vase designs in the form of plants conceived *c.* 1893 / 94: see Victor Champier, 'Un Salon d'art décoratif à la galerie Georges Petit', *Revue des Arts Décoratifs* 15 (1894–95): 235. Lachenal also designed a variant of the model on a larger scale (H 45.5 cm) in stoneware (illus. right), dating from 1895 (unsubstantiated): see Aileen Dawson, 'The Stieglitz Museum', *Apollo* (November 1984): 316, fig. 7. For stylistically similar variants in stoneware by Lachenal see A. Le Chatelier, 'Céramique d'art', *Art & Décoration* VI (1899): 182, 189. The form with its high shoulder derives from Chinese prunus vase models and is referred to as a 'gourde'. Within the firm Daum used this term for variously shaped globular vessels with thin necks. The first *triplé* (double-cased) models were developed for the 1893 Chicago World's Columbian Exposition (see cat. no. 83). The narcissus motif, rare at Daum,

makes its first appearance here, afterwards reappearing sporadically in models of entirely different design: in 1901 on model no. 1824, 'Vase oignon, narcisses festonné' (onion vase, festooned with narcissi); in 1902 / 3 as a special *intercalaire* piece for the 1903 exhibition in Paris; and in 1904 on model no. 2328, 'Vase œuf à pied triplé vert, narcisse et muguet' (ovoid footed vase, double-cased, narcissus and lily of the valley): see *Daum Tarif* I; K.H.O., 'Daum Frères – Nancy', *Deutsche Kunst and Dekoration*, 13 (1904): 125. The edition with narcissus decoration on eight different vessel shapes was not produced until 1913, as nos. 3984–91, 'Verreries à lamelles, ciselées à la roue' (marquetry glass, wheel-engraved): see *Daum Cat. aquar.* I; *Daum Tarif* I.

Lit.: Nancy 1999, cat. no. 38, illus. p. 241; Bardin 2002, vol. 1, p. 115.

83

'Tulipes' bottle and plate

Signature: *Daum ‡ Nancy* painted in burnish gold on the underside; moon, coronet, *800* stamped on the edge of the silver plate mount
Mount: Nikolaus Trübner, Heidelberg
Daum studio, Nancy
1898

Colourless glass body, double-cased in pink and bluish green. Tulip decoration in double relief etching on a rough ground; tulip relief engraved and polished, contours and markings painted in burnish gold. Originally silver-gilt mount on the foot of the bottle and rim of the plate.

Bottle H 21 Ø 9.3 cm
Plate H 2.5 Ø 18 cm
(including mounts)

Prov.: formerly Nikolaus Trübner Estate, Heidelberg

Made to order after available models, presumably part of a service. The first *triplé* (double-cased) model with tulip decoration, no. 609, was made as early as 1893 for the Chicago World's Columbian Exposition: see *Daum Tarif* I; E. Gouttière-Vernolle, 'Verrerie Lorraine', *Lorraine Artiste* (March 1893): 203; Krantz 1894, p. 29. The orders placed with Daum Frères by the Heidelberg goldsmith Nikolaus Trübner are presumably linked with his participation in the 1893 Chicago World's Columbian Exposition, where Trübner would have seen the first *triplé* pieces. As a rule, he preferred to order elaborately worked models, which he was evidently able to have combined to order from the available Daum forms, decoration and techniques before 1900. General lines in the *triplé* technique did not begin to be produced until 1898, when this glass was designed under the supervision of Henri Bergé, from model no. 1094; in the same colours, however, not until model no. 1231: see *Daum Tarif* I; *Daum Cat. aquar.* I. Plate forms similar enough for comparison made up part of the range of plates available in table services as early as 1890.

For a smaller variant of the bottle shape, with a short neck and a silver-gilt, mounted foot, dating from 1897, see Sapporo, *Daum*, 1980, no. 14. Henri Bergé continued to execute studies of various varieties of tulip until 1905.

Lit.: Karlsruhe, *Trübner*, 1993, illus. no. 4; Sylla, *Trübner*, 2000, p. 98, illus. p. 97.

84

'Clématite' (clematis) vase

Signature: *800*, half-moon, coronet and *N. TRÜBNER* deeply impressed hallmark *N. Trübner Heidelberg* engraved in cursive writing on the foot along the rocaille rim; guarantee stamp also on the mount round the lip and on the underside of the mount
Mount: Nikolaus Trübner, Heidelberg
Daum studio, Nancy
c. 1896–98

Colourless glass over pink body, cased in green. Decoration in simple relief etching on a slightly shiny, grainy ground; relief engraved and partly polished, contour lines and highlighting painted in burnish gold: the tendrils of a clematis vine growing upwards with two flowers and four buds. Foot and lip encased in silver-gilt, chased mounts: rocaille edging on the quatrefoil foot and two pairs of clematis tendrils, each of which, differently configured, grows out of two bows.

Overall height 25 cm
Glass Ø 7.6 cm
Foot W 15.1 D 15.5 cm
(including mount)

Prov.: formerly Nikolaus Trübner Estate, Heidelberg

A bespoke piece after available models. A popular vase form featured even in the first Daum catalogue (1891), where it is given the firm's internal designation of 'Charles VII', which was often used for different decoration and techniques. The motif goes back to Jacques Gruber, who exhibited a model called 'Clématites noires', which is not further described, in Nancy in 1894. The edition model based on the 'Charles VII', no. 639 (illus. below, right), is adorned with dangling clematis tendrils, with five-petalled blooms. The standing clematis motif with four-petalled blooms, as on Trübner's vase, appears from 1897 in the catalogue of models, at first on pieces in green and red and made for mounts, nos. 1058–59: see *Daum Cat. aquar.* I. In 1902 Henri Bergé did a botanical drawing of a four-petalled clematis bloom that differs considerably from the simplified decoration on the present vase: see Nancy, *Fleurs*, 1999, p. 131, cat. no. 87, illus. p. 16. For more on glass ordered by Trübner see cat. nos. 83 and 85.

Lit.: Karlsruhe, *Trübner*, 1993, illus. no. 4; Sylla, *Trübner*, 2000, p. 99, illus. p. 97.

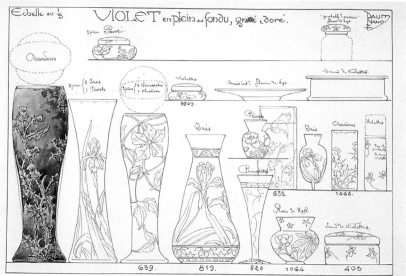

85

'Œillets' (carnations) bowl

Signature: *Daum ‡ Nancy*
painted in burnish gold on the
underside; stamped *800*, half-
moon, coronet on the foot-rim
Mount: Nikolaus Trübner,
Heidelberg
Daum studio, Nancy
1898

Colourless glass body with
double casing in red and bluish
green; lip indented in four
places. Decoration in double
relief etching with a rough
ground; relief worked over
entirely in low-relief engraving, contour lines and lip painted in burnish gold: two carnation stalks, one forked with
two buds and a bloom, the
other smaller, with a wilting
bloom. Four-footed silver-gilt
mount, chased and soldered;
on the feet and the lower
edge four *ajouré* (openwork)
designs, each consisting of bud
motifs; overlaid by garlands
of fruit in relief with wavy
hatching.

H 8.6 W 12.1 D 11.7 cm
(including mount)

Prov.: formerly Nikolaus Trübner Estate, Heidelberg

A bespoke piece after available
models. For the motif see cat.
no. 87. The same bowl form
recurs in a 1897 model with
strawberry decoration, no. 1026,
'Bol à sucre, cabossé' (sugar
bowl, indented) (illus. centre,
right), from the 'Vieux rose fondu, gravé & doré' (dusty pink,
cast, engraved & gilded) line.
To date the present piece, it must
be compared with the larger
variant of the form, without an
everted rim (W and D 15 cm),
model no. 1231, 'Bol à fraise,
cabossé à talon, triplé, doré,
œillets' (strawberry bowl, indented with the hook, double-
cased, gilded, carnations, illus.
centre, left) from the 1898
'Triplé rouge & vert fond givré,
bord doré' (double-cased, red &
green, frosted ground, gilt
edged) line: see *Daum Cat. aquar.*
I; *Daum Tarif* I. Nikolaus Trübner had ordered the pieces in
cat. nos. 83–87 together, by 1898
at the earliest.

Lit.: Karlsruhe, *Trübner*, 1993,
illus. no. 4; Sylla, *Trübner*, 2000,
p. 99f., illus. p. 97.

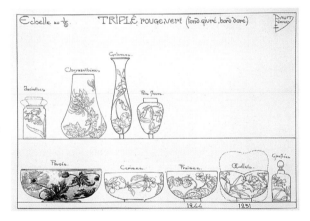

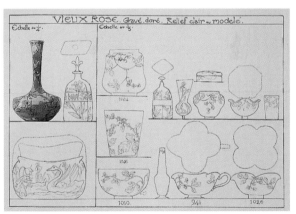

86

'Pois de senteur'
(sweet pea) plate

Signature: *Daum Nancy ‡*
engraved and rubbed with
gold on the underside
After Bergé, Nancy
c. 1897

Colourless glass casing over
two inner layers, in mauve
and semi-opaque light blue;
floor of colourless glass
applied and freely formed;
plate shaped by centrifugal
force (the inner layers are

thus turned outwards). The
rim slightly turned up. Decoration in shaded relief etching
on a glossy, smooth ground,
design within contours in
flat relief etching, partly
matt ground; ground partly
worked over with grinding
and polishing: tendrils of a
sweet pea vine.

H 3.5 Ø 24 cm

Prov.: formerly Nikolaus Trübner Estate, Heidelberg

From an edition, possibly a small
one. A plate of corresponding
size, model no. 1057, 'Assiette à
gateaux' (cake plate), from the
1897 'Vert-mousse, chèvrefeuille' (moss green, honeysuckle) edition, belongs under
the heading of special articles
to be mounted: see *Daum Cat.
aquar.* I; *Daum Tarif* I. The motif
was introduced in 1894 as the
decoration of a bottle-shaped
vase: see cat. no. 78. The botanically accurate depiction of the

wild vetchling with its pinnate
leaves points to Henri Bergé.
For a larger version (Ø 28 cm)
of the same model, without
indication of colours, see
Yoshimizu 1983, no. 555 a.
Bergé may well have been
acquainted with the unusual
dish designed by Emile Gallé
with clematis sandwiched decoration executed by Burgun,
Schverer & Co. (illus. below,
right): see M.-C. Forest, 'Verreries d'Emile Gallé au Musée
des Beaux-Arts de Lyon', *Bulletin des Musées et Monuments*

Lyonnais, no. 1 (1989): 21. For
glass ordered by Trübner see
cat. nos. 83 and 85.

87

'Œillets' (carnations)
jardinière

Signature: *Daum ‡ Nancy*
painted in burnish gold on the
underside
Mount: Nikolaus Trübner,
Heidelberg
Daum studio, Nancy
1898

Colourless glass body, double-
cased in pink and bluish
green. Carnation decoration
in double relief etching on a
rough ground; carnation
relief engraved and polished,
contours and lines within
them painted in burnish gold.
Originally silver-gilt mount
with a peacock in the round
and lilies of the valley; on the
foot, the head of Aquarius –
on the front laughing, on the
back wearing a serious expression – surrounded by sym-
metrical linear decoration
with iris and aquatic plants.

H 25.5 Ø 41; 19.7 cm
(including mount)

Prov.: formerly Nikolaus Trübner Estate, Heidelberg

Bespoke piece after available
models. The vessel form was
first listed in 1898 as model no.
1297, 'Chèvrefeuille' (honeysuckle), from the 'Triplé violet
& violet azur (ciselé ou non)'
(double-cased, mauve and
azure mauve [wheel-engraved
or not]); subsequently it was
produced in different sizes and
with various motifs and techniques, also in variations with a
broader floor and handles: see
Daum Cat. aquar. I; *Daum Tarif* I.
The carnation motif appears as
early as 1894 on a bottle-shaped
vase, 'Œillets roux', by Jacques
Gruber (illus. right), exhibited
at the Exposition d'Art Décoratif et Industriel Lorrain in

Nancy: see Nancy, *Art Décoratif*,
1894, no. 203. Gruber's motifs
for Daum were evidently reinterpreted later under Bergé's
supervision. For the same decoration, on a jug with a silver-
gilt Trübner mount, in the
Museum für Kunsthandwerk,
Frankfurt am Main, see Sylla,
Trübner, 2000, p. 102, illus.
p. 103. For glass ordered by
Trübner see cat. nos. 83 and 85.

Lit.: Karlsruhe, *Trübner*, 1993,
illus. no. 4; Sylla, *Trübner*, 2000,
p. 100, illus. p. 97.

88
'Algues et poissons' (pondweed and fish) vase

Signature: *Daum ‡ Nancy*
originally painted in burnish
gold on the underside
After Bergé, Nancy
1898

Colourless glass with powdered glass inclusions in light
bluish green, pulled in places;
partly cased with dark red, lip
pulled out and down in five
places, finished by being dip-
cased in colourless glass;
concave floor ground and
polished. Underwater decoration with dangling pond-
weed in simple, flat relief
etching on a rough, scaly
ground; contour lines of the
fish and markings within
them mainly in needle etching, supplemented with
painting in reddish brown
and black flat colour. Pondweed partly in needle etching
or on a gold ground.

H 16.6 Ø 11.6 cm

Luxury edition. Model no.
1343, 'Vase boule aplati, algues
et poissons' (vase, cup flattened, pondweed and fish)
(illus. above): see *Daum Cat.
aquar.* I; *Daum Tarif* I; preliminary painting (illus. far right).

This underwater scene differs
noticeably both from the previous one and contemporary
interpretations by other artists.
The extreme contrast in composition and design between
the foreground and the background motifs creates a fascinating atmosphere. The false
colour composition in dark
red over bluish green occurs as
early as *c.* 1889 in underwater
decoration by Rousseau and
Léveillé (see cat. no. 5). This
popular decor was also executed in the two techniques of
'triplé, ciselé, fond martelé'
(double-cased, wheel-engraved,
martelé ground) and *intercalaire*.

For the same model, dating
from before 1900, see Grover
1970, p. 106; Zurich, Wühre 9,
1986, no. 47. For the same decor,
on other forms, see Mannoni
n.d. [1986], p. 51; Suzuki,
Kitazawa, 1996, no. 305; for a
variation without overlay, on a
carinated dish, see Sapporo,

Daum, 1980, no. 15; Daum,
Dossier S.R.I.L., no. 54005433;
for an *intercalaire* vase with
high shoulder from the company collection see Daum
1980, p. 97; Sapporo, *Daum*,
1980, no. 54; Zurich, *Daum*,
1986, no. 27, illus. pp. 30–31; for
a drawing from 1899 with variants of the underwater decoration on other forms, executed
in engraving on overlay in pink
and green, see *Daum Album* I,
pl. 9, model no. 1426, 1427;
Daum 1980, p. 15.

Lit.: Ricke, *Koepff*, 1998,
p. 752f., fig. 14; Darmstadt
1999, cat. no. 349.

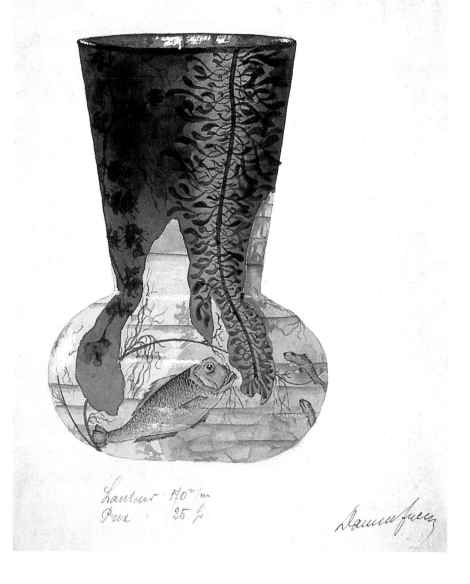

89

'Orchidées' (orchid) vase

Signature: *DAUM NANCY ǂ*
engraved on the underside
After Bergé, Nancy
1899

Colourless glass inclusions
with broad, partly overlapping swathes of white and
pink powder, with sporadic
inclusions of white with silver
content; sandwiched decoration of polychrome enamel
painting under colourless
casing with light green powdered glass fused on; floor
engraved in fine matt *martelé*
texturing. Sandwiched decoration consists of two sprays
of stylized orchid blooms in
white and pink, on the outer
wall with light green stems
and foliage suggested in shallow relief etching; the flowers
covered in places with fine
relief engraving finished in
carved texturing. The black
dots are impurities in the
green fused-on powder.

H 17.3 Ø 8.6 cm

A one-off piece, made specially
for the 1900 Paris Exposition
Universelle (illus. below), no.
96: 'Orchidées, gobelet ciselé
en affleurements' (orchids,
goblet deeply wheel-engraved),
from the 'Verrerie de grand feu
sous couvertes (décorations
intercalaires)' (high-fired sandwiched decoration) edition: see
the literature cited below. The
description of the deep cuts
disclosing the flowers lying in
the layer between is apt. This
seems to have been one of the
earliest experiments with this
technique, since later sandwiched decoration was not so
deeply embedded. In the same
section of the catalogue there
is, in no. 299, a second orchid

motif, with the addition of
entrelacs ciselés (wheel-engraved
interlacing), which, however,
cannot be the present model
with etched foliate decoration.
The vase is distinguished by
such unusually bold stylization
and freedom of handling that it
bears little resemblance to the
sandwiched painted decoration
by Désiré Christian and Burgun, Schverer & Co. in Meisenthal. For a paperweight with
the same *intercalaire* decoration, in white and pink, and
the motif described as a lady's-
slipper (Venus's slipper), see
Pertuy 1984, pp. 56, 61.

Lit.: Paris, *Daum*, 1900, p. 22,
no. 96 not illus.; Meier-Graefe
1900, illus. p. 107; J. Bloch-Dermant, *Guidargus de la verrerie*
(Paris, 1985), p. 203; Arwas
1987, p. 81; Nancy 1999, cat.
no. 46, illus. p. 179.

90

'Pluviôse' vase

Signature: *DAUM NANCY ‡*
engraved on the underside
After Bergé, Nancy
c. 1899–1902

Colourless glass with sand-wiched decoration of a wood-land scene consisting of etched, bluish-grey fused-on glass powder, overlaid with painting in black flat colour; in the floor area light green mottled fused-on powdered glass. Lip matt, rounded off by cutting with fine textur-ing. Decoration: on the outer wall raindrops falling in diag-onals in simple, low-relief etching, the ground textured in fine matt carving, the floor area engraved with *martelé* texture.

H 12.9 Ø 10.8 cm

From a luxury edition, reissued as small editions. An early model from the 'Pluviôse' (name of the fifth month in the French Republican calendar: January–February) edition was among the well-received pieces made specially for the 1900 Paris Exposition Universelle. It was followed by a number of variously shaped models, for the 1903 Ecole de Nancy exhib-ition in Paris (illus. below, right): see Paris, *Daum*, 1900, p. 22, no. 88; E. Nicolas, 'Les Verreries et cristaux d'art de MM. Daum', *Lorraine Artiste* (September 1902): 258; Paris 1903, illus. n.p.; Paris, portfolio, 1903, vol. 2, pl. 22; Daum 1980, p. 56. The present model has been cut down. The painstak-ingly matched engraving of the lip deceptively gives the impression of completeness. On closer scrutiny, however, the cuts later made through the decoration are discernible in the fine twigs hanging down from the rim with no connec-tion to the whole, an element that does not recur in later cut landscape decoration by Daum. On all known models from the 'Pluviôse' group, the woodland motif gradually dis-solves into grey cloud config-urations. In 1907 the factory donated a bottle-shaped vase with two ring handles and the same decoration to the Conser-vatoire National des Arts et Métiers, Paris: see Paris, *Arts Métiers*, 1908, p. 279, no. 14033. For a variant from the company collection with snail applica-tions, dating from 1900, see Sapporo, *Daum*, 1980, no. 27.

91

'Le Scarabée' (beetle) flacon

Signature: *DAUM ‡ NANCY d' après BUSSIÈRE* engraved on the underside
Design: Ernest Bussière, Nancy, 1899

Colourless glass over white body with silver content, double-cased in light mauve and green, dipped in colourless glass; rim matt ground flat and bevelled; floor engraved with *martelé* texture. On the front and back recurring symmetrical decoration in relief engraving, relief lightly polished in places. The stopper of the same glass is a matt ground, engraved fan-shaped knop.

H 22.5 W 9.5 D 7.6 cm

Made specially, in the small edition 'Cristaux sculptés de plein relief' (crystal glass sculpted in high relief), for the 1900 Paris Exposition Universelle: see Paris, *Daum*, 1900, p. 18, no. 82, illus. p. 20. Bussière's designs for glass derive from his successful ceramic designs, which were executed by Keller & Guérin in Lunéville in *grès métallique* and first publicly shown at the 1895 exhibition in Remiremont: see Nancy, *Bussière*, 2000, pp. 10, 60–61.

The original ceramic model, the same in form but without a stopper, was still being shown in 1903, as a 'Scarabée' vase (illus. p. 63) at the Ecole de Nancy exhibition in Paris: see Paris 1903, vol. 2, pl. 26, no. 3.

This flacon belongs to the group of Bussière designs criticised by Gustav Pazaurek for exemplifying 'cut cased glass in outlandish forms by Daum Frères' (illus. below): see Pazaurek 1901, p. 61. His criticism was not unjustified, as the adaptation or integration of plant forms did not always achieve the design effect desired, especially when glass was the material used. For the same, possibly even identical, model in the firm collection see Sterner 1969, M. Daum Collection, no. 69; Bloch-Dermant 1980, p. 149; Monte Carlo, *Daum*, 1982, no. 23, illus. pl. VI.

Lit.: Nancy 1999, cat. no. 47, illus. p. 293; Bardin 2002, vol. 2, p. 371.

92

'Les Lézards' (lizards) vase

Signature: *DAUM ‡ NANCY d' après Bussière* engraved on the underside
Design: Ernest Bussière, Nancy
1899–1900

Colourless glass with flaky white inclusions, cased in mauve; sandwiched decoration in simple relief etching, dipped in colourless and green glass; two lizard applications on the lip and shoulder formed at the kiln of solid colourless glass. *Intercalaire* decoration of delicate mauve, bare trees on the outer wall supplemented by falling pseudo-maple leaves in low-relief engraving; ground, lip and floor entirely engraved in carved and *martelé* textures; the lizard applications are matt engraved and partly undercut.

H 21 Ø 12.3 cm

A one-off piece, made specially as 'Cristaux sculptés de plein relief' (crystal glass sculpted in full relief) to be shown at the 1900 Paris Exposition Universelle (illus. below): see the literature cited below. This vase

is among the finest achievements of the factory, both in terms of aesthetics and workmanship. The supplementary woodland decor with falling leaves can probably be traced back to Henri Bergé. The almost surrealist handling shows the wood as an enchanting landscape that draws one into its luminous depths, with the mystical quality underscored by the presence of lizards. In ancient Greek and Egyptian mythology they symbolize divine wisdom, in Roman mythology death and resurrection and in Japan, marital love: see Cooper 1978, p. 42; Lurker 1985, p. 152; Düsseldorf, *Netsuke*, 1994, no. 460. The consummate craftsmanship with which this piece has been executed is all the more remarkable when one considers the risks involved in time-consuming engraving on multiple-cased glass and

the large applications in several pieces. It may have been modelled on Sino-Japanese ceramics with sculptural representations of dragons, which also inspired the ceramist Edmond Lachenal in Paris to conceive comparable creations: see Munich 1972, nos. 1165, 1168, 1169, illus. pp. 183, 189.

Bussière's glass designs go back to his successful ceramic designs, which were executed by Keller & Guérin in Lunéville in *grès métallique* and were first publicly shown at the exhibition in Remiremont in 1895: see Nancy, *Bussière*, 2000, pp. 10, 60–61. The original ceramic model, which is slightly more squat, was still being shown in 1903 as 'Gourde lézard' (illus. above), at the Ecole de Nancy exhibition in Paris: see Paris 1903, vol. 2, pl. 26, no. 3.

Lit.: Paris, *Daum*, 1900, p. 18, no. 76; Pazaurek 1901, illus. no. 84; Darmstadt 1999, cat. no. 350; Nancy 1999, cat. no. 45, illus. p. 254; Bardin 2002, vol. 2, p. 317.

93

Vase in the shape of a waterlily bud

Signature: *Daum Nancy ‡ 4* engraved and rubbed with gold on the underside
After Bergé
c. 1899–1901

Colourless glass over opaque pink body cased in green; mould-blown, solid foot of green glass, applied and freely formed. Petals engraved in fine carved texture; lip cut into shape, vessel delicately matt etched, the outer leaves lightly polished.

H 14.8 Ø 10 cm

Prov.: formerly Daum Collection, Nancy

Small luxury edition. The inspiration for the form, which is both vegetal and sculpture in the round, can be traced back to Ernest Bussière's ceramic designs: see illus. p. 63 and cat. no. 91, some of which were translated into glass at Daum Frères for the 1900 Paris Exposition Universelle. To date the present piece it will be necessary to draw on the 'Gueule de lion' (snapdragon: *Antirrhinum*) model by Bussière, presented in 1900 and technically similar enough for comparison, with light green body cased in dark green and light purple. This vase was acquired at that time by Justus Brinckmann for the Museum für Kunst und Gewerbe, Hamburg (see comparative illus. of cat. no. 91; H. Spielmann et al., *Die Jugendstilsammlung*, vol. 1: *Künstler A–F*, coll. cat., Museum für Kunst und Gewerbe, Hamburg [Hamburg, 1979], p. 288, no. 402). Viewed purely from a technical point of view, these *soufflé moulé* (mould-blown) vessels are cased glass with relief decoration created by blowing into an optic mould. The relief was, as a rule, finished with etching and engraving. A precursor of this type of design and make may have been the 'Gourde en forme d'ancolie' (bottle-gourd in the shape of a columbine) (illus. p. 64, no. 5) vase exhibited at the 1897 Brussels Exposition Internationale and subse-

quently purchased by the king of Belgium: see E. Schmitt's essay 'Daum Frères: Stepping

out of Gallé's Shadow' in the present volume. The title 'Bouton de nénuphar' (waterlily bud) given in the catalogue to the auction of the Daum Collection cannot be verified: see the literature cited below. The date 1906 cited there can be refuted since entirely different colours created with glass powder figured prominently at that time in such mould-blown vessels.

Lit.: Nancy, *Daum* III, 1979, no. 1; Monte Carlo, *Daum*, 1982, pl. XV, no. 93; J. Bloch-Dermant, *Guidargus de la verrerie* (Paris, 1985), p. 341; Charpentier et al. 1987, p. 139.

94

Footed 'pavots' (poppies) urn

Signature: *DAUM NANCY ‡*
engraved on the underside
After Bergé, Nancy
c. 1897–1900

Colourless glass over opalescent body in white with silver content partly cased in light green and purple (from rods); foot of colourless glass with the same inner layer as well as green overlay, applied and freely formed. Rim matt ground flat and exterior bevelled. Decoration in relief engraving, the ground entirely textured in fine carving and *martelé* and in places lightly polished: two poppy plants with a bud, a flower in full bloom and a fading flower. Faint traces of etching on the foot-rim indicate preliminary etching.

H 25.7 Ø 8.9 cm

A one-off piece or from a very small special edition. A high incidence of colour areas created by fusing on segments of coloured rod appeared in 1899 in red and black or green: see *Daum Album* I, pl. 23. The poppy motif is one of the earliest used as decoration at for Daum: model no. 376, *c.* 1890–92. As engraved overlay decoration for 'Pavots noirs' (illus. p. 60, no. 3) it was included among Gruber's designs for Daum shown at the 1894 Exposition d'Art Décoratif et Industriel Lorrain: see Nancy, *Art Décoratif*, 1894, p. 32, no. 192; Meier-Graefe 1896, p. 69. The shape of the vase appeared as early as the 1897 Brussels Exposition Internationale; an exemplar with daisies dating from 1897 belonged to the Daum Collection: see comparative illus. of cat. no. 80; see also Sterner 1969, no. 110. The form was represented with various elaborate decoration

schemes at the 1900 Paris Exposition Universelle and that year was registered as a luxury model, no. 1534, 'Urne à pied, sauge' (footed urn, sage), in the 'Triplé vert, pâte rose' (double-cased, pink paste) line (illus. below): see Paris, *Daum*, 1900, p. 13; *Daum Cat. aquar.* I; Pazaurek 1901, illus. nos. 83–84. Bergé's 1912 drawing of 'Pavot papavèr' (illus. above) reveals characteristic features of his interpretation of this decoration. For the same form, with 'Pavots et étoiles' (poppies and stars) in purple and a silver mount by Cardeilhac, see Schmitt, *Sammlung Silzer*, 1989, p. 84, no. 30, illus. p. 77; *Sammlung Silzer* 2003, no. 67.

Lit.: Zons 1999, cat. no. A 6, p. 143, illus. p. 49.

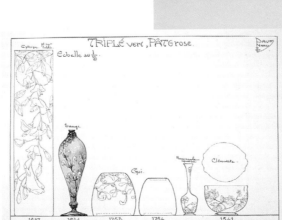

95

'Chandelles' (dandelion)

Signature: *Daum ‡ Nancy* painted in burnish gold on the underside; *TRÜBNER*, crescent moon, coronet stamped below the hinge
Mount: Nikolaus Trübner, gold and silversmith, Heidelberg
After Bergé, Nancy
1900

Colourless glass over blown-out white body, partly overlaid with powdered glass inclusions in light green and pink. Decoration in simple low-relief etching on a grainy ground; contours and markings painted in burnish gold and flat colours in black and purplish red: dandelion in its various stages of growth. Solid colourless stopper with square knop and dandelion decoration, supplemented by a dense relief dot grid on a gold ground. Hinged silver-gilt lid with chased dandelion relief.

H 13 Ø 6.2 cm
(including mount)

Prov.: formerly Nikolaus Trüb-ner Estate, Heidelberg

Serially produced. Model no. 1580, 'Flacon à sel jaspé, chandelles No. 4' (salt-cellar, mot-tled, dandelions no. 4), made in 1900: see *Daum Cat. aquar.* I; *Daum Tarif* I. The dandelion motif occurs as early as 1894, as model no. 722, with the additional designation 'Chicorée'. The form of the receptacle first appeared in 1896, as model no. 899, 'Bonbonnière Impériale mauve au chiffre du tzar Nico-las II' (imperial sweetmeat box in mauve with the cipher of Tsar Nicholas II). It was, how-ever, usually designated as a 'Flacon à sel' from 1897 and produced in four sizes (mea-surements not given), also with a domed lid, bearing various decorative programmes. A colour variant of the model was registered in 1903, as no. 2267, 'Flacon à sel 3 bleuté patiné, chandelles' (salt-cellar 3 blue-tinted patinated, dan-delion) (illus. far right). For a *jardinière* with the same decor-ation and colours from the Daum Collection, dating from 1899, see Tokyo, *Daum*, 1987,

no. 5. This piece appears in the 1900 catalogue of models as no. 1555, 'Boule cabossé jaspé, chandelles et devises' (bowl mottled, dandelion fuzz and emblems) (illus. below, left): see *Daum Cat. aquar.* I; *Daum Tarif* I.

Lit.: Karlsruhe, *Trübner*, 1993, illus. no. 4; Sylla, *Trübner*, 2000, p. 98, illus. p. 97.

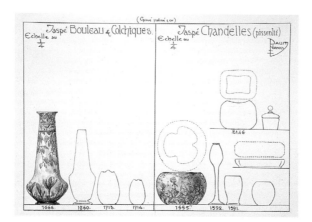

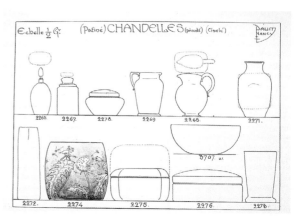

96

Cylindrical 'muguets' (lilies of the valley) vase

Signature: *DAUM ‡ NANCY* engraved and gilded on the underside
Mount: Nikolaus Trübner, gold and silversmith, Heidelberg
After Bergé, Nancy, 1900

Colourless glass over irregular, semi-opaque white body, triple-cased in white, yellowish orange and light green; lip indented to form a trefoil. Decoration in simple relief etching. Markings within contours in flat relief etching, the ground in polished *martelé* fine engraving: lilies of the valley. Removable, basket-like silver mount with four feet, *ajouré* (openwork) decoration consisting of four identical leaves.

H 15 Ø 4.7 cm

Prov.: formerly Nikolaus Trübner Estate, Heidelberg

Luxury edition. Model no. 1596, 'Petit cylindre trilobé, vert mousse, muguets' (small trilobate cylinder, moss green, lilies of the valley), 1900. The drawing that belongs to it is listed under the 'Pâte ivoire' edition, also 1900, with the wrong model number, 1592 (illus. below): see *Daum Tarif* I.; *Daum Cat. aquar.* I.

The lily of the valley motif can be verified as early as 1894 for the edition model no. 697, 'boîte à pastilles, forme basse, opale, muguets' (pill box, low form, opal, lilies of the valley) designed by the Daum studio. The shape of the vase can be traced back to Emile Gallé (see cat. nos. 26 and 43). Nikolaus Trübner tended to prefer elaborately made luxury-edition pieces.

Lit.: Karlsruhe, *Trübner*, 1993, illus. no. 4; Sylla, *Trübner*, 2000, p. 101, with illus.

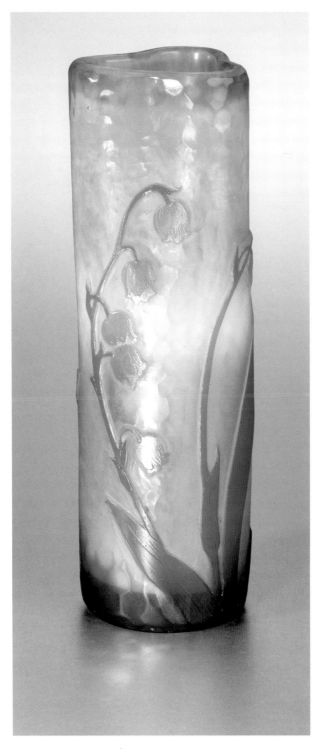

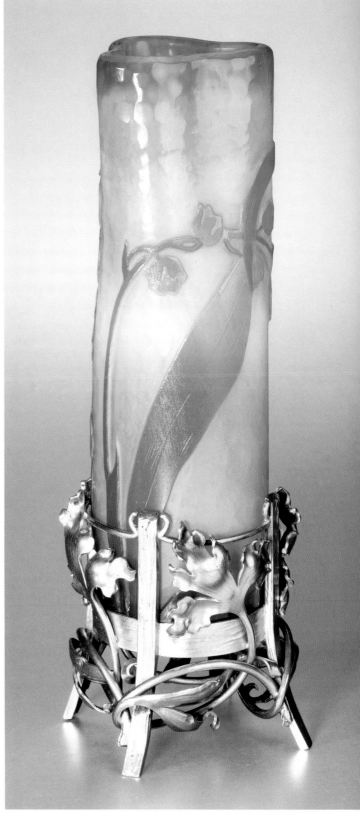

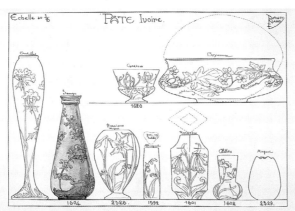

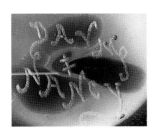

97
Vase with woodland scene and silver mount

Signature: *DAUM NANCY ‡*
engraved and rubbed with gold
on the underside
Mount: Nikolaus Trübner, gold
and silversmith, Heidelberg,
After Bergé, Nancy
c. 1900–1902

Colourless glass with zones of partly overlapping powdered glass inclusions in light green and pink, cased in delicate mauve; *intercalaire* decoration in simple relief etching; cased in colourless and mauve, low on the wall light green, high on the wall white and yellow powder with silver content fused on; floor engraved in fine-matt *martelé*. Decoration consists of a woodland scene with autumnal deciduous trees, the delicate mauve tree trunks partly in the layer in between, partly on the outer wall, supplemented with shallow matt etching. Cast, originally gilt, silver mount with hinge consisting of four faun heads interlinked by laurel wreaths.

H 16 Ø 12.1 cm
(including mount)

Prov.: formerly Nikolaus Trübner Estate, Heidelberg

Presumably a one-off piece. Bergé's *intercalaire* landscapes, often in false colours, sandwiched as decoration between casings, are among those achieving the greatest spatial depth. Nikolaus Trübner's striking silver mount dominates the delicate design of this piece (illus. below).

The *intercalaire* decoration may suggest a date between 1899 and 1904. Daum had the technique patented in 1899. Landscape decoration such as this belongs thematically to the 'Les brumes – matinales et vespérales – divers aspects de la nature – la Forêt – la Vallée – l'Etang – la Mer etc., paysages vitrifiés sous couvertes translucides, ombrées, nuagées et estompées à la roue de graveur' (morning and evening mists – various aspects of nature – the forest – the valley – the pond – the sea, etc., landscapes fused under translucent casings,

cloudy, shaded and matted at the engraving-wheel) group first presented to the public at the 1900 Paris Exposition Universelle: see Paris, *Daum*, 1900, p. 23. The elaborate method of making such pieces was not suitable for serial production even though eleven *intercalaire* models are included in the drawings for edition pieces, two of them bearing the 1901 model numbers 1822–23 (illus. p. 65, bottom right): see *Daum Cat. aquar.* I; *Daum Tarif* I; Paris, *Daum*, 1900, pp. 12–13; Paris 1903, p. 9, no. D, illus. n.p.; Nancy 1904, p. 39, no. 46, illus. LVII, colour pl. The form was used without the added stand in 1900 for model no. 1637, 'Potiche ronde, opale rose, sépia, ombelles' (covered Sino-Japanese jar, pink opal, sepia, umbels): see *Daum Cat. aquar.* I; *Daum Tarif* I. Henri Bergé drew a great many landscape studies. A large number dating from 1910 to 1914 can be found in the Daum archives.

Lit.: Sylla, *Trübner*, 2000, p. 196, not illus.

98
'Pavot noir' (black poppy) vase

Signature: *DAUM ‡ NANCY*
engraved and rubbed
with gold on the underside
After Bergé, Nancy
c. 1900–1902

Colourless glass with strewn, partly inverted, inclusion of pink powder under two layers of casing in dark red and white with silver content; *intercalaire* decoration in shaded relief etching, double-cased in colourless glass and semi-opaque grey overlay (from rod); two violet glass handles applied. Concave floor ground and polished. *Intercalaire* decoration consists of two bending poppies, a leaf and a bud. The same striking colours of silver on a copper-ruby red layer can also be achieved by painting with silver stain. Owing to the semi-opacity of the outer casing it is not possible to ascertain precisely which method was used to apply the *intercalaire* decoration.

H 13.2 Ø 11.4 cm

Presumably a one-off piece. The same form, adorned with a pond scene in the *intercalaire* technique, was shown at the 1900 Paris Exposition Universelle: see Paris, *Daum*, 1900, p. 12. The cloudy grey outer casing creates an impression of fog. A group of *intercalaire* landscape pieces was presented under this thematic heading at the 1900 Paris Exposition Universelle: see cat. no. 97. The 'Pavots noirs' first occur in Jacques Gruber's 1894 designs (illus. p. 60, no. 3). Designs typical of Henri Bergé include representations of individual leaves or flowers, which were first presented on exhibits at the 1897 Brussels Exposition Internationale: see E. Schmitt's essay 'Daum Frères: Stepping out of Gallé's Shadow' in the present volume. For related *intercalaire* decoration by Henri Bergé see cat. no. 103.

Lit.: Bloch-Dermant 1980, p. 145; Zons 1999, cat. no. A 8, p.143, illus. p. 51.

99

Baluster-shaped 'anémone' vase

Signature: *Daum Nancy ‡* engraved and partly rubbed with gold on the underside After Bergé, Nancy
c. 1900–1903

Colourless glass over opalescent body in white (powder) with silver content, double-cased in orange and green; foot-rim in *martelé* cutting, floor centre ground and polished. Decoration in simple relief etching and low-relief engraving, the ground engraved throughout in *martelé* and carved texturing, the wall graduated, markedly polished on the foot, lightly on the lip: anemones, a flower in full bloom and two buds; on the foot a small, detached bud and a leaf.

H 43 Ø 12.3 cm

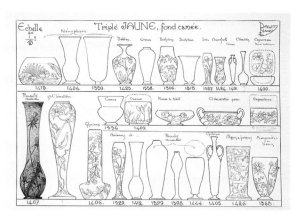

From a small luxury edition. The anemone motif was introduced in 1898 by Henri Bergé for model no. 1371. The present decoration, however, has not been found among the extant Bergé drawings. The shape of the vase was first listed in 1900, as model no. 1595. Although not included in the *triplé jaune* (three layers, double-cased, yellow) edition (illus. below, centre), it occurs until 1903 relatively often with different decoration and in different sizes, ranging from 30 to 50 cm in height (including nos. 1881, 2034, 2110, 2305, 2306, 2308): see *Daum Cat. aquar.* I, *Daum Tarif* I. For the same decoration in *triplé jaune*, on a different form, dating from 1899 (illus. below), see *Daum Album* I, pl. 6, model no. 1403, *Daum Tarif* I. In the 1899 'Anémone pluie d'or' (golden rain anemone) line, the motif is surrounded by gold tooling etched in the vertical: see *Daum Tarif* I; *Daum Album* I, pl. 31. A popular motif, it was again taken up in 1905 in the edition with red anemones (see cat. no. 107).

100

Vase with anemone

Signature: *DAUM NANCY ‡*
engraved and rubbed
with gold
After Bergé, Nancy
c. 1900–1902

Colourless glass body with mixed powder inclusions in green, mauve and traces of white; *intercalaire* decoration painted in polychrome enamel colours, cased with colourless and light mauve glass; dilated lip, matt engraved, floor ground with a matt carved texture. *Intercalaire* decoration repeated in relief engraving on the outer wall, the ground cut and engraved in large and small *martelé* texturing; the entire wall lightly polished: four standing stems of a variety of anemone or garden poppy in pinkish red, two in full bloom, a bud and a closed, wilted bloom. The type of fused powder inclusions could have been executed as on the Christmas Rose (hellebore) vase: see cat. no. 102.

H 27.3 Ø 14 cm

Presumably a one-off piece. A faulty silver mount was removed. The lozenge-shaped hallmark of the French maker corresponds to the punch mark on the bottle by Burgun, Schverer & Co. (see cat. no. 66).

The shape of the vase derives from a smaller variant of model no. 1330, 'Vase conique lys martagon' (conoidal vase, Turk's cap lily), of 1898, which was again produced in 1901, in different sizes and proportions, as model nos. 1924 and 1934, 'Iris céramique': see *Daum Cat. Aquar.* I; *Daum Tarif* I. *Intercalaire* decoration with anemones was introduced at the 1900 Paris Exposition Universelle and again at the 1903 Ecole de Nancy exhibition in Paris: see Paris, *Daum*, 1900, p. 22, nos. 47, 182–83; E. Nicolas, 'Les Verreries et cristaux d'art de MM. Daum', *La Lorraine Artiste* (September 1902): 261; Paris 1903, p. 9, Daum, section D. For *intercalaire* anemone decoration in different colours, on variously shaped footed vases dating from *c.* 1900, see Sterner 1969, M. Daum Collection, no. 29, 155; Nancy, *Daum* II, 1978, no. 38; Monte Carlo, *Daum*, 1982, no. 40, illus. pl. I; Charpentier et al. 1987, p. 139; Suzuki, *Kitazawa*, 1996, no. 358; for the same motif, on a baluster-shaped vase dating from *c.* 1900, whose colours are not indicated, see Bloch-Dermant 1980, p. 139. For *intercalaire* decoration consisting of yellow anemones on a ground coloured with powder inclusions and on a different vessel shape, as in cat. no. 102, see Tokyo, *Daum*, 1984, no. 16.

Lit.: Nancy 1999, cat. no. 51, illus. p. 293.

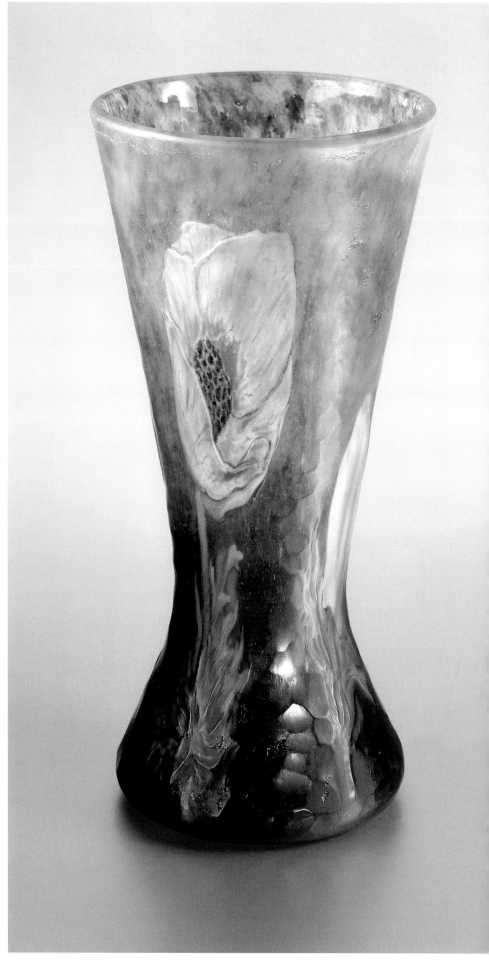

101

**'Paysage pâte grise'
(landscape in grey paste)
vase**

Signature: *Daum Nancy ‡*
engraved and partly rubbed
with gold on the underside
After Bergé, Nancy
1902

Colourless glass with partly
overlapping zones of powder
inclusions in green and
mauve, with white and green
powder fused on; two applied
handles of colourless glass
with the same powder fused
on; reduction-fired on the
pontil iron. Foot-rim ground
flat, rough matt, concave
floor centre ground and polished. Decoration in simple
relief etching with glossy
ground like frosted glass,
markings within contours in
needle etching, relief partly
engraved: a woodland scene
with deciduous trees.
Depending on the composi-
tion of the white powdered
glass, the iridescent surface
can also be created during
processing at the kiln.

H 31.6 W 10.6 D 10.4 cm
(including handles)

A 1902 edition. Model no.
2030 (illus. below), from the
'Paysage pâte grise (vitrification gravée)' (landscape, grey
paste [fused, engraved])
edition: see *Daum Cat. aquar.* I;
Daum Tarif I.

Boldly coloured, stylized landscapes such as this, which har-
monize with the shape of the
vessel, are among Daum's most
compelling creations. For the
same model, with colours not
indicated, see Pétry and Maury,
Daum, 1989, p. 177, no. 61

Lit.: Darmstadt 1999, cat.
no. 360.

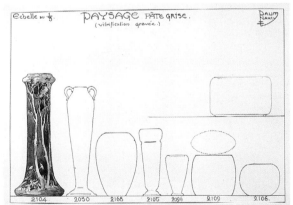

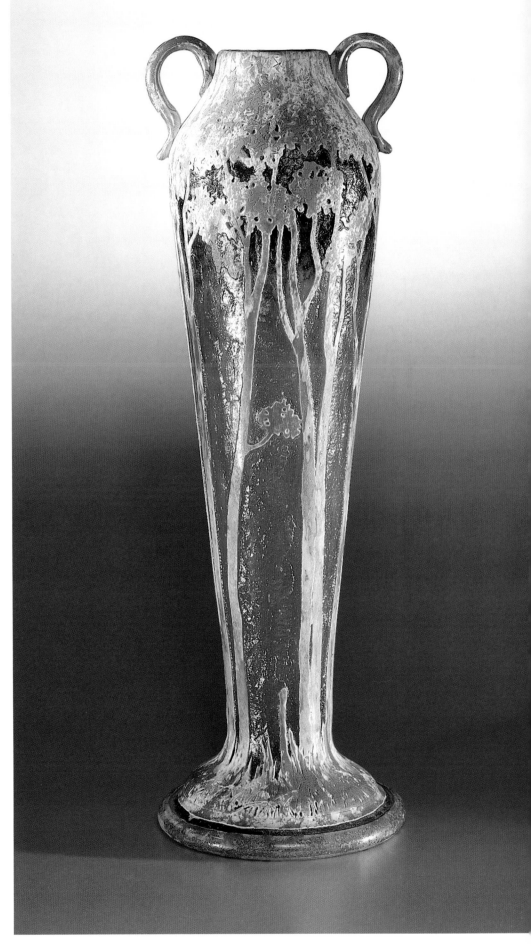

102

High-shouldered 'ellébore' or 'roses de noël' (hellebore or Christmas roses) vase

Signature: *DAUM NANCY ‡*
engraved on the underside
After Bergé, Nancy
c. 1900–1902

Colourless glass body with several powder inclusions: up to base of the neck in dense, flaky white, with superimposed, partly overlapping zones in finely scattered light green and mottled mauve rubbed into the white layer, which is still in relief; *intercalaire* decoration painted in polychrome enamel colours, the wall not entirely cased with colourless glass; floor polished and matt etched with mottled effect. *Intercalaire* decoration consisting of three Christmas roses in various phases of growth, from the bud to the fading flower, repeated on the outer wall in simple relief etching with a grainy ground; relief engraved in fine, delicately polished carved texture.

H 25 Ø 11.9 cm

Presumably a one-off piece. The Christmas rose (hellebore) was among the earliest motifs used by the Daum studio, *c.* 1890–92, for etched decoration in high relief such as model no. 368, 'Vase oblique, rosé, gravé doré, relief, rose de Noël' (oblique vase, pink, gold-tooled, relief, Christmas rose). It was often executed in different decoration techniques. Henri Bergé's studies include both species of hellebore: *Helleborus viridis* and *Helleborus niger*. The signed drawing (illus. above), owned by the Musée de l'Ecole de Nancy

(inv. no. 988.2.47, 27 x 33.6 cm), is very close in design to the present decoration. The various phases of growth, including the fading flower, are symbolic of life. A large version of this vase form appeared in 1902, as model no. 2023 (H 34 cm), in the 'Geranium, fond nacré' (geranium, nacreous ground) edition. This larger variant was also used for *intercalaire* orchid and periwinkle decoration ('Orchidée entrelacs ciselés') (orchids, interlaced, wheel-engraved) shown at the 1900 Paris Exposition Universelle: see Zurich, Wühre 9, 1986, no. 50; Zurich 2000, no. 28. Exemplars with emphatically mottled powder inclusions, created by rubbing the powder into surface depressions, were shown at the Ecole de Nancy exhibitions in Paris in 1903 and in Nancy in 1904 in Nancy (see cat. no. 103).

Lit.: Nancy, *Fleurs*, 1999, cat. no. 56, illus. p. 87.

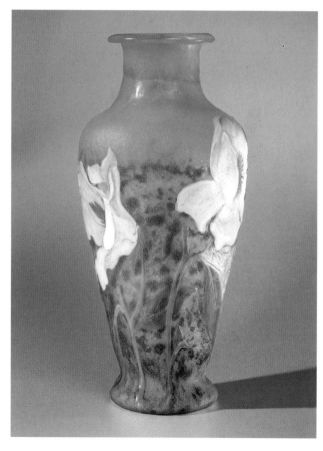

103

**'Pavots noirs'
(black poppies) vase**

Signature: *58 DAUM ‡ NANCY*
engraved on the underside
After Bergé, Nancy
c. 1902/3

Colourless glass, crackled; white, then red powder rubbed into surface depressions, cased in colourless, dark red and white glass with silver content; *intercalaire* decoration in shaded relief etching; cased in colourless glass, optic-blown into a finely ribbed optic mould with eighteen ribs, and freely formed. Lip engraved with raised ridges matt cut at the rim. Decoration between the layers: poppies with two blooms, a seed capsule and a bud, repeated on the colourless outer casing in low-relief engraving; wall and floor entirely worked over with finely engraved and carved texturing. The same striking colours of silver on a copper ruby-red layer could also have been produced by painting with silver stain. The matt-engraved texturing makes it impossible to ascertain which method was used to create the presumably etched *intercalaire* decoration.

H 16.3 Ø 14.8 cm

A one-off piece for the Ecole de Nancy exhibition in Paris in 1903 (illus. below, right) and in Nancy in 1904: see the literature cited below. The dramatic rendering of the motif, concentrated as it is on the flower, deviates noticeably from Jacques Gruber's decorative poppies (illus. p. 60, no. 3). The shape of the vessel imitates that of the poppy seed capsule, even in such details as the ribbed texture of the wall. Taking over botanical models so directly is a hallmark of Henri Bergé's designs. Powder inclusions rubbed into surface depressions are not handled in the same way on models made for serial production (see cat. no. 102).

Lit.: Paris, portfolio, 1903, vol. 2, pl. 17, no. 5; Duncan, *Salons*, 1998, p. 132; Zons 1999,

104
Vase with woodland scene

Signature: *DAUM NANCY ‡*
engraved, also a pointed oval
sticker with print effaced on
the underside
After Bergé, Nancy
1903/04

Colourless glass body with
multi-layered glass powder
inclusions, in places overlapping, in green, white with silver content and light mauve;
intercalaire decoration in
shaded relief etching, cased
in colourless glass, wider
areas of overlapping powder
inclusions in salmon and light
yellow, cased in white; lip
dilated and engraved. Ancillary decoration on the outer
wall in relief engraving, with
the wall and floor worked
over in delicate, lightly polished carved texturing: dangling foliage on lip and shoulder, low on the wall water
and waterlilies. A bubble
below the rim is disguised by
a four-legged, inset insect executed in engraving and painting with gold and black flat
colour.

H 21 Ø 11.1 cm

Presumably a one-off piece, made specially for the 1904 Ecole de Nancy exhibition in Nancy (illus. p. 216, bottom left): see the literature cited below. For Henri Bergé's landscapes in the same technique see cat. no. 97. *Intercalaire* pieces similar enough for comparison, with white engraved casing, were made for the 1900 and 1903 Paris Expositions Universelles as well as the 1904 exhibition in Nancy, and belonged to the following groups: 'Les brumes – matinales et vespérales ...' (Morning and evening mists...) (1900), the winter landscapes entitled 'Nivôse' (name of the fourth month in the French Republican calendar: December – January) and flowers, such as 'Narcisses' or 'Tulipes': see Paris, *Daum*, 1900, p. 22, nos. 81, 84, illus. p. 13; Paris 1903, p. 9, no. D, illus. n.p.; Paris, portfolio, 1903, illus. pl. 22. In 1907 Daum Frères donated an elaborately engraved Christmas rose vase of this type to the Conservatoire National des Arts et Métiers, Paris: see Paris, *Arts Métiers*, 1908, p. 279, no. 14034. For virtually the same form, with an *intercalaire* lake landscape cased in bluish white opal glass, see Hilschenz-Mlynek and Ricke 1985, p. 85, no. 53. For an *intercalaire* vase of the same kind, with white casing and a seascape with gull, and dating from 1900, see Suzuki, *Kitazawa*, 1996, no. 360.

Lit.: Nancy 1904, pl. LVII; K.H.O., 'Daum Frères – Nancy', *Deutsche Kunst und Dekoration*, 13 (1904): 122; Nancy 1999, cat. no. 52, illus. p. 179.

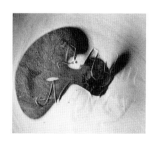

105

'Vigne et escargots' (grapevine and snails) vase

Signature: *DAUM NANCY ⧧*
(so-called triangular signature)
etched in relief on lower wall
After Bergé, Nancy
1904

Colourless glass body with powdered glass inclusions in yellow with reddish orange under dark blue as well as partly overlapping fused-on powder in white, rust and purplish red, bluish green, dark blue and yellow; on the dark blue parts several small colourless prunts, on the walls are two snails, one on either side, preformed and applied, rim not entirely dilated; floor ground fine matt. Interior of vessel matt etched. Decoration in simple low-relief etching, markings within contours in line engraving, applications and *martelé* ground worked over in engraving: blue grapes in varying degrees of relief with autumnally tinged leaves and two burgundy snails.

H 19.4 W 18.1 D 12.7 cm
(including applications)

From a luxury edition, presumably made specially for the 1905 Liège Exposition Universelle, as a variant with inwardly curved rim and *martelé* fine engraving after model no. 2439 (H 20 cm), 'Bol droit, vigne et escargots, vitrification et application' (straight-sided bowl, vine and snails, fusing and application) (illus. below, right): see *Daum Cat. aquar.* I; *Daum Tarif* I.

This vase is notable for its extraordinary richness of colour; serially produced pieces cannot compare. Indeed the superb execution of what in itself is an attractive design makes the composition a veritable masterpiece of glass art. The contrast between the undated Bergé study of grapevine leaves (illus. below, left) and the use of false colour in the design of the realized piece could hardly be greater, yet both betray the same unmistakable hand. The first snail applications as sculpture in the round appeared as early as the 1900 Paris Exposition Universelle: see Paris, *Daum*, 1900, p. 12; Pazaurek 1901, p. 96, fig. 86. For further forms from the same edition, dating from 1904, some of which are in the Daum Collection, see Nancy, *Daum* IV, 1980, no. 35; Sapporo,

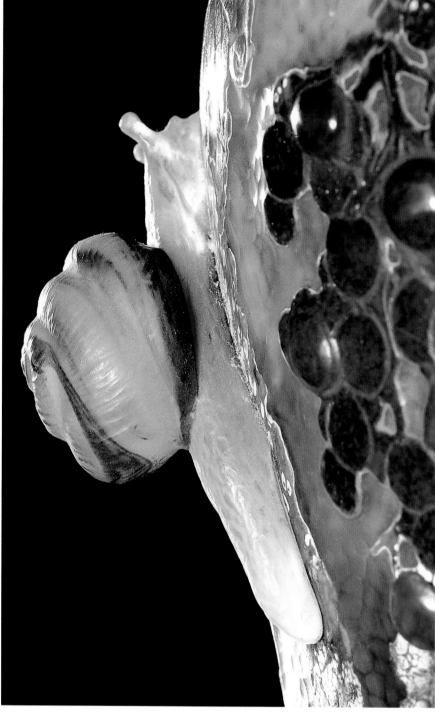

Daum, 1980, no. 32; Monte Carlo, *Daum*, 1982, nos. 82, 87, illus. pl. XIV; Brussels 1983, no. 64; Yoshimizu 1983, nos. 119, 570; Zurich, *Daum*, 1986, no. 38, illus. p. 28; Zurich, Wühre 9, 1986, no. 79; Cappa 1991, no. 178; Daum, Dossier S.R.I.L., no. 54005721.

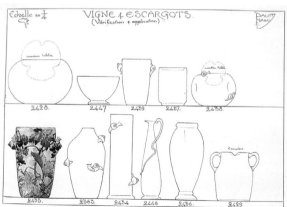

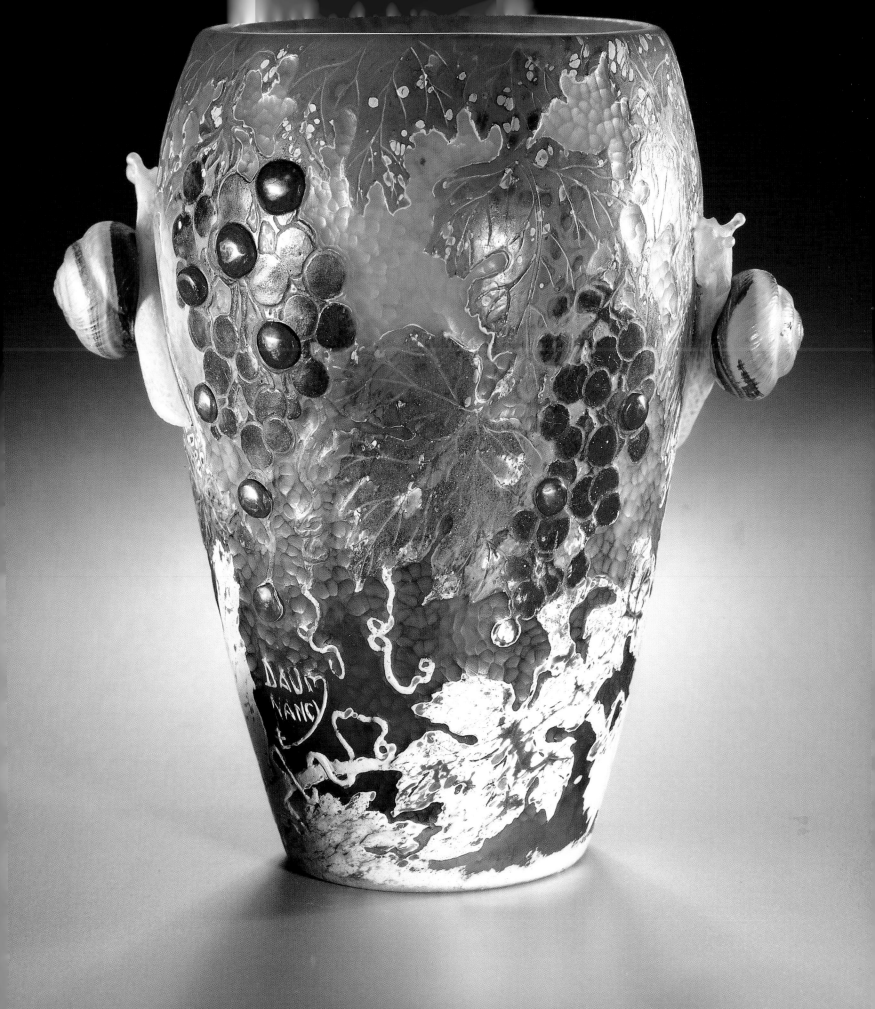

Vase with beetle

Signature: *DAUM ‡ NANCY*
engraved on the underside
Daum studio, Nancy
c. 1904/5

Colourless glass body with upwardly curving blue powder inclusions and multi-layered, fused-on powder in white, white with silver content and cobalt blue; large beetle, made up of several fitted parts and fused-on hot. Cloud decoration in flat, shaded etching. Beetle: legs and feelers of colourless glass threading segments with purple powder fused on; abdomen of colourless glass with white powder inclusions and spiralling colourless threading with mauve powder fused on; the wings of colourless glass with red powder inclusions backed with gold leaf; head and thorax of black glass, the eyes of colourless glass backed with gold leaf.

H 19 Ø 13.9 cm
Prov.: formerly Daum
Collection, Nancy

A one-off piece or from a small edition made specially, perhaps for the 1905 Liège Exposition Universelle, where Daum displayed 400 exhibits. For this design, which, for Daum, is an unusually abstract rendering of landscape, models can be found in Emile Gallé's late work. They include vessels with dragonfly or stag-beetle applications: see Paris, portfolio, 1903, pl. 6, no. 5; see also cat. no. 60 here. It has not been clarified to what extent models of this kind derive from Henri Bergé. It may instead be a creation of one of the master glass-blowers, Adolphe Claude, Camille Enel or Eugène Gall, all of whom, like Bergé, were awarded silver medals at the 1905 Liège Exposition Uni-

verselle: see Houtart 1908, p. 29. The sculptural insect applications on Daum luxury edition models (illus. p. 65 bottom left) are, as a rule, smaller and worked over with engraving; the first one had appeared by 1902: model no. 2116, 'Vase en losange à reflets, feuilles rouilles scarabées' (diaper-patterned vase with highlights, russet leaves, beetles). Most of these

were made between 1903 and 1905, with decoration including 'scarabées, mouche et araignée' (beetles, fly and spider), 'libellules' (dragonflies) and a 'cigale' (cicada); among them are model nos. 2188, 2225, 2348, 2561: see *Daum Cat. aquar.* I; *Daum Tarif* I. For a comparable beetle application, designated 'hanneton' (cockchafer), on a different vase

form and dating from
c. 1905, see Pétry and Maury, *Daum*, 1989, p. 79, no. 80 (Musée des Beaux-Arts, Nancy); Karlsruhe, *Daum*, 1995, no. 55.

Lit.: Sterner 1969, M. Daum Collection, no. 2; Bloch-Dermant 1980, p. 153; Monte Carlo, *Daum*, 1982, no. 60, pl. 1.

107
'Anémones' vase

Signature: *DAUM ‡ NANCY*
engraved and rubbed with gold
on the underside
Henri Bergé, Nancy
1905

Colourless glass body with
zones of partly overlapping
powder inclusions in mixed
yellowish orange with pinkish
red and light blue, overlaid
with fused-on marquetry
patches in white and pinkish
red, on lower wall fused-on
blackish brown powder.
Decoration in simple relief
etching, markings within contours in needle etching, on the
flowers in low-relief engraving; the upper half of the wall
worked over in fine *martelé*
cutting: three standing
anemones, two with blooms
and one with a half-opened
bud.

H 18.4 Ø 9.8 cm

Luxury edition. Model no. 2548,
'Bol à pied rond, rouille, anémones (ciselées sur plaques)'
(bowl with round foot, russet,
anemones [wheel-engraved on
marquetry patches]) (illus.
below): see *Daum Cat. aquar.* I;
Daum Tarif I.

The striking colour scheme
cannot be reconciled with
the more subtle Art Nouveau
colours. The glowing palette,
anticipating colour developments in the 1920s, had begun
to be used by 1904, in the 'Vigne
et escargots' edition (see cat.
no. 105). The commercially
viable idea of deploying a bold
palette may be traceable to the
Schneider brothers, whose work
was greatly admired by Antonin
Daum. Ernest Schneider, like
Bergé, was awarded a silver
medal at the 1905 Liège Exposition Universelle, although
Schneider had worked essentially in an administrative capacity.
The Schneider brothers continued to use virtually the same
successful colour combinations
after establishing a factory of
their own in 1918. The form was
used in 1905 in several sizes for
different editions. On the *sur
plaque* marquetry technique see
cat. no. 108. For the same model,
dating from 1898, see Zurich,
Daum, 1986, no. 23, illus. p. 29.

For further models from this
edition see Mannoni n.d.
[1986], p. 64. For exemplars
in the Daum Collection designated, among other things,
Anémones flammées', see
Monte Carlo, *Daum*, 1982,
no. 89; Tokyo, *Daum*, 1984,
nos. 82–83.

Lit.: Darmstadt 1999, cat.
no. 358.

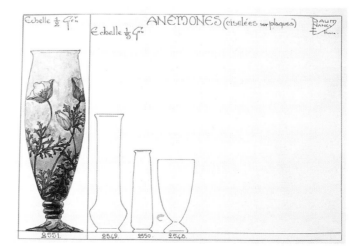

108
'Crocus' vase

Signature: *DAUM NANCY ‡*
(so-called triangular signature) in raised etching on lower wall; *MEUBLES D'ART MAJORELLE PARIS NANCY LYON* on the underside, sticker with green print
After Bergé, Nancy
autumn 1906

Colourless glass body with zones of powder inclusions in cobalt blue and white with silver content mixed with yellow and light mauve; overlaid with six fused-on white marquetry patches, four of them with red and two with mauve overlay; in the lower half greyish green powder fused on; neck freely formed. Decoration in simple relief etching, within contours in needle etching, on the blooms in low-relief engraving; the upper half of the wall in lightly polished, fine *martelé* cutting: three pairs of crocus plants, each of which features a bud.

H 30.3 Ø 12.3 cm

Luxury edition. Model no. 2909, 'Oignon, ciselé, crocus' (onion-shaped, wheel-engraved, crocus) vase: see *Daum Tarif* I.

This model must have been inspired by Emile Gallé's successful onion-shaped marquetry vase with crocuses and a long, globular neck, shown at the Salon de la Société Nationale des Beaux-Arts in 1898: see E. Molinier, 'Les Arts du Feu: Salons de 1898', *Art & Décoration* 3 (1898): 192–93. Comparison of the two crocus models shows that the designer responsible at Daum, Henri Bergé, for all his many borrowings from Gallé, nonetheless went an entirely different way with this design as the handling of colour also shows. Gallé pre-

ferred broken, sensitively nuanced colour tones and finely textured blends whereas Bergé used colour fields and colour contrasts. The undated, unsigned Bergé study (illus. right) differs from his botanical drawings in emphasizing the silhouette against a black ground, which has been retained on the vase in a reversed colour scheme. The Daum archives have no pictures of this well-known and quite frequently executed model. The technical development of decoration at the factory shows that, until 1900, the focus was on layering coloured glass and decoration. In 1900 Daum introduced his 'Colorations nouvelles, tachetées' (new colour schemes, mottled), using pow-

dered glass, which were serially produced from 1901 by *vitrification*. The marquetry technique, usually linked with engraving, patented by Gallé in 1898, was implemented by Daum on a wider range of products and called *lamellé ciselé* or *ciselé sur plaque* (lamellar, wheel-engraved or wheel engraved on marquetry patches), at the 1903 Ecole de Nancy exhibition in Paris: see *Daum Cat. aquar.* I, nos. 2303ff.; *Daum Tarif* I; Paris 1903, p. 8, no. A. For further exemplars of this model, most dating from *c.* 1899–1902, see Lausanne 1973, no. 86; Blount 1968, p. 73, no. 98; Yoshimizu 1983, nos. 123, 553; Tokyo, *Daum*, 1984, no. 25; Schmitt, *Sammlung Silzer*, 1989, p. 90, no. 37, illus. p. 87;

Schmitt, Zurich II, 1995, p. 81, no. 134; Takeda and Olivié 1996, no. 36; Daum, Dossier S.R.I.L., no. 54005690; dating from 1904–14: see Okuoka and Mizuta, Sapporo selection, 1990, no. 26; with dating corrected: *Sammlung Silzer* 2003, no. 68.

109

Goblet vase with blue hyacinths

Signature: *DAUM NANCY* ‡
engraved on the foot-rim;
72 engraved on the underside
After Bergé, Nancy
c. 1906–8

Colourless glass, full of seeds
(fine air bubbles) with streaky
white powder inclusions and
fused-on white, salmon-
coloured and light blue powder; freely formed, on the
underside two thick applied
layers of colourless glass with
green powder inclusions,
mainly to aid in freely shaping the foot, and on the upper
edge pulled up in several
places over the belly of the
vessel to form the foliage;
wall flattened on two sides,
rim dilated and engraved.
Decoration in relief etching
and engraving, which in-
cludes working over the wall
and floor: on front and back
respectively a light blue
hyacinth with lively sur-
rounding foliage, on the front
a blue butterfly.

H 21.1 W 10.9 D 8 cm
Prov.: formerly Daum
Collection, Nancy

Presumably a one-off piece,
possibly also made specially for
the 1908 Strasbourg Exhibition. Contrary to what is frequently stated in the literature,
there is no evidence of the
piece having been called
'Jacinthes sous le givre' (hyacinths under frost): see the
literature cited below. A connection may exist between the
present piece and the 'Jacinthes
bleues' (illus. far right) and
'Jacinthes rouges' editions of
autumn 1906, model nos.
2826–27, 2880–81, and the studies of plants done by Henri
Bergé in 1907, even though the
serially produced models and
the freely conceived one-off
piece have nothing in common
formally: see *Daum Tarif* I.;
Daum Cat. aquar. I. For a variant
in the same technique, with
pink tulips, dating from 1909,
see Zurich, *Daum*, 1986, no. 65,
illus. p. 36a. It may have been
Charles Schneider, who trained
as an engraver and from 1906
was employed along with

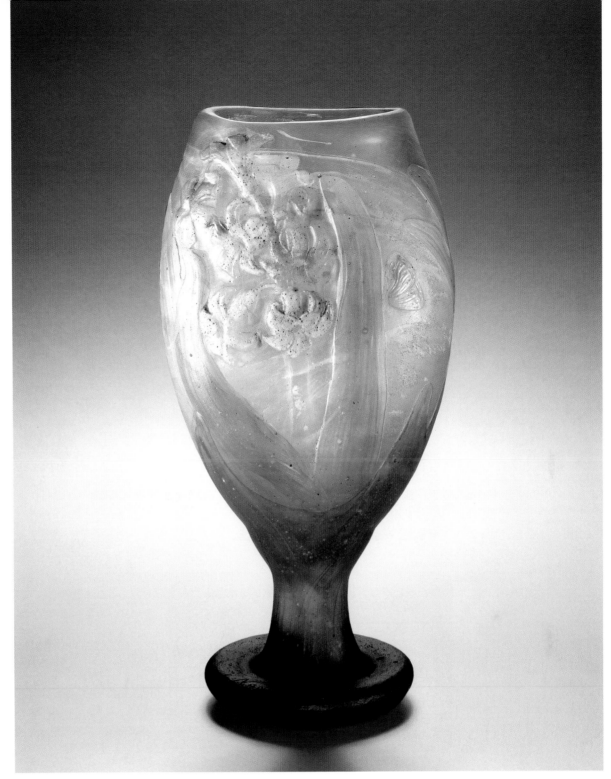

Bergé as a designer, who reinterpreted the design with
subtly engraved decoration.
On the hyacinth motif, rarely
used before 1906, see cat. no. 81.

Lit.: Monte Carlo, *Daum*, 1982,
no. 45, pl. 1.

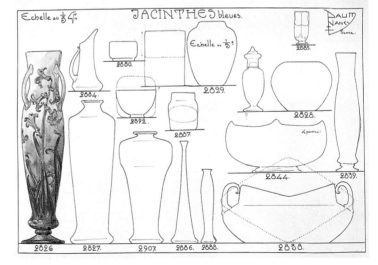

'Orchis & mouche' (orchis & fly) vase

Signature: *Daum ‡ Nancy* painted with gold on the underside
Decoration after Bergé, vessel shape after Bussière, Nancy Autumn 1906

Colourless glass body with zones of powder inclusions in white mixed with yellow and dark violet; lip freely formed; concave floor ground and polished. Decoration in simple relief etching, markings within contours executed in needle etching and painting in flat colours in rusty red, black and green; stippled gold on foot-rim: a fly above three great brown-tinged orchis (*ophrys fuciflora*) plants growing in a meadow, one depicted with buds only.

H 25.2 W 7.4 D 6.9 cm

Serially produced. Model no. 2857, 'Vase gueule de lion, orchis & mouche' (snapdragon, orchis & fly vase): see *Daum Cat. aquar.* I (illus. right); *Daum Tarif* I.

The shape of the vase derives from the snapdragon flower and, called 'Gueule de lion', is a design by Ernest Bussière, first shown in glass at the 1900 Paris Exposition Universelle (see comparative illus. of cat. no. 91) and again in 1903 at the Ecole de Nancy exhibition in Paris (illus. right): see Paris, *Daum*, 1900, p. 18, no. 77. The form is one of the criticized examples of 'cut cased glass in outlandish forms by Daum Frères': see Pazaurek 1901, p. 61. For a colour variant of the original form, in pink and light green, see Mukai, *Hida Takayama*, 1997, p. 107. The 'original shape was altered by the removal of the tubular neck

insert in 1906. For a larger example of the present model (H 32 cm), dating from 1905, see Daum 1980, p. 122. For a plant study by Henri Bergé (illus. below, right) and other vessels with the same decoration, dating from *c.* 1904–8, see Pertuy 1984, pp. 52–55. Bergé executed several studies

of orchis varieties, some dating from 1911, which in many respects recall the handling of the motif on the present piece. For further vessel shape with the same decoration see Lausanne 1973, no. 78; Klesse, *Funke-Kaiser* I, 1981, no. 412, illus. p. 524; Brussels 1983, no. 55; Cappa 1991, no. 167;

Klesse, *Funke-Kaiser* II, 1991, p. 26, no. 22; Suzuki, *Kitazawa*, 1996, nos. 379, 387–88. The form is integrated into the 1973 Salvador Dalí design 'Poisson malebranche': see Tokyo, Paris selection, 1991, no. 82.

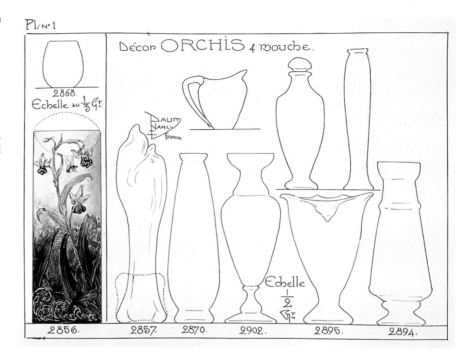

111

'Champignons' (mushrooms and toadstools) vase

Signature: *Daum ‡ Nancy*
engraved on the underside
After Bergé or Wirtz, Nancy
1907

Thick-walled, colourless glass with superimposed powder inclusions in white, yellow and pink; dilated lip, two applied handles of colourless glass with powder fused on in the same colours. Decor in shaded relief etching with frosted-looking ground, relief in flat engraving, partly with *martelé* texturing, and in painting with flat colours in red, brown, green and black: a large fly agaric, a small green toadstool, a large chanterelle, a small panther cap, a large green mushroom with a large panther cap and a low-growing fly agaric and five brown mushrooms with a cut off chanterelle.

H 21.8 W 12.5 D 12.5 cm
(including handle)

Serially produced. Model no. 2959, 'Vase basset deux anses' (pyriform vase, two handles), from the 'Champignons, clair' (mushrooms, light) edition: see *Daum Tarif* I.

Emile Wirtz, creator of the stylistically and thematically related group with mushrooms in the round exhibited in Nancy in 1909 (see comparative illus. of cat. no. 117), may also have conceived the design of this edition. A signed, undated drawing by Wirtz related to this glass sculpture is extant: see Daum 1980, p. 58; Bacri 1993, p. 108. The catalogue of models contains only sheet no. 3 from the 1907 'Champignons' edition, with a selection of vessel shapes decorated with landscapes and mushrooms in the rain (illus. below); three versions of the decoration are included in the price list: *clair* (light, nos. 2958–62, 3018, 3034–37, 3047–53), *foncé* (dark) with additional zone of dark violet powder inclusions (nos. 2963–73, 3016–17, 3054–55) and 'Pluie et champignons' (rain and mushrooms) (3019–22): see *Daum Cat. aquar.* I; *Daum Tarif* I. Comparisons of the relevant pieces show that the forms of one decor-

ation group were also occasionally used for the two other decoration variants: see cat. no. 112.

For the same model see Daum, Dossier S.R.I.L., no. 54005487; for a larger model (H 24 cm) formerly in the Daum Collection see Tokyo, *Daum*, 1987, no. 175. For further forms from this edition, including a table lamp and a long-stemmed goblet, square in section (H 40 cm), see Munich 1981, p. 32, nos. 122–23; for a bottle see Hilschenz-Mlynek and Ricke 1985, p. 96, no. 78; Munich, *Nancy 1900*, 1980, no. 476; For a beaker-shaped vase with handles see Zurich, Wühre 9, 1986, no. 82; Bacri 1993, p. 105 (Musée des Beaux-Arts, Nancy); for models in the Daum Collection see Tokyo, *Daum*, 1987, nos. 131, 148, 187.

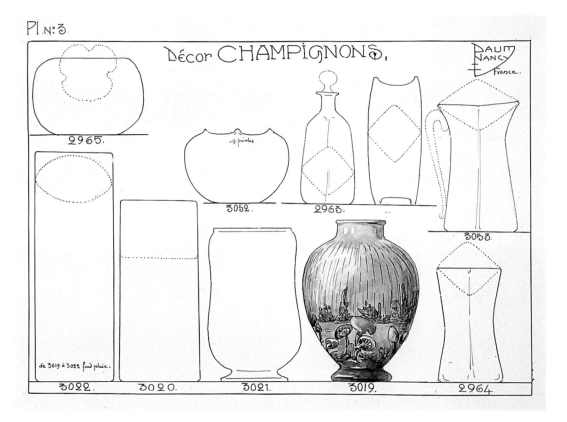

112

'Champignons' rectangular vase

Signature: *Daum Nancy ‡* engraved on the underside
After Bergé or Wirtz, Nancy
1907

Colourless glass with layered powder inclusions in white, yellow and pink; mould-blown, lip dilated and engraved on the outside. Decoration in bold, simple relief etching with a coarse, grainy, slightly glossy ground; relief in low and high-relief engraving and in painting with flat colours, in red, brown, green and black: decoration consists of fourteen, mainly poisonous, mushrooms: 1) a large panther cap, a small red-staining inocybe and a small lurid green mushroom; narrow sides 2) and 4) a fly agaric and a chanterelle on each, enlarged, with a small mushroom, 3) three red-staining inocybes, two red mushrooms and a small green one.

H 12.6 W 9.6 D 6.2 cm

Serially produced. Model no. 2967, 'Vase Claude Lorrain', from the 'Champignons, foncé' (mushrooms, dark) edition: see *Daum Cat. aquar.* I; *Daum Tarif* I.

The description *foncé* (dark) is not applicable to the present version of the model since the dark violet powder inclusions are missing; *clair* (light) should have been used instead. The same box shape with the firm's working title, 'Vase Claude Lorrain', was also employed that same year with corn-cockle decoration as model no. 2976 from the 'Nielles & mouches' (corn-cockle & flies) edition. It is among the first forms to be entered (*c.* 1890–92) in the catalogue of models, as model no. 339: see *Daum Cat. aquar.* I; *Daum Tarif* I. For more on this type of decoration and on attribution see cat. no. 111.

113

'Champignons' (mushrooms) vase

Signature: *Daum ‡ Nancy* engraved on the underside
After Bergé or Wirtz, Nancy
1907

Thick-walled colourless glass body with layered powder inclusions in white, yellow and pink; mould-blown, lip dilated and engraved on the outside. Decoration in bold, simple relief etching with a coarse, grainy, slightly glossy ground; relief in low and high-relief engraving and in painting with flat colours in red, brown, green and black: twelve, mainly poisonous, mushrooms, depicted on the sides in small groups as follows: 1) two fly agarics, 2) a small fly agaric, a mushroom with a green cap and a large panther cap, 3) four red-staining inocybes and 4) a fly agaric, a large panther cap and a small green-capped mushroom; four pine-cones dangle from the rim on to the shoulder.

H 26 W 12.2 D 12.1 cm

Serially produced. Model no. 3036, 'Vase carré, culot' (square vase, base), from the 'Champignons, clair' (mushrooms, light) edition: see *Daum Tarif* I.

For the same model in the Daum Collection bearing the title 'Champignons des bois' (wild mushrooms) see Nancy, *Daum* III, 1979, no. 5; Daum 1980, p. 83; Munich, *Nancy 1900*, 1980, no. 477, illus. p. 110; Monte Carlo, *Daum*, 1982, pl. XV, no. 67. For a cylindrical vase, with decoration supplemented by a dangling pine branch, see Mannoni n.d. [1986], p. 55; Suzuki, *Kitazawa*, 1996, no. 307. For more on this type of decoration and on attribution see cat. no. 111.

114

Four-footed 'champignons' (mushrooms) vase

Signature: *DAUM ‡ NANCY* painted on the underside in black flat colour
After Bergé or Wirtz, Nancy
1907

Colourless glass with layered powder inclusions in white, yellow and pink; mould-blown, lip freely formed, slightly inverted and engraved on the outside. Decoration in bold, simple relief etching with a coarse, grainy, slightly glossy ground; relief in low and high-relief engraving and in painting with flat colours, in red, brown, green and black: decoration consisting of twelve, mainly poisonous, mushrooms, depicted on the sides in small groups as follows: 1) two fly agarics, 2) three red-staining inocybes, 3) two panther caps and a green mushroom as well as 4) a small fly agaric, a large red-staining inocybe and a small, lurid green mushroom.

H 13.2 W 6.5 D 6.1 cm

Serially produced. Model no. 3035, 'Vase carré à pointes' (square vase with points), from the 'Champignons, clair' (mushrooms, light) edition: see *Daum Cat. aquar.* I; *Daum Tarif* I.

The form was also used in varying sizes for other editions: that same year as model no. 3090 in the 'Magnolia rose' (pink magnolia) edition, in 1908 with landscape decoration, model no. 3134, in the 'Messidor' edition, in 1910 for model no. 3405, in the 'Amarante' edition; see ibid. For more on this type of decoration and on attribution see cat. no. 111.

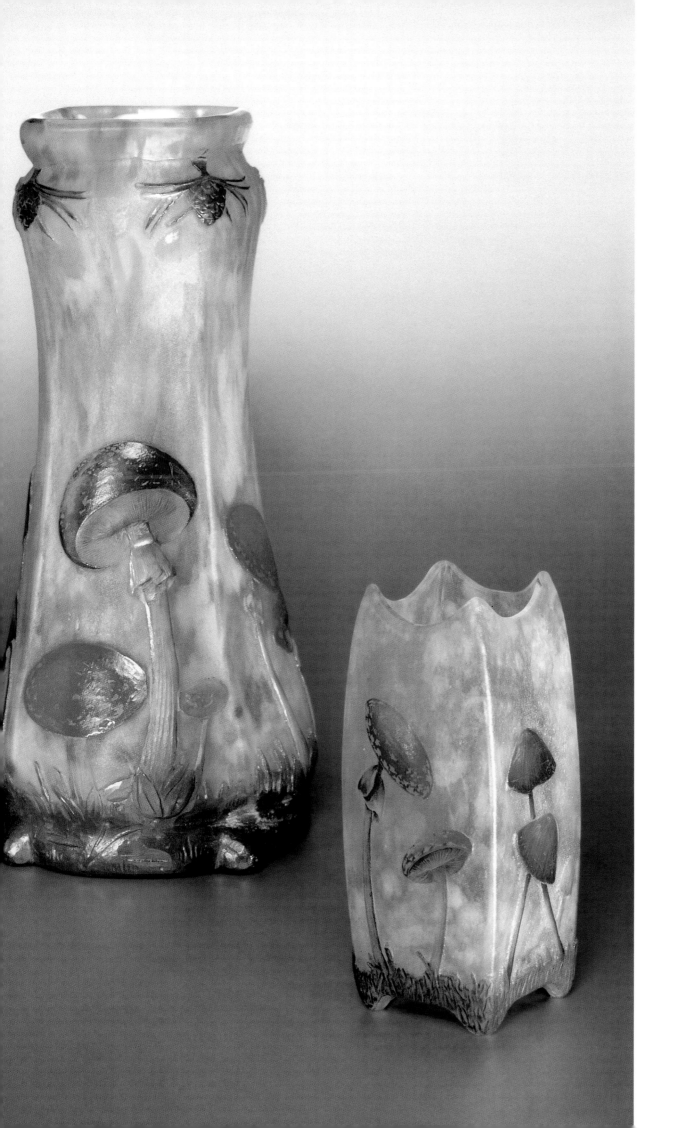

115

'Champignons'
(mushrooms) bowl

Signature: ‡ *DAum NAncy*
engraved on the underside
After Bergé or Wirtz, Nancy
1907

Colourless glass with layered
powder inclusions in white,
yellow and pink; lip inverted
at a slight incline, two handles of colourless glass,
applied with fused-on powder in the same colours. Decoration in shaded relief etching with a ground resembling
frosted glass, relief in low
and high-relief engraving,
partly with *martelé* texturing
and in painting with flat
colours, in red, brown, green
and black: eight poisonous
mushrooms, five of them on
the front, including red-staining inocybes, fly agarics and
panther caps.

H 6.1   W 17.4   D 11.5 cm
(including handles)

Serially produced. Model no.
3047, 'Petite coupe conique,
deux anses' (small conoidal
cup, two handles), from the

'Champignons, clair' (mushrooms, light) edition: see *Daum
Tarif* I.

Since the measurements are
not given in the price list, the
following model, no. 3048,
'Petit bol conique, 2 anses'
(small conoidal bowl, 2 handles), may also be considered,
yet the difference in price indicates it must be larger than the
model listed before it. A large
version of the bowl was first
made as model no. 3032,
'Saladier conique, deux anses'
(conoidal salad bowl, two handles), with edelweiss decoration: see ibid. For more on this
type of decoration and on attribution see cat. no. 111. For a
larger, covered version of the
model see Blount 1968, p. 84,
no. 124.

116

'Champignons' (mushrooms) bowl

Signature: *Daum Nancy ‡*
and *No 11* engraved on the
underside
After Bergé or Wirtz, Nancy
1907

Thick-walled colourless glass
with zones of partly layered
powder inclusions in dark
violet as well as white, yellow
and pink; applied floor of
colourless glass with dark

violet powder inclusions, lip
dilated and pulled up to form
three points. Decoration in
bold, simple relief etching
on a coarse, grainy, slightly
glossy ground; relief in low
and high-relief engraving and
in painting with flat colours,
in red, light yellow, brown,
green and black: twenty-five,
mainly poisonous, mush-
rooms, in six groups, set
against the suggestion of a
sketchily outlined horizon
and a dark forest floor with

martelé cutting, grass and
oak leaves.

H 14.1 Ø 24 cm

Serially produced. Model no.
3016, 'Saladier trois points'
(three-pointed salad bowl),
from the 'Champignons, foncé'
(mushrooms, dark) edition:
see *Daum Tarif* I.

The shape of the bowl, also
designated 'Saladier tricorne'
(three-cornered salad bowl),
was used as early as 1906, for
model no. 2844, 'Jacinthes

bleues' (see comparative illus.
of cat. no. 109): see *Daum Cat.
aquar.* I; *Daum Tarif* I. The same
model is in the Musée des
Beaux-Arts, Nancy, inv. nos.
113016 and 92-22-9. For mushrooms from the *foncé* (dark)
group on a small footed bowl
with a quatrefoil rim see
Zurich, Wühre 9, 1986, no. 58.
For more on this type of decoration and on attribution see
cat. no. 111.

117

Vase with pond scene

Signature: ‡ *DAUM NANCY*
engraved on the wall
Nancy
1908/9

Colourless glass with partly layered fused-on powdered glass in white, yellow, green and dark red; freely formed, on lower wall a lily-pad freely shaped of layers of colourless and light green glass and pulled up laterally from a rounded gather applied on the bottom to form handles; several partly preformed prunts, two dark green, four dark red and six colourless ones with dark brown centres. Rim dilated, engraved and lightly polished; vessel finished with faint matt etching. Sculptural, engraved application consisting of six colourless waterlily blooms with two green leaves, three tadpoles and stylized fish in dark red. Upper wall and applications partly polished.

H 13.7 W 21 D 11.5 cm
(including applications)

Specially made, presumably for the 1909 Exposition Internationale de l'Est de la France Nancy, where the exhibits also included the bottle-shaped vase 'Flore des marais' (marsh flora) (illus. above: left, on the improvised stand) with the same waterlily applications: see Nancy, *Daum* I, 1977, no. 58; Daum 1980, p. 78; Monte Carlo, *Daum*, 1982, no. 90; Suzuki, *Kitazawa*, 1996, no. 249. Eugène Michel developed pond scenes with sculptural waterlily and fish applications in Paris from *c.* 1898 to 1904 (see cat. nos. 11, 12, 14). His extraordinary works, which represented a real challenge to the engraver, may have been the inspiration for the present piece. Charles Schneider may have conceived the vase. Trained as an engraver, he had been employed at Daum as a designer since 1906.

Lit.: Ricke, *Koepff*, 1998, p. 753, fig. 16.

118

Gourd-shaped flacon

Signature: ‡ *DAUM NANCY* engraved on lower wall; *18* engraved on the underside; *5* diamond-point engraved on the stopper; *CASSE LYON*, sticker with white print on gold ground
Nancy
c. 1908–11

Colourless glass body with layered fused-on powder in yellow, red, bluish green and dark violet; blown into an optic mould with twelve ribs and freely formed, a colourless glass knop with gold leaf and red powder inclusions fused on. Rim matt ground. Wall partly matt etched; engraved application, undercut in several places, representing a beetle almost fully in the round, with wings open.

H 13.8 Ø 11.2 cm
(including stopper)

A one-off piece or from a small luxury edition. Small, covered vessels in the shape of fruits similar enough for comparison were shown at the exhibition in Nancy in 1909 (see comparative illus. of cat. no. 117). It has yet to be clarified whether Henri Bergé, Charles Schneider or Emile Wirtz, who presented his mushroom sculpture at that exhibition, designed vessels in the shape of fruits. The development from organic and vegetal forms had been promoted by Ernest Bussière at Daum (illus. p. 63). Since the fruit objects are mainly freely formed, glassmakers played a paramount role in their design. They received awards regularly at exhibitions between 1900 and 1914. For the same form, see 'Coloquinte' (colocynth, a bitter-apple gourd), without stopper and application, dating from *c.* 1910, in Pétry and Maury, *Daum*, 1989, p. 177, no. 63 (Musée de l'Ecole de Nancy, Nancy). More common are the large calabash and pumpkin shapes: see, for instance, Hilschenz-Mlynek and Ricke 1985, no 88. For further fruit shapes in the Daum Collection, dating from 1910, see Daum 1980, p. 57; Sapporo, *Daum*, 1980, nos. 50–51.

119

'Hépathique' (hepatica) vase

Signature: *DAUM ‡ NANCY*
engraved *18*, on the underside
engraved on lower wall
After Bergé, Nancy
c. 1910–12

Thick-walled colourless glass
with bubbly, streaky powder
inclusions in white and pink,
several overlapping segments
of colourless threading with
purplish black powder fused
on and zones of fused-on
powder in purplish black and
white with pinkish mauve;
sporadic, small light green
prunts, fused on hot; freely
formed, preformed solid
applied foot of colourless
glass with fused-on dark purple powder and traces of
white with silver content and
light green, lip cut into shape
on one side and, like the wall,
flattened on two sides. Vessel
matt etched. Decoration in
simple relief etching, flowers
and upper wall worked over
with engraving: standing liverwort flowers.

H 26.9 W 13.4 D 11.5 cm

A one-off piece or from a small
luxury edition, possibly made
specially for the 1910–12 exhibitions in Brussels, Turin or
Paris. An undated Henri Bergé
plant study (Musée de l'Ecole
de Nancy, inv. no. 988.2.36,
21.7 x 28.6 cm; illus. below)
reveals parallels with the decoration of the present footed
vase. For the same decoration,
on a slender footed vase, a vessel shape of which the incidence, like the vase form
above, increased between
1910 and 1912, see Zurich,
Wühre 9, 1986, no. 51; Suzuki,
Kitazawa, 1996, no. 410.

'Primevères' (primroses) vase

Signature: *DAUM ‡ NANCY* engraved on the foot;
4102 VX painted on the underside in etching ink or white cold colour
After Bergé and Wirtz, Nancy
1919

Colourless glass with zones of partly overlapping powder inclusions in cobalt blue and yellowish orange mixed with pink, a white glass patch and green, yellow and pink powder layers. Decoration in simple relief etching, within contours in needle etching, on the flowers in low, lightly polished relief engraving: white primrose flowers arranged vertically, on the back inflorescences.

H 19.9 Ø 5.5 cm
Prov.: formerly Daum Collection, Nancy

Luxury edition. Model no. 4102, 'Porte-bouquet pointu' (pointed bouquet vase), from the 'Primevères verreries à lamelles ciselées' (primroses, marquetry, wheel-engraved) edition (illus. below): see *Daum Cat. aquar.* I and I I; *Daum Tarif* I and II.

This model belongs to the third edition of the new product lines launched after the First World War, which imitated the successful pre-war designs in style and craftsmanship. A 1921 Bergé plant study (illus. right) reveals, unlike his earlier drawings, hardly any design parallels with the translation of the motif into decoration. The stylization can presumably be traced back to Emile Wirtz, head designer from 1919. Editions of this type remained in production until *c.* 1928 owing to high demand. For further models from this edition, dating from 1912/13, see Zurich, Wühre 9, 1986, no. 57; from the Daum Collection, dating from *c.* 1905 and 1912, see Daum 1980, p. 115; Tokyo, *Daum*, 1984, no. 17 (table lamp); Tokyo, *Daum*, 1987, nos. 124, 140, 168, 172.

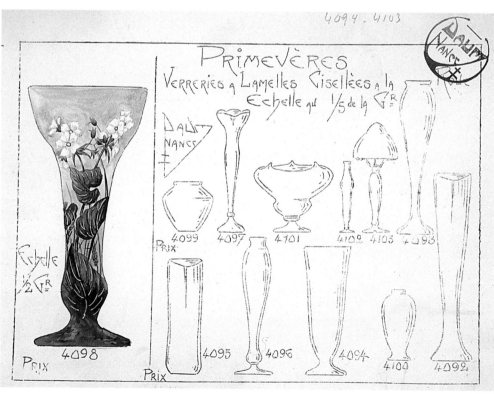

121
'Pommier' (apple tree) vase

Signature: *DAUM ‡ NANCY*
engraved on the foot-rim;
4469 painted in light green
cold colour and *15* engraved
on the underside
After Bergé and Wirtz, Nancy
1924

Colourless glass with mixed
powder inclusions in yellow,
cobalt blue and shades of
orange as well as two white
patches and green and purplish black powder fused on.
Decoration in simple relief
etching, markings within
contours in needle etching,
on the flowers in flat, faintly
polished relief engraving:
twigs with dense foliage and
three apple blossoms.

H 23.3   Ø 6.2 cm
Prov.: formerly Daum
Collection, Nancy

Luxury edition. Model no. 4469,
'Petite urne effilée' (small taper-
ing urn), from the 1924 'Pommier, verreries à lamelles ciselées
à la roue' (apple tree, marquetry,
wheel-engraved) edition (illus.
right): see *Daum Cat. aquar.* II;
Daum Tarif II.

The term *urne* (urn) used to
designate the present form was
frequently employed in firm
records for high-shouldered vessels. There is no apparent resemblance between the 1909 Bergé
study no. 38, 'Fleurs de pommier' (apple blossoms, illus.
below, right), and the translation
of the motif into design. On the
stylization see cat. no. 120. For
other models in the edition see
Hilschenz-Mlynek and Ricke
1985, p. 115, no. 116; Mannoni
n.d. [1986], p. 57; for those in
the Daum Collection see Daum,
Dossier S.R.I.L. no. 54005705;
Monte Carlo, *Daum*, 1982, no. 52,
illus. pl. X; Tokyo, *Daum*, 1984,
nos. 55–56; Tokyo, *Daum*, 1987,
nos. 75, 100, 156 (dating from
c. 1910).

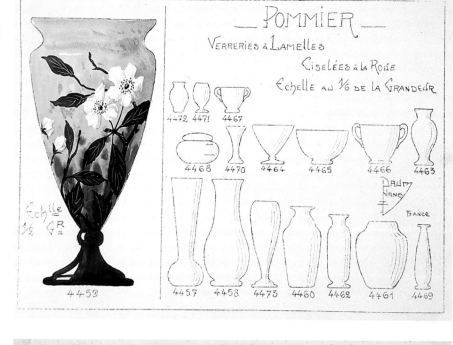

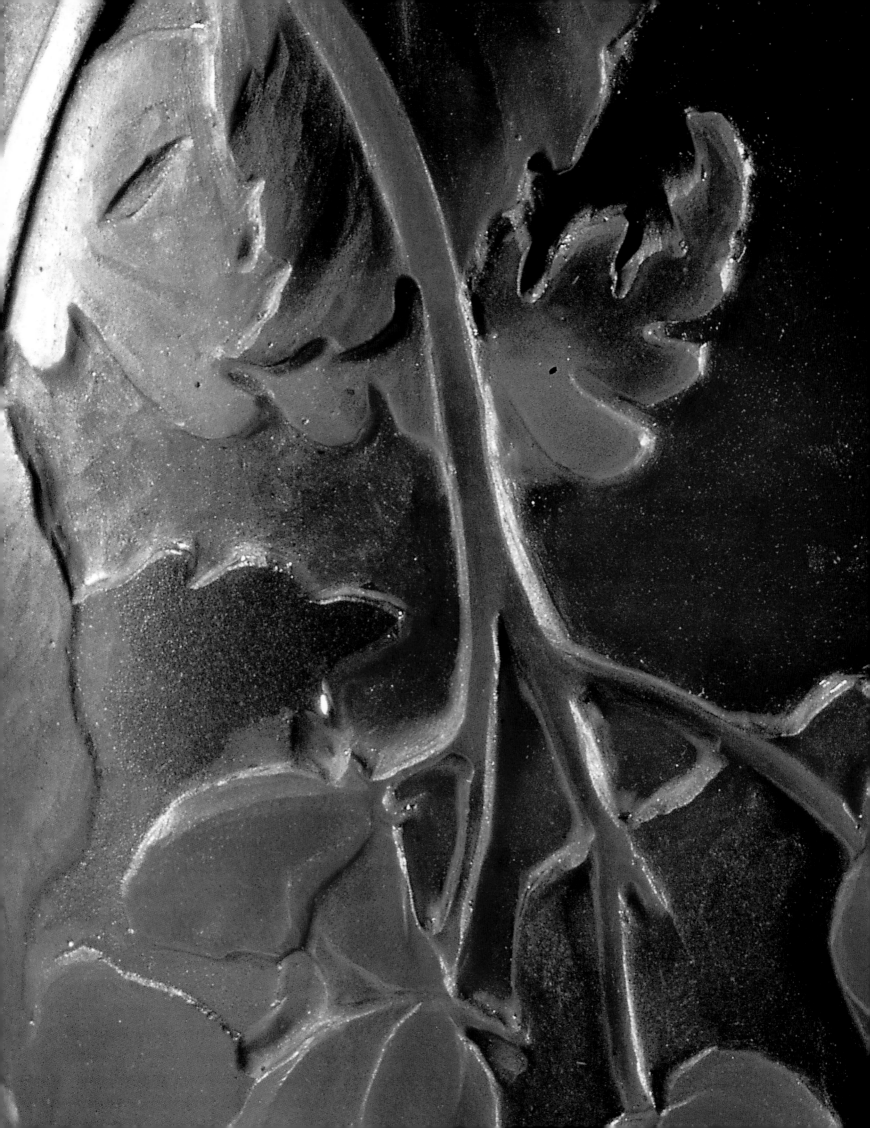

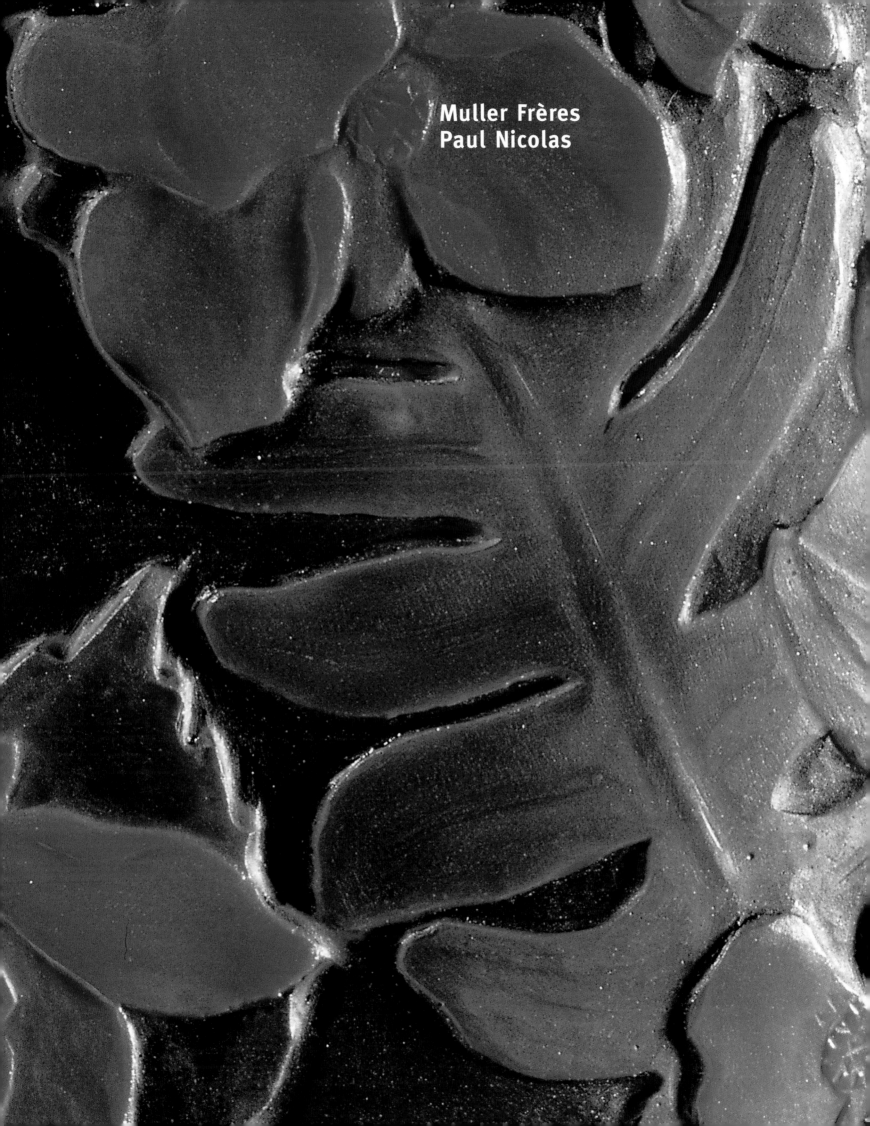

Muller Frères
Paul Nicolas

122

Vase

Signature: *J D Muller Croismare* in needle etching on the underside
Design and execution: Jean-Désiré Muller, Croismare
c. 1900–1905

Colourless glass body with simple relief decoration on one side, shallow relief engraving within the contours. Outer and inner wall painted in flecks with reduction colours primarily with silver content and lustre: plant (hibiscus) with two flowers and two open seed capsules.

H 15 Ø 7.7 cm

Luxury glass edition. Dating this factory's products is difficult since the literature of the time rarely goes into it in any depth and it has never been subjected to scholarly analysis. The relatively early date is suggested by the intricacy of the decoration, which *c.* 1905, after the powder colouring and techniques made known by Daum Frères had been adopted, tended to be handled more boldly. For comparison see a footed vase dating from 1900–1905 with waterlily buds finished in a similar technique in Schmitt, *Sammlung Silzer*, 1989, p. 266, no. 139, illus. p. 265; *Sammlung Silzer* 2003, no. 210.

This painting technique was pioneered by Amédée de Caranza and Désiré Christian.

123

Vase with cockchafer

Signature: *MULLER* etched in relief low on the wall
Attributed to Jean-Désiré and Eugène Muller
c. 1908–14

Colourless body glass with loose white powder inclusions and double casing in white and copper-ruby red-brown (striking colours of copper); rim pinched and ground down, in places to upper outer wall; small pontil mark, not ground down. Decoration in varying degrees of relief and needle etching, with silver-stain painting. Inner and outer wall matt etched, relief polished in places: a cockchafer in flight above a twig running diagonally from bottom to top with pendent cymose inflorescence and berries of the guelder-rose (*Viburnum opulus*).

H 12.7 Ø 8 cm

Serially produced. There are parallels to both the stylization of the decoration and the layering of colours in Val Saint-Lambert products, for which, according to *Carnet Muller*, Jean-Désiré and Eugène Muller were responsible from 1906 to 1908: see Brussels, *Val Saint-Lambert*, 1990, nos. 125–47, illus. pp. 64–69. For the same decoration, in different colours and on a different vessel shape, described as 'American maple in bloom', see Cappa 1991, no. 852.

124

Vase with red begonias

Signature: *MULLER FRES LUNÉVILLE* etched in relief on lower wall
Muller studio
c. 1919–25

Colourless glass body with dark purplish powder inclusions and triple casing in white with silver content, transparent green and opaque bright red; vessel wall flattened bilaterally. Decoration in relief etching, lines within the contours – except for some leaves low on the wall – in relief engraving; ground, including rim and floor, engraved with carved texture: red begonias in front of bluish green fern fronds on a brownish purple ground. The colour layers cannot be precisely determined because of the striking colours.

H 22.1 W 15 D 9.2 cm

A one-off piece or from a small luxury edition. Masterly engraving that makes the most of the play of colours. Attribution to a designer is impossible. Dated on the basis of the signature and the design of the floral decoration, which is still close to the principles espoused by the Ecole de Nancy. The factory did not adapt its product range to the contemporary Art Deco style until the late 1920s.

125

'Orchidées blanches'
jardinière

Signature: *Muller*
etched in relief on lower wall
Attributed to Jean-Désiré and
Eugène Muller
c. 1908–14

Colourless glass body with
triple casing in light green,
white and copper ruby-red-
brown (striking colours of
copper); the vessel subsequently matt etched. Decoration in low-relief etching
and in silver-stain painting:
a spray of orchids (*Oncidium*)
and stylized leaves.

H 10.2 W 15 D 11 cm

Serially produced. See cat. no.
123. For other forms with the
same motif, with a different
colour scheme, see Brussels,
Val Saint-Lambert, 1990, no.
129; Cappa 1991, nos. 855–56.
For a vase with stylized lady's-
slipper, which was formed
with the same mould, see
Hilschenz-Mlynek and Ricke
1985, p. 333, no. 454.

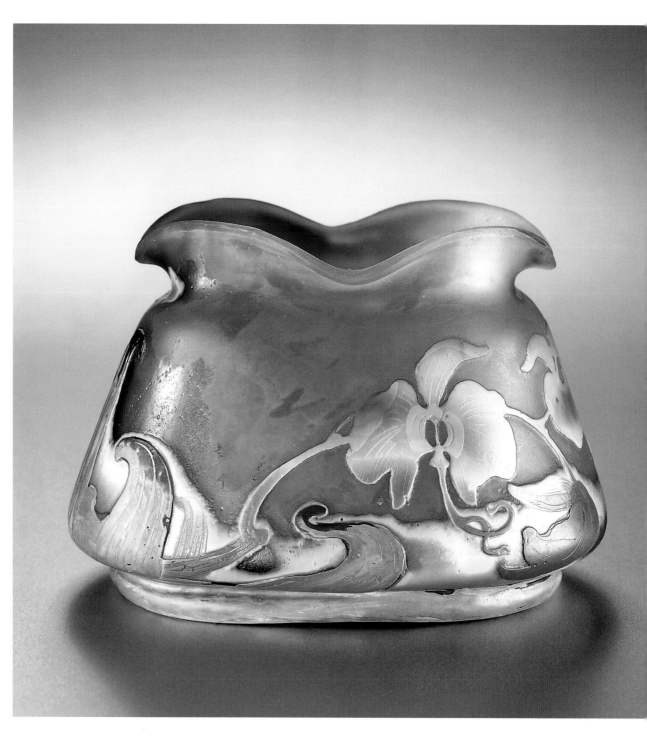

126

Vase with crab

Signature: *P. Nicolas Nancy*
diamond-point engraved on
the underside
Paul Nicolas
c. 1930–37

Colourless glass body with
scattered, partly layered
inclusions of cobalt and silver
compounds, with sandwiched
double-casing in blown-out,
opaque light blue and violet;
sandwiched decoration in
relief etching and silver-stain
painting, solid floor of
colourless glass with partly
fused powder in white and
yellow with silver content
applied, freely formed. Outer
wall, foot-rim and lip textured with matt fine carving,
the crab motif of the underwater scene in reserves relief-
cut to create a sculptural
effect and lightly polished.

H 20.8 Ø 17 cm

A one-off piece or from a small
series. The highly aesthetic
quality of the vase furnishes
convincing proof of Nicolas's
great talent, which is not easy
to discern in the etched designs
he did in the manner of the late
serially produced Gallé pieces.
The present piece may have
been inspired by a vase designed
by Daum *c.* 1920 with *intercalaire* decoration and called

'Crabe au fond de la mer'
(illus. left): see Nancy, *Daum* II,
1978, p. 29, no. 39 not illus.; Daum
1980, p. 96; Sapporo, *Daum*, 1980,
no. 73, drawing no. 4.

Lit.: Ricke, *Koepff*, p. 753, fig. 15.

Sources

Contract of 4 January 1885 concluded between Emile Gallé, the manufacturer Burgun, Schverer & Co., Meisenthal, and its glass painter Désiré Christian

The Meisenthal Glassworks hereby undertakes to manufacture for M. Gallé all glass articles, engraved or cut, based on his drawings, made with his moulds or produced according to his specific instructions, unless this lies beyond the competence of the factory. None of these models will be divulged by the factory to any other customer. The decoration will be executed by the firm's painter M. D. Christian. In exchange, and in the interests of the manufactory and its glass decorators, M. Gallé undertakes to supply the factory workshop with a regular provision of work for its painters. Further, M. Christian will remain in the position he presently occupies and pledges to both parties not to place his skills or knowledge at the service of any third party, be it with respect to the invention of processes and improvements in enamels or to other applications on glass fired in a muffle kiln. M. Christian reserves the right to do as he sees fit with innovations that he has presented to both parties and that they have rejected. Nonetheless, as in the past, the factory will enjoy every latitude in decorating his glassware, without, of course, copying, altering or imitating the *verre Gallé*. On articles described as ordinary, the firm Burgun, Schverer and Co. will concede to M. Gallé a rebate of twenty per cent (20%) with shipping gratis to the border. Enamel-decorated table services will not be treated as ordinary articles. The description 'ordinary' pertains to coloured and cut ware for which the cost of forming amounts to less than two-thirds that of the decoration. These Gentlemen, together with their travelling salesmen and other factory representatives, will exercise the utmost discretion in public with regard to M. Gallé's output.

Emile Gallé
Notes on glass production
Notice sur la production du verre

The eighth exhibition of the Union Centrale des Arts Décoratifs, entitled "La pierre, le bois, la terre et le verre", was held to showcase the achievements of France's crafts industry. Emile Gallé participated in this national event with large collections of ceramics and glass.

The following report, which Gallé submitted to the jury, is instructive in a number of ways. It illustrates the close interaction between artistic intentions and technical research, indicates the wide range of his products and gives iconographic details of his chosen subjects during his emergence as a leading figure of Art Nouveau glass art.

These extensive notes by Gallé on his glass production are augmented by comparably important comments he made on his submissions to the Paris Exposition Universelle of 1889; complete notes: Gallé, *Ecrits*, 1908, pp. 302–53.

Eighth Exhibition of the Union Centrale des Arts Décoratifs (1884)

II *Notes on glass production*

Emile Gallé, master glassmaker in Nancy, has the honour of submitting various specimens created by him to the Jury of the eighth Exposition. He kindly draws your attention: to certain technical processes of decoration and various new applications that he has recently realized; to the decorative uses to which they are put.

I *Glass decoration processes employed by Gallé*
A – New colour schemes on glass, double- and triple-cased, marbled glass, imitation of precious stones, use of metal foil, air bubbles.
B – Extending the palette of opaque enamel on glass with regard to tonal values; new colour schemes. Use of transparent and translucent enamel on glass, other than cobalt oxide enamel.
C – New and unusual decor: cased glass, new decorative engraving process. Cut and wheel-work; cameo and intaglio engraving, figurines.

New colour schemes
This year the exhibitor presents a number of hues coloured in the body (chromium oxide, ferrous oxide and various combinations of the oxides of iron, cobalt and manganese); free imitations of semi-precious stones, transparent, translucent or marbled with opaque veining. Coloration is obtained by introducing into the glass various oxides and metal salts, opal glass and gold, cuprous oxide or manganese coloured glass. He also presents glassware incorporating gold and platinum leaf, as well as double- and tripled-cased glass with a marbled layer.

Certain specimens give rise to completely new effects and unprecedented functions for which no parallels exist in modern or historic glassmaking.

In order of increasing complexity the exhibitor begs the jury to examine the following samples:

Ordinary glass age-spotted with iron oxide – Cigarette box.
  Fighting octopus.
  Cylindrical pot and tray. Cut, polished.
  Moulded cut-glass dragon, gold-mounted.

Light green prasinite glass (with potash base), slightly dichroic. – Bowl with cabochons in sapphirine or blue-quartz colour glass (composition based on potash), with translucent enamel.
Chemistry mortar; wheel-engraved, cut and polished. Same colour.

'Clair de lune' glass (with potash base). – In passing, Emile Gallé would like to note that glass coloured by a small quantity of cobalt oxide of a pretty sapphire hue, a colour since popularized by a number of French and foreign glassmakers, was already issued by him in 1878. The decorative uses derived from it have made this shade extremely fashionable. Commercialized by him under the name *clair de lune*, it has also been produced in Germany under the name *Mondschein* and in England under that of *moonlight glass*. The Musée des Arts Décoratifs exhibits a sample range of that shade bought by the Museum from Gallé in 1878.

The exhibitor presents the same sapphire tone in the following models:

Black-sapphire 'nuagé' glass.
  A crescent-moon shaped ashtray engraved with figurines.
  A round-edged square flask. Decor: woman with sickle-moon.
  Cut-glass, enameled baluster-shaped light.
Slightly dichroic green glass (with soda base). – Enamelled, lobed glass basket.
Same tone, speckled black and red heliotrope type (cuprous oxide). Vase with two handles; translucent enamel.
Vase with potash base, imitating a quartz coloured by carburized coal-based substances. – Square vase with two handles, enamelled.
Same glass, with sardonyx hue (glass flecks with cuprous oxide). – Mould-blown slender conical vase.
Same glassware, imitating riband agate. – Blue jug cast with lion relief, pressed into the mould and with polychrome enamel. Large pail with applied forms resembling the scales of a pine cone. Smoky tones, polychrome marbling.
Glass tinted with cobalt oxide, sprinkled with blue and red-coloured opal. – Leaf, festooned vase, creamer with polychrome enamel.
Clear glass with blood-red marbling, chalcedony type (cuprous oxide glass). – Oval, slender conical vase; the circles are drawn round with the iron by the glassmaker. Enamelled edges.
  Teapot with lid, blood-red dappling; cut-glass carp, gilded: fin gathered with the iron.
Glass tinted with transparent speckling, 'scale' type (manganese). – Mug with decor recalling a mount.
Clear glass, amethyst quartz type (manganese). – Paintbrush-holder, with cicadas cut into the marbling. Little pot with cut Egyptian scarabs and enamel. *Pourrissoir* tub; opaque marbling.
Clear glass, asbestos-quartz type. – Small bowl with blue and silver decor.

Clear glass, moss-agate type (copper oxide). – Small Medici vase with engraved figurines and enamel.
Clear glass, marbled, opalized quartz type, moonstone, etc. – Black-marbled bowl with intaglio and cameo engraving.
Clear glass, marbled opaque emerald green. – Covered, engraved potiche jar.
Marbled glass, cased green. – Emerald-green basin, turquoise marbling, gilt and silver-gilt engraving.
Triple-cased glass, pink opal, black marbling. – Bowl with cameo and intaglio engraving.
Triple-cased glass, marbled opal, jade type. – Bowl with cameo and intaglio engraving.
Marbled glass, whose near-crimson, bluish colouring betrays the presence of gold. In reflected light, this marbling appears yellowish; in refraction, red or pink.
  Agate-glass flat-relief flask, opalescent pebbling in reflected light; crimson in refracted. The stopper imitates a stone known as rhinestone or 'Bohemian ruby'.
  Flask of a similar shape, yellowish; stopper adorned with colourless transparent glass within opaque colour ground, high-relief engraved.
  Covered cup with intaglio Bacchanalia.
  Such colorations are interesting both from a technical and decorative point of view, with respect to the potential they offer to the artist. Unfortunately, if industrial applications alone are considered, the process does not appear to be particularly practical, the effects concerned being so variable that they result in a relatively high proportion of rejects. A number of such pieces are thus entirely devoid of artistic and commercial value. As for the finer pieces, one must have a fairly lively imagination to extract interesting subjects from their bizarre designs; the path one has to follow is similar to that in gem engraving, where, for example, an artist will try to elicit a female figure from the vein in a piece of pink agate.
  The black-marbled cup with cameo and intaglio engraving is a rare example of the value that invention can impart to a piece of impure glass. This object contained three opaque marble lines from which the artist extracted his chosen subject: night, silence, sleep.

The same occurs on the following piece:
Seedy glass, amethyst-quartz type. – On this object, the engraver takes pleasure in depicting a woman and cupids blowing soap bubbles represented in the walls of the piece by blown bubbles.

Metal foiling. – The exhibitor also presents tinted glass incorporating gold and platinum leaf that serves as a repoussoir for the enamels, and in particular for translucent enamels whose brilliance is much enhanced in this way:
  Small, flat helm; grisaille niello and enamel; gold leaf.
  Vase with polychrome enamels; platinum foil.

New colourings, translucent enamel
All decorations by the exhibitor are executed by hand. His palette has broadened and now includes painting on glass, gilding and silvering, high-relief enamelling, grisaille, painting with crystal colours on white relief, employed by the Bohemians under the name *weisse*

Email (i.e. *Reliefemail*), binders composed of tin oxide, lead oxide and flint; finally, the hard 'Arab' enamels and transparent enamels.

The fervent desire to create products with a pronounced modern and French character from enamel paint on glassware has incited the exhibitor to seek hues that neither glassmakers from Damascus and Venice, nor German painters have used in their pieces; particular reds and blues, for example, particular blacks, yellows and greens, particular crimsons, pinks and violets – and above all half-tones, broken or fine shades, some greys, flesh tones and ivory tints. Employed carefully, and being careful not to overcool the decoration of the glass, they can bestow a certain charm, and certainly adorn the materials in a most novel manner.

Finally, convergences between the decoration and the function of individual objects have encouraged Gallé in his search for translucent enamels other than the magnificent ancient cobalt blue. Since some objects are to present their decorative properties as much through reflection as refraction, we have felt it necessary to enlarge the colour range of the enamels in the direction of reduced opacity. Such are the technical means that Gallé employs regularly in decoration, and his exhibition will sometimes show them combined in one and the same piece.

Tinting and surface colouring of glass by means of silver oxide. – Slender, conical, clear-glass vessel painted yellow with silver stain, with carved reserves and opaque and translucent polychrome enamels; use of gold and platinum.

Grisaille. – Glass bowl with gold inclusions, grisaille figures and enamels.

High-relief painting – Slender, conical, clear-glass vase with blue glass foot. View of Nancy and high-relief painted ornamentation in black.

Large basin with flat sides and two handles. Decor: winter and autumn, black cameo highlighted by gilt enamel.

Liqueur service, square shape, black, high-relief engraving with transparent enamels.

Small tankards, corn-cockle and rinceaux, black cameo engraving on glass with gold inclusions. Black and white enamel over gold.

Opaque paint applied on wheel-engraved glass. – Small, clear-glass vase; crawfish and small fish, enamel edging.

Opaque white decorated with crystal colours (Bohemian technique), lacking solidity, discolours in acid. Clear-glass goblet, with Venetian ribbons, decorated with forget-me-nots (imitated by both German and Parisian workshops).

Figured *bonbonnière*.

Liqueur flask with recurring 'card' motifs.

Enamels coloured in the mass, with softer shades, applied by Gallé to the preceding style and to small, clear-glass items whose sides are ground flat. The decor is visible from both sides; vitrified, it adheres perfectly to the glass. – Paintbrush-holder. Subject: water-carriers. The decoration is drawn with a black line, the subjects filled in with enamel.

Hard batch-coloured enamels, as in the Arab or Venetian technique. – The well-documented difficulty of manufacture using this method – rediscovered by Philippe-Joseph Brocard (the obstacles are noted by Jules Henrivaux) – consists of finding a stable enamel that does not tarnish in the atmosphere or in the presence of acidity,

and yet whose composition is reasonably similar to the body receiving the decoration; in this way, crazing is avoided, without, however, the piece suffering distortion while it is fusing on account of the fact that the same basis is shared by both body and enamel. All in all then, with respect to the composition of the glass that is to receive the enamel, crucial connections between the composition and the firing of the enamel remain elusive. These enamels are not available commercially.

When he started out on this road, that is to say, around 1873, Gallé employed solely opaque red, white, turquoise and green, as well as transparent blue and gold, each outlined with a brown line to assist the painter responsible for laying in the enamel in following the design, and, above all, to provide the eye with a clear idea of this design.

Opaque enamel, various tones. – Basin with Persian decor (industrially produced). Persian jug. Woman dressed in a pale yellow enamel; grisaille head. Appearance of gold foil in glass with Persian decor.

Opaque enamels associated with iridescent colours, adapted to the Persian style. – Designed by Gallé, this decoration is based on red and black enamels, softened by a gold and platinum ground and brown rinceaux drawn with a pen, with nuanced shading, grey, pink and iridescent colours.

Goblet, foot pincered and goffered.

Oval *jardinière*.

Slender conical vase, trilobate neck.

Lobate four-foot conical vase.

Scent bottles.

Use of silver-stained glass. – Threaded flower-tub; horsemen in white enamel on gold, decoration in shimmering silver stain on gold foil.

New shades of opaque enamel. – Square box, smoked glass, polychrome enamels.

Smoked glass flacon, bird shape, turtledove-grey, gold brown, café-au-lait, flesh tint, red, black, dark blue, light blue enamels. Square-necked round vase, black, pink, ivory and gold rosettes. Vase in copper-oxide glass, black palm fronds, ivory-coloured, pink and silver. Example of the decorative use of a readily obtainable material that has been positively abused in recent years. Even in its most industrial products, Venice never debased this pretty nuance.

Opaque enamels with faded tints, with gold and silver. – Solid, clear-glass basket. Ecru-coloured glass handle. Decoration: heraldic lions in enamel of a slightly faded tone, pale blue, washed-out satin, peach, washed-out black.

Light-hued opaque enamels with plain silvered transparent enamel. – Rounded-edged square flask, amber grey; sea anemones. The purpose of this quest for a dilute colour range is to make the objects concerned appear as if underwater.

Transparent enamels. – In some of his more recent pieces Emile Gallé has introduced a totally colourless and transparent enamel. Ceremonial glass, baluster shaped, in amber grey glass with Venetian ribbons (optic moulding). Decoration composed of ivory enamel over gold, and beads of a colourless and, as it were, aqueous enamel, imitating droplets of water. The effect seen from inside these pieces is satisfactory.

Pale green glass flask, bluish glass medallions ornamented with figurines drawn in pen and filled in with a colourless enamel imitating intaglio. The property of H. M. the Queen of Italy.

Coloured transparent enamels and fluxes obtained by Gallé that do not exist on the market. – Dichroic, slender conical vase, ornamented with *sempervivum* blooms in polychrome enamel and in a transparent enamel known as 'amber-yellow enamel', of a particular yellowish hue.
Mother-of-pearl enamel. Slender conical vase adorned with an iris whose stem is in enamel imitating mother-of-pearl.
Violet transparent enamel.
Enamel applied over enamel. Crimson transparent enamel, vase with two handles, orchids. Pendulum clock: modern ornamentation. The property of H. M. the Queen of Italy.
Emerald green transparent enamel. Jug with one handle and a spout; bearing motto: *Me fleurisse la rose.*
It might be interesting to employ such colourings in small areas of stained glass for interiors. It is beyond question, however, that their proper place is rather in vases that can then be placed, if only temporarily, between the viewer and the main light source in the home. As experimented here, an interior made entirely of opaque enamel would, on the contrary, have no decorative effect.

Unusual decoration, wheel-engraving

Unusual and curious decoration. – Experiment with double glass. Instead of being cut out with the knife or diamond-point engraved on a piece of foil enclosed between the two shells when cold, the decoration is painted in gold on one of them. The solder is concealed by enamel edging.
New process of decorative engraving. – Cross of Lorraine hollowed out on a helmet-shaped vase. Unique to Gallé, it is a novel method of ornamentation that imitates certain imprints or agglomerations of fossil shells.
Use of solid crystal, the result of gemstone imitation and the attempt to ensure the solidity of glass objects. – Oval vase with two handles, smoked glass, engraved with fleur-de-lys; red and shrimp-pink enamel decor on a patinated black ground.
Round cup on foot, in solid clear glass, hollowed sides; reserves cut into rinceaux with polished facets; medallion with intaglio engraving: woman drawing a bow.
Wheel-engraving, in association with enamelling in decorating glass. – 'M. Gallé', writes Jules Henrivaux, Director of Saint-Gobain, in his book *Le Verre et le Cristal*, 'has striven to restore to popularity among a very select and, it should be conceded, very exclusive, public, an art that shone brightly in Antiquity as well as during the sixteenth and seventeenth centuries – that of engraving on glass; he manages to convey its full potential, by combining it in one and the same piece with enamel, in spite of the extraordinary perils and frequent losses involved. In recent years, colour has completely eclipsed the charming art of engraving in the affection of the public.'
At Gallé's exhibition at the Champ-de-Mars in 1878, the Musée des Arts Décoratifs purchased a small, thick, clear-glass bowl with engraved subjects – the four seasons, after Raphael – and

decorated with white, black and red enamels on relief bandeaus in imitation of the mounts of the silversmith. Gallé made this advance expressly to add warmth to the chilly decoration of clear crystal glass.
This year, he presents the following pieces, engraved or decorated in his own factory, that bear witness to even closer collaboration between the wheel and enamelling:
Enamels laid in the engraved areas, or set into deep and gilded cuts, a process that imparts the solid appearance of a mount to the decor. – Small ashtray in moss-agate glass, with the inscription: *Plaisir est fumée.* Emerald green, black-striped enamels, fringed by gilt-edged incisions. Small ashtray in amethyst- and asbestos-type glass, running border in silvered cut, painted pale blue enamel, fly with intaglio engraved wings and body in enamels set within surface engraving.
Ashtray in moss-agate glass. Engraved, gilded and enamelled dragonfly. Hyacinth branch deep cut, asbestos and enamels, white, fawn and black.
Aspersorium, gilt incisions imitating inlay and set gemstones: glass cabochons, enamelled red and blue with engraved animals.
Pendular clock: intaglio subject: Fortuna sleeping on her wheel; violet and green transparent enamels, ivory opaque enamelling.
Shell cup rock-crystal type; engraving and polychrome enamel.
Green-white jug *nuagé* gold, prettily clipped yew branches, interspersed with emerald-green and turquoise leaves; berries, red enamel, butterflies, cut, interspersed with various enamels.
Motto: *Toujours de même*, gilt incised on black enamel.
Richly decorated service, known as water glass, smoky-quartz type, polished spiral cut, animals in gilded green enamel, the design intaglio engraved.
Vase in the shape of a bag, ecru glass, bordered with laurel, alternately engraved, gilded, polychrome; blazon.
Engraving finishes. – Emile Gallé accords the greatest care to the composition of designs for wheel-engraving. He never etches with hydrofluoric acid as this can never obtain the artistic effects he desires.
All engraving is done with the wheel, with emery and lead, copper or wooden wheels. Their finish is the finest imaginable. The figurines are executed as carefully as intaglio on precious stones.

II Decorative applications derived by Emile Gallé from the manufacturing processes of his art

A. – Inventing or selecting forms that emphasize the natural qualities of glass, the most important of which being transparency and translucence; respecting the appropriateness and function of each object; exploiting decorative processes derived from glass-making.
B. – Conceiving ornamentation that accords with the laws governing glassware decoration, in particular that of transparent materials; knowledge of the styles of the past and the traditions of decoration in glassmaking; a marked preference for motifs borrowed predominantly from the flora and fauna of the country, freely interpreted and adapted to enamel work and intaglio engraving; the fruitful arrival of *feeling* in glass decoration; *verrerie parlante.*

C. – Products that, through their reasonable pricing, can stem the tide of German articles and inferior wares.

Invention or selection of forms appropriate to the function of the article

Table service. – Smoky-quartz type glass, with intaglio engraving and enamel borders. Combined apparent and actual stability. Neutral or intrinsic tones intended to avoid conveying any impression of harshness or cold. Cut areas allowing for added brilliance.

Fruit basket centrepiece. – Low-slung shape, lobed, derived from a shell. The ornamentation consists of 'Antique'-style cutwork that recalls the original form. Border with modern adornments, black and gold high-relief enamelling.

Forms derived from natural elements and transparent materials that can, in turn, be applied to glassware. – Shell- or basket-shaped container for cards, papers and flowers, in solid glass imparting stability to an office desk. The form is redolent of a number of creatures from the primeval world, such as ammonites, *Ostrea columba*; material, opalescent quartz type, *nuagé* velvety black. The intaglio engraved decor represents the return of the dove to the Ark; inscription: *Post nubila Phoebus*.

Small vase with violets. Squat, depressed form, reminiscent of certain species of beetle, the resemblance completed by a double handle and lugs in the shape of eyes. The decoration is composed of cutwork and striations.

Rose vase. Certain flowers with flexible stems and heavy blooms, such as the 'Maréchal Niel' rose, or with a stubby stalk, such as 'Magnolia Lenné', require a vase that displays them to best effect. Such is the purpose of this piece; the elongated shape is inspired by the flowers of certain labiates. Fittings. Conical vessels display the form of a slender shell stood on its tip. The central piece is an intaglio snail with leaping lion, a purely fantastic form. The decoration is borrowed from the form and appearance of the material, as limpid as spring water, or as murky as a marsh. The vase is crisscrossed by moss-green, dark blue and blackish waves. Cutwork cupids play with snails of the same shape as the vase. The snails recur in white, green and violet enamels. The piece belongs to the Président du Conseil, Jules Ferry.

Motifs borrowed from flora and fauna of the countryside

Insects. – Medallions on faded gold, adorned with small, stylized and enlarged butterflies. Border comprising insect limbs; regular ornamentation produced by iteration. The brown design is drawn in pen and filled in with enamels in a tempered pink, pearl white, golden brown, red, on ecru-coloured glass. Small scent flacon; same method. Speckled enamels and foiled in gold.

Oval vase with four cabochons. Same stylistic experiments: the history of the butterfly: caterpillar, cocoon, love. The spirals simulating silken threads tie together the motifs to bordering made of noctuid wings, in red, pink, café-au-lait and white and gold enamels.

Pitcher. Same method. Ornamentation derived from the cockchafer.

Flower-tub, Venetian ribbons (optic moulding); Persian divinity creating the insects.

Cigar-box adorned with a cameo representing a flying grasshopper, cut in solid clear crystal; light emerald-green marbling mimics the green stripes on the wings. Pink enamel. The remainder of the vase depicts Egyptian harvesters, gilt-engraved. Large, conical vase in the shape of a water-clock with polychrome enamel ring. The overall form of the cup and its foot reminds the artist of certain kinds of flower that wither just prior to full bloom, such as the dandelion; after making numerous studies of the plant, he engraved the motif (i.e. the flower as it appears in nature) on the foot and embellished the base by edging it with a loose, gilt-engraved line of leaves. The leg becomes the stem of a giant flower that is the cup itself. Cutwork lends definition to the divisions of the calyx. The edges are fringed with a regular border redolent of pistils, and interrupted intermittently. The little insects that visit these flowers (much enlarged and freely interpreted) adorn the cup, detached in relief by the engraver. Their fan-like wings are gilded, the back left treated matt and striated like a quartz knob. Slender conical vase adorned with fine gossamer, engraved, gilded. The insect, made out of a glob of glass decorated in polychrome (ivory, pale green, gold and brown) stands in relief against an apple-green inscription: *Araignée du soir, espoir.* On the base, a frieze formed by the repetition of a fly with pale green wings.

Glass patella, amber, gold-spangled. Spangles glitter through the black-speckled colourless wings of a fantastical dragonfly. The broad, flat handles are enamelled with minium on a lead ground, openwork. Deep within the bowl of the basin more dragonflies, in blue transparent enamel. Property of Antonin Proust.

Paintbrush-holder. The handles are adorned with ornamental violets in polychrome enamel over a ground ranging from red, through rosy-dawn and flesh tone, to a violet-tinged chocolate-brown. The body is in amethyst-type quartz. The engraver conjured up out of the marbling a Provençal cicada and a shimmering butterfly with extended wings.

Verrerie parlante. – Decorative motifs borrowed from legend and from French poetry:

A goblet, polychrome enamels over glass incorporating gold leaf. Subject taken from the *Ballade des Dames du Temps jadis* by François Villon: *La Reyne Blanche comme un lys, qui chantoit à voix de Sereine.*

Flower-tub. Bouquets in transparent and opaque enamels. Motto: *Me fleurisse la rose.*

Amethyst glass. *Pourrissoir* tub; dotted with dark-hued roses, engraved, leaded. Motto: *Elles ont gardé leur parfum.* Transparent enamels derived from parts of the flower.

Vase honorifique, a covered goblet. Intaglio engraving representing Fortuna on her wheel; with one hand she raises a glass. Inscription: *Vitrea fama.* Intaglio engraved rinceaux, enamelled edging incorporating wheels of fortune.

Studio compositions and designs. – Finally Emile Gallé here exhibits specimens of ornamental studies and drawings that were conceived by himself or by his pupils under his direction for glass decoration. The attention of the jury is directed to the fact that Gallé always takes nature as his point of departure and that he strives to go beyond it in his effort to achieve an expression and style all his own.

Nancy, 22 September 1884.

Notes on the production of glass and luxury crystal objects by Emile Gallé

Notice sur la production de verres et crystaux de luxe d'Emile Gallé

Extract from Gallé's commentary on his submission to the Paris Exposition Universelle of 1889

IV Industrial applications: The popularization of art

Gentlemen, in submitting to you, after artefacts of great refinement and luxury, specimens from my manufactory adapted to more modest requirements, I am confident this has been done without compromising quality. Neither my craftsmen nor I have found it beyond our power to reconcile affordable products with art; we have not felt that crystal in its commercial garb has, of necessity, to be the subject of inferior taste. After all the Orient, uninfluenced by Europe, has managed to produce the most exquisite trinkets. A sizeable, but not excessively large workforce that is conscientious, competent and equipped with plenty of tools and, more importantly, of models, and has recourse to numerous technical processes and methods as well as a design studio that imparts direction to the work in hand – such are the conditions that have allowed me to furnish goods to retailers and export traders alike at reasonable prices.

I have not been content to produce pieces that display mastery alone; I have also striven to make art accessible, so as to open a greater number of minds to more ambitious works. I have indeed propagated a feeling for nature – for the grace in a flower, for the beauty in an insect. My labours over the past twenty-four years have already spawned a rich vein of infinitely varied forms, styles, ideas and genres for the creation of fine glassware. I therefore believe I am justified in claiming that I have 'popularized' art.

You will find in my work living proof that neither art nor taste depend on costly manufacture, and that it is enough for the producer to submit his models and decorations with grace and personal commitment in accordance with the prevailing economic constraints and the practices of his craft.

In my low-cost production, I have eschewed the artificial, the cumbersome, the flimsy. I have paid particular attention to solid colours. The great mass of new works has had an effect on public taste. I have paved the way to crystal glassworking and – occasionally to my detriment – its profitable exploitation by factories devoted to high turnover. Imitations of the 'genre Gallé' have begun appearing. I am all the gladder for this.

I wish only that moderation, sobriety and good taste may preside for ever over the use to which my humble discoveries are put! And may any discoveries reap the benefit from the increased esteem in which a material of which we remain fond is held, rather than merely increase the stocks of debased and inferior products.

V The organization of a design studio, especially for crystal glass: Matter governed by art

In my factory, I have set up a special studio for composition and design in glass production. Under my direct supervision, this studio serves as the motor of all the others.

It is there that profiles for turning the wooden forms for glass-blowing are executed, the watercolours and cartoons for the enamellers, engravers and painters are made. In the factory's garden and in natural history collections, numerous models from life are always at the studio's disposal.

My own contribution resides above all in dreaming up new roles for crystal – be they pleasant or terrible; in painstakingly composing amiable- or tragic-looking faces for it; in organizing the disparate elements; in preparing well in advance for the execution of future projects; in ensuring that our techniques are adapted to the work before us; and, against the backdrop of what is after all a hazardous enterprise, in tipping the scales in favour of future success in a decisive operation that might, in former times, have been dubbed an 'opus magnum'. In other words, I set down in advance, so far as it lies in my power, the qualities that this effervescent, mutable material should, in addition to colour schemes and compositions, possess, in order to realize my dream, my idea.

Needless to say, all these calculations can be, and often are, jeopardized by unforeseen circumstances; yet it is precisely the unpredictability of a craft in which the vagaries of fire are involved that has unexpectedly led to fortuitous results.

Sometimes I even amuse myself by making flawed pieces into charming playthings, little baroque problems with which this multifarious material captures the imagination. In the same way, the eyes of a sick man turn a leaf of marbled paper into a thousand bizarre figures or a child construes clouds lit by the setting sun as an immense sheepfold, while the seaman sees in them only rolling whitecaps or a beach.

It is by dint of similar processes that hardstone engravers, the Soldis, Lemaires and Schultzes, conjure up the strangest designs from onyx or riband agate. 'What a charming art!' the eminent professor at the Collège de France, M. Guillaume, exclaimed in his *Etudes sur l'art et la nature*, a volume devoted to ancient and modern art. 'To take a gemstone as nature intended', he continues, 'with all its irregularities, its unpredictable planes, with its vast gamut of diverse colours, and extract from it compositions complete with nudes, drapery and accessories; to add nuance to the colours by carefully reducing the thickness of the various layers; to act for an instant as a servant to matter so as to force it to express an idea and so, by turning nature's tricks to our own advantage, make the final product appear like the outcome of a pre-established agreement between mere happenstance and the genius of the engraver. This kind of work is tailor-made to solicit the inventive and resourceful mind and take up all the skill of an artist.'

And, Gentleman, it is indeed a seductive art. Yet even these masters would surely envy the power that glassmakers wield as they create agates and marble with their own hands.

It has caught my fancy to make magnificent onyxes and to wrap streams of lava and pitch around a vase; to divert the Styx and the Acheron into the foot of a cup; and, armed with infernal vapours and fiery meteors, to tear, in a fulginous crystal, poor Orpheus from his fainting Eurydice.

As I have written beneath a vase of mine, 'I sow seeds of fire', and reap with my wheel paradoxical blossoms from the depths of obscure strata, where I know they lie awaiting me. It is perhaps for us that the poet has written:

Je récolte en secret des fleurs mystérieuses!
(I secretly harvest mysterious flowers).

How then could I ever consent to subjugate my art to this soulless substance that is destined to obey the glassmaker's sceptre, the conjuror's magic wand, which makes it a slave of his imaginings?

And so, Gentlemen, I am responsible not only for the design but for everything. My wish has been that crystal glass gives all that it can to the hand that plays with it, be it gently or roughly. For it is through me that it receives its expressive potential – an unquiet black or the *morbidezza* of feeble roses.

VI French crystal with an entirely modern style and feel enters collections of art and of curiosities

Gentlemen, these various occupations may never have succeeded in wholly gaining your approbation were I, in my own work, to have limited myself to applying common decorations intended for other materials, or deriving from anywhere else but my own personal fund, or had I relied on archaeological reconstitutions or even on variations of the legacy of past glassmakers.

The complaint is often aired of how people admire exclusively objects of ancient art and that this has long stifled innovation. It is my firm belief, however, that we will more surely earn the esteem of others by conceiving modern works in a French idiom instead of twiddling our thumbs and lamenting our lot. I have sought to make things that will one day serve to bear witness to their own time – our time.

It must be admitted, however, that the extraordinary quality of French crystal glass in former times even failed to interest the close-knit group whose word was then law – people of taste, sensitivity, erudition, yet eclecticism, who were entranced by unusual materials and scornful of mediocre, mechanical, infinitely blasé products, and, for that very reason, adored naivety and were moved by any expression of innocence.

The present experiments have been favourably received. I am far from suggesting that the merit redounds to me and to no one else; I have not been alone in opening to contemporary French glass the doors to museums and to no less exclusive private collections that heretofore received solely Venetian or Bohemian replicas, Arab glassware and the exquisite crystal of the Far East.

It is with gladness that you will one day observe, Gentlemen, that in 1889 a hallowed place, until then barred to the art of ennobling useful articles, finally surrendered to the renewed splendour of French crystal ware.

Selections from Emile Gallé's correspondence with the firm Burgun, Schverer & Co., Meisenthal

The Corning Museum of Glass, Corning, NY, Chambon Collection

Letter from Emile Gallé probably to the director of the manufactory, Antoine Burgun

Nancy, 11[?] August 1890
My dear Friend,

I write to offer my apologies since at the moment I fear my failing strength is not up to my attending the meeting. So it is, I'm afraid! I am just dragging myself about. I will be with you in spirit on Tuesday and will do my utmost to recover from what ails me. Be that as it may, here is a signed authority allowing me to be represented if it becomes impossible for me to appear. Would you be kind enough as to prepare the following materials so I can have them ready to hand when the proper time comes.

Pink opal caps in a soft, light tone, adaptable either to clear-type glass or white crystal (one or the other).

Amber-brown glass or crystal caps, fine hue. Remind M. Joseph Burgun that this latter clashed when applied to clear glass. It has to be brown in the thin areas.

With sincere affection,   *E. Gallé*

Nancy, le 11e [?] Août 1890
Mon cher ami,

Je viens te présenter mes excuses, car je crains que mes forces assez peu solides en ce moment ne me permettent pas d'assister à la réunion. C'est pourtant comme celà! Je me traîne partout. Je serai de cœur avec vous mardi et ferai tout mon possible pour dominer ce malaise. En tout cas, voici une procuration signée pour me représenter en cas d'impossibilité.

Tu serais bien aimable de me faire préparer les matières suivantes afin que je les trouve en temps utile.

Calottes opale rose, ton tendre-clair, cordant avec soit du verre ordre blanc, soit avec du cristal blanc (l'un ou l'autre)

Calottes verre ou cristal brun ambré foncé, beau ton. Rappeler à M. Joseph Burgun que le dernier, appliqué sur du verre blanc claquait. Il faut qu'il soit brun dans les minces.

Sincères affections   *E. Gallé*

The Corning Museum of Glass, Corning, NY, Chambon Collection, dossier 2, letter p. 1.

Letter from Emile Gallé probably to Désiré Christian

15 May 93

Please find enclosed a duplicate of my letter to M. M. [?] B. Schv & Co. concerning the shoddy production of my Thistle [Chardon] series, nos. 1 to 19 [?]. I have informed this M. M. [?] that, as this pertained also to your decoration, I would send my letter on to you. Be so kind as to see when we might set up a meeting. It is crucial that we do so as soon as possible. I am not free on Sunday; for us here it's impossible.

How is it with the subsequent series? Since I have ordered the warehouse to withdraw series P [?] 1 to 19 [?], with which there is such uncertainty as to price – those pieces are presently being ground at my factory in order to correct the meagre and meaningless *martelé* applied prior to your decor – the result is that I have nothing left; all our customers have come by to express their regret at having to take 'our' orders elsewhere. As for the pieces I am making here, all the newspapers are talking about them and that just serves to compound my problems since [?] these are de luxe one-offs made to special commission.

This then is the situation. You must agree that measures will have to be taken as we are now merely laying the foundations for our rivals' success with our own hands. Very charitable I'm sure, but it will hardly make for much work for our excellent painters, all the more since I have decided, in agreement with M. Gallé [i.e., père Charles Gallé] and the depot, that it is imperative to dispense with all earlier series each year. I am sincerely sorry, for I remain absolutely convinced that you have been exercising the same zeal and thoroughness in the present situation as you always have in the past. What is your son up to?

Cordial greetings [?]   *E. G.*

Was the information from the *Sprechsaal* used for [lathe] turning? [*Postscript in the left-hand margin*]

15 Mai 93

Je vous envoie cijoint le duplicata de ma lettre à M. M. [?] B. Schv & Cie au sujet du mauvais établist [établissement] de ma série Chardon 1 à 19 [?]. J'ai informé ce M. M. [?] que, vos décors étant en question, je vous communiquais ma lettre. Veuillez donc voir quand nous pourrons nous réunir. C'est indispensable le plus tôt possible. Je ne suis pas libre Dimanche. Nous avons impossibilité de ce côté.

Ou en est la série à la suite. Ayant donné ordre au dépôt de retirer la série P [?] 1 à 19 [?] sur laquelle nous n'avons qu'incertitude quant aux prix, – celle du thème [?] étant à la taille chez moi pour rectifier les pauvres et insignifiants martelés que l'on y a faits avant vos décors, – il en résulte que je n'ai rien; tous nos clients sont passés, désolés d'avoir à aller porter nos ordres ailleurs. Quant aux pièces que je fais ici, tous les journaux en parlent et cela augmente encore mes ennuis car [?] ce ne sont que de splendides unités faites sur commandes spéciales.

Voilà la situation. Convenez qu'il faudra prendre des mesures, car nous édifions de nos propres mains la fortune de nos rivaux. Cela est fort charitable, mais ce n'est pas ce qui me permettra de donner du travail à nos braves peintres, d'autant plus que je suis décidé, d'accord avec Mr Gallé et le dépôt à supprimer chaque année énergiquement toutes les séries précedentes.

Bien désolé, car je suis persuadé que vous mettez dans cette situation tout le zèle et le dévouement dont vous avez donné des preuves par le passé. Que fait votre fils

    Cordial salut [?]   *E. G.*

a-t-on utilisé le renseignement donné par le sprechsaal pour le tournage.

The Corning Museum of Glass, Corning, NY, Chambon Collection, dossier 2, letter p. 7.

Undated note from Emile Gallé to Désiré Christian

I am worried about the tulip-vase decorations. Herewith a few words of additional explanation. On the basis of the ones here, I note that the workshop has not fully grasped this decor. The relief is exaggerated and too many colours are mixed and juxtaposed without melding. The tones must be as shown in the models and should appear solid, incorporated and not baldly placed one on top of the other. The white spots on the foil were not patches; I wanted them to be voids to lighten the mass of the enamel. I don't like the contour lines either. It would also be as well if a number of leaves, those where the speckled enamel has not sufficiently fused, could seem as if veiled under a silver glaze.

    I have had 10 gold foils and 10 silver foils sent to you for the large vases. I've paid for them. So they should not be included.

Je suis inquiet du décor des vases tulipes. Voici encore quelques explications. Je remarque, d' après celles qui sont ici que l'atelier n'a pas compris ce décor. Il est trop en relief, il y a trop de couleurs mêlées juxtaposées, sans être fondues ensemble. Il faut que tous les tons du modèle soient bien observés et soient gras, fondus ensemble, et non sèchement posés les uns sur les autres. Les taches blanches des feuilles n'étaient pas des taches, je voulais des trous pour alléger la Masse de l'émail. Je n'aime pas non plus le cerné. Peut-être aussi serait-il bien que quelques feuilles, celles où les émaux tachés ne seraient pas assez fondus soient comme voilées par un glacis d'argent.

    Je vous ai fait envoyer 10 flles [feuilles] or 10 flles [feuilles] argent pour les gds [grands] vases. Je les ai payées. Il ne faudra donc les compter.

The Corning Museum of Glass, Corning, NY, Chambon Collection, dossier 2, letter p. 12, text 2.

Undated note from an unnamed collaborator of Gallé's in Nancy to the studio at Burgun, Schverer & Co., Meisenthal

M. Emile believes he has left his files – the duplicates of the documents that were left behind for the workshop – with M. Christian. Please return after the new vases as sent presently are added at the end of our [numbers]. Decors to follow forthwith [remark in the margins].

M. Emile croit avoir laissé chez M. Christian son dossier, Duplicata de celui laissé pour l'atelier. Prière de le retourner après y avoir ajouté à la suite les nos [numéros] des vases nouveaux envoyés à ce jour, les décors suivront incessamment

The Corning Museum of Glass, Corning, NY, Chambon Collection, dossier 2, letter p. 12, text 3.

After presenting his first marquetry pieces at the Salon des Champ-de-Mars of 1897, Gallé submitted a wide variety of works of this type to the 1898 exhibition. Many of these were designed as *verres parlantes*, bearing short inscriptions and quotations that underscored the intended mood of the pieces and encouraged the viewer to perceive them in a particular way.

In a private letter addressed to the editor of the journal *Revue des Arts Décoratifs*, Victor Champier, Gallé endeavoured to clarify his aims. The letter provides vivid testimony to Gallé's view of himself and his artistic intentions.

Emile Gallé
My Submissions to the Salon

Nancy, 29 April 1898
Dear Victor Champier,
You ask me what I am sending to the Salon. – Question marks, exclamation marks and my most humble observation that, in art as in life, the best thing is truth and the most beautiful is light. Yes, truthful materials, forms, colours, decorations emerge from the contemplation of the realities of Nature that so wonderfully conjures up the certitude of things invisible. In my factory, methods, indeed whole trades, have sprung from new imperatives of expression. After engraving, acid-etching and enamelling, they are: *marqueterie sur verre, cristal broché, intarsia crystal.* There are flower-chalices, hungry for air and daylight – as well as an anthology of all that blooms.

Braving the scorn, I persist (like artists in the Middle Ages, who relied on their faith and ideals) in furnishing my vases with texts, thereby completing the literary education of those who purchase them. How can the decorator's right to a *libretto* be denied when a composer's is conceded without further ado? Bells with no beautiful and grave words inscribed on them, which thus cannot touch our souls, are nothing but outsized door chimes.

If my glasswork resounds, it is above all because of Emile Hinzelin's invocation of the meadow saffron:

Veilleuses! ... que veillez-vous?

(Night-lights, wherefore do you light the night?)
Sully-Prudhomme, Valmore, Banville reply, and we fix their words in glass:

Quoique tu sommeilles...

(Though you slumber...),
says Hugo to the *opium flower*. Yet, 'it takes so little', the *spring crocus* replies, 'it takes so little to awaken sleeping angels...' Do you not feel that this phrase, taken from the *Trésor des humbles* (Treasure of the Humble), explains our passion for working in glass, for its aesthetic, its buoyant optimism during years of hardship and tumult? Art? Beauty? Flowers? What for?

Pour adoucir les hommes

(To soften men's hearts)
the *wood anemone* replies, or rather Sully-Prudhomme. And the *Anemone nemorosa,* with Maeterlinck, insists:

Il ne faut pas avoir peur d'en semer par les routes.

(One should not be afraid of sowing on every road.)
Of course I too hate stupid floral battles; I even hesitate before sacrificing a flower to ornament or to study. But today they have to be hurled at the feet of Barbarians! The touching grace of their death is to be paraded over the most humble artefacts. What does it matter that hundreds of pretty sprigs of life perish in the dust beneath cattle and wild beasts so long as one passer-by among the impoverished hordes on flower-strewn paths takes home a single bloom! What does the pain, what do the thousands of crushed petals matter so long as one hardened heart is for a moment touched by pity and, though tired and disgusted by all fallen things, bends down before a rose lying on the ground!

A beautiful thing cannot die without first purifying something; so says the same Maeterlinck, who believes in the miraculous virtues of beauty – an ideal element for instilling warmth and goodness.

This is what the *winter* and *alpine croci* whisper unknowingly: this is what the *solanum*, the *iris of the passion*, the *iris of Pentecost* say. The *columbine*'s grief is no less than theirs:

Tristesse, sois mon diadème (Hugo, Châtiments)

(Sadness, my diadem...)
The birch,

Le charme attristant du jour qui baisse (Charles Guérin)

(The saddening charm of a day that ends),
the lepidopteron, the lark, the star, all proclaim Nature's accord with the poets, those men of great conscience, when they affirm:

Vous savez bien que j'ai des ailes,

O vérités!

(You know very well that I have wings,

O truths!) as Hugo once more proclaims.

Moi, je n'alourdis pas mon vol de haine

(No hate weighs down my flight)
Valmore protests, while Banville asserts:

Nous monterons enfin vers la lumière

(We shall at last rise to the light).
The *Figuier* (Fig tree), however, lets human tears roll down its exalted calyx:

Car tous les hommes sont des fils d'un même Père;

Ils sont la même larme et sortent du même oeil.

(For all men come from one and the same Father;

They are but one tear and come from the same eye.)
And who proffers these dubious words – someone long forgotten, Victor Hugo. And on his cup, in the warmth of the our glassmakers' onyx, I have carved, with piety and pain, the august sign of one still more forgotten, who suffered and died for having promised that 'blessed are they which do hunger and thirst after righteousness: for they will be sated'.

That is why, my dear friend, I issued *several copies* of these vases, and it is for a communion of this kind that this gigantic drinking glass has been made as deep as possible.

'Mes Envois au Salon', *Revue des Arts Décoratifs* 18 (1898): 144–48; see also Gallé, *Ecrits*, 1908, pp. 200–203.

Emile Gallé
Symbolic Decoration
A Speech

The following is the inaugural lecture Emile Gallé gave at the public session of the Académie de Stanislas on 17 May 1900. It is published in vol. XVII of the fifth series of publications issued by the Académie de Stanislas. Gallé had been elected a member of this institution in 1891.

At this very instant, as I come to offer my thanks to the Académie de Stanislas for the honour it has shown me by admitting me publicly, I weigh my debt to your hospitality with some trepidation: soon it will be ten years! You to whom I am indebted have not exercised excessive rigour with respect to the parsimony of my contribution to your elected tasks. I know only too well your forbearance, and inadequacy of my claims to your good offices.

The delay you have so kindly allowed deprives me today of a joy, since I no longer see amongst you two friends who had served as my guarantors. M. Jules Lejeune and the Reverend Othon Cuvier are no longer with us. If I recall these two noble figures, it is least of all out of vanity; indeed I know full well that, in welcoming amongst you an artisan whose various achievements appear superficial, it is only by dint of the credit you nurture for the sentiments of these two much-venerated gentlemen, examples both for their enlightened charity and for the tolerance they showed any sincerely held conviction, as well as for their saintly endeavours to unite men in mutual esteem, study and peace. They had but to assuage the lingering doubts I had, not as to your benevolence, but as to myself. For the reverence I feel for your academy was born long ago in my youth, in the generous light of your Annual meetings, at those venerable yet hearty May Thursdays when my classmates from the Lycée at Nancy, Hubert Zaepfell and the angelic young martyr Paul Seigneret, pure victims both, would spirit us away from the boisterous pleasures of the Cours Léopold to come to this nobly appointed room to hear the likes of Lacroix, Margerie, Burnouf, Benoît, Godron, Lombard, Volland and Duchêne.

Fresh from our studies, we could there revel in a science lightly borne, an Atticism as attractive as one of Jean Lamour's golden guipures. Who then would have thought that an average pupil of the best masters who ever lived would one day take it upon himself to hold a speech, albeit belatedly, here and (thank the Lord) before several of them?

The fulfilment of my obligations will, I hope, more readily find favour through my choice of a subject familiar to me from my everyday occupations. It will be all the more sincere for it; and, perhaps, more interesting.

You have been kind enough, then, to give the floor to a composer of ornaments, to an assembler of images, who will speak to you now about Symbolism in decoration.

To dream up themes to be rendered in lines, forms, nuances, thoughts, and thus to adorn our living spaces and objects (be they useful or ornamental) and to adapt one's designs to the methods of a given manufacturing technique – to which every medium is unique, be it metal or wood, marble or cloth – is certainly an absorbing occupation. But it is at bottom more serious, more pregnant with consequences, than the ornamental designer commonly suspects.

Every application of human effort, however minute its result may appear, can be compared with a man sowing seed. For it is true that, be it unthinkingly or with some purpose in mind, the designer, too, plies the sower's trade. He throws seed onto a field reserved for a special crop: 'decoration', for which particular tools and labourers are needed and in which certain seedlings ensure a particular harvest. For all the ornaments that are born from his daily endeavours – from the most humble to the most elevated – may one day become part of what shall be a most revealing testament: *the decorative style of a period*. In effect, every artistic creation is conceived and produced under the influence of the more or less habitual daydreams and intentions of the artist: however he may desire it, it is from these that his work springs. Willingly or not, his daily concerns are like godmothers to his newborn infant, either good fairies or witches, who can cast evil spells or confer miraculous gifts. The work will invariably bear the indelible imprint of his thoughts, of the impassioned preoccupations of his spirit. It will synthesize a symbol unconsciously, making it still more profound. There runs, among the weft and woollen threads of certain Asian rugs, a silky strand of woman's hair: it is the hallmark of a task accomplished – like a faded ribbon in a closed book that marks the much-pondered or best-loved page – perhaps forever interrupted. So the *décorateur* always admixes something of himself in his work. Only later can the weave be untangled; someone will come across a whitened hair, a tear dabbed dry (Marceline Valmore's manuscripts often can hardly be read for them) and the unspeaking thing will let forth, with either a sigh of weariness and disgust – a sign the artist felt constrained, disheartened by his endeavour – or the manly *satisfecit* of the poet:

O soir, aimable soir, désiré par celui
Dont les bras, sans mentir, peuvent dire: Aujourd'hui
Nous avons travaillé!
(Oh, evening, well-beloved evening, desired by he
whose arms, without falsehood, can say: 'Today
we have done our work!')

No one knows the name of the great artist-thinker (an Egyptian sculptor, royal goldsmith or temple decorator) who, halting for a moment in rapt contemplation of a miry insect, the dung-chafer, rolling about a ball of manure in which to lay her eggs in the heat of the Libyan sand, was first struck by religious awe. He was the first to go beyond appearances to seek out the reflection of an august image, thus creating that mystical ornament, *the sacred scarab*. Between her forelegs – and later, in Phoenician imitations, between her wings unfurled – the insect carries the sun's globe, the source of all light, all heat; with her hind legs, she maternally rolls another celestial body, another globe, the Earth, in which she deposits the germ of life. Drawn by its inventor, the artist, it advances evidence of God the creator, of the providential concordance of our satellite with the source of calorific energy! Strange and ancient foreknowledge of the form of our terrestrial planet, one might say; that is a true symbol – artistic, cosmographic, religious and prophetic. But what such a masterstroke chiefly betokens is the artist's inherent quality of soul and mind – astonishingly, prophetically beautiful.

This characteristic example means you will be spared all the more or less hackneyed definitions that have been given of the symbol, of

Symbolism and of symbolic art. We can start by agreeing, can't we, that the symbol, in art, poetry and religion, *is the likeness of a thing (for the most part abstract), a sign understood by initiates*; it is – in decoration, as it is on a vase or a medal, a statue, a picture, a bas-relief, a temple as well as in a poem or a song or play – always the translation, the awakening of an idea by way of its image.

Dans le grossier symbole éclate l'idéal

.(In the crudeness of the Symbol the Ideal bursts forth),

Maurice Bouchor has written. And symbolic decoration humbly concurs with that definition; that is, with any ornamental figure, any synthesis of a drawing, of a sculptural form, of a nuance capable of rendering the subtlest abstractions. As long as the artist has something of the poet, the field is wide open; for the poet is the Symbolist par excellence. How then should the decorative artist act? A little like Bernardin de Saint-Pierre: 'I brought a rose with her thorns as the symbol of my hopes combined with my many fears.'

But it is best when the symbol is not too enigmatic. The French spirit loves clarity. As Victor Hugo says:

. *L'idée à qui tout cède est toujours clair.*

(The idea to which all yields was ever a clear one.)

And a Frenchman, gazing on some modern British florilegium (sometimes akin to a flowery charade), prides himself, like Hugo, on being finally able to decipher the riddle:

Une rose dit: 'Devine!'

Et je lui répondis: 'Amour!'

(A rose said: 'Guess'!

And I replied: 'Love'!)

Does it follow that the rose is more lovelorn than the peony? 'The weeping willow', writes the aesthetician Lévêque in his *Science du beau*, 'does not "weep" any more than any other willow; the violet is no more modest than the opium poppy.' The moral expression of the plant world is thus purely symbolic. As fellow-citizens of a truly outstanding Symbolist, Grandville, we learned how to read in his *Fleurs animées* and *Etoiles*; and we are well aware that a flower's eloquence, thanks to the mysteries of its organism and of its fate, and thanks to the synthesis of the vegetal symbol depicted with the artist's pencil, can outstrip in the strength of its power of suggestion the authority of any human figure. We know that the expressivity of our heraldic thistle, for example, derives from a defiant act; and, in other plants, from a tendency to droop, from a pensive line, an emblematic tendency – and that nuances, swelling lines, scents are all terms that Baudelaire calls:

Le langage des fleurs et des choses muettes.

(The language of flowers and of voiceless things.)

A question immediately arises: What decorative quality does the symbol possess? To quote a phrase used in the trade, can a symbol charge an ornament? Is not the Symbolist in danger of sacrificing visual pleasure to intellectual games? Certainly the symbolic sign of the noblest idea will scarcely guarantee a patch any more decorative than a common-or-garden rosette if not invigorated by an accent of line, by the emphasis and power of likeness, the wizardry of relief and colouring. No less obviously, the mere use of a symbol can never magically bestow grace on a decor conceived without skill or invention.

But who would disagree that an artist, intent on portraying a flower, an insect, a landscape, a human figure, one who strives to draw out its character, the feelings it harbours, will create a more vibrant work, a more readily communicable emotion than one whose sole instrument is the camera or cold scalpel? The most realistic image reproduced in a scientific tome fails to move us because no human soul breathes within it; whereas some still wholly natural depiction by a Japanese artist, for example, can uniquely convey an evocative motif, the mocking or melancholic features of some living creature or sentient being. Unconsciously, by dint solely of a passion for Nature, he transforms the *forest*, the *joys of springs* or the *sadness of autumn* into symbols through and through. In the art of ornament, then, the symbol acts as a point of light in the unmoving, deliberately meaningless tumult of scrolls and arabesques. The symbolic grabs one's attention; it ushers in thought, poetry, art. Symbols are the particles around which ideas can form.

Moreover, allow us to suggest that it would in truth be of little avail to discourage the use of symbols among decorative artists when they are so avidly embraced by poets. And, as long as the pen, the brush, the pencil are guided by the mind, there can be no doubt that the symbol will continue to bewitch mankind. Still more, the love of Nature will always bring Symbolism in its wake: the familiar flower that all adore will always play a leading symbolic role in ornamentation. Gutzkow recounts that a man searching for true happiness once asked it of the flower and the flower referred him to the star, whereupon the astral body answered: 'Quickly now, back to the cornflower!'

Like poets, jewellers and lacemakers cannot survive without Nature. It *legitimates their claim* to all: it is *their dominion*, it is *a source of life*! Victor Hugo, that great brandisher of symbols, confesses it freely:

Nous ne ferions rien qui vaille

Sans l'orme et sans le houx,

Et l'oiseau travaille

A nos poèmes avec nous.

(We will never do anything worthwhile

without the elm and the holly;

and the bird labours

at our poems by our side.)

Calderón pens this homage to flowers: 'If my voice is a new one, if I have received a new heart, then I owe this rebirth to the flower.' And in his eyes flowers become a symbol of his reconciliation with moral beauty, with the divine.

To ban the symbol from decoration one would first have to chase our satellite down from the firmament:

Cette faucille d'or dans le champ des étoiles!

(That golden sickle in the starry field!)

Then the Morning Star and the Evening Star would have to be extinguished; constellations would have to be obliterated. To stop the mouth of the symbol in art one would have to rub out: 'God, the sacred star that sees into the soul.' For, ultimately, only one word is behind all Nature, from eon to eon, from symbol to symbol, from reflection to reflection,

Le mot, c'est Dieu:

Les constellations le disent en silence!

(The word is God:

In silence the constellations say it is so!)

And this is precisely what makes our national art so strong, from its primitive stirrings to the touching gesture that let fly prayers from our cathedrals up to heaven. This was the source of its beauty in the lively development in the thirteenth century. It has never thrived cooped up in the studio; like ivy around an oaken trunk, it clings fast to unfettered

Nature – that is, to Symbolism itself. In grandiose manner, Baudelaire has given utterance to this conception of the harmonic resonances that underpin the immensity of Creation:

La Nature est un temple, où de vivants piliers
Laissent parfois sortir de confuses paroles.
L'homme y passe à travers des forêts de symbols,
Qui l'observent avec des regards familiers
(Nature is a temple from which living pillars
Occasionally proffer indistinct words.
Man passes through forests of symbols,
Which gaze at him with familiar looks.)

Therein resides the whole history of the applied arts in this Celtic, this Gaulish nation, the proud child of raw Nature, scion of the Druids, of the bard, forever returning – following each successive invasion (from southern, from eastern climes) and after all the intermixing, after all the transient fashions, be they Roman or Barbarian – to its nature, to Nature, to genius unshackled, to its source: to the indigenous flora and fauna, to the joy a workman finds in lovingly decorating his own home to his own taste. And thus, the vernacular decorative arts, Symbolist without knowing how or why, like Nature herself, like the holm oak and the heathland, range from the fern groves of Gavr'inis, via Besançon's floriated bronzes, to the ivy and vine-tendrils of delicate Gallo-Greek creations – if you will allow me this neologism – that characterize the output of fourth-century Attic manufactories in the regions of the Marne, Allier and Rhône. The spirit of the *terroir* was then forged into joyous toasts on historiated goblets from Rheims or Vichy that hark back to Greek chalices with mottoes and foretell of our red-blooded, Gaulish faience of the sixteenth and eighteenth centuries. Our attitude to the decorative arts is likewise a welcome return to the Celtic forest of Brocéliande, just as it was with the glorious national fronds of the thirteenth and sixteenth centuries.

For it is indeed the antique pottery of the Gauls that peers through the 'rustic *figulines*' of Bernard Palissy, moulding itself as closely on Nature as the imprint of a fossil, draping itself in lifelike colours, moistening each object in flowing enamel; and it is that which, in living and breathing copies, brings out the specific characteristics of the fronds of our myriad ferns and the features of every shell from marsh or river, of every crustacean and fish. – Yes, we know that in the past it was considered quite the thing (from high on paradox-loving cathedra and in certain prejudice-ridden cliques) to belittle the Applied Arts and the craftwork of our ancient trades. May we then seize in passing this opportunity to proclaim *the principle of the unity of art* and pay due homage to a worthy ancestor, one of the patrons in France of the art of the kiln and wheel, to a true Symbolist of the 'arts of the earth'. And it is enough to do him the justice he deserves, to recall the kinds of preoccupations that lie behind his lively clay dishes, and the French, the Gaulish invention of translucent glaze. Let him speak for himself and tell of his purpose and his goal: 'Several days after emotions subsided and the Civil War had come to an end, that is, when it had pleased God to send His peace among us, I was one day strolling through the meadow in the city of Saintes, by the River Charente. And whilst I was pondering the horrendous dangers from which God had deigned to protect me during the recent tumult, I harkened to the voices of a few girls seated in a copse of willow intoning Psalm CIV. And, because their voices were pleasant and well tuned, I set aside my earlier thoughts and, pausing for a moment to attend to the aforementioned Psalm, stopped listening to the voices and began reflecting on its meaning. And I said to myself: Most admirable goodness of God! My purpose will be to ensure that we feel the same reverence for works from your hands as David in his Psalm. And straightway I began to think of building a garden in accordance with the design, adornments and surpassing beauty of what the prophet describes in the Psalm, an amphitheatre of refuge that would be a saintly delectation and an honest labour for both body and mind.'

Herein then resides the mystery of the 'conchology that so bored Bouvard and Pécuchet', which prompted one modern French critic to let out a pedantic squib aimed at Palissy's creations[1]: 'There is no art in a pot because in it there is no purpose' – that is to say, no premeditation. The potter from Saintes, however, did clearly intend something – in reproducing Nature he nurtured the desire to inculcate men by showing them how they might perceive God through the similarities and beauty in his humblest creations.

Yet, for his part, how can a modern creator of decors summon up enough sincerity, enough faith, to turn his work into a source of reinvigorated Symbolism, of emancipated art, by progressing – through and by means of the unstinting scrutiny of Nature – to a higher, a superior ideal, one that by rights should be part of the habitual concerns of an artist?

First of all, today Nature provides him with wholly new forms: science offers him virgin, characteristic symbols, unknown to our ancestors, the sight of which is apt to surprise all those who have lost the gift for noticing familiar things. Among the ideas circulating in decorative art workshops one can see today, for example, that beneficial solanum, *Parmentier's potato*, the *Alpine paradise* or *St Bruno lily*, *mallow* and *bleeding heart*, introduced since the beginning of the century, and which, by dint of a singularly elegant and evocative cordate shape, gentle colouring, by the wing-like folds of two outermost petals, will soon come to the fore as a wholly contemporary symbol of love and friendship. The flower with a characteristic turbinate corolla; the *periwinkle*, the *herb Paris*, of questionable good faith; *bittersweet*, that illustrious offshoot of goodly poisoners, that sister of those toxic – or rather healing – *plants henbane*, *deadly nightshade* and *mandrake*. Then there's the affecting problem of *bittersweet*! A beneficial pain and a salutary ordeal, it is the emblem of an unquiet conscience.

We have a penchant for traditional plants, those our forebears were fond of. But the flowing current of modernity runs deeper, more strongly than the slumbering brook of personal preference. It carries all before it. As if for Ophelia's final nosegay, it now throws up the orchid, a plant exhibiting a richness, an unconscionable strangeness of form, species, scent, colour and whimsy, of sensual pleasure and troubling mystery…

Finally, from every side science opens new horizons for the decorative artist. Oceanography (one of its most fervent advocates is amongst us here in Nancy), like the magical diver in *A Thousand and One Nights*, like the king of the sea, spirits away his earthly favourites in his arms and shows them around his blue palaces:

Homme libre, toujours tu chériras la mer.
La mer est ton miroir, tu contemples ton âme.
Vous êtes tous les deux ténébreux et discrets.
Homme! nul n'a sondé le fond de tes abîmes.
Ô mer! Nul ne connaît tes richesses intimes,
Tant vous êtes jaloux de garder vos secrets.[2]
(Free man, you will forever cherish the sea.

The sea is your mirror, in it you gaze on your soul,
For you both are sombre and keep your counsel.
Man! None has plumbed the depths of your abyss.
Oh Sea! None knows your innermost riches,
So jealous you are of keeping your every secret.)

The secrets of the ocean are being brought up by fearless deep-sea divers who empty marine harvests into laboratories whence they progress to our workshops and cast museums. They make drawings of undreamt-of materials – sea enamels, sea cameos – and publish them for the artist's benefit. Soon enough, crystalline jellyfish will bring unheard-of nuances and whiplash lines to the belly of many a goblet.

So it is that, in tandem with novel forms and decorative schemes, to unearth the symbols of a new art, it will be enough to look about one, to strive to understand, to study and to love. For a symbol will emerge spontaneously in an ornament from a combination of these factors: from the study of Nature, from the love of one's art and from the need to express what lies in one's heart.

This is what nineteenth-century artists have all too often lost sight of. This astonishing age, so admirable in many respects, labours under the delusion that it can manufacture applied art, and has flooded the world with it on an industrial and commercial scale – doing so under very specific, most unfavourable conditions. Unlike their predecessors, those who produce interiors today are scarcely able to experience the pure joy felt by an artisan in love with his work. The designer too has dragged himself along slavishly imitating the past, making copies from which thought is entirely absent, and in which the symbols, created for an earlier period, are misunderstood by our own, which responds to different needs, to a different conception of life.

This was one of the mistakes, one of the bitter pills of the industrialized age, of the excessive division of labour and of its organization far from the domestic hearth and the family, exiled from its natural milieu and into a noxious, artificial atmosphere. The century that is about to come to a close has produced no 'popular' art – that is to say, art applied to objects of everyday life and executed spontaneously, gleefully by the artisan at his bench. Moreover, much the same conclusion has been drawn by the best-informed of our contemporaries, the most generous spirits and the most hard-working, high-minded artists.

Let us nonetheless hail the return of a healthier approach to artistic creation: William Morris, a great artist, a humanitarian philosopher, the prophet of joy in work, has declared that labour is humane, that it is good, that art has a healing effect; and that the hallowed, the salutary art is vernacular art – in short, the expression of Man's joy in working with things.

For our part, we proclaim a deeply held faith in the doctrine that assigns a function to art in the culture of humankind, in the awakening of minds and souls, by harnessing the beauty that flows through the world.

Are such high purposes to be precluded from the arts? Who would dare not to vouchsafe them in light of the heavenly calligraphy of the Alhambra, before the Loggie of the Vatican, before the walls of the Sistine Chapel, before the affable, unsophisticated, tender and fond allegories of that symbolic and exquisite art, the Christian art of the second and third centuries at the Cemetery of St. Callistus? It is not precisely because the symbol breathes and resonates through these supreme creations that they have exerted such mysterious sway over the souls of men? Such too is this decor realized by Puvis de Chavannes.

An old woman, emaciated by the vigils and sacrifices of a life of nought but piety and pity, a body that bears and holds up its fervent charity alone, leans with august solicitude upon a terrace balcony. Night falls. The stars grow wan. The city sleeps. It is her child, the woman's child: it a mother's alarm that has dragged her from her bed, that now transfixes her to the spot in the chilly morn.

St Geneviève fears of her Lutetia's destruction by fire, of the Huns outside the city gates and of the enemy within. Paris, sleep on. In the unfathomable silence, Geneviève listens. Her lamp, too, keeps vigil, and her hand is placed on the stone as if she were trying not to wake a newborn babe. This ancestral shadow is the very symbol of love. The lamp is the symbol of a vigilant soul. And each one of us takes away in his heart the silence that emanates from and envelops the work.

Allow me to pause a moment after evoking this admirable paragon of the purest symbol.

My conclusion will be then that the word *symbol* is well-nigh synonymous with that of *art*. Consciously or unconsciously, the symbol individualizes and enlivens the artwork: it constitutes its very soul. And, at the dawn of the twentieth century, it would be fitting to salute the renaissance of our national, popular art, as the herald of better times to come. 'It is the modern artist's allotted task', Charles Albert said at the Congress for Art in Brussels, 'to create an atmosphere for tomorrow'. The work should be a struggle for Justice in ourselves, for Justice around us. In that case, life in the twentieth century will no longer want for joy, art or beauty.

Notes

1 Brunetière.
2 Baudelaire.

Response of Charles de Meixmoron de Dombasle to the Candidate Emile Gallé*

Sir |...|

With the noblest elevation of thought and the greatest richness of language, you have provided us with an outline of the theory of Symbolic art and its purpose in ornamental decoration, to elicit ideas and feelings. You have warned us of the reefs against which so many of its exponents have come to grief by being insufficiently aware of its eternal symbols, damaging its signs, adulterating its ornamentation and dislodging it from its rightful place. In the most eloquent terms, your discourse has stressed an artist's duty to be sincere and truthful and talked of the joys he feels as a creator and poet, and of his mission as educator and initiator. You have defined these aspirations, these convictions, and, by the same token, your own position. All too aware of my limitations, I cannot follow you into the higher realms to which you have transported your listeners; I am to remain on what is for me more familiar ground, that of the practical application of these elevated thoughts, their use in satisfying the requirements of our lives as well as the pleasure that industrial art, which has so blossomed under your influence, can procure a mere art-lover who basks in the knowledge that he was one of your earliest admirers.

Decorating dwelling-places and furnishings has long preoccupied humanity, from the Barbarian hordes to more polished nations. There lies within every human soul an instinct for adornment and embellishment, which starts with one's person, before moving on to the home and then the objects one uses. Crude and undisciplined amongst primitive peoples, this innate sense grows more refined as civilization develops. It has mirrored its progress, remaining grave, noble and elevated among self-possessed nations, before becoming ailing and tortured as they decline. The decorative arts of every country, every epoch, every race, possess precise and individual characteristics. To speak of our country alone, the French applied arts have passed through various phases: austere in the Roman age, extraordinarily rich in the Gothic period, from the thirteenth to the fifteen century, delicately and discreetly undemonstrative under Louis XII, lively and unbridled in the Renaissance, heavy and severe under Louis XIII, majestic under Louis XIV, witty and verging on the sensual under Louis XV, of an unsophisticated and cheerful grace under Louis XVI, forbidding and chilly during the First Empire – each decorative style uniquely reflects the customs and even the history of its period.

I deliberately halted at the beginning of the nineteenth century because, in contrast with its predecessors, it has not possessed, at least for three-quarters of its duration, any significant independent decorative expression. Neither the Restoration, nor the July Monarchy, nor the Second Empire can lay claim to a truly specific style, in spite of vain attempts by several talented artists to lend form to their ideas. While the fiery breath of Romanticism was rekindling the art of painting, decoration remained shackled by copies and pastiches of the styles of yesteryear, shifting from one to the other in a perpetual struggle to assuage the vagaries of fashion, that tyrant whose victims are legion. Neo-Greek archaisms, medievalizing crotchets, the

unfurled and beribboned elegance of the eighteenth century and, worst of all, madcap amalgams of styles, successively clamored for public favour. The most sumptuous residences, the most opulent salons, amounted to little more than a farrago of furniture and furnishings of every style, original and fake. As early as 1836 Alfred de Musset railed against an anarchic eclecticism only worsened by its banality. 'We feed off debris', he exclaimed in the *Confessions d'un Enfant du Siècle*, 'as if the end of the world were nigh; we possess objects from every period – excepting our own, a thing that has never been witnessed at any other time.'

Amidst all this chaos, however, a light might be glimpsed. At the Exposition Universelle of 1867 and, more significantly, at that in 1878, there appeared objects produced in the Far East that were to bedazzle eyes made weary by this overlong phase of imitation. How could it be? So much grace in the most trifling items, so much charm, elegance, and with absolutely novel and untried means! The hackneyed acanthus, oak and laurel leaves, the eternally rehearsed Egyptian lotus flower, the scrollwork, the rinceaux and the egg-and-dart outside of which it had seemed no salvation existed could in fact be dispensed with! There existed colours other than Sèvres blue, decorations other than *bouquets de Saxe*, ornaments other than bowdlerized versions of the three Orders, shapes other than sphere, cone, cylinder and ovoid!

Sir, I will not hazard an investigation of the influence the products of this fresh and novel approach exerted upon you, coinciding as they did with the onset of your artistic career. Though interesting, gauging the reasons why an artist embarks on a chosen path and sticks with it is always a delicate matter. I would at least be willing to credit that circumstances – your entourage, your training, your own personal disposition – conspired to pave the way for the effect the marvellous innovations of the Asiatic arts had on your youthful imagination. But I would be quick to add that, if their influence impressed itself into every branch of the arts, into painting particularly, and aroused in you a deeply felt emotion, it was but a stimulant, and the conception of art you forged was something quite different. The art of China or Japan contents itself with delighting and amusing the eye: yours entertains a higher purpose; it speaks to the heart and stimulates the mind. You unearthed this art readymade, not in a school or a tradition, but within yourself. Before moving on to show my appreciation, I would first like to analyze, by way of a short biographical sketch, how the initiation into new forms of expression that has characterized the development of your talent began.

The father's side of your family came from the bonny and fertile *département* of the Oise, one of the jewels in the crown of our ancient Ile-de-France, the cradle of our fatherland. Your grandfather, M. François Gallé, an officer during the First Empire and a notable book collector, was a passionate amateur botanist. A pupil at the high school at Clermont-sur-Oise, your father, M. Charles Gallé, acted for several years as head of the soft-paste decoration studios at the celebrated porcelain manufactory in Chantilly. While away on business in Nancy, he met and married in 1845 Mlle Reinemer of a family from Lorraine, in the same year founding, together with his mother-in-law, a lead-crystal and pottery concern in which he directed the design and manufacture departments. Possessing a vivid imagination, energetic and hard-working, he decorated *blanc de Sèvres*, designed a large number of models for faience and glassware produced at Raon-l'Etape [*recte*: Saint-Clément] and at Meysenthal, restored or finished old moulds for eighteenth-century tableware and vases belonging to the faience factory of Saint-Clément and created several hundred original models. The annexation of Alsace in 1871 led him to uproot his manufacturing workshops to the Garenne, on the outskirts of Nancy, and to transfer the business to his brother-in-law, M. Dannreuther.

I regretfully cannot expound at greater length on this seminal artist, who you were fortunate enough to have constantly by your side as a valuable cooperator. His exceptional talent was much admired by M. Ch. Robert in his official report on the 1855 Exposition, praising his works for 'a pleasing originality, a personal elegance, exempt from any tendency to servility, in which boldness of execution is equalled only by the quality of the results.'

Born at Nancy in 1846, you excelled in your studies at the *lycée*, a fact supported by the many eminent colleagues to whose selflessness you have just gratefully rendered due homage. Your tastes seemed to draw you to Letters and indeed you were valiantly to carry off the grade of *bachelier ès lettres*. With this success in your pocket, your father took you under his wing, providing you with the basics of his industry. Of an evening, seated at the family table, you would leaf through volumes of illustrations that have so charmed our inquisitive youth down the ages: the *Magasin pittoresque*, which you, like our Grandville, whose pupil you might have been, enjoyed so much, various natural history collections, *Les Fleurs animées*, Bourdin's edition of *A Thousand and One Nights*, *Toppfer*, the *Tales of Hoffmann* peppered with sprightly thumbnail sketches by Gavarni, the pretty plaquettes by Havard with drawings by Bertall, Gérard Séguin and Lorentz, Sylvestre de Sacy's Bible and countless other tomes that would still find a place amongst any book-lover's list of favourites. It is these early sources that so moved you in your youth that must be held responsible for a certain mystical tinge, a taste for Oriental legend-spinning and for arabesques on glass, a touch of sentimental Symbolism, a love of the Marvellous, a passion for flowers and for the patient examination of Nature.

From this moment on, the fondness for plants that your forebears had bequeathed you – for they all adored and grew them – became a dominating factor. You were to follow courses by Professor Vaultrin and accompany the eminent Dr Godron on his walks. Your leisure time was spent herbalizing, first in the Avant-Garde near Pompey, where the Lorraine flora is so varied, then in the Haye forest in the Vosges, in the Savoy Alps and in Alsace. You studied these delicate products of Nature, not only as an artist bewitched by their charm, but as a genuine botanist. At the same time, Professor Casse and the painter Paul Pierre, who regrettably left us only a few months ago, gave you lessons on how to draw and paint in the open air.

The years 1862 to 1864 [*recte*: 1874] saw you crisscrossing Germany and England, spending your time drawing and making models at Weimar and London, learning the languages of both countries and studying music, for which you had early exhibited a strong liking.[1] A series of happy coincidences allowed you the opportunity of meeting Liszt in Weimar[2] and of hearing compositions by his illustrious son-in-law, Richard Wagner, in his house. By this time you were already the committed Wagnerian you have remained, thirty years ahead of the change in attitude that has since raised the renown of that great artist to its zenith. In Berlin and London, and then in Paris, you admired masterpieces of applied art amassed in the Brandt collec-

tions, and then in the museum at Kensington, the Musée Cluny, the Louvre and the Arts et Métiers collection.[3] You cemented a relationship with the studio glassmaker Rousseau and learned much about the aesthetics of furniture from your friends Messieurs Bonnaffé and Fourcaud.[4]

In 1864 [*recte*: 1867[5]] you returned to the paternal firm to fill a position as an industrial designer. The first steps were arduous as you failed to find – in Nancy or elsewhere – drawing lessons specially geared to the decorative arts, for ceramics, glassmaking, furniture and the composition of forms generally. This stumbling-block, however – which I might be tempted to see as presenting an advantage rather than an inconvenience, since it allowed you to preserve your individuality – was never likely to halt someone with a will as tenacious as yours: armed with profound knowledge and the stylistic awareness you had gleaned from the finest public and private collections in Europe, you went on to finish your education alone. The sheer number and variety of your works are staggering: though their rapid enumeration may appear somewhat dry, I cannot resist the temptation since the enormous labour they represent is part and parcel of the history of progress in the decorative arts in Nancy during the final quarter of the present century.

First of all came interlace lettering, armorial bearings, tableware, then high-fired earthenware lamp-stands, turned cachepots and vases, Hinduesque palms in dark-blue braided yellow and in orange fringed with blue, Rouen and Moustiers work in which personal style was quickly to supplant tradition, Turkish cups, where the nuances of the red Saint-Clément paste was used as a ground for decorative underglaze rosettes, pinkish bleeding hearts, lilacs, broad-leaved and of every turquoise hue, nocturnal birds over stormy skies, decorations on glass, Louis XVI forget-me-nots, Lorraine grasses, afterpieces in the manner of the eighteenth century. Then came a Lorraine herbal, comprising a hundred or so watercolours after nature, full of the liveliest movement, destined for dinner- or serving-plates and for vegetable dishes, in which a painter's consummate art brought out in every detail the effects to be derived from high-fire blue *camaïeu* floated on subtle tin enamel. For some egg-cups you depicted together with Victor Prouvé – at the time some thirteen or fourteen years old and already gifted with a prodigious verve for caricature – such subjects as cockerels, ducks and chickens with burlesque inscriptions. As a decor for dessert dishes you conceived a second series of watercolours, extending the Symbolism of animated flowers to other species; you added texts handwritten in an expressive lettering borrowed first from the Arab and Chinese styles, then from the fifteenth century and finally from convoluted plant tendrils.

The war of 1870, during which your patriotism spurred you on to join as a volunteer in the 23rd Regiment, constituted an abrupt interruption in your career. Back at work in 1871, you started with a series of allegories, where you gave vent to the despondency in which the misfortunes of the Nation had plunged your heart. Exhibited in London that same year through the good offices of M. du Sommerard, the French Commissioner General, these plaintive Lorraine and Alsace faiences were acquired by the Princesses of Wales, Louise and Mary, in sympathy. You then created *pièces de fantaisie* intended to complete the Saint-Clément services, knife-racks, salt cellars, knife handles, rocaille clock-cases, flambeaus and shells, all with variants modelled on cats, peacocks, outlandish owls, pitchers and tobacco pots knotted with rough and ready 'willows' whipped out of earthenware with Callotesque beggars painted *grand feu*, vases-cum-cockerels bedecked with a compendious wayside florula, enamelled stoneware cylinders with substantial blue-painted bosses depicting snowbells and their wintry carpet. Rustic *services de ferme* were sprinkled with the fluttering seeds of dandelion, hawkweed and umbellifer. On cider jugs – I avow on your behalf before the shade of the great king who presides over this assembly – you were to portray a corpulent Stanislaw strolling on the Carrière, with his legendary cane in his hand. After enamelling the diverse wickerwork of Lorraine – trugs, creels and punnets from Saizerais and Nancy; after folded papers and playing cards transformed into Lorraine faience through the application of a battery of blazons, and medieval-style illuminated texts taken from François Villon or Charles d'Orléans, together with Gengoult Prouvé, you threw yourself headlong into heraldry. From that arose haulms-cum-candlesticks, escutcheon-ashtrays and perfervid torcheres, bucking lions bearing turrets in which the energetic temperament of your collaborator disported itself. A singular individual unjustly neglected today, our fellow-citizen Jean Cayon, played a fleeting role in these activities, delivering to your studio some emblems, few, too few unfortunately, in a wonderfully elegant, very personal style.

We have reached 1874, the year in which your father entrusted you with the management of the factory. You were committed at that juncture to centralize your business activities: anticipating the retirement of the chief of glassmaking at Raon-l'Etape, M. Müller,[6] whose hospitality towards your painters and models, scrupulous delicacy, practical know-how and boundless understanding were a boon to you at the time, and also due to a rise in the duty on glass owing to the annexation of Alsace, you continued adding to the plant at Nancy. In addition to the extant drawing, composition, decoration and engraving workshops, in the Garenne you set up a research laboratory that was to serve as a focus for outsourced manufacturing and was the seed of the factory as it is today. The equipment necessary for the preparation of coloured glass, enamel glass and *verre de terre* gradually turned to producing *objets d'art*, until the day when the workshop was forced, in reaction to imitations first from Lorraine, then in Nancy itself, to organize itself on an industrial footing, without, however, its output forfeiting its personality.

As 1878 approached, a crucial year in the evolution of your taste and talent, you prepared for the Exposition Universelle by creating a host of models in the then fashionable underglaze decoration. You drew inspiration from Egyptian flora and fauna, and, simultaneously, from the Japanese, turning out massive vases, huge *jardinières* clad in metal foils under a thick, coloured glaze, sacred scarabs, lotus flowers, papyrus, locusts and scenes from Antiquity. These constituted one final concession to traditions whose preconceptions were cramping your individuality. A new era was dawning for you: a master of every process, with every tool you needed ready to hand, you felt drawn by new aspirations, not simply to bewitch the eye, but to arouse feelings, to speak to the spirit through form and decorative schemes that were informed by a guiding principle, an intellectual theme that awaited its development. Your intention now was to give inert material a soul – the great problem that the artists of the Middle Ages had solved, solutions into which you breathed new life by adapting them to modern demands.

In 1883 [*recte*: 1885; see Thiébaut, *Dessins*, 1983, p. 32] you built huge workshops for a faience manufactory, a glass factory [*recte*: glass factory built in 1894] and workshops for cabinetmaking, a new industry for you. It is against the backdrop of your splendid firm (thanks to your open-hearted hospitality, visitors are welcome) that one should see your products so as to appreciate their true variety and character. All around, lofty trees evoke thoughts of calm and peacefulness; the sense of serenity emanating from this corner of the city's outskirts is disturbed only by the occasional blast of a bugle from the nearby barracks. Once through the doors the journey continues rich in surprises and increasing contentment. In the summer months, in the courtyards, beds of decorative flowers delight the eye and every day teach your staff something new. In a main building of impressively elegant construction, the work is divided up on a rational basis. Here, the cabinetmakers select, fit, cut out and apply the thin veneers of exotic timber that adorn tables, consoles, trunks, pier-glasses and furniture of every sort mounted in a neighbouring shop. There modellers prepare and painters decorate faience pieces before they are loaded into the blazing maws of the muffles from which they will emerge all the more magnificent. Elsewhere, points and wheels engrave the glass, enriching it with delicate incisions. In another room, specialist workers cast, chisel and polish the bronze mounts that provide the finishing touches to the furniture. In the centre a room teeming with drawings, plans, fragments of glass and wood, flasks and the whole arsenal of the chemist serves as your workroom, a studious retreat where your ideas, inventions and orders can be developed and passed on to your workforce. It is there I can see you just as Victor Prouvé portrayed you, peering anxiously at the long-necked vase you are holding, seeking to tease out of its warm transparency the decoration it lacks to be perfect.

Farther off still, in a vast hall, there stand furnaces for melting down the glass that barrel chests or great press-moulds will soon transform into vases, dishes, flacons or any one of a thousand imaginings that have earned your glass such well-deserved fame. Another building houses finished specimens of all these products. I will venture no further in my investigation, as I feel it might be indiscreet to describe your private residence, those spacious halls in which you have gathered together a remarkable selection of your output, or your cheerful garden alive with the most unusual essences and plants, like a gorgeous book in which you are forever dipping into in your search for inspiration, as if from the very fountainhead of Nature. Your preference lay in three substances – earthenware, glass and wood – and it is these that have served as the framework for your entire career.

I have already mentioned the range of your endeavours as applied to faience, whose readiness to submit to the most unconventional caprices of form and colour have delighted artists since time immemorial. In our region, Strasbourg, Niederville, Sarreguemines, Aprey, Lunéville and Saint-Clément were all important centres for ceramics, and several have kept or even improved their good name. Around 1860, Pull, Deck, Jean, Ulysse, Parvillée and Havilaud had already begun regenerating that charming speciality that had declined into slavish imitation since the end of the previous century. Your role in the innovation of its processes and applications was considerable. Yet the popularity it enjoyed until about twenty years ago did not take root; public taste turned to stoneware and above all to glass that soon became the great favourite of fashion.

Glass, that noble material – invented according to certain authorities by Tubal-Cain, the eighth man after Adam, and which was, to move to less hypothetical ground, certainly known to the Egyptians more than two thousand years before Christ – was and remains the apple of your eye. Bewitched by its transparency like that of immobilized running water, by a fluidity that adapts to every transmutation, by the ease with which it alters on contact with oxides, precious metals, coal, you conquered and disciplined it, endowing it not only with outer splendour and gracefulness, but with a voice, a song, a soul. It helped make your dreams come true, to symbolize your hopes, transform lines by your favourite authors into eloquent pictures. From 1864 [recte: 1867] to 1874 you worked on glass no less passionately than on earthenware; you discovered interesting ways of gunning on decoration in the forehearth and by interposing metallic or vitrifiable colorants between the cases that instantly transformed the ordinary clear glass of our Lorraine tableware, bedecking it with the most splendid colours. Glass engraving had undergone various vicissitudes in your studios; once tinted glass had appeared, plain engraving or incised flowers of the field on crystal glass (one of your father's developments that you increased in complexity with texts, fabliaux and naturalistic touches) appeared rather cold. For a time your workshop seemed to be in danger, but the application of engraving on solid marbled glass in imitation of gemstone and edged in enamel ensured further orders. Then, studying multiple-case glass in the Gréaux collections and the Palais d'Eté, as well as your discovery of *marqueterie sur verre*, provided a fresh impetus for making crystal in your workshop (in spite of competition from acid-etched imitations), which continues to grow apace.

The exquisite art of the *ébéniste*, whose contribution to the embellishment of our homes is so precious, was bound to attract and captivate a spirit as alert as yours to fresh developments in the applied arts. Following its triumphal procession from the sixteenth to the nineteenth century, woodworking had forfeited its character by parroting the Roman style during the First Empire. Romanticism, with its indigestible and crude amalgam of Renaissance and Gothic, did little to rejuvenate the art. Later, the invasion of carved oak and the thoughtless abuse of textiles made our furniture ponderous and vulgar. Struck by the potential offered to that art by the exploitation of our French forests and by exotic timbers seasoned under the sun of the Indies or the Americas into the most sumptuous colours, you started (and I borrow the phrase from you) 'to adore the wood that until then the potter had burned'. Flanked on every side by woods whose exquisite hue your tools brought to light, you applied your mind to marrying them to elegant arabesques and to compositions appropriate to every type of article. Under your aegis, this new art blossomed to such an extent that, in spite of the recent enlargement of your workshops, you have scarcely been able to keep pace.

In approaching your work, I will limit myself to the major achievements in these three facets of artistic industry. Whether in reference to wood, glass or ceramics, the hallmark of your aesthetic is that it is an interpretation of reality with a poet's mind and a painter's eye. Unflagging in your interest in Nature, you are in love with everything her charm and evocativeness can offer: the mysterious voices that speak so orotundly to her initiates, the grandiloquent and glorious spectacles she stages, the tenderness of the fleeting hours when the world shelters behind a gossamer of shade, the magically shifting tableaux of her parts, the delicacy, strength and melancholy of her flora, the elegance of her creatures in an infinite multiplicity of species, from the bottomless abyss to the airless confines of the ether. Stirred, spurred on by a vision, a moment, by all the offspring of that inexhaustibly creative force, you translate your feelings into objects that you lend form that accords with your emotions.

> *La forme, ô grand sculpteur, c'est tout et ce n'est rien;*
> *Ce n'est rien sans l'esprit, c'est tout avec l'idée.*
> (Form, O great sculptor, is both everything and nothing;
> It is nothing without the mind, yet with the idea it is everything),

as Victor Hugo wrote long ago to the sculptor David. How aptly, how responsively, how tactfully you know how to diversify these forms, which the slightest deviation of a line might have rendered commonplace, but which, in your hands, remain ever elegant, personal, meaningful.

On this basis you went on to concoct wonderful ornamentation full of colour and detail, painting shells and algae from the depths of the sea on the sides of an opaline vase, or inlaying into a table formed from a gnarled old Lorraine vine-foot – and under the gloaming of a threatening sky evocative of the dangers that lurk in the morning frost – plants that plague our vineyards, conjuring up that infinitesimal, redoubtable army vanquished by Pasteur's genius through a vitrified paste of deep violet, or devoting a complete, magnificent piece of furniture to the humble denizens of our kitchen-gardens, thereby through a delicate intricacy or opulent harmony ratifying their hitherto contested right to a place in decoration and ornament. Wise and empathetic, you invite us to console our travails with symbols: the *Bonté de la nuit* (goodness of the night), the *Charme attristant du jour qui baisse* (dispiriting charm of a day drawing to a close), *Bonté calme des choses* (calm goodness of things), *Sourire dans les larmes* (smiling through tears), the *Diadème de la tristresse* (diadem of sadness). Elsewhere, you have celebrated the gentle land of Lorraine, the succour brought by our great woods, the pervasive melancholy of their paths moistened by autumn rains. And always, among thousands of lithe or forceful objects, your hymn to the flower continues unabated in countless variations. Your song, sometimes with a flute's murmur, sometimes in the brightness of the horn, celebrates the grace and splendour of your fondest friends: Easter anemones, Alpine soldanella, autumn crocus, saffron crocus, winter crocus, the orchids – each became stylized motifs for ideas or ornaments.

Besides the well-chosen and evocative words you find deep within your heart, you are also fond of searching for inspiration in the works of our poets. 'The masters of the word', you have written, 'the poets, are also masters of decoration; they possess the ability to envisage images and create symbols.' The immense achievement of Victor Hugo, who, with his titanic lyre, has serenaded and comprehended all things, constitutes an inexhaustible goldmine to which you owe many of your most unforgettable creations. You adore Lamartine for his mystical compassion, Alfred de Vigny for his noble, high-minded serenity, Théophile Gautier for the painterly quality of his imagery, Baudelaire and Verlaine for the acerbic love of things into which their melancholy withdrew, Théodore de Banville for his Attic inspirations and Marceline Desbordes-Valmore for the elegiac tenderness of her broken heart.

Thus you have not so much rejuvenated as renovated the industrial arts, giving them a fresh impetus that quickly communicated itself to all nations susceptible to new things. It was your initiative that created this movement – particularly in evidence here in Nancy, where the recent establishment of fine, large-scale furniture and glass factories has consolidated the rebirth and ongoing vitality of Lorraine taste. It is to you that our dear Lorraine owes her brilliant artistic crown, of which we are justly proud and which has been consecrated at the recent opening of the Exposition Universelle in Paris.

The appearance of a new piece by your hand is greeted by instantaneous and uninhibited acclaim: the most eminent critics voice their admiration in scores of articles, which gathered together would constitute a substantial tome, and, for you, a precious celebratory volume. Referring to your glasswork, M. de Fourcaud enthuses about 'the manifold allusions that seep up from these enigmatic, eloquent vases like water that mysteriously, noiselessly flows from a shaded fountain', then, concerning your furniture, about 'the tenderness beyond words of the wood you use, its tactile freshness, its marmoreal nobility, silky opulence, floral grace and unparalleled sensitivity.' M. Marius Vachon salutes with transport the artistic renaissance of the provinces your works proclaim. M. Roger Marx praises 'your unfailing respect for the laws of appropriation within the bounds of originality, for your astuteness, for the boundless love of your native soil, which you cherish with the thousand-fold tenderness of one who combines sensitivity, erudition and scholarship.' M. Henrivaux declares that 'it does not appear that the art of glass could go any further and that an artist like you recalls an alchemist extracting the quintessence, materializing the intangible, vitrifying his dreams.' M. Paul Desjardins 'has given up trying to pigeonhole your genius', averring that 'you have invented everything that can be, with the help of a kind of foresight and thanks to a special understanding you have reached with the symbolic that makes one think back to Richard Wagner, that great creator and interpreter of myth.' 'Here then', Vicômte Melchior de Vogüé has written, 'is a man who can explain the madness of art to us, just as Vasari described it among the Florentine masters. He has endowed plants with a personality, a language of their own; he has rediscovered – be it when he inlays their image in a commode or else when he bestrews it through the melt for his glassware – the mysterious laws of their attitudes.'

Yet I must limit myself to but a few passages – and in the same way I can only touch on the numerous awards, gold medals, diplomas and *grand prix* you have carried off at every exhibition in France and abroad in which you have taken part. Appointed Chevalier de la Légion d'Honneur in 1884 [*recte*: 1885] and promoted Officier in 1889, you have been a statutory member of the Société Nationale des Beaux-Arts since 1892, and a member of the Admissions Committee of your 'Section' at the Exposition Universelle. The Musée du Luxembourg, the Musée des Arts Décoratifs and the Musée de la Ville de Paris as well as the most renowned royal and princely collections of every nation vie for the honour of possessing your works.

The creation of these unique museum pieces is not your only praiseworthy achievement. I cannot myself too highly applaud an industriousness that turns out objects that, by daily example, have popularized those principles of decorative art and artistic character that is imprinted on even the humblest artefact.

Well aware of how close to your heart the subject is, I would, Sir, like to add a few words concerning your collaborators, to whose tal-

ent you have always made it a duty to give rightful acknowledgement by publishing a list of their names on the occasion of each exhibition. I have already mentioned Gengoult Prouvé, in so untimely a manner wrenched from the art of modelling in which he so excelled; his name lives on, however, in his son Victor, who today stands at the forefront of our phalanx of Lorraine artists. This impulsive, indeed impetuous, artist toiled at your side for seven or eight years. He provided cartoons and bas-reliefs for a crystal-glass clock-case now the property of the Queen of Italy and representing *Fortuna Asleep on her Wheel*; for a cup over which lay entwined the figures of Night, Silence and Sleep; for vases on which was engraved *Orpheus Lamenting for Eurydice* or a head of Joan of Arc; for a superb mosaic table with a passage from Tacitus concerning ancient Gaul; for a chess-set; for a *Prospero* and *Miranda* recalling an episode from one of Shakespeare's most astringent tragedies. I also know of and would like to make known the heartfelt gratitude that you have always acknowledged for the twenty-year collaboration of Louis Hestaux, a charming painter of the country around Nancy, a creator of a number of delightful works in which the most vivid impressions are captured with a keen sense of poetry and whose hand transpires in the elegant and steady line of many a cartoon, drawing, watercolour, flower study as well as on profiles on vases, airy patterns and borders with which he daily furnished your workshops. I should also make mention the considerable number of pupils that you have trained in the various trades you employ and who owe their taste and knowledge to your guidance: modellers, woodcarvers, inlayers, cabinetmakers, metal-chasers, glass-engravers, servitors, glassmakers, acid-etchers, enamellers, decorators and painters.

I have cited your own writings several times, and wish there were time enough to quote numerous passages from those devoted to your art, your remarks to juries, your descriptions of pieces, your official reports, your toasts, all of which evince the same qualities of elegance and subtlety, which beguiled us in your speech. I can do no better than to compare their style to that of your exquisite creations, so refined, so graceful, so novel in their ornamentation, yet without foreswearing the nobility and proud bearing of their line and design.

Pursue your work, Sir, continue to charm us, to lift our spirits by intricate, precious inventions that release us from the routine of earthly existence to immerse us in the delight of reverie, in aspirations to the otherworldly, in the mysteries of the symbolic, and to rescue us for a moment from the wretchedness of human nature. Do not cease your wonderful hymns to ennobled Nature, and encourage us to adore the gifts of our native land that the munificence of the Creator has sown so plentifully about us but that we are all too prone to pass over in the hustle and bustle of the daily round.

Some days ago, I saw in a showcase a small, mottled-glass Phoenician vase, more than two thousand years old and recently brought back from its country of origin. This contemporary of Alexander, the size of a child's fist and which one could have shattered between two fingers, had crossed the intervening centuries without so much as a crack. The town where it had been created is little more than a pile of ruins, its temples, its palaces have crumbled into dust, oxidation has tarnished the bronzes and other metals that once adorned them, the throng of mighty conquerors that once milled have yielded the field to a handful of fisher folk and shepherds – yet this fragment of glass, whose fragility would seem to have destined it to be the first to pass into oblivion, has survived as a witness to that devastated region's wealth and splendour in former times.

Our discussions, our differences are vain and pointless. Men come and go, institutions collapse and, in the silence of the tomb, ambition turns to dust. Like every manifestation of the divine gift of intelligence, art, however, has longevity on its side: if the artist encounters his moments of fatigue, his reverses and discouragements, compensation comes in the form of his joy as a creator and a sense that his works – when they are built as are yours on the indestructible foundation of a passionate love of beauty – will endure for ever.

Notes

1, 3, 4   E.-T. Charpentier suspects a typo in the dates given for Gallé's stay in Germany and England: 'Shouldn't it be 1874 instead of 1864? That would explain everything: from 1862 to 1874 was the second half of his youth. . . . Afterwards – and that is not unusual in a period of ten years – travels and visits to museums, language proficiency and experience of the world, relationships with researchers like Rousseau with similar areas of specialization, while all these activities would not have been possible in two years. Moreover, Gallé would have visited museums before they had been founded (Kensington) and Fourcaud would have been a precocious aesthetic theorist indeed had he published before reaching the age of eleven' (p. 424).

2   It was not possible for Gallé to become personally acquainted with Liszt: 'Instead I should like to talk about his contact with Franz Liszt . . . , which is utterly impossible, even if Gallé had been in Weimar from 1862 onwards, for it is documented that Liszt gave up his post in the Grand Duchy in 1861' (p. 422).

5   It was neither in 1864 nor in 1874 but instead December 1866 that Gallé returned to his parents' home: 'In my opinion this mistake can be traced back to an imprecision that was made by stretching the facts in a speech. Later it took root in the literature, thus completely falsifying even a typo or a reference to a publication with incorrectly matching supplementary information' (pp. 424–25).

6   The information given here by Meixmoron is incorrect. In fact, the collaboration with Adelphe Muller's faience factory (not glassworks) took place in Raon-l'Etape from c. 1873 to 1898.

*   'Réponse du président M. Ch. de Meixmoron de Dombasle au récipiendaire M. Emile Gallé', *Mémoires de l'Académie de Stanislas*, vol. XVII, 5th ser. (Nancy, 1900), pp. XL–LXI.

The notes refer to F. T. Charpentier, 'Remarques sur les premières biographies de Gallé parues de son temps', in *A travers l'art français: Du moyen âge au 20ème siècle*, vol. 15 (1978), pp. 419–26.

Robert de Montesquiou
The Goldsmith and the Glass Artist
(Gallé and Lalique)

To write in eulogy of Lalique simply that he is the 'Gallé of jewellery' would be entirely understandable. For an artist, what could be more rewarding than to fulfil a dream, that of hanging jewels like minute Gallé vases round the necks of beautiful women? Its most satisfactory realization is surely captured by this admirable description: 'Her earrings were two tiny sapphire scales bearing a hollow pearl filled with liquid perfume. An occasional droplet would seep through the holes in the pearl and onto her bare shoulder.'

Moreover, since we were talking of names, these two possess remarkable similarities. And the master of glass – who prizes the goldsmith's creations as those of a fellow-artist – would not gainsay me if I were to add that, had Lalique begun first, one would have been tempted to write that Gallé is the Lalique of glass. Both possess a spiritual and emotional understanding of the most subtle language of flowers, which on occasion appears in the shape of a thoughtful face: an allegory enwrapped in colours and contours – this is the captivating draught that the glassmaker pours into his divine vase – that seek to convey the same heady fragrance as drips out of Lalique's hollow pearls.

God forbid that I should here embark upon an encomium of Gallé. A judicious interruption, such as 'and now the flood-gates open!' would soon bring me to heel. For is it not apt to compare all the *faux* Gallés with a deluge? They are, incidentally, not altogether bereft of charm (how else could they have been able to swim in his illustrious wake and bask in his reflected glory?), being in fact, in spite of everything, yet another indubitable, telltale symptom of his success.

But genuine Gallé vases – it is also true that he, too, is familiar with and practices the more pleasant side of commercial production – are our murrhine bowls, brothers to those mysterious cups much-vaunted in Antiquity. Gallé prepares the batch himself according to a secret formula. His works are shot through with subtle tones that summon up symbolic plants, carved out along the projections and swellings of the crystal. His vases are signed with the master's name, under the hexagonal and decorative cells of waxy honeycomb, or filled with the inner radiance of gems ground into the mix. Their bewitching beauty sends us into a curious, indeed unsettling state of euphoria.

The slenderness, the suppleness of a spray of blooms on a delicate stem is characteristic of Venetian glass, though overtaken today by Koep[p]ing's work, dark-hued volubilis, which cannot wait to be knocked or even brushed against before shattering. Indeed, in the bosom of the vitrine and under the influence of the atmosphere alone, living and vibrant, wary, sensitive, they wither, they splinter…

Notwithstanding, to object to the forms of Gallé's glasswork, to call them massive or wish them lighter, would be a blunder of a superficial mind. For it would be to evince a total miscomprehension of what imparts their dignity: their relationship to the gemstone, the creation of simulated onyx, of artificial cornelian, with the aim of drawing from them vessels laced with dark night or rosy dawn. It is logical to treat such ersatz precious stones in the same way as the genuine article and to preserve them from all brilliance: to leave them in their native state, only slightly altered in the vitreous mass, solidified in the furnace and muffle kiln. In much the same way, old-ivory Madonnas, painstakingly carved along the curve of the tusk, distend and incurve in swelling hips, pregnancies and hydropsies.

Such Gallés are the only gifts that one can still dare to present to kings, who feel both proud and fortunate to possess them, before carrying them off protectively to the undying honour of their museums.

As the noble modesty of their creator has done nothing to make it known, much less derive advantage from it, it will be as well to remark, be it in passing, that, to erase some painful memories, it was two vases by Gallé that France chose to present to the Tsar, in addition to some priceless lachrymatories from which tears could at last well up.

Papers recently unearthed in Flemish archives allege that Verlaine descends from an ancient family from Verlaine and attest that poor Lélian – who otherwise has produced more sustainable letters of nobility – was a nobleman and in consequence a *dilettante*! A similar discovery concerning Gallé is immanent – at least this is the implication from an old glassmaking treatise, which, having first assured us that contrary to popular opinion not all glassblowers are wedded to the bottle, opines: 'The craftsmen who work at this fine and high art are all noblemen. All have obtained important, great privileges, not the least of which is exercising their trade without besmirching their title.' There then follow the genealogies of Antoine de Brossard, de Caqueray, de Virgille, de la Mairie, de Sagrier, de Bongard and of many other highborn glass men.

Boasting of having *dug up* a number of significant secrets, the author of the old book does indeed provide some startling facts concerning glass, which he dubs *transparent metal* and of which he recounts an abundance of miracles: once he turns it lamp-black ('though lugubrious is not with its own beauty'), another time milky white, peach leaf, pearly, viper-, heliotrope-coloured, blood-red or rose.

He instructs us 'how to make a fine and noble carbuncle' and to distill a yellow varnish from broom blossom; to extract essences from poppy, iris, crimson rose, violets, borage flowers, from red cabbage, gladioli, mallow, pimpernel and other herbs to make lacquers of the same colour; to *scrub up* pearls and to concoct imitation ones so skilfully 'that they are no less bright than those forged by Nature in the depths of the sea.'… But let us return to our noble glassmaker.

And yet it is not the complex, many-sided artist of whom I wish to speak, the man with leafy, bushy (should I say capillary?) ideas like sprigs of those grasses that, even when dry still seem alive, remaining sempiternally in flower; a mind to which images offer themselves in their most detailed, intricate form, crystallizing and studding them with diamonds as they enter what is a kind of Salzburg mine of the cerebellum, where they are honed into a thousand rainbow facets; a mirror whose glass always reflects and entraps arborizing fibrillae; a myopic yet lynx-sharp eye that may occasionally miss the overall picture, but for which a dragonfly's wing never splits into enough cells – or enough secrets!

I wish to speak today neither of him, nor of the erudite botanist, that Linnaeus who neither distorts nor omits a single drooping head nor a single fleeting profile; nor of the astonishing *ébéniste*, who treats wood as he does agate, drawing from its veins and streaks allegorical landscapes with earth and sky, which he treats like Matteo del Nassaro of Verona, who plumbed the red maculae of sanguine jasper to extract drops of the blood of Christ Crucified; nor even of the marvellous lead-crystal maker – *primus inter pares* of the trinity, responsible for resurrecting Chinese glass (just as Carriès was for Japanese stoneware), of the patient student in the museum at Berlin, where the finest specimens of that skill bedazzle the eye, a curious art of superposing, variously coloured layers of glass that reappear, as fancy or necessity has it, through the perspicacity of a pedestal drill.

Rather, if I am to speak again of the prestigious *verrier* (to whom, moreover, I have devoted a brief descriptive poem, which I wish were better known [the reference is to 'Loggia', published in *Le Chef des odeurs suaves*]), it will be to speak of one of those elect Stations, anxious with the anxiety that led to such noble achievements – and of which we are permitted to see only the polished and, one is tempted to say, effortless, results, divorced from the secret travails of its tortured parturition in the furnace, from its birth pangs at the blow chair, and which let fly, which set rolling before us only the finest iridized bubbles, the briolettes of the finest water, the purest milk-white pearls.

It was at the end of a visit to the splendid factories of this denizen of Nancy, to his elegant manufactories and charming laboratories. We had been admiring his many models, indeed breathing the air of great clumps of trees; rows of models and marquetry spread out before us; and the vases that take on their colours and silhouettes, and whose delicate and subtle flanks, whose transparent almost organic bellies will flower with similar, fraternal blooms, hardly to be distinguished from the shape of the vessels. Yet the thread through the labyrinth never unravelled, never snapped – and our guide's bunch of keys clinked away with one more enigmatic key that he hid yet simultaneously seemed to lay before us, with a desire to betray his secret without deliberately divulging it – to be consoled without having first to bemoan.

So if indeed, oh Gallé, the door to Bluebeard's den screeched on its hinges, it would have opened before me perhaps to reveal the skirts of women long-dead, the tunics of your defunct Muses hanging from clear-glass hooks.

Or perhaps the spangled and micaceous cast-offs from your still-born daughters, from flacons brimful of sleepless nights, *lagenae* big with dreams and pains to which you sometimes give the indubitably symbolic form of a tear moulded from countless adamantine corpses and gemstone hecatombs. And, upon these radiating rays, I recognized the preordained swellings, the original, primitive contours of those vases by your hand that stupefy us the most, the ones whose untroubled blossoms seemed to burst forth ready flowering from your brain and from your muffle, and whose cracked and split spectres, chipped and thunderstruck phantoms silently recite each fiendish stage of their fervent genesis. Ragged purple rubies, tattered azure sapphires, carbuncle shreds, pendulous and prismatic pendant-

drops (into which oftentimes you have pounded and intermixed these very gems), which a glimmer of light from the waning sun burns deep in Bluebeard's closet, set ablaze, then kindling flames and tears – like a brazier of myriad stones in which the phoenix of your creations, that fabulous bird of your fairyland, is consumed and from which, unceasingly, it rises again.

(from Robert de Montesquiou, *Roseaux pensants* [Paris, 1897], pp. 174–80 [second part of the chapter entitled 'Orfèvre et verrier (Gallé et Lalique)'])

Helmut Ricke

Drawings from Gallé's Studio

The 5 March 1898 application for design protection

The addition of *Modèle et décor déposé* to his signature can be found on many of Gallé's pieces after 1880. That this was to protect his designs from being copied was clear. What remained to a great extent unclear, however, was how the process of securing protection should be imagined, until in 1982 a large bundle of the Gallé studio's design material of unknown provenance came to light and was sold at auction by Sotheby's Monaco.[1] Comprising thirteen portfolios, this material probably came from the now defunct Conseil des Prud'hommes archives in Nancy, authorities whose responsibilities included granting and ensuring the protection of designs to companies in the region.

The drawings were done between 1880 and 1902. The majority of individual items making up this important collection of source material were acquired by The Corning Museum of Glass, Corning, N.Y.[2] The dossier of 5 March 1898[3] (illus. p. 276, top) was bought at auction by Gerda Koepff, who donated it to the Kunstgewerbemuseum, Cologne, now the Museum für Angewandte Kunst.

Brigitte Klesse, then director of the museum, did make the drawings known to specialists in 1983 in a lecture on the occasion of the ninth convention of the Association Internationale pour l'Histoire du Verre in Nancy, taking the opportunity to comment extensively on them. However, in her summary of the material she was able to show only seven of thirty-five sheets.[4] Gallé's papers accompanying them also remained unpublished.

The following list and concluding note illustrate what the application for design protection covered. All that was involved was the protection against misuse, that is, unauthorized copying of a specified number of vessel shapes, motifs, compositions, etc., by competitors. To achieve this, neither original drawings nor a logical ordering of the dossier's contents was required so that this bundle of material was left looking as if it had been haphazardly assembled.

Design protection was deemed necessary only for serially produced wares. Drawings for individual commissions or objects intended as one-off pieces in the grand genre were not registered. In such cases Gallé could be sure that it would be virtually impossible for competitors to produce convincing copies or even imitations. In this area, therefore, all that had to be protected were techniques, such as marquetry and patinage. This was accomplished by means of patents,[5] which, since they expired after fifteen years, were far more effective instruments with regard to competitors than merely the registration of design protection, which was valid for only a few years. The documents Gallé presented to the Conseil were evidently not sorted by materials and this was done deliberately, even though as a rule the drawings themselves reveal the uses for which they were primarily intended. Designs relating to furniture production are mixed with those for glassmaking. Further, original drawings on paper are included with copies on tracing paper. Moreover, decoration that should have been grouped together has in many cases been arbitrarily separated. The furniture designs shown in plates 2, 5, 8, 21, 22 and 24 have been reproduced here for the sake of completeness, but will not be addressed in the following.

Some vase designs are merely line drawings (pls. 25, 26). A vase shape inspired by the seed capsule of the primrose was, as far as can be seen today, used only for pieces executed in the marquetry technique – usually with the frequently encountered autumn crocus decoration on the vessel wall (illus. below). The vase with three apertures (pl. 26), however, was mainly made with enamel decoration in bold relief (illus. p. 274, left)[6] but occasionally also with etching. The moulded flacon form (pl. 17) was not originally intended to be decorated, but after Gallé's death the factory produced variations on it, including a long-necked vase with floral decoration.[7]

'Fruit de primulacée' vase with 'Veilleuses' (autumn crocus) marquetry decoration, pl. 25. Formerly Brugnot Collection, Paris

The drawings on tracing paper with four variants of the sunflower motif, to each of which a vase form has been assigned (pls. 27–30; illus. p. 275), are particularly painstakingly executed and bear the remark that they can also be used with other vase shapes. Gallé took advantage of this more than once.[8] The vessels have all been executed in the technique of etching on overlay. The seed capsules are formed by low cabochons with metallic inclusions. Flower petals are often backed with foil. Vessel interiors are matt etched and the entire surface acid-polished. The pieces in this group share the same signature, which encompasses Gallé's name, wavy and simple concentric rings surrounding the name and the addition of *déposé*.

A special case is the drawing in plate 12, an original drawing that, unlike the other glass designs, has been so meticulously done on paper that one might initially be inclined to think that it was for a piece to be executed in metal. The reference to the rim, which is to be ground, reveals that this drawing represents a design for glass. Gallé must have intended it to be mounted on a bronze stand. Formally speaking, it bears a striking resemblance to the marquetry vases (1898) with

columbine motifs (cat. no. 40), representing as it does the formal principle underlying that piece, but turned upside down.

The rhomboid box (pl. 31) might also have been conceivable as executed in wood intarsia, yet the *Pour Bonheur* (good luck) inscription on it relates it to the various formal possibilities provided by Gallé's new techniques of marquetry and patinage. He makes a point of referring to the patent pending on them.[9] The decoration does not seem at first sight particularly suitable for techniques not intended for serially produced wares. However, a box in the Neumann Collection in Switzerland (illus. below) proves that Gallé really did have boxes made in marquetry after the registered decoration schema.[10] Still this must be regarded as the exception. The drawing is for one of the popular *étrennes*, the stylish New Year's presents fashionable at the time, with the appropriate message.[11] The piece in the Neumann Collection does not bear an inscription; instead it is adorned with a delicate border round the edge of the lid painted in enamels and the sides of the box have been decorated with marquetry.

The designs shown in plates 19 and 20, which reveal affinities with the box design and feature inscriptions, could conceivably have been intended for enamel painting, yet they were probably meant for intarsia in wood owing to their rather astringent, highly stylized quality. The same holds for the columbine rosette (pl. 1) and presumably also for the sophisticated blend of foliage, trailing mist and moths in plate 34. Similar motifs are, however, also known in enamel painting.[12]

The motif of a group of swallows (pls. 3, 6, 7, 9 and 10) can be just as easily imagined on glass as on wood. The images themselves represent variations on the formal repertoire drawn on by the studio from the 1880s onwards.[13] Even though Gallé explicitly points out that the designs he has registered are unpublished, this does not refer in all cases to the basic idea underlying the decoration but merely to the specific form presented to the authorities. The sheet with bat studies should be viewed in this light (pl. 32), as should the variations on the columbine and pansy motifs (pls. 33, 35; 4, 23). In 1899 Gallé even took the precaution of having his celebrated early 1880s 'Claire de lune' bowl placed under protection again, possibly with a view to it being included in his

'Bouteille à 3 orifices' vase with 'Dielytra' (Bleeding Heart) decoration in relief enamel, pl. 26. Private collection

'Trèfles' (clover leaves) box, shape and decoration matching pl. 31. Neumann Collection, Château de Gingins, Switzerland

Vase with 'Hélianthe' (tall sunflower) decoration, shape and decoration matching pl. 28. King Gustav V Foundation, Stockholm

1   See Sotheby's Monaco 1982, nos. 26–58. Another bundle of material came under the hammer in the same place only five years later: auct. cat. Sotheby's Monaco, 5 April 1987, nos. 155–65. It comprised ten portfolios and a single sheet. Three of the portfolios (nos. 162, 164, 165) were identical with nos. 37, 50 and 57 of the 1982 auction and the same holds for the individual sheet (1982, no. 30; 1987, no. 161). The others were unknown prior to the second auction.

2   The following portfolios and batches are still in the library there: Sotheby's Monaco 1982, no. 26 – registered on 17 June 1880: 19 plates, 38 motifs; Sotheby's Monaco 1982, no. 27 – registered on 5 April 1895: pls. 1–52, 55–60; 58 of a total of 60 plates; Sotheby's Monaco 1982, no. 28 – registered on 14 May 1895: pls. 1–27 (except for pl. 15) and 46–48; 29 of a total of 48 plates; Sotheby's Monaco 1982, no. 38, 41–46 – registered on 23 September 1897: pls. 8–10; 22–38; 20 of a total of 50 plates. For this information we are indebted to Gail P. Bardhan and Norma P. H. Jenkins of The Rakow Library, The Corning Museum of Glass, Corning, NY.

3   Sotheby's Monaco, 1982, no. 48.

4   See B. Klesse, 'Entwurfszeichnungen aus den Ateliers Emile Gallé', summary in *Annales du 9e Congrès International d'Etude Historique du Verre*, Nancy, France, 22–28 May 1983 (Liège, 1985), pp. 375–84.

5   See Hakenjos 1982, pp. 566–84.

6   See also the drawing heightened with watercolour in Thiébaut, *Dessins*, 1993, p. 168, labelled *639 No. 4*.

7   See Hilschenz-Mlynek and Ricke 1985, no. 347 – with soliflore with begonia decoration, and reference to further variants.

8   See, for instance, Hilschenz-Mlynek and Ricke 1985, no. 238, with reference to further copies and variants.

9   Both patents were registered six weeks after the application for design protection had been submitted, on 26 April 1898.

10   See Bartha, *Collection Neumann*, 1993, p. 68.

11   See Hilschenz-Mlynek and Ricke 1985, nos. 232, 264.

12   See Kitazawa, *Gallé*, 1997, no. 27; *Gallé et Toulouse-Lautrec* 1995, no. 9.

13   For more on the swallow motif see, for instance, Klesse 1982, pp. 54, 55 – drawing for Gallé by Eugène Kremer at Meisenthal and the vase based on it. The motif of the group of swallows on a telegraph line had been used before 1875, by Theodore Deck on a ceramic plate; see Hakenjos 1982, p. 139.

14   See auct. cat. Sotheby's Monaco, 5 April 1987, no. 164, illus. p. 53; for the bowl see, for instance, Paris, *Gallé*, 1985, no. 77.

15   See Klesse (note 4), p. 380.

presentation 'L'Histoire du verre' at the 1900 Paris Exposition Universelle.[14]

The signatures reproduced in plates 11 and 18 were probably intended mainly for intarsia work in the form shown, yet they might well have been adapted – like most of these designs – to the specific conditions obtaining for painting on glass or faience.

The original drawings for stands shown in plates 13 to 16 have been executed with particular care. Such stands were developed as mounts for the marquetry pieces new at the time and were cast in Gallé's studio. Paul Holderbach and August Herbst, Gallé's employees responsible for cabinetmaking and, therefore, cast bronze fittings for furniture, may have executed these designs.[15] Three of the stands were used for pieces in the Koepff Collection (cat. nos. 36, 39, 40).

Nancy Garenne,
le Cinq Mars, 1898

Envelope for the 35 plates for
which Gallé applied for design
protection on 5 March 1898

Descriptions du présent
Album A. cessis a jour à Mon-
sieur Maxant Greffier du
Conseil des Prud'hommes de
Nancy, par E. Gallé, ft à Nancy

Pl. no. 1. *Rosace* (quart de)

Pl. no. 2. *Détails* de parties de
meubles, d'après *la plante*: a/
colonnette.

b/ fuseau avec torsion.

c/ piètement de meubles.

Pl. no. 3. *Les clochers*, décor.

Pl. no. 4. *Pensées stilisées*, "

Pl. no. 5. *Piètement de meuble
d'après la plante, avec torsion.*

Pl. no. 6. *Les hirondelles*,
Décor.

Pl. no. 7. *Les hirondelles*, Jeu de
fond.

Pl. no. 8. *Le marronier*, piètement et traverse de meuble.

Pl. no. 9. *'Conciliabule'*, Décor.

Pl. no. 10. *Voyage*, Décor.

Pl. no. 11. *Signature aux pensées.*

Pl. no. 12. *Forme de vase
lozangé*, conique, col mouluré

Pl. no. 13. *L'Etang*, socle

Pl. no. 14. *Aquilegia*, socle

Pl. no. 15. *Fausse renoncule*
Socle

Pl. no. 16. *Végétation*, Socle

Pl. no. 17. *La graine,*

a/ flacon b/ *Le bouton à fleur*,
bouchon

Pl. no. 18. *Signature au Dielytra* (a). b/ *cœur*, c/ *trèfle*
(semis)

Pl. no. 19. a/ *Couronne de
cœurs*. b/ *'Riche de cœurs'*

Pl. no. 20. c/ *" de trèfles*. d/
*'Pour bonheur'*Pl. no. 21. *'Les
Trois-Epís'*, Chaise

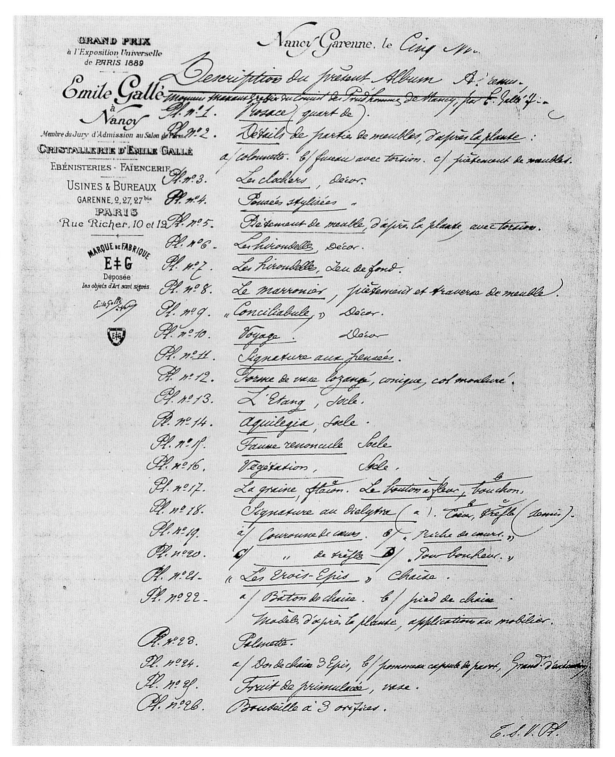

Pl. no. 22. a/ *Bâton de chaise*. b/ *pied de chaise*.

Modèles d'après la plante, applications au mobilier

Pl. no. 23. Palmette

Pl. no. 24. a/ Dos de chaise

3 Epís, b/ pommeau capsule de pavot, Grand$_r$ d'exécution

Pl. no. 25. *Fruit de primulacée*, vase.

Pl. no. 26. Bouteille à 3 orifices.

Pl. no. 27. *Hélianthe* Décor applicable à toute forme, et particulièrement à celle indiquée, 27 b.

Pl. no. 28. " " ", 28 b.

Pl. no. 29. " " ", 29 b.

Pl. no. 30. " " ", 30 b.

Pl. no. 31. a/ Boîte lozangée et D/ son couvercle, á exécuter en toutes grandeurs, matières, décors etc. – B. bordure de trêfles (oxalei acetosella)

c/ *'Le trèfle à quatre feuilles'*, décor, avec dévise: *'pour bonheur'* décor applicable à cette pièce, ou á tous autres objets, procédés notamment ceux des *'placage verrier, brochage verrier, intarsia, cristal bijou'*, procédés artistiques de mon invention, de mon secret, et que je compte faire incessamment breveter.

Pl. no. 32. *'Choses crépusculaires'* Stylisation de chauves-souris et signature stylisée de l'artiste.

Pl. no. 33. 'Ancolie' Motif de décor.

Pl. no. 34. *Stylisation* nuées, végétations, sphinx.

Pl. no. 35. *L'ancolie à longues cornes*, Stylisation.

NB: Tous ces modèles, ces décors sont des compositions de mon invention, inédites, destinées à être appliquées à la production exclusive de mes usines et ateliers, à la vente exclusive de mes débits et concessionnaires, à être exécutées en toutes grandeurs, matières, industries, coloris, procédés, notament [*sic*] ceux dits cihaut, et de même L'ébénisterie, la marqueterie, la sculpture pour le bois, pour le verre ['3 mots E.G.' added subsequently and confirmed in the margins], l'émaillage, la gravure chimique, la ciselure au touret, la taille, la peinture, la moulure, la fonte, les patines, l'impression, pour la fabrication du verre, du cristal, de la poterie, des bronzes.

Emile Gallé

Pl. n° 27. Hélianthe Décor applicable à toute forme, et particulièrement à celle indiquée, 27 b.
Pl. n° 28. " " " 28 b.
Pl. n° 29 " " " 29 b.
Pl. n° 30 " " " 30 b.
Pl. n° 31 - a/ Boîte lozangée et D/ son couvercle, à exécuter en toutes grandeurs, matières, décors, etc. — B. bordure de trèfles (oxali acetosella) c/ "Le trèfle à 4 feuilles" décor, avec devise: "pour bonheur" décor applicable à cette pièce, ou à tous autre objets, procédés, notamment ceux des "placage verrier, brochage verrier, intarsia, cristal bijou", procédés artistiques de mon invention, de mon secret, et que je compte faire incessamment breveter.
Pl. n° 32. "Choses crépusculaires" Stylisation de chauves-souris et signature stylisée de l'artiste.
Pl. n° 33. "Ancolie" Motif de décor.
Pl. n° 34. "Stylisation nuées, végétation, sphinx.
Pl. n° 35. L'ancolie à longues cornes, Stylisation.
N.B. Tous ces modèles, ces décors sont des compositions de mon invention, inédites, destinées à être appliquées à la production exclusive de mes usines et ateliers, à la vente exclusive de mes débits et concessionnaires, à être exécutées en toutes grandeurs, matières, industries, coloris, procédés, notamment ceux dits ci-haut, et de même l'ébénisterie, la marqueterie, la sculpture pour le bois, pour le verre, l'émaillage, la gravure chimique, la ciselure au touret, la taille, la peinture, la moulure, la fonte, les patines, l'impression, pour la fabrication du verre, du cristal, de la poterie, des bronzes.
3 mots E.G.
Emile Gallé

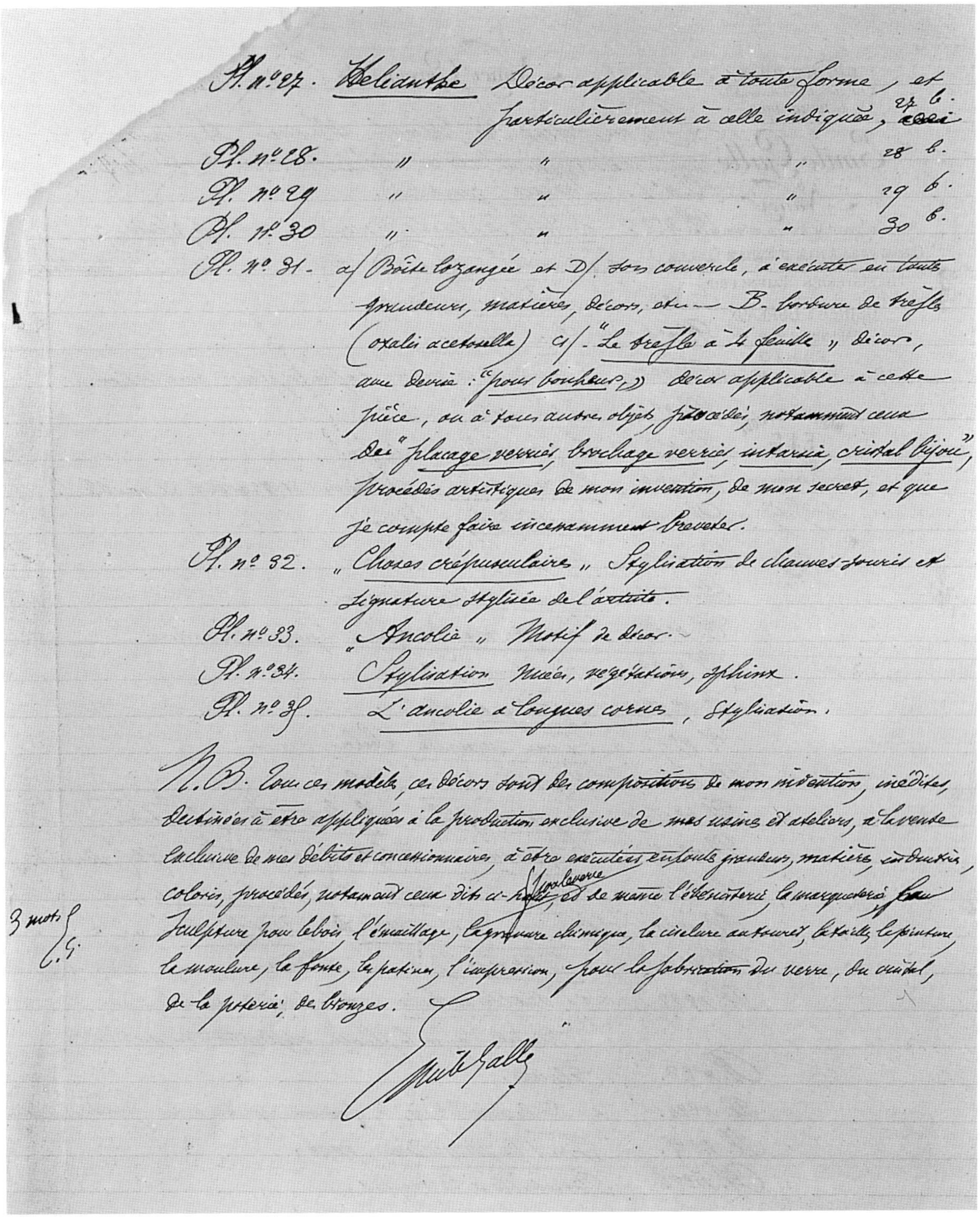

Nancy Garenne
Fifth March 1898

Descriptions of the present
Album A, submitted this day
to M. Maxant, Clerk of the
Conseil des Prud'hommes of
Nancy, by Emile Gallé,
manufacturer [?] in Nancy

1 *Rosette* (quarter)
Pen on tracing paper
27.9 x 28.1 cm

2 *Drawings of furniture
details*, modelled on plants:
a) small column
b) spindle with twist
c) leg
Pen on tracing paper
40 x 19.9 cm

1

3 *Bell-towers*, decoration
Pen on tracing paper
45.8 x 36.6 cm

4 *Stylized pansies*
Pen on tracing paper
21.1 x 22.2 cm

5 *Furniture leg* modelled
on a plant, with twist
Pencil on paper
71.4 x 16.5 cm

3

Measurements (height x
width) appear, respectively,
on the left-hand and lower
edge of each sheet.

The drawings were mounted
by Gallé's employees on
brownish paper or light cardboard in varying formats –
some of them not very carefully. Many of the sheets
show traces of folding; they
were evidently used in the
studio before being submitted to the authorities responsible for ensuring the protection of designs.

The drawings are numbered
continuously from 1 to 35
and now bear stamps with
the inscription *ATELIER
ÉMILE GALLÉ / SOTHEBY
MONACO / 24. 10. 1982.*

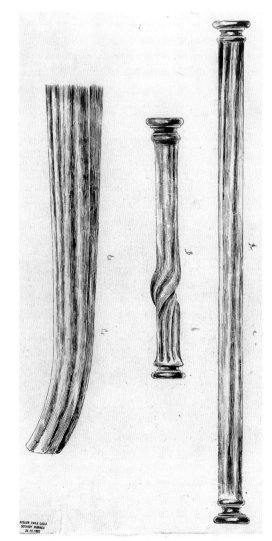

2

4

5

6 *Swallows*, decoration
Pen on tracing paper
36.3 x 58.4 cm

7 *Swallows*, playing in space
Pen on tracing paper
28.6 x 49.9 cm

8 *Chestnut*, leg, cross-strut of
a piece of furniture
Pen on tracing paper
72.7 x 59.6 cm

9 *'Secret meeting'*, decoration
Pen on tracing paper
34 x 66.5 cm

10 *Voyage*, decoration
Pen on tracing paper
19.3 x 56 cm

6

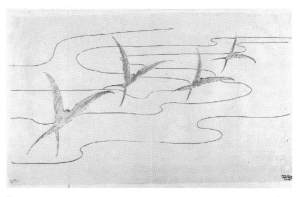

7

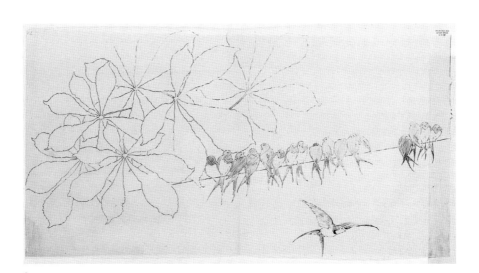

9

8

10

11 *Signature with pansies*
Pen on tracing paper
19.2 x 14.9 cm

12 *Rhomboid vase form,*
conical, rim cut
Pencil on paper
27.7 x 20.2 cm

13 *Pond,* mount
Pencil on paper
13.1 x 22.9 cm

14 *Columbine,* mount
Pencil on paper
12.2 x 16.9 cm

15 *Horn-wort,* mount
Pencil on paper
8.9 x 13.3 cm

16 *Growth,* mount
Pen on tracing paper
9.2 x 14.4 cm

11

12

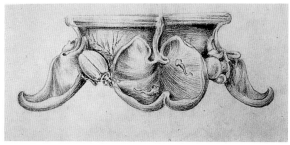

13

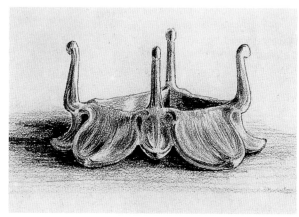

14

15

16

17

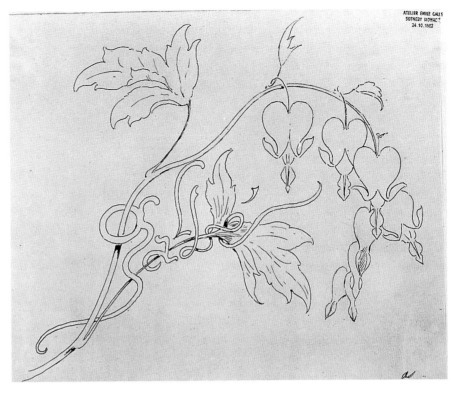

17 *Seed*
a) Flacon
b) Bud, stopper
Pen on tracing paper
18.9 x 19.7 cm

18 *Signature* with
a) Bleeding Hearts
b) Heart
c) Clover-leaf (half)
Pen on paper
a) 18.8 x 23 cm
b) 5.3 x 8.8 cm

19
a) *Coronet of hearts*
b) *'Rich in hearts'*
Pen on tracing paper
44.2 x 20 cm

20
c) *Clover-leaf coronet*
d) *'Good luck'*
Pen on tracing paper
43.5 x 20.8 cm

18

19

20

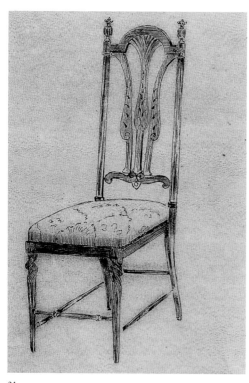

21

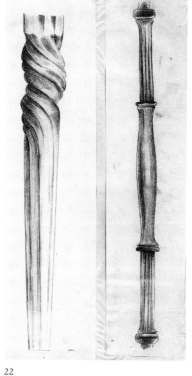

22

23

21 *'Three ears* [of grain]', chair, Pen on tracing paper
19.7 x 14.6 cm

22
a) *Cross-strut of a chair*
b) *Chair leg*
Modelled on plant life, for use with furniture
Pencil on paper
a) 45.2 x 16.8 cm
b) 42.1 x 9.6 cm

23 *Palmette*
Pen on tracing paper
12.3 x 15.1 cm

24
a) *Back of chair, 3 ears*
b) *Knob in the shape of a poppy seed capsule*, original size
Pencil on paper
63.7 x 34.4 cm

25 *Fruit of the primrose*, vase
Pen on tracing paper
29.3 x 23.8 cm

24

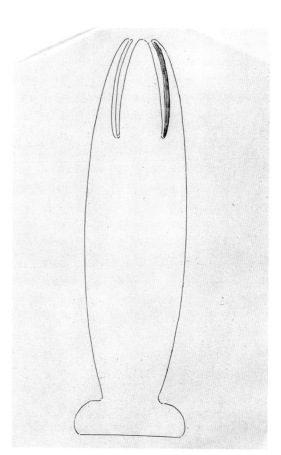

25

26 *Bottle with three apertures*
Pen on tracing paper
34.7 x 15.5 cm

27 *Sunflower*, decoration, to
be used on all vessel shapes,
especially on what is referred
to as 27 b
Pen on tracing paper
19.8 x 32.3 cm

28 *Sunflower*, decoration, to
be used on all vessel shapes,
especially on what is referred
to as 28 b
Pen on tracing paper
42.2 x 46 cm

29 *Sunflower*, decoration, to
be used on all vessel shapes,
especially on what is referred
to as 29 b
Pen on tracing paper
29.5 x 48 cm

30 *Sunflower*, decoration, to
be used on all vessel shapes,
especially on what is referred
to as 30 b
Pen on tracing paper
22 x 42.5 cm

31
a) Rhomboid box and
b) its lid, to be made in all
sizes, all materials, decoration schemes, etc. – B.
Clover-leaf border (*Oxalei
acetosella*)
c) 'Four-leaf clover', decoration with the motto 'Good
Luck', decoration to be used
on this piece or on all other
objects, processes, especially
'glass marquetry, glass brocade, intarsia, *cristal bijou*',
artistic processes I invented
that are my secret and that I
intend to have patented
forthwith.
Pen on tracing paper
14.7 x 14.4 cm

27

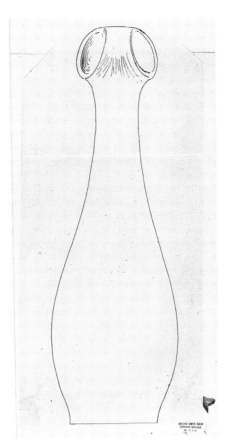

26

29

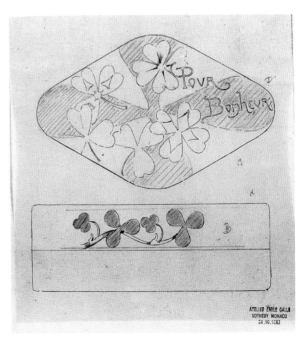

28

30

31

32 *'Things of the dusk'*, bat
motifs and stylized artist's
signature. Pen on tracing
paper, 37.2 x 35.6 cm

33 *'Columbine'*, decorative
motif. Pen on tracing paper
35.1 x 22.4 cm

34 *Stylization*, clouds,
plants, Sphinx ligustri
(Privet hawk-moth)
Pen on tracing paper
46.3 x 47.1 cm

35 *Columbine with long
spurs*, stylization
Pen on tracing paper
37.6 x 49.2 cm

32

33

Note:

All these models, these decorative programmes, are
compositions I have con-
ceived. They are unpublished
and intended for use in production solely in my factories
and studios, to be sold
exclusively in my retail outlets and by my authorized
dealers, to be executed in all
sizes, materials, crafts, colour
schemes, manufacturing
processes, especially those
listed above and also in cabinetmaking, marquetry,
wooden sculpture, enamel
painting on glass, etching,
wheel-engraving, cutting,
painting, casting, patinage,
press-moulding, the pro-
duction of glass, crystal,
ceramics and bronze.

Emile Gallé

34

35

Eva Schmitt

The Daum Factory Archives

The Cristallerie Daum archives[1] are under the auspices of the Service Régional de l'Inventaire de Lorraine in Nancy, headed by Mireille Bouvet and Jacques Guillaume, and have for the most part been made accessible to the public in the form of copies, photographs and slides. Not all the source material covering the period up to 1911 may be used for research purposes.

The study of all texts relevant to Daum in this book, entailing in essentials the comprehensive evaluation of the entire Daum archives, including the drawings from the firm's own drawing school and library, has been conducted by Christophe Bardin in his doctoral thesis, *Daum (1878–1939): Débuts, évolution et accomplissement d'une industrie d'art lorraine, Thèse pour obtenir le grade de docteur de l'Université de Nancy II*, 2 vols. (Nancy, 2002).

Important sources on production up to 1914,
examined in order to identify and date pieces in the
Koepff Collection
Catalogue of models (Catalogue aquarellé), price list (Tarif), Album I, three photographic series and individual photographs of elaborate exhibition models, some 2000 drawings of models, 152 studies of plants drawn from nature by Henri Bergé as well as the Daum sales and exhibition catalogues.

Catalogue aquarellé
is a catalogue of models consisting of 448 lithographs, some with watercolour, with for the most part numbered drawings of edition models, which as a rule are grouped on each sheet by glassmaking technique.[2] By drawing on the models and comparing prices with the price list (Tarif), one can ascertain the name of an object, when it was made, developments in its line, the formal canon drawn on and its decoration.

Neither the handwritten date 1894 on the first plate in the catalogue of models nor the date 1890 noted on the first page of the price list are reliable for dating the first issue of the catalogue of models and the price list. Detailed work with these two most important sources has revealed numerous contradictions when compared with contemporary publications on the factory's early product lines and these contradictions could be resolved only by systematic, in-depth, on-site research. The most important sources relevant to the production of editions, the Catalogue aquarellé and Tarif, were presumably issued continuously to parallel production only from autumn 1898 onwards, following the extremely successful participation in the 1897 Brussels Exposition Internationale. Products made before September 1898 were entered and dated retrospectively.

Tarif
denotes the handwritten price list of edition pieces by model number with brief descriptions of the objects. Two bound exemplars are extant and the information in them occasionally varies. The original of Tarif

No. 1 contains a variety of additional information, including technical instructions for exhibitions or references to unsigned editions. The second exemplar, which is more uniform in conception and written far more legibly, is evidently a copy in which the errors in the original have been corrected. The model numbers correspond, with a few exceptions, to those noted in the catalogue of models. The information conveyed in keywords usually amounts to a succinct object description. It includes, apart from the designation of the decoration by plant motif, numerous names used within the firm itself for both forms and techniques, which are not, however, consistently retained in the long term.

Album I
denotes a portfolio compiled in 1899 containing 45 or 46 lithograph plates, most of them with watercolour, and extant in two exemplars in the Daum archives. The portfolio was evidently intended as a pattern book for the Paris Exposition Universelle. It contains in essentials the so-called 1899 *martelé* models[3] alongside serially produced utility glass with miniature-like painted landscapes and plants. One plate shows three early models from 1894.

Photographic series
document elaborate pieces made for special purposes. These are either one-off pieces or small editions that were made for particularly important occasions, usually exhibitions, and are only rarely entered in the catalogue of models and the price list. The passe-partouts make it possible to identify three series by Henry Dufey, a Strasbourg photographer, and several individual photographs by various other photographers. It has been possible to assign the photographic series to objects with the aid of descriptions in contemporary product and exhibition catalogues and to identify the early special pieces after designs by Jacques Gruber and later by Henri Bergé.[4]
Series 1
on bluish grey cardboard with a round red Dufey stamp on the reverse; extant in two different sizes. This first series comprises the earliest exhibition models, from 1893 to 1894, which are after designs by Jacques Gruber, or an artist influenced by him.
Series 2
on chamois-coloured, rectangular matt cardboard with recessed Dufey signature in the lower zone of the photographs. This series comprises exhibits from 1894 to 1897, after designs by Gruber and Bergé or an artist influenced by them.
Series 3
on chamois-coloured, rectangular matt cardboard with recessed Dufey signature and address in the lower zone of the passe-partout. The photographs are of exhibits after designs by Henri Bergé for the Ecole de Nancy exhibitions in Paris in 1903 and in Nancy in 1904.

Individual photographs without passe-partouts are of groups of exhibits for the 1900 Paris Exposition Universelle. Other photographs are of pieces for the exhibitions from 1905 to 1910.[5] They were supplemented by reproductions of two photographs taken for the 1893 Chicago World's Columbian Exposition and the 1895 exhibition in Bordeaux from the Daum documents in the Musée Lorrain in Nancy.

Model drawings
Most of the some 2000 drawings date from after 1918. They are as a rule marked Daum Frères without designer signatures. Earlier designs occa-

sionally bear the signatures of Henri Bergé or Emile Wirtz. No signed drawings by the designers Jacques Gruber and Charles Schneider are extant.

152 Plant studies

from nature by Henri Bergé are in the Daum archives. This corpus was divided up years ago; more of these studies are in the Musée de l'Ecole de Nancy and in the Musée des Beaux-Arts in Nancy. They are drawn in pencil, pen and black or coloured ink and finished with watercolour or body colour. As a rule the artist added the name of the plant and often also a number and the studies are frequently also signed and dated. They can, however, hardly be used to date designs for decoration since they were rarely done in the same year as the designs. Used as models, these botanical studies eloquently attest to Bergé's talent as a draughtsman and the years of untiring dedication to developing new motifs at Daum.[6]

Firm catalogues and other important exhibition catalogues

Not all the catalogues mentioned by Sterner in 1969 were in the archives. They could, however, be supplemented by copies of the 1897 and 1900 catalogues from the Musée Lorrain in Nancy. The important catalogue produced by Daum for the 1895 exhibition in Bordeaux is still missing.[7] The major catalogues accompanying the exhibitions mounted by the Société Lorraine des Amis des Arts in Nancy are in the Bibliothèque Municipale in Nancy (1896 is missing).

Daum product catalogue of 1891

Daum Frères & Cie. Verreries Artistiques de Nancy: Créations de 1891 (Nancy, 1891). This is the first catalogue of its products issued by the factory, presenting in essentials the sets of drinking glasses produced up to 1891 alongside some vases, jars/boxes, etc., after designs by Antonin Daum and his decoration studio, with forms and motifs borrowing from historical and traditional Lorraine models. For a reproduction of plate 22 see p. 58 in the present volume.

Brussels, catalogue, 1897

A small catalogue in roughly half postcard format illustrated by Jacques Gruber, who presents his designs from 1893 to 1896 in individual plates. The middle section contains a picture of models by Gruber and Bergé, which are shown on the exhibition table by Louis Majorelle. For illustrations see p. 62 and cat. no. 80 in the present volume.

Paris, *Daum*, 1900

Firm catalogue, measuring roughly 14 · 11 cm, with photographs of the studio and several glass pieces. Some of the original photographs are in the Daum archives. Apart from lines in drinking glasses and dressing-table sets as well as oil lamps and electric table lamps, they also show the most important pieces made to order or for special purposes, after designs by Henri Bergé, Ernest Bussière and Jacques Gruber. Most of the exhibits shown in these pictures can be identified from the descriptions of the objects. For illustrations see cat. nos. 89, 91, 92 in the present volume.

Paris 1903

Catalogue accompanying the Ecole de Nancy exhibition in Paris, with succinct descriptions of Daum Frères pieces and several photographs from Photo series 3. Bergé is not mentioned.

Paris, portfolio, 1903

Collection of unbound plates supplementing the illustrations to the 1903 catalogue.

On the problem of dating in the price list until September 1898

The price list and the catalogue of models are the most important and comprehensive documents to be drawn on for identifying and dating edition models. In specific instances, working with these two sources and comparison with contemporary accounts or the rare dates on pieces reveals discrepancies up to c. 1910, despite the abundance of archive material. For the early editions the main criterion is the technique used to make them, which is assigned to the various models (vessel shapes and the motifs intended for them). From 1901 it is possible to trace systematic planning of product lines by motifs, which are executed in specific techniques. A sequence of forms belonging to each of these editions is given in the catalogue of models. In practice, however, forms from other editions were also used interchangeably. Such 'extra' models are usually entered separately with their own model number in the price list and they can be found if one is familiar with the names used within the firm itself for them. Moreover, other models were made to order for clients in the early years by recombining the available repertoire of decoration, forms and decoration techniques and these bespoke models are not registered in the Daum archives. They include some of the pieces in the Koepff Collection commissioned by the Heidelberg goldsmith Nikolaus Trübner: see cat. nos. 83–87, 95–97.

In the price list sections covering individual services or the section entitled 'divers' (miscellaneous) are demarcated by lines. Dates appear at the beginning of each section. Comparisons of contemporary sources and objects, however, show up discrepancies in the archive material, such as confusion of model numbers and information connected with them between the catalogue of models and the price list. It soon becomes apparent when one is working with them that, in the early years, dates were evidently entered later – in different writing – in the original price list. The first date entry in original writing reads 'Septembre 1898'. This date presumably marks the beginning of continuous entry of edition models, the year they went into production. Evidence for this conjecture is furnished by the 1898 models scattered throughout the catalogue of models, which are on the sheets showing the early editions (illus. p. 59). All date entries predating 1898 at the beginning of new sections, therefore, were added later and it has been shown that they do not tally with other reliable evidence for most models.

Bardin's doctoral thesis does not mention the correction key I appended to the price list up to September 1898 in the first German edition of the present book. In the 'Registre des modèles. 1891–1939' table appended to his dissertation, he leaves the dates from the price list as they are, occasionally adding general references to earlier dates for groups of models without, however, specifying the model numbers concerned.[8] In the important listing of all Daum decoration schemes, 'Liste des décors. 1891–1939', that follows, all the original dates are also retained although the earlier use of some of the motifs has been verified. These discrepancies are also linked with the circumstance that, in the most important Daum archive sources, the catalogue of models and the price list, only the glass produced in editions is listed, with virtually none of the pieces made specially for exhibitions or as presentation models, which, as a rule, featured new decorative motifs.

Dating in the price list up to September 1898

Model no.	Original date	Corrected date
1 – 319	1890	1889–1890
320 – 457	1893	1891–1892
458 – 601	1893	
602 – 733	1894	
734 – 836	1895	
837 – 963	1896	
964 –1244	1897	from no. 1167 new division and dating, 1898 according to Bardin
964 –1166	1897	
1167 –1389	1898	
1245 –1389	Sept. 1898	

The overview above reveals that there is a double entry for the date 1893. If one compares the number of models made each year (approx. 100–150 pieces), it becomes obvious that the first entry of 1893 cannot be correct.

1–319. The first part of the price list includes essentially sets of drinking glasses, some of which were presented in the first catalogue of products (1891). The last plates, nos. 21–22 (illus. p. 58), of this catalogue show, under the heading 'Divers' (Miscellaneous), various vases and jars/boxes that are included in the price list up to model no. 336. The date 1893, on the other hand, has already been entered in the price list at model no. 320. If one corrects this entry by correlating it with the year the first catalogue was issued, the result is that the dating of the first section of models, nos. 1–319, must be corrected to 1889–90. It extends from the onset of Antonin Daum's improvements on the design of the sets of drinking glasses in 1889 until the end of 1890, which was later entered on the first page of the price list.[9]

320–457. The correction beginning with model no. 320 undertaken by means of dating based on the 1891 catalogue applies up to the next date entry.

458–601. The date 1893 referring to model no. 458 is its second occurrence in the price list. Mainly sets of drinking glasses are entered in this section, up to 601.

602–733. From 602 the lengthy section 'Pièces diverses' (Miscellaneous Pieces), nos. 602–733, is dated 1894. However, this is where the celebrated designs for the Chicago World's Columbian Exposition (identified nos. 602, 609, 613, 621, 625, 626, 634–36, 725), which had been published by the end of March 1893, and the models for the Franco-Russian rapprochement on the occasion of the visit by the Russian fleet to France in October 1893 (nos. 644, 653), are entered. They are interspersed with models that must have been made in 1894, such as model no. 688 with the rarely occurring addition of 'fecit 1894'.[10] One can assume that these models began to be serially produced in 1894.

734–836. Services are again covered under the date 1895 and, from no. 784, 'Pièces diverses', many of which can be identified because they were exhibited at the 1897 Brussels Exposition Internationale.

837–963. The date 1896 refers up to model no. 900 to the unsigned 'Verreries jaspées ordinaires' (Ordinary streaked/mottled glass) with floral decoration, which are described only by vessel type and 'Serie N'

and are numbered consecutively from 1 to 59. Some of these are shown in the catalogue of models and can be identified. Nos. 896–900 again reveal decoration thematically related to Franco-Russian rapprochement. Services follow from 901.

964–1244. In the first 1897 section, nos. 964–1059 refer to 'Articles spéciaux pour montures' (Items specially for mounting). The following lengthy section, 'Articles divers', nos. 1060–1244, is not demarcated by a line and contains numerous models for participation in the Brussels Exposition Internationale, where Daum had made several additional deliveries, bringing the total of exhibits shown and sold to approximately 900 by October 1897. Here Christophe Bardin has added a new subsection and the date 1898 to no. 1167.[11]

Notes

1 Owned by the Société S.A.G.E.M. in Paris.
2 The first sheets bear, on the left above the border, a handwritten, later date, which tallies with the dates in the price lists.
3 *Martelé* is the descriptive term used for a pattern created by fine cutting and recalling the hammered texture of metal surfaces. This invariably pre-etched edition usually features *martelé* texturing, often polished and covering extensive surface areas whereas the relief texturing of floral motifs may be etched or traced in engraving.
4 See E. Schmitt's essay 'Daum Frères: Stepping out of Gallé's Shadow' in the present volume.
5 Among these are the models technically denoted *soufflé-moulé* (mould-blown) with landscape or vegetal decoration in relief blown into moulds, some of which were not produced on a large scale until 1910: see *Revue lorraine illustré* (1908), no. 1, n.p. For pieces made specially for the last important event hosted by the Ecole de Nancy, the 'Exposition Internationale de l'Est de la France Nancy 1909', see Charpentier et al. 1987, p. 167; for exhibits at the 1910 Brussels Exposition Universelle et Industrielle see Barrez 1912, illus. n.p. [72 a, 74 a].
6 In the account of the 'Exposition Internationale de l'Est de la France Nancy 1909', Henri Bergé is portrayed as follows: 'Bergé artiste décorateur de haute valeur d'une trop grande modestie' (Bergé, an artist decorator of high rank but too modest): see E. Nicolas, 'Le Pavillon de l'Ecole de Nancy à l'exposition de Nancy', *Art et industrie* III–V (Sept. 1909): n.p.
7 Bardin 2002, vol. 1, p. 142, n. 76.
8 Bardin 2002, vol. 2, p. 473.
9 The decoration workshops were not well equipped or staffed until 1889: see Bardin 2002, vol. 1, p. 118.
10 See Zurich, Wühre 9, 1986, no. 6.
11 Bardin 2002, vol. 2, p. 474.

KAISERLICHES PATENTAMT.

PATENTSCHRIFT

— № 92709 —

KLASSE 32: GLAS.

AUSGEGEBEN DEN 25. MAI 1897.

BURGUN SCHVERER & CIE in MEISENTHAL, Lothringen.

Verfahren zur Herstellung von bemalten Hohlglasgegenständen.

Patentirt im Deutschen Reiche vom 21. Februar 1896 ab.

Das vorliegende Verfahren bezweckt die Herstellung von Kunstgegenständen aus Glas, die das Aussehen der sogenannten echten Antiken haben.

Das Verfahren besteht darin, daſs das Muster in Emaille in bekannter Weise auf eine gut abgekühlte Glasröhre oder dergl. aufgetragen und diese nach dem Trocknen der Emaille bei sehr hoher Temperatur eingebrannt wird.

Die Glasröhre wird dann im Abkühlofen langsam aufgewärmt und hierauf mit einer Schicht flüssigen Glases überzogen.

Dieses Einbetten der Malerei zwischen zwei Glasschichten ist bereits bekannt (vergl. z. B. die Patentschriften Nr. 66924 und 74578) und wird deshalb hier nicht als neu beansprucht.

Vielmehr besteht das Wesen der vorliegenden Erfindung darin, den so vorbereiteten Glasröhren durch den Preſs- oder Blaseproceſs die beabsichtige Form zu geben, wodurch, wie bereits erwähnt, die fertigen Hohlglasgegenstände das Ansehen der bekannten echten Antiken erhalten sollen.

PATENT-ANSPRUCH:

Verfahren zur Herstellung von bemalten Hohlglasgegenständen, gekennzeichnet durch die Anwendung des Blase- oder Preſsverfahrens auf solche Glashohlkörper (Röhren oder dergl.), welche zwischen zwei Glasschichten eine Malerei tragen.

Patent application registered by the firm BURGUN, SCHVERER & CO. for a 'Process for Decorating Hollow Glassware'

Mémoire descriptif déposé à l'appui d'une Demande de Brevet d'Invention formée par La Maison sociale Burgun, Schverer & Co. pour un 'Procédé pour la Décoration d'Objets en Verre Creux'

Decoration is applied in enamel on a thoroughly cooled cap.

The caps are slowly reheated in the lehr and, once at the requisite temperature, are covered with a layer of glass taken directly from the furnace. Reheated, the whole unit is then blown into a mould.

CLAIMS
In brief, I claim the invention of the following:
A process for decorating hollow glass objects as described above.

Paris, 13 March 1897
p.p. the Firm of Burgun, Schverer & Co.,

Patent application for a new decoration method termed 'High-fired Insert Decoration' for crystal, glassware, etc., registered by the firm Daum Frères for the duration of fifteen years.

Mémoire Descriptif déposé à l'appui de la Demande d'un Brevet d'Invention de quinze ans pour une 'Nouveau mode de décoration dit: "Décoration Intercalaire à grand feu" pour cristaux, verreries, etc.' par la Société Daum Frères

This patent application concerns a new method of decorating objects in glass, crystal, etc., which we call 'high-fired *intercalaire* [sandwiched] decoration'. We designate by this term a decor previously cold-worked onto a glass body of any shape whatever (open or not at both ends) that may be fired without shattering, which is then annealed until soft so as it can be flashed inside and/or outside with several coats of molten glass, before the vase or other object is made into the shape required.

The decoration thus lies between the layers of glass.

The initial body is prepared and worked while hot like a normal blank and can comprise several layers of coloured glass (double-, triple-case, etc.); it may receive in the rough additional ornamentation (applied work, cabochons, gadroons; of all shapes and colours).

The decoration of the body is then cold-worked, just like a finished product, by means of enamel paint, acid-etching, wheel-engraving or any other standard process.

It is then reheated until soft. By applying various coatings the vessel is formed into its final shape; this [in turn] can be subjected to any decorative process whatsoever (enamel, paint, engraving, etc.), whether or not these are cut through to the insert motif or not.

The aim of this patent is to ensure possession of exclusive rights to any motif, subject or decoration interposed between cases of a glass object by way of a cold-worked body subsequently reheated such as we have just described, whatever the decorations of the body or object concerned.

We enclose with this description two illustrations showing respectively a decorated vessel body and the vase with the resulting *intercalaire* decoration.

IN BRIEF [...]

Paris, 23 June 1899

Appendix

Manufacturers and Artists

For participation in exhibitions see also 'Selected Exhibitions', p. 322.

General Remarks

The literature cited in this section is limited to references supplementing those in Schmitt, *Sammlung Silzer*, 1989, and Schmitt, Zurich II, 1995, as well as to publications since 1995.

■ = Publication of major importance.

For participation in exhibitions see also 'Selected Exhibitions', p. 322.

Appert Frères
Paris

1832

The firm 'Appert', which produces enamels and pigments for glass and ceramics ('Emaux, cristaux et couleurs vitrifiables'), is founded by Louis-Adrien Appert (d. 1866), from 1824 to 1830 ironmonger in Paris, at 50, rue des Arcis. The eldest son of Pierre Antoine Sulpice Appert and his wife, Germaine Thérèse Fiche, Louis-Adrien Appert marries Eulalie Legras in 1824, with whom he has a daughter, Eulalie Caroline; in 1831 he marries his second wife, Esther Eugénie Laurent, with whom he has two sons, Adrien-Antoine (1836–1902) and Léon-Alfred Appert (1837–1925).

1836/1837

Address: rue St-Maur 45 ter (10e arrondissement).

1839–1841

Address: 57, rue du Temple (3e arrondissement).

from 1842

Private and business address (rental): 151, Faubourg St-Martin (10e arrondissement); from 1853 owner of a house, let out, at 56, ave. Montaigne.

from 1857

Youngest son, Léon-Alfred, production manager. In 1857 producer of chemicals for glassmaking as well as enamels, coloured crystal glass, enamels for gold, enamels for painting china, glass, crystal glass and coloured crystal glass and enamel, gold, silver and prepared fluxes ('préparateur de chimie, fabrique de produits vitrifiés, émaux et cristaux coloriés, émaux pour or, couleurs à porcelaine, à verre, à cristal et à émail, or, argent et fondants préparés').

Léon-Alfred Appert, engineer, studies from 1853 to 1856 at the Ecole Centrale des Arts et Manufactures in Paris, where of 250 students he is the third best in his final examinations and best in chemistry. From 1857 member, 1895–97 vice-president of the Société d'Encouragements pour l'Industrie Nationale; in 1889 president of the Société des Ingénieurs Civils de France. His inventions make the firm develop into the most important manufacturer producing materials for the various branches of ceramics, enamel and glass production. Léon-Alfred Appert receives numerous awards, including the platinum medal of the Société d'Encouragements pour l'Industrie Nationale in 1877; the Chevalier in 1878 and the Officier de la Légion d'Honneur in 1886; the Officier de l'Instruction Publique in 1882; the Monthyon Prize from the Academy of Science, Paris, in 1887. In 1901 made honorary president of the Chambre Syndicale des Maîtres de Verrerie de France and in 1909 of the Chambre Syndicale des Souffleurs de Verre, etc. Further awards in Portugal, Russia, Belgium and Italy, in the 1880s.

from 1858

Trades under the name 'Appert & Fils' after conversion to a public company by Louis-Adrien Appert and his sons, Adrien-Antoine and Léon-Alfred; factory address: La Villette, 6, rue Royale (19e arrondissement; today rue de l'Ourcq). From 1862 a second outlet in Paris, at 28, rue de Notre-Dame-de-Nazareth (3e arrondissement), where the society 'Appert, Lengelé et Cie.' is founded on 2 May 1861. (Appert & Fils is, despite an entry in the 1852 registry-office rolls, not involved in this.) From 1862 production of powdered coloured glass and frit for porcelain, faience, glass, crystal and enamels ('chimiste, couleur broyée à l'eau pour porcelaine, faïence, verre, cristal et émail', *Almanach du Commerce*, 1863).

from 1865

Trades under the name 'Appert Frères' after being taken over by Adrien-Antoine and Léon-Alfred Appert; business address: 6, rue Royale. Louis-Adrien Appert retires. In 1867 the business registered in the rolls of important businesses, the 'Notables Commerçants du Département de la Seine', in Paris and the Seine district. Around 1871–77 – possibly even as early as 1867/68 – years of collaboration begin with →Eugène Rousseau (1827–1890), which is presumably continued after 1890 by his successor, →Ernest Léveillé (1841–1913) and his employee, →Eugène Michel (1848–1904). In 1873 the firm participates for the first time in a World's Fair, the Vienna Weltausstellung, with simulated hardstone, etc., where it is awarded honorary diploma and two medals.

From 1875 Appert Frères is involved in restoring windows of the most important churches in France.

from 1878

Glass factory built in Clichy-La Garenne: 5, chemin des Chasses. Business addresses in Paris: 66, rue Notre-Dame-de-Nazareth and 151, rue de Faubourg St-Martin. Production of basic ingredients used in the following trades: enamellers of jewellery and crafts, painters of watch dials of all kinds, miniature painters, bronze-founders, sign-painters on tinplate, painters of porcelain, crystal, flat and hollow glass, artificial pearls, artists who used powdered glass or frit, gold and silver leaf, etc. as well as makers of photographic enamel pictures (lithophanes). Also made artificial hardstones and fantasy articles in glass, flat glass with multiple casing, opal glass for lamps and glass parts for physical and chemical laboratory equipment, lights, etc., such as for lighthouses or optical glass for export. In 1880 first patent application registered by Léon-Alfred Appert, for blowing and processing glass with mechanically compressed air ('Soufflage et travail du verre par l'air comprimé mécaniquement'). In 1885 second patent application registered, for perforated glass panes for ventilation ('Verre perforé. Procédé de fabrication. Air et lumière').

from 1888

Head office and business in Paris: 66, rue Notre-Dame-de-Nazareth; factory: 34, rue de Chasses in Clichy-la-Garenne, Seine. Manufacture of coloured glass, optical glass and perforated flat glass for ventilation systems in addition to the original product range of pigments and raw materials for glassmaking and the manufacture of vessels blown with compressed air. In 1889 development of a special casting technique as a combination of casting and pressing into the mould either by mechanical means, such as a plunger, or with compressed air. Participation in the 1889 Paris Exposition Universelle with mosaics for the French pavilion in the park in collaboration with Edmond Coignet (1856–1915). In 1890 and 1916 Léon-Alfred Appert is president of the Chambre Syndicale des Maîtres de Verrerie de France.

1893

Participation in the Chicago World's Columbian Exposition, primarily with technical glass, some of it very large vessels, such as carboys, and battery jars, which were square in section. Patent application registered for safety glass ('Verre et glace armés. Procédé de fabrication dit sandwich, adopté par la Cie. de St-Gobain et aux Etats-Unis par la Mississippi Glass Company').

1898

Founding of the American branch: Appert Glass Company, in Port-Allegany, PA.

1900

Participation in the 1900 Paris Exposition Universelle, as in 1889 hors-concours, with an outstanding line of large glass tubing and flat glass in a wide range of colours.

1902–1931

Firm managed by the sons, Maurice-Adrien (1869–1941) and Léopold-Antonin Appert (1867–1931), who have worked for the firm for some time and remain members of the Chambre Syndicale de la Céramique et de la Verrerie until 1931. Léon-Alfred Appert retires and assumes honorary duties, including membership of the Ministry of Trade Commission for Industrial Hygiene in 1910, honorary councillor of the Board of Trade in 1912 and technical glass consultant for the Conservatoire National des Arts et Métiers, Paris, in 1918.

1905

The firm participates in the Liège Exposition Universelle, with special glass for microscopes, physics, chemistry and medicine, perforated glass for ventilation systems, coloured flat glass of all kinds for leaded stained-glass windows, etc.; enamel pigments of all kinds, also for various metal applications and also the manufacture of pins. The firm receives a Grand Prix; the employees Louis Etter and Léon Hoefflinger are awarded silver medals. In 1915 the firm registers a

patent for spotlight glass moulding ('Moulage du verre pour réflecteurs, moulage méthodique').
after 1918
Paris address: 20, rue de Paradis. Participation in the 1925 Paris International Exposition as purveyors of flat glass for windows designed by artists.
1930
As in 1905 factory and head office: Clichy, 34, rue des Chasses, showrooms in Paris: 30, rue Notre-Dame-de-Nazareth. Continues manufacture of glass for special purposes: for watches and clocks, black glass as protection from the sun and heat, glass to protect against X-rays and other dangerous radiation, hard glass and glass with trademarks: Cralix, Gamma, Lambda, Nextra, Rubiphore and Serax.
1931
The company is dissolved.

Exhibitions
1883
Amsterdam, Exposition Coloniale et d'Exportation Générale – gold medal
1908
London, Franco-British Exhibition – hors-concours, member of the jury
1925
Paris, Exposition Internationale des Arts Décoratifs et Industriels Modernes (exh. cat.)

Léon-Alfred Appert's writings:
Several scientific treatises and reports for the Academy of Science and the Société d'Encouragements pour l'Industrie Nationale in Paris; 'Le Verre', *Revue des Arts Décoratifs* 5 (1884–85): 419–50; Appert and Henrivaux 1893, pp. 353–54; Appert and Henrivaux, *Verre et verrerie* (Paris, 1900); *La Verrerie depuis vingt ans* (Paris, 1902).

Archival documents and literature
Marriage Appert and Legras, 17 Sept. 1824, Archives de Paris, Fichier des mariages parisiens 1795–1862, vol. 4, p. 84; *Almanach du Commerce*, 1827, pp. XXII, 195; ibid., 1830, pp. XXII, 50; marriage certificate Appert and Laurent, 28 May 1831, Archives de Paris, V2E, no. 8505; birth certificate Léon-Alfred, 28 March 1837, ibid., 5 MI1 and 443, no. 3712; *Almanach du Commerce*, 1836, pp. XXII, 106; ibid., 1839, pp. XXIII, 127; ibid., 1841, p. 76; Cadastre 151, rue de Faubourg St-Martin, Archives de Paris D1P4, 1852, no. 421; Cadastre 28, rue N. D. de Nazareth, ibid., D1P4, 1852, no. 807; *Almanach du Commerce*, 1855, p. 573; ibid., 1857, pp. 71, 579; articles of foundation of the Société Appert, Lengelé et Cie. dated 2 May 1861, Archives de Paris, D32U3, no. 40; Cadastre 151, rue de Faubourg St-Martin, Archives de Paris, D1P4, 1862, no. 424; Cadastre 56, ave. Montaigne, ibid., D1P4, 1862, no. 747; *Almanach du Commerce*, 1863, pp. 100, 754; ibid., 1865, pp. 101, 824; death certificate of Louis-Adrien Appert, 31 Jan. 1866, Archives de Paris, 5MI4 and 10, no. 364; succession L.-A. Appert 1866, ibid., succession après décès DQ7, 10591, no. 729; 1873 Vienna Exhibition, *Amtliches Verzeichnis der Aussteller, welchen von der internationalen Jury Ehrenpreise zuerkannt worden sind* (Vienna, 1873), p. 304, no. 106; Cohausen and Poschinger 1874, p. 83; ■ documents on Léon-Alfred Appert's candidacy for the Légion d'Honneur 1878, Archives Nationales nos. FI2 and 5082; Didron and Clémendot 1880, pp. 32, 34–35, 64; Garnier 1886, pp. 345–46; Rousset 1888–90, p. 338; Henrivaux 1889, p. 171; Gerspach, 'La Mosaïque décorative à l'exposition universelle de 1889', *Revue des Arts Décoratifs*, 10 (1889–90): 265; Appert and Henrivaux 1893, pp. 354, 390–96; Krantz 1894, pp. 25–26; Houtart 1902, pp. 142, 145, 149, 163, 166, 184; Houtart 1908, pp. 12, 19–20, 26, 29; *Almanach du Commerce*, 1910, pp. 1677, 1829; Paris 1910, p. 30; Turin, France, 1911, p. 299, no. 1; *Exposition Internationale des Arts Décoratifs et Industriels Modernes: Catalogue général officiel*, issued by the Ministère du Commerce et de l'Industrie, des Postes et des Télégraphes (Paris, 1925), pp. 78, 162, 200, 238, 749; Hogrel 1930, pp. 15, 71, 304, 322, 421, 442; ■ Bascou and Thiébaut, Orsay, 1988, p. 228.

→ Jean, Léveillé, Michel, Rousseau

Henri Marie Joseph Bergé
called Henri or Henry Bergé

Diarville, Nancy, 15 Oct. 1870–Nancy, 26 Nov. 1937

Son of the lace manufacturer Marie Joseph Bergé (d. 31 Jan. 1871) and wife, Marie Joséphine, née Maudru.
1888–1892/93
Studies decoration painting and printmaking at the Ecole des Beaux-Arts, Nancy; pupil of Jules François Marie Joseph Larcher (1849–1920). In 1890 awarded a first and two third prizes at the Jacquot competition. Thought to have trained afterwards in Paris as a teacher at higher secondary schools (Lycée, Collège).
1895–1914
At first freelance, from 1897 head designer with formative influence at →Daum Frères, where he supervises the firm's drawing school for apprentices from 1896/97 to *c*. 1930. Apart from model designs, Bergé executes hundreds of botanical studies, numerous landscapes and some studies of animals, marine fauna and serpents for Daum models while freelancing on the side. From 1895 regular participation in the Salon de Nancy exhibitions mounted by the Société Lorraine des Amis des Arts in Nancy, from 1898 a member of that association. Shows oil paintings, watercolours and designs for Daum Frères as well as, in 1902, a plaster bust of a child and, in 1903, a design for a frame. Moreover he designs fabric and graphic art, including posters and illustrations in books and magazines. In 1903 he conceives 22 window designs for the dining room of an inn, La cure d'Air Trianon in Maxéville, and another for a private flat in Maxéville. Address in Nancy in 1896: 3, rue Eugène Ferry. On 20 March 1897 marries Anne Marie Joséphine Rougieux; witnesses: →Jacques Gruber and Jules Larcher, his former teacher. From now on he lives with his in-laws, at 126, rue de Strasbourg. Secretary of the Association des Artistes Lorrains from 1898 to 1902.
from 1899
Teaches applied and decorative art at the Ecole Professionnelle de l'Est, at the invitation of the director, Robert Herborn. In 1901 Bergé becomes a member of the board of directors of the Alliance Provinciale des Industries d'Art, called the Ecole de Nancy (est. 1901). In 1902 he is commissioned by the Ecole de Nancy to give courses in ornamental composition to workmen. In 1905 signs a contract with Daum Frères under the following terms: 'Il est tenu à aucune continuité mais à un acte de présence journalier d'au moins une heure pour recevoir les ordres et assurer l'execution des études ou travaux commandées' (He is not obliged to continual employment but instead to the act of being present daily for at least one hour to receive instructions and to ensure that studies or bespoke pieces are being executed).
from 1906
Most important designer of objects and small sculpture made according to the *pâte de verre* technique developed for Daum from late in 1903 by Amalric Walter (1870–1959). In addition designs for Mougin Frères, china manufacturers, in Montreville near Nancy. At the competition held by Alphonse Cythère, at the Société des Produits Céramiques de Rambervillers in 1906, Bergé's design for a *bonbonnière* (sweatmeat or comfit box and jar) is the only piece actually executed. The press evaluates his work as a 'scrupuleuse observation de la nature' (conscientiously precise observation of nature), regretting at the same time that it lacked boldness in execution ('il est regretté une certaine timidité dans l'execution').
1909
Awarded a Médaille vermeil (silver-gilt medal) for ten years of teaching at the Ecole Professionnelle de l'Est; in 1923 appointed Officier de l'Académie and in 1932 Officier de l'Instruction Publique.
1915–1919
Professor for drawing from models at the Lycée Poincaré.
1919–*c*. 1930
Works less for Daum & Cie. and freelances for Amalric Walter, who has been self-employed since 1919, working in *pâte de verre* in his own studio in Nancy, at first at 20, rue Claudot, later 31, rue Eugène Ferry.
1925
Bergé receives his last official award for his designs for Walter, in the pre-1914 Ecole de Nancy style.

Exhibitions

1897
Paris, Champs-Elysées, Salon des Artistes Français (exh. rep.)
1925
Paris, Exposition Internationale des Arts Décoratifs et Industriels Modernes – Gold medal for Bergé's designs for Amalric Walter

Archival documents and literature

Nancy 1895, p. 54, nos. 41, 722; marriage certificate Bergé and Rougieux, 20 March 1897, Archives Municipales de la Ville de Nancy, Mariages 1897, no. 163; Brussels, *Daum*, 1897; V. Champier, 'L'Exposition universelle de Bruxelles', *Revue des Arts Décoratifs* 17 (1897): 394; Nancy 1897, p. 63, nos. 30–34, p. 106, no. 435, p. 133, no. 667; *Bulletin des Sociétés artistiques de l'Est* (April 1897): 55; Nancy 1898, p. 64, nos. 22–24, p. 112, nos. 457–58; Association des Artistes Lorrains, *Bulletin des Sociétés artistiques de l'Est* (August 1898): 109; Nancy 1899, p. 64, nos. 23–24; Nancy 1900, pp. 25, 65, nos. 30–32, p. 109, nos. 417–18; 'Récompenses de l'exposition de 1900', *La Lorraine* (Sept. 1900): 60; 'Les Arts décoratifs à l'Ecole professionnelle de l'Est', *Lorraine Artiste* (Feb. 1901): 89–90; Nancy 1902, p. 145, no. 712; Nancy 1903, p. 156, no. 789; Nancy 1904, p. 39, nos. 44–48, illus. pls. LVI–LVII, colour pl. n. p.; Houtard 1908, p. 29; Commandant Lalance, 'L'Ecole de Nancy à Strasbourg', *Bulletin des Sociétés artistiques de l'Est* (May 1908): 64; Strasbourg, 1908, pp. 16–17, nos. 71–74; Paris 1910, pp. 18, 22; Barrez 1912, p. 78; death certificate of Henri Bergé, 26 Nov. 1937, Mairie de la Ville de Nancy, Décès 1937, no. 2370; ■ Charpentier et al. 1987, pp. 124, 135, 141, 165, 167, 206, 216, 306, 307, 311; Aptel et al. 1989, pp. 69, 74, 116, 117, 252, 271; ■ M. Bouvet, Y. Gawlik., J. Guillaume, C. Bardin and V. Ayrolles, *Collaborateurs de Daum*, manuscript S.R.I.L 1997; Epinal 1997, cat. no. 99, pp. 110, 137, 142, 153; Darmstadt 1999, pp. 283, 305, 307, 309, illus. pp. 283, 335–47; ■ Nancy 1999, pp. 57, 121, 138, 180, 217, 240–41, 243, 246–47, 259, cat. no. 15, illus. pp. 56, 121, 221, 266; ■ Nancy, *Fleurs*, 1999, p. 13, 47–51, cat. nos. 28–29, 39–41, 44, 46, 48, 50, 52–53, 55, 57, 59, 61, 86–96, 130, illus. pp. 15–16, 50, 68–69, 72–74, 76, 78–91, 108–10, 119; ■ Bardin 2002, vol. 1, pp. 25, 39, 42, 72, 73, 78–79, 80–81, 83–86, 90–97, 100, 146, 150, 154, 170, 180–81, 196, 213–14, 221, 229, illus. pp. 71, 90, 91, 97, 106, 108, 110–14, 220; ibid. vol. 2, pp. 250, 262, 293, 297, 300, 338, 342, 343, 353, 453, 497, 510.

→Daum Frères, Gruber

Burgun, Schverer & Co.
Verreries de Meisenthal
Meisenthal, Lorraine

1704
Glass factory built by Sébastien Burgun, Martin Stenger and the brothers Jean-Martin, Jean-Nicolas and Etienne (Stephan) Walter on the premises of the former glassworks in Meisenthal. Building permission granted on 2 Sept. 1702 by Duc Léopold.

1704–1792
State lease of the glassworks in Meisenthal renewed in 1727 and 1762.

1711–1823
Trades under the name 'Verreries de Meisenthal', with a workforce of 15. In 1721 lease for building a branch in Götzenbruck concluded with Jean-Georges Poncet, who transfers his rights under the terms of the agreement to the four sons of the Meisenthal firm founders, Stephan Stenger, and the brothers Niklaus, Stephan and Martin Walter. In 1789 in Götzenbruck: 1 wood-fired furnace and 12 pots, workforce of 53, including 20 glassmakers, grinders and engravers. Meisenthal: 18 shareholders. 1 wood-fired furnace and 12 pots, workforce of 56, including 12 specialist glassmakers. Both factories manufacture watch and clock glass; drinking glasses make up one-third of the total output. By decree of the National Assembly the founders' heirs become proprietors of the glassworks leased in Götzenbruck and Meisenthal on 30 July 1792. By 1800 there are 18 joint heirs to the glassworks.

1824–1900
Trades under the name 'Burgun Schverer & Co. (until 1870 the French abbreviation 'Cie.') Verreries de Meisenthal', production at the expanding branch in Götzenbruck begins to produce clock and watch glass exclusively. In 1830 the Götzenbruck branch breaks away from the Meisenthal firm, becoming 'Walter, Berger & Co.' in 1909.

1830–1855
Directors: Adam Burgun, Nicolas Schverer (b. 1776) and Clément Burgun (d. 1858). Burgun, Schverer & Co. takes part in the 1834 Metz exhibition with high-quality crystal glass noted for its 'regularity of form and precision cutting'.

1854–1861
Together with →Verreries Réunies de Vallerysthal et Portieux, a warehouse is established in Paris at Toutain Guérard et Cie., 32, rue de Paradis, Poissonnière (10e arrondissement).

1855–1889
Director: Nicolas Mathieu Burgun (1825–1889). Participation in the 1855 Paris Exposition Universelle with, among other exhibits, large 'vases of opaque glass' and table services of top 'quality and purity', workforce of 250. From 1860/61 business links with →Charles Gallé-Reinemer (1818–1902) in Nancy (first invoices under customer account number 179 in January 1861), who buys blanks as well as finished glass. Between 1861 and 1867, depending on certificate status in his training as a glass painter, →Désiré Christian begins work for Gallé-Reinemer. From 1867 growth in orders through →Emile Gallé's (1846–1904) work at the family firm, leading to his becoming head designer. All painted Gallé decoration executed in Meisenthal; the Gallé-Reinemer workshop in Nancy is mainly responsible for engraving. Franco-Prussian War (1870–71) causes collaboration to cease, afterwards resumption of the tried and tested business links between Burgun, Schverer & Co. and Gallé-Reinemer. In 1878 Eugène Jacques (also called Eugen Jakob) Kremer (8 May 1867–7 Feb. 1941) begins training as a glass painter. What is up to now the earliest written record of settlements between July 1881 and June 1882 furnishes evidence of considerable sums having been paid to Christian for 'Gallé decorations' and glass production for Gallé 20 days a month from January to March 1882.

1885
Secret contract is concluded between Emile Gallé, Désiré Christian and Burgun, Schverer & Co. concerning the production of utility and luxury glass for Gallé according to his instructions, with Christian responsible for execution. Further terms of the contract: Gallé pledges to pay commissions on a regular basis and Christian reserves the right to use his own designs and inventions should they not be needed by the signatories of the contract.

1889–1903
Director: Antoine Mathieu Burgun (1861–1906), son of Nicolas Mathieu Burgun. Until his own glassworks began operations, in May 1894, the following worked for Emile Gallé: glass painters Nicolas Schmitt (1823–1892), his son, Joseph Schmitt (1855–1912), Joseph Basilius Winckler (b. 1859), François Pierre Christian (b. 1863), Eugène Jacques Kremer (1867–1941) and Alfred Jean-Marie Schaeffer (1869–1918); engravers Joseph Maas (1867–1904), Emile Maas (b. 1864), Antoine Walter (b. 1856); master glassmakers Georg Franckhauser (1843–1900) and Jacques Joseph Stenger (1849–1916); glassworks foreman and head glass-blower Joseph Rémy Burgun (1843–1921).

In 1893, almost as in 1886: workforce of 450 (1886: 350), with 150 employees in the steam-grinding division. Two Boëtius anthracite-fired furnaces and 24 (1886: 20) covered pots. Manufacture of crystal and half crystal, pressed glass items. Workshops for painting, gilding and engraving. Branches in Hamburg, Paris (27, rue de Paradis) and London (21 Hatton Garden); showrooms also in Berlin, Alexandria and Beirut from 1894 to 1897. Participation at the Leipzig Messe (Trade Fair).

from 1894
Burgun, Schverer & Co. makes its own art glass under Désiré Christian's management. Signature: *B., S. & Co.*, also in combination with the cross of Lorraine and a thistle, occasionally with *Meisenthal* and sun. In 1895 participation in the Strasbourg Exhibition with 'table glass, crystal glass, etched, engraved and cut glass, cased glass, fantasy articles, such as vases and jugs decorated with etched and engraved scenes'. Among these wares are glass with sandwiched decoration in enamel painting executed under Désiré Christian's supervision. The firm is awarded an honorary diploma and medals and Christian receives his first official personal distinction as a 'master painter' alongside the glassmakers Jacques Joseph Stenger and Georg Franckhauser. 1895/96 signature: *Verrerie d'Art de Lorraine Burgun, Schverer & Co.* with cross of Lorraine and thistle. Patent applications are registered for sandwiched decoration in enamel painting by Burgun, Schverer & Co. in Germany on 21 Feb. 1896 under no. 92709 and in France on 13 March 1897 under no. 264948 ('Procédé pour la décoration d'objets en verre creux'). Around 1897/98 Christian becomes self-employed.

from 1897/98

Eugène Jacques Kremer, Christian's pupil and assistant, becomes head of the decoration studio. In 1900 silver medal and bronze medals for employees at the 1900 Paris Exposition Universelle for exhibits with floral sandwich gold glass decoration.

1900–1919

Trades under the name 'Burgun Schverer & Co. Verreries de Meisenthal Kommanditgesellschaft auf Aktien' after conversion to a joint-stock company, presumably as early as from 1900 two directors, as mentioned in 1902 in firm records: Antoine Mathieu Burgun and Albert Emil Wanner (1861–1916). Workforce of approx. 500. Two Boëtius furnaces, 2 coal-fired tanks and 24 covered pots. Makes smooth and cut hollow glass. Steam-grinding division employs a workforce of 28. Speciality: arts and crafts products. Branches in Paris, Milan, Saargemünd, Berlin, Hamburg, Leipzig (from 1904), Buenos Aires and Mexico (from 1905).

1903–1916

Director: Albert Emil Wanner, personally liable partner. Glass art is now made to order, except for some speciality pieces. Production concentrates on freely blown and pressed utility glass. Before 1916, however, the factory announces that arts and crafts products are a speciality, alongside table services in half and special crystal. Member of the Vereinigung deutscher Hohlglasfabriken G.m.b.H. in Bonn. From 1908 to 1915 designs are executed by the versatile and prolific artist Jean Désiré Ringel d'Illzach (1847–1916), made to order in pressed glass after his own method, which made it possible to reproduce precisely the most delicate textures. From 1914 to 1918 full-time operations cease on account of the war; in 1915 the factory is closed down.

1916–1924

Factory is reopened. Director: Jean-Baptiste Eckert.

1919–1939

Trades under the name 'Verreries de Meisenthal Société par Actions'. After 1922 financial difficulties set in.

1924–1935

Director: Pierre Gilliot (b. 1888), workforce of approx. 600. In 1930 products are marketed in Paris by Gaston Drot (2 & 32, rue de Paradis), Gustave-Désiré Le Bouc (22, rue de la Fidélité) and Ferdinand Lefort (197, rue du Faubourg-Saint-Denis); in Lille, Nord, by Gérard Dumont (73, rue Meurein). In 1934 financial straits owing to worldwide economic crisis.

1935–1961

Director: Antoine Maas (1894–1969). From 1939 to 1965 trades under the name 'Verreries de Meisenthal Société Anonyme'. 1944–45 War leads to cessation of operations; sustains severe damage. After 1945 production of pressed glass and mainly handmade utility and ornamental glass, including containers and utility glass for restaurants.

1961–1969

Director: Marie-Antoinette Maas (b. 1921). In 1963 2 furnaces with 6 and 12 pots, respectively. Work force of 253, including 123 glass-blowers, 110 engravers, grinders, cutters and painters. Branches in Paris and Saarbrücken.

1965–1969

Trades under the name 'CRISTALLERIE Verrerie de Meisenthal Société Anonyme'. On 31 Dec. 1969 the firm ceases operations, with a workforce of approx. 300.

Exhibitions

1819

Paris, Louvre, Ve Exposition des Produits de l'Industrie Française (exh. rep.)

1826

Metz, Exposition Départementale de l'Industrie et des Beaux-Arts – 1st prize, again in 1834

1861

Metz, Exposition Universelle de Metz

1886

Leipzig, Messe (Trade Fair), regular participation until 1914

1900

Stuttgart, Technologische Glasausstellung (Technical Glass Exhibition)

Archival documents and literature

Supplementing Schmitt, Zurich II, 1995, p. 279: *Almanach du Commerce*, 1859, pp. 589, 874; exh. corresp., Strasbourg 1895, pp. 7, 11; A. T. Stoll (ed.), *Strassburger Industrie- und Gewerbeausstellung für Elsass-Lothringen, Baden und die bayerische Rheinpfalz* (Schlettstadt, Alsace, 1896), p. 59; Strasbourg 1897, pp. 49–50; Strasbourg 1901, pp. 97–98; T. Knorr, 'Das lothringische Glas', *Die wirtschaftliche Entwicklung Elsass-Lothringens 1871–1918* (Frankfurt am Main, 1931), pp. 316, 332; Stenger 1988, p. 136; Debize 1989, pp. 14, 80; Cappa 1991, pp. 322–29; *Miller's Antiques Checklist* (London, 1992), pp. 44–45; Thiébaut, *Dessins*, 1993, pp. 28–29; Netzer, Berlin, 1994, pp. 54–57, nos. 6–7; Ricke 2002, p. 167; Schmitt, Zurich II, 1995, p. 278–79; nos. 127–28; Takeda and Olivié 1996, no. 42; additions made by Susanne Brenner in 1997; ■ Meisenthal 1999; ■ Nancy 1999, pp. 67, 172, cat. nos. 17–19, illus. pp. 83, 172, 288; F. Montes de Oca, *L'Age d'or du verre en France 1800–1830. Verreries de l'empire et de la restauration* (Paris, 2001), p. 464.

→D. Christian, F. Christian, Gallé, Vallerysthal

Ernest Bussière

Ars-sur-Moselle 30 July 1863–Nancy 22 Aug. 1913

Son of the metalworker (turner) Louis Edmond Bussière (d. 1869) and his wife, Anne Adeline, née Henry (1838–1898); an elder brother, Louis Pierre (b. 1860), later town councillor and commercial representative.

1869

After father's death, family moves to Nancy, where they remain.

1877–1881

Attends Ecole Municipale de Dessin in Nancy, where he studies modelling under the sculptor and portraitist Charles Pêtre (1828–1907). Concomitantly minor modelling commissions for the renowned cabinetmaker Auguste Majorelle. First participation in an exhibition, the Salon de Nancy (Société des Amis des Arts) of 1878, where he shows a portrait medallion of his mother.

7 Dec. 1882–1889

Studies sculpture at the Ecole Nationale des Beaux-Arts in Paris; pupil of Augustin-Alexandre Dumont (1801–1884), later of Jean-Marie Bonnassieux (1810–1892) and Gabriel-Jules Thomas (1824–1905). In 1883 work from first year of study accepted; takes part for the first time in the Salon des Artistes Français in Paris, showing a bust of his mother. His fellow students include the painters Victor Prouvé (1858–1943) and Emile Friant (1863–1932) of Nancy. On recommendation of his friend Friant he is awarded a bursary amounting to 1200 Frs from the city of Nancy. Nov. 1884–85: national service in Commercy, where he breaks his leg in an accident.

In 1887 recommended for Grand Prix de Rome competition.

Public commissions: 1885, Sommervillers, Place de l'église, monument to mayor Félix Noël; 1887–89, Nancy, St. Epvre, marble tombstone for Monseigneur Trouillet, for which he receives an 'honorable mention' in 1889 at the Salon des Artistes Français in Paris.

1889–1913

Teaches modelling at the Ecole des Beaux-Arts in Nancy. His pupils include Alfred Finot (1876–1946) and Joseph Mougin (1876–1961). Also freelances as a medal-engraver and sculptor. Public and private commissions for portraits, war monuments, tombstones, busts and bas-reliefs as well as architectural sculpture, including some 208 ceramic pieces. In 1895 Bussière and Louis Majorelle become vice-presidents of the Association Amicale Lorraine des Anciens Elèves de l'Ecole Nationale et Spéciale des Beaux-Arts, Nancy. In 1896 Bussière is appointed Officier d'Académie, Nancy. That year he marries Anne Collet (1874–1958), with whom he has four children. Before 1900 he teaches modelling at the Ecole Professionnelle de l'Est, at which →Henri Bergé also teaches from 1899.

Public commissions: 1892, Nancy, Institut des Jeunes aveugles de Santifontaine, monument to Abbé Gridel; 1893, Nancy, Parc de la Pépinière, monument to Grandville; 1895, Roville-devant-Bayon, Place de l'église, monument to Mathieu de Dombasle; 1899, Fontenoy-sur-Moselle, war monument commemorating the Franco-Prussian War of 1870–71, together with the architect Lucien Weissenburger; 1902, Lunéville, Parc du château, monument to Emile Erckmann; 1903, Nancy, Ecole de Pharmacie, monument to Gustave Bleicher; 1904, Nancy, Cours du lycée Loritz, monument to H. Loritz, and Vittel, Place de l'église, monument to mayor Ambroise Bouloumié; 1908, Lunéville, Place Stanislas, monument to Ernest Bichat, founder of the vocational school; 1912, Longwy-Haut aux trois sièges de Longwy, cemetery, war monument.

1895–c. 1903

Collaborates with the Keller & Guérin ceramics factory in Lunéville on the recommendation of the head of the art division (from 1885), Maurice Ravinelle (1842–1896). Bussière models in 'faïences aux reflets métalliques' (faience with metallic sheen), approx. 31 highly sculptural, non-functional vessels, taking as his point of departure the forms of mainly endemic flora and fauna, two in combination with human figures. The factory develops a special clay body (pipe-clay) for firing at low temperatures and a glaze with a high aluminium content for his supple modelling. (In contemporary reports the term *grès*, although erroneous, is used quite frequently.) In 1896 his 'Mélancholie de l'automne' pottery, first shown at the Paris Salon is praised as a 'novum'. At the 1900 Paris Exposition Universelle Bussière shows pottery and glass designs for →Daum Frères after some of his own works of pottery.

1901–1913

Member of the board of the Alliance Provinciale des Industries d'Art, known as the Ecole de Nancy (est. 1901). In 1902 he is commissioned by the Ecole de Nancy to instruct workmen in modelling and sculpting. In 1903 he is appointed Officier de l'Instruction Publique. Shows terracotta and marble sculpture at the Ecole de Nancy exhibition in Paris, where he also exhibits the pottery executed by Keller & Guérin in Lunéville. His marble sculpture *Le Sommeil* is again exhibited in Nancy, where it is purchased by donors for the museum. In 1904 he shows a ceramic relief of a recumbent female nude in *grès flammé*, for Alphonse Cythère, Société des Produits Céramiques de Rambervillers, at the Ecole de Nancy exhibition in Nancy. In 1908/9 designs and executes the official plaque for the 1909 exhibition in Nancy. Last architecturally related sculptures are made in 1909–11: *Opera* and *Comedy* for the theatre in Lunéville. Address in 1913: 12–14, rue Félix Faure.

1923–1925

Pierre (1880–1955) and Joseph Mougin (1876–1961) from Montreville near Nancy are commissioned by Edouard Fenal to reissue Bussière's ceramic designs. The proprietor of the Badonviller faience factory, Fenal, takes over Keller & Guérin in Lunéville in 1923, where he has the reissued models executed with different glazes. Usually signed *Bussière*, the reissued designs are also occasionally signed *grès Mougin Nancy*.

Exhibitions

1878
Nancy, Grande Salle de l'Université, Société des Amis des Arts, again in 1884 and 1886

1883
Paris, Champs-Elysées, Salon des Artistes Français, again in 1884, 1887, 1889, 1890, 1892 and 1894

1896
Paris, Grand Palais, Salon des Artistes Français, again in 1899, 1902, 1906 and 1910

Archival documents and literature

Rolls of the Ecole des Beaux-Arts, Archives Municipales de la Ville de Nancy, Régistre matricule Ecole nationale des Beaux-Arts, AT 52 322, no. 236; Nancy 1890, p. 34, nos. 102–9; Nancy 1892, p. 33, nos. 81–82; Association Amicale Lorraine des Anciens Elèves de l'Ecole Nationale et Spéciale des Beaux-Arts, *Bulletin des Sociétés artistiques de l'Est* (Jan. 1895): 11; 'Exposition de Remiremont', ibid. (Sept. 1895): 111, suppl.; F. Malterre, 'L'Art décoratif au Salon des Champs-Elysées', *La Plume* (1896): 354; Nancy 1898, p. 137, no. 677; Nancy 1899, p. 126, nos. 604–6, p. 130, no. 634; G. S., 'Les Vases de Bussière', *Lorraine Artiste* (Aug. 1900): 26–27, with illus.; Nancy 1901, p. 141, nos. 737–40; Nancy 1902, p. 145, nos. 714–17; J. Rais, 'L'Ecole de Nancy et son exposition au Musée des arts décoratifs', *Art & Décoration* 13 (1903): 137; Nancy 1903, p. 8, illus. n.p.; Paris, portfolio, 1903, vol. 2, pl. 25, nos. 1–2, pl. 26, nos. 1–3, pl. 27, nos. 1, 7; Nancy 1905, p. 141, nos. 649–53; Nancy 1906, p. 134, nos. 579–82; Nancy 1909, p. 94, nos. 638–41, p. 106, nos. 149–51; Lafitte 1912, p. 856; Nancy 1913, p. 79, nos. 677–88; death certificate, Mairie de la Ville de Nancy, Décès 1913, no. 1881; Bénézit 1976, vol. 2, p. 417; ibid., vol. 8, p. 260; Munich, *Nancy 1900*, 1980, p. 364, nos. 409–410, with illus.; Horst Makus, *Keramik aus Historismus und Jugendstil in Frankreich mit Beispielen aus anderen europäischen Ländern: Ausgewählte Objekte aus zwei Privatsammlungen*, exh. cat., Staatliche Kunstsammlungen, Kassel (Kassel, 1981), pp. 82, 144; ■ Charpentier et al. 1987, pp. 51, 135, 167, 224, 249, 306; Aptel et al. 1989, pp. 19, 20, 196, 197, 198, 200, 272; Debize 1989, pp. 31, 48–49, 66, 70, 85–86, 88, 114, 145, 151, illus. pp. 17, 75, 89; ■ *Allgemeines Künstlerlexikon* 1996, vol.

12, p. 573; ibid., 1997; vol. 15, p. 345; Epinal 1997, pp. 110–11, 163, no. 61; Duncan, *Salons*, 1998, pp. 28, 459, illus. pp. 11, 74–75, 260–61; Darmstadt 1999, pp. 305, 309, 352, illus. pp. 280, 350; ■ Nancy 1999, pp. 126, 180, 189, 241, 253, cat. nos. 20–24, illus. pp. 105, 253–55, 289; ■ I. Hiblot, *Catalogue raisonné des œuvres d'Ernest Bussière 1883–1913: Statuaire et céramiste – Maîtrise d'Histoire de l'art* (MA, History of Art), Université de Nancy II, Année universitaire 1999–2000 (Nancy, 2000); ■ Nancy, *Bussière*, 2000; Nancy 2001, pp. 116–17; Bardin 2002, vol. 1, pp. 31, 33, 41, 43, 102, 175; vol. 2, pp. 297, 322, 337, 341–44, 347, 353, 498, illus. pp. 370–71, 381.

→Daum Frères

Désiré Jean Baptiste Christian
called Désiré Christian

Lemberg 23 May 1846–Meisenthal 19 Jan. 1907

Son of a forester and later innkeeper, Jean-Baptiste Christian from Lemberg near Meisenthal and wife, Odile, née Lutz; one of nine children. Probably worked at the →Burgun, Schverer & Co. glassworks in Meisenthal, even as a boy; trains as a glass painter in Meisenthal and possibly also near Paris (Christian took a trip to Paris in May 1863).

between 1861 and 1867

Between these years, depending on when he completed his training as a glass painter, Désiré Christian begins to work for the Gallé-Reinemer studio at Burgun, Schverer & Co. The two firms have maintained business links since 1860/61. About 1867 Christian begins to work directly with the son of Charles Gallé-Reinemer, →Emile Gallé (1846–1904), who is exactly the same age; Emile had begun to work in 1867 on a regular basis and later in a management capacity as a designer for the family firm. The Franco-Prussian War of 1870–71 causes production to be interrupted; afterwards, however, it is resumed and the tried and tested collaboration between Burgun, Schverer & Co. and Gallé-Reinemer is intensified.

1873

Désiré Christian marries Juliane Lina Hilt, with whom he has a son, Armand Antoine (24 July 1874–13 Nov. 1953), and a daughter, Marie Augustine (7 June 1880–8 May 1942).

1877/78–1894

Christian manages the Meisenthal studio for Emile Gallé, who becomes the managing director of the family firm in Nancy in 1877. The earliest document, a settlement of accounts from July 1881 to June 1882, furnishes written evidence of considerable sums having been paid to Christian for 'Gallé decorations' and glass production for Gallé twenty days a month from January to March 1882. In 1885 secret contract is concluded between Emile Gallé, Désiré Christian and Burgun, Schverer & Co. concerning the production of utility and luxury glass for Gallé according to his instructions, with Christian responsible for execution. Further terms of the agreement: Gallé pledges to pay commissions on a regular basis and Christian reserves the right to use his own designs and inventions should they not be needed by the other signatories of the contract. The agreement confirms Christian's status as an independent designer, technical inventor and production coordinator for Gallé. His close associates include primarily the following specialists from the decoration workshops at Burgun, Schverer & Co.: glass painters: Nicolas Schmitt (1823–1892), his son, Joseph Schmitt (1855–1912), Joseph Basilius Winckler (b. 1859), →François Pierre Christian (b. 1863), Eugène Jacques (also called [Eugen Jakob] Kremer) (1867–1941) and Alfred Jean-Marie Schaeffer (1869–1918); engravers: Joseph Maas (1867–1904), Emile Maas (b. 1864), Antoine Walter (b. 1856). Between 1891 and 1896 Christian purchases property in the Meisenthal 'Strumpf', Route de Soucht, with the intention of building a house of his own there.

from 1894

Head of glass-art production at Burgun, Schverer & Co. after premature termination of the secret contract following Gallé's building a glassworks of his own in Nancy. In 1895 Burgun, Schverer & Co. exhibits glasses with sandwiched decoration in enamel painting, in Strasbourg. Apart from the firm being awarded an honorary diploma and medals, Christian, too, receives his first official personal distinction as a 'master painter' alongside the glassmakers Jacques Joseph Stenger (1849–1916) and Georg Franckhauser (1843–1900). In 1896 and 1897 patent applications are registered by Burgun, Schverer & Co. in Germany and France for sandwiched decoration in enamel painting developed by Désiré Christian and his assistant, Eugène Jacques Kremer. Christian notes that he is living in Nancy in September 1896. He may have been there in connection with work for Emile Gallé, but a link with →Daum Frères in connection with the inclusive patent for sandwiched decoration, also referred to as the *intercalaire* technique, for which Daum applied in 1899, is also possible.

1897/98–1907

Désiré Christian is self-employed, working with his youngest brother, François Pierre, and his children, Armand Antoine and Marie Augustine. Blanks are procured from Burgun, Schverer & Co., later presumably also from the Cristallerie de St.-Louis in Saint-Louis-lès-Bitche and from the →Vereinigte Glashütten Vallerysthal since the same forms, some in the same colour combinations, are used by both Christian and the above-named glass manufacturers. In September 1898 Christian notes that he is living in Vallerysthal. Collaboration with the Vereinigte Glashütten Vallerysthal cannot be verified. The painted decoration used at that glassworks, particularly its technical sophistication, would, however, seem to support an attribution to Christian.

1899

Earliest evidence of the firm 'D. Christian & Sohn' in Meisenthal appears in the records of the annual Munich Exhibition at the Royal Glass Palace, in which the firm takes part. Although also known to have traded under the name 'Christian frères & fils, Meisenthal', there is no evidence of this in the exhibition records.

1899–1900

Establishes a decoration studio in his own house in Meisenthal. Four men and a woman are employed to work there in addition to Désiré Christian and his son, Armand Antoine. The following also work occasionally for the studio: his brother, François Christian, and his brother-in-law, Joseph Schmitt (1855–1912), both previously glass painters at Burgun, Schverer & Co., as well as Aloïs Stébe and Aloïs Schounn and from 1899 to 1902 the engraver Johann Nicolaus Illig (b. 1879), trained at Cristallerie de Saint-Louis. Christian participates in the 1900 the Paris Exposition Universelle, showing 'vessels decorated between the layers'; silver medal for Christian, employee distinction for Illig.

1901–1906

Successes at international exhibitions, where he receives numerous awards, including one in 1904 at the St. Louis Louisiana Purchase Exhibition, where he shows engraved cased glass and sandwich-glass decoration, also ornamental glass in Charles Spindler's *Herrenzimmer* in St. Leonhardt near Börsch; in 1906 participation in Strasbourg with cased glass. Christian offers the following products: glass art and faience art, fantasy pieces after specially conceived designs, mounted items, table services. The factory mark or signature is *C* with a cross of Lorraine, aligned in the horizontal with the *C*: left *D*, right *F*, below them *A*. General distributor in 1901: Bader-Nottin, Strasbourg, 23 Blauwolkengasse. Christian also sells earlier Gallé objects to museums; in 1906 makes Gallé glass available for an exhibition at the Kaiser Wilhelm-Museum, Krefeld, 'Erstlingsarbeiten Emile Gallés' (Early Works of Emile Gallé). In 1906 he sells both 'early Gallé' and 'early Meisenthal' glass in Metz. In 1907 Armand Antoine Christian works from January on for 'Burgun, Schverer & Co.' in Meisenthal as a 'factory official'; his father dies on 19 Jan. 1907.

1907–1909

The firm 'Désiré Christian & Sohn, Meisenthal' continues to be represented after Désiré Christian's death: in 1907 at the Elsässisches Kunsthaus in Strasbourg; in 1909 in the German Glass Industry Directory; and at exhibitions in 1907 (Berlin), in 1908 (Stuttgart).

Archival documents and literature

Supplementing Schmitt, *Sammlung Silzer*, 1989, p. 54: electoral rolls in Meisenthal: 1890/91, 2AL230; 1893, 2AL243; 1903 2AL279; 1907 2AL295, Archives Départementales, Saint-Julien-les-Metz, citizens' records: 243Q125, p. 78; 95Q155, p. 3; 243Q134, p. 72; 243Q131, p. 49, Archives Départementales, Saint-Julien-les-Metz, exh. corresp., Strasbourg 1895, pp. 7, 11; Munich 1899, Königlischer Glaspalast, Münchener Jahresausstellung 1899, p. 187, nos. 2463–77; Otto N. Witt, *Weltausstellung in Paris: Amtlicher Katalog der Ausstellung des Deutschen Reichs – Redaktion und Einführung zu Glasindustrie und Keramik* (Berlin, 1900), pp. 348, 424, no. 4286; Munich 1900, Königlischer Glaspalast, Münchener Jahresausstellung 1900, p. 185, nos. 2058–67; Dresden 1901, Ausstellungshalle an der Stübelallee, Internationale Kunstausstellung, p. 130; Strasbourg 1901, pp. 99–100, nos. 610–25; Houtart 1902, pp. 169, 175; Munich 1902, Königlischer Glaspalast, Münchener Jahresausstellung 1902, p. 201, nos. 2609–32; St. Louis, MO, 1904, Louisiana Pur-

chase Exposition, *Official Catalogue of the Exhibition of the German Empire*, ed. Wagner, applied arts section: Julius Lessing, pp. 454, 465, nos. 2705, 2992; Dresden 1906, Ausstellungshalle an der Stübelallee, Internationale Kunstausstellung, *Offizieller Katalog*, p. 102; *Die Werkkunst*, vol. 1906/7, p. 367; death certificate of Désiré Christian, 19 Jan. 1907, copy in the possession of Yvon Fleck, Meisenthal; *Deutschlands Glasindustrie, Adressbuch sämtlicher Deutschen Glashütten*, issued by Die Glashütte (Dresden, 1909), p. 378, no. 1262; Debize 1989, p. 14, illus. p. 90; Schmitt, *Sammlung Silzer*, 1989, pp. 12, 369, 375, 381, 388, nos. 52–57, with illus.; Venzmer and Mendelssohn, Mainz, 1990, nos. 25–27, with illus.; Schmitt 1990, pp. 47, 48, 51, 53, 54, illus. no. 10; Bartha, Neumann Collection, 1993, p. 110; Thiébaut, *Dessins*, 1993, pp. 28–30; Netzer, Berlin, 1994, nos. 6–7, with illus.; Ricke 2002, p. 168, no. 261, with illus. Supplementary research Susanne Brenner 1997; ■ Meisenthal 1999, pp. 18–23, 24–31, cat. nos. 47, 56, 85–87, 89–91; Nancy 1999, p. 67, cat. nos. 27–29, illus. p. 64.

→Burgun, Schverer & Co., Gallé, Vallerysthal

François Pierre Christian

Bissenberg-Eguelshardt (parois Bitche) b. 12 April 1863
Son of a forester and later innkeeper Jean-Baptiste Christian from Lemberg near Meisenthal and his wife, Odile, née Lutz; one of nine children, youngest brother of →Désiré Christian.

1870/71

François Christian is said to have moved to Paris with his brothers Antoine (b. 1855) and Emile (b. 1861) for political reasons (Meisenthal belonged from 1871 to the part of Lorraine annexed by the German Empire).

1882

Resident of Aubervilliers – possibly to train at Verreries d'Aubervilliers, the local glass factory.

before 1890–c. 1905/6

Lives in Meisenthal; works as a glass painter and designer, possibly also as a porcelain painter. Until *c.* 1899 works for →Burgun, Schverer & Co. in the decoration studio managed by his brother, Désiré Christian, until *c.* 1897/98, where until 1894 primarily ornamental and utility glass was painted for →Emile Gallé in Nancy.

from c. 1899–c. 1905/6

François Christian is employed at his brother's firm. He signs pieces, some of which he has designed, *F. Christian, Meisenthal/Lothringen*; *François Christian, Meisenthal, Lothringen*; or *Geb. Christian, Meisenthal, Lothringen*. Although François Christian is known to have worked for his brother's firm as early as 1901, the studio, also known as 'Geb. Christian & Sohn, Meisenthal/Lothringen' participates in public exhibitions as 'Désiré Christian & Sohn, Meisenthal, Lothringen'.

after 1905

François Christian is said to have left Meisenthal for Cologne (although there is no evidence of him in the directories there), where he continued to practise his profession. He is thought to have retreated to Brittany during the First World War, where he is said to have died, although the place and name are unknown.

Archival documents and literature

Birth certificate, Mairie de la Ville de Bitche; envelope, Musée du Verre et du Cristal Meisenthal; documents: 423Q825, 423Q984, 19E113, Archives Départementales, Saint-Julien-les-Metz; Meisenthal electoral rolls: 1890 and 91, 2AL230; 1893, 2AL243, Archives Départementales, Saint-Julien-les-Metz; letter paper: 21J21, Archives Départementales, Saint-Julien-les-Metz; Pazaurek 1901, p. 121; P. Schulze, 'Erstlingsarbeiten Emile Gallés', *Die Werkkunst* (1905–6): 236; Klesse, *Funke-Kaiser* I, 1981, pp. 106–7; Schmitt, *Sammlung Silzer*, 1989, pp. 52–53; Debize 1989, illus. p. 90; Venzmer and Mendelssohn, Mainz, 1990, pp. 66–69; ■ Meisenthal 1999, p. 31, cat. nos. 92–100.
Susanne Brenner 1997

→Burgun, Schverer & Co., D. Christian

Daum Frères Verreries de Nancy
Nancy

22 June 1873
Inquiry related to the building of the Verreries Sainte-Catherine glass factory for window glass in Nancy, Faubourg Sainte Catherine, by Guillaume Avril (b. 1829), founder of Verreries de Trois-Fontaines, his son-in-law, Victor Josué Bertrand (b. 1843), an engineer, and the brothers Eugène and Jean-Baptiste Auguste Villaume, owners of the premises.

13 Feb. 1874
Building permission granted to the company 'Villaume Avril et Bertrand'.

Aug. 1875
Production of watch and clock glass and drip-pans for candelabra instead of window glass as originally specified in the inquiry about building permission. Financial straits owing to withdrawal of the Villaume family from the partnership, preventing the completion of the buildings as planned. Trades under the name 'Verreries Sainte-Catherine Société industrielle Avril Bertrand et Cie.'; director: Victor Josué Bertrand.

1876–1878
More buildings are erected and the glassware line is extended to include watch glass, flacons, container and lighting glass, which is made possible by two loans from Jean Daum (23 June 1825–10 Feb. 1885), notary public from Bitsch (now Bitche en Moselle), who has lived with his family in Nancy since 5 Oct. 1876 as a consequence of the Franco-Prussian War. Jean Daum had married Marie-Louise-Cordule Isenmann (1828–1901), with whom he has seven children: Louise (1852–1891), Auguste (1853–1909), Charles (1856–1897), Jeanne (1858–1927), Fanny (1863– 1927), Jean-Antonin (1864–1930) and Léon (1857–1858) who died young.

23 March 1878
Jean Daum takes over the factory since Avril and Bertrand are unable to return the money he has lent them. The Villaume family, however, continues to own the premises. From 12 August continuation of the original product range, with manufacture to order of watch and clock glass, until 1927/28, when the Picard factory in Lunéville closes down. New staff members include Adolphe Claude (b. 1848), later head gaffer (glass-blower), and the new foreman of the glassworks, Eugène Marquot (b. 1822), who by 1880 builds up the most important line at the factory: 'sets of glasses, monochrome, cut, engraved and mould-blown in half crystal; speciality: utility glass for restaurants'.

from 1879
Managing director: Jean-Louis-Auguste Daum (1853–1909), called Auguste Daum, who broke off legal training as a notary public for this reason. In 1883 he marries Jeanne Constantin (1858–1921), with whom he has five children: a daughter, Louise (1884–1940), and four sons, Jean (1885–1916), Léon (b. 1887), Paul (1888–1944) and Henri (1889–1965). From 1884 member of the recently founded Société Industrielle de l'Est; in 1886 member of the Société Centrale d'Horticulture de Nancy; in 1890 member of the Commission Administrative du Bureau de Bienfaisance and the Société des Amis des Arts; in 1897 Chevalier de la Légion d'Honneur; in 1906 officer of Nicham-Iftikhar; in 1903 and 1905 president of the Tribunal de Commerce (commerce and trade court) in Nancy, where he has been a judge since 1897; in 1908 president of the Friends of Nancy University. On 1 Jan. 1882 Auguste Daum establishes a company fund for emergency care in case of accidents.

26 Dec. 1883
Founds a joint-stock company, to exist from 1 Jan. 1884 to 1 Jan. 1896, with Jean Daum and his son, Auguste, as partners, after the latter has married into money. Trades under the name 'Verrerie de Nancy Daum & Fils, Nancy, Faubourg Sainte Catherine, 2, rue du pont de la croix'.

1885–1887
Following Jean Daum's death the firm trades under the name 'Verrerie de Nancy Daum & Cie.', with Auguste Daum as director. His mother, brothers and sisters are shareholders. In 1886 he opens a primary school at the glass factory for orphans working there.

from 1887
Trades under the name 'Verrerie de Nancy Daum Frères & Cie.' owing to the employment (under the terms of the contract concluded in 1883) of Jean-Antonin Daum, called Antonin, Auguste's youngest brother, who had trained as an engineer at the Ecole Centrale in Paris. Antonin Daum modernizes the technical side of the company, introducing a gas-powered cracking off and fusing machine in 1888.

In 1898 he marries Anne-Marguerite Didion (1876–1914), with whom he has two daughters, Antoinette (b. 1899) and Françoise (b. 1902), and a son, Michel (1900–1986). From 1894 a member of the Société Lorraine des Amis des Arts and on the Comité de l'Association des Artistes Lorrains; in 1900 made a Chevalier; in 1910 Officier de la Légion d'Honneur; in 1901 vice-president of the Alliance Provinciale des Industries d'Art, called the Ecole de Nancy, as well as a member of the Société Centrale d'Horticulture. In 1926 is made Commandeur de la Légion d'Honneur and appointed a member of the committee of the Musée des Arts Décoratifs, Paris, to succeed his friend, the late Louis Majorelle; in 1928 made a member of the Académie de Stanislas, Nancy.

1889–1891
Antonin Daum extended the firm's line to include more luxury sets of glasses. In 1891 the first Daum Frères & Cie. catalogue is issued with sets of glasses and some vase models with historicist forms and decoration, executed in cutting, engraving, etching and painting with burnish gold. In the same year the glass painter Emile Dufour (b. 1860) is hired. From 1891 a special division for luxury glass is established with select employees, some of whom remain on the job until the 1920s and 1930s, ensuring continuous high standards: head of the decoration studio: Brutus Camille Dammann (b. 1841), called père Dammann, with the firm from 1889; head of the engraving workshop Jules Marchand; head of the cutting and grinding workshop Sévère Winckler; head gaffers (glass-blowers): Adolphe Claude (b. 1848) and Jean-Baptiste Gall (1868–1938), who began as an apprentice in the firm in 1884, in 1921 was made an Officier d'Académie and in 1926 Chevalier de la Légion d'Honneur.

from 1893
Freelance work by →Jacques Gruber (1870–1936), who had trained as a painter in Paris and, until he left the firm in 1897/98, is responsible for designing elaborate exhibition pieces. Participation in the Chicago World's Columbian Exposition, showing historicist services and the first group of glass art from the Daum studio as well as a few Gruber designs, which were singled out for special mention, resulting in an increased production of glass art. In 1894 factory premises bought. Beginning of long-term collaboration and friendship with Louis Majorelle (1859–1926), whose first commission for Antonin Daum is to design the furniture for the exhibition in Nancy. The engraver Emile Maas is hired in the glass-art division. In 1895 Antonin Daum succeeds →Emile Gallé (who has stepped down) on the Conseil de Surveillance et de Perfectionnement de l'Ecole des Beaux-Arts. The painter →Henri Bergé (1870–1937) begins to work for Daum. From 1897/98 he is head designer and head of the firm's drawing school. Fire in the glassworks. Five successful exhibitions, at which Gruber's designs are singled out for praise. Gruber designs the first piece on commission, a vase presented to Princess Hélène d'Orléans by the ladies of Lorraine.

1896
The 'Société Daum et fils' is dissolved; Auguste Daum becomes the proprietor of the factory and guarantor of all company debts. Work is shown at the Galerie Georges Petit in Paris, where the ceramist →Edmond Lachenal (1855–1948), who occasionally designs for Daum from 1897, also has pieces on display. First official acquisitions of Daum pieces by museums and the French state. Closer collaboration with Louis Majorelle, including joint participation in exhibitions and shared advertisements.

1897
Enormously successful at the 1897 Brussels Exposition Internationale, purchases by the king of Belgium and royal museums. Henri Boucher, Minister of Trade and Industry, visits the factory. First mention of the firm's drawing school. About 1897–98 Charles Schneider (1881–1953) begins an apprenticeship as an engraver at Daum, while studying at the Ecole des Beaux-Arts in Nancy. From 1904 to 1906 he attends the Ecole des Beaux-Arts in Paris, in 1905 supported by a bursary from the city of Nancy, for which he had been recommended by Antonin Daum. From 1897 to 1900 warehouse and showrooms in Frankfurt am Main, Germany.

20 March 1898
'Verrerie de Nancy Daum Frères & Cie.' is founded as a joint-stock company, with Auguste and Antonin Daum as co-directors, for a period of fifteen years. The official contract is linked with Antonin Daum's marriage, which has brought him a great deal of money. On the occasion of his marriage, the staff presents him with the first Daum (non-electric) table lamp, 'Eglantine' (wild rose), made of wrought iron and glass and designed by Gruber, which leads to a new product line in collaboration with Majorelle's smithy. That year sees the

realization of a prize-winning crocus vase by the sculptor Louis Fuchs (Musée des Arts Décoratifs, Paris). Emile-Hippolyte-Marius Wirtz (19 Dec. 1884–Nov. 1953), called Emile Wirtz, starts an apprenticeship as a glass painter while studying painting at the Ecole des Beaux-Arts in Nancy, an artist who would later become Antonin Daum's closest associate.

1899

Beginning of serial production of oil and candle-burning lamps, from 1901 electric lamps and from 1903 lamps designed by Louis Majorelle, in whose workshop the wrought-iron mounts are made. Application for a patent on sandwiched decoration is submitted on 23 June 1899 under no. 290213 ('Nouveau mode de décoration intercalaire à grand feu, pour cristaux, verreries etc.'). This patent, unlike those of 1896 and 1897, which →Burgun, Schverer & Co. had had registered in Germany and France on enamel painting between casings, encompasses all kinds of sandwiched decoration, be it painting, etching, engraving or cutting.

1900

Enormously successful at the 1900 Paris Exposition Universelle, with approx. 375 exhibits, including dressing-table sets and sets of glasses as well as elaborate multiple-cased glass art engraved with the new fused-on and fused-in powdered glass or with iridescent surfaces as well as *intercalaire* glass with decoration between casings. Special exhibits include large vases up to 95 cm high and the first five electric lamps. Apart from Bergé as head designer, the freelance artists →Jacques Gruber (figurative designs) and →Ernest Bussière are represented with vessels after some of his ceramic models. Workforce of 300, including 50 in the decoration studio; two furnaces with 12 pots. Coloured glass by Appert Frères. Outlets in Paris, 32, rue de Paradis, and in Frankfurt am Main, Kaiserstrasse 73.

from 1901

Antonin Daum is made vice-president of the Alliance Provinciale des Industries d'Art, called the Ecole de Nancy, founded that year. In 1902 he is commissioned by the Ecole de Nancy to give courses for workmen in the theory of ornamental composition and practical courses in ceramics and glass.

Participation in exhibitions: at St Petersburg in 1901 and Turin in 1902; exhibits included *intercalaire* models, some of which were already shown at the 1900 Paris Exposition Universelle.

from 1903

Ernest Schneider (1877–1937) is hired to relieve Antonin Daum of some administrative tasks. From late 1903 to 1914 the development and production of *pâte de verre* objects and vessels by Amalric Walter (1870–1959), a graduate of the Ecole Nationale de Céramique in Sèvres; from 1906 usually after models by Henri Bergé. In 1903 a service of glasses is designed by Edmond Lachenal (1855–1948). In 1904 the first catalogue of lamps. From 1906 to 1913 Charles Schneider, formerly an engraver's apprentice at Daum, works as a designer, along with Henri Bergé. In 1906/7 Antonin Daum gives lectures on the occasion of awarding prizes to pupils of the Ecole Professionnelle de l'Est in Nancy.

1907–1914

Employment of Jean Daum, Auguste Daum's eldest son, who is trained in the firm, conscripted in 1914 and falls at Verdun in 1916. Posthumously made a Chevalier de la Légion d'Honneur. In 1907 and 1911 buildings added, designed by the architects Louis Marchal and Emile Toussaint of Nancy. In 1909 the firm participates (hors-concours) in the Nancy exhibition, showing its first *pâte de verre* objects and windows designed by Walter.

from 1909

Trades under the name 'Daum & Cie.' following Auguste Daum's death in compliance with the terms of the contract that had been concluded by the brothers in 1898. Director: Antonin Daum. Successful participation at the 1910 Brussels Exposition Universelle, where approx. 600 exhibits are shown; special mention is made of small sculpture and windows in *pâte de verre*. Antonin Daum is made an Officier de la Légion d'Honneur.

from 1911

Paul Daum, chemical engineer and youngest son of Auguste Daum, is employed at the firm. In 1912 his youngest brother, Henri Daum (1889–1965), joins the firm after finishing his studies in corporate law. The sculptor Jules-Elie-Edouard Cayette (1884–1953), called Jules Cayette, takes part in the Société Lorraine des Amis des Arts exhibition in Nancy with designs for glass lamps made at Daum. In 1913 the Schneider brothers leave Daum to found a glass factory of their own. That year the Daum factory is awarded the Grand Prix at the Ghent Exposition Universelle.

1914–1918

Jean, Paul and Henri Daum, like many members of the staff, serve in the war; the factory is closed down sporadically and is even temporarily used as a field hospital. From 1915 to 1918 production of glass for laboratories. In 1916 first trials of what were called *vases ferronnés*, glass of the *verres de jade* type blown into mounts designed by Louis Majorelle.

from 1919

Directors: Antonin, Paul and Henri Daum. Resume production of glass art, continuing and developing lines established before the war. Head designer: Emile Wirtz (1884–1953), pupil and successor of Henri Bergé, who continues to work in a limited capacity. In 1923 Wirtz is made an Officier d'Académie and in 1952 Chevalier de la Légion d'Honneur. Head of the design studio: Léon Thincelin (b. 1875), from 1897 glass painter at the factory. In 1920 Antonin Daum becomes a member of the Société des Artistes Décorateurs in Paris.

1919–1928

Dual production of newly conceived Art Nouveau editions and new models gradually adapted to the stylistic trend of Art Deco: until 1922 stylized, mainly applied floral decoration, in opaque enamel colours or in relief etching on overlay as well as *vases ferronnés* and *verres de jade* with coloured powdered glass fused in between layers and inclusions of precious metal foil, which is also used for the *vases ferronnés*, the *vases à décor de résille* with a reticulated mould-blown decoration between casings with coloured glass powder rubbed in and the *vases bullés* with inclusions of irregular air bubbles or air bubbles induced by optic moulding.

from 1923

Collaboration with such well-known Paris artists as Edgar Brandt (1880–1960), Paul Follot, André Groult (1884–1967), Nic Frères and Max Verrier, who have the glass for the lamps they design made at Daum and also occasionally design for Daum. In 1922–23 lawsuit with the André Delatte glass factory (est. 1921) over the copying of Daum designs. In 1923 Pierre Froissart, Antonin Daum's son-in-law, becomes business partner and employee. In 1925 participation in the Paris Exposition Internationale, showing a glass mosaic with quite large tesserae in the main concourse of the Nancy pavilion, with lighting after designs by André Groult and Louis Majorelle, smoky glass with stylized figurative etching and the first decoration in fine matt cutting; in addition represented by the Paris shops L'Acropole, proprietor Jean de Gaudart d'Allaines (8, rue de Caulaincourt), and D.I.M. (40, rue du Colisée), a business selling modern interior decoration.

from 1925

Employment of Michel Daum, chemist and son of Antonin Daum. In 1926 Médaille du travail awarded to thirty long-term employees. Paul Daum gradually steps into the shoes of his uncle, Antonin Daum. Collaboration with Emile Wirtz on creating a consistent line in the trend-setting Art Deco style. Apart from editions featuring simple forms and markedly stylized figurative and floral motifs, some of which are based on geometric forms, editions with purely geometric decoration in bold relief etching are launched increasingly, from 1929 also with usually polished cutting on transparent, thick-walled glass in the following colours: straw (yellow), blue, aquamarine, grey, smoky brown, red, black and three different greens.

1925–1935

A new factory, 'Verrerie de Belle-Etoile and Lorrain Verreries d'Art', which is designed for serial production, is erected in Croismare and Meurthe-et-Moselle by architect Raphael Oudeville of Nancy, who also builds the Nancy workshop (1930) for grinding off pontil marks. First director of the branch is a former glass-works foreman at →Muller Frères, Hublin, who is succeeded in 1926 by Paul Daum, who remains in the position until 1930. In 1927 pressed glass production gets underway. 'Lorrain' agency is opened in Paris. Head of glass production from 1928 to 1932: André Rosemberg (b. 1897), from 1909 foreman in Nancy. Employed by the firm from 1928 to 1934 is artisan Pierre d'Avesn, pseudonym of Pierre Girre (23 Oct. 1901–19 June 1989), designer of pressed-glass models, pupil and former employee of René Lalique. In 1932 the furnaces are extinguished owing to the worldwide economic crisis and on 16 Dec. 1934 operations cease entirely.

1930–1939

Directors: Paul, Henri and Michel Daum following Antonin Daum's death. Paul Daum (28 Oct. 1888–17 Feb. 1944) becomes artistic director in Nancy. He has been committed to municipal politics since 1919 as a town councillor; in 1931 and 1933 serves as deputy mayor; in 1921 made a Chevalier de la Légion d'Honneur; in 1930 member, from 1937 president of the Chambre Syndicale des Cristalliers et Verriers de l'Est. The worldwide economic crisis begins to be felt in the Nancy factory, which from 1930 gradually reduces working time in the decoration studios and wages. In 1935 major commission for the transatlantic luxury liner *Normandie*, consisting of sets of glasses and carafes (50,000 pieces). Michel Daum develops the crystal glass for it. From September 1936 to April 1937 cessation of production for eight months owing to workers' strike. Blanks bought from other firms.

from 1937

Production of crystal glass exclusively. Participation in the 1937 Paris Exposition Internationale. In 1938 first thick-walled vessels in flowing forms with bold applications, which continue to be developed in 1948, with 1950s forms being based on them. From 1938 to 1943 Paul Daum is founder-president of the Fédération des Chambres Syndicales de l'Industrie du Verre et l'Union Syndicale des Verreries (glass industry federation).

1939–1945

Glassworks is shut down because of mobilization although the grinding and cutting workshop continues to operate until 1940, headed by Henri Daum. Paul Daum acquires (jointly with the Cristallerie St-Louis) the Verrerie de Blérancourt and Aisne glassworks so that production, managed by Michel Daum, can continue. On 24 Feb. 1943 Paul Daum, a member of the Résistance, is arrested by the Gestapo. He dies at Neue-Bremme concentration camp near Saarbrücken on 17 Feb. 1944.

from 1945

Trades under the name 'Cristallerie Daum'; directors: Henri and Michel Daum; technical director: Antoine Froissart; sales director: Jacques Daum. Production focuses on fine colourless crystal table glass. In 1947 the office building is rebuilt by the architects Fernand Pierron and Laxou in Nancy, but in December the firm premises are flooded. In 1948 Michel Daum designs thick-walled glass with applications and air bubbles; from 1950 to *c.* 1955 colourless, freely formed, thick-walled crystal glass sculptures and vessels are produced. Employees: Guy Petitfils and Jean-Pierre Demarchi (design); Jean Martin, head gaffer; Louis Gisquet, foreman of the engraving workshop. In 1952 Michel Daum is made a Chevalier de la Légion d'Honneur. Henri Daum retires in 1960.

from 1962

Trades under the name 'Cristallerie Daum S. A.' after conversion into a public corporation; president: Michel Daum. Designers *c.* 1964: Philippe Desforges, Guy Petitfils and Janine Dausse.

1965–1976

President: Jacques Daum (b. 1909), Auguste Daum's grandson, who initiates productive collaboration with contemporary artists. The firm is a member of Group 21, an association of twenty firms worldwide making products designed by artists that have been judged by an international jury. In 1966 enlargement of the workshop for grinding off pontil marks. In 1968 resumption of *pâte de verre* production in limited editions after designs by Jacqueline Badord, Robert Couturier (until 1974), Salvador Dalí (until 1970), Jean-Pierre Demarchi, Pierre Dmitrienko (until 1970), Maurice Legendre, Claude Lhoste; in 1969 by Bernard Citroën, Thomas Gleb (until 1970), Claude Goutin, Paolo Santini; in 1970 by Guy Petitfils, Claude Wetzstein; in 1971 by Pierre Sulmon; in 1974 by Roy Adzak, et al. From 1969 designs by César for cast figurines of colourless and coloured glass, launched in 1970 at the Eurodomus III trade fair in Milan.

from 1976

President: Pierre de Chérisey (b. 1936), Antonin Daum's grandson. *Pâte de verre* designs: Olivier Brice (1976); Dan Dailey (1981); Tony Morgan (1982); Hilton McConnico (1987), et al.

from 1986

Financial straits. In 1994 the firm is bought by the city of Nancy, glassworks in Nancy closed down.

1996–2003

The firm is taken over by the Société S.A.G.E.M. in Paris. Studios for *pâte de verre*, engraving, grinding and cutting in operation in Nancy.

Exhibitions

1895

Brussels, Maison d'art, 'Toison d'or', again in 1896 and 1899

1896

Paris, Georges Petit, annual exhibition (exh. rep.)

1899

Poitiers, Industrial Exhibition – Grand Prix (mentioned exclusively in Paris, *Daum*, 1900, p. 2)

1902

Mülhausen, Alsace, Ausstellung des Industrieverbandes Mülhausen

1903

Paris, Galerie Georges Petit, Daum, Lachenal, Majorelle (exh. rep.)

1907

Bordeaux, Exposition Maritime Internationale de Bordeaux

1909

Copenhagen, Exposition d'Art Décoratif

1910

Lyons, Salon de Lyon

1915

Casablanca, Exposition de Casablanca

1919

Lyons, Foire de Lyon, regular participation until 1939

1921

Luxembourg, Exposition Lorraine-Luxembourgeoise d'Arts Appliqués, de Peinture et de Sculpture

Paris, Pavillon de Marsan, Salon de la Société des Artistes Décorateurs – participation of Antonin Daum, again in 1923–25, 1928–30

Paris, Grand Palais, Salon d'Automne, again in 1927, 1929, 1930 with Antonin Daum retrospective

1922

Marseilles, Exposition Coloniale – Grand Prix

1923

Barcelona, Exposition Internationale – Grand Prix

Mulhouse, Alsace, Exposition de la Société des Arts

Paris, Musée Galliera, Exposition de la Verrerie et l'Emaillerie Moderne (exh. rep.)

1924

Geneva, Musée d'Art et Histoire (solo exh.) (exh. rep.)

1925

Paris, Exposition Internationale des Arts Décoratifs et Industriels Modernes – hors-concours; Antonin Daum member of the jury and chairman, Class 12: Glass

1926

Minneapolis, MN, Modern Glass from Abroad, touring exhibition in the United States

1927

Dresden, Modernes europäisches Kunstgewerbe (Modern European Applied Arts) (exh. rep.)

Copenhagen, International Exhibition – Grand Prix

Leipzig, Grassi-Museum, Europäisches Kunstgewerbe (European Applied Arts) (exh. cat.)

Madrid, Exposition Internationale – diplôme d'honneur

Paris, Pavillon de Marsan, Salon de la Société des Artistes Décorateurs – participation of Paul Daum, again in 1931, 1933–37, 1942

1929–1930

New York, Metropolitan Museum of Art, International Exhibition – Contemporary Glass and Rugs, touring exhibition; Boston, MA, Museum of Fine Arts; Philadelphia, PA, The Pennsylvania Museum; Chicago, IL, The Art Institute of Chicago; Pittsburgh, PA, Carnegie Institute; Dayton, OH, Dayton Art Institute; Cincinnati, OH, Cincinnati Museum Association; Baltimore, MD, The Baltimore Museum of Art (exh. cat.)

1930

Budapest, International Trade Fair

Liège, Foire Internationale de Liège – participation hors-concours, Paul Daum member of the jury; distinctions awarded to employees: silver medal to Emile Wirtz (head designer), Emile Poulet and Emile Toussaint (glass-blowers) and Paul Racadot (engraver)

Lyons, Foire de Lyon, again in 1938

Monza, Villa Reale, IVa Mostra Internazionale delle Arti Decorative

Paris, Musée Galliera, Le Décor Moderne de la Table (exh. rep.)

1931

Paris, Bois de Vincennes, Exposition Coloniale – hors-concours, Paul Daum vice-president of Class 73; distinctions awarded to employees: diplôme d'honneur to Emile Wirtz (head designer); gold medals to Emile Poulet and Emile Toussaint (glass-blowers) and Paul Racadot (engraver)

1932

Leipzig, Messe (Trade Fair)

1933
Paris, Pavillon de Marsan, Le Décor de la Vie sous la IIIe République de 1870 à 1900 (exh. cat.)
1934
Paris, 2e Salon de la Lumière (exh. rep.)
Paris, Musée Galliera, Le Verre, la Mosaïque et l'Email dans la Décoration moderne (exh. rep.)
1936
Milan, Palazzo dell'Arte, VIth Triennale, again in 1951, IXth (exh. cat.), 1954, Xth (exh. cat.), 1957, XIth (exh. cat.), 1960, XIIth (exh. cat.) and 1973 XVth Triennale with special exhibition I Cinquant'anni della Triennale. 1923–73 Mostra storica (exh. cat.)
1937
Paris, Champ-de-Mars, Exposition Internationale des Arts et Techniques dans la Vie Moderne (Exposition Internationale) (exh. cat.) – participation hors-concours, Paul Daum member of the jury
Paris, Pavillon de Marsan, Le Décor de la Vie de 1900 à 1920 (exh. cat.)
1939
New York, World's Fair – Building the World of Tomorrow (exh. cat.)
San Francisco, CA, Golden Gate International Exposition (exh. cat.)

Writings by Antonin Daum:

'L'Art avec l'industrie', *L'Immeuble et la Construction dans l'Est* no. 23 (7 Oct. 1906): 165–67; 'L'Ecole de Nancy à l'Exposition de 1909', *Bulletin des Sociétés Artistiques de l'Est* (August 1910): 92–93; ibid. (September 1910): 99–103; 'Verrerie d'art de Nancy', *Nancy et la Région Lorraine* (1925): 168–72; 'Les Industries d'art à Nancy avant et depuis la guerre', *Mémoires de l'Académie Stanislas, Années 1924–1925*, vol. XXII, CLXXV (Nancy, 1925), pp. 55–63; 'Verriers d'autrefois', inaugural address on appointment to the Académie de Stanislas on 24 May 1928 in ibid., vol. XXIV, CLXXVII, Nancy 1928, pp. LVI–LXX.

Writings by Paul Daum:

'French Crystal and Glassware', *Céramique et Verrerie de France* (31 Aug. 1939).

Writings by Michel Daum:

'Les Parts respectives de l'invention et de l'observation dans la création des formes en verrerie', *Glastechnische Berichte*, no. VIII (1959): 64–67, with illus.

Writings by Noël Daum:

Daum: Maîtres verriers 1870–1980 (Lausanne, 1980).

Archival documents and literature

Supplementing Schmitt, Zurich II, 1995, pp. 284–85: death certificate of Jean Daum, Archives Municipales de la Ville de Nancy, Décès 1885, no. 247; Rousset 1888–90, pp. 343, 140; Daum 1891; *Daum Cat. aquar.* I; E. Gouttière-Vernolle, 'Verrerie Lorraine', *Lorraine Artiste* (March 1893): 201–2; André 1894, pp. 12-13; ■ Krantz 1894, pp. 28–29; Nancy 1894, pp. 21, 109, nos. 636–44; 'Nancy', *Art Décoratif* (1894): 32, nos. 189–213; ■ Rev., Est, Daum, 1894; 'Nancy', *Art Décoratif* (1894): 39, nos. 44–48, illus. pls. LVI–LVII, colour pl. n.p.; Nancy 1895, p. 120, no. 722; 'Exposition de Remiremont', *Bulletin des Sociétés artistiques de l'Est* (Sept. 1895): 111, suppl.; Meier-Graefe, 1896, p. 69, illus. pp. 68–69; *Chronique du mois, Revue des Arts Décoratifs* 16 (1896): 371; Brussels, *Daum*, 1897; Brussels, catalogue, 1897; ■ V. Champier, 'L'Exposition universelle de Bruxelles', *Revue des Arts Décoratifs* 17 (1897): 394; Nancy 1897, p. 133, no. 667; ■ Rev., Est, Daum, 1897; Nancy 1898, p. 141, no. 708; *Daum Album* I, 1899; Frantz-Jourdain, 'En Vue de l'exposition de 1900: Le Deuxième concours ouvert par l'union centrale des arts décoratifs', *Revue des Arts Décoratifs* 19 (1899): 118, illus. p. 114; E. Hinzelin, 'L'Art en Lorraine', *Lorraine Artiste* (March 1899): 12–13, illus. pp. 3, 7, 9, 14; Nancy 1899, p. 145, no. 780; Paris, *Daum*, 1900; G. S. [Gaston Save], 'La Verrerie d'Art de MM. Daum Frères', *Lorraine Artiste* (Oct. 1900): 106–9; (Nov. 1900): 118–20; (March 1901): 97–99; G. S. [Gaston Save], 'Lampes en verrerie d'art Daum frères: Exposition de la maison Majorelle', ibid. (April 1901): 133–35, with illus.; A. Sandier, 'La Céramique à l'exposition II', *Art & Décoration* 9 (1901): 64–65; Bernard 1902, pp. 26, 67–68; G. Geoffroy, *Les Industries artistiques françaises et étrangères à l'exposition universelle de 1900* (Paris, n.d. [1902]), p. 32, illus. p. 33, pls. 61–62; E. Nicolas, 'Les Verreries et cristaux d'art de MM. Daum', *Lorraine Artiste* (Sept. 1902): 258–63; Paris 1903, pp. 8–9, illus. n.p.; Paris, portfolio, 1903, vol. 2, illus. pls. 17, 22; J. Rais, 'L'Ecole de Nancy et son exposition au musée des arts décoratifs', *Art & Décora-*

tion 13 (1903): 136, illus. p. 135; 'Nos Industries d'art à Paris', *Lorraine Artiste* (Jan. 1904): 26–27; Nancy 1904, p. 39, nos. 44–48, illus. pls. LVI–LVII, colour pl. n.p.; Strasbourg 1908, pp. 16–17, nos. 71–74; E. Nicolas, 'L'Ecole de Nancy à Strasbourg', *Bulletin des Sociétés artistiques de l'Est* (March 1908): 32; Commandant Lalance, 'L'Ecole de Nancy à Strasbourg', ibid. (May 1908): 64; Nancy 1910, p. 120, no. 456; Paris 1910, p. 18; Nancy 1911, p. 44, no. 371; Barrez 1912, pp. 72–73, 76, 78, 79, 80, illus. pp. 72a, 74a [n.p.]; Lafitte 1912, pp. 36, 38, 473, 873, illus. pls. VIII, XX; Nancy 1912, p. 60, nos. 423, 430; *Daum Cat. aquar.* II; Nancy 1920, p. 63, nos. 519–20; Octave Maus 1926, p. 187; R. Papini, *Arte d'oggi* (Milan, 1930), nos. 619–20; G. Renard, 'Eloge funèbre de M. Antonin Daum, Membre Titulaire', in *Mémoires de l'Académie Stanislas, Années 1929–1930*, vol. XXVII, CLXXX (Nancy, 1930), pp. X–XIV; Paris 1937, pp. 126–27, nos. 1043–56; San Francisco, CA, 1939, Golden Gate International Exposition, exh. cat., *Decorative Arts*, no. 413; H. Daum, *Histoire de la verrerie*, typescript, 1964, supplemented by Michel Daum 1970, pp. 1–42; Sterner 1969; 'Eurodomus 3', *Domus* (1970): nos. 488, VII and 7, with illus.; Nancy, *Daum* I, 1977; Nancy, *Daum* II, 1978; Nancy, *Daum* III, 1979; ■ Daum 1980; Nancy, *Daum* IV, 1980; ■ Sapporo, *Daum*, 1980; Munich 1981; Nancy, *Daum* V, 1981; ■ Monte Carlo, *Daum*, 1982; Yoshimizu 1983, nos. 99–130, 548–90; ■ Tokyo, *Daum*, 1984; ■ Zurich, *Daum*, 1986; ■ Zurich, Wühre 9, 1986; ■ Charpentier et al. 1987; ■ Tokyo, *Daum*, 1987; Tokyo, *Style floral*, 1988, nos. 60–95; Aptel et al. 1989; Debize 1989; ■ Pétry and Maury, *Daum*, 1989; Brunhammer and Tise 1990, p. 272; *Glass Fantasy* 1990; Bouvier, *Majorelle*, 1991, pp. 54, 56, 74, 80, 86, 98, 102, 105, 107, 109, 126, 134, 188, 194, 199, 206–7, illus. pp. 50, 133, 188–89, 196, 205–7; Cappa 1991, pp. 24–25, 96–134, 516–17; Cappa 1991, pp. 24–25, 96–134, 516–17; Duncan 1991, pp. 28, 38, 40, 43, 52, 126, 145–49, 155–56, 160, illus. pp. 43, 144–45, 210–18; Yoshimizu and Klesse 1992, nos. 71–85, 187, 188; Bartha, Neumann Collection, 1993, pp. 28–48; Karlsruhe, *Trübner*, 1993; P. Thiébaut, *Etude architecturale: Verrerie Daum Lorraine, puis usine de blanchiment*, Service régional de l'inventaire de Lorraine (Nancy, 1993); P. Thiébaut, *Etude architecturale: Verrerie Ste-Catherine, puis Daum*, Service régional de l'inventaire de Lorraine (Nancy, 1995); *Dictionnaire Biographie 1933–95*, vol. 10, p. 275; Karlsruhe, *Daum*, 1995; Schmitt, Zurich II, 1995, pp. 81–87, 181–84, 284–85, nos. 133–45, 309–15; Suzuki, *Kitazawa*, 1996, nos. 28–52, 231–429, 501; Takeda and Olivié, 1996, nos. 30–39; ■ M. Bouvet, Y. Gawlik, J. Guillaume, C. Bardin, V. Ayrolles, *Collaborateurs de Daum*, manuscript S.R.I.L 1997; Daum, Dossier Service Régional de l'Inventaire de Lorraine, 1997; Mukai, *Hida Takayama*, 1997, pp. 92, 104, 107, 109, 127, 150; Duncan, *Salons*, 1998, pp. 35, 38, 460, illus. pp. 8, 33, 36, 38, 122–37; ■ Bardin 1999; Darmstadt 1999, pp. 272–73, 302–10, 356, illus. pp. 269–70, cat. nos. 348–71, with illus.; ■ Nancy 1999, pp. 135–36, 140, 145, 147, 172–73, 176–77, 180–82, 239–47, 279, cat. nos. 34–69, 265–71, 291, illus. pp. 45, 83, 206, 219, 238, 248–49, 254–55, 281, 330–31; Sylla, *Trübner*, 2000, pp. 97–106, 191–96, illus. pp. 97, 101, 103–5, 192–93, 195; ■ Bardin 2000; Nancy 2001, pp. 22–25, 50–51, 86–91, with illus.; ■ Bardin 2002, vols. 1–2; ■ C. Bardin, 'Autour de la coupe au serpent, le rôle des frères Schneider à la manufacture Daum', in B. Chavanne and N. Tailleur, *Schneider: Une Verrerie au XXe siècle*, exh. cat., Musée des Beaux-Arts de Nancy (Nancy, 2003), pp. 23–39.

Oral information on Pierre d'Avesn from Marcel Smigielski, Munich, 1997. Written information from Christophe Bardin, 2003.

→Bergé, Bussière, Gruber, Lachenal, Muller

Escalier de Cristal
Pannier-Lahoche et Cie.
Pannier Frères
Paris

from 1806
Philippe-Auguste Charpentier (Châlons-sur-Marne 21 Nov. 1781–Paris 5 Jan. 1815), son of the goldsmith Henry Charpentier of Châlons-sur-Marne and his wife, Marie Madeleine Mérat of Paris, works as a metal engraver in Paris, at 4, place de Grève (then 9e arrondissement, now place de l'Hôtel de Ville, 4e arrondissement; registered in 1807 in the *Almanach du Commerce* de la Ville de Paris, the trade and commerce annual of the city of Paris).
Until 1809
Additional training as a gem-cutter and crystal-glass cutter under Romain-Vincent Jeuffroy (1749–1826), a celebrated Paris gem-cutter, who teaches at the Institut Impérial de Gravure sur Pierres Fines in Paris from 1811. From 1807 Charpen-

tier has a second address (registered in the *Almanach du Commerce*, 1808): 133, Palais du Tribunat (from 1809 identical with the old name, Palais-Royal, the 2e, now 1er arrondissement).

10 June 1809

At her suggestion Philippe-Auguste Charpentier establishes a private company with his sister, Jeanne-Marie Rosalie Desarnaud, née Charpentier (b. Châlons-sur-Marne 3 Sept. 1775), who lives with her second husband, Barthélémy Desarnaud (Bordeaux 1758–Paris 1810), a businessman, at 154, rue du Lycée (formerly 2e arrondissement, now rue de Valois 1er arrondissement), accessible from the Palais-Royal garden. Jeanne-Marie Rosalie Charpentier had been divorced in 1802 in Paris from Pierre Renaud, the father of her two children. On 9 July 1803 she marries, on the advice of her father, Henry Charpentier, with a prenuptial agreement providing for separation of property. Her financial share in the business of her brother, Philippe-Auguste Charpentier, may have enabled him to move to new sales rooms under the Palais-Royal arcades, where he also offers engraved glass for the first time.

1809–1811

Trades under the name 'Charpentier', engraver of gems, crystal glass and metals; address: 153, Palais-Royal, Galerie de Pierre (registered from 1810 to 1812 in the *Almanach du Commerce*). On the death of her second husband, on 8 Aug. 1810, Jeanne-Marie Rosalie Desarnaud inherits, on 1 May 1811, the handsome fortune of 10,398 Frs. She invests a considerable portion of it in the joint business and now has a two-thirds majority in the firm. A month later, on 1 June 1811, her brother, Philippe-Auguste Charpentier, draws up his will in his own hand, making his sister his sole legatee and successor.

from 1812

Charpentier is no longer registered as an engraver but instead as a specialist shop for crystal glass, at 153, Palais-Royal, Galerie de Pierre (*Almanach du Commerce*, 1813). The firm name Charpentier includes Mme Desarnaud since widows generally used their maiden names at that time.

22 April 1813

Charpentier applies for a patent at the Comité Consultatif des Arts et Manufactures on the use of crystal glass in furniture-making, but is refused one. The application describes a procedure for integrating cut crystal glass elements, vessels and objects with ormolu mounts on furniture and objects such as clocks, candelabra, etc. No Christian name is on the patent application so that it may also refer to Charpentier as a business entity. The new combination of crystal glass with gilded ormolu mounts would contribute substantially to the growing renown of the business.

from 1813

Trades under the name 'Charpentier & Comp.' with the addition of 'à l'Escalier de Cristal'. The business is enlarged to accommodate the sale of porcelain and alabaster wares in the neighbouring Palais-Royal arcade. The added name refers to the shop's staircase with its new banister made from polished crystal glass and gilded fittings. The address previously cited in connection with the business remains unchanged (*Almanach du Commerce*, 1814).

Jeanne-Marie Rosalie Desarnaud, née Charpentier, runs the business after her brother's death, on 5 Jan. 1815. The new name, 'Desarnaud Ve., née Charpentier, à l'Escalier de Cristal, graveur du duc de Berry', with the old address, is registered from 1816 to 1828 in the *Almanach du Commerce*. According to the will as executed on 13 Dec. 1815, Mme Desarnaud receives her brother's furnishings and his one-third share in the business. The value of the entire stock of crystal glass is estimated at 18,665 Frs. She signs this document as 'Rosalie Charpentier Ve. [widowed] Desarnaud' and gives as her profession 'marchande de cristaux' (retailer of crystal glasswares) and that of her late brother's as 'ouvrier graveur en cristaux' (crystal-glass engraver workman).

from 1818

Mme Desarnaud is designated as purveyor of crystal glass to three courts, 'Fournisseur de cristaux du duc de Berry, du Garde-Meuble de la Couronne, et du roi', after several applications to the ministers and officials responsible at the Court and the Court furniture repository ('Garde-meuble de la Couronne').

1819

Experiences enormous success at the fifth Exposition des Produits de l'Industrie Française in Paris, where she is awarded a gold medal. The exhibition report describes Mme Desarnaud as the first to have decorated crystal glass with ormolu and gives the Aimé-Gabriel d'Artigues glass factory in Vonêche as her supplier of blanks. The most important pieces in her sumptuous range of luxury wares are made for members of the aristocracy in France and abroad. They include a mantel clock for Naples, a dressing-table with mirror and matching chair of cut crystal glass for the Queen of Spain, four candelabra for Russia, a washstand for Etruria and mantel decorations for the Duke of Brunswick.

1823

Participation in the sixth Exposition des Produits de l'Industrie Française in Paris, which notes an increase in exhibitors showing similar luxury articles of crystal glass and ormolu. The report on the exhibition written by Charles Malo in the *Bazar Parisien* in 1824 in part repeats what was stated in the 1819 report, describing her product range as follows: 'Desarnaud (dame veuve), Cristallerie, Palais-Royal no. 153, est la première qui ait fabriqué des candelabres, pendules, grands et petits vases d'ornement pour les cheminées et des meubles en cristal ornés de bronze. Les cristaux mis en œuvre par madame Desarnaud, et qu'elle exposa au Louvre en 1819, parurent tellement remarquables, les uns par la grandeur de leur dimension, les autres par leur beauté et le goût qui avait présidé à leur taille, que le jury d'examen lui décerna la médaille d'or.' (Mme Desarnaud [a widow], maker of crystal glass at 153, Palais-Royal, is the first to make candelabra, table clocks, ornamental vases large and small for mantel-pieces and crystal glass furniture decorated with ormolu. The crystal glass pieces that Mme Desarnaud has commissioned to be made, and that she exhibited at the Louvre in 1819, appear so remarkable, some for their imposing size and others for their beauty and the taste that governed their cut decoration, that the examining jury awarded her the gold medal).

1828–1838

The glass and gem-cutter Jacques Boin takes over the business. He is registered from 1818 in the *Almanach du Commerce* and from 1819 to 1829 at 120, Galerie de Valois, Palais-Royal (the name was changed from Galerie de Pierre to Galerie de Valois in 1828). Boin's address had been, since the first registration of a business (in 1798), the studio of Antoine Bucher, engraver of gemstones and crystal glass. On 14 Nov. 1817 Boin had married Bucher's daughter, and had worked since 1818 in the studio (which his wife had taken over in 1816), having been head of it from 1820. Presumably Boin and his studio worked for Mme Desarnaud before taking over her business. From 1829 Boin is registered as 'A l'Escalier de Cristal, tailleur et graveur, successeur de Mme Desarnaud, Palais-Royal'. From 1830 he appears in the *Almanach du Commerce* as follows: '152 & 153 Galerie de Valois and Palais-Royal. Tailleur et graveur, services en cristal pour la table, cristaux pour orfèvres, porcelaine pour la table, objets de fantaisie pour étrennes' (Cutter and engraver, services in crystal glass for the table, crystal glass for gold- and silversmiths, porcelain for the table, fantasy objects as New Year's presents). In 1839 Boin is no longer listed in the *Almanach du Commerce*.

from 1839

Pierre-Isidore Lahoche (Beuvraignes 1805–Saint-Germain-en-Laye 1892) takes over the business, according to the 1840 *Almanach du Commerce*, as 'Lahoche, succ. de Boin', and in 1841 as 'Lahoche-Boin', at 152 & 153, Galerie de Valois and Palais-Royal. Unlike his predecessor, Boin, from 1844 Lahoche shows work at international exhibitions and is successful. His first awards are bronze medals he receives in Paris in 1849 and in London in 1851, re-establishing the original exclusive status of the business. About 1844 registered as 'Lahoche' at a different address (possibly only due to a change in the numbering of the building): 162–64, Galerie de Valois and Palais-Royal.

1852–1866

Trades under the name 'Société Lahoche et Pannier' owing to the marriage of Lahoche's daughter, Célina, to Emile Augustin Pannier (Paris 1828–Paris 1892), whose father, Augustin Benjamin Pannier (Paris 1800–Paris 1859), has been head of the faience wholesaler A. Pannier-Launay, rue Sainte-Marguerite, since 1829. In 1853 awarded a silver medal at the New York World's Fair and in 1855 another at the Paris Exposition Universelle as well as a bronze medal at the 1862 London International Exhibition. In 1866 Pierre-Isidore Lahoche retires.

from 1866

Trades under the name 'Pannier-Lahoche et Compagnie' after conversion into a public company on 1 Sept. 1866 by Emile Augustin Pannier and a former shop employee, Camille Joseph Gabriel Bourdier, living in Paris, at 11, rue Royer Collard, whose share amounted to 50,000 francs, a quarter of the total capitalization. The contract is valid for a twelve-year period, expiring on 1 Sept. 1878 (in it Pannier's first and second names are given as Augustin Emile). Pannier's application for permission to be an exhibitor at the 1867 Paris Exposition Universelle contains an abbreviated addition: 'Nt en porcelaine et cristaux', which stands for 'Notables

Commerçants du Département de la Seine en porcelaine et cristaux' (Reputable dealers, Seine Dépt., in porcelain and crystal glass), which means that he was in the rolls of important businesses in Paris and the Seine Département. In his application Pannier gives his trade as 'ornementiste' (not modern usage since 'ornemaniste' is now the term for 'decoration painter'), who commissioned numerous studios for porcelain and glass painting, engraving, bronze casting and mounting in vermeil (silver-gilt) at addresses in Paris listed without workshop names. In the German report on the 1867 Paris Exposition Universelle his 'much admired exhibits' are among 'the best France has to show' and 'the porcelain painting especially is among the finest in this genre'.

from 1872

The business moves to the corner house at 6, rue Scribe and 1, rue Auber, near the Opera (the old sale rooms from the ground floor to the third floor were given up in 1873). At the 1878 Paris Exposition Universelle shows Venetian luxury glass in the antique style and glass made by French crystal factories. From 1881 places regular orders with Baccarat. In the 1880s markets glass art by →Emile Gallé (1846–1904) and →Eugène Rousseau (1827–1890) et al.

1885–1923

The business is managed by sons Georges (Paris 1853–Paris 1944) and Charles Emile Henri Pannier (d. 1935 Paris), who is a designer. Trades under the name 'Société Pannier Frères & Cie.' after a limited partnership was established on 27 Nov. 1885. From 1891 the firm advertises luxury furnishings, designed by artists and made of sumptuous woods with bronze mounts and fittings, integrating oil paintings, etc., which are executed in collaboration with reputable workshops. They are launched at the Galerie Georges Petit in 1894. Shows bronzes, furniture, porcelain and glass at the 1900 Paris Exposition Universelle and is awarded a gold medal.

1923

The business is closed down.

Exhibitions

1819
Paris, Louvre, Ve Exposition des Produits de l'Industrie Française – gold medal (exh. rep.), participates again in 1823 (exh. rep.), 1844 and 1849 – bronze medal
1894
Paris, Galerie Georges Petit, Art Décoratif Moderne
1933
Paris, Pavillon de Marsan, Le Décor de la Vie sous la IIIe République de 1870 à 1900 (cat.)

Archival documents and literature

Birth and baptismal certificate of Philippe-Auguste Charpentier, Archives minicipales de Châlons en Champagne, GG 13 (Paroisse St. Alpin); marriage contract no. 250, Desarnaud and Charpentier, 20. messidor an 11, with addition on 10. messidor an 11, Archives départementales de Bordeaux 3E24479, no. 250; marriage certificate no. 259, Desarnaud and Charpentier, 23 messidor an 11, Archives municipales de Bordeaux 2E41, no. 259; *Almanach du Commerce*, 1805, p. 140; ibid., 1807, pp. 143, 170; ibid., 1808, pp. 145, 174; ibid., 1809, pp. 164, 195; ibid., 1810, pp. 173, 210; registration of death, Décès 1810, no. 96 Desarnaud, Archives de Paris DQ8 and 360; settlement of succession, Déclaration de succession Barthélémy Desarnaud 1 May 1811, no. 919, Archives de Paris DQ7 and 2204; *Almanach du Commerce*, 1811, pp. 188, 229; ibid., 1812, pp. 189, 223; ibid., 1813, p. 192; ibid., 1814, p. 172; registration of death, Décès 1815, no. 20, Charpentier Archives de Paris DQ8 and 402; settlement of succession, Déclaration de succession Philippe Auguste Charpentier 13 Dec. 1815, no. 1164, Archives de Paris DQ7 and 2997; *Almanach du Commerce*, 1816, p. 149; C. Malo, *Bazar Parisien ou choix raisonné des produits de l'industrie parisienne* (Paris, 1824), p. 144; *Almanach du Commerce*, 1827, p. 331; ibid., 1828, p. 346; ibid., 1829, pp. 124, 108; ibid., 1830, p. 81; ibid., 1836, p. 91; ibid., 1840, p. 103; ibid., 1841, pp. 221, 428; ibid., 1857, pp. 588, 804; contract concluded between Pannier and Bourdier of 1 Sept. 1866, Archives de Paris, D32U3, no. 258; application for permission to participate in the 1867 Paris Exposition Universelle, Demande d'admission, no. 434, Groupe 3, classe 17, Pannier-Lahoche, Archives Nationales F12 3041; W. Hamm, *Illustrirter Katalog der Pariser Industrie-Ausstellung von 1867* (Leipzig, 1868), p. 115, with illus.; Cadastre Galerie de Valois 162–64, Archives de Paris D1P4, 1862, no. 1170; Didron and Clémendot 1880, p. 43; Archives de la Cristallerie de Baccarat, *Livre de commandes* (1881), vol. 4, p. 226; Paris 1910, p. 7; Paris 1933, p. 184, nos. 1463–64; J. Jantzen, *Deutsches Glas aus fünf*

Jahrhunderten, issued by the Kunstmuseums der Stadt Düsseldorf (Düsseldorf, 1960), p. 59, no. 181, illus. no. 88; ■ F.-A. Dreier, 'Geschnittene Gläser von Charpentier: Ein Beitrag zum Pariser Glasschnitt des Empire', *Glastechnische Berichte* 34, no. 5 (1961): 282–85; Bloch-Dermant 1980, pp. 46–47, with illus.; Klesse, *Funke-Kaiser* I, 1981, p. 13, no. 102, illus. p. 176; Arwas 1987, p. 252; ■ Bascou and Thiébaut, Orsay, 1988, p. 230; → Paris, *Japonisme*, 1988, p. 324, cat. 382; ■ Thiébaut 1988; documentation Musée d'Orsay, Paris; W. Spiegl, *Pariser Glasschnitt im Empire: Die sogenannten Charpentier-Gläser*, rev. version of essay of 23 Feb. 2002, same title, in *Die Kunst* 5 (1987): 393–97; ■ F. Montes de Oca, *L'Age d'or du verre en France 1800–1830: Verreries de l'empire et de la restauration* (Paris, 2001), pp. 48, 58, 62–64, 172, 266–70, 426–44, 452–59, 464, 466, illus. pp. 269–70, 441, 452, 457–59.

→Gallé, Rousseau

Emile Charles Martin Gallé
called Emile Gallé

Nancy 4 May 1846–Nancy 23 Sept. 1904
Son of the porcelain painter Charles Louis Edouard Gallé, called Charles Gallé (Paris 3 Dec. 1818–Nancy 3 Dec. 1902) and wife, Fanny Reinemer (Nancy 24 Oct. 1825–Nancy 13 April 1891).

1846–1877

Charles Gallé works from 1846 in the glass and ceramics business run by his mother-in-law, Marguerite Reinemer (1801–1869), in Nancy (1, rue de la Faïencerie), which he takes over in 1854. From 1855 trades under the name 'Gallé-Reinemer'. From 1852 to 1872 success at eight international and two national exhibitions with awards. From 1854 purveyor to the court of Napoleon III, initially of engraved glass services. Collaborates with several firms to realize his naturalistic and historicist designs, including the porcelain factories in Sèvres, Limoges and Paris and the following glass factories: Choisy-le-Roy, St. Denis et Pantin, Baccarat and St. Louis. To facilitate long-term business collaboration – as with the →Burgun, Schverer & Co. glass factory in Meisenthal (1860/61–1894), with the St. Clément faience factory (1864–76) and with Adelphe Muller, faience manufacturer in Raon-l'Etape (c. 1873–98) – partner firms place studios and select employees at Gallé's disposal to work exclusively for Gallé-Reinemer. In 1866 Charles Gallé is appointed purveyor to the court. In 1866/67 establishes an engraving workshop of his own in Nancy with four engravers: Emile Lang père (b. 1842), Pierre Mercier père, Guy Anaïs (b. 1843) and Ferdinand Schmitzberger from Bohemia. In 1873 the Gallé family moved into the villa they have had built at 2, avenue de la Garenne, which houses a design and decoration studio as well as a ceramics storeroom. Ceramics occasionally executed by the freelance ceramist Jules-Dominique Thiéry in Nancy and Paul Décelles in Saint-Dié. In 1874 outlet in Nancy is given over to Charles Gallé's brother-in-law, Henri Dannreuther (1827–1881), a glass and porcelain merchant from Colmar, who, with his family, takes French citizenship following the Franco-Prussian War of 1870–71.

1857–1877

Emile Gallé's career: 1857–65 attends Lycée Impérial in Nancy, finishes with classes in rhetoric and philosophy. In 1864 first designs for faience. From autumn 1865 to Dec. 1866 studies in Weimar, including at private institutes, under Dr. Troebst (mineralogy, chemistry and botany) as well as Franz Jäde and Carl Stegmann (draughtsmanship and modelling); also travels in Germany and Bohemia. On his return to France he prepares for the 1867 Paris Exposition Universelle, where he first shows work, jointly with his father. From 1867 head designer of faience and glass in his father's firm, linked with brief stays for work in Meisenthal and St. Clément. Around 1867 begins to work with the glass painter →Désiré Christian, who is the same age as Gallé, at the Gallé-Reinemer studio for Burgun, Schverer & Co. In 1870 Emile Gallé volunteers for military service in the Franco-Prussian War but is not sent to the front. War leads to interruption in collaboration with Meisenthal. In 1871 Gallé represents his father in London for several months at the trade fair organized by Edmond du Sommerard, Curator at the Musée Cluny in Paris, 'Art de France'; while in London visits museums and studies botany at Kew Gardens. Afterwards studies in Paris, including stone-cutting at the Louvre and glass under Philippe-Joseph Brocard and →Eugène Rousseau. Until 1877 Emile Gallé's designs for faience with white tin glaze on conventional shapes include detailed depictions of plants, insects, fish and birds, often rendered in motion, as well as monograms, coats of arms or hunting scenes, also linked with landscape vignettes or banderoles with thematically apt quotations from proverbs, songs and poems. From the 1870s forms and decoration are Chinese and Japanese-inspired. His glass designs usually entail utilitarian forms of colourless or transparent coloured glass with engraved decoration or opaque enamel painting in red, white, turquoise, green and blue in combination with usually dark brown contours in flat colour: delicate floral decoration with insects, forget-me-nots, ribbons and bows in the Louis XVI style as well as pastoral genre scenes. From 1874 the painter and draughtsman →Louis Hestaux (1858–1919) is occasionally employed by Gallé, from 1876 on a regular basis, becoming head of the drawing studio in 1878. In 1875 Emile Gallé marries Henriette Grimm (Clesbourg 1848–Nancy 1914), a pastor's daughter from Bischviller, Alsace, with whom he has four daughters: Thérèse (1877–1966), Lucile (1879–1981), Claude (1884–1950) and Geneviève (1885–1966). From 1876 to 1879/80 collaboration with the Claire-Fontaine faience factory in Haute-Saône. In 1877 additional execution of faience forms by the Paris modellers Charles Rigollot and Henri Giraud. The Gallé-Reinemer workforce comprises approx. 20 glass painters and engravers.

1877–1904

Emile Gallé, head of the firm, from 1878 trades under his name; his father remains in management until 1898. At first continues to work with previous business partners, also with the Burgun, Schverer & Co. glass factory in Meisenthal, which since 1871 has been in the part of Lorraine annexed by Germany. Emile Gallé travels to Switzerland and northern Italy. First publication of writings on botany, later on his own work and on the state of arts and crafts. Co-founder and secretary-general of the Société Centrale d'Horticulture de Nancy, from 1891 vice-president. Develops a style of design in glass increasingly influenced by Chinese and Japanese art, initially in sophisticated enamel painting with precious metals and flat colours used to outline and for integrated grisaille or en camaïeu paintings; also engraving and cutting. Just as previously, designs and most engraving executed in Nancy, blanks and enamel painting in Meisenthal. At the 1878 Paris Exposition Universelle first official recognition of his glass and ceramic designs. Special mention for breaking new ground in enamel painting. Membership of the Société Nationale d'Horticulture de France and the Chambre de Commerce de l'Est. From 1879 to 1896 represented in Paris by Marcelin Daigueperce (1843–1896), 34, rue des Petites-Ecuries, from 1886: 10–12, rue Richer. First applications for patents on his own faience designs and signatures (E cross of Lorraine G). Lawsuits filed in 1879–80 against the Keller & Guérin faience factory in Lunéville and Claire-Fontaine in Haute-Saône for using Gallé's designs without his permission. In 1880 organization of and catalogue compilation for 'Géographie botanique', the first exhibition of its kind, in Nancy. Concludes a contract for work with A. Thomas & P. Bardenat, faience factory in Choisy-le-Roi. Trips to Belgium to study in the museums in Brussels and Antwerp. In 1881, 1882 and 1885 participation in the Exposition Partielle de la Société d'Horticulture de Nancy. In 1883 Gallé travels in Switzerland. In 1882 first glass with inclusions of coloured powdered glass or granules. Before 1884 incorporation of more colours used in stained glass, such as yellow silver stain and lustre as well as coloured overlay, transparent coloured glass in purple, smoky brown and forest green, sometimes with precious metal inclusions. Decoration in the oriental and Japanese style, some with picture reserves. First integrated martelé textures in polished engraving. In addition to modified Roman and medieval forms also angular and carinated vessels modelled on Chinese pieces and organic natural forms. In 1883/84 a friend, the painter Victor Prouvé (1858–1943), submits first designs for glass, followed by others for glass and furniture for the 1889 and 1900 Paris Expositions Universelles. In 1884 Emile Gallé is made an honorary member of the Société d'Horticulture de Genève and a member of the Commission de Surveillance (Invigilators Committee) de l'Ecole de Dessin de Nancy. Enormously successful at the 8th exhibition of the Union Central des Arts Décoratifs in Paris, 'Le Pierre, le Bois de Construction, la Terre et le Verre' (stone, wood in construction, terracotta and glass). Gradually enlarges the firm's premises.

1885

Begins to produce furniture and faience after his own designs in Nancy following the construction of a kiln and new workshops at 27, avenue de la Garenne, to which a second office for Gallé as well as design and finishing workshops for glass are added. Contracts concluded for collaboration with long-term business partners Adelphe Muller in Raon-l'Etape and Nicolas Mathieu Burgun (1825–1889), director of the Meisenthal glass factory Burgun, Schverer & Co., as well as Désiré Christian (1846–1907), who has headed his Meisenthal decoration studio for

many years. The contract regulating the execution of glass art in Meisenthal contains Christian's proviso in which he reserves to do as he chooses with his own technical and artistic innovations insofar as they are not needed by Gallé or Burgun. Emile Gallé becomes a member of the Société Botanique de France. Friendship with Tokuzō (also Hokkai) Takashima (1850–1931), who holds a bursary from the Japanese government to study forestry until 1888 at the Ecole Forestière in Nancy. In April Gallé spends two weeks in Berlin studying the extraordinary collection comprising approx. 350 pieces of antique and contemporary Chinese glass acquired by the Kunstgewerbemuseum through the mediation of the Imperial envoy in Peking, Max von Brandt. Gallé is made a Chevalier de la Légion d'Honneur, in 1889 Officier and in 1900 Commandeur de la Légion d'Honneur. Begins to work with Ismaël Soriot, who has previously worked as an engraver for Baccarat.

1886

In Limoges first participation in an exhibition with three crafts: ceramics, glass and furniture with intarsia inlay. Installation of a muffle kiln and establishment of an experimental laboratory in Nancy. After a two-year break, first business trip to Meisenthal, followed by four others by April 1888.

1886–1894

Technical and artistic innovations in furniture, faience and glass, including the integration of sculptural elements in furniture design and the development of a harder white faience paste as a suitable body for polychrome painting under transparent coloured glazes. Further development of elaborate decoration methods, such as émaux-bijoux (jewelling) – enamel painting on bright gold – and émaux champlevés – ground grooves filled with enamelling. Began to use pre-etched or partly etched glass editions with floral decoration, at first still combined with elaborate enamel, gold, silver-stain and lustre painting. New coloured glass in amber yellow, opaque jade and simulated agate as well as black casing. New expressive possibilities are created by combining engraving and cutting techniques to form sculptural relief work on walls with Impressionist surface texturing. Figurative representation is still carried out in classical copper-wheel engraving but only occasionally after 1889. In 1887 Gallé shows work at the Exposition Générale d'Horticulture de Nancy; appointed secretary and treasurer of the Comité Départemental de l'Exposition Universelle de 1889. In 1888 appointed representative correspondent of the Chambre Syndicale de la Céramique et de la Verrerie. Emile Gallé's glass art, furniture and ceramics are enormously successful at the 1889 Paris Exposition Universelle. Gallé's new, versatile way with glass design is both technically and aesthetically innovative. Especially acclaimed are his Symbolist works with literary quotations, called verreries parlantes. Meets the poet Count Robert de Montesquiou, through whom he makes numerous contacts with such celebrities as the actress Sarah Bernhardt and the novelist Marcel Proust and other distinguished contemporaries, including Countess Elisabeth de Greffulhe and Princess Marthe de Bibesco. Works on editing the bulletin of the Société Nationale d'Horticulture de Nancy. In 1890 made an honorary member of the committee for the botanical exhibition in Brussels. In 1891 his mother dies. Gallé shows 'objets d'art' at the first Salon de la Société Nationale des Beaux-Arts in Paris exhibition, from 1892 a member, from 1893 on the jury for 'objets d'art'. Member of the Académie de Stanislas in Nancy. In 1892 visits the Wagner Festival in Bayreuth, Germany, which inspires him to design a Grail chalice, exhibited at the 1894 Paris Salon. Designs the 'Vase Pasteur', commissioned by the Ecole Normale Supérieur on the occasion of Louis Pasteur's 70th birthday It is presented to the chemist in April 1893. In 1893 enlarges furniture workshops to include a sales room. On the occasion of the visit by the Russian fleet to Paris the Lorraine delegation presents the Tsar with, among other things, a Gallé table, 'Gardez les cœurs qu'avez gagnés'.

from 1894

His own glassworks (27, ave. de la Garenne). Glassworks foreman Joseph Rémy Burgun (1843–1921) and the glass painter Alfred Jean-Marie Schaeffer (1869–1918) are the sole employees of the Meisenthal studio to continue working in Nancy in the early years when the business is being built up. Applies for registered trademarks for products made in Nancy. Founding member of the Société des Arts Décoratifs Lorrains de Nancy. Streamlines serially produced objects by using etched overlay relief decoration over entire surfaces and by gradually limiting painting techniques to enamelling and gilding. Until 1896 red coloured glass predominant, often in opaque reddish-brown striking colours. Continues to make special one-off pieces developed on the basis of cost-intensive technical experimentation. In 1896 death of Paris business partner of many years, Marcelin

Daigueperce, whose son, Albert (1873–1956), succeeds to the business, remaining the Gallé representative. Two Gallé vases, with mounts by Lucien Falize, are the official gift of the city of Paris to Tsar Nicholas II and his wife. In 1897 Gallé becomes a member of the juries at the Ghent Exposition Quinquennale d'Agriculture et d'Horticulture and the Exposition de la Société Nationale d'Horticulture de France and joins the Comité à l'Union Centrale des Arts Décoratifs and the Comité à l'Ecole Guérin in Paris. Opens an outlet in Frankfurt am Main, at 38 Kaiserstrasse. Participates in the inaugural exhibition of the Kaiser Wilhelm-Museum, Krefeld. The French Minister of Trade and Industry, Henri Boucher, visits Gallé's factory. In 1898 Gallé becomes treasurer and a founding member of the Nancy Chapter of the Human Rights League. Committed to the cause of Alfred Dreyfus, the Jewish officer who is unjustly charged with treason. Auguste Herbst (b. 1878) begins to work as a draughtsman. The Raon-l'Etape faience factory closes down. Employees of the Nancy ceramics studio, which closed in 1901: Emile Munier (b. 1866), Emile Villermaux (b. 1874) and Auguste Martin (b. 1858). On 26 April 1898 Gallé applies for a patent on the techniques of marquetry and patinage. In 1899 founding member of the Nancy Adult Education College.
1900
Becomes a member of the St Petersburg Exhibition Committee. Gives lecture entitled 'Le Décor symbolique' on acceptance by the Académie de Stanislas. Declines the position of vice-presidency of the jury for the Paris Exposition Universelle because he wishes to take part in it. Again receives highest award there, a Grand Prix for glass and furniture as well as distinctions for several employees. Participates in the special presentation 'Histoire de Verre Français' with reissues of earlier designs. Marquetry decoration and applications that modify vessel forms are now dominant in Gallé's glass. His firm employs a workforce of approx. 150, including approx. 70 furniture-makers and metalworkers. The draughtsmen in the decoration studio supervised by Louis Hestaux include: 1895–1919 Paul Nicolas (1875–1952), 1898–1931 Auguste Herbst (b. 1878); Rose Wild (d. 1904), Philippe Partagé (b. 1848), Frédéric Deshayes (b. 1883), Jacques Pfoh (b. 1873), Raymond Koenig, Daniel Schoen (b. 1873) and the furniture designer Henri Hazard (b. 1872). Modellers and form turners supervised by Paul Holderbach (b. 1867): Hans or Jean Cordier (b. 1845), Michel Antoine (b. 1878), Eugène Chamaut (b. 1878), Alia Hardy, née Jacquet, Hippolyte Pertusot, Ernest Vigneron, (b. 1881) and Alphonse Weisse (b. 1874). Foreman of the glassworks from 1898: Julien Roiseux (b. 1857); head gaffer of 12 glass-blowers, including Philippe Meyer (b. 1861) and Georges Raspiller. Technicians for making coloured glass batches: Julien Gillet (b. 1872) and Nicolas Meyer. Most important engravers: L. or E. Diebold (b. 1873), Emile Lang père (b. 1842), Pierre Mercier (b. 1877), Ferdinand Schmitzberger (b. 1847), Ismaël Soriot (b. 1856) and Eugène Windeck (b. 1874). Cutters and grinders: Victor Bourst (b. 1871), Nicolas Gross (b. 1871). Head enameller: Emile Munier (b. 1866), formerly painter of decoration on faience. Employees in furniture-making who receive awards at the Paris Exposition Universelle, such as intarsia layers and carvers: Jules Beix (1854–1901), Edouard Dignon (b. 1861), Hippolyte Dubois (b. 1872), Emile Guy, Abel Pierrat (b. 1876) and carpenters and joiners Jacques Bour (b. 1848), Auguste Dumini or Dermigny (b. 1849), Chrétien Karcher (b. 1863), G. Mansuy and Adolphe Wendler (b. 1862).
1901–1904
Further development of vessel form into sculpture in the round, which is largely formed at the kiln and worked over with engraving similar to cutting. Emile Gallé becomes founding president of the Alliance Provinciale des Industries d'Art, also called the Ecole de Nancy, an association of Lorraine craftsmen committed to the 'genre Gallé', with Antonin Daum as vice-president. Gallé outlets in London: 13, South Molton Street, Bond Street. Symptoms of Emile Gallé's terminal illness (leukaemia) worsens, spa cures at Plombières and Bussang, again in 1902. Louis de Fourcaud (1853–1914), professor of aesthetics and art history at the Ecole Nationale des Beaux-Arts in Paris visits Gallé in preparation of his biography of the glass artist. In 1902 Gallé's father dies. In 1903 made honorary vice-president of the Société Centrale d'Horticulture de Nancy. Last designs for the Ecole de Nancy exhibition in Paris. Fire breaks out in the factory, gutting the decoration studio and the showrooms. In 1904 destroyed rooms are rebuilt. Spa cures in Luxembourg and Baden-Baden. Glass bought by the city of Nancy. Emile Gallé dies on 23 Sept. 1904.
1904–1914
Emile Gallé's widow, Henriette Gallé-Grimm, manages the Gallé factories Cristallerie & Ebénisterie d'Art, from 1906 jointly with her son-in-law, Professor Paul Perdrizet (1870–1938), an archaeologist and art historian; artistic director until

1919: Louis Hestaux; managing director until 1936: Emile Lang, Jr. Production of the cost and time-intensive glass introduced by Emile Gallé is discontinued. Glass production is restricted to the serial production of etched cased glass with plant and landscape decoration. Continuation of furniture-making. From 1904 to 1913 property is bought to enlarge factory premises, remodelling of buildings and modernizing of workshops. In 1908 Henriette Gallé-Grimm and Paul Perdrizet publish Ecrits, Emile Gallé's writings on botany and art. The firm now employs a workforce of 176, including 22 women and 28 children. Henriette Gallé-Grimm dies on 22 April 1914. The factory is taken over by her daughters Thérèse Gallé-Bourgogne, Lucile Gallé-Perdrizet and Geneviève Gallé-Chevalier, with Claude Gallé as managing director.
1914–1936
Director: Professor Paul Perdrizet, although appointed to a chair at Strasbourg University in 1919. From 1914 to 1918 production ceases in Nancy on account of the war. Limited production by a few employees at Pantin and in 1917/18 at the Schneider factory in Epinay-sur-Seine (information imparted in conversations conducted with Ernest Schneider, Jr., and Gérard Bertrand).
from 1918
Trades under the name 'Etablissements Gallé'. Louis Hestaux dies and is succeeded by Auguste Herbst in 1919 as artistic director. New buildings, some of them for etching. Colour scheme limited in products made after the war. Glass usually colourless with one or two casings in contrasting colours. Decoration almost silhouette-like, flattened and more smoothly etched than before 1914. The few new developments include vases with white crazed casing and, in 1925, floral overlay glass, mould-blown with compressed air into metal moulds and worked over with etching. In 1924 and 1925 last enlargements of premises.
1925–1936
Trades under the name 'Société Anonyme des Etablissements Gallé' after conversion into a joint-stock company. Principal shareholders are the heirs, Claude Gallé and her married sisters, who transfer their functions that year to their husbands: Professor Paul Perdrizet, Professor Lucien Bourgogne and Robert Chevalier. In 1926 sales rooms remodelled. In 1928 the director, Professor Paul Perdrizet, changes his name to Perdrizet-Gallé. In 1930 member of the Chambre Syndicale de la Céramique et de la Verrerie in Paris. Wares sold in Nancy by Cristaux d'Art, rue du Pont cassé, in Paris by Mohrenwitz, 12, rue Richer. In 1931 furnaces are extinguished owing to the worldwide economic crisis, yet available stocks of blanks continue to be finished and decorated. In 1934 the business in Nancy closes down. On 27 Aug. 1936 stock, plant and moulds, etc., are sold at auction. Towards end of the year the firm buildings and premises also sold.

Exhibitions
Charles Gallé, from 1855 on Charles Gallé-Reinemer:
1852
Luxembourg, Exposition de Luxembourg – silver medal
1861
Metz, Exposition Universelle de Metz – silver medal
1865
Bordeaux, Exposition de Bordeaux – silver medal for ceramics
Chaumont, Exposition de Chaumont – honorary diploma
1868
Nancy, Société des amis des arts de Nancy

Emile Gallé and Charles Gallé-Reinemer:
1871
London, International Exhibition, 'Art de France' section – bronze medal
1872
Lyons, Exposition Universelle et Internationale de Lyon – gold medal for ceramics and glass

Emile Gallé (not including botanical exhibitions):
1879
Paris, Musée des Arts Décoratifs, Exposition d'Art Contemporain
1880
Nice, Exposition de Nice
1886
Limoges, Hôtel de Ville, Exposition des Sciences et Arts Appliqués à l'Industrie (exh. cat.) – 1st participation, with furniture

1891
Moscow, Industrial Exhibition, 'Art de France' section
1894
Nantes, Exposition d'Art Décoratif (organized by the Société des Amis des Arts de Nantes)
1895
Paris, S. Bing, L'Art Nouveau, group show again in 1896
1896
Mülhausen, Ausstellung des Kunstvereins
Toulouse, Exposition d'Art Décoratif Moderne (organized by La Dépêche de Toulouse)
1897
Breslau, Museum, Glass Exhibition
Krefeld, Kaiser Wilhelm-Museum, 1897 art exhibition (exh. cat.), again in 1898
Paris, Le Cent Epreuves (organized by Le Figaro)
Stockholm, Konst och industriutställningen (Art and Industry Exhibition)
1898
Darmstadt, Kunsthalle, First Exhibition by the Freie Vereinigung Darmstädter Künstler (exh. rep.)
Göttingen, 3rd Kunstverein Exhibition
Karlsruhe, Kunstgewerbe-Ausstellung (Arts and Crafts Exhibition)
Munich, Littauer's Kunstsalon, Glass and Ceramics Exhibition
1900
Bordeaux, IIe Exposition de la Société d'Art Moderne
1901
Paris, Salon de La Plume
Paris, Musée Galliera, Exposition d'Art Appliqué
1902
Mülhausen, Musée des Beaux-Arts, Exposition de la Société Industrielle
1904
Reichenberg (Liberec), Lamp Competition – gold medal
1906
Krefeld, Kaiser Wilhelm-Museum (solo exh.) Erstlingsarbeiten (Early Work)
1923
Paris, Musée Galliera, Exposition de la Verrerie et de l'Emaillerie Modernes (exh. rep.)
1925
Paris, Exposition Internationale des Arts Décoratifs et Industriels Modernes (exh. cat.) – participation in Pavillon de Nancy without mention of firm
1933
Paris, Pavillon de Marsan, Le Décor de la Vie sous la IIIe République de 1870 à 1900 (exh. cat.)

Writings by Emile Gallé:

Ecrits pour l'art, floriculture, art décoratif, notices d'exposition (1884–1889) (Paris, 1908). A total of 58 titles on the following subjects: botany, glass, ceramics and furniture, the state of contemporary arts and crafts, in Hakenjos 1982, pp. 861–69.

Literature

Supplementing Zurich 1995: Paul Arène, 'Huitième Exposition de L'Union Centrale: Pierre, bois de construction, terre et verre – La Céramique', *Revue des Arts Décoratifs* 5 (1884–85): 176–77; Edmond Bazire, 'La Verrerie et la cristallerie', ibid.: 193–94; L. de Fourcaud, 'Rapport général', ibid.: 260–61, illus. p. 260a; Garnier 1886, pp. 344–45, illus. pp. 345–46; Limoges 1886, *Exposition des Sciences et Arts appliqués à l'industrie*, exh. cat., collectively compiled, sect. 3, Louis Bourdey, p. 54, nos. 404–20, pp. 104–5, nos. 1033–38, no. 1037, p. 108, nos. 1045–48; L. de Fourcaud, 'Les Arts Décoratifs au Salon 1892: Champs-Elysées et Champ-de-Mars', exh. rev., *Art Décoratif* 13 (1892–93): 7–10; L. E. Day, 'Une Exposition française d'art décoratif jugée par un anglais', *Revue des Arts Décoratifs* 14 (1893–94): 222; André 1894, pp. 10, 12; Paris 1903, p. 10, illus. n.p.; Paris, portfolio, 1903, vol. nos. 1–15, 82–86, illus. pls. 1–15, vol. 2, illus. pls. 3–6; Strasbourg 1908, p. 17, nos. 79–95; Emile Nicolas, 'L'Ecole de Nancy à Strasbourg', *Bulletin des Sociétés artistiques de l'Est* (March 1908): 32; Commandant Lalance, 'L'Ecole de Nancy à Strasbourg', ibid. (May 1908): 63, 64; Paris 1910, p. 19; Jean 1911, pp. 298–301, illus. pp. 299–300; Octave Maus 1926, p. 203; F.-T. Charpentier and P. Husson, *La Céramique de Gallé conservée au musée*, coll. cat., Musée de l'Ecole de Nancy (Nancy, 1984); Paris, *Gallé*, 1985; Charpentier et al. 1987, pp. 5–10, 15–16, 18, 21–22, 26–28, 31, 41, 43–44, 46,

49, 51–53, 55, 59, 63–65, 67–68, 70–101, 103–4, 106, 109–10, 112–13, 118–29, 131–33, 135, 137–39, 150–51, 153–54, 159–62, 165, 167–68, 170, 173–74, 176, 180, 183–85, 187–88, 194–96, 202, 204, 208, 219, 222, 228–29, 234, 242, 248, 250, 252–55, 258, 260, 262–66, 269, 275, 279, 282, 289–94, 296, 298–303, 308–11; Aptel et al. 1989, pp. 14, 19, 21, 22, 23, 25–30, 33, 34, 36, 38, 41–42, 44–46, 48, 50, 52–53, 56, 59, 62, 65–66, 69–70, 72–74, 76, 78, 81, 83, 86–87, 110, 112, 132–33, 155, 157, 159–60, 163–66, 168, 170, 172, 175, 178, 182, 184, 187–88, 192, 194–98, 206, 208, 215–16, 221, 230, 234, 241, 245–46, 263, 273; Debize 1989, pp. 9–16, 18–21, 23, 25–29, 33–34, 36, 39–41, 43–45, 51–53, 55–57, 64, 66, 68–74, 76–77, 80, 82, 85–86, 88, 90–91, 93–96, 98, 100, 102–6, 112, 114, 142, 150, 152, illus. pp. 7, 8, 11, 13, 14, 17, 22, 24, 28, 60, 61, 65, 67, 72, 74, 87, 105; ■ Thiébaut, *Dessins*, 1993; ■ F.-T. Charpentier, 'Gallé après Gallé', *Arts Nouveaux, Bulletin de l'Association du Musée de l'Ecole de Nancy*, no. 10 (spring 1994): 18–24, title illus., pp. 18–22, 24; ■ Le Tacon 1995; Duncan, *Salons*, 1998, pp. 32–35, 39, 43, 460, illus. pp. 8, 34–35, 39–40, 42, 200–37; ■ Le Tacon 1998; Darmstadt 1999, pp. 267–72, 284–91, 302–10, 360, illus. pp. 277, 281, 288–89, 303, 305–6, 308, 310, cat. nos. 282–90, 300–347, with illus.; ■ Le Tacon and De Luca 1999; ■ Meisenthal 1999, pp. 15–31, cat. nos. 1–42; ■ Nancy 1999, pp. 67–85, 91–92, 95–101, 121, 122, 135–49, 151–67, 169–83, 203–5, 215–16, 271, 277–78, cat. nos. 78–186, illus. pp. 40, 46, 50–51, 54, 63, 66, 86, 89, 94, 102, 104, 109, 112–13, 124, 141, 150, 152–54, 158, 161, 163, 165, 168, 184–85, 202, 213, 216, 219, 223–25, 264, 270, 276, 279; ■ Nancy, *Fleurs*, 1999, pp. 13, 19–20, 31–32, 35–36, 39–45, cat. nos. 2–17, 25–27, 32–38, 63–67, 69–80, 82–83, 103, 105–14, 117–23, 127, 131, 133–35, illus. pp. 18–19, 24, 34, 37–44, 54–62, 66–67, 70–71, 66–107, 112–15, 120–21; Le Tacon, *Solvay Gallé*, 2000; ■ Sapporo 2000; F. Le Tacon, 'Les Sciences végétales en Lorraine au dix-neuvième siècle', *Sciences et techniques en Lorraine à l'époque de l'Ecole de Nancy: Actes des conférences données du 4 mars au 8 avril 1999 à la MJC Pichon de Nancy* (Nancy, 2001), pp. 185–88; F. Le Tacon, 'Emile Gallé: botaniste et scientifique', ibid., pp. 207–24; Nancy 2001, pp. 8, 18, 32–41, 56–81, 92–95, 98–103, with illus.; V. Thomas, R. Bouvier, B. Lauwick and J. Perrin, *Emile Gallé et Victor Prouvé: Une Alliance pour le mobilier*, exh. cat., Musée de l'Ecole de Nancy (Nancy, 2002).
→Hestaux

Jacques Gruber

Sundhausen, Alsace 25 Feb. 1870–Paris 1936
Son of Emile Gruber and wife, Madeleine, née Mathis.

1877
Mother and son move to Nancy; father lives separately from them, also abroad in the United States and Germany. In 1902 the parents live in Berne, Switzerland.
1885–1890
Studies painting at the Ecole des Beaux-Arts in Nancy; pupil of Jules François Marie Joseph Larcher, called Jules Larcher (1849–1920), and Louis Théodore Devilly (1818–1886), school director from 1871 and formerly cartoon draughtsman for the reputable firm of C.-L. Maréchal (est. 1839), glass painters and makers of leaded windows, in Metz.
1889–1893
Holder of a bursary from the city of Nancy to study at the Ecole des Arts Décoratifs and the Ecole des Beaux-Arts in Paris; pupil of Elie Delaunay (1828–1891), his successor, Gustave Moreau (1826–1898), and the glass painter Pierre Victor Galland (1822–1892). His friends includes the painter Simon Bussy and the architect Paul Charbonnier. In 1893 medal for painting at the competition for decorative composition for the three divisions of the Ecole des Beaux-Arts.
c. 1891–1893
National service in Nancy, for some of the term of service is with his cousin, Ferdinand Baldensperger, professor of literature; commissioned by the commanding officer of his regiment to design and execute murals for the regimental mess. In 1893 first designs for →Daum Frères for the Chicago World's Columbian Exposition.
Dec. 1893–1914
Teaches decorative composition and style as Jules Larcher's successor where he had trained, the Ecole des Beaux-Arts in Nancy. Gruber's most important pupils include Jean Lurçat (1892–1966), Alfred Levy and Paul Colin (b. 1892). Also freelances as an artist for Daum Frères and Louis Majorelle (1859–1926), contributing substantially to their early success. Until 1895 Gruber was the sole designer for Daum Frères, but afterwards and until c. 1897/98 shares this work as well as giving drawing lessons to employees with →Henri Bergé (1870–1937), who, how-

ever, does most of the teaching. From 1894 Gruber is a member of the Société Lorraine des Amis des Arts in Nancy and often shows paintings, pastels and work in the decorative and applied arts in several different media at their exhibitions. Gruber also designs book covers for René Wiener. In 1895 he is made treasurer of the Association Amicale Lorraine des Anciens Elèves de l'Ecole Nationale et Spéciale des Beaux-Arts. Sells a work in pastels at the exhibition in Remiremont.

from 1897

Designs etched overlay plates of glass for furniture and from 1898 stained-glass windows. In 1898 designed his first table lamp, 'Eglantine' (wild rose), for Antonin Daum's wedding and this leads to the launching of a new product line at →Daum, in collaboration with Majorelle (who makes the wrought-iron lamp feet). Gruber's address in Nancy: 29, rue Eugène Ferry; from 1900: 5, rue des Jardiniers. He also designs textiles (executed by Charles Fridrich, Nancy), ceramics (executed by Alphonse Cythère, Société des Produits Céramiques de Rambervillers), sculpture (executed by Justin Ferez, Nancy), book covers, carpets and wooden frames. In 1901 founding member of the Alliance Provinciale des Industries d'Art, known as the Ecole de Nancy. Designs glass panes for furniture by Eugène Vallin (1856–1922) in Nancy. On 9 May 1902 marries the painter Suzanne Elisa Jeanne Jagielski (b. 1874), with whom he has two sons, Jean-Jacques and Francis (1912–1948). Antonin Daum and Jules Larcher (his former teacher) are witnesses at the wedding ceremony. Gruber's wife has also exhibited for years at the exhibitions mounted by the Société Lorraine de Amis des Arts in Nancy, showing her pastels as Suzanne Jagielska (the marriage certificate does not indicate her profession).

Gruber is given architecturally related commissions: windows, executed by Charles Gauvillé in Malzéville: in 1901–2 the ceiling windows of the Crédit Lyonnais in Nancy; in 1902 the dining-room of the Villa Majorelle in Nancy.

1904–16

Flat glass studio in Nancy: 4 & 6, rue de la Salle; works as an artist with his wife. His employees: Jules Cayette (1882–1953) for sculpture and modelling; Violat for painting decoration; Grandemange, Koenig, Nachin and Poubel for working on flat glass; and Neiss for cabinetmaking. In 1910 Gruber shows six windows and a wooden stove screen with glass set in copper cames at the exhibition mounted by the Musée Galliera.

Architecturally related commissions for windows as well as numerous private commissions, including the following: 1907, Euville near Commercy, the Town Hall, and Nancy, Magasins Réunis – both in collaboration with Maréchal-Champigneulle, makers of flat glass in Bar-le-Duc; 1909, Nancy, Chambre de Commerce; 1910, Nancy, Restaurant Excelsior; 1911, Nancy, the house of the architect Paul Charbonnier.

from 1916

Flat glass studio in Paris; address: 10, villa d'Alésia, IIIter, rue d'Alésia (14e arrondissement). From 1920 new departure in design: stylized and later geometric floral and figurative decoration; windows after 1925 mainly with sacral motifs for churches, exotic landscapes and scenes as well as motifs with the theme of work, technology and industry. In 1928 collaborates with the architect Michel Roux-Spitz. In 1929 lighting for the luxury liner *Ile-de-France*. After 1930 his two sons, Jean-Jacques and Francis, work for him, conceiving designs as well.

Important architecturally related commissions for windows, from 1922 mainly for churches, including: 1916–18, Louis Corbin's Château d'Ecrennes, Brie; 1922, Paris, Saint-Christophe-de-Javel; 1925, Paris, windows for several pavilions at the Exposition Internationale des Arts Décoratifs et Industriels Modernes; 1926–28, Bar-le-Duc, post office; 1928, Nancy, Fonderies de Pont-à-Mousson, and Nancy, Caisse d'Epargne (Savings Bank); 1933, Verdun, Cathedral.

Exhibitions

1895

Paris, Champs-Elysées, Salon de la Société des Artistes Français

1896

Gérardmer, Exposition de Gérardmer

1911

Paris, Grand Palais, Salon de la Société des Artistes Français – gold medal

1919

Paris, Grand Palais, Salon des Artistes Décorateurs, again in 1920–27, 1929, 1930, 1932 and 1933

1920

Nancy, Salle Poirel, Société Lorraine des Amis des Arts Ie Exposition (exh. cat.), again in 1922, 1924 and 1928

1921

Luxembourg, Exposition Lorraine-Luxembourgoise d'Arts Appliqués, de Peinture et de Sculpture

1922

Paris, Salon d'Automne, again in 1924, 1930, 1932 and 1933

1923

Paris, Musée Galliera, Exposition de la Verrerie et de l'Emaillerie Modernes

1925

Paris, Exposition Internationale des Arts Décoratifs et Industriels Modernes (exh. cat.) (exh. rep.) – hors-concours, president of Class 6

1927

Madrid, International Exhibition

1929

Barcelona, Palacio de Artes Industriales y Decorativas, Exposición Internacional de Barcelona

Paris, Musée Galliera, L'Art Religieux

1929–30

New York, Metropolitan Museum of Art, International Exhibition – Contemporary Glass and Rugs, touring exhibition: Boston, MA, Museum of Fine Arts; Philadelphia, PA, The Pennsylvania Museum; Chicago, IL, The Art Institute of Chicago; Pittsburgh, PA, Carnegie Institute; Dayton, OH, Dayton Art Institute; Cincinnati, OH, Cincinnati Museum Association; Baltimore, MD, The Baltimore Museum of Art (exh. cat.)

1933

Paris, Salon des Industries d'Art: Lorraine à Paris

1936

Paris, Salon du Vitrail

Archival documents and literature

André 1894, pp. 11, 12; Nancy 1894, p. 109, nos. 636–44; Nancy, *Art Décoratif* (1894): 32, nos. 189–213, p. 49, no. 351; Association Amicale Lorraine des Anciens Elèves de l'Ecole Nationale et Spéciale des Beaux-Arts, *Bulletin des Sociétés artistiques de l'Est* (Jan. 1895): 11; 'Expostion de Remiremont', ibid. (Sept.): 111; ibid. (Oct.): suppl.; ibid. (Nov.): 139; Nancy 1895, p. 66, nos. 162–63, p. 103, nos. 567–68, p. 120, no. 722; Nancy 1897, p. 77, no. 151, p. 115, no. 521, p. 133, nos. 667–69; Nancy 1898, p. 120, nos. 527–28, p. 142, nos. 515–718; S. Sontag, 'L'Art décoratif nouveau en Lorraine: II Les vitraux gravés', *Bulletin des Sociétés artistiques de l'Est* (April 1898): 58–61, with illus.; Nancy 1899, p. 78, no. 143, p. 110, nos. 447–51; Nancy 1901, p. 122, nos. 551–58, p. 148, nos. 808–11; marriage certificate Gruber and Jagielski, 9 May 1902, Mairie de la Ville de Nancy, 1902, no. 327; Nancy 1902, p. 127, nos. 552–54, p. 150, nos. 748–49, 794; ■ Emil Nicolas, 'Les Vitraux de M. J. Gruber', *Lorraine Artiste* (1903): 232–33; Nancy 1904, p. 43, nos. 143–52; Nancy 1905, p. 149, nos. 701, 703; Nancy 1906, p. 86, nos. 114–20, p. 142, nos. 665–68; Nancy 1907, p. 87, nos. 107–8, p. 111, nos. 334–35, p. 127, nos. 492–96; Nancy 1908, p. 136, no. 515; Emile Nicolas, 'L'Ecole de Nancy à Strasbourg', *Bulletin de la Société artistique de l'Est* (March 1908): 32; Commandant Lalance, 'L'Ecole de Nancy à Strasbourg', ibid. (May 1908): 64; Strasbourg 1908, pp. 20–21, nos. 98–119; Nancy 1909, p. 136, no. 515; Nancy 1910, p. 121, no. 463; Paris 1910, pp. 19–20; Nancy 1911, p. 36, nos. 237–40, p. 44, no. 388; ■ René D'Avril, 'Les Vitraux de Jacques Gruber', *Revue Lorraine illustré* (1912): 41–48, with illus.; Nancy 1912, p. 62, nos. 454–55; Nancy 1920, p. 57; Paris 1925, pp. 29, 62, 66, 78, 79, 86, 96, 101, 127, 139, 161, 200, 201, 219, 232, 238, 766; New York 1929, *International Exhibition: Contemporary Glass and Rugs*, exh. cat., Metropolitan Museum of Art, compiled by Charles R. Richards (New York, 1929), no. 106, with illus.; Hogrel 1930, pp. 368, 383, 391; ■ J.-L. Vallières, 'Jacques Gruber: Le Régénératuer du vitrail', *La Vie en Alsace* (1936): 6–12, with illus.; Hans Hofstätter, *Gustave Moreau* (Cologne, 1978), pp. 185, 188, 193, 194; Munich, *Nancy 1900*, 1980, p. 326, nos. 355–57; ■ Brussels, *Gruber*, 1983; ■ Charpentier et al. 1987; Brunhammer and Tise 1990, p. 275; Bouvier, *Majorelle*, 1991, pp. 46, 102–3, 109, 111, 136, 156, illus. pp. 103, 110, 112, 117, 135, 156, 188, 197; Duncan 1991, pp. 11, 28, 52, 119–20, 124, 156, illus. p. 116, pls. 6–7; Vollmer 1992, vol. 2, p. 322, vol. 3, p. 274; Epinal 1997, cat. nos. 11, 22, 23, 26, 27, 68, 72, 172, 174, 176, pp. 112–13, 130–33, 135, 139, 144, 161–65; Darmstadt 1999, pp. 9, 268, 270, 273, 275–76, 291, 305–6, 362, illus. pp. 268, 282, 299, 306, 335; ■ Nancy 1999, pp. 138, 257, cat. nos. 192–204, illus. pp. 111, 226, 263, 278; Nancy 2001, pp. 82–83, 104–5, 107, with illus.; Bardin 2002, vol. 1, pp. 25, 61, 72, 78, 80–81, 86–92, 104–5, 123–24, 133, 137, 145–46, 148, 150, 154–55, 170, 213, 229, vol. 2, pp. 322, 337, 339–44, 347, 353, 405, 440, 448, 504, illus. pp. 87, 146, 368–69.
→Daum Frères

Harant & Guignard
Maisons Toy & Le Rosey
Paris

11 May 1888
Harant & Guignard is founded as a commercial enterprise to take over 'Toy', a shop at 6, rue Halévy (9e arrondissement), by the specialist dealer in English porcelain, Louis Pierre Henry Harant (1854–1925), called Louis Harant, and an employee, François Louis Georges Guignard, who is married to Henriette Louise Rose Harant, Louis Harant's sister. Registered in the *Almanach du Commerce* from 1836, 'Toy' specializes in English china and especially Minton since 1841 but even before the takeover it was also selling faience and crystal glass services.

c. 1892
Entered in the list of important firms, 'Notables Commerçants du Département de la Seine', in Paris and the Seine Déptartement. Special models are made to order for one of the services it produces.

from 1897
Louis Harant is president, from 1905 honorary president, of the Chambre Syndicale de la Céramique et de la Verrerie. Participates in the Salon du Champ-de-Mars in Paris, in 1898 together with the engraver →Eugène Michel. In 1897 and 1900 Harant & Guignard, described as decorators, are hors-concours at the Brussels and Paris Expositions Universelles; Harant is on the jury. The 1900 Exposition report made special mention of the sets of cut and engraved glasses after the firm's own designs as 'indubitably charming and in the best of taste' (d'un charme indiscutable et du goût le plus sûr). In 1900 Harant is made a Chevalier de la Légion d'Honneur and in 1901 he joins the committee for the St Petersburg International Glass and Ceramics Exhibition.

c. 1900
Takes over 'Le Rosey', at 11, rue de la Paix (2e arrondissement), a business with a proprietary decorating studio for finishing upmarket porcelain services. In 1901 'Le Rosey / Harant & Guignard successeurs, XI, rue de la Paix' applies for protection of its 'Service Muguet' under no. 11166 of 7 Aug. 1901, with matt engraved lily of the valley decoration arranged like a bouquet, with the stems growing up out of the floor and the floral design developed on the bowls of the pieces. Shows elegant china and glassware at the St Petersburg exhibition.

27 March 1903
Takes over the business owned by →Ernest Baptiste Léveillé (1841–1913), including all designs by Léveillé and →Eugène Rousseau. Subsequently trades for a time under the name 'Maisons Toy et Léveillé réunies', also singly as 'Léveillé' and 'Toy'; address: 10, rue de la Paix.

1903–1910
Harant & Guignard runs two businesses, 'Toy', at 10, rue de la Paix, and 'Le Rosey', at 11, rue de la Paix (2e arrondissement). Until the First World War, 'Toy' sells both original Léveillé and Rousseau models and variations on them. The celebrated faience 'Rousseau' service of 1866/67 with etchings by Félix Bracquemond (1833–1914) after Japanese coloured woodcuts by Katsushika Hokusai (1760–1849) and Hiroshige (1797–1858) is made until 1938.

In 1905 again hors-concours at the Liège Exposition, where they show sets of glasses and fantasy articles in crystal glass and coloured or flashed and cased glass, engraved or painted after their own designs. In 1910 shows a large collection of Léveillé and Rousseau designs as 'Toy' at the Musée Galliera. That year also successful at the Brussels Exposition Universelle with, among other exhibits, variations on engraved overlay vases after Léveillé and Rousseau.

1911–1925
Address of Le Rosey: 5, bd. Malesherbes (8e arrondissement), after the two businesses separate to operate independently. Maison Toy stays in the old shop at 10, rue de la Paix.

1926–1931
Trades under the name 'Toy (Maisons Toy et Le Rosey réunies)'; address: 10, rue de la Paix. In 1930 Mlle Harant becoming managing director, like Louis Harant before her, a member of the Chambre Syndicale de la Céramique et de la Verrerie. The range of wares remains unchanged: editions, table services, glass art, faience, models are made to order.

from 1932
Address: 61, rue d'Anjou (8e arrondissement), until the business closes down in the 1960s.

Archival documents and literature

Almanach du Commerce 1893, pp. 424, 1261; L. de Fourcaud, 'Les Arts décoratifs aux Salons de 1897: Le Champ-de-Mars II – Les Arts intimes', *Revue des Arts Décoratifs* 17 (1897): 232; V. Champier, 'L'Exposition universelle de Bruxelles', ibid.: 394, illus. p. 393; E. Molinier, 'Les Arts du Feu: Salons de 1898', *Art & Décoration* 3 (1898): 191; 'Tablettes', *Art & Décoration* 8 (Sept. 1900): 1, suppl.; G. Kahn, 'Le Cristal taillé et gravé', *Art & Décoration* 11 (1902): illus. p. 61; Houtart 1902, p. 162; Bernard 1902, pp. 26, 68–69; Houtart 1908, pp. 8, 11, 18, 26, 29–30; Paris 1910, pp. 4–5, 7, 12–13; Turin, *France*, 1911, p. 300, no. 13; Barrez 1912, pp. 35, 63–64, with illus.; Hogrel 1930, pp. 9, 19, 380–81; ■ B. Lainé, Chr. Filloles-Alex and M. Rousset, *Objets 1860–1910: Dessins et modèles de fabrique déposés à Paris*, exh. cat., Archives de Paris (Paris, 1993), pp. 180–81; Duncan, *Salons*, 1998, p. 463, illus. pp. 305–7; documentation Musée d'Orsay, Paris.

→Léveillé, Michel, Rousseau

Louis Hestaux

Metz 27 May 1858–Nancy 22 June 1919
Eldest son of the printer Benoît Hestaux (d. 1907) and wife Anne-Marguerite, née Pinet (d. 1902).

1871
The Franco-Prussian War causes parents, who take French citizenship, to move to Nancy, at 30, rue du Montet.

1873–1876
Employed at lithography studio of printers Berger-Levrault, also attends evening classes in painting at the Ecole Municipale de Dessin in Nancy taught by Louis Théodore Devilly (1818–1886), school director from 1871. At the age of 15, Hestaux receives a silver medal in his first year, 1873, and in 1875 a gold medal, Prix d'Excellence de l'Ecole Municipale de Dessin et de Peinture. Friendship develops with fellow pupils Victor Prouvé (1858–1943) and Emile Friant (1863–1932).

1874–1919
At first occasional employment, from 1876 employed on a regular basis and from 1878 made head of →Emile Gallé's (1846–1904) decoration studio. Hestaux also continues to work freelance as a painter, printmaker and designer of arts and crafts in wood, leather, fabric (execution: Charles Fridrich, Nancy) and metal, including jewellery. His work reveals considerable talent and individuality. His simple, elegant furniture designs draw attention to his sculptural decoration. From 1884 member of the Société Lorraine des Amis des Arts (est. 1833) in Nancy, taking part regularly in its exhibitions with oil paintings and watercolours, mainly landscapes with the occasional genre painting. Until 1899 also shows sculptural wood objects and furniture. 3 Oct 1889 marries Jeanne Victorine Emilie Ferry (1869–1944), with Emile Gallé as one of the witnesses. The couple has three children: Lucien (b. 1890), André (b. 1901) and Alice (b. 1903). New address: 116, rue du Montet, from 1895: 130, rue du Montet.

from 1895
Exhibits work at the Salon of the Société Nationale des Beaux-Arts in Paris in the applied arts section. Member of the second artists' association (est. 1892) in Nancy, the *Société des Artistes Lorrains*. Receives three awards at the 1900 Paris Exposition Universelle: a gold and silver medal as a Gallé employee and a bronze medal for his own creations. In 1901 made a member of the board of directors of the recently founded Alliance Provinciale des Industries d'Art, known as the Ecole de Nancy. In 1902 (also mentioned in 1898) appointed associate member of the Société Nationale des Beaux-Arts in Paris. In 1903/4 participates in Ecole de Nancy exhibitions in Paris and in Nancy as a Gallé employee and with his own designs for metal panelling and fabrics (execution: Charles Fridrich, Nancy).

1908–1919
Regular trips to Brittany for health reasons, to Quiberon, Concarneau and Pouldu. From 1914 to 1918 studio and flat in Paris while the Gallé factory is closed during the war. Returns to Nancy in 1919.

Exhibitions
1884–1887
Nancy, Grande Salle de l'Université, Société Lorraine des Amis des Arts

1920
Nancy, Salle Victor Poirel, Société Lorraine des Amis des Arts l'Exposition (exh. cat.) – first retrospective
1933
Nancy, Salle Victor Poirel, Centenaire de la Société Lorraine des Amis des Arts

Literature

Nancy 1890, p. 54, nos. 398–94; Nancy 1892, p. 53, nos. 330–38; André 1894, p. 11; Nancy 1894, pp. 26, 60, nos. 153–58; 'Nancy', Art Décoratif (1894): 45, nos. 322–24, p. 52, nos. 387–92; Nancy 1895, p. 67, nos. 175–82; 'Exposition de Remiremont', Bulletin des Sociétés artistiques de l'Est (Sept. 1895): 111, suppl.; Nancy 1897, p. 78, nos. 156–61, p. 115, nos. 527–28, p. 133, nos. 670–78; G. Soulier, 'Les Arts de l'ameublement aus Salons', Art & Décoration 4 (1898): 16, 18, illus. p. 21; Nancy 1898, p. 82, nos. 162–67, p. 142, no. 719; Nancy 1899, p. 79, nos. 152–59; Nancy 1900, p. 79, nos. 146–50; Nancy 1901, p. 85, nos. 170–75, p. 124, nos. 572–77; Nancy 1902, p. 88, nos. 196–202, p. 129, nos. 565–70; Nancy 1903, p. 90, nos. 204–9, p. 130, nos. 566–69; Nancy 1904, p. 44, nos. 158–63; Nancy 1905, p. 94, nos. 187–89, p. 127, nos. 514–19; Nancy 1906, p. 87, nos. 132–33, p. 119, nos. 428–30; Nancy 1907, p. 88, nos. 114–15, p. 112, nos. 343–51; Nancy 1908, p. 87, nos. 114–17, p. 115, nos. 350–56; Emile Nicolas, 'L'Ecole de Nancy à Strasbourg', Bulletin des Sociétés artistiques de l'Est (March 1908): 34; Commandant Lalance, 'L'Ecole de Nancy à Strasbourg', ibid. (May 1908): 63–65; Strasbourg 1908, pp. 17, 22, nos. 130–43; Nancy 1909, p. 54, no. 163, p. 82, nos. 483–84; Nancy 1910, p. 74, nos. 91–93, p. 101, nos. 305–8; Paris, SNBA, p. LIX, nos. 2473–74; Nancy 1911, p. 27, nos. 62–64, p. 37, nos. 248–51; Lafitte 1912, pp. 38, 473, 873, illus. pl. VII; Nancy 1912, p. 32, no. 82, p. 49, nos. 274–78; Nancy 1913, p. 39, nos. 112–13, p. 37, nos. 380–83; Archives Municipales de la Ville de Nancy, death certificate, 1919, no. 1636; Nancy 1920, p. 63; ■ T. Charpentier, Louis Hestaux: Collaborateur de Gallé, exh. cat., Musée de l'Ecole de Nancy (Nancy, n.d. [1982]); Charpentier et al. 1987, pp. 16, 42, 53, 57, 79, 83, 84, 87–91, 95, 99, 103, 110, 136, 141, 154, 168, 279, 291, 309, 310; Nancy 1993, Musée des Beaux-Arts, De Charles de Meixmoron à Etienne Cournault: Centenaire de l'Association des Artistes lorrains – Rétrospective 1892–1950, compiled by Claude Pétry and Clara Gelly-Saldias (Nancy, 1993), pp. 43–44, cat. nos. 22, 28; Dictionnaire Biographie 1933–95, vol. 17, p. 1167; Aptel et al. 1989, pp. 16, 28, 74, 81, 160, 178, 195, 221, 224, 228, 230, 241, 252, 263, 275; ■ Thiébaut, Dessins, 1993, pp. 39–40, illus. pp. 40, 86–87, 108, 122, 140, 177; Darmstadt 1999, pp. 266, 289, 303, 360, 362, illus. p. 267; Le Tacon and De Luca 1999, pp. 12–13, illus. p. 13; ■ Nancy 1999, pp. 121, 138, cat. nos. 209–11, illus. p. 120; Nancy 2001, pp. 18–19, 34–35.

→Gallé

Ste Marie François Augustin Jean, called Auguste or Augustin Jean

Paris 19 Jan. 1829 – Vierzon-Village 3 Nov. 1896
Son of the tapestry weaver or upholster ('tapissier aux gobelins') and later director Antoine Théodore Jean and his wife, Jeanne Virginie, née Héronville.

before 1856
Trains and works as a porcelain painter.
18 June 1856
Marries Claire Roux, with whom he has three children, one daughter and two sons, Maurice (b. 1861) and Charles, both of whom are later employed at the family firm; address in Paris: 350, rue St-Jacques (5e arrondissement).
from 1859
Freelance maker of faience (to his own specifications). In 1861 first mentioned in the Almanach du Commerce, address: 11, rue de Sèvres. Jean is not mentioned in the registry of the building belonging to the city of Paris from 1861 and torn down in 1863.
1863–1867
Studio address: 32, rue d'Assas (6e arrondissement). Participates in the 1862 London International Exhibition, showing faience in the ancient Greek and the Renaissance style; recipient of sole medal awarded to a French ceramist, though some critics call the work 'dull and not original enough'. In 1864 first mention in Sageret's building and professional registry in Paris with the following description of products: 'Faience art: artistic faience in all styles, all periods. Speciality architecturally related faience for interiors and exteriors, including religious motifs, imitations of Luca della Robbia [1399–1482] of all sizes, both sculpture in the round and reliefs, also tiles, flagged flooring and panels. All painting stoved at high temperature and permanent' (Faïences d'art: faïences artistiques de tous les styles et de toutes les époques. Spécialité pour l'intérieur des bâtiments et l'extérieur. Faïences monumentales et religieuses, imitations de Luca della Robbia de toutes grandeurs, ronde bosse et bas-reliefs. Dallages, carrelages et panneaux de toutes les dimensions. Toutes les peintures sont cuites au grand feu ce qui les rend inaltérables).
1865–1878
Outlet in London, at 211, Regent Street; from 1877: 81a, Newman Street and Oxford Street.
1866–1871
Paris shop: 39, bd. Malesherbes (8e arrondissement).
from 1868
Own studio for faience with a shop and flat in Paris-Vaugirard: 61, rue Dombasle (15e arrondissement). A new building, with a 3-m-high brick chimney, is also equipped with machinery for making faience paste, two large (1.8-m-high) muffle kilns, each covering a floor area of 1 sq m, a mould-making workshop and a forge as well as a galvanizing bath. Shop and drawing studio on the upper floor. In 1869 Jean is entered as a member in the rolls of the Chambre Syndicale de la Céramique et de la Verrerie (est. 1868). From 1870 furnaces extinguished on account of the Franco-Prussian War.
    First patent registered on 8 Nov. 1872 Bulletin no. 97101, for the 'Application de la galvanoplastie à la décoration de tous les produits de la céramique'. This patent was presumably the first of its kind, describing how the non-conducting surfaces of ceramics, faience and porcelain can be made to conduct, which is necessary for galvanized decoration. The technique produces long-lasting results since the conductivity is achieved by stoving stains containing copper, gold or silver. In 1874 Jean is first mentioned in Sageret under the heading 'Artistes Peintres Décorateurs', in 1877 with the additional entry '24 medals at various exhibitions'.
18 April 1876
Liquidation proceedings are concluded (begun on 26 Aug. 1875) owing to the firm's dire financial straits brought on by the 1870–71 Franco-Prussian War and the Communard revolts, when all wares in the shop at 39, bd. Malesherbes, worth 18,000 Frs, are destroyed and Jean receives no compensation because he misses the date by which he would have been entitled to claim it.
from 1876
Intensive preoccupation with painting on hollow glass in enamels and lustre as well as precious metals, also works on developing his glass technology with →Appert Frères.

Application for second patent registered (represented by his son, Maurice, living at 61, rue Dombasle) on 30 April 1877, Bulletin no. 118301, for 'Verre métallisé'. The patent describes how to make glass surfaces iridescent by reduction firing of batch containing silver nitrate or acetate and bismuth. At the 1878 Paris Exposition Universelle shows 'iridescent glass made according to his method, with enamel painting and engraving'; also, with other ceramist, commissioned to make tiling for the partitions designed by the exhibition architect, Hardy. Jean's participation at first rejected but his son Maurice succeeds in his being approved.

1880–1883
Builds new workshops on leased premises: 142, rue de l'Abbé Groult (15e arrondissement), from 1881 storeroom, 64, rue d'Hauteville (10e arrondissement), and shop at 45, rue des Petites Ecuries (10e arrondissement). Glass also sold by T. Ducy, 53, rue de Châteaudun (9e arrondissement).

8 Jan. 1884
Second liquidation concluded (begun 27 March 1883): insolvency caused by new investment related to glass design, which cannot be financed because of commitments to pay off debts from the first insolvency.

1884/85–1887/88
Sons Maurice and Charles Jean, who have worked for the factory as ceramists for years, become joint directors. The firm trades under the name 'Jean M. & C. Fils' (Sageret, 1885–87). Initially continues to make artistic faience as well as architectural ceramics. In 1887/88 moves to Vierzon-Village with son Maurice, first entry in electoral rolls in 1888.

1888–1896
Studio and flat in the Châtaignier section of Vierzon-Village, rue du Sergent Bobillot, together with son Maurice, who is mayor from 1893 to 1896. In 1889 patent application registered by son Charles (living in Paris, at 63, rue du Château d'eau, Hôtel de l'Union), on 12 Feb. 1889, Bulletin no. 196013, for 'Teinter ou métalliser le tout ou en partie le verre, cristal et tout ce qui a rapport à la verrerie et à la céramique en général, dans le cours de la fabrication ou une fois les pièces terminées, par le vaporisateur ou tout autre appareil à vent, ayant pour base l'air' (Tinting or metalizing the whole or part of glass, crystal and anything related to glass and ceramics in general in the course of manufacture or after completion of pieces by vapour deposition or any other compressed air spraying device based on air). The patent describes the use of compressed-air spraying devices to be used for colouring or metalizing whole or part ceramics, glass and crystal surfaces during manufacture or afterwards. (One of Jean's former employees, Ernest Baudin, is awarded a silver medal at the 1889 Paris Exposition Universelle.)

Archival documents and literature
Supplementing Schmitt, Zurich II, 1995, p. 300: birth certificate Archives de Paris V2E and 2774; marriage Jean and Roux on 18 June 1856, ibid., Fichier des mariages parisiens 1795–1862, vol. 131, p. 40; Cadastres 10–12, rue de Sèvres, ibid., D1P4,1852, no. 1097; *Almanach du Commerce*, 1861, pp. 323, 770, 1540; Cadastre 61, rue Dombasle, Archives de Paris, D1P4, 1862, no. 351; J. B. Waring, *Masterpieces of Industrial Art and Sculpture at the International Exhibition 1862* (London, 1863), p. 294; *Almanach du Commerce*, 1863, pp. 339, 818, 1194; Sageret 1864, pp. 123, 214; ibid., 1865, pp. 75, 136; ibid., 1866, pp. 79, 146, 442; *Almanach du Commerce*, 1867, pp. 330, 747, 905; ibid., 1868, pp. 52 (Liste de Récompensés, 1867), 749; Sageret 1868, pp. 85, 159, 515; 'Chambre syndicale de la céramique et de la verrerie, Liste des adhérents', *Moniteur de la céramique, de la verrerie et des industries qui s'y rattachent*, no. 1 (1869): 38; Sageret 1874, pp. 103, 201, 436, 660; Sageret 1875, pp. 111, 465; Mascret 1874–82, JOS 61, faillites 26 Aug. 1875–1 May 1876; ■ documents of insolvency, 26 Aug. 1875–18 April 1876, Archives de Paris, D11U3 and 813, no. 997; Sageret 1877, pp. 114, 227, 505; enquiry about participation in the 1878 Paris Exposition Universelle: Archives Nationales F21 3367–68; Sageret 1879, pp. 121, 245, 771; Hauteville address in *Revue Universelle: Le Commerce et l'industrie* III (1880): 84; Sageret 1881, pp. 126, 259, 580, 815; *Union Centrale des Arts Décoratifs: Catalogue illustré officiel du Salon des arts décoratifs* (Paris, 1882), p. 97, nos. 395–401; ■ insolvency documents, 27 March 1883–1 Aug. 1884, Archives de Paris D11U3 and 1090, no. 13397 (contains, like the first set of insolvency documents, 26 Aug. 1875–18 April 1876, contradictory information, including mother's name, date of marriage, year factory was built); Sageret 1883, pp. 139, 290, 640; L. de Fourcaud, 'Rapport général', *Revue des Arts Décoratifs* 5 (1884–85): 252; Sageret 1885, pp. 310, 675; Sageret 1887, p. 335; death certificate of Marie Augustin Jean, Service Patrimoine de Vierzon, Décès 1896, no. 145; Paris, *Arts Métiers*, 1908, p. 265, no. 9400 (Cristallerie de Pantin); *Glass Fantasy* 1990, p. 60; E. Schmitt, *Europäisches Jugend-*stilglas aus der Glassammlung Silzer and Leihgabe Deutsche Bank, exh. cat., State Tretyakov Gallery, Moscow (text in Russian) (Moscow, 1991), nos. 4–5, illus. pp. 22–23; documentation Musée d'Orsay, Paris; information imparted in writing by Frédéric Morillon, Service Patrimoine de la Ville de Vierzon, 1997.

→Appert Frères

Edouard Achille Lachenal
called Edmond Lachenal

Paris 3 June 1855–Paris 10 June 1948
Born out of wedlock as Edouard Achille Gaucher, to Jean-Pierre Lachenal (commanditaire) and Armantine Louise Gaucher; recognized as son and renamed Edouard Achille Lachenal through parents' marriage on 19 July 1860

1867
Begins a potter's apprenticeship near Paris.
1870–1880
Trains under the ceramist Théodore Deck (1823–1891) in Paris, bd. St-Jacques (14e arrondissement), whose employees, Léon Henri Loire (1821–1898) and Joseph Victor Ranvier (1832–1896), are among Lachenal's most important teachers. After 1873 Lachenal becomes head of the decoration studio. About 1879/80 marries Anne Marie Cloarec, who becomes his closest working associate in the years that follow. The couple has two sons, Jean-Jacques (1881–1945) and Raoul Pierre (1885–1956).
1880–1885
Studio in Malakoff, Seine: 23, rue Augustin-Dumont. In 1882 listed for the first time in Sageret, the Paris directory of buildings and trades with the following entry: 'Ex-chef de l'atelier de la maison d' Deck. Faïence d'art architecturale, seule maison faisant toutes les fabrications, faïence ordinaire et artistique au prix ordinaire. Solidité garantie' (Former head of the studio at Deck. Architectural art faience, sole firm making all types of faience, both ordinary and artistic, at normal prices. Durability guaranteed). In 1885 his wife dies.
from 1885
Studio in Châtillon-sous-Bagneux, Seine: 32, rue du Ponceau. From 1885 the artist advertises his speciality, matt faience, in Sageret. From 1886 showed work regularly at the annual exhibitions hosted by Georges Petit. Awarded a bronze medal in 1887 at the ninth exhibition mounted by the Union Central des Arts Décoratifs, L'Invention, la Forme et la Décor for his invention of what are called matt enamels with a velvety finish. Awarded a gold medal for work he shows at the 1889 Paris Exposition Universelle. In 1890 sells a large vase to the Musée des Arts Décoratifs, Paris. About 1893 begins what would be years of collaboration with the Swedish craftswoman and sculptor, Agnès de Frumerie-Kjellberg (1869–1937). In 1894/95 works with Keller & Guérin in Lunéville on experiments with engobes (slip) with a metallic content on stoneware. By this time he may have come into contact with →Ernest Bussière (1863–1913) and other artists from Nancy since they also work then for Keller & Guérin. It is also possible that he already knows →Antonin Daum, who exhibits jointly with Lachenal in 1896 at the annual Georges Petit exhibition in Paris.
from 1895
Member of the Société Nationale des Beaux-Arts. Intensive work on modelling; also executes sculpture by other artists, including Pierre Félix Fix-Masseau (1869–1937) and Auguste Rodin (1840–1917). From 1896 concentrates on stoneware. His first vase designs for →Daum Frères in Nancy are shown at the 1897 Brussels Exposition Internationale. In 1899 publishes drawings. In 1900 faience decoration on furniture and work in wood by Colin and Paul Bec, known as *ligno-céramique*. Made a Chevalier de la Légion d'Honneur. In 1901 develops pottery vessels trimmed with silver and gold decoration, known as *métallo-céramiques*. His son Raoul Pierre (1885–1956) begins to work for him. At the Georges Petit exhibition in 1903/4 shows sets of glasses he has designed, 'Crocus' and 'Gui', which are executed by →Daum Frères. Lachenal also uses the mistletoe decoration of the latter in designs for faience and precious metals.
from 1904
Works in cast pewter by Edouard Lachenal, from 1907 also in bronze. Edouard Lachenal's address in Paris from 1905 to 1910: 15 & 17, rue Auber (9e arrondisse-

ment: according to Sageret 1906–11). In 1911 Raoul Pierre Lachenal, youngest son and most important employee, founds a studio of his own in Boulogne-sur-Seine, 102, ave. Victor Hugo.

c. 1912

Edouard Lachenal again designs for the Keller & Guérin pottery factory in Lunéville.

1914

Gives the studio to his eldest son, Jean-Jacques, who has also worked for years in his father's studio. Edouard Lachenal becomes interested in the theatre; lives at Châtillon-sous-Bagneux, Seine.

5 June 1917

Marries his second wife, Marguerite Barety, in Paris.

c. 1930

Lives in Versailles, 1, rue Delaunay.

before 1948

Lives in Paris, at 22, rue de Verneuil (7e arrondissement).

Exhibitions

1885

Antwerp, Palace of Industry, International Exhibition

1886–1903

Paris, Galerie Georges Petit (solo exh.)– shows work regularly at annual exhibitions, in 1896 jointly with Daum, in 1903 with Daum and Majorelle

1896

Paris, Galerie S. Bing, Lachenal, Dalpayrat et Lesbros

1898

Berlin, Kunstgewerbemuseum, Moderne Kunsttöpferei (modern pottery) (exh. rep.)

1901

Paris, Salon de la Vie Moderne

Vienna, Museum für Kunst und Industrie (E)

1904

Düsseldorf, Städtischer Kunstpalast, Internationale Kunstausstellung mit Sonderausstellung von künstlerischen Gefässen für Blumen und Obst (Municipal Art Palace, International Art Exhibition with Special Exhibition of Art Vessels for Flowers and Fruit) (cat.) – with La Maison Moderne (Delrue & C.),

Paris, Magasin Majorelle (E)

Archival documents and literature

Birth certificate (1855) with further documents on the second marriage and death: Archives de Paris V2E no. 6699; Sageret 1882, pp. 131, 270; P. Arène, 'Huitième Exposition de L'Union Centrale: Pierre, bois de construction, terre et verre – La Céramique', *Revue des Arts Décoratifs* 5 (1884–85): 177; Sageret 1885, p. 310; R. Marx, 'La Décoration achitecturale et les industries d'art à l'exposition universelle de 1889', *Revue des Arts Décoratifs* 11 (1890–91), illus. p. 38; Sageret 1892, p. 399; L. de Fourcaud, 'Les Arts décoratifs au Salon 1892: Champs-Elysées et Champ-de-Mars (troisième et dernière article)', *Revue des Arts Décoratifs* 13 (1892–93): 12, illus. p. 6; L. E. Day, 'Une Exposition française d'art décoratif jugée par un anglais', ibid. 14 (1893–94): 221; L. de Fourcaud, 'Les Arts décoratifs au Salon 1894: Champ-de-Mars (troisième et dernière article)', ibid. 15 (1894–95): 6, 13, illus. p. 6; V. Champier, 'Un Salon d'art décoratif à la galerie Georges Petit', ibid.: 233, illus. pp. 235–36, 392; L. de Fourcaud, 'Les Arts décoratifs au Salon 1896: Champ-de-Mars', ibid. 16 (1896): 230; 'Chronique du Mois', *Revue des Arts Décoratifs* (Feb. 1896): 59; 'Chronique du Mois', ibid.: 371, illus. p. 371b; 'L'Ecole Guérin, les céramiques de Lachenal et Dalpayrat', *Art & Décoration* 1 (1897): 24; L. de Fourcaud, 'Les Arts décoratifs au Salon 1897: Champ-de-Mars II – Les Arts intimes', *Revue des Arts Décoratifs* 17 (1897): 231, 341; E. Molinier, 'Les Arts du Feu', *Art & Décoration* 1 (1897): 111; E. Molinier, 'L'Exposition de céramique', ibid. 2 (1897): 4; E. Molinier, 'Les Arts du Feu: Salons de 1898', ibid. 3 (1898): 196; L. Enault, 'L'Exposition Lachenal', *Revue des Arts Décoratifs* 18 (1898): 335–38, with illus.; M. S., 'Korrespondenzen: Berlin', *Dekorative Kunst* 2, no. 9 (1898): 129; A. Le Chatelier, 'Céramique d'art', *Art & Décoration* 6 (1899): illus. pp. 182–83, 188–89; G. Soulier, 'L'Ameublement à l'exposition', ibid. 8 (1900): 148, illus. p. 149; A. Sandier, 'La Céramique à l'exposition', ibid.: 195; 'Tablettes', ibid. (Sept. 1900): 1, suppl.; A. Sandier, 'La Céramique à l'exposition II', ibid. 9 (1901): 62, illus. p. 58; E. Molinier, 'Les Objets d'art aux Salons III', ibid. 10 (1901): 47; G. Geoffroy, *Les Industries artistiques françaises et étrangères à l'exposition universelle de 1900* (Paris,

n.d. [1902]), pp. 5, 14, 31; F. Jourdain, 'Les Meubles et les teintures murales aux salons de 1901', *Revue des Arts Décoratifs* 21 (1901): illus. p. 208; F. Minkus, 'Edmond Lachenal', *Kunst und Kunsthandwerk* (1901): 390–98, illus. from p. 386; E. Belville, 'Daum, Lachenal, Majorelle à la Galerie Georges Petit', *L'Art Décoratif* (Jan. 1904): 33; 'Nos Industries d'art à Paris', *Lorraine Artiste* (Jan. 1904): 26–27; Düsseldorf 1904, p. 153; Sageret 1906, p. 637; ibid., 1911, p. 719; marriage certificate Lachenal and Barety, 5 June 1917, Mairie du 17e Arrondissement de la Ville de Paris, Mariages 1917, no. 749; excerpt from registry of deaths Edouard Lachenal, Mairie du 7e Arrondissement de la Ville de Paris, Décès 1948, no. 750; ■ H.-J. Heuser, *Französische Keramik zwischen 1850 und 1910*, coll. cat. M. and H.-J. Heuser (Munich, 1974), pp. 92–93, nos. 29–33, with illus.; Bénézit 1976, vol. 6, p. 359; Munich, *Nancy 1900*, 1980, p. 362, nos. 405–8, with illus.; ■ H. Makus, *Keramik aus Historismus und Jugendstil in Frankreich mit Beispielen aus anderen europäischen Ländern: Ausgewählte Objekte aus zwei Privatsammlungen*, exh. cat., Staatliche Kunstsammlungen, Kassel (Kassel, 1981), pp. 105–15, with illus.; ■ Carl Benno Heller, *Europäische Keramik 1880–1930: Sammlung Silzer*, exh. cat., Hessisches Landesmuseum, Darmstadt (Darmstadt, 1986), pp. 91, 116–21, with illus.; Debize 1989, p. 88; Brunhammer and Tise 1990, p. 277; *Dictionnaire Biographie* 1933–95, vol. 18, p. 1506; Bardin 2002, vol. 1, p. 102, illus. p. 115, vol. 2, pp. 297, 455; documentation Musée d'Orsay, Paris.

→Daum Frères

Ernest-Baptiste Léveillé
called Ernest Léveillé

Paris 2 Feb. 1841–Vaucresson 25 March 1913

Son of Jean François Léveillé (1808–1882) and his wife, Arsène Clémence Henry (1812–1886), living at 12, rue de Thiroux (different name today); an elder sister, Marie Clémence (b. 1836).

Father, Jean François Léveillé, works from 1835 in specialist porcelain shop of same name, at 12, rue de Thiroux (first mention in 1836 in the *Almanach de Commere*, the trade and commerce annual of the city of Paris), branch opened in 1838/39, 357bis, bd. St-Honoré (8e arrondissement). The firm was probably owned by his father or uncle since the following entries are in the 1841 *Almanach du Commerce*: Thérèse Léveillé, widow, under the addresses of both shops; Léveillé nephew, faience and porcelain, under 12, rue de Thiroux; Léveillé, eldest son (aîné), faience specialist (aîné faïencier) under 357bis, bd. St-Honoré (8e arrondissement).

before 1869

Nothing is known about Ernest Léveillé's personal career or the history of the Léveillé firm. Whether the entries in the 1867 and 1868 *Almanach du Commerce* 'Léveillé, artist, draughtsman; address: 10, Grenelles St-Germain' (7e arrondissement) have anything to do with him has yet to be determined.

from 1869

Ernest Léveillé is director of the specialist shop for porcelain and glass he founds under his name at 74, bd. Haussmann (9e arrondissement). On 1 Feb. 1872 marries Philippine Emilie Mairet (17 June 1852–29 Aug. 1905), with whom he has four daughters: Jeanne Louise, Alfrède Clémence, Marie Jeanne and Suzanne Louise Eulalie.

c. 1871–1887

Branch: 131, rue de Provence (9e arrondissement); moves c. 1884 to: 3, rue de Rome (8e arrondissement).

16 Dec. 1885

Takes over stocks from →Eugène Rousseau (1827–1890), including his designs and moulds.

1886– c. 1892

Trades under the name 'Maisons Rousseau et Léveillé réunies, 74, bd. Haussmann' (in *Almanach du Commerce* until 1893). Collaboration with Rousseau, who introduces him to glass design. Participates with Rousseau in the 1889 Paris Exposition Universelle, where he is awarded a gold medal. Critics attribute the 'new decoration method of relief etching of cased glass in combination with engraving' to Léveillé. His first designs for glass include vases with detailed underwater scenes and vases modelled on Chinese work with spiralling tendril motifs in polished mitre cutting, mainly on colourless glass. (This decoration scheme is taken over by →Emile Gallé and patented in 1895 with only slight modifications.)

from c. 1892

Reversion to original name of 'E. Léveillé' after Eugène Rousseau's death. 1892–97 annual participation in the Salon du Champ-de-Mars exhibitions jointly with the glass cutter →Eugène Michel, who engraved for Rousseau. Using glass bodies created by Rousseau, Léveillé develops new, in part increasingly sculptural relief decoration with flora and fauna motifs, which are subsequently also interpreted by →Gallé and especially →Daum in Nancy. They include: maple or chestnut leaves, bats, ravens, pine martens, snakes, an octopus on the seabed, tropical plants, palms and maize. At the 1893 Chicago World's Columbian Exposition shows services in historicist manner, with period styles including Louis XV and Louis XVI as well as glass art after Rousseau: including decoration in the Japonist style, such as peach blossoms on opaque copper red casing in sunk or raised gold tooling or in white and pink enamel painting heightened with gold and a square *jardinière* with inclusions and what is known as lion-skin decoration over gold-leaf inclusions; in 1895 shows work at the Liège Exhibition of Applied Arts.

1899–1902

Business address: 140, Faubourg St-Honoré (8e arrondissement). At the 1900 Paris Exposition Universelle shows 'vases [that are] multiple-cased in several colours and carved', etc., where he is awarded a gold medal. In 1901 designs for glasses, historicist in combination with prunts that lend the walls new form. In 1902 new shapes with polished line cutting or mat floral engraving.

27 March 1903

Léveillé sold his stock as well as his and →Rousseau's designs to Louis Harant (1854–1925), head of →Harant & Guignard Maison Toy, 10, rue de la Paix (2e arrondissement).

Exhibitions
1891
Moscow, Industrial Exhibition, 'Art de France' section
1895
Liège, Exposition d'Art Appliqué
1933
Paris, Pavillon de Marsan, Le Décor de la Vie sous la IIIe République de 1870 à 1900 (exh. cat.)

Archival documents and literature
Supplementing Schmitt, Zurich II, 1995, p. 311: *Almanach du Commerce*, 1836, pp. CCXVII, 258; ibid., 1839, pp. CCXL, 142; birth certificate Ernest Baptiste Léveillé 2 Feb. 1841, Archives Départementales de la Ville de Paris V2E 4209; *Almanach du Commerce*, 1841, pp. 244, 455; ibid., 1867, p. 379; ibid., 1868, p. 389; marriage certificate 24 Feb. 1872, ibid., V4E 3377; *Almanach du Commerce*, 1880, p. 995; sale agreement Rousseau and Léveillé 1885, Archives nationales, Minutier Central, LXVI, 1689, 16 Dec. 1885, *Vente de matériel et marchandises par M. Rousseau à M. et Mme Léveillé*; exhibits 'Maison Léveillé 1889', *Supplément à la Revue des Arts Décoratifs* (Nov. 1889): H. VII, n.p.; exhibits 'Maison Léveillé 1889', ibid. (July and Aug. 1890): XII, n.p.; R. Marx, 'La Décoration achitecturale et les industries d'art à l'exposition universelle de 1889', *Revue des Arts Décoratifs* 11 (1890–91): 37–39; succession Eugène Rousseau, Archives de Paris, succession après décès 17 Oct. 1890, DQ7, 10930; exhibits 'Maison Léveillé 1893', *Supplément à la Revue des Arts Décoratifs* 21 (July 1894): n.p.; L. de Fourcaud, 'Les Arts décoratifs au Salon 1892: Champs-Elysées et Champ-de-Mars', *Revue des Arts Décoratifs* 13 (1892–93): 10, illus. p. 3; *Almanach du Commerce*, 1892, pp. 1265, 1425; Paris, Salon du Champ-de-Mars 1892, no. 76; *Almanach du Commerce*, 1893, pp. 511, 1261, 1419; Paris, Salon du Champ-de-Mars 1893, nos. 337–40; L. E. Day, 'Une Exposition française d'art décoratif jugée par un anglais', *Revue des Arts Décoratifs* 14 (1893–94): 220; Paris, Salon du Champ-de-Mars 1894, nos. 441–49; Krantz 1894, pp. 27–28; L. de Fourcaud, 'Les Arts décoratifs au Salon 1894: Champ-de-Mars (troisième et dernière article)', *Revue des Arts Décoratifs* 15 (1894–95): 4; 'Paris, Salon du Champ-de-Mars 1895', no. 294; ibid., 1896, no. 316; L. de Fourcaud, 'Les Arts décoratifs aux Salons de 1896: Le Champ-de-Mars III', ibid. 17 (1897): 231; L. de Fourcaud, 'Les Arts décoratifs aux Salons de 1897: Le Champ-de-Mars II – Les Arts intimes', ibid. 17 (1897): 342; Paris, Salon du Champ-de-Mars 1897, no. 297; E. Molinier, 'Les Arts du Feu', *Art & Décoration* 1 (1897): 114; E. Molinier, 'L'Exposition de céramique', ibid. 2 (1897): illus. p. 5; Marx 1900, p. 54; G. Kahn, 'La Verrerie: Verrerie usuelle – Les Services de table', *Art & Décoration* 10 (1901): 131, 138–39, illus. pp. 130, 138; G. Kahn, 'Le Cristal taillé et

gravé', ibid. 11 (1902): 62, illus. pp. 58, 60–61; G. Geoffroy, *Les Industries artistiques françaises et étrangères à l'exposition universelle de 1900* (Paris, n.d. [1902]), p. 32; *Almanach du Commerce*, 1910, pp. 537, 1373, 1678; Paris 1910, pp. 4–5, 7, 12–13; *Almanach du Commerce*, 1911/12, vol. 1, pp. 542, 1408; ■ Bascou and Thiébaut, Orsay, 1988, pp. 160, 232, nos. OAO 308–9; Tokyo, *Style floral*, 1988, no. 97; Schneck 1990, p. 456; Yoshimizu and Klesse 1992, nos. 7–9; Schmitt, Zurich II, 1995, no. 175, p. 108, p. 311; ■ documentation Musée d'Orsay; Paris.

→Rousseau, Michel, Harant & Guignard

Eugène Michel

Lunéville (Meurthe et Moselle) 9 Aug. 1848–Paris 6 Nov. 1904
Third and youngest child of Joseph Michel (b. 1814), a tailor, and his wife, Anne Joséphine, née Marchal (b. 1814), a sewing-maid (*lingère*), 147, pl. St-Jacques; an elder sister Eléonore (b. 1845). The first sister of that name died in 1844, four months after birth. Grandfather, Dominique Michel, was a gardener in Lunéville, maternal grandfather, Joseph Marchal, a farmer.

before 1868

Nothing specific can as yet be said about Eugène Michel's education and training. The archives of the Cristallerie de Baccarat, approx. 30 km from Lunéville, make no mention of this. Likely to have trained in Paris since stone and glass cutting had developed there from the early nineteenth century, affording numerous training opportunities.

c. 1867/68–70 or 1872/73

Begins working with →Eugène Rousseau (1827–1890), 41, rue Coquillière (1e arrondissement), executing the latter's designs for engraving and cutting. By 1868 Michel lives in Paris, for it was there that he enlists in the national service, and petitions for exemption as the only son of a widowed mother.

1870

Address in Paris: 237, rue St-Denis (2e arrondissement). Though the registry of buildings does not mention Michel, it does refer to one Letheux, a landlord letting furnished rooms, and informtion on changes in lodgers. Michel is exempted from national service but with the remark 'Bon pour la garde mobile'. He does not appear in the 1871 Paris electoral rolls.

c. 1874–1876

Eugène Michel marries Adèle Eugénie Perrin (1854–1940), with who he has two daughters, Jeanne (1876–1956) and Lucie Léonie (b. 1886), both of whom later marry and live in Paris's 14e arrondissement. Jeanne marries the architect Paul Denis before 1904; Lucie Léonie marries Marie Albert Jouve, secretary in the Ministry of Finance, in 1912.

1876–1904

Eugène Michel's Paris address: 20, rue de la Michodière (2e arrondissement); from 1893 registered in the *Almanach du Commerce* as an independent studio; c. 1900–1904 private address: 18, rue des Capucines (2e arrondissement). After 1885 also engraver for Rousseau's successor, →E. Léveillé (1841–1913), with whom he first shows work, in 1892, at the Salon du Champ-de-Mars; in 1898 shows work there with →Harant & Guignard 'Maison Toy' (6, rue Halévy, from 1903: 10, rue de la Paix). Participates in the 1900 Paris Exposition Universelle in the special show mounted by the Union Centrale des Arts Décoratifs.

1902

Article in the journal *Art & Décoration* on the structuring of fairly large art workshops under the heading 'L'Idée de corporation'. The discussion is carried on by Eugène Michel, reputable Paris firms such as Christofle and Vever and the artists Auguste Rodin (1840–1917), Alexandre Charpentier (1856–1909) and Eugène Grasset (1841–1917). According to Michel, he has several engravers working for him in his studio. Head engravers share proceeds, in addition to their wages. Apprentices have to master their craft to be accepted to work there. They receive the usual wages and continue their training individually with experienced employees according to Eugène Michel's ideas of how this should be done. (M. Michel, graveur sur cristaux, réalise la corporation ou l'atelier corporatif chez lui. Il crée une participation aux bénéfices pour ces principaux ouvriers. Il prend comme apprentis, des ouvriers qui savent déjà travailler, leur donne le salaire auquel ils sont accoutumés, et leur apprend le métier tel qu'il l'entend. Il couple, dans ses ateliers, un ouvrier nouveau avec un ancien ouvrier, et obtient ainsi une instruction mutuelle, une mise au courant progressive, qu'il juge suffisante.) [M. Michel, glass engraver, is realizing the corporation or the corporate studio in his own business. He has set up a profit-sharing scheme for his chief workmen. He takes as apprentices workers who already know how to work, gives them the wages to which they are accustomed and teaches them the trade as he understands it. In his studios he pairs off a new workman with an experienced one, thus securing mutual instruction, continually keeping informed about things to the degree he considers sufficient.)

before 1904

Artistic collaboration with Eugène Lelièvre, at 12, rue Debelleyme (3e arrondissement), who designs metal mounts, as well as Edmond Enot (b. 1848), manufacturer of bronze mounts at 13, rue des Pyramides (1e arrondissement).

1904

Retrospective at the first exhibition mounted by the Société des Artistes Décorateurs at the Petit Palais in Paris.

1905–1910

His widow, Adèle Eugénie Michel, continues to manage the studio at what has been the private address: 18, rue des Capucines (2e arrondissement).

c. 1910–1911

Studio is taken over by the engraver L. Parot, at first trading under the name 'L. Parot succ. Michel'. After 1918 Parot is listed at a different address.

Exhibitions

1903

Paris, Grand Palais, Salon de la Société des Artistes Français

1933

Paris, Pavillon de Marsan, Le Décor de la Vie sous la IIIe République de 1870 à 1900 (exh. cat.)

Archival documents and literature

Supplementing Schmitt, *Sammlung Silzer* 1989, pp. 12, 254, no. 135, illus. p. 255: marriage certificate of Joseph Michel and Anne Joséphine Marchal, Archives Municipales de Lunéville, Archives communales postérieures à 1790 Série E Section 5, no. 53 acte de mariage 1843, no. 73; birth certificate and date of death of Eléonore Michel (6 Jan. 1844–14 May 1844), ibid., Naissances 1844, nos. 4 and 54; birth certificate Eléonore Michel 24 Feb. 1845, ibid., 1845, nos. 43 and 55; birth certificate Eugène Michel 9 Aug. 1848, ibid., 1848, nos. 173 and 58; Cadastre 1852, 1876 (1900 missing), 18, rue des Capucines, Archives de Paris D1P4 and 185; Tableaux de recensement de classe de 1868, Tirage fixé Canton Nord 26 Jan. 1869, Archives Municipales de Lunéville Serie H1, no. 97; Tableaux de recensement des classes de 1866–70, Canton Nord, ibid., Serie H1-Section 29–1° 21, no. 37; birth certificate Jeanne Michel, 2 July 1876 with note of death date as 30 May 1956, Archives de Paris 5MI3 and 26, no. 926; birth certificate Lucie Léonie Michel, 20 Feb. 1886 with note of marriage to Marie Albert Jouve, ibid., 5 Mi 3 and 1066, no. 215; L. de Fourcaud, 'Les Arts Décoratifs au Salon 1892 Champs-Elysées et Champ-de-Mars', *Revue des Arts Décoratifs* 13 (1892–93): 10, illus. p. 3; *Almanach du Commerce*, 1893, pp. 559, 1512; L. de Fourcaud, 'Les Arts décoratifs aux Salons de 1897: Le Champ-de-Mars III', ibid. (1897): 232; E. Molinier, 'Les Arts du Feu. Salons de 1898', *Art & Décoration* 3 (1898): 191; Pazaurek 1901, p. 99; G. Kahn, 'Les Objets d'Art aux Salons', ibid. 12 (1902): 25, 29; 'L'Idée de corporation, Opinions de MM. Auguste Rodin, Alexandre Charpentier, Eugène Grasset, Christofle, Siot-Decauville, Vever, Michel, Gaudin', ibid. (May 1902): 2, 4, suppl.; death certificate of Eugène Michel, Archives Mairie 7e Arrondissement de la Ville de Paris 1904, no. 1639; letter written by Michel's widow to André Saglio, commissioner of the 1904 St. Louis, MO, World's Fair concerning the theft of two vases: no. 2755 'marins' and 2257 'vigne vierge'; Archives Nationales, Paris Serie F 21 4068; Paris 1910, pp. 7, 10, 20, 22; *Almanach du Commerce*, 1910, pp. 605, 2081; ibid., 1911–12, vol. 1, p. 612; marriage certificate of Marie Albert Jouve and Lucie Léonie Michel, Archives Mairie 14e Arrondissement de la Ville Paris 1912, no. 1871, p. 109; Paris 1933, p. 184, nos. 1461–62; Brunhammer and Tise 1990, p. 279, illus. p. 25; Cappa 1991, pp. 332–33, with illus.; Yoshimizu and Klesse 1992, no. 86; Ricke 1995, p. 168, no. 262, illus. p. 169; Suzuki, *Kitazawa*, 1996, no. 434; Mukai, *Hida Takayama*, 1997, p. 105; Duncan, *Salons*, 1998, pp. 30, 32, 462, illus. pp. 44, 334–37; information imparted in writing in 1997 by Janine Milliard, Archives Municipales de Meudon Direction de la Photothèque; documentation Musée d'Orsay, Paris.

→ Harant & Guignard, Léveillé, Rousseau

Muller Frères
Grandes Verreries de Croismare
Croismare and Lunéville
France

22 Aug. 1894

Arrival of Nicolas Muller (b. 1833), butcher, from Montbronn-lès-Bitche, in Nancy with a family of nine (originally ten) children. The family is naturalized in France on 29 April 1895, his son, Jean, in 1896. Nearly all the brothers and sisters train as glass decorators: Emile, Camille, Jean and Auguste at the Cristallerie de Saint Louis in Saint Louis-lès-Bitche. Decorative cutters: Emile (6 Nov. 1866–12 March 1923) and Nicolas-Camille, called Camille (24 Sept. 1869–20 Feb. 1922). Engravers: Jean (1872–29 Jan. 1954), Auguste (b. 7 June 1874) and Jean-Pierre, called Pierre (12 Nov. 1875–29 Jan. 1946). Glass painters: Jean-Désiré, called Désiré (1877–1952), and Eugène (1883–1917). Désiré may have been a pupil of Désiré Christian's in Meisenthal. Henri-Victor, called Henri (1868–1936), works in an office. There is no information on the training of Victor (b. 1880) and Anne Marie Catherine (1881–4 May 1964).

1894–1897

Emile, Camille, Jean, Auguste and Henri works at the glass factory recently opened by →Emile Gallé. In 1896 Henri leaves to organize a firm of his own, including the establishment of a glass refinery in Lunéville, at first at rue Sainte-Anne, then rue de la Barre. In 1898 the Muller family moves to Croismare.

1897–1918

Trades under the name 'Muller et Cie. Verreries d'art de Croismare'. Director: Henri Muller, who has procured important documents at Emile Gallé's factory. Finishing and decorating in Lunéville, rue de la Barre; production of blanks in collaboration with the glass factory in Croismare founded in 1858 by Guerner, a glassmaker, and Stenger, a chemist, from Vallerysthal; from 1865 trades under the name 'Guerner & Bailly' and from 1893, after conversion into a joint-stock company, as 'S.A. des Grandes Verreries de Croismare'. The Muller brothers produce glass in the manner of →Emile Gallé, →Désiré Christian and →Daum Frères, but much more cheaply and usually with floral overlay decoration, some of it elaborately crafted and meticulously worked. The engraved decoration is usually of a high quality. Pieces painted with stain and lustre stand comparison with similar work by Désiré Christian and Amédée de Caranza. Decoration or techniques used by Gallé and Daum are often copied without much modification.

1906–1908

Désiré and Eugène Muller work as artisans at Cristalleries du Val Saint-Lambert in Belgium, responsible for numerous models with floral and landscape decoration in etched overlay, also in combination with silver-stain painting.

1910

Decoration studio moves in Lunéville to 11, rue d'Hénaménil. In 1911 Emile Muller, originally trained as a decorative engraver, becomes head engraver at the Houdaille & Triquet glass factory in Choisy-le-Roi, under the auspices of which he participates in the Exposition Internationale des Industries et du Travail in Turin, where he is awarded a silver medal.

1914–1918

Glass production in Croismare and Lunéville interrupted by war. In 1917 Eugène Muller falls on the front. His brothers Camille, Jean and Auguste work occasionally for the Cristallerie de Sèvres, Landier & Fils.

from 1919

Trades under the name 'Muller Frères Lunéville' following the takeover of the 'S.A. des Grandes Verreries de Croismare' glassworks, which belonged from 1905 to Hinzelin, a brewer. Firm address: Lunéville, rue de la Vézouze, since the finishing and decoration workshop is there. In the early 1920s etched overlay glass is still being made there in the manner of industrially produced Gallé glass, most of it with floral or landscape decoration. Colour schemes and style changed between the mid- and late 1920s to contrasting colour combinations with stylized flower and animal motifs and geometric designs in enamels or relief etching, also with mica inclusions. Production centres on lamps, which are free-blown or mould-blown with compressed air.

from 1923

Victor and Désiré Muller found a glass refinery, 'Verrerie Muller' in Lunéville, at 16, rue Sébastien Keller. Employing a workforce of approx. 32 in 1926, it merges with the joint-stock company in Croismare in 1927.

Trades under the name 'S.A. des Grandes Verreries de Croismare et Verreries d'Art Muller Frères Réunies'. On 6 May 1929 development and application for patent registration of a sandwich glass decoration, under no. 674.628, for the 'Procédé de décoration d'objets dans l'épaisseur du verre entre deux ou plusieurs couches au moyen d'intercalaires décoratifs' (Technique of decorating objects throughout the thickness of the glass between two or more casings by means of decorative intercalation). Sold in Paris by Blondiaux, 40, rue de Paradis. In 1932 the business is in debt as a consequence of the worldwide economic crisis. In 1934 the glass refinery in Lunéville, 16, rue Sébastien Keller, closes down and the buildings are requisitioned by the municipality in 1940 for military purposes. In 1935 the glass factory in Croismare ceases production and the buildings are taken over in 1937 by a forge, 'Forges et Ateliers de la Vezouze'.

1935–1939

Georges and Marcel Muller continue to run a small decoration studio in Lunéville, Faubourg d'Einville.

1945–1952

Georges and Désiré Muller run a small studio in Lunéville, place du Château, which closes in 1952 on the death of Désiré Muller.

Exhibitions

1908
London, Franco-British Exhibition
1925
Paris, Exposition Internationale des Arts Décoratifs et Industriels Modernes (exh. cat.)

Archival documents and literature

Supplementing Schmitt, Zurich II, 1995 p. 326: Nancy 1901, p. 150, no. 828; Paris 1910, pp. 7, 11; exh. cat., Turin 1911, *Parco del Valentino: Exposition internationale des industries et du travail – Catalogue spécial officiel de la section française* (Paris, 1911), see Houdaille & Triquet; ■ F. Borga, 'La Prestigieuse signature des frères Muller: Maîtres verriers', *Trouvailles*, no. 59 (Aug. and Sept. 1986): 50–51, with illus.; ■ J.-P. Carciofi, 'Les Frères Muller: Maîtres-verriers à Lunéville 1895–1952', *La Revue Lorraine Populaire*, no. 71 (Aug. 1986): 256–59, with illus.; Tokyo, *Style floral*, 1988, no. 98; Aptel et al. 1989, pp. 78, 88, 277; Debize 1989, pp. 31, 36, 49, 56, 66, 70, 78, 89–91, illus. pp. 30, 88; *Glass Fantasy* 1990, pp. 25, 93, 183–84, 187, 200; Cappa 1991, 344–47, 470–71; ■ P. Thiébaut, *Etude architecturale: Usine de gravure et de décoration sur verre, dite Verrerie Muller*, Service Régional de l'Inventaire de Lorraine (Nancy, 1992); Bartha, Neumann Collection, 1993, p. 112; ■ P. Thiébaut, *Etude architecturale: Verrerie Guerner, puis Muller Frères, puis Forges et Ateliers de la Vezouze*, Service régional de l'inventaire de Lorraine (Nancy, 1993); Schmitt, Zurich II, 1995, pp. 109, 218, 326, nos. 176, 379; Suzuki, *Kitazawa*, 1996, nos. 53–57, 430–32; Takeda and Olivié 1996, nos. 40–41; ■ F.-T. Charpentier, 'Gallé après Gallé', *Arts Nouveaux: Bulletin de l'Association du Musée de l'Ecole de Nancy*, no. 10 (spring 1994): 15–18, illus. pp. 16–17; Schmitt, Zurich II, 1995, pp. 109, 218, 326, nos. 176, 379; Suzuki, *Kitazawa*, 1996, nos. 53–57, 430–32; Takeda and Olivié 1996, nos. 40–41; Le Tacon and De Luca 1999, p. 22; Meisenthal 1999, p. 20; Nancy 1999, p. 182, cat. nos. 286–88, illus. pp. 268, 334.

→Gallé

Paul Jean Baptiste Nicolas

Laval-devant-Bruyères, Vosges 25 May 1875– Nancy 21 Feb. 1952
Son of a gardener, Jean Pierre Nicolas, and wife, Marguerite Catherine, née Jacques; younger brother of Emile Nicolas (1871–1940), well-known art critic and later president of the Académie de Stanislas in Nancy, who supports him.

1885–1892

Attends higher secondary school; completes architecture studies at the Ecole des Beaux-Arts in Nancy.

1893–1914

Works in →Emile Gallé's decoration studio after one year, gaining experience as an architect. Trains in etching, painting floral decoration and as an engraver. Also designs ceramics (executed by the Société des Produits Céramiques de Rambervillers) and textiles (executed by Charles Fridrich, Nancy). In 1896 national service. Before 1900 deputy of →Louis Hestaux (1858–1919), most important artist working at Emile Gallé's decoration studio and head of it. Participation in the 1900 Paris Exhibition as a privileged member of Gallé's staff. From 1901 member of the Alliance Provinciale des Industries d'Art, otherwise known as the Ecole de Nancy.

1904–1914

Assistant to Louis Hestaux, who becomes artistic director of the Gallé factories 'Cristallerie & Ebénisterie d'Art' on Gallé's death. About 1905 marries Madeleine Marie Lantche, with whom he has three sons, including Paul (b. 1907). Occasionally does illustrations for the journal *La Lorraine Artiste* and designs embroidery patterns for his wife. In 1908 participates in the Strasbourg Exhibition with glass, embroidery, bronze fittings, wrought iron and stoneware vessels executed by Alphonse Cythère, Société des Produits Céramiques de Rambervillers. Address in Nancy: 80, rue de Laxou.

1914–1918

Military service and cessation of operations at the Gallé factories.

1919–1923

Own studio for decorating glass in Nancy, at 64, rue de la République; engraving and cutting workshop on the ground floor of his private dwelling, with a separate etching workshop in the garden. Until 1923 collaborates with three former employees of the Etablissement Gallé: the engravers Pierre Mercier, Eugène Windeck and Emile Villermaux; trades under the name 'Les Graveurs réunis'. Signatures *D'Argental* with cross of Lorraine and *L'Art Verrier* with or without the addition of *SL*. In 1920 participates in the Nancy exhibition, showing 12 engraved crystal vases under the auspices of the Société des Graveurs sur Cristaux; designer: Paul Nicolas; employees: E. Windeck, E. Villermaux, Guy Roger, H. Windeck; blanks procured from the 'Cristallerie de Saint-Louis' in Saint-Louis-lès-Bitche. Produces etched, also engraved overlay decoration with floral motifs and landscapes in the manner of the Etablissement Gallé. In 1923 studio co-operative disbands when employees rejoin their former firm.

1923–1952

Trades under the name 'Paul Nicolas Cristaux d'Art', retains studio: 64, rue de la République; from 1928/29 signature *Paul Nicolas*. Also freelances at 'Cristallerie de Saint-Louis' in Saint-Louis-lès-Bitche, at first mainly continuing the Art Nouveau style and collaborating with a select group of glassmakers. Until *c.* 1931 employs a workforce of 14 in the studio, then lays off some employees owing to the worldwide economic crisis. Work sold in Nancy by Galerie Moser, 43, rue Saint-Dizier, and in Paris by Rigaut, rue de Paradis; exports to Argentina, Japan, the United States and Morocco. In 1925 designs for engraving and cutting on colourless crystal glass, *c.* 1930 on cased glass, with geometric designs in the 1920s style. From 1926 to 1933 son Jean is employed by the firm. From 1930 to 1938 glass with colours and decoration of high quality between casings that, unlike similar work by contemporary artists and firms, recalls Art Nouveau glass in the handling of form, colour and liveliness of representation. Particularly fine stylized underwater scenes, also in combination with elaborate engraving. In 1932 vase commissioned by the Société Centrale d'Horticulture for Albert Lebrun, President of the Republic. In 1936 awarded the distinction of 'Meilleur Ouvrier de France' for a vase with red fish in sandwiched decoration. In 1938 glass vessel commissioned by Lorraine artists as a present for the Grand Duchess of Luxembourg.

1940–1952

Enamel painting on blanks by →Daum Frères, stoved by Nicolas in the kiln owned by his friend, Amalric Walter (1870–1959).

Exhibitions
1920
Nancy, Salle Victor Poirel, Société Lorraine des Amis des Arts (exh. cat.), again in 1929 (exh. cat.) and in the 1930s
1925
Paris, Exposition Internationale des Arts Décoratifs et Industriels Modernes (exh. cat.) – honorary diploma
1934
Paris, Musée Galliéra, Le Verre, la Mosaïque et l'Email
1937
Paris, Champ-de-Mars, Exposition Internationale des Arts et Techniques dans la Vie moderne (international) – diploma and gold medal

Archival documents and literature
Supplementing Schmitt, Zurich II, 1995, p. 327: birth certificate, Archives Municipales de Laval, 1875, no. 11; Nancy 1902, p. 137, nos. 647–49; Nancy 1908, p. 140, nos. 556–57; Emile Nicolas, 'L'Ecole de Nancy à Strasbourg', *Bulletin des sociétés artistiques de l'Est* (March 1908): 33; Commandant Lalance, 'L'Ecole de Nancy à Strasbourg', ibid. (May): 63, 64–65; Strasbourg 1908, p. 15, no. 52, p. 25, nos. 167–73; Nancy 1912, p. 52, no. 329; Lafitte 1912, p. 43; Nancy 1913, p. 67, no. 456; Nancy 1920, p. 58, no. 446; Nancy 1929, p. 73, no. 917; death certificate, Archives Municipales de la Ville de Nancy, 1952, no. 305; Charpentier et al. 1987, pp. 83, 138, 154, 155, 164, 259, 300, 310; Aptel et al. 1989, pp. 74, 81, 197, 252, 277; Debize 1989, pp. 37, 56, 70, 78, 91, illus. p. 90; Yoshimizu and Klesse 1992, nos. 195–97; F.-T. Charpentier, 'Gallé après Gallé', *Arts Nouveaux, Bulletin de l'Association du Musée de l'Ecole de Nancy*, no. 10 (spring 1994): 15, illus. p. 14; Schmitt, Zurich II, 1995, pp. 218, 327, no. 379; Epinal 1997, cat. no. 61, pp. 115–16; Nancy 2001, cat. no. 68, illus. p. 95; ■ A. Chambrion, 'Un Grand Décorateur sur cristaux Paul Nicolas', *Arts Nouveaux: Magazine de l'Art Nouveau en Lorraine et dans le Monde: Association des Amis du Musée de l'Ecole de Nancy* (Dec. 2002): 22–26.

→Gallé

François Eugène Rousseau called Eugène Rousseau

Paris 17 March 1827–Paris 12 June 1890
Eldest son of Joseph Rousseau (12 June 1797–2 Oct. 1855) and his wife, Alexandrine Henriette Cochet (d. 11 Aug. 1838); a younger brother, Ernest Paul Rousseau (b. 29 April 1833). Joseph Rousseau, specialist dealer in faience, leases in December 1824 a shop for porcelain and faience (est. 1753 by Louis-François Picard-Duban) at 41, rue Coquillière (1er arrondissement). From 1827 his advertisements bear the title of purveyor to the court ('Faïencier du Roi et des Princes') of porcelain, faience, stoneware, crystal and utility glass as well as flooring tiles, garden urns, bottles, stoppers, etc.

from 1855
Eugène Rousseau manages the family firm after his father's death; his younger brother, Ernest Paul, is employed there. In 1856 Eugène Rousseau marries Ernestine Bourg (d. 1901), with whom he has two daughters, Geneviève (d. 1934) and Marguerite. In a complex comprising an inner courtyard surrounded by housing tracts, Rousseau rents business space on the ground floor and several flats at 41, rue Coquillière.
from 1861
Works as a designer, at first of porcelain painting, executed by 'Creil et Montereau' in Paris and such freelance porcelain painters as Alphonse Walter, father of the glass artist Amalric Walter, and from 1871 Henri Lambert, both from 1859 painters in the Sèvres porcelain factory. Successfully shows porcelain and stoneware with decoration in the antique style, including putti, ornaments and plants, at the 1862 London International Exhibition. In 1863–67 porcelain design, decorated in the *pâte sur pâte* technique in collaboration with Marc-Louis-Emmanuel Solon (1835–1913), who works at the Sèvres factory as a specialist in this technique and signs his work for Rousseau with the pseudonym Milès.
from 1864
Founding member of the Union Centrale des Beaux-Arts Appliqués à l'Industrie. From 1866 to 1868 collaborates with Félix Bracquemond (1833–1914), who does

etchings after Japanese colour woodcuts by Katsushika Hokusai (1760–1849) and Hiroshige (1797–1858) as models for the first faience dining service designed by Rousseau. Known as the 'Service Rousseau', launched at the 1867 Paris Exposition Universelle, it is still regarded as a milestone of Japonist design in France, which gave rise to new impulses in the decorative arts.
c. 1867/68
Begins to have glass made after his own designs, at first presumably at several different studios (see on this pp. 25–26). Among the first models are two pieces with enamel painting acquired in 1869 by the Victoria & Albert Museum in London. About 1867/68–1870 or 1872/73 begins to collaborate with →Eugène Michel (1848–1904), who executes cut and engraved decoration. In 1869 Rousseau is in the rolls of the Chambre Syndicale de la Céramique et de la Verrerie (est. 1868). About 1871–77, presumably as early as 1867/68, collaboration with the Paris glass factory →Appert Frères, at 6, rue Royale (19e arrondissement), for blanks after his own designs.
from 1874
Successful with Japanese-inspired glass designs, including crystal glass in rock crystal engraving, at exhibitions, first at the IVe Exposition de l'Union Centrale des Beaux-Arts Appliqués à l'Industrie in Paris. In 1877 reduces the number of sales rooms he has leased at 41, rue Coquillière. Begins to work with Alphonse Reyen, a known specialist in etching on cased glass. Participates hors-concours in the 1878 Paris Exposition Universelle, at which 'Cristalleries de Baccarat' and →Emile Gallé also shows Japanese-inspired designs. By then Rousseau has exhibited his first 'strass glass'. In 1884 participates in the eighth Union Centrale Exhibition, showing opaque colour glass for the first time, also as overlay engraved like Chinese glass as well as 'strass glass' with powdered glass inclusions, particles of gold or metallic compounds and 'strass craquelé' variants in combination with fissures on the inner wall created by crazing as well as a vase with a relief of a leaping carp taking up half of one face. Further motifs: a vase with two elephant-head appliqués, chrysanthemums with 16 petals, a pond scene with butterflies and a sphinx. Rousseau's innovative exhibits spark off controversy among experts. In 1885 is made a Chevalier de la Légion d'Honneur.
16 Dec. 1885
Sells his business, including all stock, his designs and his cast-iron moulds, to →Ernest Léveillé (1841–1913).
1885–1889
Collaboration with Léveillé, whom he instructs in his glassmaking techniques. Participating jointly in the 1889 Paris Exposition Universelle, they were awarded a gold medal.

Exhibitions
1869
Altona, Altonaer Industrieverein von 1845 (organization), Schleswig-Holsteinische Landes-Industrie-Ausstellung: Internationale Ausstellung für Industrie, Gewerbe, Landwirtschaft, Fischerei, Bergbau und Viehzucht [Schleswig-Holstein State Industrial Exhibition: International Exhibition for Industry, Crafts, Agriculture, Fishing, Mining and Stock-Farming] – silver medal
1871
London, International Exhibition, 'Art de France' section – medal
1933
Paris, Pavillon de Marsan, Le Décor de la Vie sous la IIIe République de 1870 à 1900 (exh. cat.)

Archival documents and literature
Supplementing Schmitt, Zurich II, 1995, pp. 340–41: *Almanach du Commerce*, 1827, pp. CCLXXII, 95; Inventaire après décès d'Alexandrine Henriette Cochet du 28 Aug. 1838, Archives Nationales Minutier central, XV, 1890; Cadastre 1852, 41, rue Coquillière, Archives de Paris, D1P4, 1852, no. 299; Contrat de Mariage Rousseau and Bourg, 31 May 1856, Archives Nationales Minutier central, LXVI, 1334; Cadastre 1862, 41, rue Coquillière, Archives de Paris, D1P4, 1862, no. 300; 'Chambre syndicale de la céramique et de la verrerie, Liste des adhérents', *Moniteur de la céramique, de la verrerie et des industries qui s'y rattachent*, no. 1 (1869): 38; *Union centrale des beaux-arts appliqué à l'industrie, Quatrième exposition 1874: Catalogue des œuvres et des produits modernes exposés au Palais de l'industrie* (Paris, 1874), p. 104; P. Burty, *Rapport présenté par le jury de la IVe section art appliqué à la céramique et à la verrerie, Union centrale des beaux-arts appliqué à l'industrie* (Paris, 1875), pp. 8, 13; Cadastre 1876, 41, rue Coquillière, Archives de Paris, D1P4, 1876, no. 300; enquiry

about participation in the 1878 Paris Exposition Universelle, Questionnaire 1878, classe 19, Archives Nationales F 12 3367; Didron and Clémendot 1880, p. 43; drawing by Bracquemond for the 'Service Rousseau', *Revue des Arts Décoratifs* 1 (1880–81): illus. p. 216; Josse, 'L'Art japonais, à propos de l'exposition organisée par M. Gonse. Lettres', ibid.: 333; P. Arène, 'Huitième Exposition de L'Union Centrale: Pierre, bois de construction, terre et verre – La Céramique', ibid. 5 (1884–85): 172; ■ E. Bazire, 'La Verrerie et la cristallerie', ibid., p. 193, illus. pl. p. 194a; ■ L. de Fourcaud, 'Rapport général', ibid.: 259–60, illus. p. 258a; sale agreement Rousseau and Léveillé 1885, Archives nationales, Minutier Central, LXVI, 1689, 16 Dec. 1885, *Vente de matériel et marchandises par M. Rousseau à M. et Mme Léveillé*; Garnier 1886, pp. 343–44, illus. nos. 57, 59, 64–65; exhibits 'Maison Léveillé 1889', *Supplément à la Revue des Arts Décoratifs* VII (Nov. 1889): n.p.; exhibits 'Maison Léveillé 1889', ibid. XII (July and Aug.): n.p.; Eugène Rousseau succession, Archives de Paris, succession après décès 17 Oct 1890, DQ7, 10930; R. Marx, 'La Décoration achitecturale et les industries d'art à l'exposition universelle de 1889', *Revue des Arts Décoratifs* 11 (1890–91): 37–39; ■ V. Champier, 'Nécrologie Eugène Rousseau: Céramiste et verrier', ibid.: 86–92; Marx 1900, p. 54; Paris 1910, pp. 4–5, 7, 10, 12–13; Jean 1911, pp. 296–97; Munich, *Nancy 1900*, 1980, p. 145, no. 5; ■ Schneck 1988; ■ Schneck 1990; *Glass Fantasy* 1990, p. 46; Yoshimizu and Klesse 1992, nos. 1–6; Bartha, Neumann Collection, 1993, p. 113; Schmitt, Zurich II, 1995, pp. 41, 340–41, nos. 57–58; Suzuki, *Kitazawa*, 1996, no. 436; Mukai, *Hida Takayama*, 1997, p. 72; documentation Musée d'Orsay, Paris; information on the exhibition in Altona from 27 Aug. to 27 Sept. 1869 imparted in writing by Meike Annuss, Altonaer-Museum, Hamburg, on 20 May 2002; Hendrik Eder, Staatsarchiv, Hamburg, on 19 May 2003 and 11 June 2003.

→Harant & Guignard, Léveillé, Michel

Verreries Réunies de Vallerysthal et Portieux
Anonyme Gesellschaft der Vereinigten Glashütten von Vallerysthal & Portieux
Vallerysthal, Lorraine

1838

The Vallerysthal glass factory is built in Val de Vallery by Baron Auguste François Eléonore de Klinglin (16 July 1785–26 June 1863), from 1833 proprietor of the 'Plaine de Walsch' glassworks (est. 1707). Permission to build is granted by King Louis Philippe on 17 May 1838. The first furnace is fired up on 4 Nov. 1838 in the presence of Eugène de Fontenay, director of the Plaine de Walsch glassworks and also in charge of Vallerysthal. Plaine de Walsch is known in the early nineteenth century for the purity of its glass. After 1833 production also includes laboratory glass, such as test tubes, as well as 'Bohemian glass' (half crystal, coloured and cut flashed glass). Incorporation of Baron Klinglin's Plaine de Walsch and Vallerysthal factories as 'Verreries de Plaine-de-Walsch et Vallerysthal'. Receives awards as early as 1839, 1844 and 1849.

1841

Workforce of 250; product: lead-free clear and coloured glass as well as utility glass. Marketed in France, Spain and the United States.

1842–1854

Director: Guérard Toutain. Gradual move of the Plaine de Walsch glassworks to Vallerysthal, which closes down in 1855/56. On 14 July 1854 the limited-liability company 'Société des verreries de Plaine-de-Walsch et Vallerysthal' is established. At the end of 1854 Guérard Toutain becomes managing director of the merged outlets and warehouses of the →Burgun, Schverer & Cie. and Vallerysthal glassworks in Paris, at 32, rue Poissonnière, trading under the name 'Toutain Guérard et Cie.'.

1855

Director: Auguste Lefebvre Dollement (until 15 Oct.). Workforce of 506. Foremen: 12 (overseers); 144 glassmakers; 173 glass cutters and grinders; 12 painters and engravers; 63 specialist grinders (watch and clock glass); 114 craftsmen and unskilled labourers; 75 woodcutters.

end of 1855–1858

Director: Auguste Adolphe Duponchel.

from 1856

Trades under the name 'Société anonyme des verreries de Plaine-de-Walsch et de Vallerysthal' after conversion into a joint-stock company with five directors on the board; Baron de Klinglin now holds only one-third of capitalization. In 1857 a third furnace goes into operation. The inventory lists 400 copper and iron moulds and 30 different types of 'pigments', making possible a broad range of coloured and opal glass products.

1859–1877

Director: Adrien Thouvenin. In 1861 only the Paris outlet with warehouse, after withdrawal of Burgun, Schverer & Cie. continues to operate, managed jointly by Auguste Adolphe Duponchel and Louis Auguste Gosse. About 1863 new Siemens furnaces installed. By 1870 Vallerysthal is one of the largest European makers of hollow glass, producing a wide range of pressed glass as well as handmade pieces. In 1871 workforce of 622: 60 female workers; 80 boys aged between 12 and 14; 92 boys and 21 girls aged between 14 and 16. Three furnaces (two made by Siemens with 12 pots each; a Boëtius with 10 pots).

1871–1918

The Franco-Prussian War of 1870–71 leaves Vallerysthal in the part of Alsace-Lorraine ceded to Germany.

from 1872

Trades under the name 'Société anonyme des verreries réunies de Vallerysthal et Portieux' and 'Vereinigte Glashütten von Vallerysthal & Portieux' after acquisition of the Portieux glassworks (est. 1705), located from 1870 in the French part of Alsace-Lorraine. The board of directors of the 'Société anonyme des verreries de Plaine-de-Walsch et de Vallerysthal' decides on 30 Aug. 1871 and 14 Sept. 1872 to continue to maintain business links with France without levying customs-related surcharges. Apart from the sales rooms with warehouse in Paris, similarly structured branches in Bordeaux, Lyons and Strasbourg. From 1874 etched glass made. In 1875 it becomes one of the first European glass factories to establish company health-care and set up pensions for employees.

1877–1887

Director: Paul Thouvenin, son of Adrien Thouvenin. At 1878 the Paris Exposition Universelle shows services engraved with floral decoration and silver inclusions, large painted vases simulating porcelain, lacquer and hardstones. About 1882 various technical innovations, including the building of a facility to house new furnaces, which begin production in 1885. From 1885 employee housing built. In 1886 workforce of 1230. Plant: 4 anthracite-fired glass furnaces (Siemens system), 36 open pots. Workshops for painting and grinding (water and steam grinding). Products: half crystal in all colours, glass for watches and clocks. Outlets in Leipzig and Offenburg. Showrooms in Paris, Bordeaux, Strasbourg, London and Constantinople.

1887–1892

Director: René Verdelet. In 1891 workforce of 871 workmen and 279 women employed in the making of hollow glass.

1892–1913

Directors: Camille Bricka (glass technology) and Richard Böhmer (administration and sales management). From 1898 to 1899 production of glass art after designs by Charles Spindler (1865–1938), an artisan, and by F. A. Otto Krüger (b. 1868) and Bruno Paul (1874–1968), painters associated with the Munich Vereinigte Werkstätten. In addition, links with →Désiré Christian in Meisenthal.

1900–1909

By 1901 fifth furnace built in a new facility. In 1902–9 workforce ranges from 1300 to 1400. Three anthracite-fired glass furnaces (Siemens system), 40 open pots. Two anthracite-fired tank furnaces (Klettenhoff system); by 1905 only three in operation (Stenger 1988, p. 149). Two steam-powered machines. Products: smooth, cut, etched, engraved and decorated hollow glass; pressed-glass articles; glass for watches and clocks; flat glass. Speciality: matt and satin glass. Showrooms and stock samples in 1902 in Paris, Strasbourg, Berlin and Hamburg, in 1903 also in Bordeaux, London, Constantinople and Cologne. About 1910 concentration on the serial production of glasses; glass art no longer sold.

1913–1914

Director: François Schwaller, conscripted in 1914.

1914–1918

The glassworks is under sequestration during the war. From December 1915 Wilhelm Neu, director of the Gebrüder Röchling Bank in Saarbrücken, acts as managing director. Production management: Eduard Cropsal. About 1915 workforce of 1500. Plant: 4 Siemens glass furnaces, both anthracite and press-coal-fired, and 46 open pots; water and steam grinding facility. Products: sets of tableware in finest special and half crystal; decoration: guilloché, etched, cut and gilded; *Römer*, beakers, crystal and white pressed glass, painted jars, clock pendulums, glass for barometers, clock glass for chemical uses and preserving jars. Show-rooms in Berlin and Hamburg. In Oct. 1917 workforce of 870 employed in Vallerysthal.

1919–1938

Director: André Lacombe. Years of renovation and modernization of plant and facilities begins. In 1920 a grinding workshop is closed because a number of grinders are transferred to the new grinding workshop established by the Cristallerie Baccarat in Rambervillers. In 1929 four-month strike. In 1930 trades under the name 'Société anonyme des verreries mécaniques de Vallerysthal et Portieux'. In 1931 the factory employs a workforce of 960. Owing to the worldwide economic crisis from 1929 successive redundancies, especially in the decoration workshop. In 1933 former head gaffer, Victor Berton, who has been with the business since 1868, is made a Chevalier de la Légion d'Honneur. In 1935 four furnaces make 'gobeleterie et moulure' (goblets and moulding), a furnace is reserved for clock and watch glass. Joseph Stenger designs the successful pressed glass 'Pensée' (pansy or heartsease) service.

1938–1939

Director: Edmond Hanus.

1939–1945

Again under German administration. War forces factory to cease operations, except for one furnace; production comes to a standstill sometimes on account of raw materials shortages and bomb damage.

1946–1953

Director: Paul Schweizer. Two furnaces fired up in Sept. 1946, a third in April 1949. In 1950 the glassworks employs a workforce of 480. Machine-made glasses made with tank furnace in Portieux from 1949 to 1955.

1953–1960

Director: Col. of Reserves Hallouin.

1960–1972

Director: Joseph Stenger. From 1960 to 1974 training centre for glassmakers and glass cutters and grinders, run from 1974 by the Lycée d'enseignement technique in Sarrebourg.

1970

Trades under the name 'Compagnie Française du Cristal' after merger of Vallerysthal-Portieux, Vannes-le-Châtel and Bayel-Fains. From 1971 it becomes obvious that Vallerysthal will be shut down. 360 redundancies.

1 May 1977

Vallerysthal ceases operations with a workforce of 130. Portieux continues to exist because the workforce registers a complaint, in 1983 switching to glass art and trading under the name 'Art de Portieux'. Designers includes such world-famous artists as Jean-Paul van Lith (b. 1940), Monica Damian-Eyrignoux (b. 1936) and Matei Négréanu (b. 1941).

Exhibitions

1838

Nancy, Industrial Exhibition – gold medal

1839

Paris, 9e Exposition des Produits de l'Industrie Française –gold medal, again in 1844 –gold medal and in 1849 –gold medal and 3 medals (platinum, bronze and silver) from the Société d'Encouragements pour l'Industrie Nationale

1840

Besançon, Industrial Exhibition –silver medal

1886

Leipzig, Messe (Trade Fair): regular participation until 1916

1906

Metz, Lothringer Keramische Ausstellung (Lorraine Ceramics Exhibition) – medal

Archival documents and literature

Supplementing Schmitt, *Sammlung Silzer*, 1989, p. 324: lists of objects and letterhead, Archives Departementales St-Julien-les-Metz, 21J19; 21J21; ancillary records for factory statistics, Archives Departementales du Bas-Rhin, Strasbourg, 87AL4780; M. Tresc. et al., *Visite à l'Exposition Universelle de Paris en 1855* (Paris, 1855), p. 674; *Almanach du Commerce*, 1857, pp. 589, 874; *Welt-Ausstellung 1873 in Wien – Amtliches Verzeichnis der Aussteller, welchen von der internationalen Jury Ehrenpreise zuerkannt worden sind* (Vienna, 1873), p. 308, no. 226; Cohausen and Poschinger 1874, pp. 68, 70; exh. rep., *Paris: Glass 1878/1879*, p. 428; *Deutschlands*

Glasindustrie: Verzeichnis sämmtlicher deutscher Glashütten mit Angabe ihrer Fabrikate, ed. J. Fahdt, 5th ed. (Dresden, 1886), pp. 5–6; ibid., 8th ed. (Dresden, 1893), pp. 6–7; A. T. Stoll (ed.), *Strassburger Industrie- und Gewerbeausstellung für Elsass-Lothringen, Baden und die bayerische Rheinpfalz* (Schlettstadt, Alsace, 1896), p. 59; Strasbourg 1897, p. 52, nos. 222–25.; 'Gläser aus Vallerysthal', *Dekorative Kunst* 1, no. 3 (1899): 45–46, illus. pp. 58–59, 243; Strasbourg 1901, pp. 87–88, nos. 493–504; 'Die Lothringische Glasindustrie', *Das Kunstgewerbe in Elsass-Lothringen* 2 (1901–2): 32, 34; *Deutschlands Glasindustrie: Verzeichnis sämtlicher deutscher Glashütten mit Angabe ihrer Fabrikate*, ed. J. Fahdt, 11th ed. (Dresden, 1902), p. 7; *Adressbuch der Keram- und Glasindustrie in Deutschland und Österreich and Ungarn* (Coburg, 1903), p. 10; *Deutschlands Glasindustrie: Adressbuch sämtlicher deutscher Glashütten*, issued by the editors of *Die Glashütte*, 18th ed. (Dresden, 1915/16), p. 8; T. Knorr, 'Das Lothringische Glas', *Die wirtschaftliche Entwicklung Elsass-Lothringens 1871–1918* (Frankfurt am Main, 1931), pp. 313, 319, 332; *L'Art du verre*, exh. cat., Musée des Arts Décoratifs, Paris, compiled by L. Amic (Paris, 1951), pp. 26, 149–50, nos. 719–35; *Union centrale des arts décoratifs, 1ère Triennale d'Art Contemporain, Art et Technique – Formes utiles*, essay by F. Carnot (Paris, 1956), s.p. Vallerysthal with illus.; Liège 1958, *Aspects de la verrerie contemporaine*, exh. cat., Musée Curtius, Liège, compiled by R. Chambon and P. Joseph (Liège, 1958), pp. 60–61, nos. 255–56, illus. no. 255; *Verrerie européenne 1958–1963*, exh. cat. Musée du Verre, Liège, compiled by J. Beguin and J. Philippe (Liège, 1963), pp. 51–52, nos. 202–13, illus. nos. 207, 210; ■ Stenger 1988, pp. 128–59, 229–30, 232–33, 234; Schmitt, *Sammlung Silzer*, 1989, pp. 13–14, 322–25, nos. 165–66, illus. pp. 323, 325; Venzmer and Mendelssohn, Mainz, 1990, nos. 345–59, with illus.; E. Schmitt, 'Malerei auf Hohlglas: Grundlagen der Glaskunst im Jugendstil', *Kunst & Antiquitäten* 5 (1990): 51–52; Klesse, *Funke-Kaiser* II, 1991, p. 90, no. 130, with illus.; Michel Drouot and Alban Fournier, *Histoire de la Verrerie de Portieux* (Epinal, 1991), pp. 109, 129–44; Cappa 1991, pp. 458–62; Netzer, Berlin, 1994, pp. 58–59, 108–9, nos. 8, 33.

Susanne Brenner and Eva Schmitt

→Burgun, Schverer & Co., Désiré Christian

Signatures

Paris before 1900

Emile Gallé

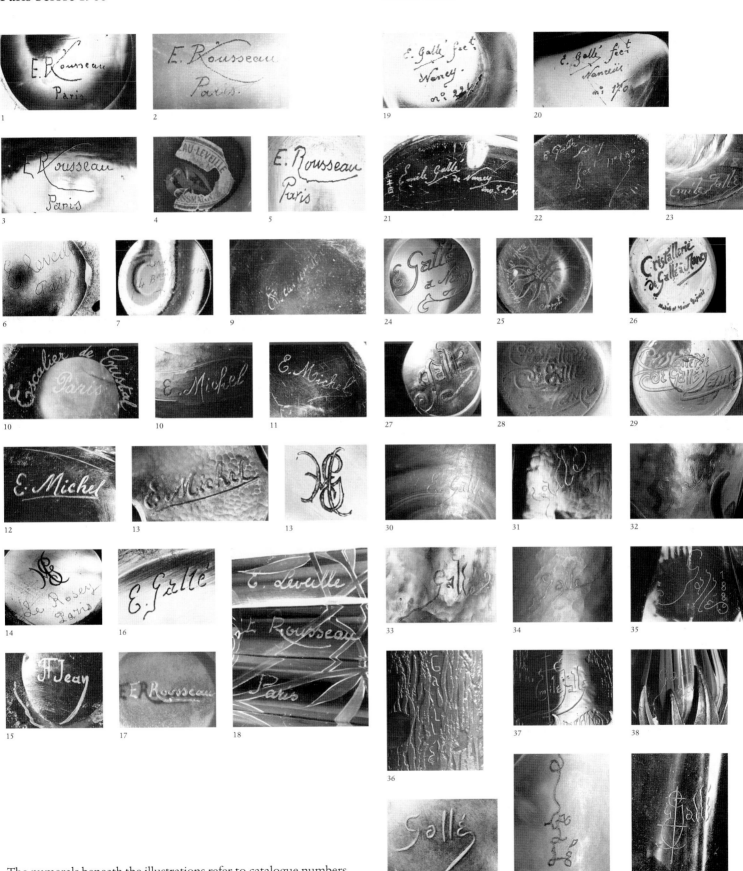

The numerals beneath the illustrations refer to catalogue numbers in this book.

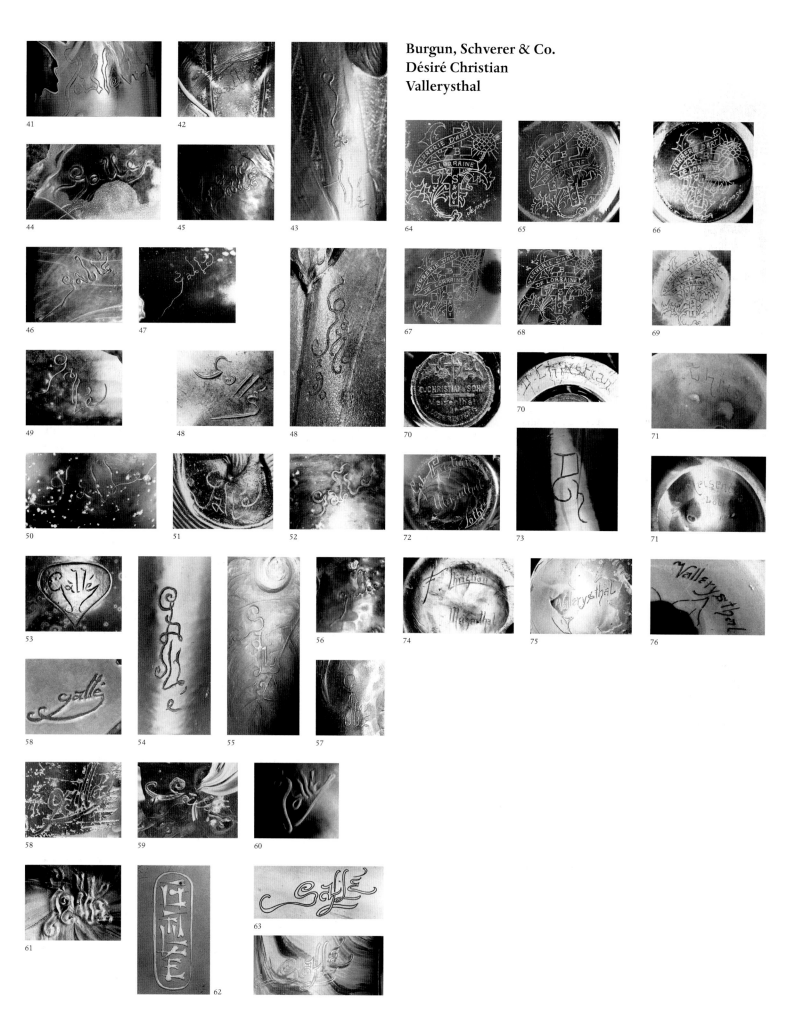

Burgun, Schverer & Co.
Désiré Christian
Vallerysthal

41

42

44

45

43

46

47

49

48

48

64

65

66

67

68

69

70

70

71

50

51

52

72

73

71

53

54

55

56

58

57

74

75

76

58

59

60

61

62

63

Daum Frères

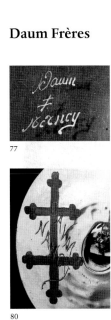
77

78

79

108

109

110

80

81

82

111

112

113

114

115

116

117

118

83

85

86

87

119

120

121

88

89

90

91

Muller Frères
Paul Nicolas

92

93

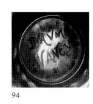
94

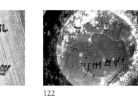
95

122

123

124

96

97

98

99

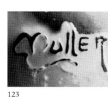
125

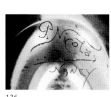
126

100

101

102

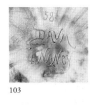
103

104

105

106

107

Selected Exhibitions

1851
London, The Great Exhibition of the Works of Industry of All Nations (1st London Exh.)
Burgun with Toutain and Guérard et Cie.; Escalier de Cristal – Bronze medal, Vallerysthal with Toutain and Guérard et Cie.

1853
New York, World's Fair of the Works of Industry of All Nations
Escalier de Cristal – Silver medal

1855
Paris, Exposition Universelle
Burgun – Honourable mention; Escalier de Cristal – Silver medal; Charles Gallé – Honourable mention; Vallerysthal – Medal, 1st class

1862
London, International Exhibition (exh. rep.)
Escalier de Cristal – Bronze medal; Jean – medal, showed faience; Rousseau – Medal, showed faience and porcelain

1863
Paris, Palais de l'Industrie, Union Centrale des Beaux-Arts Appliqués à l'Industrie
Rousseau – Bronze medal

1865
Paris, Palais de l'Industrie, Union Centrale des Beaux-Arts Appliqués à l'Industrie
Rousseau

1867
Paris, Exposition Universelle
Burgun – Silver medal for drinking glass; Charles Gallé-Reinemer – Honourable mention; Emile Gallé – 1st participation in an exhibition; Escalier de Cristal – Bronze medal; Jean – Bronze medal; Rousseau – Hors-concours, member of the jury; Vallerysthal – Medal, 1st class

1869
Paris, Palais de l'Industrie, Union Centrale des Beaux-Arts Appliqués à l'Industrie
Rousseau

1873
Vienna, Weltausstellung (Vienna International) (exh. rep.)
Appert – Diplôme d'honneur and 2 medals for merit; Lachenal with Théodore Deck – Employee medal; Rousseau – Diploma, showed porcelain; Vallerysthal – Progress medal

1874
Paris, Palais de l'Industrie, Union Centrale des Beaux-Arts Appliqués à l'Industrie
Rousseau – Gold medal, 1st participation with glass

1878
Paris, Exposition Universelle (exh. rep.)
Appert – Gold medal; Escalier de Cristal; Gallé – Bronze medal for glass, silver and bronze medals for ceramics; Jean – Bronze medal; Rousseau – Hors-concours, member of the jury; Vallerysthal – Gold medal

1882
Paris, Union Centrale des Arts Décoratifs, Salon des Arts Décoratifs (exh. cat.)
Jean

1884
Paris, Palais de l'Industrie, VIIIe Exposition de l'Union Centrale des Arts Décoratifs: La Pierre, le Bois de Construction, la Terre et le Verre (exh. rep.)
Gallé – Gold medals for ceramics and glass; Lachenal – Silver medal; Rousseau – Hors-concours

1887
Paris, Palais de l'Industrie, IXe Exposition de l'Union Centrale des Arts Décoratifs: L' Invention, la Forme et le Décor
Lachenal – Bronze medal

1888
Copenhagen, Landbrugs-, Kunst- og Industriudstilling (Agriculture, Art and Industry Exhibition)
Gallé
Nancy, Galeries Poirel, Société Lorraine des Amis des Arts XXVe Exposition
Bussière; Hestaux

1889
Nancy, Galeries Poirel, Société Lorraine des Amis des Arts
Hestaux
Paris, Exposition Universelle (exh. rep.)
Appert – Hors-concours, member of the jury; Bussière – Honourable mention; Gallé – Grand Prix for glass, gold medal for ceramics and silver medal for furniture; Hestaux with Gallé; Lachenal – Gold medal; Léveillé and Rousseau – Gold medal

1890
Nancy, Galeries Poirel, Société Lorraine des Amis des Arts XXVIIe Exposition (exh. cat.)
Bussière; Hestaux

1891
Nancy, Galeries Poirel, Société Lorraine des Amis des Arts
Bussière; Hestaux
Paris, Champ-de-Mars, Salon de la Société Nationale des Beaux-Arts
Gallé; Lachenal

1892
Nancy, Galeries Poirel, Société Lorraine des Amis des Arts (exh. cat.)
Bussière; Hestaux
Paris, Champ-de-Mars, Salon de la Société Nationale des Beaux-Arts
Gallé; Lachenal; Léveillé with Michel

1893
Chicago, IL, World's Columbian Exposition (exh. rep.)
France hors-concours Appert; Daum with Gruber, first participation with glass art; Gallé represented by exhibits from the Musée des Arts Décoratifs in Paris; Léveillé – Commemorative medal
London, Grafton Gallery, French Decorative Art
Gallé; Lachenal; Léveillé
Nancy, Galeries Poirel, Société Lorraine des Amis des Arts (exh. cat.)
Bussière; Hestaux
Paris, Champ-de-Mars, Salon de la Société Nationale des Beaux-Arts
Gallé; Léveillé with Michel

1894
Antwerp, Exposition Internationale d'Anvers
Gallé
Brussels, Pour l'Art
Gallé
Lyons, Exposition Internationale et Coloniale
Daum with Gruber – Grand gold medal
Nancy, Galeries Poirel, Exposition d'Art Décoratif et Industriel Lorrain (exh. cat.)
Daum with Gruber; Gallé with Hestaux; Gruber; Hestaux
Nancy, Galeries Poirel, Société Lorraine des Amis des Arts (exh. cat.)
Daum with Gruber; Gruber; Hestaux
Paris, Champ-de-Mars, Salon de la Société Nationale des Beaux-Arts
Gallé; Lachenal; Léveillé with Michel

1895
Bordeaux, La Société Philomathique de Bordeaux (organ.)*, 13ème Exposition de l'Industrie et des Beaux-Arts, des Arts Industriels et de l'Art Ancien*
Daum with Gruber – Diplôme d'honneur
Brussels, La Libre Esthétique (exh. rep.)
Daum with Gruber
Nancy, Galeries Poirel, Société Lorraine des Amis des Arts (exh. cat.)
Bergé; Bussière; Daum with Bergé and Gruber; Gallé with Hestaux; Gruber; Hestaux
Paris, Champ-de-Mars, Salon de la Société Nationale des Beaux-Arts
Bergé; Gallé; Hestaux; Lachenal; Léveillé with Michel
Remiremont, Exposition de Remiremont
Bussière – 1st participation with ceramics; Daum with Gruber – Purchase by the Committee; Gruber – Purchase of a pastel; Hestaux

Strasbourg, Industrie- und Gewerbe-Ausstellung Elsass-Lothringens, Badens und der bayerischen Rheinpfalz
Burgun – Diplôme d'honneur with medal; awards for employees: Désiré Christian (master painter), Joseph Stenger and Georg Franckhauser (glassmakers); Vallerysthal

1896
Brussels, 3ième Exposition de la Libre Esthétique (exh. rep.)
Gallé
Nancy, Galeries Poirel, Société Lorraine des Amis des Arts
Bussière; Gruber; Hestaux
Paris, Champ-de-Mars, Salon de la Société Nationale des Beaux-Arts
Gallé; Hestaux; Lachenal; Léveillé with Michel

1897
Brussels, Exposition Internationale de Bruxelles (exh. cat.)
Daum with Bergé; Gruber and Lachenal – 2 Diplômes d'honneur, 2 gold medals and 6 medals for employees; Harant & Guignard – Hors-concours, member of the jury
Dresden, Ausstellungshalle an der Stübelallee, Internationale Kunstausstellung (exh. cat.)
Gallé
Munich, Königlicher Glaspalast, VII. Internationale Kunstausstellung
Gallé – Medal, 1st class
Nancy, Galeries Poirel, Société Lorraine des Amis des Arts (exh. cat.)
Bergé; Daum with Bergé and Gruber; Gruber; Hestaux
Paris, Champ-de-Mars, Salon de la Société Nationale des Beaux-Arts
Gallé; Harant & Guignard; Hestaux; Lachenal; Léveillé with Michel
Paris, Palais des Beaux-Arts au Champ-de-Mars, Exposition Nationale de la Céramique et de tous les Arts du Feu
Gallé; Lachenal; Léveillé
Strasbourg, Hôtel de Ville, Exposition d'Art 1897 (exh. cat.)
Burgun; Gallé; Vallerysthal

1898
Munich, Königlicher Glaspalast, VIII. Internationale Kunst-Ausstellung (organ. by the Secession)
Gallé
Nancy, Galeries Poirel, Société Lorraine des Amis des Arts (exh. cat.)
Bergé; Bussière; Daum; Gallé; Gruber; Hestaux
Paris, Champ-de-Mars, Salon de la Société Nationale des Beaux-Arts
Gallé; Harant & Guignard with Michel; Hestaux; Lachenal

1899
Munich, Königlicher Glaspalast, Münchener Jahresausstellung 1899 (exh. cat.)
Christian
Munich, Königliches Kunstausstellungsgebäude am Königsplatz, Internationale Kunst-Ausstellung des Vereins bildender Künstler A.V. 'Sezession' 1899 (exh. cat.)
Daum
Nancy, Galeries Poirel, Société Lorraine des Amis des Arts (exh. cat.)
Bergé; Bussière; Gruber; Hestaux
Paris, Champ-de-Mars, Salon de la Société Nationale des Beaux-Arts
Gallé; Hestaux
St Petersburg, Museum Stieglitz, International Exposition (organ. by Mir Iskousstva)
Gallé

1900
Munich, Königlicher Glaspalast, Münchener Jahresausstellung 1900 (exh. cat.)
Christian
Nancy, Galeries Poirel, Société Lorraine des Amis des Arts (exh. cat.)
Bergé; Gruber; Hestaux
Paris, Exposition Universelle (exh. rep.)
Appert – Hors-concours, member of the jury; Burgun – Silver medal; bronze medals for employees: Eugène Kremer, Jacques Stenger and Joseph Maas; Bussière – Honourable mention, participation with glass for Daum and with ceramics; Christian – Silver medal; Daum – Grand Prix and awards for employees: Silver medal for Bergé (head designer); Bronze medal for Adolphe Claude (glass-blowing), père Dammann (glass painting), Jules Marchand (engraving) and Sévère Winckler (cutting); Honourable mention for Eugène Gall (glass-blowing); Escalier de Cristal – Gold medal; Gallé – Grand Prix for glass and for furniture, respectively; awards for employees: Gold medal for Louis Hestaux

(glass); Silver medal – Louis Hestaux (furniture), Paul Holderbach (glass), Emile Munier (glass painting) and Julien Roiseux (glass-blowing); Bronze medal for Jacques Bour (furniture), Hans Cordier (glass), Diébold (glass engraving), Hippolythe Dubois (furniture), Julien Gillet (glass technology), Auguste Herbst (furniture), Nicolas Meyer (glass technology), Philippe Meyer (glass-blowing), Paul Nicolas (glass, erroneously awarded to his brother, Emile), Ferdinand Schmitzberger (glass engraving), Daniel Schoen (glass), Ismaël Soriot (glass engraving), Adolphe Wendler (furniture) and Rose Wild (glass); Honourable mention for Joseph Beix (furniture), Victor Bourst (glass cutting), Edouard Dignon (furniture), Auguste Dumini (Dermingy) (furniture), Emile Guy (furniture), Henri Hazard (furniture), Chrétien Karcher (furniture), G. Mansuy (furniture), Pierre Mercier (glass engraving), Abel Pierrat (furniture), Nicolas Roth (metal) and Eugène Windeck (glass engraving); Gruber with Daum; Harant & Guignard – Hors-concours, member of the jury; Lachenal – Gold medal; Léveillé – Gold medal; Michel and Rousseau in Union Centrale des Arts Décoratifs special exhibition
Paris, Champ-de-Mars, Salon de la Société Nationale des Beaux-Arts
Gallé; Hestaux

1901
Darmstadt, Die Ausstellung der Künstlerkolonie Darmstadt 1901
Gallé
Dresden, Ausstellungspalast an der Stübelallee, Internationale Kunstausstellung (exh. cat.)
Christian; Gallé; Muller
Nancy, Galeries Poirel, Société Lorraine des Amis des Arts (exh. cat.)
Bussière; Daum; Gruber; Hestaux; Muller
Paris, Champ-de-Mars, Salon de la Société Nationale des Beaux-Arts
Gallé; Hestaux; Lachenal
St Petersburg, Imperial Society for the Promotion of the Arts, St Petersburg International Art Exposition (exh. rep.)
Christian – Silver medal; Daum; Gallé; Harant & Guignard; Lachenal – Gold medal
Strasbourg, Kunstausstellung im Alten Schloss (Art Exhibition in the Old Palace) (exh. cat.)
Burgun; Christian; Vallerysthal

1902
Munich, Königlicher Glaspalast, Münchener Jahresausstellung 1902 (exh. cat.)
Christian
Nancy, Galeries Poirel, Société Lorraine des Amis des Arts (exh. cat.)
Bergé; Bussière; Gruber; Hestaux; Nicolas
Paris, Champ-de-Mars, Salon de la Société Nationale des Beaux-Arts
Gallé; Hestaux
Turin, Prima Esposizione Internazionale d'Arte Decorativa Moderna (1st International Exhibition for the Modern Decorative Arts)
Burgun; Christian – Certificate of recognition; Daum; Vallerysthal

1903
Nancy, Galeries Poirel, Société Lorraine des Amis des Arts (exh. cat.)
Bergé; Bussière; Hestaux
Paris, Pavillon de Marsan, Exposition de l'Alliance Provinciale des Industries d'Art: Ecole de Nancy (exh. cat.)
Bussière; Daum; Gallé; Gruber; Hestaux
Paris, Champ-de-Mars, Salon de la Société Nationale des Beaux-Arts
Gallé; Harant & Guignard / Toy with Léveillé; Hestaux; Lachenal

1904
Nancy, Galeries Poirel, Société Lorraine des Amis des Arts: Ecole de Nancy – Exposition d'Art Décoratif Moderne (exh. cat.)
Bussière with Alphonse Cythère; Daum with Bergé and E. Schneider; Gallé with Hestaux and Nicolas; Gruber; Hestaux
Paris, Petit Palais, 1er Salon de la Société des Artistes Décorateurs
Lachenal; Majorelle; Michel – 1st Retrospective
Paris, Champ-de-Mars, Salon de la Société Nationale des Beaux-Arts
Gallé; Hestaux; Lachenal
St. Louis, MO, Louisiana Purchase Exposition (exh. rep.)
Christian – Gold medal; Daum; Gallé; Léveillé; Michel

1905

Liège, Exposition Universelle et Internationale (exh. cat.; exh. rep.)
Appert Frères – Grand Prix; Daum – Grand Prix and awards for employees: Silver medal for Henri Bergé, Adolphe Claude, père Dammann, Camille Enel, Eugène Gall, Jules Marchand, Emile Maas, Ernest Schneider and Julien Stoop; Honourable mention for Madame Ganné and Madame Jaladis; Harant & Guignard – Hors-concours, member of the jury; awards for employees: Gold medal for Eugène Lavezard and Maurice Macé; Silver medal for Mr Herbert, Charles Kaulfusz, Emile Thiaucourt; Bronze medal for J. Kaulfusz
Nancy, Galeries Poirel, Société Lorraine des Amis des Arts (exh. cat.)
Bussière; Gruber; Hestaux
Paris, Champ-de-Mars, Salon de la Société Nationale des Beaux-Arts
Harant & Guignard / Toy with Léveillé; Hestaux; Lachenal

1906

Dresden, Ausstellungspalast an der Stübelallee, III. Deutsche Kunstgewerbeausstellung (exh. cat.)
Christian
Milan, Esposizione Internazionale del Sempione (International Exhibition on the Occasion of the Inauguration of the Simplon Tunnel)
Appert Frères – Hors-concours; Daum – Grand Prix and awards for employees: Gold medal for Henri Bergé, Adolphe Claude, père Dammann, Jules Marchand, Emile Maas and Ernest Schneider; Silver medal for Camille Enel and Eugène Gall
Nancy, Galeries Poirel, Société Lorraine des Amis des Arts (exh. cat.)
Bussière; Gruber; Hestaux
Paris, Champ-de-Mars, Salon de la Société Nationale des Beaux-Arts
Hestaux
Paris, Pavillon de Marsan, Salon de la Société des Artistes Décorateurs
Lachenal

1907

Nancy, Galeries Poirel, Société Lorraine des Amis des Arts XLIIIe Exposition (exh. cat.)
Gruber; Hestaux
Paris, Champ-de-Mars, Salon de la Société Nationale des Beaux-Arts
Hestaux
Paris, Pavillon de Marsan, Salon de la Société des Artistes Décorateurs
Lachenal

1908

Nancy, Galeries Poirel, Société Lorraine des Amis des Arts (exh. cat.)
Gruber; Hestaux; Nicolas
Paris, Salon d'Automne
Gruber
Paris, Champ-de-Mars, Salon de la Société Nationale des Beaux-Arts
Hestaux
Strasbourg, Palais de Rohan, Exposition d'Art Décoratif de l'Ecole de Nancy à Strasbourg (exh. cat.)
Daum with Bergé and E. Schneider; Gallé; Gruber; Hestaux; Nicolas

1909

Nancy, Galeries Poirel, Société Lorraine des Amis des Arts: Peinture, Sculpture, Architecture (exh. cat.)
Bussière – Participated in the *Exposition Rétrospective pour les Peintres Lorrains H.C. et les Sculpteurs Lorrains Récompensés aux Salons Parisiens*; Gruber; Hestaux
Nancy, Parc Ste-Marie, Exposition Internationale de l'Est de la France Nancy 1909 (exh. rep.)
Bussière – Hors-concours, member of the jury; Daum – Hors-concours, member of the jury; awards for employees: Diplôme d'honneur for Henri Bergé, Eugène Gall, Charles Schneider and Ernest Schneider; Gold medal for Adolphe Claude, père Dammann, Jules Marchand and Hippolyte Wirtz; Silver medal for Emile Dufour, Camille Enel, Jules Georges (engraver), Emile Maas and Paul Porta (glass-blower); bronze medal for Odalbert Langevin, Hilaire Stein and Paul Vautrin; Gallé – Hors-concours, Henriette Gallé member of the jury; Gruber; Hestaux with Gallé; Nicolas
Paris, Champ-de-Mars, Salon de la Société Nationale des Beaux-Arts
Hestaux

1910

Brussels, Exposition Universelle et Industrielle de Bruxelles
Daum – Grand Prix and awards for employees: Diplôme d'honneur for Henri Bergé, Eugène Gall, Charles Schneider, Ernest Schneider and Amalric Walter; Gold medal for Adolphe Claude, père Dammann and Jules Marchand; Silver medal for père Ricard and Emile Wirtz; Bronze medal for Chambreuil, Eugène Dammann, Emile Dufour, Camille Enel, Georges Friedel, Mme Ganné, Jules Georges, Odalbert Langevin, Emile Maas, Victor Marchand, Paul Porta, Rouchon, Basile and Hilaire Stein, Thincelin and Paul Vautrin; Harant & Guignard / Toy – Grand Prix and silver medals for employees Herbert, Guillou and Emile Thiaucourt
Nancy, Galeries Poirel, Société Lorraine des Amis des Arts (exh. cat.)
Daum; Gruber; Hestaux
Paris, Champ-de-Mars, Salon de la Société Nationale des Beaux-Arts
Harant & Guignard / Toy with Léveillé; Hestaux
Paris, Musée Galliera, La Verrerie et la Cristallerie Artistique (exh. cat.)
Appert Frères; Daum with Bergé, Charles Schneider and Amalric Walter; Escalier de Cristal; Gallé; Gruber; Harant & Guignard with Léveillé and Rousseau; Michel; Muller

1911

Nancy, Galeries Poirel, Société Lorraine des Amis des Arts (exh. cat.)
Daum; Gruber; Hestaux
Paris, Champ-de-Mars, Salon de la Société Nationale des Beaux-Arts
Hestaux
Paris, Pavillon de Marsan, Salon de la Société des Artistes Décorateurs
Gruber
Turin, Parco del Valentino, Esposizione Internazionale delle Industrie e del Lavoro (International Exhibition for Industry and Work) (exh. cat.)
Appert Frères; Paris – Grand Prix; Daum; Gruber – Award for a window; Harant & Guignard

1912

Nancy, Galeries Poirel, Société Lorraine des Amis des Arts (exh. cat.)
Gruber; Hestaux; Nicolas

Paris, Champ-de-Mars, Salon de la Société Nationale des Beaux-Arts
Hestaux
Paris, Pavillon de Marsan, Salon de la Société des Artistes Décorateurs
Daum; Gruber
Paris, Grand Palais, Salon d'Automne
Daum

1913

Ghent, Exposition Universelle et Internationale de Gand
Daum – Grand Prix
Nancy, Galeries Poirel, Société Lorraine des Amis des Arts (exh. cat.)
Bussière – Retrospective; Hestaux; Nicolas
Paris, Champ-de-Mars, Salon de la Société Nationale des Beaux-Arts
Hestaux
Paris, Pavillon de Marsan, Salon de la Société des Artistes Décorateurs
Lachenal

1914

Paris, Champ-de-Mars, Salon de la Société Nationale des Beaux-Arts
Hestaux
Paris, Pavillon de Marsan, Salon de la Société des Artistes Décorateurs
Lachenal

Selected Bibliography

■ = Publication of major importance

Allgemeines Künstlerlexikon
Allgemeines Künstlerlexikon: Die bildenden Künstler aller Zeiten und Völker. Vol. 1f. Munich and Leipzig, 1983f.

■ *Almanach du Commerce* 1797ff.
1797–1818: Almanach du Commerce de la ville de Paris par La Tynna. Ed. de la Tynna; *1819–1838: Bottin du Commerce de Paris, des départements de la France et des principales villes du monde,* ed. Sébastien Bottin; *1839–1856: Annuaire général du commerce et de l'industrie, de la magistrature et de l'administration ou almanach des 500.000 adresses.* Issued by Firmin Didot, since 1857 issued by Didot & Bottin. Paris, 1797ff.

André 1894
C. André. *Exposition des arts décoratifs lorrains: Discours prononcé à la séance d'inauguration du 22 juin 1894.* Nancy, 1894.

Antiquitätenzeitung. Munich (972ff.).

Appert and Henrivaux 1893
L. Appert and J. Henrivaux. 'La Verrerie à l'exposition universelle de 1889'. Exh. rep., Champ-de-Mars, Paris. *Revue Technique de l'Exposition de 1889* 10 (1893): 353–54.

Aptel et al. 1989
C. Aptel, H. Claude, C. Coley et al. *Nancy 1900: Rayonnement de l'Art Nouveau.* Ed. Gérard Klopp. Thionville, 1989.

Art & Décoration. Paris (1897ff.).

■ *Art of Gallé* 1988
Art of Gallé: 108 Masterworks in Glass. Auct. cat. Habsburg, Feldman S.A. and Finarte, Geneva, 27 June 1988.

Arwas 1987
V. Arwas. *Glass: Art Nouveau to Art Deco.* London, 1977 (2nd ed. 1980).

Bacri 1993
C. Bacri, N. Daum, C. Pétry et al. *Daum: Masters of French Decorative Glass.* London, 1993.

■ Bardin 1999
C. Bardin. 'Les Débuts de la verrerie Daum à Nancy'. *Revue de l'Art* 3, no. 125 (1999): 64–70.

■ Bardin 2000
C. Bardin. *Daum: Collection du Musée des Beaux-Arts de Nancy.* Intro. Béatrice Salmon. Nancy, 2000.

■ Bardin 2002
C. Bardin. *Daum (1878–1939): 'Débuts, évolution et accomplissement d'une industrie d'art lorraine'.* 2 vols. Ph.D. Diss., Université de Nancy II, 2002.

Barrez 1912
C. Barrez. *Exposition universelle et internationale de Bruxelles 1910: Section française, classe 73, groupe XII, verres et cristaux.* Paris, 1912.

■ Bartha, *Collection Neumann,* 1993
G. de Bartha. *L'Art 1900: La Collection Neumann.* Pref. Wolf Uecker. Lausanne and Paris, 1993.

■ Bascou and Thiébaut, *Orsay,* 1988
M. Bascou, M.-M. Massé and P. Thiébaut. *Catalogue sommaire illustré des Arts Décoratifs.* Coll. cat. Musée d'Orsay, Paris. Paris, 1988.

Bénézit 1976
E. Bénézit. *Dictionnaire critique et documentaire des peintres, sculpteurs, dessinateurs et graveurs de tous les temps et de tous les pays par un groupe d'écrivains spécialistes français et étrangers.* 10 vols., 3rd enlarged ed. Paris, 1976.

Bernard 1902
M. Bernard. *Exposition internationale artistique de Saint-Petersbourg 1901–1902: Section française.* Paris, 1902.

■ Bing, *Formenschatz,* 1888–91
Japanischer Formenschatz. Compiled by S. Bing. 36 nos., 6 vols. Leipzig, n.d. [1888–1891] (printed approx. six months after the French original edition, *Le Japon artistique: Document d'art et d'industrie,* April 1888–April 1891).

Bloch-Dermant 1980
J. Bloch-Dermant. *The Art of French Glass, 1860–1914.* London, 1980. Originally published as *L'Art du Verre en France 1860–1914.* Lausanne and Paris, 1974.

Blount 1968
B. and H. Blount. *French Cameo Glass.* Des Moines, IA, 1968.

Bouvier, *Majorelle,* 1991
R. Bouvier. *Majorelle: Une aventure moderne.* Paris, 1991.

Bröhan 1976
K. H. Bröhan. *Kunst der Jahrhundertwende und der zwanziger Jahre: Katalog der Sammlung K. H. Bröhan.* Vol. 2, part 1: *Jugendstil, Werkbund, Art Déco: Glas, Holz, Keramik.* Coll. cat. Bröhan-Museum, Berlin. Berlin, 1976.

Brunhammer 1976
Y. Brunhammer et al. *Art Nouveau Belgium-France.* Exh. cat. Institute for the Arts, Rice University, Houston, TX, and The Art Institute Chicago. Houston, TX, and Chicago, 1976.

Brunhammer and Tise 1990
Y. Brunhammer and S. Tise. *French Decorative Art: The Société des Artistes Décorateurs, 1900–1942.* Paris, 1990.

Brussels 1965
H. Fettweis. *Art verrier 1865–1925.* Exh. cat. Musées Royaux d'Art et d'Histoire, Brussels. Brussels, 1965.

Brussels 1983
G. Cappa. *100 ans d'art verrier en Europe.* Exh. cat. Société Générale de Banque, Brussels. Brussels, 1983.

■ Brussels, catalogue, 1897
Verreries artistiques de Nancy Daum Frères & Cie. Handwritten inventory of exhibits, including pieces delivered later to the Brussels International Exhibition. Fond Daum; owner: SAGEM, Paris. Copies: Service Régional de l'Inventaire de Lorraine S.R.I.L. Nancy, 1897.

■ Brussels, *Daum,* 1897
Daum Frères & Cie. Verreries artistiques de Nancy. Exh. cat. Exposition de Bruxelles 1897. Ed. Jean-Louis-Auguste and Jean-Antonin Daum; illus. Jacques Gruber. Nancy, 1897.

Brussels, *Gruber,* 1983
F. Dierkens-Aubry, F. Roussel, A. Kennes-Roolant, C. Coley, J. Choux and D. Maniewska. *Jacques Gruber (1871–1936): Ebéniste et maître-verrier.* Exh. cat. Musée Horta, Brussels. Brussels, n.d. [1983].

Brussels, *Val Saint-Lambert,* 1990
M. Thiry. *Val Saint-Lambert: Art & Design 1880–1990.* Exh. cat. Banque Bruxelles Lambert, Brussels. Brussels, 1990.

Bulletin des Sociétés Artistiques de l'Est. Journal of the following artists' associations: Société Lorraine des Amis des Arts, Association des Artistes Lorrains, Société des Architectes de l'Est, Association amicale des anciens Elèves de l'Ecole des Beaux-Arts. Nancy, 1895.

Burty 1866
P. Burty. *Chefs-d'œuvre des arts industriels: Céramique, verrerie et vitraux, émaux, métaux, orfèvrerie et bijouterie, tapisserie.* Paris, 1866.

Cappa 1991
G. Cappa. *L'Europe de l'art verrier des précurseurs de l'art nouveau à l'art actuel.* Liège, 1991.

Champier 1889–94
V. Champier. *Les Industries d'art à la fin du XIXe siècle d'après les œuvres ayant figuré à l'exposition universelle de 1889 et aux expositions de Chicago 1893, Lyon et Anvers 1894. Mobilier, bronze, orfèvrerie, bijouterie, joaillerie, céramique, verrerie, vitraux, papiers peints, étoffes, tapis, dentelles, éventails, armes de luxes, instruments de musique etc.* Paris, 1889–94.

Charpentier 1978
F.-T. Charpentier. *Emile Gallé industriel et poète 1846–1904.* Nancy, 1978.

Charpentier, *Biographies,* 1978
F.-T. Charpentier. 'Remarques sur les premières biographies de Gallé parues de son temps'. *Archives de l'art français* XXV (1978): 419–31.

Charpentier et al. 1987
F.-T. Charpentier, C. Debize, M. Herold et al. *L'Art nouveau a L'Ecole de Nancy.* Paris, 1987.

Chavance 1928
R. Chavance. *L'Art français depuis vingt ans: La Céramique et la verrerie.* Paris, 1928.

Cleveland, *Japonisme,* 1975
G. P. Weisberg et al., *Japonisme: Japanese Influence on French Art, 1854–1910.* Exh. cat. The Cleveland Museum of Art, Cleveland, OH. Cleveland, OH, 1975.

Cohausen and Poschinger 1874
O. von Cohausen and G. von Poschinger. 'Industrie der Stein-, Thon- und Glaswaaren'. *Offizieller Bericht der Deutschen Kommission, Weltausstellung Wien.* Braunschweig, 1874, p. 83.

Cooper 1978
J. C. Cooper. *An Illustrated Encyclopaedia of Traditional Symbols.* London, 1978.

Corning 1984
Emile Gallé: Dreams into Glass. Compiled by
W. Warmus. Exh. cat. The Corning Museum of
Glass, Corning, NY. Corning, NY, 1984.

Darmstadt 1898
Darmstädter Kunst- und Gewerbe-Ausstellung. Exh.
cat. Darmstadt, 1898.

Darmstadt 1999
R. Ulmer (ed.). *Art Nouveau, Symbolismus und Jugend-
stil in Frankreich.* Authors: I. Becker, U. Berger, R.
Bouvier, C. Debize, J. Döring, R. Joppien, B. John-
Willeke, G. Lacambre, V. Losse, H. Makus, E.
Schmitt, P. Thiébaut. Exh. cat. Mathildenhöhe,
Darmstadt. Stuttgart and New York, 1999.

Daum 1891
*Daum Frères & Cie. Verreries Artistiques de Nancy: Créa-
tions de 1891.* Sales catalogue. Nancy, 1891.

■ Daum 1980
N. Daum. *Daum: Maîtres verriers 1870–1980.* Lausanne, 1980.

■ *Daum Album* I
*Verreries artistiques de Nancy: Daum Frères Album No. 1
– Extrait de la collection de dessins.* Two virtually identical exemplars with 45 and 46 pls., respectively,
showing approx. 120 models between no. 688 and
no. 1521 from 1894 to 1899. An album with cover,
presumably prepared as a catalogue for the 1900
Exposition Universelle. Fonds Daum; owner:
SAGEM, Paris. Copies: Service Régional de l'Inventaire de Lorraine S.R.I.L. Nancy, 1899.

■ *Daum Cat. aquar.* I
*Verreries artistiques de Nancy Daum Frères: Catalogue
aquarellé.* Vol. I: *1893–1923.* 2 vols. with 448 lithographs of models from 1893, some in watercolours.
Fonds Daum; owner: SAGEM, Paris. Copies: Service
Régional de l'Inventaire de Lorraine S.R.I.L. Nancy,
1923.

■ *Daum Cat. aquar.* II
*Verreries artistiques de Nancy Daum Frères: Catalogue
aquarellé.* Vol. II: *1923–1939.* Fonds Daum; owner:
SAGEM, Paris. Copies: Service Régional de l'Inventaire de Lorraine S.R.I.L. Nancy, 1939.

Daum, Dossier S.R.I.L., 1997
J. Guillaume, Y. Gawlik et al. *Dossier de la collection de
la Cristallerie Daum, Nancy.* Service Régional de l'Inventaire de Lorraine. Nancy, 1997.

■ *Daum Tarif* I
*Verreries artistiques de Nancy Daum Frères: Catalogue de
production et tarif.* Vol. 1: *1890–1923.* Two handwritten books of models, which, with a few exceptions,
concur, with occasional contour sketches. Fonds
Daum; owner: SAGEM, Paris. Copies: Service
Régional de l'Inventaire de Lorraine S.R.I.L. Nancy,
1923.

■ *Daum Tarif* II
Verreries artistiques de Nancy Daum Frères: Tarif. Vol.
II: *1923–1939.* Handwritten book of models, beginning with the copy of vol. I from 1911, enlarged by
the addition of contour sketches. Fonds Daum; owner: SAGEM, Paris. Copies: Service Régionale de l'Inventaire de Lorraine S.R.I.L. Nancy, 1939.

Debize 1989
C. Debize. *Guide: L'Ecole de Nancy.* Nancy, 1989.

Dictionnaire Biographie 1933–95
J. Balteau, M. Barroux, M. Prevost et al. *Dictionnaire
de biographie française.* Paris, 1933–95.

Didron and Clémendot 1880
E. Didron and L. Clémendot. *Exposition universelle et
internationale de 1878 à Paris: Rapport sur les cristaux,
la verriere et les vitraux.* Exh. rep. Champ-de-Mars,
Paris. Paris, 1880.

Ducuing 1867
F. Ducuing. *Exposition universelle de 1867 illustrée:
Publication internationale autorisée par la commission
impériale.* Exh. rep. Champ-de-Mars, Paris. 2 vols.
Paris, n.d. [1867].

Duncan 1991
A. Duncan. *Louis Majorelle: Master of Art Nouveau
Design.* London, 1991.

Duncan, *Salons,* 1998
A. Duncan. *The Paris Salons, 1895–1914.* Vol. IV:
Ceramics and Glass. Woodbridge, 1998.

Duncan and de Bartha 1984
A. Duncan and G. de Bartha. *Glass by Gallé.* London,
1984.

Düsseldorf 1904
*Internationale Kunstausstellung mit Sonderausstellung
von künstlerischen Gefässen für Blumen und Obst.* Exh.
cat. Städtischer Kunstpalast, Düsseldorf. Düsseldorf,
1904.

Düsseldorf, *Netsuke,* 1994
*Netsuke: Japanischer Gürtelschmuck des 18.–
20. Jahrhunderts aus einer westdeutschen Privatsamm-
lung.* Compiled by P. Jirka-Schmitz. Kunstmuseum
Düsseldorf. Düsseldorf, 1994.

Eck 1866
C. Eck. *L'Art et l'industrie: Influence des expositions sur
l'avenir industriel.* Paris, 1866.

Epinal 1997
F. Bertrand. *Grès flammés de Rambervillers: Art Nouveau dans les Vosges.* Exh. cat. Musée Départemental
d'Art Ancien et Contemporain, Epinal. Epinal, 1997.

L'Estampelle. Fontaine-Lès-Dijon (1969–89).

Fourcaud 1903
L. de Fourcaud. *Emile Gallé.* Paris, 1903.

Franzke 1987
I. Franzke. *Jugendstil: Glas, Graphik, Keramik, Metall,
Möbel, Skulpturen und Textilien von 1880 bis 1915.*
Coll. cat. Badisches Landesmuseum, Karlsruhe.
Karlsruhe, 1987.

Frauberger 1878
H. Frauberger. *Die Kunstindustrie auf der Pariser
Weltausstellung 1878.* Exh. rep. Champ-de-Mars,
Paris. Leipzig, 1879.

Fred 1900
W. Fred. 'Glas und Keramik auf der Pariser
Weltausstellung'. Exh. rev. *Kunst und Kunsthand-
werk* 3 (1900): 379–89.

Gallé 1898
E. Gallé. 'Mes envois au Salon'. *Revue des Arts Décoratifs* 18 (1898):144–48.

■ Gallé, *Ecrits,* 1908
E. Gallé. *Ecrits pour l'art: Floriculture, art décoratif,
notices d'exposition 1884–1889.* Paris, 1908; repr. Marseilles, 1980.

■ *Gallé's Gallé* 1993
Y. Kikuchi, K. Suzuki and Y. Tsuchiya. *Gallé's Gallé:
The Masterpieces of Emile Gallé.* Shikosha, Kyoto,
1993 (text in Japanese, list of works in English).

■ *Gallé et Toulouse-Lautrec* 1995
*Exposition Emile Gallé et Toulouse-Lautrec: Lumière et
Couleurs de la Belle Epoque.* Exh. cat. The Suntory
Museum of Art, Tokyo. Tokyo, 1995.

■ Garner 1976
P. Garner. *Gallé.* London, 1976.

■ Garner, *El Fituri,* 1982
P. Garner. *The Catalogue of the El Fituri Collection.*
Geneva, 1982.

Garnier 1886
E. Garnier. *Histoire de la verrerie et de l'émaillerie.*
Tours, 1886.

Glass Fantasy 1990
Glass Fantasy: From Art Nouveau to the Present-day.
Kyoto Shoin. Kyoto, 1990 (text in Japanese, intro-
ductions also in English).

Gonse 1883
L. Gonse. *L'Art japonais.* 2 vols. Paris, 1883.

Grover 1970
R. and L. Grover. *Carved and Decorated European Art
Glass.* Rutland, VT, and Tokyo, 1970.

■ Hakenjos 1982
B. Hakenjos. *Emile Gallé: Keramik, Glas und Möbel des
Art Nouveau.* Ph.D. Diss. Cologne, 1982.

Havard 1878
H. Havard. 'Les Arts industriels: La Verrerie'. *L'Art et
l'industrie de tous les peuples à l'exposition universelle de
1878: Description illustrée des merveilles du Champ-de-
Mars et du Trocadéro par les écrivains spéciaux les plus
autorisés.* Exh. rep. Champ-de-Mars, Paris. Paris,
1878, pp. 299–321.

Heller 1982
C. B. Heller. *Jugendstil: Kunst um 1900.* Coll. cat. Hes-
sisches Landesmuseum, Darmstadt, Kataloge des
Hessischen Landesmuseums, no. 12. 3rd rev. ed.
Darmstadt, 1982.

Henrivaux 1889
J. Henrivaux. 'La Verrerie à l'exposition universelle
de 1889'. Exh. rep. Champ-de-Mars, Paris. *Revue des
Arts Décoratifs* 10, no. 6 (1889): 169–85.

■ Hilschenz-Mlynek and Ricke 1985
H. Hilschenz-Mlynek and H. Ricke. *Glas – Historismus, Jugendstil, Art Déco.* Vol. 1: *Frankreich: Die Sammlung Hentrich im Kunstmuseum Düsseldorf.* Coll. cat.
Kunstmuseum, Düsseldorf. Düsseldorf, 1985.

Hogrel 1930
J. Hogrel. *Annuaire des Céramistes et Verriers de France.*
Paris, 1930.

Houtart 1902
E. Houtart. *Rapports du jury international, groupe XII: Décoration et mobilier des édifices publics et des habitations, Ministère du commerce, de l'industrie, des postes et des télégraphes.* Vol. 2: *Classe 73 – Cristaux et Verreries.* Paris, 1902.

Houtart 1908
E. Houtart. *Exposition universelle & internationale de Liège 1905: Section française.* Exh. rep. Parc de la Boverie, Liège. Paris, 1908.

Jean 1911
R. Jean. *Les Arts de la terre.* Paris, 1911.

Karlsruhe, *Daum*, 1995
I. Franzke, Claude Pétry, Pierre Valck and Clotilde Bacri-Herbo (eds.). *Daum-Glas des Jugendstils und Art Déco aus dem Musée des Beaux-Arts in Nancy.* Exh. cat. Badisches Landesmuseum Museum beim Markt, Karlsruhe. Karlsruhe, 1995.

Karlsruhe, *Trübner*, 1993
S. Esser. *Der Grossherzoglich-badische Hofgoldschmied Nikolaus Trübner.* Brochure. Badisches Landesmuseum, Karlsruhe. Karlsruhe, n.d. [1993].

■ **Kitazawa, *Gallé*, 1997**
Emile Gallé: Meditation of the Fin de Siècle. Catalogue of Gallé glass in the Kitazawa art museums in Suwa and elsewhere. Japan, 1997 (text in Japanese).

■ **Klesse 1982**
B. Klesse. *Auf den künstlerischen Spuren Emile Gallés.* Exh. cat. Kunstgewerbemuseum, Cologne. Cologne, 1982; see also *Wallraf-Richartz Jahrbuch.* Vol. XLII. Cologne, 1981.

Klesse, *Funke-Kaiser* I, 1981
B. Klesse and H. Mayr. *Glas vom Jugendstil bis heute, Sammlung Gertrud und Dr. Karl Funke-Kaiser.* Coll. cat. Kunstgewerbemuseum, Cologne. Cologne, 1981.

Klesse, *Funke-Kaiser* II, 1991
B. Klesse. *Glas und Keramik vom Historismus bis zur Gegenwart, Schenkung Gertrud und Dr. Karl Funke-Kaiser.* Coll. cat. Kunstgewerbemuseum, Cologne. Cologne, 1991.

Klesse and Reineking von Bock 1973
B. Klesse and G. Reineking von Bock. *Glas: Kataloge des Kunstgewerbemuseums Cologne.* Vol. 1. Coll. cat. Kunstgewerbemuseum, Cologne. 2nd enlarged ed. Cologne, 1973.

■ **Krantz 1894**
C. Krantz. *Exposition internationale de Chicago en 1893: Rapports comité 22. Cristaux et verrerie.* Exh. rep. Chicago International Exhibition. Paris, 1894.

Lafitte 1912
L. Lafitte. *Rapport général sur l'exposition internationale de l'est de la France Nancy 1909.* Paris, 1912.

Lausanne 1973
L'Art verrier à l'aube du XXe siècle. Exh. cat. Galerie des Arts Décoratifs, Lausanne. Lausanne, 1973.

■ **Le Tacon 1995**
F. Le Tacon. *Emile Gallé ou le Mariage de l'Art et de la Science.* Paris, 1995.

■ **Le Tacon 1998**
F. Le Tacon. *L'Œuvre de Verre d'Emile Gallé.* Paris, 1998.

■ **Le Tacon and De Luca 1999**
F. Le Tacon and F. De Luca. *L'Usine d'art Gallé à Nancy.* Nancy, 1999.

Le Tacon, *Solvay Gallé*, 2000
F. Le Tacon. *Solvay Gallé & Art Nouveau.* Nancy, 2002.

Liesville 1878
A.-R. de Liesville. 'La Verrerie'. *Exposition universelle de 1878: Les beaux-arts et les arts décoratifs.* Exh. rep. Champ-de-Mars, Paris. Ed. Louis Gonse. Vol. 1: *L'Art moderne*, pp. 424–31. Paris, 1879.

La Lorraine Artiste. Nancy (1888ff.).

Lurker 1985
M. Lurker (ed.). *Wörterbuch der Symbolik.* 3rd ed. Stuttgart, 1985.

Mannoni n.d. [1986]
E. Mannoni. *Les Pâtes de verre.* Paris, n.d. [1986].

Marshall 1990
J. Marshall. *Glass Source Book: A Visual Record of the World's Great Glass Making Traditions.* Secaucus, NJ, and London, 1990.

Marx 1900
R. Marx. 'La Décoration et les industries d'art'. Exh. rep. Champ-de-Mars, Paris. In Bénédite, Léonce et al. *Exposition universelle de 1900: Les Beaux-arts et les arts décoratifs.* Paris, (n.d.) [1900], pp. 459–520.

Marx 1911
R. Marx. 'Emile Gallé: Psychologie de l'artiste et synthèse de l'œuvre'. *Art & Décoration* (Aug. 1911): 233–52.

Mascret 1863ff.
H.-F. Mascret. *Dictionnaire des faillites, séparations de biens, nominations de conseils judicaires, interdictions prononcées par les tribunaux de Paris d'après les journaux judicaires.* Paris, 1863ff.

Meier-Graefe 1896
J. Meier-Graefe. 'Modernes Kunstgewerbe in Nancy: I. Die Gläser'. *Zeitschrift des bayrischen Kunstgewerbevereins* (1896): 68–71, with illus.

■ **Meier-Graefe 1900**
J. Meier-Graefe. 'Das künstlerische Gewerbe auf der Weltausstellung'. In J. Meier-Graefe (ed.). *Die Weltausstellung in Paris 1900.* Paris and Leipzig, 1900, pp. 105–28, with illus.

■ **Meisenthal 1999**
F. Le Tacon, P. Franckhauser and Y. Fleck. *Meisenthal Berceau du verre Art nouveau.* Exh. cat. Musée du Verre et du Cristal, Meisenthal. Meisenthal, 1999.

Monte Carlo, *Daum*, 1982
Daum Nancy. Auct. cat. Ader Picard Tajan, Hôtel Hermitage, Monte Carlo, 17 April 1982. Monte Carlo, 1982.

Mukai, *Hida Takayama*, 1997
T. Mukai. *Guide to the Hida Takayama Museum of Art.* Coll. cat. Museum of Art, Hida Takayama. Hida Takayama, Japan, 1997 (text in Japanese, intro. in English).

Munich 1898
Offizieller Katalog der Internationalen Kunst-Ausstellung des Vereins bildender Künstler A. V 'Secession'. Exh. cat. Munich, 1898.

Munich 1972
S. Wichmann, M. Goedl-Roth, F.-W. von Hase et al. *Weltkulturen und moderne Kunst.* Exh. cat. Haus der Kunst, Munich. Munich, 1972.

Munich, *Daum*, 1981
G. Fahr-Becker-Sterner. *Daum: Verrerie d'Art – Glas aus Frankreich um 1900.* Exh. cat. Museum Villa Stuck, Munich. Munich, 1981.

■ **Munich, *Nancy 1900*, 1980**
J. A. and H. Schmoll genannt Eisenwerth. *Nancy 1900: Jugendstil in Lothringen.* Exh. cat. Stadtmuseum, Munich. Munich, 1980.

■ **Nancy 1890 (1892, 1895, 1897–1903, 1905–13, 1920, 1929)**
Société lorraine des amis des arts. Exh. cats. Galeries Poirel, Nancy. Nancy, 1890, 1892, 1895, 1897–1903, 1905–13, 1920, 1929.

■ **Nancy 1904**
Société lorraine des amis des arts: Ecole de Nancy – Exposition d'art décoratif moderne. Exh. cat. Galeries Poirel, Nancy. Nancy, 1904.

■ **Nancy 1999**
R. Bouvier, H. Claude, F. Loyer, J.-L. Olivié, F. Roussel, B. Salmon, P. Thiébaut, V. Thomas, V. Ayroles, F. Bertrand and E. Decker. *L'Ecole de Nancy, 1889–1909: Art nouveau et industries d'art.* Exh. cat. Galeries Poirel, Nancy. Paris, 1999.

Nancy 2001
R. Bouvier, V. Thomas, F. Parmantier and J. Perrin. *Musée de l'Ecole de Nancy: La Collection.* Paris, 2001.

■ **Nancy, *Art Décoratif*, 1894**
Exposition d'art décoratif et industriel lorrain. Exh. cat. Galeries Poirel, Nancy. Nancy, 1894.

■ **Nancy, *Bussière*, 2000**
V. Thomas, F. Parmantier, I. Hiblot, F. Sylvestre and E. Wambach. *Céramiques végétales: Ernest Bussière et l'Art nouveau.* Exh. cat. Musée de l'Ecole de Nancy. Nancy, 2000.

Nancy, *Daum* I, 1977
Daum: Cent ans de verre et de cristal. Exh. cat. Musée des Beaux-Arts, Nancy. Nancy, n.d. [1977].

Nancy, *Daum* II, 1978
Daum: Cent ans de création dans le verre et le cristal. Exh. cat. Musée des Beaux-Arts, Nancy. Nancy, 1978.

Nancy, *Daum* III, 1979
Daum: Cent ans de verrerie d'art 'trois styles'. Exh. cat. Musée des Beaux-Arts, Nancy. Nancy, 1979.

Nancy, *Daum* IV, 1980
Daum: Verre et cristal d'art. Exh. cat. Musée des Beaux-Arts, Nancy. Nancy, 1980.

Nancy, *Daum* V, 1981
Daum: Verre et cristal. Exh. cat. Musée des Beaux-Arts, Nancy. Nancy, 1981.

■ **Nancy, *Fleurs*, 1999**
J.-P. Bouillon, V. Caray, M.-B. Bouvet, A. Hamon, F. Hirtz, J.-P. Midant, P. Raguin, V. Thomas and

P. Valck. *Fleurs et ornements: 'Ma racine est au fond des bois'*. Exh. cat. Musée de l'Ecole de Nancy, Nancy. Nancy, 1999.

Netzer, Berlin, 1994
S. Netzer. *Glas der Moderne 1880–1930*. Selection from the collection owned by the Kunstgewerbemuseums SMPK Berlin. Exh. cat. Haus der Wissenschaft, Bonn-Bad Godesberg. Berlin, 1994.

Newark 1989
T. Newark. *Emile Gallé*. Secaucus, NJ, 1989.

■ Nicolas 1900/1901
E. Nicolas. 'M. Emile Gallé à l'exposition de 1900: La Verrerie'. *La Lorraine Artiste* (1900): 97–100, 113–16, 163–67; (1901): 5–9, 25–30, 49–54.

Octave Maus 1926
M. Octave Maus. *Trente années de lutte pour l'art: Les XX, 1884–1893: La Libre Esthétique, 1894–1914*. Brussels, 1926.

Okuoka and Mizuta, Sapporo selection, 1990
S. Okuoka, Y. Mizuta and M. Tomana. *Prism of Fantasy – 200 Works from the Glass Collection of Hokkaido Museum of Modern Art*. Coll. cat. Hokkaidō Museum of Modern Art, Sapporo. Sapporo, 1990 (text in Japanese).

■ Olivié, *Gallé*, 1995
J.-L. Olivié. 'The Discovery of an Unknown Collection of Emile Gallé Glass', in *Royal Glass: An Exhibition of Four Centuries of Table Glass, Glass Services, and Goblets*. Ed. Ole Villumsen Krog. Exh. cat. Christiansborg Palace, Copenhagen. Copenhagen, 1995, pp. 232–59.

Orléans 1987
F. Demange, E. Fontan and J.-L. Olivié. *Transparences: L'Art du verre en France de 1914 à 1960*. Exh. cat. Musée des Beaux-Arts d'Orléans, Orléans. Paris, 1987.

■ Osaka 1987
Emile Gallé. Exh. cat. Navio Museum, Osaka. Osaka, 1987 (text in Japanese).

■ Paris 1903
Exposition de l'alliance provinciale des industries d'art: Ecole de Nancy. Exh. cat. Pavillon de Marsan, Paris. Paris, 1903.

Paris 1910
E. Delard. *Exposition de la verrerie et de la cristallerie artistiques*. Exh. cat. Musée Galliera, Paris. Paris, 1910.

Paris 1933
F. Carnot. *Le Décor de la vie sous la IIIe République de 1870 à 1900*. Exh. cat. Musée des Arts Décoratifs, Pavillon de Marsan, Paris. Paris, 1933.

■ Paris 1937
Le Décor de la vie de 1900 à 1925. Exh. cat. Musée des Arts Décoratifs, Pavillon de Marsan, Paris. Paris, 1937.

Paris, *Arts Métiers*, 1908
Catalogue officiel des collections du conservatoire national des arts et métiers: Quatrième fascicule – Arts chimiques, matières colorantes et teinture, céramique et verrerie. Paris, 1908.

■ Paris, *Daum*, 1900
Verreries & Cristaux Artistiques de Nancy: Agence générale & exposition permanente à Paris – 32, rue de Paradis: Verreries de Nancy Daum Frères – Katalog zur Weltausstellung 1900 in Paris. Title page illus. by Henri Bergé. Nancy, 1900.

■ Paris, *Gallé*, 1985
T. Charpentier and P. Thiébaut. *Gallé*. Exh. cat. Musée du Luxembourg, Paris. Paris, 1985.

Paris, *Japonisme*, 1988
M. Bascou, G. Lacambre, A. Mabuchi, C. Mathieu, S. Takashina and F. Heilbrun. *Le Japonisme*. Exh. cat. Galeries Nationales du Grand Palais, Paris; Musée National d'Art Occidental, Tokyo. Paris, 1988.

Paris, Marx Collection, 1914
Catalogue des objets d'art moderne: Porcelaines, grès, verres, cristaux, pâtes de verre, étains, émaux translucides, émaux cloisonnés, faisant partie de la collection Roger Marx. Auct. cat. Galerie Manzi and Joyant. Paris, 1914.

■ Paris, portfolio, 1903
Exposition Lorraine: L'Ecole de Nancy. Ed. Armand Guérinet, portfolio. Vol. 1: *Le Mobilier*. Vol. 2: *Objets d'art, verrerie, céramique, cuirs d'art, bronzes etc*. Paris, 1903.

Paris, *Rousseau*, 1988
J.-P. Bouillon, C. Shimizu and P. Thiébaut. *Art, industrie et japonisme: Le service 'Rousseau'*. Les dossiers du Musée d'Orsay 20. Paris, 1988.

Paris, Salon, 1912
Société du salon d'automne: Exposition de 1912: Catalogue des ouvrages de peinture, sculpture, dessin, gravure, architecture et art décoratif. Exh. cat. Salon d'automne Champ-de-Mars, Paris. Paris, 1912.

Paris, Salon du Champ-de-Mars, 1891–1914
Extracts from exhibition catalogues of the Société Nationale des Beaux-Arts in the artists' documentation centre at the Musée Orsay.

■ Pazaurek 1901
G. E. Pazaurek. *Moderne Gläser*. Leipzig, n.d. [1901].

Pertuy 1984
J. and M. Pertuy. *A la Recherche des orchidées dans l'Ecole de Nancy: La Société française d'orchidophilie*. Paris, 1984.

■ Pétry and Maury, *Daum*, 1989
C. Pétry and N. Maury. *Daum dans les musées de Nancy*. Exh. cat. Musée des Beaux-Arts, Nancy; Musée de l'Ecole de Nancy, Nancy. Nancy, n.d. [1989]

Philadelphia 1876
International Exhibition 1876: Official Catalogue. Exh. cat. Fairmount Park, Philadelphia, PA, issued by the United States Centennial Commission. Philadelphia, PA, 1876.

Polak 1962
A. Polak. *Modern Glass*. London, 1962.

Prague, Paris selection, 1991
J.-L. Olivié and Y. Brunhammer. *Mistrovská díla sklářství ve francii od 19. století po dnešek* [French Glass Art from the 19th Century to the Present]. Exh. cat. Museum of Applied Arts, Prague. Prague, 1991.

■ *Rev. Est*, Daum, 1894
'Exposition industrielle des arts décoratifs à Nancy: Le Problème d'une société nouvelle'. *Revue industrielle de l'Est*, no. 138 (26 Aug. 1894): 6–9.

■ *Rev. Est*, Daum, 1897
'Visite à Nancy de M. Henri Boucher, Ministre du commerce et de l'industrie, des postes et télégraphes: A la verrerie Daum Frères & Cie. *Revue industrielle de l'Est* (24 Oct. 1897): 5–8, suppl.

■ *Revue des Arts Décoratifs* (Paris 1880–1902f).

Ricke 2002
H. Ricke. *Glass Art: Reflecting the Centuries – Masterpieces from the Glasmuseum Hentrich in the museum kunst palast, Düsseldorf*. Munich, Berlin, London and New York, 2002.

Ricke, *Koepff*, 1998
H. Ricke. 'Teichlandschaften und Unterwasserwelten: Art Nouveau Gläser der Sammlung Gerda Koepff'. *Weltkunst*, no. 4 (April 1998): 749–53.

Rousset 1888–90
C. Rousset. *Annuaire de la verrerie et de la céramique*. Paris, 1888–90.

■ Sageret 1862–1900
Sageret. *Annuaire du Bâtiment des Travaux Publics et des Arts Industriels* (issued annually except in the war years). Paris, 1862–1900.

Sammlung Silzer 2003
Auct. cat. Fischer, no. 138. *Sammlung Silzer*. Heilbronn, 2003.

Sapporo 1978
[*The Beauty of Glass: Emile Gallé and the Ecole de Nancy*]. Exh. cat. Hokkaidō Museum of Modern Art, Sapporo. Sapporo, 1978 (text in Japanese).

Sapporo 1991
H. Ricke. *Glas: Jugendstil und Art Déco*. Exh. cat. Hokkaidō Museum of Modern Art, Sapporo. Sapporo, 1991 (text in Japanese and German).

■ Sapporo 2000
P. Thiébaut, K. Suzuki, M. Ido, Y. Mizuta and Y. Tsuchiya. *Emile Gallé*. Exh. cat. Hokkaidō Museum of Modern Art. Sapporo, 2000.

Sapporo, *Daum*, 1980
Centenaire de Daum au Japon. Exh. cat. Hokkaidō Museum of Modern Art, Sapporo. Sapporo, 1980 (text in Japanese and French).

Schmitt 1990
E. Schmitt. 'Malerei auf Hohlglas: Grundlagen der Glaskunst im Jugendstil'. *Kunst & Antiquitäten*, 5 (1990): 46–55.

■ Schmitt, *Sammlung Silzer*, 1989
E. Schmitt. *Glas – Kunst – Handwerk 1870–1945: Glassammlung Silzer*. Exh. cat. Augustinermuseum, Freiburg. Freiburg, 1989.

■ Schmitt, Zurich II, 1995
E. Schmitt. *Museum Bellerive: Glas*. Vol. II: *Historismus Jugendstil Zwanziger Jahre*. Exh. cat. Museum Bellerive, Zurich. Zurich, 1995.

■ Schneck 1988
K. Schneck. *François Eugène Rousseau: Keramik und Glas an der Schwelle zum Jugendstil*. MA thesis, Kunst-

historisches Institut der Freien Universität, Berlin. Berlin, 1988.

■ Schneck 1990
K. Schneck. 'François Eugène Rousseau (1827–1890): Céramique et verrerie à l'aube de l'Art Nouveau'. *Annales du 11e Congrès de l'Association Internationale pour L'Histoire du Verre*. Basel 1988; Amsterdam, 1990, pp. 449–58.

Seoul 1986
J.-L. Olivié. *100 ans d'art du verre en France*. Exh. cat. Hoam Art Museum, Seoul. Seoul, 1986 (text in Korean and French).

Sotheby's Monaco, 1982
Emile Gallé: Vases, lampes et projets. Auct. cat. Sotheby Parke Bernet Monaco, 24 Oct. 1982. Monte Carlo, 1982.

■ Stenger 1988
A. Stenger. *Verreries et verriers au pays de Sarrebourg: Chronique Historique*. Sarrebourg, 1988.

Sterner 1969
G. Sterner. *Die Vasen der Gebrüder Daum*. Ph.D. Diss. Munich, 1969.

Strasbourg 1897
Exposition d'Art. Hôtel de Ville, Place Broglie, Strasbourg. Strasbourg, 1897.

Strasbourg 1901
Katalog der internationalen Kunstausstellung im Alten Schloss. 20 June–20 July. Strasbourg, 1901.

Strasbourg 1908
Exposition de l'Ecole de Nancy à Strasbourg. Exh. cat. Palais de Rohan, Société des Amis des Arts de Strasbourg. Strasbourg, 1908.

■ Sun Kurino 1995
[*Catalogue Emile Gallé*], no. 1, Sun Kurino Museum of Art, Atami. Japan, 1995 (text in Japanese).

■ Suzuki, *Kitazawa*, 1996
K. Suzuki. *Glass of Art Nouveau*. Catalogue of the Kitazawa Art Museums in Suwa and elsewhere. Japan, 1996 (text in Japanese, Foreword in English).

Sylla, *Trübner*, 2000
S. Sylla. *Nikolaus Trübner (1849–1910): Ein badischer Hofgoldschmied*. Ph.D. Diss., Ruprecht-Karls-Universität, Heidelberg, 2000.

Takeda and Olivié 1996
A. Takeda and J.-L. Olivié. *Ouvrages sélectionnés dans la collection de verrerie*. Coll. cat. Jukēn Museum of Art, Hiroshima. Hiroshima, 1996 (text in Japanese).

■ Thiébaut 1988
P. Thiébaut. 'Contribution à une histoire du mobilier japonisant: Les Créations de l'Escalier de Cristal'. *Revue de l'Art*, no. 85 (1989): 76–83.

■ Thiébaut, *Dessins*, 1993
P. Thiébaut, *Les Dessins de Gallé*. Coll cat. Musée d'Orsay, Paris. Paris, 1993.

Tokyo 1974
Emile Gallé. Exh. cat. Takashimaya, Tokyo Nihombashi, Tokyo. Tokyo, 1974 (text in Japanese).

Tokyo, *Daum*, 1984
J. P. Camard. *Collection Daum Nancy*. Auct. cat. Ader

Picard Tajan, Tokyo, Hotel Okura, 15 March 1984. Tokyo, 1984 (text in Japanese and French).

Tokyo, *Daum*, 1987
J. P. Camard and F. Marcilhac. *Collection Daum Nancy: 3ème et dernière vente*. Auct. cat. Ader, Picard Tajan, Hotel Okura, Tokyo, 7 Oct. 1987. Tokyo, 1987 (text in Japanese and French).

■ Tokyo, *Gallé*, 1980
Exposition Emile Gallé, org. par le Nihon Keisai Shimbun. Exh. cat. Nagoya, Tokyo. Osaka and Tokyo, 1980 (introductory texts in Japanese, catalogue in Japanese and French).

Tokyo, Paris selection, 1991
J.-L. Olivié. *Chefs d'œuvre de la verrerie et de la cristallerie française au Musée des arts décoratifs, 1800–1990*. Exh. cat. Suntory Museum of Art, Tokyo. Tokyo, 1991 (text in Japanese and French).

Tokyo, *Style floral*, 1988
Le Monde de l'art nouveau: Style floral. Exh. cat. Odakyu Grand Gallery, Tokyo. Tokyo, 1988 (text in Japanese, short intro. in French by F. Marcilhac).

Traub, *Christian*, 1978
J. S. Traub. *The Glass of Désiré Christian: Ghost for Gallé*. Chicago, 1978.

Turin, France, 1911
Exposition internationale des industries et du travail: Catalogue spécial officiel de la section française. Exh. cat. Parco del Valentino, Turin. Paris, 1911.

Uhland 1880
W. H. Uhland (ed.). *Illustrirter Katalog der Pariser Weltausstellung von 1878: Erster Theil Kunstindustrie*. Exh. rep. Champ-de-Mars, Paris. Leipzig, 1880.

Venzmer and Mendelssohn, Mainz, 1990
W. Venzmer and G. Mendelssohn. *Jugendstil im Landesmuseum Mainz*. Coll. cat. Mittelrheinisches Landesmuseum, Mainz. Mainz, 1990.

Vienna 1873
Welt-Ausstellung 1873 in Wien: Officieller General-Catalog. Exh. cat. Prater, Vienna. Vienna, 1873.

Vollmer 1992
H. Vollmer (ed.). *Allgemeines Lexikon der bildenden Künstler des XX. Jahrhunderts*. 6 vols. Taschenbuchausgabe. Leipzig, 1992.

■ Wichmann, *Japonisme*, 1981
S. Wichmann, *Japonisme: The Japanese Influence on Western Art since 1858*. Trans. Mary Wittall. London, 1981, repr. 1985. Originally published as *Japonismus: Ostasien – Europa: Begegnungen in der Kunst des 19. und 20. Jahrhunderts*. Herrsching, 1980.

Weisberg, Bing, 1986
G. P. Weisberg. *Art Nouveau Bing: Paris Style 1900*. New York, 1986.

Yoshimizu 1983
T. Yoshimizu. *Glass of Art Nouveau*. Tankōsha, Kyoto. 1983 (text in Japanese).

■ Yoshimizu 1985
T. Yoshimizu. *The Glass Art of Emile Gallé*. Gakken, Japan, 1985 (text in Japanese, bibliography and short catalogue in English).

Yoshimizu 1988
[*Glass: Art Nouveau and Art Déco*]. Tokyo, 1988 (text in Japanese).

■ Yoshimizu and Klesse 1992
T. Yoshimizu and B. Klesse (eds.). *The Survey of Glass in the World*. Vol. 3: *Art Nouveau and Art Déco*. Tokyo, 1992 (text in Japanese).

Zons 1999
H. Blum-Spicker. *Mohn: Mythos – Symbol – Gestalt*. Authors: S. Barten, H. Dietrich, P. R. Franke, G. Götte, H. Schadewaldt. Exh. cat. Kreismuseum Zons, Dormagen. Dormagen, 1999.

Zons 2002
H. Blum-Spicker. *Iris: Mythos – Symbol – Gestalt*. Authors: I. Becker, H. Dietrich, B. Frederking, C. Kiehs-Glos, A. Kossatz-Deissmann, M. Mrass. Exh. cat. Kreismuseum Zons, Dormagen. Dormagen, 2002.

■ Zurich 1980
S. Barten and B. Hakenjos. *Emile Gallé: Keramik, Glas und Möbel des Art Nouveau*. Exh. cat. Museum Bellerive, Zurich. Zurich, 1980.

Zurich 2000
G. de Bartha. *Daum Frères – Verreries de Nancy: Glaskunst aus der Zeit 1892–1914*. Coll. cat. Galerie Katharina Büttiker, Zurich. Zurich, 2000.

Zurich, *Daum*, 1986
S. Barten. *Daum Nancy: Glas des Art Nouveau und Art Déco*. Exh. cat. Museum Bellerive, Zurich. Zurich, 1986.

Zurich, Wühre 9, 1986
H. Spaček. *Daum Frères – Verreries de Nancy: Glaskunst aus der Zeit 1892–1935: Sammlung Katharina Büttiker-Weber*. Exh. cat. Galerie Wühre 9, Zurich. Zurich, 1986.

Glossary
of Technical Terms

annealing Gradually lowering the temperature of glass after an object has been made at the furnace. Serves to soften or relax the internal stress that is caused by differences in temperature between the cooler outer wall and the layers inside. → annealing furnace

annealing furnace, also called lehr Glass oven that gradually cools molten glass, at a temperature of approx. 450–500°C. There are two types of annealing furnace: the batch-worked oven, in which the temperature is gradually lowered, and the continuous oven with a conveyor belt of wire netting on which the hot glass is gradually moved into lower-temperature zones.

application Raised decorative element that is fused on to the glass surface while being → hot-worked.

bevelled rim Flat ground rim, the edges of which have been cut such that they are sloping.

blowing out Technique of glass-blowing employed to regulate the distribution of coloured glass applied to a vessel, creating sharply defined or diffuse colour areas.

blowpipe Metal tube about 1.3 to 1.8 m long and approx. 10 mm in diameter with a welded end-piece of fire-resistant steel. The blowpipe is used to pick up a molten gather and to form it by blowing. → pontil

bright gold, silver or platinum Decorating technique whereby a thin, highly glossy layer of precious metal is applied to a glass body. After being covered with a solution of precious metal chloride mixed with sulphur balsam (with platinum alcohol), lavender oil and a dash of bismuth compounds (as a fluxing agent) the piece is allowed to dry and then fired (at a temperature of at least 500°C). The resulting finish has a precious metal content ranging from 6 to 12 per cent. After firing, pieces with a smooth ground that are produced in this manner are extremely glossy on the exterior and on the underside. On a matt ground, or after having been carefully worked over with a glass brush, the exterior acquires a matt finish and the underside remains glossy. As a rule the layers of gilding are very thin and consequently not as durable as layers of → burnish gold. Gold and platinum are preferred in glass painting since silver tends to tarnish black (sulphur oxidation) and reacts with the glass (yellowing).

burnish or burnishing gold, silver or platinum Decorating technique whereby a thin, matt layer of precious metal created by the application of a suspension of turpentine, powdered precious metal, lead and bismuth compounds, dried and fired (at 600°C), which is burnished to a high gloss with an agate tool and a polishing agent. Viewed from the underside, the lustre appears in matt colours, with gold showing up yellow to ochre, silver appearing white and platinum greyish black. The precious metal content of the solution ranges from 12 to 40 per cent. When fired, the layer of burnished lustre is from three to six times thicker than glossy lustre (→ bright gold). The addition of powdered silver causes burnished gold lustre to take on a greenish tinge. Tarnishing is prevented in silver lustre by the addition of gold and platinum. Platinum lustre is hardly ever used because it is so costly.

carving → Engraving or → cutting a glass surface to give it a carved look. The various traces left by the engraving wheels used in this technique, which was invented by Emile Gallé, underscore the sculptural quality and the design of the decoration and surfaces.

casing Generic term for the often highly sophisticated processes entailed in covering a glass body with a thin coating of glass. → overlay

casting Shaping a large glass mass by allowing it to solidify in a mould. The molten glass is ladled into the mould, smoothed out and, after initial solidification, is removed, still hot, from the mould and allowed to cool slowly in an → annealing furnace.

coloured glass → glass, coloured

crackle or crazed glass → crazing

crazing Submerging molten glass in water to create crackle glass, the surface of which is notable for its network of fine fissures. Crazing can be enclosed in the wall by being → cased.

crystal glass → glass, crystal

cutting → grinding

cutting, edge → Engraving or cutting technique executed with the sharp strap wheel, creating L-shaped grooves in the glass.

cutting lathe Implement used to → grind decoration, which, like the → engraving tool, consists of a fixed, horizontal drive shaft and vertically rotating, interchangeable cutting wheels.

cutting, mitre → Engraving or cutting technique executed with the mitre wheel, creating V-shaped grooves in the glass.

cutting, olive or printy → Engraving or cutting technique executed with the olive or printy wheel, creating oval-shaped or rounded grooves in the glass.

dilating Technique whereby the lip of a vessel is widened with pincers or similar → glassmaking tools.

dipping Submerging the → parison or glass body in the batch to add another layer of glass. This process is employed primarily to enlarge the parison, but also to add a layer of → coloured glass from the pot.

enamel colours, also called vitreous enamel or enamel Composed of → pigment and → flux, which fuse in the course of firing to bond with the support substance. They are mixed cold as pulverized coloured glazes or as a mixture of flux and pigment with a solvent (for instance, turpentine) to create a smooth paste, which is applied with a brush. After drying, the glass body is fired at temperatures ranging from 490 to 580°C in a → muffle kiln. Enamel colours are subdivided into three groups: opaque enamel, transparent enamel and → flat colours.

enamel painting Painting with → enamel colours.

engraving Mechanically removing part of the glass surface, for decoration purposes, with the → engraving tool, which is operated by rotating copper wheels of varying diameter (approx. 0.5–10 cm), and a mixture of oil and emery with → grains of varying size to create nuances of texture. The three-dimensional effect of a cut is determined by the interplay of surface textures, forms and depth of cut. A distinction is made between → relief or cameo engraving and hollow or intaglio engraving. The terms cameo and intaglio cutting are usually used in reference to figurative motifs. The traditional, labour-intensive method of copper-wheel engraving was gradually replaced after the First World War by → cutting with carborundum wheels.

engraving, diamond-point Incising ornamentation or inscriptions on glass with a stylus that is fitted with a diamond or tungsten carbide point.

engraving, line → Engraving or → cutting that forms angular grooves in the glass surface. The width of the line produced is determined by the inclination of the mitre wheel.

engraving, relief, also called relief cutting Engraving technique used to produce raised decoration.

engraving, rock-crystal In glass decoration a term for engraving that is entirely polished, including the surrounding wall, to a high gloss.

engraving tool Implement with a fixed, horizontal drive shaft, interchangeable spindles and copper wheels. → engraving

etching Decorating a glass surface by corroding it with hydrofluoric acid. Depending on the concentration, additives (e.g., sodium compounds or potash, sulphuric acid, hydrochloric acid or nitric acid), temperature and time of exposure, the acid bites into the glass more or less strongly, creating various textures. Etching over large surfaces is achieved by dipping a piece in an acid bath; etching over small areas by the application of a mordant (biting) solution or paste. The composition of the acid bath depends on the sort of etched texture desired on the glass surface. The parts of the decoration that are not meant to be etched are usually covered with a resist, an acid-resistant, non-porous lacquer made up of wax or tallow mixed with bitumen or colophonium (rosin) in an organic solvent. To create stepped relief decoration, the resist is partly removed and the glass submerged again in the acid bath. One of the by-products of this process is the formation of fluoride compounds, which form a residue, preventing further etching where they have been deposited. The glass must, therefore, be taken out of the acid bath several times to remove the residue until the desired depth of etching has been reached.

etching, needle Etching technique used to create fine, shallow decoration. The resist layer (only possible with lacquer or lead foil) is incised with a steel etching needle or an etching knife.

etching, relief Etching technique used to produce raised decoration.

fine matt Term used for the satin matt surface finish achieved by fine grinding or matting by hand.

finishing, also called refining techniques Term used for decoration techniques executed on cold glass, such as → cutting, → engraving, → etching and painting.

flat colour Glossy or matt, flat → enamel, in transparent or opaque colour tones, applied with a brush or draughtsman's pen. Flat colour contains a more fluid enamel and a higher → pigment content than opaque or transparent enamel. The composition of the enamel is very similar to that of transparent → enamel. Owing to its physical properties – comparable to watercolour – it is applied in thin layers. Flat colours are suitable for contour drawings, priming grounds and decoration executed with a spraying device.

flux Very soft, colourless glass with a low melting point, composed of quartz sand, lead oxide, boric- and bismuth compounds, ground to a powder to obtain → enamel colours.

freely forming Crafting hot glass at the furnace with various → glassmaking tools and piece moulds.

gather Hot glass collected from the furnace on a → blowpipe or → pontil. → parison

glass-blowing → glassmaking

glass, coloured Transparent, uniformly tinted glass of one colour, achieved by mixing the batch with → metallic compounds. The most beautiful colours are attained in glass with a lead content. Potassium silicate is least suited. Coloured glass mixed with agents to look → opalescent, semi-opaque or opaque is specified as such in the catalogue.

glass, crystal Glass free of air bubbles and streaks with a high potassium and lead content. Nowadays the EU norm requires a potassium and lead content of 10 per cent.

glassmaking, also called glass-blowing or hot-working Processing a molten, viscous batch at the furnace with → glassmaking tools at temperatures of about 1200 °C. The simplest process begins by inflating the → parison. By → dipping it, a larger amount of glass can be preformed, depending on the processes to follow, which may be → mould blowing or → freely forming. For the lip to be → dilated, the glass body must be attached at the bottom to a → pontil so that it can be cracked off the → blowpipe. The plug formed between the mould and the end of the pipe is broken off by dripping water on to it, and the lip thus created is cut into shape and dilated after heating. The finished vessel is cracked off the pontil iron and placed in the → annealing furnace to cool. → hot-working

glassmaking tools The most important glassmaking tools are the → blowpipe, the → pontil, dilating tools, the blocking wood, pincers, shears, tongs, the → marver, the smoothing iron and calipers for measuring.

glass-painting colours Subdivided into cold and firing colours. Cold painting entails merely applying the paint (watercolour, tempera, oil or lacquer paints etc.) and letting it dry, which makes it not very durable. Colours for firing are subdivided into four groups:
1. → Enamel (opaque enamel, transparent enamel and → flat colour)
2. Precious metals (→ bright or → burnish gold, silver or platinum)
3. → Stain and → reduction colours
4. → Lustre

Firing colours are applied, dried and then fired in a → muffle kiln at temperatures between 500 and 600 °C. They are of highly varying durability, depending on how they bond with the surface of the glass body. Stain is the most durable and lustre the least.

glory hole Small furnace used to carry out special operations during the glassmaking process, including → reduction firing, which creates → iridescence, etc.

granules Coarse glass powder of variously sized grains, ranging from approx. 1 to 10 mm in diameter.

grinding Mechanical removal of glass from a surface for decorative purposes by means of natural and synthetic stone grinding wheels of variable particle size and profile under a continual stream of water. Grinding is carried out in four stages: rough cutting, smoothing, fine cutting and → polishing. Roughing involves the initial working in of a decoration with an iron or coarse-grained silicium carbide disc, which is also used, with finer emery particles, for the next stage, smoothing. A corundum disc is used for fine matt cutting.
Matt-finished decoration is lent three-dimensionality through the different grain size on the surface of the discs.

grinding flat Mechanical removal of glass to create flat, even surfaces. Grinding is done on a horizontal grinding wheel. It is used primarily to work the floor and lips of vessels. Facet decoration can be executed on cylindrical vessels by this means.

grinding, relief Grinding to produce raised decoration.

hot-working, also called working at the furnace Generic term covering all methods of decorating and forming glass at the furnace. → glassmaking

inclusion Any type of glass, air bubble or foreign material, such as → metallic compounds or foils, ceramic materials or minerals, embedded between the layers of glass, which may be either deliberate elements of decoration or flaws.

intercalaire Proprietary name used by Daum Frères for their → sandwich-glass decoration,

patented on 23 June 1899. See the description in the patent application in the 'Sources' section of the Appendix.

iridescence Finish created by vaporizing molten, red-hot glass in a → glory hole with mixtures of metallic compounds, such as zinc chloride, arsenic, bismuth, barium or strontium nitrate, which forms a shimmering layer of iridescence on the surface of the glass body.

lehr → annealing furnace

liver colour → Striking colours of gold and copper in opaque reddish-brown tints.

lustre pigments One or more metal resonates (gold, silver, platinum, bismuth, copper, lead, iron etc.) mixed with volatile oils (e.g., lavender, rosemary or peppermint oil), which can be applied in a thin coating with a brush to an object, dried and then fired at 550–600 °C. Colourless or coloured, lustre is of limited durability since it cannot bond with the glass surface. Its durability can be increased by applying it to a → matt-finished glass surface.

marquetry, *marqueterie de verre* Concept taken from cabinetmaking and applied by Emile Gallé to glassmaking, specifically to the technical decoration process, patented on 26 April 1898, entailing → fusing and inlaying preformed patches of glass and segments of glass threading. Objects executed in the marquetry technique are usually finished with → engraving. After 1900 Daum Frères began to simplify the process. From 1903 onwards the technique used for luxury series by Daum is referred to as *lamellé ciselé* or *ciselé sur plaque*.

martelé A term introduced by Daum Frères in Nancy for the texturing of surfaces that have a hammered look, recalling engraving or cutting consisting of rows of honey-combs or irregular depressions. *Martelé* cutting formed part of Emile Gallé's repertoire of special engraving techniques as early as 1884. Daum occasionally employed it in 1894, but did not use it more frequently until 1898/99.

marver Formerly a polished marble slab, today a sturdy flat cast-iron block on which the → gather is rolled and slightly preformed or applications to be hot-worked are preprocessed.

matt iridescence Finish created by reheating → iridescent glass in a moderate → oxidizing fire or by vapour-coating with certain chemicals. The cracks and fissures thus created in the iridescent layer lend it a matt appearance. The colours produced in the iridescent layer are determined by firing temperature and the duration of the firing process. Matt-firing increases the durability of iridescence.

matt finish Generic term for all finishing techniques creating matt glass surfaces. They include → engraving, → cutting, sandblasting, → etching and even matt painting with matt, colourless → flat colour.

metal foil Usually applied as → inclusions. Metals used for this purpose must have a melting point above the firing temperature of the glass (1000–1200°C). The only metal that can be used in this way without posing any difficulties is platinum (melting point 1772°C). Since gold and silver foil melt at 1064.4 and 961.9°C, respectively, the surface of the molten glass must be cooled slightly before the foil is fused on. Aluminium (melting point 660.4°C) and tin foil (an alloy of lead, tin and silver) cannot be used because their melting points are too low. Silvery metal foils can also be of white gold (an alloy of gold, silver and copper with a melting point of approx. 1050°C).

metallic compounds Often oxides but also sulphites, selenites, nitrates, chromates etc.

mould blowing Technique whereby the glassmaker blows the glass into a mould – usually consisting of two parts if unpatterned, or two or more if the shape is complex – in order to produce the entire form in one operation.

mould, optic Small, hinged mould with a handle, used in pattern-moulding; when the molten glass is blown into the mould the glass is pressed into a relief pattern. Common patterns take the form of ribs, diamond diapering, balls, rings and reticulation. The optic mould is a dip mould, but, unlike it, is usually part-size and is a one or at most two-piece mould because as a rule the → gather is still small when blown into the optic mould and has not yet taken on its final form.

mould, ribbed → Optic mould with parallel, vertical fluting and ribbing.

muffle kiln Furnace for firing → glass-painting colours with a separate firing compartment – a muffle – of fireclay, which is heated from outside the compartment.

needle etching → etching, needle

opalescent glass, also called opal glass Slightly cloudy to semi-opaque glass with varying tints, depending on whether it is viewed from above or looked through.

optic moulding Blowing glass into an → optic mould. Afterwards the piece is either blown into another mould or is freely blown.

optic mould → mould, optic

overlay Layer of usually monochrome coloured glass, as a rule thinner than the glass body over whose surface it is evenly applied. → casing

oxidizing fire (firing) Kiln atmosphere rich in oxygen.

parison The first → gather taken from the furnace and blown.

patinage Term coined by Emile Gallé for the decorative techniques involved in making semi-opaque or opaque glass, which he had patented on 26 April 1898. Gallé's patinage is carried out either on the body surface, in between casings or on both levels. In addition to fusing on extremely fine

powdered glass, metallic compounds and impurities, such as coal dust, ash or ferrous oxide from the blowpipe, the hot glass was also quenched briefly in water to create very fine → crazing. The different techniques were often combined. The processes described above are linked with the creation of extremely fine air bubbles (seeds), causing additional cloudiness. Patinage is usually associated with the → marquetry technique.

pigment Metallic salts or → metallic compounds melted into the batch and distributed as ions or colloids. Certainty about the type of pigment used can be arrived at only by chemical and physical analysis. In the present catalogue, therefore, only colours are described. Mention is made of colouring agents only when it has been possible to establish the use of particular ones on the basis of irrefutable criteria.

pinching Forming the lip of a glass vessel in the opposite way to → dilating it, by narrowing it or indenting it with pincers.

polishing Mechanical brightening of matt glass surfaces in two stages: 1. preliminary polishing with pumice and discs of poplar wood or cork, 2. burnishing with brush, felt or padded discs and polishing agent. Small → engraved surfaces are polished with a lead wheel.

pontil, punty Iron rod used for attaching and cracking off a hot body of glass so that the lip can be worked. → pontil mark → blowpipe

pontil mark Mark full of cracks where the → pontil has been removed from the glass body.

powder, fused-on Flecked, usually bubbly decoration created by applying → glass powder of variable grain size to a hot glass body, which is fused either on to large surfaces or is concentrated in particular areas.

powder, glass, also called powdered or pulverized glass Fine → coloured glass powder, available in particle sizes ranging from approx. 0.1 to 0.5 mm in diameter.

pressed glass Semi-mechanically or mechanically made hollow glass blown into patterned moulds or pressed into them with the aid of a plunger.

reduction colours Colour produced by → reduction firing glass that has been → stained.

reduction firing Manner of firing whereby the air in the furnace is smoky and low in oxygen. In contact with hot glass it produces the chemical reaction known as reduction: electrons are absorbed by metal particles in the glass, causing extremely thin, iridescent metal deposits to form on the surface.

relief cutting → engraving, relief

relief etching → etching, relief

relief grinding → grinding, relief

ribbed mould → mould, ribbed

rock crystal engraving → engraving, rock crystal

rod, also called coloured rod Solid rod of coloured glass (approx. 20–30 cm long and 3–5 cm thick) used

to make colour → gathers and → parisons or partial casing. The amount needed is cut off from the rod, which is first preheated at the furnace vent, and taken up by the → blowpipe or a → pontil.

sandwich glass, also called sandwiched decoration Decoration sandwiched between two layers of glass. In Art Nouveau glass this was usually done by combining → hot-working methods with → finishing or refining techniques. Among these is painting in enamel colours between layers of glass, often on coloured glass beneath a colourless glass casing. The process was a speciality of Burgun, Schverer & Co. in Meisenthal, which had it patented in Germany on 21 February 1896 and in France on 13 March 1897. See the 'Sources' section of the Appendix. → *intercalaire*

silver stain → Glass-painting colour, usually yellow, that bonds with the surface of the glass on the basis of an inorganic silver compound. Because it is relatively easy to handle and has so many applications, silver stain is the most frequently used stain. The intensity of hue, which can range from greenish yellow, golden yellow to a cognac colour and ultimately reddish brown, depends on the silver compound used, its concentration when applied, firing temperature and duration as well as the composition of the batch. The following are used: silver oxide, sulphide, carbonate, chloride or nitrate, usually mixed with distilled water (for large surfaces also with gum arabic) and ochre (a fine-earth mixture of clay, brown iron ore, quartz and lime) as a dispersion agent. These are applied to the glass surface, allowed to dry and then fired, depending on the physical properties of the charge, at 530–600°C. Metallic compounds in the glass, like arsenic, aluminium, antimony, iron, copper, cobalt, manganese and selenium, are of paramount importance in determining the bonding strength of silver stain and, as a result, intensity of hue. They reduce silver ions to silver atoms, which stain the glass yellow. The presence of several fluxing agents can lead to diminishing the intensity of the hue or to colour changes. The presence of oxide of antimony, for instance, turns the glass surface a saturated red when silver stain is fired. Special experiments with lead borosilicate glass and silver stain produced, depending on the oxide of aluminium and antimony content, a diverse palette, ranging from orange and red to purple and blue. → Striking colours of silver stain create patina-like tints that tend towards blues when the layer is thin and, when it is thicker, range from ivory and ochre to greyish green and silvery metallic precipitates. They are created by long firing times at a high temperature, a high silver concentration applied directly, without dispersion agents, by application on coloured glass with reducing metallic compounds such as copper, cobalt, manganese, iron or selenium compounds and by mixing with one or more metallic compounds with a reducing effect, which can be done within one firing or in several layers in the course of several firings. Silver stain does not produce striking colours on transparent gold-ruby red even when highly concentrated, but does weaken the colour tone, with the bluish red ruby colour becoming orange. On → liver-coloured gold-ruby red, silver stain immediately turns to striking colours. In → reduction firing the transparent silver stain layer takes on a golden → iridescent sheen at the furnace or in the muffle kiln, which can be rendered → matt iridescent. The entire range of colour changes through silver staining is encountered in numerous pieces of Art Nouveau glass, including work by Amédée de Caranza, Désiré Christian, Emile Gallé and Muller Frères.

stain Transparent → glass-painting colour that bonds with the surface of the glass to a greater or lesser degree depending on the inorganic silver or copper compounds used and their combination with bismuth compounds. → silver stain

striking colours Term used for colour changes in glass when the colour is not, or is only incompletely, created while the batch is in the molten state, but instead is induced by subsequent treatment (cooling or repeated heating) involving colouring agents. Most striking colours contain colloidal dispersed colouring agents that clump together to form larger particles (aggregation process) during the striking process. Changes in particle size alter the light absorption of the colloid and, therefore, the colour of the glass. This process – to which coloured glass, such as yellow with ferrous sulphate anions that are not colloidal dispersed, is subjected – usually takes place during cooling. Examples of well-known striking colours are:

	as an ion	as a colloidal suspension
gold-ruby red	yellowish	reddish purple, opaque brick red, opaque reddish brown*
copper-ruby red	green-yellow	red, dark red, opaque dark reddish brown to black
silver	colourless	yellow, honey, yellow ochre to grey with metallic precipitates
selenium ruby	colourless	yellow, orange, fiery red, dark red, black
antimony ruby	colourless	yellow, dark red, black
yellow with ferrous sulphate anions	yellow to brown	

* thin layers appear bluish when held up to the light

vitreous enamel → enamel colours